D0820696

3 0450 01089 4443

Tudor Rule and Revolution

G. R. ELTON
Professor of English Constitutional History in the University of Cambridge and Fellow of Clare College.
Photograph: Ramsey & Muspratt, Cambridge

Tudor Rule and Revolution

Essays for G. R. ELTON from his American friends

Edited by
DELLOYD J. GUTH
and
JOHN W. McKENNA

CAMBRIDGE UNIVERSITY PRESS
Cambridge
London New York New Rochelle
Melbourne Sydney

Published by the Press Syndicate of the University of Cambridge
The Pitt Building, Trumpington Street, Cambridge CB2 1RP
32 East 57th Street, New York, NY 10022, USA
296 Beaconsfield Parade, Middle Park, Melbourne 3206, Australia

First published 1982

Printed in Great Britain at The Pitman Press, Bath

Library of Congress catalogue card number: 82 – 4266

British Library Cataloguing in Publication Data

Tudor rule and revolution: essays for G. R. Elton
from his American friends.
1. England – History – Tudors, 1485–1603
– Addresses, essays, lectures
I. Guth, Delloyd J. II. McKenna, John W.
III. Elton, G.R.
942.05 DA315

ISBN 0 521 24841 8

PP

Contents

Notes on contributors

THOMAS G. BARNES studied at Harvard and received the D.Phil. from Oxford under the supervision of R. B. Wernham. He has taught at Lycoming College and, since 1960, at the University of California, Berkeley, where he is Professor of History and Law. An authority on the later Court of Star Chamber, he has published widely on topics in English local government and done comparative research on the French Conseil Privé under Henri IV.

W. HAMILTON BRYSON received an LL.B. from Harvard Law School and Ph.D. from Cambridge, under the supervision of D. E. C. Yale. Following post-doctoral study at the Max-Planck-Instituts für Europäische Rechtsgeschichte he joined the faculty of the University of Richmond where he is Professor of Law. In addition to his study of *The Equity Side of the Exchequer*, he has made substantial contributions to Anglo-American legal bibliography.

CHARLES H. CARTER graduated from Columbia University with a Ph.D. under the supervision of Garrett Mattingly whose *Festschrift* he edited. He has taught at Long Island University, at the University of Oregon, and at Tulane University where he holds a professorship in Anglo-Spanish history. An authority on European diplomatic history, he has written on *The Secret Diplomacy of the Habsburgs, 1598–1625* and on Jacobean politics with particular reference to international relations.

MARIA L. CIONI received a Ph.D. from Cambridge where she studied under the supervision of G. R. Elton. After returning to Canada she worked with the federal government and is currently liaison manager of the Telidon and Education Project of the Ontario educational broadcasting channel. Her current activities involve research and writing in the field of videotex technology.

JAMES S. COCKBURN studied at the University of Leeds, from which he received the LL.B. and LL.M. under the supervision of P. S.

James and G. C. F. Foster. He has taught at the University of London and at the University of Maryland where he is Professor of English History. His work in legal history includes editions and calendars of indictments and *A History of English Assizes, 1558–1714*.

DAVID CRESSY was educated at Clare College, Cambridge where he received the Ph.D. under the supervision of R. S. Schofield. He has taught at St John's College in Santa Fe and at the Claremont Colleges. Following his studies of Tudor and Stuart education, and of *Literacy and the Social Order*, he is now doing research on England and New England in the seventeenth century.

CHARLES M. GRAY studied at Harvard University and received the Ph.D. under the supervision of Wilbur K. Jordan. He has taught at the Massachusetts Institute of Technology, at Yale, and at the University of Chicago where he is Professor of History. In addition to a study of *Copyhold, Equity and the Common Law*, he has explored numerous aspects of medieval and early modern jurisprudence.

DELLOYD J. GUTH worked under G. R. Elton at Clare College, Cambridge and completed the Ph.D. at the University of Pittsburgh. He has taught at the University of Michigan, the University of Lancaster, and the University of Illinois at Urbana-Champaign. He currently holds visiting appointments in the Faculties of Law, University of British Columbia and Victoria University. In addition to his researches on pre-Reformation law, he has published bibliographies on late medieval English history and on the John F. Kennedy assassination.

RUDOLPH W. HEINZE studied at Concordia College, DePaul University and at the University of Iowa for the Ph.D. under the supervision of Robert M. Kingdom. He has taught at Ohio State University, Concordia College in Illinois and is now Professor of History at Oak Hill College, London. His researches on *The Proclamations of the Tudor Kings* and on numerous aspects of Tudor and Stuart legal history include forthcoming work on the proclamations of James I.

J. H. HEXTER studied at the University of Cincinnati and Harvard University where he received the Ph.D. under the supervision of W. C. Abbott. He has taught at MIT, at Queen's College, CUNY, at Yale, where he is Director of the Yale Center for Parliamentary History, and at Washington University, St Louis. There he is Director of the Center for the Study of Law, Liberty and Justice, with the possibly unique title of

Distinguished Historian in Residence *in absentia* while on leave as Mellon Senior Fellow at the National Humanities Center, North Carolina. His numerous books include *The Reign of King Pym*, studies of More's Utopia and of historiographical traditions, and works on the history of political theory.

DALE E. HOAK studied at the College of Wooster, the University of Pittsburgh and at Clare College, Cambridge where he received a Ph.D. under the supervision of G. R. Elton. He has taught at Chatham College, Carnegie-Mellon University, Florida Atlantic University and at the College of William and Mary where he is Professor of History. His work on Renaissance history and society includes studies of iconography and witch-hunting and a volume on *The King's Council in the Reign of Edward VI*.

STANFORD E. LEHMBERG was educated at the University of Kansas and at Cambridge where he received the Ph.D., having studied history with G. R. Elton and Christopher Morris, literature with C. S. Lewis and organ music with Boris Ord. He has taught at the University of Texas and is currently Professor of History at the University of Minnesota. In addition to biographies of Sir Thomas Elyot and Sir Walter Mildmay he has published studies of the Reformation Parliament and later parliaments of Henry VIII.

MORTIMER LEVINE studied at New York University and at the University of Pennsylvania, where he received the Ph.D. under the supervision of Conyers Read. He has taught at Brooklyn College and at West Virginia University where he is Professor of History. His published work includes a bibliography of Tudor history, studies on Tudor dynastic problems, and a volume on *The Early Elizabethan Succession Question*.

WALLACE T. MACCAFFREY was educated at Reed College and at Harvard University where he received the Ph.D. under the supervision of Wilbur K. Jordan. He has taught at UCLA, at Haverford College and at Harvard, where he is Francis Lee Higginson Professor of History. His studies of Elizabethan local and national politics include a monograph on Exeter, a study of the Elizabethan regime, and *Elizabeth I and the Making of Policy*.

JOHN W. MCKENNA studied at Amherst College, at Columbia with Garrett Mattingly, and at Cambridge where he received the Ph.D. under the supervision of Edward Miller and G. R. Elton. He has taught at

Brooklyn College, the University of California, Riverside, and at Haverford College where he held the Scull Professorship of English Constitutional History. He has published studies of later medieval constitutional issues, royal iconography, political cults, and continues to explore Anglo-French kingship and political propaganda.

ELLIOT ROSE studied at Cambridge, where he received the M.A., and is Professor of History at the University of Toronto where he has taught since 1955. His wide-ranging interests in Tudor-Stuart society and culture embrace studies of witchcraft, the contemporary perceptions of social rank and mobility, and the analysis of *Cases of Conscience*.

ARTHUR JOSEPH SLAVIN was educated at Louisiana State University and at the University of North Carolina where he received a Ph.D. under the supervision of Stephen Baxter. He has taught at Bucknell University, UCLA, the University of California, Irvine, and at the University of Louisville where he is Justus Bier Distinguished Professor. His work on early Tudor England includes a biography of Sir Ralph Sadler, editing *Tudor Men and Institutions*, and studies of Thomas Cromwell and Thomas Wriothesley.

FREDERICK A. YOUNGS, JR studied at Tulane University, DePaul University, and at Cambridge where he received the Ph.D. under the supervision of G. R. Elton. He has taught at California State University, Long Beach, and at Louisiana State University where he is Professor of History. In addition to his work on *The Proclamations of the Tudor Queens* he has published various studies including a guide to English local administrative units.

Introduction

This volume began as a birthday book, a collection of related studies presented to Geoffrey Rudolph Elton on his sixtieth birthday, 17 August 1981, by some of his many friends and former students now resident in North America. No scholar of his generation has been more influential in furthering what Geoffrey himself calls 'the practice of history.' No historian in this century has taught more consistently, or demonstrated more effectively, the need for a continuing return to manuscript evidence and the re-examination of archival records. His compelling vision of early modern institutions has been all the more influential for his restatement of the centrality of rule and revolution in that early modern society which is largely our shared past. His emphasis on the origins and consequences of secular and religious changes in the sixteenth century has redirected research outward from the Henrician age, both in time and geography. These essays attest to the breadth of that research and the far-reaching effects of those prolific writings. Each relates directly to issues or problems which Geoffrey Elton has dealt with in his own work, yet some reach well back to the later middle ages and others stretch forward into the Stuart era. This diversity has invariably been inspired and occasionally provoked by the range of the Eltonian canon. Since that energetic activity continues unabated, this volume must be considered not a *Festschrift* in the ordinary sense but a *florilegium*, the celebration of a friend and colleague in mid-career from whom we confidently expect many happy scholarly returns.

These studies, therefore, have a common theme and a shared purpose both professional and personal. For almost three decades Geoffrey and Sheila Elton have opened their home and their hearts to innumerable students and fellow historians. For some this personal relationship was their introduction both to the delights of English history and to the splendid vagaries of the 'other' Cambridge. All enjoyed that mixture of learning, wit, and hospitality which has earned the Eltons such a remarkable assemblage of friends on several continents. These ties, renewed by frequent visits to the United States and Canada, have been strengthened by that indefatigable correspondence for which Geoffrey is justly famous. Many more of our colleagues would have liked to join in this expression of esteem and affection. Some were prevented by previous commitments or for reasons of health. Others, even more numerous, work in fields outside the limits of this gathering. We are joined, therefore, by absent friends.

The essays presented here were restricted in length so as to include a larger number of contributors, and some of the authors plan to expand on their offerings at a later date. Mr William Davies and the staff of Cambridge University Press have made our task both pleasurable and possible. At their suggestion the texts follow American orthography both for the sake of uniformity and to substantiate our transatlantic collegiality. Through the kindness of Geoffrey Elton and so many of his countrymen many North American scholars have come to regard Britain as their second homeland. All the more fitting, therefore, that we should salute one who, himself an adopted child of Britain, has demonstrated time and again his notable mastery of the English language and of England's history.

D.J.G.

J.W.McK.

Abbreviations

APC	*Acts of the Privy Council*, ed. by John R. Dasent (32 vols., London, 1890–1907)
BL	British Library
CJ	*Journals of the House of Commons* (232 vols., London, 1803–1975/6): I, 8 Nov. 1547–2 March 1628; and II, 13 April 1640–14 March 1642 (London, 1803)
CPR	*Calendars of the Patent Rolls Preserved in the Public Record Office* (London, HMSO, various dates)
CUP	Cambridge University Press
DNB	*Dictionary of National Biography*, ed. by Leslie Stephen and Sidney Lee (63 vols., plus Supplements, New York, Macmillan and Co., 1885–1900)
EETS	Early English Text Society
HMC	*Historical Manuscripts Commission* (London, HMSO, various dates)
HMSO	Her Majesty's Stationery Office
LP	*Letters and Papers, Foreign and Domestic, of the Reign of Henry VIII*, ed. by John S. Brewer, James Gairdner, and R. H. Brodie (21 vols., London, HMSO, 1862–1932).
MS/MSS	Manuscript/Manuscripts
OED	*Oxford English Dictionary*, ed. by James A. H. Murray, Henry Bradley, W. A. Craigie, and C. T. Onions (11 vols. in 18 parts, Oxford, Oxford University Press, 1888–1933; corrected reissue in 13 vols., 1933; 3 vols. Supplement by R. W. Burchfield, 1972–)
PRO	Public Record Office, London
RP	*Rotuli Parliamentorum, ut et Petitiones et Placita in Parliamento* (11 vols., London, Record Commission, 1810–28)
SP	State Papers, unpublished and in the PRO
SR	*Statutes of the Realm, 1101–1713*, ed. by Alexander Luders, T. E. Tomlins, J. Raithby, *et al.* (11 vols., London, Record Commission, 1810–28)

STC *A Short-Title Catalogue of Books Printed in England, Scotland, & Ireland, And of English Books Printed Abroad 1475–1640*, compiled by Alfred W. Pollard and Gilbert R. Redgrave (London, The Bibliographical Society, 1926); 3 vols. Supplement by W. A. Jackson, F. S. Ferguson, and Katharine F. Pantzer (2 vols., London, Oxford University Press, 1976–)

VCH *Victoria History of the Counties of England*, ed. by H. A. Doubleday, William Page, Louis F. Salzman, and Ralph B. Pugh (London and Westminster, 1900–34; London, Institute of Historical Research, 1935–)

Part one

An Era of Reformations

The Tudor Revolution and the Devil's Art: Bishop Bonner's printed forms

ARTHUR J. SLAVIN

Studies in the Tudor Revolution have moved outward from an earlier emphasis on changes in the working of government to embrace the history of the Reformation. Professor Elton and others have published shelves of work on government, law, and administration.[1] They have also explored much else in what Dr Bradshaw recently dubbed 'Elton's Era.'[2] Focus has now shifted from the machinery of government to church reform and to the mid-Tudor political crisis.[3] Nowhere is this shift more marked than in the character of the two general narratives by Professor Elton himself: *England Under the Tudors* (1955) and *Reform and Reformation* (1977).[4]

Professor Elton has touched the contribution which printing made to

[1] See extensive bibliographical notes in Jennifer Loach and R. Tittler (eds.), *The Mid-Tudor Polity, 1540–1560* (London, Macmillan, 1980), and G. R. Elton, *Reform and Reformation: England, 1509–1558* (Cambridge, Mass., Harvard University Press, 1977).

[2] 'It looks as if Tawney's century is yielding place to Elton's era': in Brendan Bradshaw, 'The Tudor Commonwealth: reform and revision,' *The Historical Journal*, XXII (1979), 455.

[3] John A. Guy, *The Cardinal's Court* (Totowa, N. J., Rowman and Littlefield, 1977), and *The Public Career of Sir Thomas More* (New Haven, Yale University Press, 1980); Brendan Bradshaw, *The Irish Constitutional Revolution of the Sixteenth Century* (Cambridge, CUP, 1979); Dale Hoak, *The King's Council in the Reign of Edward VI* (Cambridge, CUP, 1976); David M. Loades, *The Reign of Mary Tudor* (London, St Martins, 1979); Rosemary O'Day and Felicity Heal (eds.), *Continuity and Change: Personnel and Administration of the Church in England, 1500–1642* (Leicester, The University Press, 1976) and by the same editors *Church and Society in England: Henry VIII to James I* (London, Macmillan, 1977); Felicity Heal, *Of Prelates and Princes* (Cambridge, CUP, 1980); Rosemary O'Day, *The English Clergy: The Emergence and Consolidation of a Profession, 1558–1642* (Leicester, The University Press, 1979); James K. McConica, *English Humanists and Reformation Politics* (Oxford, The Clarendon Press, 1965); Arthur B. Ferguson, *The Articulate Citizen and the English Renaissance* (Durham, N.C., Duke University Press, 1965) and his *Clio Unbound* (Durham, N.C., Duke University Press, 1979); W. R. D. Jones, *The Tudor Commonwealth, 1529–1559* (London, Athlone Press, 1970); and P. S. Donaldson, *A Machiavellian Treatise by Stephen Gardiner* (Cambridge, CUP, 1979).

[4] Bradshaw, 'The Tudor Commonwealth,' 463, predicts a lively debate on this shift. My own reading of it is being prepared for publication under the title 'Telling the story: G. R. Elton, narrative, and the Tudor age.'

that governmental revolution.[5] His work has stimulated the study of Cromwellian propaganda, of opposition ballads and broadsides expressing dissent and rebellion,[6] and of the spreading of Protestant ideas under license in bibles and formularies of the faith.[7] The result has been to restore printing to the place it held as an agent of change among contemporaries, recalling Foxe's dictum:

> The lord began to work for his church not with sword and target to subdue his exalted adversaries, but with printing, writing and reading . . . How many printing presses there be in the world . . . that either the Pope must abolish knowledge and printing or printing will at length root him out.[8]

This theory of progress through technology fascinated Elizabethans. Bacon said printing, gunpowder and the mariner's compass had changed 'the whole face and state of things throughout the world.'[9] Hakewill asserted the superiority of Moderns over Ancients on the same bases: *His tribus tota Antiquitas nihil par habet.*[10] While all English writers welcomed advances in navigation some regarded printing and gunpowder as devilish forces. The poet Daniel condemned them as fatal instruments contrived 'the one to publish, th'other to defend impious Contention and proud Discontent.'[11] Pessimists lamented a lost unity and order, but all agreed on the transforming power of the new technologies.[12]

[5] There is little discussion on the subject in either *The Tudor Revolution in Government* (Cambridge, CUP, 1953) or *England Under the Tudors* (London, Longmans, 1955). *Policy and Police* (Cambridge, CUP, 1972), 171–216, signalled a vigorous interest in propaganda, printers and booksellers. For an earlier definition see, G. R Elton, 'The problems and significance of administrative history in the Tudor period,' *Journal of British Studies*, IV (1965), 18.

[6] G. R. Elton, 'Reform and the "Commonwealth-Men" of Edward VI's reign,' in Peter Clark, A. G. R. Smith, and N. Tyacke (eds.), *The English Commonwealth, 1547–1640* (London, Athlone Press, 1979), 23–38; also C. S. L. Davies, 'The Pilgrimage of Grace reconsidered,' *Past and Present*, XLVIII (1970), 3–78; David M. Loades, 'The press under the early Tudors,' *Transactions of the Cambridge Bibliographical Society*, IV (1964), 29–50; and Jennifer Loach, 'Pamphlets and politics,' *Bulletin of the Institute of Historical Research*, XLVIII (1975), 31–45.

[7] E. R. Riegler, 'Printing, Protestantism and politics: Thomas Cromwell and religious reform' (University of California, Los Angeles, Unpublished Ph.D. thesis, 1978).

[8] S. R. Cattley and G. Townshend (eds.), *Acts and Monuments* (8 vols., London, Josiah Pratt, 1837–41), III, 718–22, and IV, 252.

[9] J. Spedding, R. L. Ellis and D. D. Heath (eds.), *Collected Works of Sir Francis Bacon* (14 vols., London, 1857–74): *Novum Organum*, VIII, 162 and 140–3; *Advancement of Learning*, VI, 128.

[10] George Hakewill, *An Apologie of the Power and the Providence of God in the Government of the World* (London, 1627); the quote from Cardanus is in the second edition (1630), 275.

[11] See Arthur B. Ferguson, 'The historical thought of Samuel Daniel: a study in Renaissance ambivalence,' *Journal of the History of Ideas*, XXXII (1971), 185–202; the quote is from L. Michel (ed.), *The Civil Wars* (New Haven, Yale University Press, 1958), VI, 37.

[12] Samuel Lilley, 'Robert Recorde and the idea of progress,' *Renaissance and Modern Studies*, II (1957), 3–37; see also Paolo Rossi, *Philosophy, Technology, and the Arts in the Early Modern Era* (New York, Knopf, 1970).

It is therefore surprising to find in the literature on 'Elton's Era' little discussion of the impact of printing on the conduct of routine royal business.[13] Few inventions seemed to promise more efficiency and immunity against both fraud and forgery, more effective translation of policy into practice. This we see readily by two examples: the development of the 'print' or stamp for royal warrants under Henry VIII,[14] and the issue by Henry VII of a printed proclamation regulating currency, in which the margins contained woodcut pictures illustrating valid coins.[15] In both cases ease of reproduction was perhaps of less significance than the ability to convey reliable information.[16] Such applications need further study, but my purpose here is to examine the earliest English government use of printed forms for routine administration.

True bureaucratic government has as an essential feature the use of sets of forms structured or patterned to organize information for the convenience of government. Such forms provide a blank space or 'window' to be filled up by whatever particulars will be required to activate it. The first English printed items answering to this description are a printed tax receipt from 1538, now in the Bodleian Library,[17] and a set of seven similar forms of slightly later date in the Public Record Office.[18]

There was, of course, medieval usage of so-called 'blank charters' as part of the tradition of manuscript forms, and they remained in use alongside the printed ones in both royal and ecclesiastical practice. In this context I shall examine the relationship between the Oxford rarity and the PRO set. My conclusions will then address a matter of basic importance to the Tudor Revolution, particularly in the wider world of Reformation government: why did such printed forms vanish from the tool kit of royal

[13] G. R. Elton, 'The sessional printing of statutes, 1484–1547,' in Eric W. Ives, R. Knecht *Wealth and Power in Tudor England: Essays Presented to S. T. Bindoff* (London, Athlone Press, 1978), 68–86.

[14] On the history of the wet and dry stamps see David R. Starkey, 'The King's Privy Chamber, 1485–1547' (Cambridge University, Unpublished Ph.D. thesis, 1974), 339–52.

[15] Paul L. Hughes and James F. Larkin (eds.), *Tudor Royal Proclamations* (3 vols., New Haven, Yale University Press, 1964–9), I, 60–1, No. 54; on printed proclamations see, *ibid.*, I, xxxviii–xliii, and Rudolph W. Heinze, *The Proclamations of the Tudor Kings* (Cambridge, CUP, 1976), 21–4.

[16] The efficacy of chain letters is clear from French and English examples: Joseph R. Strayer and Charles H. Taylor, *Studies in Early French Taxation* (Cambridge, Mass., Harvard University Press, 1939) and also Martin Wolfe, *The Fiscal System of Renaissance France* (New Haven, Yale University Press, 1972), 93–8 and 255–87. Under Henry VIII the government was able to distribute 600 copies of an order with pendant seals together with printed copies for posting, on short notice: Heinze, *Proclamations*, 22–4.

[17] Bodleian Library, MS Arch. A.B. 8, vol. 36; see, Rowan Watson, 'Some early printed receipts for clerical taxation,' *Journal of the Society of Archivists*, VI (1978), 96–8; also, Ida Darlington, *ibid.*, III (1965–9), 575–6.

[18] PRO, *SP* 1/169, fol. 21; 1/175, fol. 126; 1/183, fol. 59; 1/197, fol. 1; E 135/8/43, nos. 2, 3 and 4.

administration, only to reappear a generation later when their use had become common elsewhere? Was this yet another example of the fate that other innovations suffered after Thomas Cromwell's death?

I

Shakespeare's audience knew forms with blanks had been used by the government in the past and were in common use in their own day. King Richard II, intending war against rebels in Ireland and mindful of his too liberal largesse, put into effect a scheme to have his agents in England use

> . . . blank charters,
> Whereto, when they shall know what men are rich
> They shall subscribe them for large sums of gold
> And send them after to supply our wants . . .[19]

Behind the poet's lines is some disputed evidence on the king's policy.[20]

The scene between Alice Ford and Mrs Page in *The Merry Wives of Windsor* occasions no such dispute. Alice shows to Mrs Page a letter revealing a proposal of marriage, a woman's path to knightly dignity, asking 'Did you ever hear the like?' Mrs Page answers:

> Letter for letter, but that the name of Page and Ford differs! To thy great comfort in this mystery of ill opinions, here's the twin brother of thy letter . . . I warrant he hath a thousand of these letters writ with blank spaces for different names, sure more, and these are of the second edition. He will print them, out of doubt, for he cares not what he puts into the press, when he would put us two . . .[21]

Theatrical language gains authority from a correspondence between the stage-world and the experience of the audience.[22] Before Shakespeare there existed a rich stock of references running together the meanings of the words blank, form, opening, and window. Caxton used the word

19 *Richard II*, Act I, iv, ll. 42–52.

20 Anthony Steel, *The Receipt of the Exchequer, 1377–1485* (Cambridge, CUP, 1954); R. H. Jones, *Royal Policy of Richard II* (Oxford, The Clarendon Press, 1968); and Gerald L. Harriss, 'Fictitious loans,' *Economic History Review*, 2nd series, VII (1955), 187–99 and 'Preference at the medieval Exchequer,' *Bulletin of the Institute of Historical Research*, XXX (1957), 17–40. Three of the thirty-three charges against Richard mentioned unlawful taxation: *RP*, III, 416–22, aa. 14, 15, and 21. The Evesham and Walsingham chroniclers wrote about the loans, but only the Croyland Continuator states flatly: '*Quandam alba charta vocata Blankechartre . . . quod utique Regis Ricardi in posterum causa exitii magna fuit,*' W. Fulman (ed.), *Historiae Croylandensis continuatio*, in *Rerum Anglicarum scriptores veterum* (Oxford, 1684), I, 493.

21 Act II, i., ll. 70–81.

22 Terence Hawkes, *Shakespeare's Talking Animals: Language and Drama in Society* (Totowa, N.J., Rowman and Littlefield, 1973), 9–36.

'form' in a general sense to indicate a set pattern for making a thing and specifically to mean a fixed body of type.[23] The word 'blank' designated the forms from which coins were struck at the Mint, as well as certain coins.[24] In 1310 there was already a use of 'window' to indicate a place of display. By 1463 the use of form and window could be synonymous, and there was a close association between the notion of a form and the frame of a window.[25] The relationship between sign and the thing signified was that of the common image of a form as the general framework of a thing. Hence over the course of more than two centuries the notion of an opening to be fulfilled up became signified by words of widely different origins with a shared core of experience: that of making, shaping or impressing metal, wood, or paper and vellum.[26] The closely related idea of a form of words had an even longer history in both Latin and English diplomatic formulae.[27]

My concern here is with the form as verbal framework containing a blank or window to be filled. In manuscript materials examples are not so rare that mere curiosity should attach to them. Hall provided instances from thirteenth century inquests but over the next two centuries found few examples. Henry VI received hundreds of certificates attached to original warrants for the taking of homage, each being made cursively by the clerk in a superscript. One form Hall did produce was more likely a precedent-book copy for Chancery clerks.[28] Edward IV raised money by loans through deliveries of blank privy seal writs.[29] Hall compared royal forms with the blank papal indulgences already familiar in England, while pointing to a French-language precedent in the practice of Henry VI.[30] What is especially valuable about the Henrician item is that the departmental clerk who subscribed the form also annotated it. He provided

[23] See *The Fable of Poge* (ed. London, 1634), 213, and also *The Book of Travellers* (London, 1483), sig. 24 B: 'At Westminstre by London in Formes imprynted.' For current Tudor usage see *OED*, V, 458–60.

[24] The blanc or blank was in origin a small French coin of silver, later minted in copper and struck by Henry V in parts of France under his control. The word had already appeared in English in 1399 (*OED*, I, 902) and later in Caxton (1480) and Lord Berners (1523). See J. Lafaurie, *Les monnaies des rois de France: Hugues Capet à Louis XII* (Paris, Chalmette, 1951), and Christopher E. Challis, *The Tudor Coinage* (Manchester, The University Press, 1978), 17–21.

[25] *OED*, V, 460, no. 19a and XIX, 164, nos. 2a–c.

[26] For my linguistic assumptions, see Philip Pettit, *The Concept of Structuralism* (Berkeley and Los Angeles, University of California Press, 1977), 1–30.

[27] Hubert Hall, *A Formula Book of English Historical Documents*, pt I: *Diplomatic Documents* and pt II: *Ministerial and Judicial Records* (Cambridge, CUP, 1908–9) provides a wide selection; see also John S. Purvis, *An Introduction to Ecclesiastical Records* (London, St Anthony's Press, 1953), 10–12. The earliest official English usage derives from the troubles of 1399; *RP*, III, 424, col. a.

[28] Hall, *A Formula Book*, II, 138, 141; I, 74. [29] *Ibid.*, I, 93. [30] *Ibid.*, I, 98.

three paragraphs of instruction to guide other clerks in the use of the proper style of address in the blanks, distinguishing landed classes, communities, townsmen, and the higher clergy.[31]

Hall was certainly right in supposing that such royal forms derived inspiration from papal instruments. Numerous bundles in the Miscellanea of Chancery and the King's Remembrancer in Exchequer provide examples of an early date from the class loosely called Indulgence Letters.[32] We need only examine them long enough to link this manuscript evidence of papal revenue administration in England with the development of printed Indulgence forms.[33]

Of the various types of Indulgence documents the most important was the confessional letter. These form a series from 1319 until the abrogation of papal authority in England. They originally provided relief *a pena* but not *a culpa* for the powerful. Their wider availability in the fifteenth century owed much to the Jubilee Indulgences of Clement VI who extended benefits to those who could not make the Roman journey but who would make a money composition. Royal license was necessary to carry money out of the realm for pilgrimage or for the distribution of confessional letters in England.[34] A provision to divide the alms payment between a Roman cause and a needful English foundation, perhaps even reserving all income to some ruinous English church or chapel, stimulated a thriving business.[35] Some letters were administered by papal agents while other fell under wholly local management.[36] The record shows continuous popularity of confessional letters at all social levels before the break from Rome.[37]

Indulgences issued by local authorities in England yield evidence about administrative practices and the problems encountered by officials. Episcopal collectors disputed the accounts of pardoners. Confessional let-

[31] PRO, C 81/1326, bearing the date 21 July, 22 Edward IV.

[32] PRO, C 47/15–21 and E 135/1–25.

[33] See, William E. Lunt, *Studies in Anglo-Papal Relations During the Middle Ages*, vol. II: *Financial Relations of the Papacy with England, 1327–1534* (Cambridge, Mass., The Medieval Academy of America, 1962), 9–12.

[34] On royal licensing see *CPR, 1348–1350* (London, HMSO, 1905), 571. Lunt, *Studies*, II, 462 and 588–9.

[35] The popularity of such letters can be seen in the affairs of a London grocer and his wife, Henry and Katherine Langley, who supported several foundations: PRO, E 135/6/56; and PRO, C 47/15/6; and, BL, MS C. 11. b. 11 (1). For later examples see Lincoln Archives Office, MS Registrum Longland, fol. 97; PRO, E 135/6/64, 70; BL, MS Harleian 670, fols. 113 and 113*v*.; BL, MSS 1A 55127 and 55128; and PRO, C 47/15/25–6.

[36] Lunt, *Studies*, II, 447–71, 525–76 and also 473–524.

[37] *Ibid.*, II, 588–602, summarizes a 1502 schedule of charges rated for incomes from £2000 to 10 shillings. In 1530 the future Lord Chancellor Wriothesley invested in a letter of pardon from all penalties of sin: Vatican Library, Armario XL 30, fol. 339.

ters to benefit a hospital, chapel, order, or private person often became controlled by the beneficiaries, which tempted some to fraud or forgery.[38] Synods and convocations dealt with such problems,[39] resorting to the appointment of examiners and to improvements in methods of book-keeping.[40] More important was the use of teams of assessors, deputy-collectors and collectors who worked closely with auditors.[41] Most important of all was the introduction of methods of enforcement through ecclesiastical courts: mandates, summons, sequestrations, and the issuance of proper acquittances.[42]

Receipts gave particular aggravation. Papal practice had developed out of small taxes such as Peter's Pence and procurations. The writing of an acquittance or receipt for a penny tax involved as much time and materials as for a much larger payment. The payee had to purchase the receipt[43] and without it had no protection against a second claim in courts Christian or at common law.[44] This was a hapless situation, in which the receipts cost more than the tax owed or the payment made for annual renewal of

[38] *LP*, IV, appendix, 5, 20 August 1533; also Vatican Library, Armario XL 11, fol. 218, 27 March 1526; Ernest F. Jacob (ed.), *The Register of Henry Chichele, Archbishop of Canterbury, 1414–1443*, Canterbury and York Society, XLVI (Oxford, 1945), III, 93; Borthwick Institute (York) MS Registrum Wolsey, fols. 133 and 133*v*.; *LP*, I, 632 (3); and Bodleian Library, MS Arch. A. b. 8 (36). For forgeries see Hereford and Worcester Record Office (Worcester) MS b 716. 093–BA. 2648/8 (i); Registrum Silvestro de' Gigli, fols. 199*v*.–200; and BL, MS Harleian 670, fol. 113; *LP*, VI, 636, records the arrest of two pardoners for fraud.

[39] Nicholas Paulus, *Geschichte des Ablasses im Mittelalter* (3 vols., Paderborn, F. Schöningh, 1923), III, 268–9; Chichele sponsored legislation in Convocation: Jacob, *Reg. Chichele*, III, 93; *CPR 1429–1436* (London, HMSO, 1907), 247. The Ely Synod issued a decree as late as 1528: *LP*, IV, ii, 4351.

[40] Dean Colet served as an examiner and attracted Erasmus' attention for so doing: PRO, C 47/15, pt 6/22, 23; *LP*, II, ii, 3992; see also PRO, *SP* 1/229, fol. 17.

[41] Durham Cathedral Library, MS Locellus XIX, 107; Lincoln Archives Office, Dean and Chapter MS Bj. 2.5; Westminster Abbey Muniments, MS WAM 5774; BL, MS Harleian 862, Walter Melford's account book as papal collector, 1418–20. The fullest of all Tudor descriptions and accounts of the system is in the account book of Peter Griphius: Vatican Library, MS Ottobono Lat. 2948, covering the years 1508–11; see, Michele Monaco (ed.), *Il 'De Officio Collectoris In Regno Angliae' di Pietro Griffi da Pisa (1469–1516)*, Uomini e Dottrine, XIX (Rome, Edizioni di Storia e Letteratura, 1973).

[42] Lunt, *Studies*, II, 3–7, outlines the process after 1327; for a summons and trial see, Edmund Hobhouse (ed.), *Calendar of the Register of John de Drokensford, Bishop of Bath and Wells, 1309–1329*, Somerset Record Society, I (London, 1887), fol. 279*v*.; BL, MS Harleian 862, fol. 61*v*. provides an instance of sequestration of a deceased collector's goods in 1362; for a conflict over goods with a royal escheator see, John W. Willis-Bund (ed.), *Register of the Diocese of Worcester during the Vacancy of the See, registrum sede vacante, 1301–1435*, Worcestershire Historical Society (1897), II, 266–7.

[43] BL, MS Harleian 862, fol. 76; Westminster Abbey Muniments, MSS WAM 29498, 29500, 29502–4; Francis C. Hingeston-Randolph (ed.), *The Register of John de Grandisson, Bishop of Exeter* (3 vols., London and Exeter, 1897–9), II, 895–6; Westminster Abbey Muniments, MSS WAM 30480, 30396 and 9437; and Bodleian Library MS Charters, Berkshire a. 2a, no. 139.

[44] Guy, *Sir Thomas More*, 70–3.

membership in a confessional gild. Moreover, where a tax was at issue, failure either to pay or to prove payment raised the threat of penalties as severe as sequestration of goods and excommunication. One priest who owed a mere two pennies and three farthings was sequestered and excommunicated.[45] Such treatment could stimulate clerical grievances as well as lay resentments, and the two came together in traditional condemnations of papal collections and pardoners.[46]

Similar difficulties later attached to printed confessional letters and tax mandates, after Caxton's introduction of them in 1476.[47] While it may be argued that the standardization achieved by printed forms discouraged forgery on grounds of expense, making it possible to issue receipts more cheaply, the evidence is ambiguous concerning indulgences and negligible for gathering taxes before the expulsion of Roman collectors.[48] Most bishops relied on their household staff for all revenue administration, and there was little evidence among them of competence and even less of efforts of improvement.[49] Bishop Bonner of London was exceptional in his sophisticated management of his own estates[50] and the thorough manner in which he administered taxes.[51]

If we turn from ecclesiastical to royal usage the road we travel is hardly an ascending one. Tudor kings sometimes used true manuscript forms[52] but were conservative in utilizing printed forms. The government did use

[45] There is a writ of excommunication in the Griphius accounts: Vatican Library, MS Ottobono 2948, fol. 70; for a case of sequestration and excommunication reversed by a bishop see Hingeston-Randolph, *Reg. Grandisson*, II, 896.

[46] R. Franks, 'The Pardon Scene in Piers Plowman,' *Speculum*, XXVI (1954), 318–24; Simon Fish, *Supplication for Beggars* (London, 1529), sig. A, 10–11 (BL, Shelfmark C. 21. b. 45), and Christopher St Germain, *Treatise Concernynge the Division betwene the Spiritualitie and the Temporalitie*, in Arthur I. Taft (ed.), *The Apologye of Syr Thomas More, Knyght*, EETS, CLXXX (London, Oxford University Press, 1930), 206–8 and 231–2; see also *LP*, VII, 1383.

[47] Colin Clair, *A History of Printing in Britain* (Oxford, Oxford University Press, 1966), 16. There is a printed list of all reported instances from 1476 through 1533, in *STC*, 14077 *c.* 1–*c.* 154.

[48] Clair, *History*, 2–34; PRO, SP 1/229, fol. 17, a printed slip of indulgence, with the receipts in hand on the dorse. Lunt, *Studies*, II, 702, questions whether the power to issue a mandate entailed the power to give receipts.

[49] Heal, *Of Prelates and Princes*, chs. 2–4, 8 and 11; esp. see 199 and 309.

[50] Gina Alexander, 'Victim or spendthrift? The Bishop of London and his income in the sixteenth century,' in Ives, *Wealth and Power*, 128–45.

[51] London Guildhall Library, MS Registrum Bonner 9531/I, fol. 47*v*.; generally for Bonner's career in Mary's reign, see Merill F. Scherr, 'Bishop Edmund Bonner: a bibliographical essay,' *The University of Newcastle (Australia) Historical Journal*, III (1975), 3–10.

[52] Albert F. Pollard, *The Reign of Henry VII from Contemporary Documents* (3 vols., London, Longmans, 1913–14), II, 44–7; J. B. Sheppard (ed.), *Christ Church Letters*, Camden Society, new series, XIX (London, 1877), 62; James Gairdner (ed.), *Letters and Papers . . . Richard III and Henry VII*, Rolls Series, XXIV (2 vols., London, HMSO, 1861–3), II, 372; *LP*, IV, i, 214, 417, appendix no. 37; *LP*, III, 2483; also *LP*, IV, i, 1200, 1284, 1305–6, 1311 and 1321: examples of forced loans, benevolences and the 1525 Amicable Grant. For

the press for proclamations and resorted early on to printing legal papers, statutes, manuals for local administrators, and guides to the ways of such central organs as the Exchequer.[53] Yet there was no show of interest in printing for routine administration. Wolsey was exceptional among early Tudor ministers in grasping the full potential of the new technology, but the surviving evidence does not show him able to translate his practice from episcopal to royal administration.[54] When Cranmer controlled the Faculty Office he required his registrar William Potkyn to send a collation to fill a benefice, stipulating that the device 'have a window expedient to set what name I will therein.'[55] Dr Chambers found no evidence that this became a general practice. On the contrary, the transfer of the dispensing functions from papal officials to royal agents did nothing to improve inefficiency and long delays despite direct intervention by Cromwell.[56]

Cromwell was no stranger to printed forms, even in the 1520s before his rise to power. Among English foundations enjoying the benefits of confessional letters and briefs of confraternity, none was more privileged or popular than the Gild of St Mary the Virgin in St Botolph's in the Lincolnshire town of Boston. Chaucer and early Tudor critics had condemned Pardoners who came hot from Rome with wallets 'bret full' of letters.[57] Cromwell nonetheless helped the Boston men win a renewal

allegedly forged obligations: *LP*, IV, i, 59, and iii, 6798; see the discussion in Gerald L. Harriss, 'Aids, loans and benevolences,' *Historical Journal*, VI (1963), 1–19.

53 *STC*, nos. 7706, 7766, 7767, 7726, 7696, 865, 7687, 10112, 10326, 14862, 16700, printed between 1505 and 1547.

54 Westminster Abbey Muniments, MS WAM, 12788, a broadside printed by Richard Pynson stating Wolsey's intention to make a legatine visitation in 1525. It is a true form, with a window for the name of the mandated institution and dated 30 May 1525. *STC* records no other blank certificates. As early as 1512 Wolsey issued the printed form of an *inspeximus* absolving Louis XII's French subjects from allegiance: *STC* 25947.7.

55 See Rosemary O'Day, 'The role of the registrar in diocesan administration,' in O'Day and Heal, *Continuity and Change*, 77–94. Potkyn began his career under Morton in 1495 and there is a steady record of his work through the 1530s: Claude Jenkins, 'Cardinal Morton's register,' in *Tudor Studies Presented . . . to Albert Frederick Pollard*, ed. by Robert W. Seton-Watson (London, Longmans, Green & Co., 1924), 27–9; see also *LP*, VI, 311, 881, 1315, 1341 and 737 (7); David S. Chambers, *Faculty Office Register, 1534–1549* (Oxford, The Clarendon Press, 1966), 92 and 152. BL, MS Harleian 6148, fol. 26*v*. is the blank collation.

56 Chambers, *Faculty Office Register*, xiv–lxvi, esp. xxii, xxv, xxxvii–xliv, for Cromwell, and li–lv, for the delays.

57 On the benefits of this gild between 1401 and the renewals and enlargements of 1505–6, 1518 and 1525–6, see Lunt, *Studies*, II, 495–8; also, *Calendar of . . . Papal Letters*, V (1396–1404), 391, and *ibid.*, X (1447–55), 86, 235 (London, HMSO, 1904 and 1915); Francis A. Gasquet, *Henry VIII and the English Monasteries* (2 vols., London, John Hodges, 1902), I, 82; and my notes 60–62 below. The charges were 13s. 4d. for admission and 8d. annual dues; the privileges could be attached to portable altars for an additional 6s. 8d. For letters and notices of payment, see PRO, C 47/16 pt 6, no. 18 and Bodleian Library, MS Arch. A. b. 8, no. 29; Lunt called the gild's privileges 'the most elaborate set of indulgences, indults and dispensations administered in England.'

and enlargement of their privileges from Pope Julius II,[58] provoking Gasquet to charge that Cromwell's prosperity in London after 1520 owed much to the sale of forged indulgences.[59] Cromwell had certainly negotiated a further enlargement of gild privileges in 1517 and 1518.[60] And in 1523 Cromwell arranged with Pynson to print an edition of 4000 confessional letters and a like number of blanks for admission to the gild.[61] Thereafter he acted for the gild and its officials on many occasions.[62]

What is remarkable about Cromwell's relations with the Gild of St Mary and its famous Boston Pardons is not any sacrilege but the evidence yielded about his early knowledge of printed forms and their use in large-scale enterprises. More remarkable perhaps is his reluctance or refusal to transfer this experience into his work for the Crown. I have already cited the evidence from the Faculty Office. Later, Cromwell may have positively inhibited the routine printing of a form or 'Declaration' designed by Bishop Longland to ease the burden of complying with royal orders in his vast diocese in 1535.[63] Then, in 1538, when Longland made his printed form of receipt for clerical taxes, at the high-point of Cromwell's power, it remained a mere curiosity, an isolated example with an obvious context; but it ushered no bold step in the Tudor Revolution.[64]

58 Foxe, *Acts and Monuments*, II, 419–34, sets the visit in 1510. I am preparing for publication a paper entitled 'Thomas Cromwell and the Boston pardons,' which includes a chronology of Cromwell's Italian visits.

59 Gasquet, *Henry VIII and the English Monasteries*, I, 381–2; also BL, MS Sloane 2495, fol. 24.

60 These are set forth in Leo X's register: Vatican Library, MS Reg. Vat. 1194, fols. 14*v*.–15*v*. and 1197, fols. 18–19. Cromwell went to Rome twice in 1517–18 on the business of the gild with Dr Nicholas Bradbridge, Chancellor of Lincoln: BL, MS Egerton 2886, fols. 22, 26*v*.–27, 42, 48*v*.–49, 79 and 180–181*v*.

61 *LP*, III, ii, 3015.

62 Lambeth Palace Library, MS Lambeth 181, fol. 1; on many occasions: *LP*, III, ii, 2411, 1324; IV, ii, 2760, 5080, 5437 and 5460; V, 1285 (vi), 554 and 1122(6); VIII, 259; IX, 585; XI, 625 and 658; PRO, E 315/232, fols. 8 and 12, and E 101/631, fol. 35.

63 When the bishops were ordered to proclaim the king's new title and style in 1534 and 1535 and to make declaration and admonition to the clergy, Longland complained that 'all the clerks I have are not able to write them in long process of time.' He therefore printed 2000 copies of a *Declaration* and sent one up to Cromwell, with an inquiry asking permission to circulate them ('if it please you to have it sent in this form?'): BL, MS Cleopatra E VI, fol. 260 (25 June 1535). Elton takes this letter as evidence of the great care Cromwell took to get the job right, speculating that Longland's form might have been a variation of draft articles by Cromwell now in PRO, SP 6/5 fols. 165–72: *Policy and Police*, 223–31. What needs more comment is the fact that no copy of Longland's form survives and that there is no evidence of Cromwell's affirmative reply. Longland was suspect in matters of religion.

64 Bodleian Library, MS Arch. A. b. 8, fol. 36; see p. 13, note 72 below.

II

That remained for Bishop Bonner to do, when he issued the receipts now bound into the large folio volumes of SP 1 in the Public Record Office. The Calendar[65] gives them no consistent notice and makes no connection among them despite the fact that their common recipient was William Latymer,[66] Master of the College of Corpus Christi within the City parish of St Laurence Pountney.[67]

Random survival of the set is improbable and cannot explain their location. Their current PRO class is a notoriously artificial one. Hence further search seemed necessary, assuming the receipts survived because of deliberate action, perhaps as evidence in some lawsuit. That search proved fruitful in the miscellaneous bundles of the King's Remembrancer in the Exchequer, producing four more Latymer receipts. Three were printed;[68] the fourth, significantly, was in manuscript.[69] Other PRO classes and various episcopal archives produced no new examples,[70] but the *Short-Title Catalogue* yielded the one printed receipt given by Bishop Longland in 1538.[71]

The discovery of this unique Longland form in a precedent-book has somewhat clarified matters.[72] There was a link between the two episcopal experiments and the familiar application of printing for papal administration in England. The forms testified to the immediate influence on administrative practice of the Henrician acts abrogating Roman authority in

[65] *LP*, XVII, 73; XVIII, i, 101; XIX, i, 82; XX, i, 2.

[66] This Latymer is not to be confused with the much older Oxford tutor and classical scholar (1460–1545) listed in *DNB*, XXXII, 181. The younger man was born in 1498 and died in 1583. See John and J. A. Venn, *Alumni Cantabrigienses* (4 vols., Cambridge, CUP, 1922–7), III, 50, and Charles H. and T. Cooper, *Athenae Cantabrigienses* (2 vols., Cambridge, CUP, 1858–61), I, 481, and the wills in PRO, PROB 11/30/38 and 11/66/28. For some of the younger Latymer's later doings, see Mortimer Levine's essay, below, 121–2.

[67] H. B. Wilson, *A History of the Parish of St Laurence Pountney* (London, Rivington Bros., 1831).

[68] PRO, E 135/8/43, nos. 2–4. [69] *Ibid.*, no. 1.

[70] PRO, C 33, 47, 78, 89, 147, 256, 260, 262, 264, 269 and 270; PRO, DEL 1–11; PRO, E 36, 179, 334, 336 and 359; PRO, REQ 2; and PRO, LR 2. London Guildhall Library, MSS 10123, 10124, 3907/1, 9235/1, 2968/1, 1239/3, 4871, 3907, 5159–67, 18318, and the registers 9531/11 (Stokesley) and 9531/12, pts 1 & 2 (Bonner). Mr Yeo produced MSS deposited by the St Paul's Dean and Chapter, not yet assigned numbers: W.D. 26, Receivers Accounts Box B/91 and 94, and the registers of Deans Nowell and Sampson. Greater London Record Office: MSS DL/C 3–5, 206–7, 330–1, 357 and 607; MSS LPL, 292, 711 and 2007, and Cartae Miscellaneae I/55–65 and 67–83; II/15–20, V/10, VI/103, and VIII/8–14.

[71] *STC*, no. 16794.

[72] Originally bound in Bodleian Library, MS Fol. Theta 657 (3), removed by Mr D. M. Rose and placed in the Conservancy volume containing Tudor printed forms, Arch. A. b. 8; the receipt is fol. 36.

England and transferring to the Crown many aspects of that authority. Moreover the enlarged series of eight forms seemed to verify the assumption made about their survival. The forms had at one time been kept together in E 135, and each one had been marked there in the same hand before removal of some to be bound in SP 1.[73]

Each point made here requires some enlargement.

Dr Heal has rightly stressed that the Henrician revolution extended clerical liability for taxes and greatly augmented the responsibility of the bishops as agents in collecting taxes for the Crown. After 1534 bishops became chief agents for gathering annates as well as first-fruits and tenths, replacing papal tax-collectors. These burdens added to episcopal handling of special levies on the clergy and of clerical subsidies.[74] The new work proved onerous, and bishops had no immunity from the consequences of careless or unlawful actions by their deputy-collectors or other officers.[75] Reliance on trusted members of the episcopal *familia* often produced ineptness and sometimes a betrayal of trust. More than one bishop took on heavy debts as a result.[76] Bonner himself did not escape this common Reformation legacy.[77]

Nonetheless, Bonner had shown zeal in shaping a reliable system for levying taxes on the king's behalf. This we know from the orders he gave on 27 October 1543, in connection with a special levy to defend Christendom against the Turk. His mandates to deans in his diocese instructed them in detail about how to proceed. Churchwardens were to take the tax from their parish priests and to pay the sum to their sheriffs for transfer to the Cofferer of the Household. Deans should assist by assembling wardens and priests at central points. To assure ease and uniformity of collec-

[73] With regnal date in the upper left of the printed side. The hand is not the one marking the placement of the removed items in *LP* (Sp 1).

[74] Felicity Heal, 'Clerical tax collection under the Tudors,' in O'Day and Heal, *Continuity and Change*, 99–103; and Heal, *Of Prelates and Princes*, 89–90, 109, 133–4, 147–9, 156–60, 196–8, 231–6, 250–4 and 280.

[75] Heal, 'Clerical tax collection,' 103–5; J. J. Scarisbrick, 'Clerical taxation in England, 1485–1547,' *Journal of Ecclesiastical History*, XI (1960), 41–54.

[76] Parliamentary statute 7 Ed. VI, c. 4 made sub-collectors responsible for their own arrears: *SR*, IV, pt i, 167–8. For irregularities and the debts of bishops, see PRO, E 347/11/5, 336/27 and SP 11/1/2; also, Lambeth Palace Library, MS CM I/83; and BL, MS Add. Rolls 1248.

[77] Bonner was behind in his personal obligations: PRO, E 334/4/8 and 7/86; E 337/2/45 and SC 6/194/3. When his deputy-collector Alexander Chibborne died without clearing his accounts, over £400 remained due for clerical tenths and other London taxes. The account was annotated with the query: was the bishop to pay or should Chibborne's estate? (PRO, SP 10/16, fol. 32). Bonner fought a long battle for exoneration: PRO, SP 10/16, fols. 91–5; PRO, SP 12/2, fol. 391 and the judgment in Bonner's favor in E 337/3/43 (3 Elizabeth I). For other evidence of Bonner's problems see E 179/43/275, fol. 1; E 336/27/1, fol. 5 and 27/2, fols. 19*v*., 20 and 32; E 318/1685, m.2; E 315/66, fol. 33; and SP 1/223, fol. 1. Bonner opposed the crown's tax on first-fruits: *LP*, XXI, ii, 70.

tion the wardens should have acquittance with receipts 'preparid aftre such a forme as we send owte to you herewith and beforehand.' Bonner attached lists of all obligated churches and chapels in each deanery, 'none lefte owte so as remaynith onelie the somes to be wrytten yn as it amountith, not nombre but in lengthe accordying to the forme of the Mynte.'[78] This form Bonner also attached. As collector-general for this levy, Bonner ordered all ecclesiastical commissioners to use the processes mandated for London. Their clerks had sufficient warning to have the forms 'before mayde readie and the names of all your churches and chapelles wrytten, onelie a glasse wyndowe lefte to wryte in the sheriffs or hys officers name, your deputies name, and as well the place and time.' Bonner said this would make for simplicity of routine at the actual points of collection, where there might otherwise be much confusion.[79]

Bonner's rigor stood against the background of a more general Tudor effort to improve all tax levies. Some training in the process had been ordered for collectors and receivers.[80] Henrician statutes required that receipts be made in writing and under seal.[81] But Bonner had issued receipts for clerical rents and subsidies in printed form as early as 1542. In the general levy against the Turks he had no fund against which to make omnibus charges, if he had wanted to resort to the press. And the absence of provincial presses would have made it all but impossible to extend the practice from his London diocese elsewhere.[82]

Bonner's interest in printing was no new thing in 1542. He had long admired good printing. If he was not 'an exceptionally cultured man,'[83] then perhaps his borrowing of Cromwell's Petrarch and Castiglione show this admiration.[84] No surmise was necessary in a second instance. Bonner had bought some engravings of human anatomy. He valued them, he said, even the woman's figure about which he was no expert, because the printing had been done exquisitely.[85] Cromwell recognized this curiosity and uncommon knowledge, when the printing of the Great Bible in Paris

[78] Croke's account is in PRO, E 179/43/275 (i); Bonner's orders are in London Guildhall Library, MS 9531/12, pt I, fols. 46*v*., 47–47*v*.

[79] London Guildhall Library, MS 9531/12, pt I, fol. 47–47*v*.

[80] Roger Schofield, 'Parliamentary lay taxation, 1485–1547' (Cambridge University, Unpublished Ph.D. thesis, 1963), 160–215.

[81] Parliamentary statute 26 Henry VIII, c. 3 (16): *SR*, III, 497, which stipulated that acquittances be accepted in all courts 'as if they were made in the Kynges name under his greate seale.' See also, 32 Henry VIII, c. 23 (5): *SR*, III, 777–8.

[82] Costs of collection were charged locally against the yield: PRO, SP 1/86, fols. 170–81.

[83] Gina Alexander, 'The life and career of Edmund Bonner, Bishop of London to 1549' (University of London, Unpublished Ph.D. thesis, 1960), 54.

[84] PRO, SP 1/57, fol. 80.

[85] PRO, SP 3/2, fol. 39; also, BL, MS Add. 48036, fols. 176 and 189; Lambeth Palace Library, MS Tenant 25.

reached its critical stage. Cromwell had sent Bonner to replace Gardiner in Paris and then asked him to oversee the work of the English printers there. Bonner exceeded his charge. He often took meals in Regnault's shop and spent long hours watching the printers and talking with them.[86] Upon his return, to occupy the London see to which he had been appointed *in absentia*, Bonner had as near neighbors on the North side of Paul's Yard most of the City's printers. Some were his tenants.[87] One who was in Cromwell's trust was probably the bishop's cousin.[88]

When Bonner resorted to the Devil's Art, he had experience and knowledge as well as motive and opportunity. Of course, the press could be a worrisome thing. This he knew at first-hand, from the heretical books and broadsides he had made strong efforts to suppress.[89] It could also be a powerful new force in government in concerns divorced from propaganda and the control of opinion.

This he proved in issuing the Latymer receipts. The first in the series contained the basic printed form of the set: an address to interested parties; a statement of authority to levy and to acquit; citation of the king's title and style; the blank or window in which to set the payee's name, the property taxed, and the amount paid; and a clause to date the levy.[90]

While there may have been some influence from Longland's form, Bonner's was less clumsy in design and more specific in intent. Longland had recited every conceivable liability of a clergyman: tenths, annates, oblations, subsidies, first-fruits, farms, pensions, reserved rents, and to be on the safe side then included an omnibus clause (*et aliorum proficuum*

86 Inner Temple Library, MS Petyt 47, fols. 1–7; Foxe, *Acts and Monuments*, v, 410; *LP*, XIII, ii, 336, 557 and 1085; G. Ribier (ed.), *Lettres et Memoires D'Estat Des Roys . . . 1537–1559* (2 vols., Paris, J. Hotot, 1666), I, 3897–3900.

87 *LP*, XIV, ii, 435 (10); London Guildhall Library, MS Registrum Sampson, fols. 78 and 183.

88 The man called 'Bonnar the printer' in *LP*, XIV, ii, 315, had important partners and did much work for the government: Edward G. Duff, *Westminster and London Printers, 1476–1535* (Cambridge, CUP, 1906), *passim*. The bishop was a bastard of the prominent Savage family and had close connections with other bastard Savages. The evidence on the link is presented in Christopher A. Haigh, 'A mid-Tudor ecclesiastical official,' *Transactions of the Historic Society of Lancashire and Cheshire*, CXXII (1970), 1–24; PRO, SP 12/8, fol. 41 and SP 1/236, fol. 140; also, London Guildhall Library, MS 9531/12, pt 2, fol. 460; Inner Temple Library, MS Petyt 538/47, fol. 3; BL, MSS Cottonian, Vitelius B XXI, fol. 136 and Caligula E IV, fol. 21*v*.; and PRO, C 78/27/17, mm. 19–24*v*. Some nieces and nephews took the bishop's name: Walter H. Frere (ed.), *Registrum Matthei Parker 1559–1575*, Canterbury and York Society, XXXV (Oxford, Oxford University Press, 1928), 46. The printer's daughter Alice married a Savage: Henry R. Plomer (ed.), *Abstracts from the Wills of English Printers and Stationers from 1492 to 1630* (London, 1903), 13–14.

89 London Guildhall Library, MS 9531/12, pt 1, fols. 25–25*v*. and 32–32*v*. and pt 2, fol. 369; DL/C/3 & 4; PRO, C 85/127 and SP 1/237, fol. 38; Foxe, *Acts and Monuments*, v, 443–51; Alexander, 'The life and career of Edmund Bonner,' 374–91.

90 PRO, SP 1/169, fol. 21 (1 February 1542) meets the requirement exactly, using the Chancery style throughout.

tam spiritualium quam temporalium). He had provided a very small blank far down the block of print and had taken over many scribal marks and rubrics from the manuscript tradition of abbreviation. His form had acknowledged process by deputy, however.[91] Bonner's form was retrograde in this, asserting the receipt was given by the bishop's hand; in fact all the known examples were subscribed by deputies. Also, Bonner's deputies misused the early forms, entering subscript notes of receipt for purposes foreign to the printed block.[92]

The examples in the set issued after the first one show rapid movement from experimentation toward perfection of a bureaucratic instrument. The 1543 issue was for a single purpose, gathering reserved rents.[93] A year later Bonner issued receipts for a new subsidy,[94] and these were models of bureaucratic clarity. There were two main clauses or entry sections, each with its own blank space: one for the annual rents and another for the first installment of the subsidy. The flow of information became more direct. In 1545 the receipts for the second installment of the subsidy levied in 1543 went further toward spelling out cleanly each operative word.[95] Later in 1545 the levy of the third installment of the 1543 subsidy produced a new improvement: a third blank space allowed the collector to set in the date of execution.[96] In the earliest versions this had been done by subscript notation.

By 1546 Bonner could issue clear and concise receipts for any appropriate purpose. In April he published one form for the first payment of a new subsidy.[97] Eight months later he had another printed for the collection of clerical tenths.[98] This last form in our series marked the completion of bureaucratic transition from the mental habits of a scribal culture to those of a print culture. It was the first English printed form of which we have knowledge using no scribal abbreviations in the block of print. It bore the date 1 January 1547. It was also the last to be made for many years. Within a month Henry VIII was dead, and within the year Edward VI's first parliament had dissolved the chantries. Their overthrow would have brought the Latymer–Corpus Christi series to an end, but the fall of the chantries cannot by itself explain why Bonner's perfected experiment left no further marks on government practices until a generation had passed. But the forms gave witness to the troubled relationship between Latymer and his bishop, and in that relationship we may find an explanation for the *lacuna*.

[91] Bodeian Library, MS Arch. A. b. 8, fol. 36.
[92] PRO, SP 1/169, fol. 121, 1/183, fol. 59 and 1/197, fol. 1.
[93] PRO, SP 1/175, fol. 121. [94] PRO, SP 1/183, fol. 59. [95] PRO, SP 1/197, fol. 1.
[96] PRO, E 135/8/43, no. 2. [97] *Ibid.*, no. 3. [98] *Ibid.*, no. 4.

William Latymer's early career had no apparent distinction. He attracted Cromwell's attention in 1538, when he was already forty years old, and then began accumulating benefices in and around London. These derived from the rich Mastership once held by Cromwell's client Thomas Starkey.[99] Thereafter the main notice we have of him is the receipts issued in Bonner's name from 1542 to 1547. And to these some suspicion of fraud and forgery adheres.

This suspicion rests chiefly on the single *manuscript* form in our series.[100] It acquits Latymer of the reserved rent on the College for more than £7 and the third installment of the subsidy then due, also a little over £7. The peculiarity about this receipt is that at its foot there are two signatures of execution purporting to be John Croke's, a man who served Bonner as vice-collector on more than one occasion. We have many examples of his autograph.[101] Matching the lower of the two signatures with Croke's genuine autograph tells against it. Moreover, the signature entered immediately above the dubious one is genuine, put there as if to show up the forgery below. A further piece of evidence supporting a suspicion of fraud and forgery is the printed form of receipt issued for the same obligations. The upper blank was filled in by Croke, acknowledging payment of the reserved rent. But the lower blank was marked with this notation for the subsidy: '*de Collegio nihill quia promisit solvere ante festam natalis*.'[102] The manuscript version bears the date of receipt 8 January 1546, while Croke dated the printed form 27 July 1545.

That sequence might seem to allow argument for the genuineness of the manuscript form. Because of the financial pressures of war in 1545 the government had advanced the date for the payment of the subsidy install-

99 The College had rich endowments, including London rents and manors, advowsons in five churches outside London, the City parishes of Little All Hallows and St Mary Abchurch as well as the Rectory of St Laurence Pountney appropriated to the College. The Master had sole control of the College seal. Latymer filled the London churches himself under license to hold incompatible benefices and also got Speldhurst in Kent: London Guildhall Library, MSS 9531/11, fol. 39, 9531/12, pt 2, fols. 318, 451*v*. and 465*v*.; Kent Archives Office, MS DRc/R/7, fols. 181*v*. and 193; BL, MS Lansdowne 444, fol. 3; and *LP*, XII, ii, 35.

100 PRO, E 135/8/43, no. 1.

101 Examples: PRO, E 179/43/275 (i); E 101/225/16, m. 10; SP 1/197, fol. 1; and E 135/8/43, nos. 2–4. Bonner's collectors were officials in his diocese: Croke (commissary and later chancellor), Johnson (registrar), Smith (notary) and Staunton (Receiver); see, London Guildhall Library, MS 9531/12, pt 1, fols. 114–58 and 221–42.

102 Latymer had not paid the Benevolence on time either; see PRO, E 135/8/43, no. 2 and E 179/43/275 (i). Bonner had a dispute over payment with the rector of St Dunstan's: E 179/43/275, fol. 1*v*. But Croke had put a unique mark against Latymer's name in the Benevolence Roll. For cases of forged obligations and also suits for exoneration see *LP*, IV, iii, 6798 and E 159/326 as well as E 359/42 and 44.

ment.[103] Latymer was under pressure not only of taxes but of some unusual expenses in his churches, making it plausible that he sought deferral on the subsidy until the time appointed in the statute but no claim to be excused from it.[104] It would then be possible to argue that he made the late payment to a collector whose stock of forms had been exhausted. But the dual signatures argue against that possibility.

So, too, does evidence not directly connected to the forms. Bonner had problems preventing illicit dealing in London chantry goods during the making of the surveys in 1546 and 1548.[105] Latymer may well have trafficked in such goods. He certainly failed to provide required accounts, and the chantry certificates and inventories showed losses. Latymer was also derelict in other ways, dealing in lead off the College roof as well as in its lands, both as a middleman and for his own gain. The historian of his collegiate benefice condemned the Master for sacrilege.[106]

There is a third piece of evidence. When the Delegates tried Bonner in 1549 on charges that led to his deprivation, the witnesses who made the main complaints were said to have been John Hooper and Hugh Latimer.[107] They alleged that the bishop did not properly maintain the

[103] Parliamentary statute 37 Henry VIII, *c.* 25 set the date of collection at 6 February 1546; for the pressures behind advancing the date see Schofield, 'Parliamentary lay taxation,' 312; also, Lincoln Archives Office, MS L 1.1/1, no. 2, an exhortation by Lincoln commissioners on the emergency in royal finances.

[104] On the great pressures from royal taxation and the rise in arrears after 1541 see Schofield, 'Parliamentary lay taxation,' 138–46, 252–5 and 341. Latymer's heavy expenses included half the costs of repairing Little All Hallows after a serious fire and also very extensive work on the fabric of the magnificient but decaying College: PRO, E 117/4/44 and London Guildhall Library, MS 3907/1, fols. 8–16*v*.

[105] For a good discussion see, C. J. Kitching (ed.), *London and Middlesex Chantry Certificates 1548*, London Record Society, XVI (London, 1980), Introduction. Churchwardens' accounts reflect the problem: London Guildhall Library, MSS 9235/1, 2968/1 and 1239/3. Bonner's own concerns are clear from *ibid.*, 9531/12m fol. 269.

[106] In Latymer's London churches there were great losses of jewels, books and vestments, plate and other objects. Wardens at St Mary Abchurch were unable to trace the disposition of money because accounts had not been kept. At St Laurence, Latymer had taken money for repair of bells without having the work done; his London churches had 838 communicants but he failed to provide a curate in two of them; he failed to make inventories on the bishop's command; and, he did not provide 30 sacks of coal for the poor as required by College charter. There is also much evidence of his land deals; see, PRO, E 117/4/13, 16 and 44; E 301/34, mm. 13d–16; E 301/88; and, LR 2/241, fols. 23–4 (chantry returns); also E 101/75/21, and London Guildhall Library, MS W.D. 26, fols. 3–5. For the land transactions, see BL, MS Lansdowne 1216; also the transcripts in Wilson, *History of St Laurence Pountney*, 60–71 and 217–18.

[107] Wilbur K. Jordan, *Edward VI* (2 vols., Cambridge, Mass., Belknap Press, 1968–70), I, 217, follows the so-called scholarly edition (1841) by Cattley and Townshend, who had accepted eighteenth century changes by abridgers who 'improved' on Foxe, usually erroneously. All editions from the first in 1563 through the fourth in 1641 correctly identified Latymer, but in subsequent editions the mistake appears; see *Acts and Monuments*, V, 747, where a section on Bonner is headed 'The denunciation of John Hooper and Hugh Latimer, against Bonner.'

king's authority in his minority and that he did maintain popish beliefs.[108] That left a story for another telling, but here I must correct the accepted version on some key points. It was in fact William Latymer, not the more famous martyr, who signed the complaint against Bonner.[109] This he did only after being solicited by Mr Secretary Smith, Bonner's arch-enemy in the Council.[110] Bonner challenged Latymer's appearance against him on this and other grounds. According to the bishop, Latymer was a notorious heretic, a Sacramentarian holding conventicles and also preaching heresy openly in London and its suburbs. Bonner spoke contemptuously of Latymer, referring to him also as 'that merchant,' heaping scorn on him in a manner resonant of the other troubles we have traced.

The bishop was outraged to be held on charges brought by a man he perhaps thought to be a forger, certainly a dealer in church lands and goods, and a heretic to boot.[111] But he was deprived, and after being restored by Queen Mary he took revenge on Latymer to the extent he could.[112] He also began again to use the printing press to help manage his diocese, but we are ignorant as to whether he resorted to it for routine business such as tax collections.[113]

III

The evidence brought together here ties together two theses about revolution in the sixteenth century. One we associate with Professor Elton's work. The second has been made popular in the phrase 'Gutenberg's Galaxy.' The first thesis set forth a revolution in the state that reached out to embrace the revolution in belief created by the Reformation. The

108 Foxe, *Acts and Monuments* (London, J. Daye, 1563), 697b–726b (BL, MS C 37 h.2) placed the trial in the Court of Delegates (710, col. a).

109 The process in Delegates does not survive in its archives (PRO, DEL 1–11); see the analysis of this archive in G. I. O. Duncan, *The High Court of Delegates* (Cambridge, CUP, 1971), 209–31. Bonner's officers had access to the trial record and exhibits and copied them into his Register: London Guildhall Library, MS 9531/12, pt 1, fols. 219*v*.–242*v*.; for the complaint see, fols. 222*v*.–223.

110 *Ibid.*, MS 9531/12, pt 1, fols. 226*v*.–228, 232–233*v*., esp. fol. 233*v*. For Smith's arrogance and bias see, Mary Dewar, *Sir Thomas Smith* (London, Athlone Press, 1964), 43–4.

111 For Bonner's comments and Latymer's reply see London Guildhall Library, MS 9531/12, pt 1, fols. 223*v*.–225, 228*v*.–229, 232*v*. and 240 *v*. ('thys marchaunte Latymer'). Crome thought Latymer unfit to preach (fol. 102*v*.), but his name does not appear among the many in various lists of suspected heretics: fols. 25, 25*v*. and 51; PRO, C 85/127, nos. 4, 12, 16–21, 24–6, 28 and 30; or, PRO, DL/C/614. In 1541 Latymer had a Sacramentarian, George Parker, as curate in Little All Hallows: PRO, SP 1/237, fol. 78.

112 The sentence of deprivation is in London Guildhall Library, MS 9531/12, pt 1, fol. 240. The ousting of Latymer from London benefices appears in fols. 451 and 465. Grindal restored Latymer (*ibid.*, MS 9531/13, fol. 11); he became a favorite of Queen Elizabeth who promoted him Dean of Peterborough.

113 *STC*, 1289, 3281–5 and 10249; also BL, MS Lansdowne 116, no. 32.

second thesis set forth in Professor Eisenstein's massive study argues that the press was itself the most radical force for change in the early modern era.[114]

I have tried to connect these two theses by asking why, in a revolutionary era, the use of the press to transform methods of government was so slow to develop after it had been put into the tool kit. Longland had been moved mainly by the sheer size and geographical diversity of his diocese. Bonner perhaps responded to the density of settlement in and around London. Each followed a long line of ecclesiastics who had pioneered in the development of the law courts, chancery and fiscal administration. Within a generation of Bonner's experiment a French writer took for granted the importance of printing for the effectiveness of government.[115] And in England blank forms were in use for a wide variety of purposes by governments at every level: both to license puritans to preach and to permit women to keep the London ale-houses that those preachers condemned; to issue most court writs; to grant the right to burial at variance with the law. James I's government printed forms to collect the farms of borough and reserved rents.[116] And monopolists wrangled over the profits to be made in government job-printing.[117]

The old system of inscribed writs, orders and receipts in the history of administration was the equivalent of the manuscript book in the history of ideas. When we find printed forms first expediting routine tasks, it is attractive to argue that this happened for the same reasons that printed books replaced literary manuscripts as increasing literacy put pressure on scribal capacity. We adduce the saving of human labor, as Bishop Longland did, supposing that the *scriptoria* produced neither as fast nor as accurate as the press. In the context of printed forms, the Tudor Revolution might impel one to find the tendency toward large-scale data collection by government giving the *ars artificialiter scribendi* many advantages over the *ars scribendi*. It has been argued that printed paper then seemed less perishable than vellum or parchment, which could be erased for re-use or

114 Elizabeth L. Eisenstein, *The Printing Press as an Agent of Change: Communications and Cultural Transformations in Early Modern Europe* (2 vols., Cambridge, CUP, 1979).

115 Louis Le Roy, *De La Vicissitude ou Variété des Choses en l'Univers* (Paris, 1575), sig. A.2.

116 Southampton Borough Record Office, Chamberlain's Accounts, 1621, fols. 23 and 24; see also J. West, *Symboleography* (London, J. Day, 1606), for London ale-houses and other City licenses; for ecclesiastical practice, see William E. Tate, *The Parish Chest* (Cambridge, CUP, 1960), 67, 153–5 and 202–3.

117 Walter W. Greg, *Companion to Arber* (Oxford: Clarendon Press, 1967), 173, gives details of the patents and also the conflict between the monopolists.

recycled for less honest purposes. In the Tudor age *ars typographia artium omnium conservatrix* became a commonplace.[118]

Yet, some drawbacks in such ahistorical reasoning may explain why Bonner's innovation did not succeed. One great inertial force was the attitude of clerks who saw the press as a threat to their private economies. Henrician laws commended the virtue of receipts by hand and under seal only. Another was also economic: in England parchment was possibly cheaper than paper throughout the sixteenth century. Many early English printers regarded that craft as a by-employment while styling themselves primarily glovers and pouch-makers. Pynson even printed government work on parchment.[119] Also, the spread of the new technology beyond London was a very slow process, inhibited by governmental fears and the fact that no native paper mill existed before 1589. The first English type foundry did not open until 1597. So the materials for printing were largely imported. Foreign printers and machinery came in as well to meet a demand not supplied domestically.[120] Bonner and Cromwell explained the printing of the Great Bible in Paris by saying English technology lagged the French in a woeful way.[121] Moreover, the argument that contemporaries saw in standardization through printing a proof against deception must remain suspect. Expert modern bibliographers still cannot always tell apart printed Tudor broadside from hand copy.[122]

Much remains to be done, therefore, before we integrate the study of the revolution in printing into our study of the Tudor Revolution. What is required now is a wide search to throw light on the press as a tool for bureaucratization. The great utilitarian advantages of printing could be seen in the first document from an English press, Caxton's 1476 In-

[118] The motto is discussed by Elizabeth Eisenstein, 'The advent of printing and the problem of the Renaissance,' *Past and Present*, XLIV (1969), 29. See, *The Printing Press as an Agent of Change*, I, 46–113, for the general argument; also, Paul Saenger, 'Colard Mansion and the evolution of the printed book,' *Library Quarterly*, XLV (1975), 405–18, and C. C. Willard, 'The MSS of Jean Petit's *Justification*,' *Studi Francesi*, XXXVIII (1969), 271–80.

[119] *LP*, II, i, 1465, 1467 and 1469 (Royal Accounts); on relative costs see Clair, *History of Printing*, 3; on scribal interests see H. Lehmann-Haupt, *Peter Schoeffer of Gernsheim and Mainz* (Rochester, L. Hart, 1950), 53–4; and Curt Bühler, *The Fifteenth Century Book: The Scribes, The Printers, The Decorators* (Philadelphia, University of Pennsylvania Press, 1960), 15–17, 23, 33, 44 and 53. For another reading on the survival of scribes, Mariano Fava and Giovanni Bresciano, 'I Librai ed i cartai di Napoli nel Renascimento,' *Archivo Storico per le province Napoletane*, XLIII (1968), 89–104.

[120] Clair, *History of Printing*, 2.

[121] Arthur J. Slavin, 'The Rochepot affair,' *The Sixteenth Century Journal*, X (1979), 9–10.

[122] William Ivins, *Prints and Visual Communications* (Cambridge, Mass., Harvard University Press, 1953), 53; Eisenstein, *Printing as an Agent of Change*, I, 80–0; Lehmann-Haupt, *Peter Schoeffer*, 37–8.

dulgence.[123] A century passed before this technology became widely applied in government. Why this was true we cannot say with certainty, but the circumstances of Cromwell's work habits and the reaction to his regime do not supply an answer. We may hope to gain answers to questions about the force of printing in the Tudor Revolution only by applying to our inquiries the same patient study Professor Elton teaches us to apply in his own studies of how governmental innovations took hold in practice.[124]

[123] See Plate no. 2 in *Printing and the Mind of Man: The Exhibition at Earl's Court and the British Museum* (London, HMSO, 1963), and the discussion in Norman F. Blake, *Caxton and His World* (London, Deutsch, 1969), 79–80 and 232–3.

S. H. Steinberg, *Five Hundred Years of Printing* (Bristol, Pelican Books, 1961), 139, comments that the printing of 18,000 copies of an indulgence in 1498 may be compared with the printing of income tax forms by HMSO.

[124] I wish to thank Dr M. L. Zell, Dr J. Block, Dr E. Riegler, Dr Mary Robertson, Dr C. A. Haigh and Professor Eisenstein for the references they so kindly sent.

How God became an Englishman

JOHN W. McKENNA

Charles V, it was said, prayed to Him in Spanish, though he spoke Italian to women, French to men and German to his horse. Joan of Arc's interrogators shrewdly wondered what language her heavenly voices had employed. The frequency of such stories suggests that the nationality of God was a touchstone of European nationalism from its earliest manifestations at the close of the middle ages. James Joyce knew the signs that the old nationalism was waning when he mused in the person of his *alter ego* Stephen Dedalus:

> God [he thought] was God's name just as his name was Stephen. *Dieu* was the French for God, and that was God's name too; and when anyone prayed to God and said *Dieu* then God knew at once that it was a French person that was praying. But though there were different names for God in all the different languages in the world and God understood what all the people who prayed said in their different languages still God remained always the same God and God's real name was God.[1]

In England none had claimed God's language and God's loyalties more strenuously than the Elizabethan and Stuart Puritans who from John Aylmer to John Milton argued mightily that God was English and England His Elect Nation. It has generally been supposed that these generations of patriotic dissenters inaugurated the durable notion of God and His Englishmen.[2]

The historians of medieval France have steadfastly reinforced this misapprehension by claiming that God, to the end of the middle ages, maintained a decided partiality towards the kingdom of France. From the mid-thirteenth century French royal publicists had developed what Ernst Kantorowicz called a 'political theology' which exploited the twin con-

[1] James Joyce, *A Portrait of the Artist as a Young Man* (corrected edn, New York, Viking Press, 1964), 16.

[2] William Haller, *Foxe's 'Book of Martyrs' and the Elect Nation* (London, Jonathan Cape, 1963); also, John E. Christopher Hill, *God's Englishman: Oliver Cromwell and the English Revolution* (New York, Dial Press, 1970).

cepts of sacred kingship and the special piety of France to hasten the emergence of a unified French state.[3] P. E. Schramm and J. R. Strayer have traced the careers of these late Capetian and Valois publicists who created and sustained a 'religion of monarchy' from the reign of Louis IX onward, utilizing religious symbols and ideas as political propaganda to subordinate local loyalties to the realm.[4] This regal mythology celebrated the Most Christian Kings of France who worked miraculous cures, were anointed with the heaven-sent oil of Clovis and cherished the distinctive insigne of the fleur-de-lys.[5] Such miraculous royal attributes easily generated a corresponding 'religion of nationalism' which emphasized the devotion of the French people and their special status before God and the Church as the new Chosen People, the heirs of Israel. The bull *Rex gloriae,* which Clement V issued in August 1311, marked the emergence of the French king Philip the Fair as a complete sovereign in his own kingdom, but it also confirmed earlier papal pronouncements that the French were 'like the people of Israel . . . a peculiar people chosen by the Lord to carry out the orders of Heaven.'[6] Medieval French publicists had celebrated rulers' pre-eminence in the affairs of the Church, and in the act of consecrating France to God they reserved God for the French.[7]

[3] These ideas have been discussed most recently in Joseph R. Strayer, 'France: The Holy Land, the Chosen People, and the Most Christian King,' in *Action and Conviction in Early Modern Europe*, ed. by Theodore K. Rabb and Jerrold E. Seigel (Princeton, Princeton University Press, 1969), 3–16, repr. in Joseph R. Strayer, *Medieval Statecraft and the Perspectives of History* (Princeton, Princeton University Press, 1971), 300–14. The heavy Dominican contribution to this royal ideology was studied in Hildegard Coester, 'Der Königskult in Frankreich um 1300 im Spiegel von Dominikanerpredigten' (Frankfurt, Unpublished Ph.D. thesis, 1935/6). Professor Strayer thought that this thesis, directed by Kantorowicz, was lost among his papers, but happily it has been rediscovered in the Princeton University Library by Professor Thomas Bisson. I am much indebted to Professor Elizabeth A. R. Brown for the loan of her copy.

[4] Percy E. Schramm, *Der König von Frankreich* (2 vols., Weimar, H. Böhlaus nachf., 1939); Helene Wieruszowski, *Vom Imperium zum nationalen Königtum* (Munich and Berlin, R. Oldenbourg, 1933); Hellmut Kämpf, *Pierre Dubois und die geistigen Grundlagen des französischen Nationalbewusstseins um 1300* (Leipzig and Berlin, B. G. Teubner, 1935).

[5] The fundamental study of these ideas is, of course, Marc Bloch, *Les rois thaumaturges* (Strasbourg, Librarie Istra, 1924), and English trans. as *The Royal Touch: Sacred Monarchy and Scrofula in England and France* (London, Routledge & Kegan Paul, 1973). On the history of the fleur-de-lys see Sandra Hindman and Garielle M. Spiegel, 'The fleur-de-lys frontispieces to Guillaume de Nangis's Chronique Abrégée: political iconography in late fifteenth-century France,' *Viator*, XII (1981), 381–407 and figs. 1–10.

[6] '. . . sicut israeliticus populus . . . [sic regnum Francie] in peculiarem populum electus a Domino in executione mandatorum celestium . . .': Strayer, *Medieval Statecraft*, 313, fn. 51, quoting *Registrum Clementis Papae V* (Rome, 1885–92), no. 7501, and a similar bull of Gregory IX in 1239. On the larger significance of *rex gloriae* see Robert Fawtier, *The Capetian Kings of France* (London, Macmillan, 1960), 95.

[7] This was the distant underpinning for the national sentiment which would unify France in the fifteenth century: Edouard Perroy, *The Hundred Years' War* (London, Eyre & Spottiswoode, 1951), 279–89; Dorothy Kirkland, 'The growth of national sentiment in France

It is less generally recognized, however, that late-medieval English publicists sought to usurp this French status as most favored nation. Edward III, who claimed the French crown itself, intensified a rivalry with the French kings over thc mystical attributes of regality. In so doing he laid the foundation for a distinctively English political theology which could support and underlay both Henrician assertions of autonomous national sovereignty and Elizabethan assurances of Britannic godliness. The scattered traces of this English royal ideology in the fourteenth and fifteenth centuries have often intrigued and sometimes puzzled English political historians and the historians of English literature. Failing to look beyond the Channel for the origins of these ideas, they have attempted to explain this ideology as an indigenous political and literary phenomenon wholly related to the pressures of the Hundred Years' War, the rise of a proto-nationalism, and the emergence of English as a literary language.[8] All of these factors assuredly contributed to the nascent national sentiment which so strikingly infused the politics and the literature of late medieval England. The strains of war, however, had only amplified a continuing English royal campaign, evident since the twelfth century, to match the sacerdotal attributes of the Frankish dynasty. When the publicists of Edward III added to this repertoire with new claims of English national piety, it was the English who became godly as God became an Englishman.[9]

I

The mimetic quality of this English political ideology appeared early and ran deep. The twin national monarchies of England and France, facing each other across the 'narrow sea,' were often at war and always in competition. In a sense their rivalry was familial: within the intertwined dyn-

before the fifteenth century,' *History*, XXIII (1938–9), 12–24; Georges Grosjean, *Le sentiment national dans la Guerre de Cent Ans* (Paris, Bossard, 1928); Bloch, *The Royal Touch*, 140–1.

8 See, e.g., the excellent accounts in V. J. Scattergood, *Politics and Poetry in the Fifteenth Century* (London, Blandford Press, 1971), 35–106, and John Barnie, *War in Medieval English Society: Social Values in the Hundred Years' War, 1337–99* (Ithaca, N.Y., Cornell University Press, 1974).

9 The contemporary lay image of God, however, was sometimes quite bizarre. In his famous devotional tract Henry, duke of Lancaster drew analogies between medieval remedies and spiritual experiences. The most striking of these analogies describes God as the healing broth produced when a capon is steamed in an earthenware pot. Clearly, to this model chivalric intellectual of the fourteenth century, God could be described as chicken soup: Emile J. Arnould (ed.), *Le Livre de Seyntz Medicines . . . of Henry of Lancaster*, Anglo-Norman Text Society, II (Oxford, B. Blackwell, 1940), 194, and trans. by Alec R. Myers (ed.), *English Historical Documents*, vol. IV: *1327–1485* (Oxford, Oxford University Press, 1969), 813.

asties and the intermingled peerage of both realms France was the mother country with claims to seniority in the Latin West and priority of its ancient dynasty over the king–dukes of the English. Through the twelfth and thirteenth centuries the symbols of that rivalry were still dynastic, as the kings of the lion throne attempted to match the sacral and thaumaturgic attributes of the senior dynasty which boasted the lilies of Clovis, the holy oil of Rheims, the wondrous power to cure the king's evil by royal touch, magical banners for peace and war, and that special autonomous sovereignty which recognized no superior under God.[10] The English kings coveted these distinctions and copied them shamelessly, grafting the sacred symbols of French monarchical authority to native Saxon roots. When the French kings of the twelfth century chose Rheims as their royal cathedral and St Denis as their burying place, Henry III confirmed the status of Westminster Abbey as the seat of the English monarchs in life and death.[11] The same monarch, the first native-born English king, named his children after Anglo-Saxon saints, and retranslated Edward the Confessor as a royal patron to rival the ostentatious piety of the Capetians.[12] Most notably, as Marc Bloch demonstrated so fully, the English kings from Henry I rivalled their French counterparts in miraculous curative powers.[13] Even the holy oil of Clovis which was generally supposed to confer unique distinction on the French kings began to have a rival when Edward II unsuccessfully sought papal sanction for an oil delivered by the Virgin to Thomas Becket for the coronation of English kings who would then conquer the Holy Land. When Henry IV and his successors adopted this novel English unction they closed the circle on over a century of imitative mystical kingship.[14]

This competition between the two Western monarchs in the outward

[10] This cluster of royal attributes as it descended to the later Valois kings is described in Malcolm G. A. Vale, *Charles VII* (London, Eyre Methuen, 1974), 194ff. My argument for its English equivalent, which can only be summarized here, will be advanced elsewhere *in extenso*.

[11] On the special place of Westminster Abbey as a royal mausoleum the partisan and now venerable account of Dean Stanley is still valuable: Arthur P. Stanley, *Historical Memorials of Westminster Abbey* (London, John Murray, 1896), 97–144.

[12] The first translation had been on 13 October 1163.

[13] In addition to the royal touch for scrofula, English kings from the thirteenth century (and continuously from the reign of Edward II) blessed coins and the so-called cramp rings for the healing of spasms and epilepsy. Bloch, noting the analogy to ceremonies practiced by French magicians, commented rather harshly that 'in France and in England this commonplace prescription became the perquisite of a special class. In France, it was appropriated by quacks; in England, by the royal line': Bloch, *The Royal Touch*, 102.

[14] Leopold G. Wickham Legg (ed.), *English Coronation Records* (Westminster, Archibald Constable, 1901), 69–76; Percy E. Schramm, *History of the English Coronation* (Oxford, Clarendon Press, 1937), 131ff.; Bloch, *The Royal Touch*, 137–9; John W. McKenna, 'The coronation oil of the Yorkist kings,' *English Historical Review*, LXXXII (1967), 102–4.

signs of sacral kingship distinguishes the fifteenth century dialogue known as the *Debate of the Heralds*. The French herald in that exchange praises the independence of his king from all overlordship whereas, he says, the English king holds from the See of Rome. Moreover, the Frenchman boasts that his king can show the fleur-de-lys, the sainte ampoulle, and the oriflamme or sacred war banner as evidence of France's pre-eminence.[15] This French treatise, a relic of the dispute at Constance, was considered sufficiently important for publication as late as 1517 and was answered by the Englishman John Coke in 1550.[16] Well into the Tudor age the rivalry between England and France for primacy in sacerdotal sovereignty was a lively topic of debate.

It was against this backdrop of the century-old competition for the mystical attributes of personal monarchy that Edward III laid claim in 1337 to the French throne itself. Presenting himself as the last legitimate heir of the Capetians, Edward henceforth styled himself king of England and France, adopting new royal arms which quartered the English lions with the sacred lilies of France to symbolize that dynastic claim. This heraldic pilfering was a conclusive step in the long struggle by which English kings asserted autonomous territorial sovereignty in Aquitaine and transformed a feudal conflict into dynastic war. The continuing dispute over those lilies was fundamental to the medieval understanding of the kingship itself.[17] Somewhat tongue-in-cheek May McKisack even suggested that, in one sense, Edward and Philip were merely two gentlemen quarreling over the right to bear the same arms, with the Hundred Years' War merely a protracted trial by combat in the court of world chivalry.[18] In asserting title to the French Crown Edward III laid claim as well to that whole package of mystical powers and attributes with which the French monarchy had been embellished. English publicists, however, continued to create a parallel ideology drawn largely from the French tradition. The old French royal myth had been created to unify the

[15] *Le débat des héraults d'armes et d'Angleterre* (Paris, Firmin Didot et Cie., 1877), and trans. by Henry Pyne (ed.), *England and France in the Fifteenth Century* (London, Longmans, Green, 1870). Internal evidence appears to date the tract to around mid-century.

[16] 'The Debate betwene the Heraldes of Englande and Fraunce, compyled by Iohn Coke, Clarke of the Kynges recognysaunce, or vulgerly called Clarke of the Statutes of the Staple at Westmynster, and fynyshed the yere of our Lorde 1550,' *STC* 5530 (London, Rycharde Wyer, 1550).

[17] The background to the dynastic claim is summarized in John Le Patourel, 'The origins of the war,' in *The Hundred Years' War*, ed. by Kenneth Fowler (London, Macmillan, 1971), 28–50. The changes in Edward's title, arms, great seal and manner of dating his regnal years were initiated in the *parlement* held at Ghent in February 1440: Perroy, *The Hundred Years' War*, 105.

[18] May McKisack, *The Fourteenth Century, 1307–1399* (Oxford, Oxford University Press, 1959), 127ff.

kingdom and rival the Empire; its English counterpart was conceived and sustained to rival the French. Just as the French 'religion of nationalism' grew from a cult of monarchy, so the new English reputation for divine sanction sprang from wholly dynastic pretensions grounded on the tradition of exalting royalty but soon infused with the abundant elements of patriotism and xenophobia. A purloined ideology of mystical kingship underlies the first great age of vernacular English political and literary patriotism and the new language of nascent English nationalism.

This imitative tradition goes far to explain that curious development by which the formidable and somewhat vicious Englishmen of the fourteenth century began to emphasize their special devotion to peace in the very midst of an aggressive expansion on the Continent, and the imaginative pretense that the English were fighting a war to end war, so that they could go on to lead the long-delayed crusade. The Plantagenet royal mystique gave richly symbolic force to the myth of English military invincibility which arose following the great victories at Crécy and Poitiers. During the heyday of the Avignon papacy, as Dr Barnie has pointed out, a popular French joke held that 'the Pope has become French and Jesus has become English.'[19] The chronicler Knighton regarded this as mockery of the seemingly miraculous victories of the English, but it was perhaps also a pointed comment on the splendid new English coin, the gold *noble*, that impressive and ubiquitous advertisement for Edward III's conquests. The face of the *noble* displayed the king standing in a ship, brandishing his sword and displaying the new royal arms, surrounded by the king's new title to both realms. On the reverse a new motto appeared: 'But Jesus, passing through the midst of them, went his way.'[20] The new English coinage, which soon supplanted the *florin* as a premier trading coin, was a formidable reminder of the English pretensions to divine sanc-

[19] Joseph R. Lumby (ed.), *Henry Knighton's Chronicon*, Rolls Series, XCII (2 vols., London, 1889–95), II, 94, quoted in Barnie, *War in Medieval English Society*, 12; see also, William H. Dunham, Jr.'s remarks on this passage in his review of Barnie's volume in *Speculum*, LII (1977), 344–7.

[20] 'Jesus autem transiens per medium illorum ibat': Luke 4:30. For a discussion of the coin's political significance see W. J. W. Potter, 'The gold coinages of Edward III: I. Early and pre-treaty coinages,' *Numismatic Chronicle*, 7th series, III (1963), 110ff. and plates 8–10; see also, George C. Brooke, *English Coins*, 3rd edn, rev. (London, Methuen, 1950), plate XXV, and the discussion in Barnie, *War in Medieval English Society*, 113, fn. 51. Doubts expressed by some scholars as to whether the inscription was intended to have political significance might be resolved by considering that the so-called 'Treaty period' *nobles* struck between 1380 and 1389 altered the Latin motto as well as the royal title. In accordance with the terms agreed upon at Brétigny, coins of this period subtracted the kingship of France from Edward's title, and substituted the inscription 'Domine ne in furore tuo arguas me' [Psalms 6:1]. Significantly, the treaty *nobles* did not drop the French royal arms from the English arms, though that might seem a logical corollary to the other alterations. For Edward III's new title of 'King of the Sea' see *RP*, II, 311.

tion. Even so, until the end of Edward III's long reign the development of an English royal mystique went unmatched by that corresponding sanctification of the land and people which was so intrinsic to the idea of France as a Holy Land and the French as the Chosen People. English chroniclers and poets could maintain that God favored their cause, blessed their enterprises and even led their armies to victory, but this providential message was still only an extension of St Paul's words to the Romans: 'If God be for us, who can be against us?'[21]

II

The tone of English propaganda had altered, however, when the aged Edward III's parliament met in the fiftieth year of his reign and the last year of his life. The parliament of 1377, presided over by the king's young heir and grandson Richard, became a public forum for the consolidation of John of Gaunt's power and an elaborate arena for the glorification of monarchy. The chancellor's opening address laid out a full English equivalent to the French doctrines of royal authority. Richard, the chancellor said, was sent to preside over them just as God had sent His beloved Son into the world; the king was God's vicar or legate over them on earth, and his grandson Richard was the long-awaited heir prefigured by Simeon in the Temple. England was the new Israel:

> And thus you have that which Scripture tells us, '*Pacem super Israel*,' peace over Israel, because Israel is understood to be the heritage of God as is England. For I truly think that God would never have honored this land in the same way as He did Israel through great victories over their enemies, if it were not that He had chosen it as His heritage.[22]

This apotheosis of monarchical glorification combined the twin roots of England's new political doctrine: the Prince as a Christ-type, and his loyal followers as the new Chosen People. Some scholars have regarded this passage as an anomalous and even extreme anticipation of John Milton's famous statement that God reveals His wishes first to His Englishmen.[23] In a more immediate sense, however, it was the necessary

[21] On the national psychology of these years see McKisack, *The Fourteenth Century*, 150–1.

[22] *RP*, II, 362: 'Et issint vous avez ce que l'Escripture dist, "Pacem super Israel," paix sur Israel, pur quel Israel est a entendu l'eritage de Dieu, q'est Engl[eterre]. Qar je pense vraiement, que Dieux ne voussist unques avoir honurez ceste Terre par manere come il fist Israel, par grantes Victories de lour Enemys, s'il ne fust q'il l'ad choise pur son heritage': Barnie, *War in Medieval English Society*, 102–3.

[23] *Ibid.*, 103: '. . . God is decreeing to begin some new and great period in his Church, ev'n to the reforming of Reformation itself: what does he then but reveal Himself to his servants, and as his manner is, first to his English-men'; John Milton, 'Areopagitica,' ed. by Ernest

last step in that long process by which the English usurped the unique mystical attributes of the French monarchy and people, claimed the French throne itself, and repatriated God. Thereafter the persuasive analogy between England and Israel became the favored theme for a whole host of arguments designed to emphasize the new English primacy in the West. Thomas Brinton, the bishop of Rochester in the 1370s and 1380s, suggested in one sermon that because of their sins 'God who was accustomed to being English will abandon us.'[24] The Cambridge theologians of 1393 attacked the pacifist views of the Lollard William Swynderby by pointing out that 'God Himself has vindicated just wars of this kind, and, indeed, often ordered His chosen people to fight, as is made plain by a reading of almost the whole of the Old Testament.'[25] Given this heavenly partiality for the English cause, the Lollard refusal to fight for the king's 'heritage' in France became a notable heresy, singled out in the heresy trials at Norwich and elsewhere.[26] Meanwhile the concept of the elect nation had presumably been absorbed into the stock rhetoric of parliamentary sermons. The fortunate survival of Bishop Russell's several drafts for his sermon to the intended parliament of Edward V employ the same analogy: England is there compared with Israel, though the king had to be content with mirroring Moses and Aaron.[27] Throughout the fifteenth century the crucial equations of the royal publicists survived political chaos: for Lancaster, for York and for Henry Tudor it was equally true that England was the new Holy Land and the

Sirluck, in Don M. Wolfe (ed.), *Complete Prose Works of John Milton* (7 vols., New Haven, Yale University Press, 1953–66), II, 553. See also the review by William H. Dunham, Jr, *Speculum*, LII (1977), 344–7.

[24] Sister Mary A. Devlin (ed.), *The Sermons of Thomas Brinton, Bishop of Rochester (1373–1389)*, Camden Society, 3rd series, LXXXV–LXXXVI (2 vols., London, 1954), I, 47. I am grateful to Brother Patrick Horner of Manhattan College for calling this passage to my attention.

[25] Quoted from William W. Capes (ed.), *The Register of John Trefnant, Bishop of Hereford, (A.D. 1389–1404)*, Canterbury and York Society, XX (London, 1916), 377–8, by Christopher T. Allmand (ed.), *Society at War: the Experience of England and France during the Hundred Years' War* (Edinburgh, Oliver & Boyd, 1973), 20–1.

[26] The Lollards, resisting the current notions of a just war, were really rejecting the royal propaganda; some of the later Lollards and their persecutors framed their differences in the terms used by Lancastrian publicists to promote the war. Lollards in the Diocese of Norwich, for example, were often accused of refusing to fight [even] 'for heritage', and it was alleged against the parchment-maker John Godesell that he believed 'quod nullo modo licitum est pugnare pro regno vel pro iure hereditario . . .': N. P. Turner (ed.), *Heresy Trials in the Diocese of Norwich, 1428–31*, Camden Society, 4th series (London, 1977), 160ff. I read 'heritage' here as meaning the king's asserted right to France, despite a gentle admonition from Dr Margaret Buxton that the term may not sustain that interpretation.

[27] Stanley B. Chrimes, *English Constitutional Ideas in the Fifteenth Century* (Cambridge, CUP, 1936), 172–3.

English king was a simulacrum, however feeble, of his heavenly counterpart.

The parliamentary sermon of 1377 came after the first age of conquest, and although it gave the highest sanction to the myth of God's Englishmen that myth could not be fully developed until an English conqueror would again take arms against the French. Neither the reign of Richard II nor that of the cousin who overthrew him to reign as Henry IV provided the opportunity for a true revival of the dynastic competition which had stimulated this ideology. But by the accession of Henry V in 1413 a new and decidedly nationalist feeling could support the revival of that war with a full-fledged political theology. The linguistic element which had long been a shadowy aspect of English patriotism took on new meaning as a tangible proof of the merged feudal and early national loyalties. At the Council of Constance a fierce if petty rivalry for preferential seating led the English representatives to declare that:

> whether a nation be understood as a people marked off from others by blood relationship and habit of unity, or by peculiarities of language (the most sure and positive sign and essence of a nation in divine and human law) . . . or whether nation be understood, as it should be, as a territory equal to that of the French nation, England is a real nation.[28]

Professor Du Boulay rightly cautions against imagining that English political nationhood had thus emerged 'in the minds of a handful of professors,' but it is true nevertheless that the vernacular chroniclers hailed this conciliar victory as a singular triumph for England's status among the European nations.[29] Henceforth the older feudal loyalties to the person of the king existed alongside a growing adherence to the concept of an English nation unified by geography and language. That king was most successful who could embody both sorts of loyalty, as did Henry V and Edward IV, and the Crown continued to be most prosperous when it seemed to exemplify the realm.

Throughout the fourteenth and fifteenth centuries England's self-conscious new dignity in the affairs of the West required an ever more

[28] Francis R. H. Du Boulay, *An Age of Ambition: English Society in the Late Middle Ages* (London, Thomas Nelson & Sons, 1970), 20. As Professor Du Boulay comes close to suggesting, the persistent doubts of English historians about the existence of a true nationalism in this period are wholly unfounded. Galbraith's useful distinctions between nationalism and patriotism, which unwittingly encouraged this timidity, were drawn from an earlier and far different age: Vivian H. Galbraith, 'Nationality and language in medieval England,' *Transaction of the Royal Historical Society*, 4th series, XXIII (1941), 113ff.

[29] See, e.g., Thomas Hearne (ed.), *Vita et Gesta Henrici Quinti Anglorum Regis* (Oxford, The Clarendon Press, 1727), 90.

vigorous defense of English pretensions to autonomous sovereignty independent of alien overlordship. The loss of the duchy of Normandy during the reign of John had cast a shadow which was finally lifted by Edward III's refusal to do homage to the French crown for Aquitaine. The great statutes of Provisors and Praemunire severely limited papal control over the English church, though they did not end those French taunts that the English remained subject to the papacy. Early on, France and the Empire had secured papal immunity from other temporal powers and then found means to liberate themselves from papal domination. French kings, ever since the bull *Per venerabilem* of 1202, could boast the assurance of Innocent III that they were 'emperors in their own kingdom' and recognized no temporal superior.[30] During the reign of Henry V the English moved towards closing this ideological gap, spurred by the pugnacity of the king's younger brother, Humphrey of Gloucester. Humphrey, who became the popular champion of English autonomous sovereignty, is reputed to have prevented the Emperor Sigismund from landing at Dover in 1416 until he had extracted a promise that no imperial authority would be claimed within the realm of England.[31]

The ubiquitous problem of papal jurisdiction bedeviled every English monarch. In February 1486 the justices who had gathered in the parliament chamber to discuss papal excommunication of English subjects began to trade stories about earlier royal defiances of the papacy. The chief justice maintained that Edward I and his barons had rejected papal claims to the overlordship of Scotland. The bishop of London recalled an incident during the reign of Henry VI when Humphrey of Gloucester had seized papal letters insulting to the king and thrown them into the fire.[32] Heartening as they were, such irreverent traditions hardly constituted legal precedents, but they reinforced a new sense of what full sovereignty was or ought to be. Step by step, in defying the authority of the French king, the pope and the Emperor, late medieval English kings were moving toward that autonomous regality of which their French counterparts had long boasted. The new English emphasis on God's direct and special favor was not a form of corporate mysticism but rather a forthright rejection of authority derived from temporal and spiritual intermediaries.

30 André Bossuat, 'La Formule "Le Roi est empereur en son royaume": Son emploi au xve siècle devant le Parlement de Paris,' *Revue historique du droit français et étranger*, 4th series, XXXIX (1961), 371–81.

31 Charles L. Kingsford (ed.), *The First English Life of the King Henry the Fifth* (Oxford, Clarendon Press, 1911), 67. This is an edn of the 1513 English version of the text by Titus Livius de Frulovisiis.

32 Chrimes, *English Constitutional Ideas*, 52–3, 379–80.

III

The appeal to providential guidance is nowhere clearer than in the propaganda generated by Henry V's two invasions of France. There the insistence on Henry's God-given 'heritage' of Normandy[33] shaded perceptibly into the cognate theme of England's heritage of the French crown, not least perhaps because the second Lancastrian could not sustain a strictly logical claim to have inherited Edward III's pretensions to France.[34] The dubious lineage of the usurping dynasty which had overthrown Edward III's grandson was glossed over by Lancastrian publicists who were doubtless glad to merge Henry V's claim into a more generalized regnal or even national title to France. After Agincourt one poet celebrated Henry's exploits 'his owne right for to have' but also made clear that Henry represented the kingdom:

> Our Kyng ordeyned with all his myght,
> For to amende that is amys,
> And that is all for Englond ryght,
> To geten agen that scholde it ben his;[35]

At the beginning of his poem the author asks God to 'save Engelond for Mary sake' but at Agincourt he has Henry V ask Christ, 'This day me save for Ingelond sake.'[36] In the old feudal sense the king personified the kingdom; now he had begun as well to represent the rights and aspirations of the nation. The carefully contrived myth that Henry V's victory at Agincourt was really the victory of God supposedly explained the king's well-publicized refusal to be honored personally on his return from France. Henry insisted that he was no more than the instrument of God's will and the vicar of God's people. The refrain of that master publicist John Lydgate's *Prayer for England* expressed the sentiment exactly:

[33] Charles L. Kingsford, *Henry V: The Typical Mediaeval Hero* (London, G. P. Putnam's Sons, 1923), 126ff.; 'John Page's poem on the Siege of Rouen' in James Gairdner (ed.), *Historical Collections of a Citizen of London*, Camden Society, new series, xvii (London, 1876), 30. Page's verse shows Henry V enjoying the style of 'imperator in regno suo': 'And he ys kyng excellent,/and unto non othyr obedyent,/That levythe here in erthe be ryght,/ But only unto God almyght,/With-yn hys owne Emperoure,/And also kyng and conqueroure, . . .': *ibid.*, 24. I propose to discuss elsewhere the complex development of English imperial claims and aspirations.

[34] 'The title of King of France was one of England's stage properties. Henry adorned himself with it and went on parading it from force of habit. No one dreamed of justifying it: it was part of the succession': Perroy, *The Hundred Years' War*, 213.

[35] Nicholas H. Nicolas, *The History of the Battle of Agincourt* (London, Johnson & Co., 1832), 303.

[36] *Ibid.*, 321; see also Henry's supposed injunction: 'Thynke on ryzt of merye Englond': *ibid.*, 320.

And ay preserue vnder thy myghty honde
The kynge, the quene, the people, and thy londe.

As the refrain is repeated, the phrase becomes 'thy people and thy londe.'[37] The king's heritage had become England's heritage, and England's heritage had become God's heritage.

This faith that England was God's land and the English God's special people was never clearer than in that masterpiece of war propaganda which is known as the *Gesta Henrici Quinti*. This anonymous Latin chronicle, written in the winter or spring of 1416–17, publicized what its editors have called 'the official program' of the reign and above all the theme that Henry V was carrying out a divine plan. The anonymous chronicler told how the 'God of Warriors,' 'gracious and merciful to His people,' had led the English into battle to recover Henry's 'divine right and claim.'[38] This account faithfully reflects Henry's near-fanatical insistence that his mission was not only blessed by God but indeed was God's particular work for which the king himself deserved no personal credit. Even the French chroniclers had recorded Henry's statement to the prisoners at Agincourt that they had been defeated not by him but by God.[39] Time and again the righteous Henry had justified his severity to besieged French towns by citing the Law of Deuteronomy on condign retaliation for their rejection of his rightful inheritance.[40] The *Gesta* even suggests that Henry V consciously imitated 'God's chosen people' of Israel by augmenting the services of the chapel royal 'to the praise and glory of God Who had so marvelously deigned to receive His England and her people as His very own.'[41]

Upon the sudden death of Henry V in 1422 the brief revival of English military glory rapidly gave way to demoralizing losses to the armies of Charles VII, newly emboldened by an inspired wave of French national

[37] Rossell H. Robbins (ed.), *Historical Poems of the XIVth and XVth centuries* (New York, Columbia University Press, 1959), 235, 238.

[38] Frank Taylor and John S. Roskell (eds.), *Gesta Henrici Quinti: The Deeds of Henry the Fifth* (Oxford, Clarendon Press, 1975), 88ff.; the account begins by describing Henry V as 'verus electus dei': *ibid.*, 2.

[39] Nicolas, *Agincourt*, 141, discusses Henry's apparent belief, reflected in the *Gesta*, that God had turned His face away from the French in punishment for their sins.

[40] Taylor and Roskell, *Gesta Henrici Quinti*, 155 and xxx.

[41] *Ibid.*, 121; the author also speaks of 'God Who had so visited and wrought the redemption of His people': *ibid.*, 151 (a reference to Luke 1:68). The chronicle gives an extended account of Beaufort's sermon to the war parliament on the theme that Henry's victory at Agincourt, following Edward III's victories at Sluys and Poitiers, meant a definitive judgment by God in the dispute since, as is emphasized, no earthly power could judge between two powers 'having no superior under Heaven': *ibid.*, 122–3.

sentiment. Publicists of the infant Henry VI attempted to capitalize on that monarch's unique claim to rule a dual monarchy of both realms. Critics of the regime cited that old lament from Ecclesiastes, 'woe to the land when the king is a child,' but a barrage of Anglo-Norman propaganda likened the infant monarch to the Christ child as a savior of both realms.[42] After the English defeat at Orléans an impartial observer in the 1430s might well have concluded with Joan of Arc that God had restored His favors to the French. The erosion of English territorial gains in France, the failure of their European alliances and increasing lawlessness at home persuaded many English moralists, as similar events had moved Bishop Brinton decades earlier, to regard England's political situation as a fall from godliness. Reform-minded poets and pamphleteers soon echoed this melancholy message:

> God be with trewthe, qwer he be.
> I wolde he were in this cuntre![43]

None quite dared to suggest, though, that God and truth might again have crossed the Channel. By 1460 a Yorkist poet would turn the motif of England's elect status to a new task by suggesting that Lancastrian misgovernance had transformed God's Englishmen into Satan's subjects:

> 'Regnum Anglorum regnum Dei est,'
> As the Aungelle to seynt Edward dede wyttenesse.
> Now regnum Sathane, it semethe, reputat best.
> For filii scelerati haue broughte it in dystresse.[44]

The message of the famous Anglo-Saxon vision had apparently been revived in late medieval England, though dynastic disputes might cast occasional doubts on the heavenly decree that 'the kingdom of the English is the kingdom of God.'[45]

[42] John W. McKenna, 'Henry VI of England and the dual monarchy: aspects of royal political propaganda, 1422–32,' *Journal of the Warburg and Courtauld Institutes*, XXVIII (1965), 145–62 and plates 26–9. With the rival coronations of Henry VI and Charles VII the competition over the French royal lilies became quite fierce. One epigramatic 'débat' had the French side claim: 'Lilia Francorum, rex Karole septime regum,/Sint tua cum regno, si qua est reverentia legum.' The 'justa responsio' of the English was: 'Lilia Francorum decensu progenitorum/Jam sunt Anglorum, si lex valet ulla priorum': Thomas Wright (ed.), *A Collection of Political Poems and Songs . . . from . . . Edward III to . . . Henry VIII*, Rolls series, XIV (2 vols., London, 1861), II, 130.

[43] Printed as a separate couplet heading a popular carol from BL, MS Sloane 2593, in Robbins, *Historical Poems*, 146.

[44] Printed in Wright, *Political Poems*, II, 267–70 and Robbins, *Historical Poems*, 207–10.

[45] The saying derives from an Anglo-Saxon vision of Bishop Beorhtweald in which St Peter, consecrating a bachelor king, was asked who would succeed him in the kingdom. Peter replied that 'The kingdom of the English is the kingdom of God, and God has been pleased to make provision for its future.' See on this Frank Barlow, *Edward the Confessor* (London, Eyre Methuen, 1970), 60; Rudolph Brotanek, *Mittelenglische Dichtungen, aus der*

Henry VI's troubled reign, beset by factional strife and demands for political reform, must have taxed severely the ingenuity of the royal publicists. Those seeking to please the king, though, could now incorporate into their rhetoric some newly won epithets which might once have seemed extreme. The notion of God's special and particular favor, once the unique boast of France and its kings, had now entered the realm of English political jargon. Addressing Henry VI some time in the 1440s, the author of one political sermon counselled the king to particular devotion to God 'who has raised you over His people, that special tribe the English, and over all other Christian kings.'[46] Within relatively few generations the English kings had embraced almost all of those much-vaunted mystical attributes which Clement V's bull of 1311 had confirmed to the Capetians and their people.

IV

One final royal distinction remained to be usurped, and the reign of Henry VI appears to have sealed that aggrandizement, too. In death, and perhaps during his later years as well, Henry VI's reputation for personal piety was as extravagant as that of any monarch since Henry III.[47] His penchant for religiosity, combined with the king's claim as heir to his French grandfather Charles VI, may have lent a certain plausibility to his assumption of the traditional French royal style 'Most Christian King.'[48] Here again, as with the claim to be God's chosen people, the English were asserting that their realm deserved parity with the dignity accorded to the

Handschrift 432 des Trinity College in Dublin (Halle, M. Niemeyer, 1940), 206. Brotanek draws attention to the currency of this saying in such late-medieval sourcebooks as the *Nova Legenda Anglie*, printed by Wynkyn de Worde in 1516, Latin edn., *STC* 4601 and the English edn by Richard Pynson, also in 1516, *STC* 4602.

46 'Igitur, christianissime Rex, . . . debetis, oracionibus ac sanctis meditacionibus, deo omnipotenti, qui tantum vos dilexit et super populum suum, peculiarem gentem, scilicet anglicanam, ac super omnes alios reges christianos taliter exaltavit, omni vestri cordis desiderio corditer deservire': Jean-Philippe Genet (ed.), *Four English Political Tracts of the Later Middle Ages*, Camden Society, 4th series, XVIII (London, 1977), 112.

47 It has recently been suggested that this reputation is due almost entirely to posthumous Tudor propaganda: Ralph Griffiths, *The Reign of King Henry VI* (Berkeley, University of California Press, 1981), 248–9. One wonders, however, whether the Tudor publicists were not simply making the best case for a rather weak subject, creating a legend of piety from pietistic styles and substituting religious benefaction for what may have been somewhat theatrical religiosity in Henry's later years.

48 The reign of Charles V had been the high-point of French propaganda reinforcing royal ideology with this style: Noël Valois, 'Le roi très chrétien,' in *La France chrétienne dans l'Histoire*, ed. by Alfred P. Baudrillart (Paris, Firmin-Didot, 1896), 317ff.; Bloch, *The Royal Touch*, 78–9; Strayer, *Medieval Statecraft*, 306–7, suggests that the title 'rex Christianissimus' which was monopolized by the French during Charles V's reign, had become almost as common under Philip the Fair.

Most Christian Kings of France. Again, the English apparently acted in shameless imitation of the rich symbolic tradition of the French kings. Although the new title may have been suggested by Henry VI's French pretensions, it was freely applied to him in his capacity as king of both realms with no regard for the unique status of this royal style. The same ecclesiastics who had incorporated the myth of God's Englishmen into his tract also lavished a variety of grandiose titles on the king. These ingenious honorifics were often related to the author's specific injunctions to Henry: the king is 'Most imperial majesty' when the title turns to his twin realms, but when God's special love for the English people is mentioned Henry becomes 'Most Christian King,' and the topic of discord in Christendom produces the style 'Most Christian of Christian Kings.'[49] The English use of this familiar French royal trademark was by no means invariable, but Henry's own ambassador Thomas Beckynton was among those who characteristically saluted him in diplomatic correspondence as 'Moost excellent and moost Christian Prince.'[50] Even Henry's political opponents sometimes employed the phrase as a stock title: in his *Ballade set on the Gates of Canterbury* a Yorkist poet of 1460 referred to 'Harry, our soueryne and most Crystyne kyng.'[51]

Henry Tudor, always eager to justify his dubious title to the Crown, assumed the same style both in private addresses and in public pageantry. He was, praying God, 'the highest and most Christian King and prince of the world' in Caxton's epilogue to the *Faytes of Arms* of 23 January 1489, a translation commissioned by the king himself and presumably sensitive to the preferred forms of addressing royalty.[52] The elaborate and carefully prepared pageantry for the reception of Catharine of Aragon in 1501 included one address to the princess which was richly stocked with the symbolic attributes of English regality. The pageant character Prelacy took as his theme the biblical parable that 'the kyng of hevyn is lyke an erthly kyng, That to his Sone preparid a weddyng':

[49] This series of royal styles comes from the same Latin treatise, Genet, *Four English Political Tracts*, 81: 'imperialissimam maiestatem'; 112: 'christianissime Rex'; 71: christianorum christianissime Rex.; also 85. This political sermon is a model for suiting ornate forms of address to the particular injunction of the moment.

[50] Beckynton and Robert Roos address him as 'Moost excellent and moost Christian Prince': Nicholas H. Nicolas (ed.), *A Journal by One of the Suite of Thomas Beckynton, during an Embassy to Negotiate a Marriage between Henry VI and a Daughter of the Count of Armagnac, A.D. 1442* (London, 1828), 7. Other reports in the same series call Henry 'moost christian Prince' (p. 7) and 'Most Christian and moost gracious Prince, oure moost dred Sovereign Lord' (p. 49).

[51] Reprinted in Robbins, *Historical Poems*, 208.

[52] Walter J. B. Crotch (ed.), *The Prologues and Epilogues of William Caxton*, EETS, original series, CLXXVI (London, Oxford University Press, 1928), 103–4; also, Norman F. Blake, *Caxton's Own Prose* (London, André Deutsch, 1973), 82–3.

And Rygth soo as qwir Soverayn lord the kyng
May be Resemblid to the kyng Celestyall
As well as any prynce erthly now lyvyng,
Syttyng among the sevyn candstykkys Royall
As he whom It hath pleasid God to accept & call
Of all honour & dygnyte, unto the heyth
Most Crysten kyng and most stedffast in the ffeyth.[53]

In ceremonial rhetoric, at least, Henry VII could be called the equal of any temporal king. His royal publicists had indeed come a long way from their restrained predecessors in the early fourteenth century.

The anonymous author of those pageant speeches of 1501 had ascribed to God the gift of Henry's style as 'Most Crysten kyng and most stedffast in the ffeyth,' though the old French title was used both by a petitioner in the parliament of 1485 and by the speaker in the Commons of 1504.[54] The Tudors were aware, however, that if God had conferred this title He had neglected to inform the papacy, which was still under the impression that it belonged to the Valois kings of France. From this point the tale is well-known: Henry VIII wanted to rival both the French king and his in-laws their Most Catholic Majesties of Spain, and to that end sought papal approval for a distinctive English title. At first he hoped to secure the old French title by Roman fiat. With the Holy League of 1511 Henry secured papal and Spanish support to reopen the Hundred Years' War. Julius II, to encourage this effort against the schismatic Louis XII, issued a secret brief of 20 March 1512 conferring on Henry of England the 'name, glory and authority' of king of France. An explicit section of that papal promise bestowed upon Henry the title of Most Christian King of France. The grant, however, was both secret and conditional upon Henry's conquest of France.[55] Although some knowledgeable cardinals and courtiers anticipated Henry's victory by referring to him as 'christianissimus rex,'

[53] The reference is to Matthew 22: 1–2; the text of the welcoming ceremony (College of Arms, MS 1st M. 13, fols. 27–74*v*.) is, *inter alia*, in Francis Grose and Thomas Astle (eds.), *The Antiquarian Repertory* . . ., 2nd edn (4 vols., London, Edward Jeffery, 1807–9), II, 276. The prefatory passages to this account refer to 'o[r] owne most Cristen regiowne of Englond, fulfilled and occupied w[t] most goodly people . . .': *ibid.*, II, 250. See on this pageant, Sidney Anglo, *Spectacle, Pageantry and Early Tudor Policy* (Oxford, Clarendon Press, 1969), 87–8. Anglo regards this panegyric of Henry VII as a reference to the king's reception of several marks of papal favor.

[54] *RP*, VI, 289; the draft protestation of the speaker is printed in Nicholas Pronay and John Taylor (eds.), *Parliamentary Texts of the Later Middle Ages* (Oxford, Clarendon Press, 1980), 200, and 198, fn. 7.

[55] See on this the account in J. J. Scarisbrick, *Henry VIII* (London, Eyre Methuen, 1968), 115ff.; Anglo, *Spectacle*, 173–4.

two unsuccessful royal expeditions in as many years frustrated English territorial aspirations and effectively nullified the sly papal gift.

Henry VIII doubtless needed no papal titles to encourage him to attack France, but Julius II's promise may well have given Henry the idea of seeking an analogous papal style for himself. In September 1515 Wolsey attempted to have his king named Protector of the Holy See, assuring the pope that such an honorable title would cost nothing.[56] The search for a distinctive English royal style was on, and by January 1516 the title *Ecclesiae Defensor* was favored. By May of that year *Defensor Fidei* had been mentioned, and negotiations continued. As late as June 1521, the College of Cardinals was still debating the merits of the titles *Apostolicus* and Protector. Some of this activity was perhaps consolation for Henry's failure to secure the imperial crown of Germany. In the end the king's authorship of the famous tract against Luther gave Leo X an excuse to confer on Henry in 1521 his style of 'Defender of the Faith.'[57] At long last England had a unique royal style to set against the royal titles by which other European monarchs advertised their piety. Tudor historians have generally viewed this as the culmination of Henry's efforts over a decade, but it was in fact the very end of a two-hundred-year search for an outward symbol of England's sovereign aspirations.

The later medieval and early Tudor publicists, like their French counterparts a century and more earlier, could call upon a whole host of symbolic proofs of God's special favor toward the English and their king. Earlier Englishmen had constantly invoked the blessings of the Deity upon their cause, claimed divine favor for their side and pointed to every triumph as the workings of divine providence in the affairs of men. But this was no more than the old and pious medieval commonplace, the mainstay of every crusade and every feudal clash, adapted to the ideology of successive generations. In borrowing the cluster of French royal attributes and the sanctity of the Frankish kingdom, English publicists of the fourteenth and fifteenth centuries established, in the symbolic language of the age, a new mythology of England's parity with, and eventually its superiority to, the other nations of the West.

This creation of a royal mystique in England led inexorably, as it had in

[56] *LP*, II, 887, 894, quoted in Anglo, *Spectacle*, 174.

[57] Scarisbrick, *Henry VIII*, 116; G. R. Elton, *Reform and Reformation: England, 1509–1558* (Cambridge, Mass., Harvard University Press, 1977), 75–6. The fullest discussion of Henry VIII's search for a royal style is in Mandell Creighton, *A History of the Papacy*, rev. edn (London, 1901), VI, 374ff.; T. Mainwaring-Brown, 'Henry VIII's book . . . and the royal title of "Defender of the Faith,"' *Transactions of the Royal Historical Society*, 1st series, VIII (1880), 242ff. The Pope intended the title as a personal style, but Henry chose to regard it as hereditary: *LP*, III, 1659; Scarisbrick, *Henry VIII*, 117, fn. 2.

France, to the development of a national political theology in which the providential myth was a central element. In fifteenth century England opposing dynastic factions claimed equal religious approbation just as rival popes had confused their followers with rival saints and sanctions in the previous century. When the followers of Lancaster revived memories of their sainted ancestor earl Thomas their opponents erected a cult of the murdered bishop Scrope of York. When the Yorkists claimed to march under a papal banner, as William I had done in 1066, the Lancastrians made a saint of their incompetent martyr Henry VI.[58] When both sides claimed divine sanctions for their cause the disunity of the realm argued against any real sense that God was in control of the kingdom. That belief was easily restored, however, with the Tudor providential message that their dynasty fulfilled a divine plan to unite the warring houses and restore the rightful line. Fittingly, the papal bull of 2 March 1486 by which Henry Tudor procured a dispensation to marry Elizabeth of York spoke of the Roman See's special affection for England in words reminiscent of the bull of 1311 which had confirmed the ancient French priority in the West.[59]

V

In the sixteenth century this late medieval revival of mystical kingship could serve as a powerful precedent for new claims of autonomous sovereignty free from the overlordship of emperors, kings, or popes. Not long after Henry Tudor's revolution of 1485 an astute Italian diplomat reported that England, though independent of *the* Empire, remained sub-

[58] The image of the Christ-like king and various analogies based on that concept had retained a steady if discontinuous popularity with the more hyperbolic orators and chroniclers. The poem praising Henry V in Digby MS 102 represents the extreme of this tradition: 'God ȝeueþ his doom to alle kynges þat be;/As a god, in erþe a kyng haþ myȝt': in Robbins, *Historical Poems*, 48. The chronicler Hardyng likened Edward III's maternal claim to France to Jesus's descent from the House of David through His mother, and drew a comparison of Henry V with Christ: Henry Ellis (ed.), *John Hardyng's Chronicle* (London, 1812), 337, 387, and see also 335 and 17. The political manipulation of popular religious cults is described in John W. McKenna, 'Popular canonization as political propaganda: the cult of Richard Scrope,' *Speculum*, XLV (1970), 608–23, and McKenna, 'Piety and propaganda: The cult of King Henry VI,' in *Chaucer and Middle English Studies in Honour of Rossell Hope Robbins*, ed. by Beryl Rowland (London, George Allen & Unwin, 1974), 72–88. On earlier aspects of that phenomenon see Josiah Cox Russell, 'The canonization of opposition to the king in Angevin England,' in *Haskins Anniversary Essays in Medieval History*, ed. by Charles H. Taylor and John L. La Monte (Boston, 1929), 279–90.

[59] That is, 'inter alia Christianorum Regna Peculiare & carisimum semper habitum & reputatum fuit, . . .': Thomas Rymer (ed.), *Foedera, Conventiones, Letterae. . .* (20 vols., London, A. & J. Churchill, 1727–35), XII, 294b–295a.

ject to the papacy.[60] The final expression of national sovereignty, in defiance of papal authority, waited upon another Tudor revolution in the 1530s. England's claim as the elect nation could thereafter be revived as a plausible political theology. The influence of that mighty idea can be read in the works of John Foxe, the words of John Aylmer, the Golden Speech of Elizabeth I and the chauvinist rhetoric of John Milton. The English role as the chosen people was already firmly fixed, however, in the political and literary traditions of the last medieval war. Those generations of Englishmen who had witnessed England becoming a nation had imagined their land as the successor to the land of Israel, the special object of God's interest and affection. It was said of them that

> The English are great lovers of themselves, and of everything belonging to them; they think that there are no other men than themselves, and no other world but England; and whenever they see a handsome foreigner they say that 'he looks like an Englishman,' and that 'it is a great pity that he should not be an Englishman';[61]

At the very end of the middle ages the English had looked at God and decided that he must surely be an Englishman. It is not altogether certain that they have since altered that opinion.[62]

[60] Charlotte A. Sneyd (ed.), *A Relation . . . of the Island of England . . . about the Year 1500*, Camden Society, original series, XXXVII (London, 1847), 53–4.

[61] *Ibid.*, 20–1.

[62] Earlier versions of this paper were delivered as the annual Visiting Scholar lecture at the University Center in Georgia, 1980, and by invitation of the Modern Language Association of America, general session of the Middle English section, at its annual meeting in New York City in December 1978. I am obliged to members of those audiences for numerous helpful suggestions and comments on this material.

The reformation of choirs: cathedral musical establishments in Tudor England

STANFORD E. LEHMBERG

The impact of government policy and parliamentary legislation on the musical establishments of the English cathedrals remains one of the unstudied aspects of the English Reformation. It is generally recognized, of course, that the Acts of Uniformity introducing the vernacular Books of Common Prayer forbade the continued use of old Latin texts.[1] Clauses providing penalties for those who did not 'sing or say' the services according to the form set out in the Prayer Book obviously dictated abandonment of existing musical settings of the Mass and other liturgies and eventually stimulated the composition of the marvelous Elizabethan anthems and services. What has so far escaped scrutiny is the way in which the lives of the professional musicians in the service of the church were altered by the suppression of the monasteries, the dissolution of the chantries, and the rejection of mandatory clerical celibacy. This essay, which is intended as a study in social history rather than musicology or liturgics, chronicles the changes in the organization of cathedral choirs during the sixteenth century. It reveals a Reformation of choirs quite as profound as the theological Reformation or the Tudor Revolution in government.[2]

[1] See 2 & 3 Edward VI, c. 1: *SR*, IV, pt I, 37–9; 5 & 6 Edward VI, c. 1: *ibid.*, 130–1; 1 Elizabeth I, c. 2: *ibid.*, 355–8.

[2] This study, a preliminary exploration of a topic which I intend to treat more fully in due course, is based on printed works and a selection of manuscript materials. I am grateful for advice and assistance provided by Anne M. Oakley at Canterbury; Claire Cross and W. J. Shiels at York; the Rev. Chancellor and Mrs John Nurser at Lincoln; Dorothy Owen at Cambridge (the repository for Ely MSS); the Very Rev. Dean and Mrs John Arnold at Rochester; Howard M. Nixon, Librarian, N. H. MacMichael, Keeper of the Muniments, and T. G. M. Keall, Headmaster of the Choir School at Westminster Abbey; the Rev. Canon Frederick Busby at Winchester; and A. R. B. Fuller, Librarian of St Paul's. Earlier examples of the social history of music include E. D. Mackerness, *A Social History of English Music* (London, Routledge & Kegan Paul, 1964) and Walter L. Woodfill, *Musicians in English Society from Elizabeth to Charles I* (Princeton, Princeton University Press, 1953). Neither deals with cathedrals at length. The present study is not concerned with parish churches, for with few exceptions they did not employ trained musicians. For an account of music in the parishes see Nicholas Temperley, *The Music of the English Parish Church* (2 vols., Cambridge, CUP, 1980).

I

The importance of the changes brought by the Reformation can be understood only in the context of pre-Reformation cathedral constitutions and their provisions for choral establishments. In the early Tudor period there were nineteen cathedral churches in England. Nine of these – Salisbury, Lincoln, York, Exeter, Hereford, Lichfield, Chichester, Wells, and St Paul's in London – were secular cathedrals, served by a dean, chapter, and inferior clergy who were in holy orders but not monks. The remaining ten cathedrals were monastic in organization. Canterbury, Winchester, Worcester, Rochester, Durham, Ely, Norwich, Coventry, and Bath were Benedictine priories, while the cathedral at Carlisle was staffed by Augustinian canons.[3] The older monastic cathedrals owed their structure to the influence of Lanfranc, who brought the monastic rule to bishops' sees which antedated the Conquest. In all of these houses the duties of a cathedral were grafted onto the normal monastic arrangements; the monks' common life centered around the choir services, the refectory, the library, and the dormitory. Secular cathedrals followed a different pattern, also established in Normandy before 1066. In these, secular canons lived in separate houses and enjoyed individual incomes derived from landed estates, but joined in the religious life of the cathedral.

By the later middle ages music had become an exceedingly important part of cathedral services. Secular cathedrals employed vicars choral who were chosen primarily for their musical abilities. At Salisbury, for instance, a statute of *c.* 1256 ordained that 'hereafter none shall be presented to the office of vicar in this church unless he has a good and musical voice and skill in plainsong, besides the merits of character required in such instances.'[4] In monastic cathedrals the daily round of sung services consumed most of the energy of the choir monks. Secular clerks especially skilled in singing joined the staff of some monastic cathedrals, for instance Worcester, and boys' voices were added to the men's, in some places as early as the eleventh century. The monastic hours continued to be sung in plainsong by men only, but as polyphonic singing developed Lady Masses sung by men and boys were introduced in the Lady Chapels of monastic cathedrals, while polyphonic 'pricksong' became a usual part of worship in secular cathedrals. In 1423 John Whethamstede, the famous

[3] See Frank Ll. Harrison, *Music in Medieval Britain* (London, Routledge & Kegan Paul, 1958), 2–17; Kathleen Edwards, *The English Secular Cathedrals in the Middle Ages* (Manchester, Manchester University Press, 1949), 11–12; Alexander Hamilton Thompson (ed.), *The Statutes of the Cathedral Church of Durham*, Surtees Society, CXLIII (Durham, 1929), xxv.

[4] Quoted in Harrison, *Music*, 5.

abbot of St Albans, ordered the appointment of at least two professional singers if the monks themselves were not capable of performing polyphony.[5] Song schools for the training of choristers grew up, somewhat earlier in secular cathedrals than in monastic ones.[6] Organs took their place during the middle ages, too, with enormous primitive instruments like that whose 'iron voice batter[ed] the ear' at Winchester[7] being supplemented or supplanted by smaller, more sensitive instruments located in various parts of the great buildings.

Late-medieval choirs were often amazingly large but were not, by modern standards at least, very well balanced. In the secular cathedrals most of the senior canons were not resident; the vicars choral were originally appointed to serve as their deputies. As a general rule there were as many vicars choral as there were canons in the cathedral chapter. Thus Lincoln, Wells, and Salisbury had (in theory at least) more than fifty vicars, York thirty-six. At St Paul's there were twelve minor canons who sang alongside the vicars of the thirty major canons. Chichester and Lichfield, the smallest of the secular cathedrals, still had more than twenty vicars.[8] It is likely, however, that the actual number of singing men serving at any given time was smaller than the number ordained by statute. A visitation of 1437 revealed that there were only thirty-four vicars choral at Wells, not the full fifty-four. Salisbury had only thirty-one in 1468, Lincoln twenty-five in 1501; York could afford only twenty in 1509.[9] When John Colet became Dean of St Paul's in 1505 he found that the thirty vicars had dwindled to six.[10] Still, the choirs of men seem large when compared to the miniscule number of boys. Fourteen choristers were provided for in the fifteenth century at Salisbury and Exeter, twelve at York, Lincoln, and Lichfield, but Wells had only six and Hereford five.[11] Colet's statutes, drafted with the intention of reforming St Paul's but never in fact adopted, mention only eight, although other documents

[5] See A. Hamilton Thompson, *Song-Schools in the Middle Ages* (London, Society for Promoting Christian Knowledge, 1942).

[6] D. H. Turner, Rachel Stockdale, Dom Philip Jebb, and David Rogers, *The Benedictines in Britain* (London, British Library, 1980), 42.

[7] Harrison, *Music*, 205, quoting the monk Wulstan (d. 963).

[8] Edwards, *English Secular Cathedrals*, 33–5; Harrison, *Music*, 8–9; G. E. Aylmer and Reginald Cant (eds.), *A History of York Minster* (Oxford, Clarendon Press, 1977), 86.

[9] Harrison, *Music*, 9; A. R. Maddison, *A Short Account of the Vicars Choral, Poor Clerks, Organists, and Choristers of Lincoln Cathedral* (London, no pub., 1878), 3; Aylmer and Cant, *York Minster*, 93.

[10] W. R. Matthews and W. M. Atkins (eds.), *A History of St Paul's Cathedral* (London, John Baker, 1957), 110.

[11] Harrison, *Music*, 10; Edwards, *English Secular Cathedrals*, 313–14; Maddison, *Lincoln Cathedral*, 21. Prior to the fifteenth century York had only seven choristers: Aylmer and Cant, *York Minster*, 88.

from the early Tudor period refer to ten.[12] The monastic cathedrals, where the whole body of monks might be involved in the liturgy, generally had even fewer boys. The indenture appointing Thomas Ashwell choirmaster at Durham in 1513 required him to train eight boys as well as 'such monks of the house as may be chosen,' and a later account refers to the Lady Mass sung daily in the Galilee 'by the master of the song schole, with certaine decons and quiristers, the master playing upon a paire of faire orgaines.'[13] Only two *pueri de capella* are mentioned at Worcester in 1392, *octo pueri cantoris* at Canterbury in 1454.[14]

One of the most interesting aspects of the cathedral musical establishments prior to the Reformation is the provision of living accommodation in colleges of vicars choral. Obviously this development affected only the secular cathedrals. Originally the vicars were attached to specific canons and lived in their houses. As more and more canons became totally non-resident, however, other quarters had to be found. It is likely, too, that some sort of common order had to be provided for the younger vicars: the most junior were normally twenty or twenty-two and might well require further training and discipline.

The oldest college of vicars choral was the famous Bedern at York. Here the vicars acquired land near the east end of the Minster as early as 1248. Residential accommodation, in the form of small chambers for individual vicars and a common dining hall, followed shortly. A chapel was added in the fourteenth century, and a pedestrian bridge was constructed so that the vicars could walk to and from services without facing the interference of traffic or the temptations of worldly life.[15] Similar halls of residence were provided at St Paul's in 1289, at Wells, Hereford, Lincoln, Exeter, and Chichester during the fourteenth century, and at Salisbury in 1407.[16] The sixteenth century records of the Bedern are unusually interesting – reference will be made to them later – and the site has been of interest, too, since recent excavations at York revealed the foundations of the buildings, shortly to be covered again by a modern housing development. Nearly complete sets of medieval vicars' buildings still survive at Wells and Hereford. At Wells a series of small houses was erected beginning in 1354. A refectory was provided at the south end of this Vicars Choral Close, a chapel and library were built at the north,

12 Harrison, *Music*, 13–14.

13 Dom David Knowles, *The Religious Orders in England* (3 vols., Cambridge, CUP, 1959), III, 17, 136 (quoting the anonymous *Rites of Durham*).

14 Harrison, *Music*, 39–43.

15 Aylmer and Cant, *York Minster*, 89–93; Frederick Harrison, *Life in a Medieval College* (London, John Murray, 1952), 29–33.

16 Edwards, *English Secular Cathedrals*, 282–3; Maddison, *Music*, 8.

and in 1457 Bishop Beckington connected the refectory to the cathedral by constructing a covered way above the Chain Gate. At Hereford twenty-seven sets of lodgings erected about 1470 stand around a beautiful cloister; they are of two storeys, one room on each floor, with fireplaces in both. There were also a kitchen, hall, and chapel.[17]

Suitable arrangements had to be made for the housing and education of choristers as well. Boys had been present in the Anglo-Saxon and Anglo-Norman monasteries, sometimes as a result of the practice of infant oblation, and in the later middle ages monastic almoners were required to provide for choristers in the monastic cathedrals. By the end of the fourteenth century song schools had arisen, either as part of the almonry or as separate establishments, with lay masters engaged especially to teach music. Similar arrangements, rather surprisingly, were made at St Paul's. In other secular cathedrals the choristers were under the care of the precentor or his deputy, the succentor. The earliest choristers' house was founded at Lincoln by Bishop Gravesend in 1264 – it still survives, although much altered and now put to different uses – and similar establishments followed at Salisbury, Wells, and Lichfield. In addition to singing, boys often read lessons. They participated in such authorized festivities as the rule of the Boy Bishop on St Nicholas' or Holy Innocents' Day and in unauthorized frivolities such as playing at 'le tenez' in Lincoln (1530) or football games in the close at York (1409). After their voices broke choristers generally proceeded to the grammar schools operated under the supervision of the Chancellor. Sometimes they remained in the service of the cathedral, acting as 'altarists' or 'poor clerks' assisting the priests at mass and providing supplies of bread, wine, and wax at the altars. After a year or so they might become vicars choral. At age twenty-two they became eligible for ordination as subdeacons. At some cathedrals – Lincoln is an example – there was a distinction between junior vicars choral or vicars of the second form, who were not yet priests, and senior vicars of the first form, who were. At Lincoln, too, there was a full complement of four residence halls or colleges, for choristers, poor clerks, junior vicars choral, and vicars of the first form, and one can trace the progress of some of the musicians. One Hamo Thwyng, for instance, was a poor clerk prior to 1491, when he was appointed a vicar and promised to be diligent in learning the organ, descant, and grammar. He is listed as an acolyte in 1492, subdeacon in 1497, deacon in 1501, and priest later in the same year. He died in 1510. It is not certain that Thwyng

[17] William Page (ed.), *VCH: Somerset* (5 vols., London, Constable and Co., 1911), II, 167; Marcus Binney, 'Hereford Cathedral Close,' *Country Life*, CLXVIII (25 September 1980), 1026–9.

had been a chorister, but his older colleague Thomas King had been. King was admitted as a poor clerk in 1467 and took priest's orders in 1479.[18] Another former chorister to become a vicar choral was William Smith, admitted as a vicar of the second form in 1544.[19]

A number of the greater monasteries maintained musical establishments comparable to those of the cathedrals. Since several of these were converted into cathedrals by Henry VIII, they are of some relevance here. Of greatest interest, both because of its prominence in national affairs and because of some unusual surviving documents, is Westminster Abbey. Here an almonry school founded in the fourteenth century provided boys for the choir which sang elaborate polyphonic music – the great antiphons of Our Lady after Compline as well as the Lady Mass and some chantry masses. At the beginning of the Tudor period William Cornysh was master of the choristers. Active from 1479 to 1491, he was probably the father of the more famous William Cornysh junior, master of the children in the Chapel Royal during the earlier years of Henry VIII's reign, whose antiphons survive in the Eton Choirbook and still merit performance. During the later years of Henry VIII's reign the choir included five minor canons who were laymen and five lay singing men as well as the choristers.[20]

One of the special privileges of the abbey, shared only by the Chapel Royal and ratified by royal warrants such as that issued by Henry VII in 1497,[21] was the power of impressing outstanding men and boys from other choirs.[22] A fascinating instance of this perquisite in operation is provided in the account book of William Fyttz, subalmoner in the early sixteenth century. On 10 November 1512 Fyttz travelled from

[18] Edwards, *English Secular Cathedrals*, 309–24; Knowles, *Religious Orders*, III, 16; Aylmer and Cant, *York Minster*, 88–9; Matthews and Atkins, *St Paul's*, 116; Maddison, *Lincoln Cathedral*, 20–6, 68, 70–1, 76–8, 83, 88; R. E. G. Cole (ed.), *Chapter Acts of the Cathedral Church of St Mary of Lincoln, A.D. 1520–1536*, Lincoln Record Society, XII (Horncastle, 1915), 133, 156.

[19] R. E. G. Cole (ed.), *Chapter Acts of the Cathedral Church of St Mary of Lincoln, A.D. 1536–1547*, Lincoln Record Society, XIII (Horncastle, 1917), 88. In 1545 Smith was in trouble because he often spent the night outside the Vicars' Close and was remiss in rising for Mattins; 'with downcast countenance' he promised to reform (112).

[20] C. S. Knighton, 'Collegiate foundations, 1540 to 1570, with special reference to St Peter in Westminster' (Cambridge University, Unpublished Ph.D. thesis, 1975), 342.

[21] Printed in Edward Pine, *The Westminster Abbey Singers* (London, Dennis Dobson, 1953), 27–8.

[22] Other musicians may have done the same thing without authorization; in 1519 Richard Bramston, a former organist of Wells who had become master of the Lady Chapel choir at St Augustine's Abbey in Bristol, returned to Wells 'in privie and disguised apparel' to kidnap a boy called Farr, 'one of our best choristers': L. S. Colchester, Roger Bowers, and Anthony Crossland (eds.), *The Organs and Organists of Wells Cathedral* (Wells, Friends of Wells Cathedral, 1974), 16.

Westminster to London 'to take too chyldren w[t] the comyssyon, the tone callyd Richard Bemond, the other callyd Wyllyam ffynnes.' Parents had to be mollified, as several entries show:

Item gevyn to Wyllyam ffynes Master lying seke by cause he had no body to help hym yn his syckenes iij[s] iijd[d]
Item to tyhc samc W. ffyncs modcr to haue hyr good wylle xij[d]
Item to Richard Bemondes master by cause of hys good wylle xij[d]
. . .
Item spent of Ric/ Bemonde ffader & moder & W ffynes moder when the came to Westminster to se the children xij[d]

Later another boy, Peter Best, was recruited from St Olave's church; his father, the parish clerk, obtained 2s. 6d. for his good will, and subsequently (together with Fynes' mother and sister) he received another payment, probably for expenses in visiting at Westminster. When one of the boys (W. White) fell ill, 10s. was paid to his father 'for his surgery & phisyk in y[e] tyme of his seknes,' and Robert Medellan's wife received 8s. 'for kcpyng of W. Whygt, onc of thc syngyng chyldcrn, viij wcks.' A bill from the 'potycary' amounted to 5s. 2d.

Once the boys were recruited they had to be clothed. The accounts record:

Item a russet cape for W. ffynes xij[d]
Item a russet cape for Ric/ Bemonde xij[d]
. . .
Item the xvj for my expenses to london to by fustyon & lynyng for the syngyng chyldren xij[s]
Item for iij halfe peces of Russet fustyon p the yard viij[d] xxx[d]
Item for xxxij yardes of wyet coton for lynyng to ther cottes per the yard vj[d] summa xvj[s]
Item to Wyllyam Taylor for makyng of iij gouns & iij cottes xj[s]

Other entries reflect payments for shirts and shoes (the boys seem to have required an amazing number of new pairs), hose, purses, and caps. The barber was given 12d. 'for Rowndyng [tonsure] of the chyldern,' and 5s. was paid for washing their clothes. There were normal allowances 'for brekfast for the chyldern' and for other meals; 'a barrel of whyght heryng for the chyldern' and 'pesyn' were purchased during the winter, while items listed the following summer include strawberries, cherries, spices, and wafers. Presumably the five boys and their master, as well as the four singing men, attended the 'drynkyng at the fest of the nat[ivity] of Seynt John baptist a[o] xiij[to] R H viij,' for which sugar jelly, 'comfettes jelly,' and white bread were provided along with four gallons of wine. Disbursements related more closely to music include 5s. 'for a prycksong book of Masses antems & other songs' and 2s. 8d. 'for a peyr of clavycors.' On two occasions money was paid 'for wryttyng of a play for the chyldern'; the boys of St Paul's were not the only ones involved in drama. Receipts suggest some of the special religious services performed by the boys; they sang 'diryges' for Queen Eleanor, Richard II, Henry V, and Henry VII.[23] In this little account book, perhaps more than in any other source, one feels close to the daily life of the singing men and boys on the eve of the Reformation.

II

The initial step in the Reformation of choirs resulted from the dissolution of the monasteries. This necessitated the reorganization of the monastic cathedrals, and it produced a number of additional cathedral establishments.

The first monastic cathedral to be converted into a secular foundation was Norwich. Here a charter dated 2 May 1538 transformed the monastic prior and convent into a secular dean and chapter. The last prior, William Castleton, became the first dean; five monks were named prebends, and sixteen more were made canons. The dean and chapter were given power to make their own statutes (they did not get around to doing so until the seventeenth century) and to allocate revenues for the support of the clergy and choristers.[24]

Other foundations followed after the parliament of 1539 passed acts legalizing the suppression of the larger monasteries and authorizing the erection of new bishoprics.[25] The remaining monastic cathedrals were refounded between March 1541 and January 1542. Generally, as at Norwich, the prior became dean, but secular clergy as well as ex-monks were named prebends, and there were no arrangements for former monks to become canons.[26]

But the refoundation of monastic cathedrals became enmeshed in

[23] Westminster Abbey Muniments, MS WAM 33301, fols. 2–20. Some extracts are quoted in Pine, *Abbey Singers*, 30–6.

[24] *LP*, XIII, i, 408; Hamilton Thompson, *Durham Statutes*, xxvi–xxx; Noel Boston, *The Musical History of Norwich Cathedral* (Norwich, Friends of Norwich Cathedral, 1963), 34–5. The suffragan bishop of Thetford also became a prebend, so the full chapter numbered twenty-two.

[25] 31 Henry VIII, cc. 13, 9: *SR*, III, 733–9, 728; Stanford E. Lehmberg, *The Later Parliaments of Henry VIII, 1536–1547* (Cambridge, CUP, 1977), 61–4, 66–7.

[26] *LP*, XVI, 678 (g. 53), 779 (g. 6), 878 (gg. 15, 25), 947 (g. 35), 1226 (g. 11); *LP*, XVII, 71 (g. 28); Hamilton Thompson, *Durham Statutes*, xxxii–xxxiii. The number of prebends varied from twelve at Canterbury, Winchester, and Durham to six at Rochester.

Henry VIII's scheme of new bishoprics. The idea of creating additional sees, probably originally Wolsey's, gained force when the revenues of the religious houses became available for their support, and the prospect of finding a continuing use for the great monastic buildings was obviously appealing as well. For a time the government toyed with the idea of establishing a large number of new bishoprics, at such places as St Albans, Burton-on-Trent, Shrewsbury, Gisburn, Thornton, Waltham, Colchester, Dunstable, Bodmin, and Fountains. Eventually these grandiose schemes were abandoned, no doubt because they were too elaborate and too costly, and in the end only six new cathedrals were established, the abortive one at Westminster and permanent foundations at Gloucester, Peterborough, Chester, Bristol, and Osney (this see, just outside Oxford, was transferred to Christ Church in 1546).

Documents which survive among the Augmentations papers in the Public Record Office provide details of the financial arrangements suggested for the new and refounded cathedrals. The original scheme for Canterbury, for instance, called for eight 'Peticanons to sing in the quere,' twelve 'laye men to sing also & serue in the quere,' and ten choristers. There was also provision for a provost, twelve prebends, six preachers, sixty scholars to be taught Latin and Greek in the grammar school, twenty students to be supported at Oxford and Cambridge, five readers of divinity, 'humanite,' physic, and civil law in the Universities, a 'M^{r} of Childerne,' and a master and an usher for the grammar school. The revenues of Canterbury exceeded £2387, so that even with this lavish establishment, costing in all £1963, the government would reap a profit of £419 13s. 4d. Winchester was also to be allowed eight minor canons, twelve lay singers, and ten choristers, Durham eight minor canons, ten laymen, and ten boys. Rochester, a poorer foundation, was to make do with six minor canons, six singing men, and eight choristers. Musical establishments consisting of eight or ten canons, six or eight laymen, and eight choristers were also envisioned at Ely, Worcester, Gloucester, Peterborough, St Albans, and Shrewsbury; still smaller choirs were thought adequate for Carlisle, Osney, and Waltham, with the smallest establishment (eight men and six boys) recommended for the cathedral at Chester.[27]

Another set of papers, evidently drafted by or for Stephen Gardiner, is more generous, allowing such large choral establishments as twenty-four men (half lay) and ten boys at Canterbury and Winchester, eighteen men and twelve boys at Worcester. Even minimal establishments, such as those proposed for Dunstable, Bodmin, Waltham, Osney, and Foun-

[27] PRO, E 315/24, fols. 1–34 (*LP*, xiv, ii, 429).

tains, were to have twelve men and six boys.[28] Throughout these accounts the rates of pay remain nearly uniform, minor canons ordinarily being given £10 per year, lay singing men £6 13s. 4d., and choristers five marks. These allowances may be compared to the £6 which was the normal pension for ex-monks.

The transitional stage for monastic choirs is particularly well illustrated by some unusually full documents for Westminster Abbey. Here twelve minor canons were allowed; four of those listed by name are identified as former monks and four as secular priests, with (presumably) four vacancies. Nine laymen 'to syng and serue in the Quyer daylie' are named, a total of twelve being authorized, with five choristers listed and (again presumably) five more to be recruited. It is interesting to note, too, that two of the forty scholars are designated 'late querister,' while five of the twenty students in divinity are 'late monkes.'[29] Both surviving Erection Books for Westminster as a cathedral foundation agree in calling for twelve minor canons (£120 p.a.), twelve singing men (£96), and ten choristers (£33 6s. 8d.).[30]

Thirteen of the new cathedrals and refounded monastic establishments were given new statutes in 1544. In contrast to the unique case at Norwich, these regulations were imposed from without; the statutes were compiled by Nicholas Heath, bishop of Worcester, George Day, bishop of Chichester, and Richard Cox, the future bishop of Ely, now archdeacon of that diocese. Although there are a few local variations – special provision for preachers at Canterbury, for instance, and for the grammar school at Worcester – these statutes have a basic common text. Appointments to the deanery and canonries were placed in the gift of the Crown, an important difference from the arrangements at the old secular cathedrals, where the bishop appointed the canons and the chapter elected the dean. Canons of the new cathedrals had no individual rights or revenues but rather became part of the corporation of the dean and chapter. Minor canons, lay clerks, and choristers were provided for; the statutes mention skill in singing as an essential qualification but provide no mechanism for dismissal if vocal abilities faltered. Constitutionally the position of these musical establishments differed markedly from that of the vicars choral of the old secular cathedrals, since the colleges of vicars choral formed separate legal corporations with property

[28] PRO, E 315/24, fols. 37–80. This is endorsed 'The bookes of the creation of all the newe houses as they came from the busshop of Winchester.'

[29] PRO, E 315/24, fols. 81–4.

[30] BL, Add. MSS 40061, fols. 2–5; Westminster Abbey Muniments, MS WAM 6478, fols. 1–5; Knighton, 'Collegiate Foundations,' 26–40.

and revenues of their own, apart from the endowments of the dean and chapter.

In cathedrals of the new foundation the precentor was the chief of the minor canons and was specifically charged by statute with the care of all choir books and the maintenance of attendance records. The number of lay clerks and choristers is also specified, in keeping with the schemes already in effect, and there are provisions for a master of the choristers, who also served as organist, and for schoolmasters, cooks, butlers, and porters. Members of the choir were to dine in the common hall, where the minor canons sat at the high table, the lay clerks at the second, and the choristers at the third. The services of the church remained much as they had been in the past, with the daily office, masses, and obits, but there is an express exemption from the monastic practice of midnight Mattins.[31]

In secular cathedrals, now often referred to as cathedrals of the old foundation, the first serious blow fell with the dissolution of the chantries in 1547. Most of the senior vicars choral held office as chantry priests in addition to singing in the choir, and they derived a large part of their revenue from chantry endowments. At Lincoln, for instance, the vicars choral were paid £5 16s. 5d. apiece in 1536, but they received additional amounts ranging from 13s. 5d. to £7 9s. 2d. for chantries and other special masses. Even the choristers received £5 9s. 2d. from obits.[32] There were already four vacant vicarages, the remaining vicars choral simply dividing their revenues among themselves; with the elimination of chantry income numbers declined still further, until the senior vicars were reduced from twenty-five to twelve. Few new admissions are recorded during the reign of Edward VI, while four of the old vicars were pensioned off with annuities of about £4 in 1549. At least four vicars choral married, thus weakening the communal life which seems to have been on shaky ground already. Arrangements for choristers were altered as well. In 1549 the number of choristers on the old foundation was cut from twelve to four, but seven or eight 'Burghersh Chanters' were instituted, on the endowment from a chantry left by Bartholomew Burghersh in 1345.[33] At Salisbury no such endowments were available, and the number of boys dropped from fourteen to eight.[34] At York the number of vicars choral

[31] Hamilton Thompson, *Durham Statutes*, xxxviii–lii; Canterbury Cathedral Library, MSS E. 34, 37.

[32] Cole, *Lincoln Chapter Acts, 1536–1547*, 176, 192–3 (figures based on the *Valor Ecclesiasticus*).

[33] *Ibid.*, 195; R. E. G. Cole (ed.), *Chapter Acts of the Cathedral Church of St Mary of Lincoln, A.D. 1547–1559*, Lincoln Record Society, xv (Horncastle, 1920), 40, 42, xxiii–xxiv. The Burghersh Chanters continue to the present, there being a dozen of them in 1981.

[34] Dora H. Robertson, *Sarum Close* (London, Jonathan Cape, 1938), 124.

fell from twenty-one in 1530 to ten in 1558, although twelve choristers were maintained throughout, and there was a threat to the continued existence of the Bedern: the vicars were harassed by the commissioners for the dissolution of chantries and colleges but managed to convince them that the Bedern was part of the cathedral establishment and thus exempt from the dissolution statute.[35] Since there were so few junior vicars choral at Lincoln, and since the poor clerks or altarists could no longer serve a useful function at chantry masses, the two groups were amalgamated in a new college of thirty poor clerks, sometimes referred to as the 'poor clerks choral.' Ten such clerks were admitted in 1556; with ages between fifteen and twenty they formed a link between the choristers and the remaining vicars, but it is doubtful that they helped much with the cathedral music.[36]

The liturgical reforms of Edward's reign had a great impact on choirs as well. In February 1548 the English Litany was chanted at St Paul's and the Epistle and Gospel were read in English.[37] As the Chronicle of the Grey Friars relates, 'After Ester beganne the servis in Ynglyche at Powles at the commandment of the dene at the tyme, William May, and also in dyvers other pariche churches.'[38] The last Latin mass at St Paul's was sung on the second Sunday in Lent 1549; Coverdale preached, and after the service the dean 'commandyd the sacrament at the hye autre to be pullyd downe.'[39] Westminster Abbey was another center of liturgical experimentation. At the mass before the opening of parliament in November 1547 and at the obit for Henry VIII in May 1548 the ordinary of the mass was sung in English, possibly to music from the Wanley Part-Books.[40] A set of injunctions delivered by royal visitors at Lincoln Cathedral decrees that 'they shall from hensforthe synge or say no Anthemes off our lady or other saynts but only of our lorde, And them not in laten but choseyng owte the beste and moste soundyng to cristen religion they shall turne the same into Englishe, settyng therunto a playn and distincte note, for euery sillable one, they shall singe them and none other.'[41] Archbishop Holgate's injunctions for York Minster (1552) emphasize the desire for

[35] Aylmer and Cant, *York Minster*, 200, 398; York Minster Library, MS H 3/3.
[36] Cole, *Lincoln Chapter Acts, 1547–1559*, xxiv, 131, 145, 149.
[37] H. H. Milman, *Annals of St Paul's Cathedral* (London, John Murray, 1868), 212.
[38] J. G. Nichols (ed.), *Chronicle of the Grey Friars of London*, Camden Society, LIII (London, 1852), 55.
[39] *Ibid.*, 58.
[40] Knighton, 'Collegiate Foundations,' 126–7; Peter le Huray, *Music and the Reformation in England, 1549–1660* (London, Herbert Jenkins, 1967), 172–81.
[41] Henry Bradshaw and Christopher Wordsworth (eds.), *Statutes of Lincoln Cathedral* (2 vols., Cambridge, CUP, 1892), II, 592.

simple music even more clearly. 'We will and command,' he wrote, rather peremptorily, 'that there be none other note sung or used in the said church at any service there to be had, saving square note plain, so that every syllable may be plainly and distinctly pronounced, and without any reports or repeatings which may induce any obscureness to the hearers.'[42]

The first Book of Common Prayer came into general use in June 1549. Performance of Latin service music now became illegal, and in December an attempt was made to call in 'all antiphoners, missales, grayles, processionales, manuelles, legendes, pies, portaises, journalles, and ordinalles' so that they could never be used again.[43] Psalms were still sung – in English of course – and the accounts for Canterbury record the payment of 50s. 'for xxvj psalters of the gretter sort for the quere' in 1550.[44] Other cathedrals, too, must have made a desperate attempt to secure new music for the new services, although one suspects that the Prayer Book was not used as uniformly as the government wished. The Grey Friars' Chronicle testifies to the diversity of practice even in London:

> [At] the Assumpcion of our Lady was soche devision thorrow alle London that some kepte holy day and some none. Almyghty God helpe it when hys wylle ys! for this was the second yere, and also the same devision was at the fest of the Nativitie of our Lady.[45]

The Edwardian reformers regarded organs with almost as much horror as elaborate Latin polyphony. In 1550 Dean May ordered that the instruments at St Paul's be removed; apparently they were silenced but not actually taken down, since they were played again on the accession of Queen Mary.[46] Ridley's injunction prohibiting organ playing in London was echoed at York by Holgate, who decreed 'that there be no more playing of the organs, either at the Morning Prayer, the Communion, or the Evening Prayer within this Church of York, but that the said playing do utterly cease and be left.'[47] All in all the prospects for cathedral musicians could hardly have been bleaker.

III

Much of this changed with the death of Edward VI. Immediately upon the accession of Mary Tudor the organ at St Paul's pealed out and the

[42] Walter H. Frere and W. M. Kennedy (eds.), *Visitation Articles and Injunctions*, Alcuin Club, XIV–XVI (London, 1910), II, 318.
[43] *Ibid.*, II, 856.
[44] Canterbury Cathedral Library, MS MA 40 (unfoliated).
[45] Nichols, *Chronicle of the Grey Friars*, 67.
[46] Milman, *Annals of St Paul's*, 227.
[47] Frere and Kennedy, *Visitation Articles*, II, 320.

choir sang a Te Deum of rejoicing. Liturgical processions were resumed – a splendid one on St Paul's Day, 25 January 1554, included fifty priests in copes of cloth of gold, all singing *Salve Festa Dies.* Prior to the arrival of Philip II the rood was restored; such an audience as was never before present is reported to have attended the reception of Cardinal Pole, with the choir of the Chapel Royal joining in the festive music.[48] A surviving account book for Mary's reign lists regular payments for singing the Psalm *De profundis* and the anthem *O Sapientia*; the ten choristers were treated to apples on St James's Day and special 'refections' on St Paul's Day, All Saints, St Erkenwald's Day, the feast of the Conception of Our Lady, and Christmas.[49] At Westminster the organ was restored and enlarged by John Howe, the celebrated organ maker. New books containing the coronation service were written out, at a cost of £2, and an old antiphoner was bought back from one of the singing men who had hidden it away. But it had to be rebound, at a cost of 19s. 4d.[50]

The accounts for this period at Canterbury reveal an extraordinary number of expenditures for music, and many of these provided an opportunity for cathedral musicians to earn additional income. Robert Coleman, one of the singing men, was paid 10s. 'for prycking of iiij bookes to set forthe the olde services.' Other items include a 'Saltar booke of parchement for ye quere,' 5s.; 'a procession,' 16d.; 'a Journall to serve the quere,' 20d.; 'two Antiphons and a Legend,' bought in London for £4, plus 8d. for carrying them from Faversham to Canterbury; 12d. 'for an Anthem of our Lady in v partes'; 3s. 4d. 'paid to John Marden [a singing man] for the prickyng of gloria in excelsis & Agnus & Sanctus in the Red Book'; and 53s. 4d. to Thomas Bull, the organist, 'for dyvers Songes necessary as Appereth by an Inventory of his owne hande prepared.' Marden was also paid 13s. 4d. 'for prickynge of St. Thomas storye and correcting and mending of dyvers other bokes in ye quere.' A pair of new organs was erected in 'our Lady quere' at a cost of £6 18s. 4d., and there were further expenses for tuning and for mending the bellows. Additional organs appear to have been borrowed for Cardinal Pole's visit, since 'iiij Laborers' received 8d. 'for feching the carydg of a paire of organs from St. Georges & thether againe.' The singing men must have been pleased when they were given their old accustomed 2s. 'vppon Christemas Day in the Morning.'[51]

[48] Milman, *Annals of St Paul's*, 233–9. [49] St Paul's Cathedral Library, MS W. D. 32.
[50] Westminster Abbey Muniments, MSS WAM 37634, 37437; Knighton, 'Collegiate foundations,' 150–1.
[51] Canterbury Cathedral Library, MSS MA 39, 40.

All was not sweetness and light, however. Rather ironically, the choir at Westminster saw its worst days under Mary: there were only eight boys in 1553, and the allocation for choristers' expenses was reduced from £33 6s. 8d. to £27 18s. 4d. It was suggested that the number of lay singing men be cut in half, from twelve to six. This was not done, but the choir remained small, with only eight men and five boys at the time of Mary's death. The restoration of monastic life in 1556 made little difference to the choir, whose members continued to serve through all the changes and vicissitudes of mid-century.[52] Presumably they enjoyed the five quarts of muscatel bought for them 'accordyng to the old custome' on Palm Sunday, and the boys may have thought it a lark to strew baskets of flowers. But there was dissension. One wonders whether it was sharp differences about religion which led 'ser Hamond pryste' to 'breake John Wodes heade, being one of the clerkes, with a pote' in 1556. Hamond was banished to the gatehouse for three days, and poor Wood was given 40s. 'for the healinge of his heade.'[53]

IV

With Elizabeth's accession the quarrel over the character of church music came to a head, and the very existence of trained choirs was threatened. The 1559 Prayer Book came into compulsory use on 24 June and the restored Latin services were eliminated once more, this time permanently. Shortly thereafter the Puritan disdain for elaborate music reappeared very strongly. In the Convocation of 1563 the more precise Genevans proposed that 'the use of organs and curious singing be removed': they favored only unaccompanied, unison singing of metrical Psalms, and that by the whole congregation, without a professional choir. This was too extreme to pass, but a majority of members present in the Lower House did support the silencing of organs. Cathedral musicians, if they knew what was going on in London, must have rejoiced when such radical propositions failed.[54]

But the Queen was on the side of the choirs. An accomplished musician herself, Elizabeth included a famous pronouncement encouraging choral

[52] A good example is Christopher Brickett. Originally a chorister in the monastic Lady Chapel choir, he became a scholar in the grammar school in 1540 and a singing man in 1549, continuing to serve in the choir until his death at age 77 on Ascension Day 1596. See Knighton, 'Collegiate foundations,' 349.

[53] Westminster Abbey Muniments, MSS WAM 33604, 37646B, 37716, 3319E, and Act Book, 1542–1609, fol. 98*v*.; Knighton, 'Collegiate foundations,' 147–64, 349–50.

[54] William P. Haugaard, *Elizabeth and the English Reformation* (Cambridge, CUP, 1968), 168–9.

music in her first Royal Injunctions. Characteristic of the Queen at her most moderate and attractive, this section is often cited in part but is worth quoting here in full, especially because it refers to financial support for the choirs.

Item, because in divers collegiate and also some parish churches heretofore there hath been livings appointed for the maintenance of men and children to use singing in the church, by means wherof the laudable science of music hath been in estimation, and preserved in knowledge; the Queen's majesty neither meaning in any wise the decay of anything that might conveniently tend to the use and continuance of the said science, neither to have the same in any part so abused in the Church that thereby the Common Prayer should be the worse understanded of the hearers, willeth and commandeth that first no alteration be made of such assignments of living, as heretofore hath been appointed to the use of singing or music in the Church, but that the same so remain. And that there be a modest and distinct song, so used in all parts of the Common Prayers in the Church, that the same may be as plainly understanded, as if it were read without singing. And yet, nevertheless, for the comforting of such that delight in music, it may be permitted, that in the beginning, or in the end of Common Prayers, either at morning or evening, there may be sung an hymn, or such-like song, to the praise of Almighty God, in the best sort of melody and music that may be conveniently devised, having respect that the sentence of the hymn may be understanded and perceived.[55]

Episcopal injunctions issued throughout Elizabeth's reign tended to echo her own statement, sometimes with Puritan overtones. In 1562 Bishop Horne insisted that 'no other note be sung' at Winchester 'but such as every syllable thereby may be both plainly and distinctly pronounced . . . and well understanded.' Nine years later he charged the choir to eliminate 'repeating of notes'; their music should not 'draw out . . . or shorten any word or syllable otherwise than by the nature of the word it is pronounced in common speech.' Parkhurst told his colleagues at Norwich to use no 'ditties' which had not been authorized by the government or the ordinary. The Lambeth Articles of 1561 called for the destruction of all old service books, and in 1565 Bishop Bentham repeated the charge, telling the people of Coventry and Lichfield to 'cast away your Mass books, your portesses and all other books of Latin service.'[56] In 1565 the Queen herself was distressed to hear that 'sondrie varieties & novelties in opinions & in externall ceremonies & rites' persisted. She sought 'vnitye quietnes & concord amongest her . . . ministers' and straitly charged all in authority to secure conformity. Her letter was forwarded to the dean and chapter of Lincoln by Archbishop Parker; they replied that they could

[55] Frere and Kennedy, *Visitation Articles*, III, 22–3. [56] *Ibid.*, III, 136, 319, 317, 96, 166.

'fynde none to offend in anie parte of such disorder,' and they sent a certificate of conformity.[57]

The daily schedule for vicars and singing men was fixed in royal injunctions for Exeter, and similar orders were sent to several other cathedrals. A bell was to be rung at 6 a.m. summoning the choir members to sing the Litany. 'All vicars and singing men shall be present in the choir in their habits one quarter of an hour before eight of the clock,' the injunctions continue, 'and then to begin the Common Prayer according to the order of the book for the morning service.' At 9 o'clock they were to attend divinity lectures (Monday, Wednesday, and Friday) or readings from the Paraphrase (Tuesday, Thursday, and Saturday), concluding with the singing of the Lord's Prayer in English, and at 10 the vicars and singing men were to commence the Communion. At Carlisle all ministers of the choir were to communicate together at least eight times a year, while singing men at Westminster were fined if they did not communicate monthly. The vicars choral of York were required (by Grindal, in 1572) to attend divinity lectures and be examined on their content by the Chancellor; they were to study St Paul's Epistles, with those under the age of forty memorizing a chapter a week. Choristers were to be examined in the English catechism three times a quarter. Lay clerks and choristers at Winchester were admonished to 'give their diligent attendance to every sermon to be made in the said church.' They were to have an English New Testament, and choristers were to memorize a chapter from the Gospels or the Acts of the Apostles each fortnight.[58]

The need for musical settings of English texts is reflected in the account books from several of the cathedrals. Once again there was an opportunity for some singers to receive extra pay. At Canterbury George Juxon, one of the lay clerks, was given 10s. 'for makyng and pryckyng certen songes for the quere' in 1575, while John Ward received £7 in 1600 and £2 in 1602 for pricking services.[59] The fragmentary treasurer's books for Rochester record the purchase in 1591 of two 'communion and service books' as well as paper and ink, possibly for transcribing music.[60] Just after Elizabeth's death 26s. 8d. was allowed at Ely 'for pricking of Churche songes.'[61] Money was spent caring for the organs too: the ubiquitous

[57] Lincolnshire Record Office, MSS Dean and Chapter A/3/7, fols. 42–3, and A/3/8, fols. 21–2.

[58] Frere and Kennedy, *Visitation Articles*, III, 41–3, 339, 347–8, 351, 138–9; Westminster Abbey Muniments, MS Act Book, 1542–1609, fol. 106.

[59] Canterbury Cathedral Library, MS MA 41.

[60] Kent Archives Office (Maidstone), MS DRc/FTb6.

[61] Ely Cathedral Archives, Cambridge University Library, MS EDC 3/1/2, fol. 7.

John Howe was paid a retainer of 12s. a year at Westminster, 13s. 4d. at St Paul's, and 5s. 8d. at Rochester, while a less prominent builder named Blackard was able to charge £2 for 'mendyng the organs' at Canterbury in 1580.[62]

V

Throughout Elizabeth's reign cathedral choirs struggled with problems in finance, discipline, and morale. It is not easy to calculate the income of singing men and choristers, since they were usually entitled to housing and meals as well as their nominal salaries. Some cases are clearer than others. At Canterbury, an unusually well financed foundation, twelve lay clerks received annual stipends of £10, and ten choristers were allowed £4 each. But the full number of singing men could only be made up by bringing in musicians from the town. Westminster (now no longer technically a cathedral, but refounded in 1560 as a collegiate church exempt from episcopal jurisdiction) paid £8 apiece to its vicars choral (ten in 1562, twelve by 1580) and £3 6s. 8d. to the ten choristers. Eight pounds was also the fee of the eight men at Rochester. The number of vicars choral at Lincoln was cut from twelve to nine in 1558, but even so they were allowed only £4 apiece; in 1561 there was complaint that there was not enough money for the seneschal of the choristers to buy adequate food for them. Under these conditions it was probably impossible to attract new vicars choral, and in 1594 the dean and chapter entered into an agreement with John Cheseman to serve as a stipendiary in the place of a vicar choral, the vicars paying him £10 a year. The resulting inequity was not resolved until 1598, when all the senior vicars choral were granted an augmentation of £4 and Cheseman (now a vicar) agreed to satisfy himself with the resulting salary of £8. Some vicars were able to supplement this wage by holding additional positions; George Hudleston, of whom more later, was sacrist at Lincoln in the 1590s, and the succentor was drawn from the ranks of the vicars choral or singing men in most of the cathedrals. At Salisbury the revenues designated for altarists were given, improperly, to lay vicars as a supplement to their salaries. At Ely the eight lay clerks received 40s. a quarter (£8 p.a.): some idea of their social status can be gleaned from the fact that the dean's quarterly stipend was £30, while even the six poor almsmen ('pauperes') received 33s. 4d. Only 16s. 8d. was allowed for each of the eight choristers. Considering the rampant

[62] Westminster Abbey Muniments, MSS WAM 33618–19; St Paul's Cathedral Library, MS W. D. 32, fol. 77*v*.; Kent Archives Office, MS DRc/FTb3; Canterbury Cathedral Library, MS MA 41.

price inflation it seems clear that the economic status of cathedral musicians declined, perhaps disastrously, in the sixteenth century.[63]

The financial distress of the singing men was compounded by the fact that most of them were now married, with families to support and no desire to avail themselves of the opportunities for communal living which remained as a legacy of the middle ages. The problem of vicars choral preferring to live outside their college or close was not new with Elizabeth's reign: as early as 1542 three junior vicars at Lincoln were reprimanded for lodging in taverns or the houses of lay people, and one finds similar entries elsewhere.[64] But the advent of clerical marriage, coupled with the more frequent employment of lay singers, greatly increased the difficulty.

Some remarkable surviving documents for the Bedern at York vividly chronicle these changes. Here the individual houses were unsuitable for wives and certainly too small for families; the records refer to them as 'cubicles,' probably similar to the rooms occupied by students at Oxford and Cambridge. As the number of vicars choral declined, outsiders came to rent the surplus chambers, so that most of the lodgings were not actually occupied by the vicars. Still, the vicars choral continued to take one meal together each day. Their 'Kitchen Book,' beginning in 1563, lists the main courses served. During the second and third weeks in November 1567 they were:

Sunday	Goose	Roast beef
Monday	Beef	Mutton
Tuesday	Mutton	Veal
Wednesday	Haddock	Lampreys
Thursday	Rabbit	Rabbit
Friday	Whiting	Whiting
Saturday	Milk & eggs	Milk & eggs

Other entries give expenses. A roast goose cost 5s. 3½d., a pig 4s., 'capons roste' 4s. 5d. Salmon was less, only 2s. 11d. In all, the charges for a typical week's food amounted to 54s. 1d.[65] Considerable 'Howshoulde stoof'

[63] Canterbury Cathedral Library, MSS MA 40–41; Frere and Kennedy, *Visitation Articles*, I, 153; Westminster Abbey Muniments, MSS WAM 33619, 33640, and Royal Charter LXXXVII; Kent Archives Office, MSS DRc/Aool/1, DRc/Ao12, DRc/FTb6; Lincolnshire Record Office, MSS Dean and Chapter A/3/7, fols. 11*v*., 120*v*., and A/3/9, fols. 1–3; Ely Cathedral Archives, Cambridge University Library, MSS EDC 3/1/1–2; and, Robertson, *Sarum Close*, 144.

[64] Cole, *Lincoln Chapter Acts, 1536–1547*, 63.

[65] York Minister Library, MS Vicars Choral Kitchen Book, 1563–1644, fols. 1–22.

was needed to prepare and serve these dinners. An inventory compiled in 1564 lists, among other things:

In primis xix sylver spones. Item one masure, lased about with silver with a cover and a knope of silver.
Item one drinking cuppe of silver and a cover of silver.
Item one pece of silver with a cover parcell guilt.
Item four iugges and xv drinkinge pottes.
Item two dosen of trenchers.
Item iiij basens, four vres, and four candlesticks, four saltes peuter and one skeele.
Item one stampe with xxx counters. And a paire of waightes, with Calvens institutions [*sic*].[66]

According to a statute accepted by eleven vicars late in Edward's reign those who were 'absent and furthe of commons' were to be fined 2d. a week. Even if they were sick they were to pay a penny.[67] These payments are recorded in the Kitchen Book, which shows that only four or five of the older vicars (presumably the unmarried ones) dined regularly in the early 1570s.[68] The end came in 1574, when a melancholy entry states:

M^d^ that the subchaunter Burlande, Sr Kay, Swaine, Iverson, Richardson, Hunter, Lee and Burges bretheren and felowes of the Colledge called the Bederne, did geve vpp howse kepinge or kepinge of commons together in the hall this weeke vppon Satturday the xxvij^th^ day of June Anno Dni 1574 by all ther consentes for so long tyme as they shoulde thinke goode therof.

A further note in another hand explains that:

This commons was broken vp by the sute of the maryed men being vicars chorall to the Deane called Mathew Hutton who gave license so to do, for that the maryed men shuld not be duble charged. Wherfore all the hoole company of the sayd vicars chorall dyd so agre vnto the same as is afore sayd.[69]

The property of the college was divided among the vicars beginning in 1577, although some silver spoons remained as late as 1591, when it was decided to give each vicar two and the subchanter three.[70] Similar events, less well documented, occurred elsewhere; at Norwich the common table was out of use by 1608, although there was talk of restoring it, and the same thing seems to have been true at Salisbury and Exeter.[71]

Under these conditions it is not surprising that discipline was hard to

66 *Ibid.*, fol. 23*v*.
67 York Minster Library, MS Vicars Choral Statute Book, 130.
68 York Minster Library, MS Vicars Choral Kitchen Book, fols. 144–81.
69 *Ibid.*, fol. 193.
70 *Ibid.*, fol. 202; Frederick Harrison, *Life in a Medieval College*, 218–25.
71 Boston, *Norwich Cathedral*, 51; Woodfill, *Musicians in English Society*, 138.

maintain. Nearly everywhere the Elizabethan records are shot through with complaints about laxity and drinking. In 1560 the subchanter at Canterbury admitted to the commissioners visiting the cathedral that there was negligence in coming to service and some drunkenness and quarreling among the minor canons.[72] The royal injunctions for Carlisle (1564) threatened expulsion of petty canons who were 'tavern or alehouse haunters, common drunkards dicers [or] carders.'[73] Thomas Smythe, the master of the choristers at Salisbury, was such a common drunkard and dicer; he had rows with the organist, and the boys openly mocked him. He was removed by Bishop Jewel but was later pardoned and finally became organist himself.[74] Some of the singers at Canterbury and Carlisle were suspected of papistry; they were to be examined and the certificate sent to Archbishop Parker.[75]

The vicars choral of Lincoln seem to have been a particularly quarrelsome lot – or, perhaps, their disputes merely happen to be better documented than most. In 1576 a junior vicar was accused of quarreling with one of his senior colleagues; he was admonished and placed under supervision for a quarter. In 1583 two more junior vicars charged with contempts and violent wrongs were threatened with expulsion. In 1584 the organist's salary was sequestered temporarily because of his negligence in teaching the boys, and he was accused of 'insignem negligentiam' again in 1595, primarily because he was not teaching the boys to play the organ. In 1594 one of the vicars was deprived because of his long absence from the cathedral. Another vicar, accused of infamous living and 'impregnacione cuiusdam mulieris infra ca[thedralem] Lincoln,' was expelled but later restored. (He seems to have married the woman.) The vicars were involved in a long controversy over the dean's right to claim payment for residence – if this were disallowed the vicars would share in the distribution of revenues. Even a letter written by the bishop in 1601 in support of the dean did not settle the matter. One of the vicars choral, George Hudleston, appears to have been especially lazy, argumentative, rash, and nosey. He was examined by the archdeacon in 1594 to ascertain 'How he came to y[e] knowledge of the contents of a certayn lettre sente by hym [the archdeacon] to M[r] Deane elected And how much therof he knew'; Hudleston claimed that he had merely found a scrap of paper in the body of the church. In 1599 the dean and chapter had a full discussion of the 'intollerabil negligens' of the vicars choral, poor clerks, and

[72] Frere and Kennedy, *Visitation Articles*, I, 153.
[73] *Ibid.*, III, 147.
[74] Robertson, *Sarum Close*, 139.
[75] Frere and Kennedy, *Visitation Articles*, III, 234, 339.

choristers and sent the head vicar a stern warning.[76] Things seem to have improved after 1600, although there is still a reference to the vicars' absence from divine service in 1602.[77]

VI

By the time of Elizabeth's death choral establishments had been reconstructed along new lines. Communal living arrangements, whether monastic or otherwise, had gone. Financial resources had eroded. One senses a lack of religious devotion and a generally secular attitude. Cathedral singers were now, probably with few exceptions, men with musical gifts rather than religious vocations. They lived as members of the urban middle classes, less well off than merchants or skilled craftsmen.

But they must have continued to sing amazingly well. The mere fact that they could manage to perform the difficult works of William Byrd and the other great Elizabethan composers is one argument for musical quality. Another derives from listeners' comments. It is true that virtually none of these have survived for the Queen's reign itself. But things were probably much the same in the 1630s, and we are fortunate in having a number of descriptions from that decade. Lieutenant Hammond's travel diary for 1635, for instance, records favorable experiences at several cathedrals. At Rochester 'her Organs though small, yet are they rich and neat; her Quiristers though but few, yet orderly and decent.' At Canterbury he 'saw and heard a fayre Organ sweet and tunable, and a deep and rauishing consert of Quirsters.' At Winchester 'they sing sweet and heauenly Anthems' and the organist is one of the rarest in the land. Exeter possessed 'a delicate, rich, and lofty Organ which has more additions than any other, as fayre Pipes of an extraordinary length, and of the bigenesse of a man's Thigh'; although the 'melodious and heauenly Harmony [was] able to rauish the Hearers Eares.' Only at Chichester and Peterborough was the singing indifferent.[78] Services could be moving experiences. For years the worthy George Herbert made his way twice a week to the cathedral at Salisbury, 'and at his return he would say, that his time spent in prayers and cathedral music elevated his soul, and was heaven upon earth.'[79]

[76] Lincolnshire Record Office, MSS Dean and Chapter A/3/7, fols. 81*r*., 95*r*., 97*v*., 120; A/3/9, fols. 3, 6–20; Bj 3-3, *passim*.

[77] *Ibid*., A/3/9, fol. 26*v*.

[78] [? Hammond], 'A relation of a short survey of the Western Counties,' ed. by Leopold Wickham Legg, *Camden Miscellany XVI,* Camden Society, 3rd series, LII (London, Royal Historical Society, 1936), 9. 11, 34, 46, 74, 87.

[79] Izaak Walton, 'The life of Mr George Herbert,' in *The Works of George Herbert* (London, Frederick Warne, n.d.), 35.

Despite troubles created by parliamentary legislation, government rapacity, Puritan disapproval, inflation, and indifference, cathedral choirs survived the Reformation, providing the church with new English services and anthems no less beautiful than the medieval Latin masses and motets. Problems indeed remained, and the civil war was shortly to prove even more unsettling than the break with Rome. By 1603, however, the Reformation of choirs was complete. Within the cathedrals a new Anglican musical tradition had taken firm root.

The Age of Debt, the Reformation and English law

DELLOYD J. GUTH*

All law is based on property, and all legitimated rights and obligations find their roots in essentially proprietary concepts. This dogma embraces our right to life, as well as our right to any realty and moveables that we might inherit or choose to acquire or divest. It follows, both logically and historically, that the single most pervasive concept in law is debt. *Meum et tuum*, what's mine is mine and what's yours is yours, binds all criminal and civil pleadings into the one proprietary base. It also strongly urges moral obligation, that mine and yours are in their respective places 'rightfully' until we agree, individually or mutually, to make a change of place. Any claim that *meum et tuum* has been dislocated – a life lost by homicide or wronged by negligence, a promissory note defaulted – therefore must be determined true or false and then restitution adjudged. At common law this requires a jury, to determine the fact, and a judge, to determine the relevant law and its remedy. With debt at the law's center, it is easy to see the natural conjoining of the legal with the moral: 'to owe' and 'to ought' are two sides of the same debt. That dual reality for debt flourished in late medieval law and society, but it did not long survive the Reformation era and what we might call the 'de-moralizing' of debt.[1]

* In more rudimentary form, I read this essay to the Canadian Conference on the History and Philosophy of Law, at the University of Windsor, 9–11 June 1980. For that invitation I happily thank Professor John Underwood Lewis of Windsor's Department of Philosophy. In this effort I have also had constant encouragement from Professor J. C. Smith of the Faculty of Law, the University of British Columbia.

Since then, extensive revisions have been made with help from: (*a*) an exhaustive critique of my original paper by Professor Charles Donahue, Jr, of Harvard Law School; and (*b*) an American Council of Learned Societies' Travel Grant for a June–July 1981 visit to England for further research and reinforcement. I gratefully acknowledge both for their generous support, reserving to myself all responsibility for this essay's final form, argument, and research.

1 The theme of debt raises issues fundamental to history, law, and jurisprudence that I can only suggest here. This essay is one more part of my comprehensive study of late medieval law courts and litigation, begun at Clare College, Cambridge, under the regular scrutiny of Professor Elton. Though my continuing obligation to him remains self-evident, this

Within this historical context, the Tudor era can be viewed as a pivotal point for the centrality of debt in English legal development. If the two centuries following the civil war brought the 'Age of Contract,'[2] then one might label the preceding three centuries the 'Age of Debt.' By Henry VIII's reign, the judicial system available to Englishmen interwove the king's common law across the crazyquilt of local customary and ecclesiastical jurisdictions. Debt, with its correlative action of trespass, had come to dominate late medieval litigation.[3] This courtroom reality, in fact, only mirrored a broader social truth: late-medieval language and its metaphors were supersaturated with the imagery of debt.

I

'Give us this day our daily bread. And forgive us our debts even as we forgive our debtors.' So read the English version of the Lord's Prayer in use from the fourteenth through the sixteenth centuries, from Wycliffe in 1390[4] through Bishop Pecock's biblical paraphrases in the 1450s[5] to the Geneva Bible of 1557.[6] The Scottish version in Matthew's Gospel was 'And forgif to us our dettis, as we forgef to our dettouris,' while Luke's more succinct text became 'And forgeve to us our synnis: as we forgeve to ilk man that aw to us.'[7] Bishop John Fisher of Rochester, shortly before

brief study is written 'For all honest det suld be Quyt with possibilite': *The Original Chronicle of Andrew of Wyntoun*, ed. F. J. Amours for the Scottish Text Society, L. (Edinburgh, William Blackwood and Sons, 1903), II, bk I, 7 (ll. 65–6).

2 P. S. Atiyah, *The Rise and Fall of Freedom of Contract* (Oxford, Clarendon Press, 1979). I admit to a slight fiddling with Professor Atiyah's periodization but I believe that I remain constructively within the meaning of his superbly argued synthesis. He sees 'an Age of Property' (90, 398) ending in 1770, when both 'The Age of Freedom of Contract' (217ff.) and 'An Age of Principles' (345,649) begin. His emphasis on social contract theorists and on a case law following the Statute of Frauds (1677) argue significantly for a developmental period in contract law from the 1660s. His perspective on 'Property' comes mainly from lawyers' literature while mine on 'Debt' comes from court records of litigation. He does discuss property with a focus on the action of debt (138–53 and esp. 189–93).

3 DeLloyd J. Guth, 'Enforcing late-medieval law: patterns in litigation during Henry VII's reign,' in *Legal Records and the Historian*, ed. by J. H. Baker (London, Royal Historical Society, 1978), 80–96; and, C. W. Brooks, 'Litigants and Attorneys in the King's Bench and Common Pleas, 1560–1640,' *ibid.*, 41–59.

4 *The Holy Bible . . . in the Earliest English Versions Made from the Latin Vulgate by John Wycliffe and His Followers*, ed. Josiah Forshall and Frederic Madden (Oxford, The University Press, 1850), IV, 14 (Matthew 6: 11–13). The Latin Vulgate: *Et dimitte nobis debita nostra, sicut et nos dimittimus debitoribus nostris.* This version survives in the King James's Translation, *The Holy Bible* (London, Robert Barker, 1611).

5 William C. Greet (ed.), *The Reule of Crysten Religioun, by Reginald Pecock*, EETS, original series, CLXXI (London, 1927).

6 *The Bible* (Geneva, Rouland Hill, 1560), Matthew 6: 12. This follows verbatim the Myles Coverdale translation published in 1535.

7 *The New Testament in Scots, Being Purvey's Revision of Wycliffe's Version Turned into Scots by*

joining Sir Thomas More at the Tower block in 1535, preached on Christ's Passion and reinforced this meaning: 'But the dampned sinner that must paye his own debtes in hell, shal suffer everlasting death . . . [and] shalt come to that place to pay thy debtes of thine own sinnes . . . [so] that the debtes of thy sinnes shall be throughly payde.'[8] A common theological manual added that the Seventh Commandment against stealing applied to those 'that nell not pay hare dette that thei oweth.'[9]

Debt thus carried with it the most personalized idea of contractual obligation, where it became primarily an internal matter of conscience, an external matter of morally right behavior and, of course, ultimately of salvation or damnation. 'And of a trewe man, be-heste [promise] is dette.'[10] Being as good as your word, harmonizing act with assurance, provided the reason for repayment. Debt meant promise, not in binding future performance but to bind past exchanges into the present where the debt, like sin, survived until formally repaid or absolved. Thus one could deny the validity of an obligation when previously unforeseen circumstances changed its nature: 'Allso if that impossible were thy promise . . . I calle never suche a promyse to be a dette.'[11] That might not have convinced a late-medieval court of law; but the action of debt on a written obligation did allow certain defenses in that direction, where defendant claimed that the deed *non est factum suum*, alleging a variety of reasons related to the debt's origins.[12] None of this meant a contract in the modern or even seventeenth century sense of a judicially enforceable future obligation. Rather, as the morality play *Everyman* had it, 'Promise is duty' in the continuing present and 'Wyll ye breke promyse that is dette?'[13]

This all gave the simplest, most popular understanding for the debtor–creditor obligation, relating sin directly to debt and duty. It

Murdoch Nisbet c. 1520, The Scottish Text Society, XLVI (Edinburgh, William Blackwood and Sons, 1901), I, 34–5, 237–8.

[8] John E. B. Mayor (ed.), *The English Works of John Fisher*, EETS, extra series, XXVII (London, 1876), 426 (ll. 10–12) and 427 (ll. 14–16, 33–4). The work is 'A Sermon verie fruitfull . . . unto the Passion of Christ.'

[9] J. H. L. Kengen (ed.), *Memoriale Credencium: A Late Middle English Manual of Theology for Lay People edited from Bodley MS Tanner 201* (Nijmegen, The Netherlands, Department of Middle English [1980]), 45 (ll. 18–19).

[10] Thomas Hoccleve, *Works*, vol. III: *The Regement of Princes*, ed. Frederick J. Furnivall, EETS, extra series, LXXII (London, 1897), 64 (l. 1772), written *c.* 1412.

[11] Charlotte D'Evelyn (ed.), *Peter Idley's Instructions to His Son*, Modern Language Association, Monograph Series VI (Boston, D. C. Heath and Company, 1935), 89 (ll. 484 and 488), written 1445–50.

[12] John H. Baker, *An Introduction to English Legal History* (London, Butterworths, 1971), 180.

[13] A. C. Cawley (ed.), *Everyman* (Manchester, Manchester University Press, 1961), 8 (l. 248) and 25 (l. 821).

placed reliance entirely on forgiveness of debt (sin), for anyone seeking restitution (salvation), and it made God the Great Creditor, the final accountant for each and every human, specifically at the Doomsday reckoning for final debts. In this context the pervasiveness of debt, and even of usury, after 1200 literally created the need for 'the birth of purgatory' in late-medieval Christian orthodoxy.[14] There mankind could find a way station after death but before one's heaven-or-hell destination, in order to make restitution for debts (sins) '. . . till that the Raunsom for them be truly payde.'[15] All of this enriches one fifteenth century *Good Wife's* aphoristic sigh.' 'At es [ease] he lyves that awe no dette.'[16]

It is also easy to see why debt became a common metaphor for death. 'By the comune lawe of nature every man muste paye his mortal tribute . . . Whenne thou shalt paye unto our lorde thy dette of naturale dethe.' In this way Anthony Woodville, earl Rivers, translated for Caxton's press in 1479 from the French version of Denis le Chartreux's *De quatuor novissimis*.[17] Robert Fabyan's *Chronicle* reported in 1509 that: 'This magnyficente and excellent prince Henry the. vii. thus payed to deth his dette of nature.'[18] A century later in *The Tempest*, Shakespeare made Trinculo exclaim 'O forgive me my sins!' only to be rebuffed by Stephano: 'He that dies, pays all debts.'[19] If man received life on credit from his maker, then death marked cancellation and final reckoning for that debt.

With typical Middle English variety, debt also had a sensual meaning, sanctioning sexual pleasures. Geoffrey Chaucer's Wife of Bath asserted 'that a man shall yelde to his wyf hire dette,'[20] referring to his obligation

[14] Jacques Le Goff, 'The usurer and purgatory,' *The Dawn of Modern Banking*, ed. Fredi Chiappelli (New Haven, Yale University Press, 1979), 43–52. Following Le Goff, I mean this 'birth of purgatory' in the sense of popular theological necessity; but in place of his explicatory emphasis on mercantile usury I urge the contemporary focus on debt. As to the place itself, various pre-1200 writers and preachers at least hint at purgatory, perhaps as far back as Augustine. Dante Alighieri's *Divine Comedy* will, of course, graphically embed it in Christian consciousness from the start of the fourteenth century.

[15] Mayor, *John Fisher*, 362 (ll. 26–7), in 'A spiritual consolation.'

[16] Tauno F. Mustanoja (ed.), *The Good Wife Taught Her Daughter* (Helsinki, Annales Academiae Scientiarum Fennicae, 1948), 220 (ll. 161–2), written *c.* 1350.

[17] Anthony Woodville, *Cordyal* (London, William Caxton, 24 March, 19 Edward IV) [fol. 8, ll. 1–2, and fol. 137, ll. 2–3], based on Jean Mielot's version; *STC* 5758. This raises to mind the broad thematic color and gloom in Johan Huizinga, *The Waning of the Middle Ages* (London, Edward Arnold, 1937).

[18] Robert Fabyan, *Chronicle*, 2nd edn (London, William Rastell, 1533), fol. 482: *STC* 10660.

[19] Alfred Harbage (ed.), *William Shakespeare: The Complete Works*, 'The Tempest,' ed. by Northrop Frye (Baltimore, Penguin Books, 1969), 1387: Act III, ii, ll. 127–8.

I cannot resist the reminder that Socrates' final words, as he died of the hemlock, were: 'Crito, we owe a cock to Asklepios; pray do not forget to pay the debt'; R. Hackforth (ed.), *Plato's Phaedo* (Cambridge, CUP, 1955), 190.

[20] Walter W. Skeat (ed.), *The Complete Works of Geoffrey Chaucer* (Oxford, The Clarendon Press, 1894), IV, 324 (l. 130). This entire topic is now lucidly explored by Thomas N.

to have sexual intercourse with his wife whenever she so desired. This derived from St Paul's First Letter to Corinthians, 7, as found in all English and Scottish translations before and after the Reformation: 'ye woman paie her fleisch dette to her husbond asking it, and biddeth ye husbond paie his fleischli dette to his wiyf asking it.'[21]

No better example than William Langland's *Piers the Plowman* has summed up late-medieval society's fascination with the debtor's metaphor. At the point where Christ gave his final charge to Peter, alias Piers, Langland's scriptural paraphrase continued:

> And after this, Christ taught his apostles how to live the life of Do-Best, and gave Piers authority to dispense pardon and mercy and forgiveness to all men. He granted him power to remit all kinds of sins, but only on condition that men gladly acknowledged his Pardon and fulfilled its condition, *Redde quod debes* – Pay back that which thou owest. So, provided that condition is carried out, Piers has the power to bind and unbind both on earth and in heaven, and absolve men from every sin except debt. As soon as these things were accomplished, Christ ascended into heaven, to dwell there until the Last Day, when He will come again and reward to the full whoever 'pays back that which he owes' – and paye it honestly and completely. And those who do not pay their debts He will punish.[22]

Here, restitution was a prerequisite for absolution, putting debt, and only debt, outside of priestly authority until the debtors (sinners) had restored themselves *status quo ante*. Salvation itself had come to be expressed in a mercantile vocabulary. Words associated with commercial obligation, money-lending, and book-keeping had come to be applied directly to the business of heaven-seeking (supervised, may we presume, by Recording Angels?).

II

Did this metaphorical reality, equating debt with both obligation and wrongdoing, express in any way the judicial reality of pre-Reformation England? The short answer is an emphatic yes. If we take common law, ecclesiastical, and local customary jurisdictions as a unitary judicial system – which was the view of any potential litigant seeking legitimated remedies – then all courts produced records clogged by actions of debt.

Tentler, *Sin and Confession on the Eve of the Reformation* (Princeton, Princeton University Press, 1977), 170–86.

21 This is the most lively translation that I have found: Greet, *Pecock's Reule of Crysten Religioun*, 347. The Latin Vulgate has it: *Uxori vir debitum reddat: similiter autum et uxor viro.*

22 William Langland, *Piers the Ploughman*, ed. J. F. Goodridge (Baltimore, Penguin Books, 1959), 236. *Redde quod debes* is in Matthew 18: 28; Wycliffe renders it 'Yelde that thou owest,' while the King James version is 'Pay mee that thou owest.'

Late medieval actions of debt rested upon notions of obligation and wrongdoing that complemented contemporary literal usages.

In a distinction as old as Roman law, debt was a personal action (*in personam*), not a real action (*in rem*).[23] In the England of 1500, personal actions offered litigants the means for suing cases that involved movables (chattels), mainly by actions of debt or of trespass. These two had virtually driven out all real actions, which had traditionally provided the means for suing cases that involved realty (land). This did not mean that litigation in 1500 no longer concerned land, only that personal actions had become the preferred procedure for claims involving either movables or realty. The action of debt dominated judicial business because it quintessentially defined late medieval obligation, both legal and moral, and because medieval law had no formalized law of contract, in the modern sense of exchanges based on future promises. English contract law would not emerge until the seventeenth century. Before that, debt was available in practice for all cases involving money (or some *res fungibiles*); and this included all claims based on an obligation or where any formal exchange of benefits had occurred.[24] Obviously where money represented payments for land, the transaction created a debt that could be prosecuted as such. And in all actions of debt, 'the ground of the action is a duty.'[25] This judicial dictum reiterated the moral root of debt's legal obligation.

In personal actions, three stages emerged: (1) the plaintiff claimed a debt for-some amount or for an unfulfilled obligation, or he claimed a trespass done against his property; (2) the court, in turn, then offered a mesne process with writs designed to secure the defendant's person into the court (*venire facias*), even to seize (*capias*) his body before the court, and ultimately to declare his contumacious person an outlaw (*utlagatum*); and, (3) most importantly for an action of debt, if the lawsuit reached stages where issue had been joined and verdict rendered, the court's judgment could be enforced by imprisonment until repayment had been made with damages. This clearly was the procedural route that litigants, and pre-

23 Fritz Schulz, *Classical Roman Law* (Oxford, The Clarendon Press, 1951), 32–4, shows how far the English distinction strayed from the classical; also, W. W. Buckland and Arnold D. McNair, *Roman Law and Common Law*, 2nd edn, rev. by F. H. Lawson (Cambridge, CUP, 1965), 89–98. Discomfort in applying the distinction to common law was clearly defined by Frederick Pollock and Frederic William Maitland, *The History of English Law*, 2nd edn (Cambridge, CUP, 1968), II, 570–2; F. W. Maitland, *The Forms of Action at Common Law*, ed. by A. H. Chaytor and W. J. Whittaker (Cambridge, CUP, 1948), 73–5.

24 C. H. S. Fifoot, *History and Sources of the Common Law: Tort and Contract* (London, Stevens & Sons Limited, 1949), 225–33; Baker, *English Legal History*, 174–5; S. F. C. Milsom, 'Sale of goods in the fifteenth century,' *Law Quarterly Review*, LXXVII (1961), 257–84.

25 *Year Book*, 7 Henry VI, fol. 5, pl. 9: for 1428; also, *Year Book*, 37 Henry VI, fol. 8, pl. 18: for 1458; and, Fifoot, *History and Sources of the Common Law*, 401–2, esp. fn. 30.

sumably their lawyers, preferred from the thirteenth into the sixteenth centuries.

Personal actions, in theory at least, pertained only to movables (*catalla*), so late medieval litigants had the other general choice of real actions whenever their claim concerned land. There was certainly no dearth of real actions available in late medieval legal quivers. One could rain a variety of original writs at one's opponent, claiming title and possession for lands, tenements, commons, rents, and the more abstract hereditaments attached to land in potential perpetuity like annuities, profits, advowsons, and franchises. Littleton's *Tenures* sought to clarify all of this land law *c.* 1470.[26] But mesne process in real actions, to get a defendant's court appearance, was both less effective than in personal actions and more menacing to such a property-based society: the original writ summoned the defendant (tenant) and, failing that, the land (but not the person) could be seized by the king and then ultimately lost by default to the plaintiff.

What had happened since the formation of the elaborate twelfth century system of writs of right, writs of entry, of the possessory assizes, and of proprietary actions for land and hereditaments? Constitutional and legal history textbooks have schooled generations to believe that all that we value in the English, as well as continental, legal traditions grew from private real property and the real actions designed to protect it. By presuming that pre-modern, meaning pre-industrial, law followed the land = wealth formula, everything from the trial jury to the franchise and the constitutional monarchy itself, whether in Magna Carta or the Glorious Revolution, has been made to owe existence to noble landlords tailoring land law to suit their own immediate interests. If we wish to cling to such presumptions, then those real actions must be found somewhere other than in the actual law courts, perhaps only in the lawyers' literature, because they are decreasingly used by litigants. After the thirteenth century, the legal protection for all property, movables and real, had shifted clearly to the personal actions: debt and trespass. If the lawyers did not lead, perhaps their clients forced the change.

But land law, real actions, real property are what constitutional historians have mistakenly made their centerpiece for the age of debt and often into the age of contract.[27] In doing so they have relied upon the

[26] *Littleton's Tenures in English*, ed. by Eugene Wambaugh (Washington, D.C., John Byrne & Co., 1903).

[27] DeLloyd J. Guth, 'How legal history survives constitutional history's demise: the Anglo-American traditions,' *Ius Commune, Sonderhefte 7: Rechtsgeschichte und Quantitative Geschichte*, herausgegeben von Filippo Ranieri (Frankfurt-am-Main: Vittorio Klostermann, 1977), 117–53.

late-medieval lawyers who had continued to emphasize real actions, even while those same lawyers busied themselves mainly with actions of debt. They still wrote about and studied real actions because these were far more complex than personal actions, and therefore open to an infinity of professional debates and interpretations that only lawyers could understand. Moreover, most fifteenth century law readings at the Inns of Court, the training schools for lawyers, centered on statutes grounded in matters of real property and real actions.[28]

Modern legal historians, led by Milsom, Baker, and Fifoot, have helped to correct the constitutional historian's preoccupation with realty and real actions, but the centrality of debt in all of this has remained seriously under-appreciated and usually overlooked.[29] There is here a methodological point of fundamental importance: only the evidence from law courts, carefully quantified, will provide accurate descriptions of legal realities for any time and place. To this must be added the broader social and literary evidence, if only for metaphorical reinforcement and context. This will produce a more empirical, more functional analysis of law which runs counter to the traditionally presentist and deductive approach, borrowed from the lawyers' own methodology, whereby law is taught from present, so-called modern, procedures and categories backwards into the past. The law cannot be fully understood by reading simply what interested the lawyers, their manuals and *Year Books* and *Law Reports*. These contained only pre-selected sets of cases sorted out by precedent-hunting lawyers. Primary use of such precedental evidence may produce a useful case-book for lawyers but it has also imposed a profoundly non-historical method on legal scholars. Such an approach could never have identified the pattern, the fact, and certainly the metaphor of debt in late medieval law.

The dramatic shift to personal actions, under the noses of contemporary lawyers and most modern historians, in no way suggested that the substance for litigation ceased to be land. Nor did it signify that fewer lawsuits, quantitatively speaking, arose out of conflicts involving realty. It only meant that after 1300 the personal action of debt, plus that of trespass, increasingly offered remedy enough. Because most lawsuits never reached judicial resolution (and still do not, in modern courts), the

[28] Samuel E. Thorne (ed.), *Readings and Moots at the Inns of Court in the Fifteenth Century*, Selden Society, LXXI (London, Bernard Quaritch, 1954).

[29] S. F. C. Milsom, *Historical Foundations of the Common Law* (London, Butterworths, 1969). Fifoot, *History and Sources of the Common Law*, strikes something of a balance; but all three, including Baker, *English Legal History*, overemphasize the importance of trespass for this time, perhaps because they know as lawyers and as historians that trespass will have a more interesting and influential future than debt.

mesne process in personal actions worked best to secure the defendant's person for a formalized confrontation inside the courtroom. That often provided sufficient intimidation for an out-of-court settlement. And where debt's remedy – restitution and damages for payments owed – would not suffice, trespass offered various writs designed ultimately to define liability where some wrong against real and personal property had been committed. For both personal actions, of debt and trespass, the contemporary language was imbued with a moral sense of right–wrong, of obligation, and of duty. This is a theme constant to late medieval law and it can be seen graphically in operation when litigation in the whole judicial system has been counted and analysed.[30]

III

Common law, meaning royal law common to the entire realm, divided itself from the thirteenth century into courts of Common Pleas, King's Bench, and Exchequer. Their plea rolls have survived from the 1190s. By the pre-Reformation era three hundred years later, the court of Common Pleas produced parchment plea rolls one foot thick for each of any year's four law terms (Michaelmas, Hilary, Easter, Trinity).[31] In Easter term, 12 Edward IV (1473), two-thirds of the 4970 case entries were actions mainly of debt or scatterings of detinue, another twenty percent alleged trespass, and less than one lawsuit in ten qualified directly as a real action. Ten years later in the same Common Pleas, Michaelmas term 1482 generated 6204 case entries on its roll, 71 percent being actions of debt, 20 percent were for trespass and only 5 percent were real actions.[32]

If we look to the other two common law courts of King's Bench and Exchequer, real actions were all the more absent. In King's Bench, litigants battled mainly over allegations of trespass, with actions of debt noteworthy but a distant second in quantity. On the plea side of the King's Bench roll for Michaelmas 1507, there were a total of 782 case entries: 509, or two-thirds, were actions of trespass, to which one can add 121 so-called *quare* actions, better known to lawyers as trespass on the case. This left only 44 actions of debt, 6 percent of the total, but even fewer real actions were on the record.[33] In Henry VII's Exchequer, the

[30] DeLloyd J. Guth, 'Enforcing late-medieval law,' 80–96. On case-counting for an earlier era, with reservations: J. M. Kelly, *Studies in the Civil Judicature of the Roman Republic* (Oxford, The Clarendon Press, 1976), 71–92.

[31] *Guide to the Contents of the Public Record Office* (London, HMSO, 1963), I.

[32] Margaret Hastings, *The Court of Common Pleas in Fifteenth-Century England* (Ithaca, N.Y., Cornell University Press, 1947), 28.

[33] PRO, KB/27/985, Plea Side only.

action of debt accounted for virtually all litigation, not a surprising figure since it was the royal revenue-chasing court. There the King's Remembrancer annually enrolled less than two hundred prosecutions, usually against smugglers evading customs duties.[34] Common law courtrooms at Westminster Hall, then, mirrored accurately the England that contemporary writers so inexorably immersed in metaphors of debt.

Pre-Reformation real actions in royal courts, in fact, had come to be prosecuted in two rather 'unreal' ways. The first was by those personal actions of trespass, especially in King's Bench, which often masked 'self-help' attempts to recover land, sometimes even by joint effort with the defendant. Obviously one could not trespass on one's own realty, so at some point in proceedings the issue of title suggested itself, once allegations of forcible entry, removal of chattels, assaults, and so forth had been made. Personal actions of trespass then became, in effect, 'real' actions concerning that land. They also carried a sense of moral obligation akin to that for debts, since trespass meant a private 'wrong' done to another.[35] In some cases, the goal was simply to use trespass to secure irrefutable royal record at common law for what, in actuality, merely registered a transfer of title, or even a land divestiture for cash, between the litigants. Trespass, like debt, could be stretched to cover a multitude of wrongs and purposes.

The second 'unreal' avoidance of real actions took place in royal courts of equity. In Yorkist and early Tudor England, the Lord Chancellor's court received an increasing number and variety of lawsuits, mostly for matters of real property enforcing a *cestui que use*. There, and in Henry VII's conciliar courts of Star Chamber, Requests, the Council Learned, and the Duchy of Lancaster's Chancery, various wildly embellished accusations of forcible entries, riot and violence usually put a forceful construction on non-violent conflicts involving land. Most cases rapidly reduced themselves to issues of title and possession, once the conciliar subpoena produced the defendant. This effectively was equity's competitive answer to common law trespass, offered presumably at less cost, less potential delay, and no trial by corruptible jury. The largest remaining group of cases throughout the equity courts amounted to pleas of debt.[336]

34 DeLloyd J. Guth, 'Exchequer penal law enforcement 1485–1509' (University of Pittsburgh, Unpublished Ph.D. thesis, 1967). These prosecutions were all initiated as actions of debt, for statutory penalties generally, see below, 152–4.

35 In this sense, trespass would be the root for the modern law of tort; Baker, *English Legal History*, 224.

36 Guth, 'Enforcing late-medieval law,' 89; this entire mass of bills, answers, replications, rejoinders, and depositions are still being tabulated and studied.

These royal courts presented central, Westminster justice in civil pleadings but most litigants served their interests adequately in local customary court provided a cheaper way to register loan and credit transactions. Presheriffs. Here debt dominated, if only because filing an action in the local court provided a cheap way to register loan and credit transactions. Presumably if one repaid on schedule the action never proceeded, which would explain why most local litigation ended with the prosecution dropped or court permission for the parties to agree. In an age and realm without institutionalized banks, customary courts could provide a major commercial service. If prosecution became necessary, accused debtors in local courts could defend themselves by wager of law, obtaining dismissal if they could produce the court's specified number of witnesses to support their denial.[37] By 1500, there were over five hundred incorporated boroughs, mainly identifying a wide variety of small-scale urban centers of market commerce.[38] Debt, and imprisonment for convicted debt defaulters, became the business of borough and other local courts, including the two sheriffs' courts in London.[39]

The third network of law courts in the late medieval judicial system belonged to the church. In the twelfth century, and parallel with England's shaping of the common law, the church had organized a mass of conciliar and synodal legislation, as well as papal decretals, around principles derived in great measure from Justinian's sixth century compilations of Roman law. An elaborate edifice of church courts, from local deanery to archidiaconal, episcopal, and papal jurisdictions, attempted to translate canon law, often by exposé and public purgation, into everyday Christian living.[40] But a look at late medieval church court records, mainly those from the bishop's consistory court, reinforces our picture of a general preoccupation with debt. Because common law forbade competition from church courts in actions of debt, English

[37] This was also available at common law but I have found very few examples there; see, DeLloyd J. Guth, 'Notes on the early Tudor Exchequer of Pleas,' *Tudor Men and Institutions*, ed. by Arthur J. Slavin (Baton Rouge, Louisiana State University Press, 1972), 116–18.

[38] M. W. Beresford and H. P. R. Finberg, *English Medieval Boroughs: A Handlist* (Newton Abbot, David & Charles, 1973); and, R. A. Griffiths (ed.), *Boroughs of Medieval Wales* (Cardiff, University of Wales Press, 1978).

[39] Philip E. Jones and Raymond Smith, *A Guide to the Records in the Corporation of London Records Office and The Guildhall Library Muniment Room* (London, English Universities Press Ltd, 1951), 64–7; Philip E. Jones (ed.), *Calendar of Plea & Memoranda Rolls . . . of the City of London at the Guildhall, a.d. 1458–1482* (Cambridge, CUP, 1961), *sub* 'Debt,' 185.

[40] The general description is available in various scholarly works, for example, Robert E. Rodes, Jr, *Ecclesiastical Administration in Medieval England* (Notre Dame, University of Notre Dame Press, 1977), 141–51; for examples from various jurisdictions, Guth, 'Enforcing late-medieval law,' 89–91.

ecclesiastical ingenuity encouraged litigation for debt under an action *perjurij sive fidei laesio* (i.e. perjury or broken faith with a creditor).[41] Most were matters of simple debt for relatively small amounts, in which the moral obligation of one's 'word' regarding a monetary bargain had allegedly been broken. Such cases are liberally scattered throughout the consistory records for Hereford, Canterbury, Chichester, and Lincoln, right up to the Reformation of the 1530s.

Royal prerogative also helped to put early Tudor lives under the shadow of debt, by way of an elaborate system for bonds, recognizances, and sureties for keeping the king's peace. By the Yorkist era these had been prime tools for royal social control and for individual self-protection. Justices could impose bond or surety whereby an individual had the threat of a fixed monetary penalty if he violated his word, his duty, or someone else's peace and property. For Henry VII, bonds became a cornerstone for building central power and stabilizing society on royal terms.[42] The bond meant a debt on an obligation which, as Professor Milsom has explained, took over from the older action of covenant.[43] The point here was that courts of law effectively created debts, or the threat of debts, as a means for maintaining legitimated order.

IV

Having suggested dimensions for the age of debt, both in the literature and litigation of late medieval England, one still needs to search for the obligatory concept behind the word. That takes us directly to debt's Latin root and into Roman law. *Debeo, debere* (to owe), hence the *debitum* (debt), derived directly from *de* and *habere*, meaning to have some thing from another, to be obligated, or to possess that which actually belongs to another.[44] *Debere* also was the direct source for the French verb *devoir* and thus the old Anglo-French words *dû* and *dueté*, which remained in English

[41] Richard H. Helmholz, 'Debt claims and probate jurisdiction in historical perspective,' *The American Journal of Legal History*, XXIII (1979), 68–82, esp. 77–8, regarding declines in consistory court lawsuits for debt just prior to the Reformation.

[42] J. R. Lander, 'Bonds, coercion and fear: Henry VII and the peerage,' in his *Crown and Nobility 1450–1509* (London, Edward Arnold, 1976). I do not share Professor Lander's hostility for the king or the technique, but I do share Lander's discomfort over certain applications of that technique.

[43] Milsom, *Historical Foundations*, 218–19; and, Milsom, 'Account stated in the action of debt,' *Law Quarterly Review*, LXXXII (1966), 534–45.

[44] *OED*, III, 82–3; *Oxford Latin Dictionary* (Oxford, The Clarendon Press, 1969), Fascicle II, 486–7; *Harper's Latin Dictionary*, rev. by Charlton T. Lewis and Charles Short (New York, American Book Company, 1907), 515.

The jurisprudential point is made superbly by J. C. Smith, *Legal Obligation* (Toronto: University of Toronto Press, 1976), 53–7.

as 'duty.'[45] Similarly, in old German the noun *Schuld* united the meaning of debt with duty.[46] This strongly suggests that the complementary meaning of debt, as both legal and moral obligation, to owe and to ought, existed throughout post-Roman, early medieval law and language.[47]

Debt is central to the Anglo-Saxon dooms which from the seventh century record schedules of elaborate fines (wer-geld) for homicide and theft weighted entirely to the victim's status. Every Anglo-Saxon had his price, as did every part of him.[48] These violent acts thus created clear indebtedness, with the wer-geld being a money substitute for vengeance, *lex talionis*, as well as for any stolen goods. Debt had been made an instrument for the control of violence with all values translated to a money standard. These early medieval dooms spoke with one voice from the perspective of debt and duty. With the arrival of eleventh century feudalism, and its mainly unwritten military, personal, and mutual sets of obligations, the concept of debt-duty must have penetrated even deeper into ordinary human consciousness.

We do not know when the formal action of debt entered English legal process. When it did, certainly before the twelfth century, it brought with it that traditional duality of legal and moral imperative. Maitland certainly saw how powerful the *idea* of debt had been, how central debt as an expression of obligation had been in developing medieval real actions designed to protect property (especially writs of right).[49] By the end of the thirteenth century the action of debt came to be used strictly for

45 *Dictionnaire de L'Académie Française*, Sixième Édition (Paris, Imprimerie et Librairie de Firmin Didot Frères, n.d.), I, 542–3; E. Littré, *Dictionnaire de la Langue Française* (Paris, Librairie Hachette et Cie., 1873), II, 1139–41.

46 *Langenscheidts Enzyklopädisches Wörterbuch, Deutsch–Englisch* (Berlin, Langenscheidt, 1975), II, 1358–9; the legal action of debt was 'die Schuldklage.' The meaning is common to other European languages, e.g., 'deber' in *Diccionario Enciclopédico de la Lengua Castellana* (Paris, Garnier Hermanos, 1905), I, 777–8.

47 In Roman law, see Otto Gradenwitz *et al.*, *Vocabularium Iurisprudentiae Romanae* . . . (Berlin, Walter de Gruyter and Co., 1903–39), II, cols. 53–82, for 'debeo'; II, cols. 82–93, for 'debitor'; II, cols. 93–6, for 'debitum'; and, IV, fasc. II, cols. 367–73, for 'obligatio.' On the arrival of '*satisfactio*' into English, by way of French *c.* 1300, and subsequent changes of meaning, from 'debt' to 'a state of mind' in the seventeenth century: David Daube, *Roman Law: Linguistic, Social and Philosophical Aspects* (Edinburgh, Edinburgh University Press, 1969), 58. Equally fascinating and pertinent, regarding '*mutuum*,' is Jacques Michel, *Gratuité en Droit Romain* (Bruxelles, Institut de Sociologie, Université Libre de Bruxelles, 1962), ch. VI, 103–27.

48 *Sources of English Constitutional History*, rev. edn by Carl Stephenson and Frederick G. Marcham (New York: Harper & Row, 1972), 2–4, all based on Felix Liebermann (ed.), *Die Gesetze der Angel-Sachsen* (Halle, 1903–16; 3 vols.). The man-price for killing or robbing a bishop or lay nobleman might be three or more times that for acts against an ordinary freeman. Compensations for injuries followed similar schedules: loss of an ear = 12s., a fingernail = 1s., an eye = 50s., a big toe = 10s.

49 Pollock and Maitland, *History of English Law*, II, 203–7.

money debts, for what modern lawyers term a liquidated sum (in Roman law, a *condictio certa*).[50] This marked the opening of the age of debt; then the personal action of detinue split off from the action of debt, with detinue henceforth employed whenever identifiable chattels, not money or *res fungibiles*, were allegedly due. In late-medieval law, 'the seller could sue in Debt for the price and the buyer in Detinue for the [specific] goods.'[51] Detinue remained a minor action, as litigants increasingly went for the money. At the very least, the expanding use of debt by litigants and lawyers clearly reflected the growth of a monetary based late-medieval economy and society. When in 1352 a parliamentary statute allowed use of writs of *capias* (seize the defendant's body) in mesne process for personal actions, debt became even more attractive.[52]

So the floodgates had opened by which debt, as well as trespass, quickly swamped the other actions available in the Writ Registers, both real and personal. In fifteenth century law, debt and trespass had almost universal elasticity, in concept and in fact. Trespass offered assessments of liability and remedy to its plaintiff-victims, much like the modern law of tort. As we have seen, it could be stretched to 'real' actions; and, as I have emphasized elsewhere, trespass also remained a popular means for victims of 'crime' seeking recoveries, rather than seeing the offense prosecuted as felony where the victim received no compensation.[53] Late medieval actions of debt were strictly recuperative, offering restitution and damages for a whole host of moneyed relationships: on obligations, on sales, on promises, on contracts, on loans.[54] And as the literary evidence illustrates, the writers and leaders of late medieval, pre-Reformation England constantly hammered the metaphors of debt, *Redde quod debes*, into the heads of all who could read or hear. In this respect little had changed for a thousand years, from Roman law through early medieval dooms and codified canonical decrees to English common and customary law: legal and moral formed a united base in debt, defining the essence for human obligation. 'To owe' and 'to ought' were inseparable. Debt-duty triumphantly ruled in and out of the law courts before 1500.

[50] *Ibid.*, II, 173–5, 210–16; Baker, *English Legal History*, 177; Fifoot, *History and Sources of Common Law*, 26–8; Schulz, *Classical Roman Law*, 611–17.

[51] Fifoot, *History and Sources of Common Law*, 228. Detinue thus presumed 'owning,' not just 'owing,' because a particular thing had to be returned, not simply its worth.

[52] *SR*, I, 322; 25 Edward III, st. 5, c. 17.

[53] Guth, 'Enforcing late-medieval law,' 86–7.

[54] Milsom, *Historical Foundations*, 219–27, 292–7; Fifoot, *History and Sources of Common Law*, 217–33; Baker, *English Legal History*, 177–81.

V

What happened to dethrone debt (duty), as well as trespass (wrong), and ultimately lead to an age of contract three centuries later can only be outlined here. Central to this legal development was the English Reformation, specifically the attendant impulses it unleashed in royal administration and parliaments to organize, redefine, and especially further to formalize and to secularize polity and law. The fact that debt and trespass had multiplied into common denominators for litigation left both actions vulnerable to demands for more precise and specific legal protections. The resort to equity, with its early Tudor judicialization and its expanded Elizabethan respectability, was only symptomatic of the common law's problem with such a simple system of remedies.

In fact both debt and trespass showed clear signs of fragmentation by 1500. Expanding and more complex mercantile activities created pressures on law for clearer, more precise formalization of contractual obligations, pressures which debt could not accommodate. Late medieval debtors and creditors were not necessarily more virtuous than earlier or later counterparts, so the mere consciousness of moral obligation gave no guarantee that debts were paid and credits received. One could argue that the growth in actions of debt signified the many failures to do what one ought and certainly that more and more refused to forgive their debtors. Similarly the broad area of negligence, against those evading their obligations to orderly and legitimate procedures, was seen to need definition and enforceable remedies well beyond those found in ordinary writs of trespass. New actions of assumpsit and of case developed respectively and, in the course of the Tudor era, would spin off even more specific actions leading to what modern lawyers recognize as contract, tort, and ejectment.

From 1529, parliaments intervened increasingly to help to shape legal actions and remedies. The First Bankruptcy Statute of 1543 dramatically attempted to rationalize and delimit debt by protecting creditors from fraud and delay.[55] Where personal actions of debt and trespass had effectively replaced real actions, the parliaments after 1529 began to lead in developing real property protections. The abortive Statute of Uses (1535), the Statute of Enrollments (1536), and the more welcomed Statute of Wills (1540) directly addressed security of realty and promoted separate

[55] W. J. Jones, 'The foundations of English bankruptcy,' *Transactions of the American Philosophical Society*, LXIX, pt 3 (1979), 11–18.

developments for what became the law of trusts.[56] The two Henry Tudors presided over fundamental shifts at common law and equity, as well as the firm restricting of ecclesiastical law.

What the sixteenth century witnessed was the steady erosion of the debt-duty base for moral obligation that had overtly buttressed the English legal system. Obligation remained in law, to be sure, but it gradually came to be defined, in a sense secularized, as contractual and consensual agreements enforceable *per se* by the common law and customary courts. Simple obligations made in debt, whether oral or written, had previously been made for accomplished exchanges of benefits, usually money for goods; such obligations had to be translated, in the eyes of later law, into formalized contracts based on future performance. By the seventeenth century and the later age of contract, obligation was strictly limited to this world, where benefit and promise could be measured in terms of enforceability and where the obligation remained personally externalized, no longer one reserved to moral duty and conscience.

To be sure, the actions of debt and trespass remained in active use as common law remedies, in 1707[57] and well into the nineteenth century;[58] but they were no longer rooted in any moral force of obligatory duty, where a 'promise [to pay or repay] was binding of its own inherent validity.'[59] In the post-Reformation era, the obligation in debt and in trespass would be transplanted from moral conscience to self-interest, from a matter of the next world's eternal judgment to a matter of definable this-worldly benefit. As duty quietly, slowly disappeared, actions of debt came to require what the lawyer's labelled 'consideration': the identity of a benefit, a material cause or *quid pro quo*, some consideration that must be present to explain why the debt existed, why the obligation merited enforcement. This first appeared in the common law in 1536 and developed thereafter[60] as evidence that lawyers and judges, not just religious reformers, could no longer function comfortably with late medieval debt.

[56] Eric W. Ives, 'The genesis of the Statute of Uses,' *English Historical Review*, LXXXII (1967), 673ff.

[57] PRO, KB 122/31 (6 Anne), Plea Side, contains 633 case entries: 418 are actions of debt (66%), 151 are trespass on the case (24%), and 42 ordinary trespass actions (6%). PRO, KB 29/366 (6 Anne), Rex Side, contains 327 case entries: 231 are simple actions of trespass (70%), 74 are actions of detinue (22%), 26 involve deaths (murder = 9, misadventure = 9, suicide = 4, divine visitation = 4), with only two actions of debt.

[58] Maitland, *Forms of Action*, 80–1. Most real actions were abolished in 1833 (3 & 4 William IV, c. 27), but the actions of debt and detinue continued until the Judicature Acts of 1873–5, which mandated one general writ of summons.

[59] Fifoot, *History and Sources of Common Law*, 398.

[60] John H. Baker (ed.), *The Reports of Sir John Spelman*, Selden Society, XCIV (London, 1978), 288–92; and, Baker, 'Origins of the "doctrine" of consideration, 1535–1585,' *On the Laws*

Again, the history of ideas provided suggestive correlations with legal realities, for the Reformation century and its aftermath. Martin Luther's pessimism about man's irrevocable unworthiness before God had made it impossible for man to connect his salvation with repayment of debts, whether before or after death. It was also Luther who led rejection of the more crass application of debtor metaphors, peddled in the theology of Tetzel and the pre-Reformation papacy. No doubt Luther and later English reformers, particularly so-called 'covenant' theologians like Bullinger and the early seventeenth century Puritans, were appalled by purgatorial, debt-ridden beliefs that made God the Final Accountant. By the Elizabethan era, Calvin's doctrine of double predestination made purgatory an unnecessary abomination because debts could neither damn the debtor to hell nor could repayment ever provide the cachet into heaven, whose inhabitants God must know (even will?) to be there.[61]

The metaphors of debt, along with the dominance of the action of debt, gave way to newer metaphors associated with the emerging law of contract. If one may speculate further, these new legal realities accompanied, and perhaps made necessary, the seventeenth century's creation of 'society' in earth-bound minds, as the reason and root for enforcing obligations. The transcendancy of moral duty in the nature of pre-Reformation debt gave way to the grounding, after the sixteenth century, of post-Reformation contractual obligation within 'society'. It was no accident, then, that Thomas Hobbes, John Locke, Adam Smith, and others articulated social contract theories,[62] in much the same metaphorical way as William Langland, Robert Fabyan, Bishop John Fisher and others had written about debt. The age of contract would be a word of formalized obligation, of temporal and defined mutuality, of concrete and tangible terms based on future promise and specific performance that could even allow such contractual debts to be discounted and negotiable.[63]

and Customs of England: Essays in Honor of Samuel E. Thorne, ed. by Morris S. Arnold, Thomas A. Green, Sally A. Scully, and Stephen D. White (Chapel Hill, The University of North Carolina Press, 1981), 336–58.

61 On the fate of hell: D. P. Walker, *The Decline of Hell: Seventeenth-Century Discussions of Eternal Torment* (Chicago, The University of Chicago Press, 1964). The 'Realist *vs.* Nominalist' arguments in late medieval philosophy and theology held implications basic for all law, especially for a legal system that tried to accommodate moral law, natural law, custom, legislation, church law, and case law into a unified jurisprudence: the Universalist's Justice and Responsibility (Reason) countered by the Nominalist's focus on Judiciary and Enforceable Obedience (Will).

62 Ernest Barker (ed.), *Social Contract: Essays by Locke, Hume, Rousseau* (Oxford, Oxford University Press, 1947), provides a convenient starting place. Hobbes denied that 'society' as such existed but argued for its artificial necessity. Locke accepted the reality of 'society' as a spontaneous, pre-existing, self-adjusting combination of property owners.

63 P. S. Atiyah, *An Introduction to the Law of Contract*, 2nd edn (Oxford: The Clarendon Press, 1971), 1–3.

Where the age of debt had moral duty and ultimately heaven-or-hell to enforce obligation, the new age of contract settled for formalized rules limited to the context of mundane 'society.' Social obligation would replace moral obligation as the rationale and force behind debt; and for jurisprudence, the breakthrough now existed that could lead in turn to utilitarianism, legal formalism, and legal positivism (or American 'realism'). Just as debt, *meum et tuum*, remained central in one form and another to English, and by extension American, legal development, so too does our modern law owe its debt to the Reformation era and the 'Tudor Revolution in Government.'[64]

[64] On the status of the action of debt in the United States: *Corpus Juris Secundum* (Brooklyn, N.Y., The American Law Book Co., 1956), XXVI, 18–22.

Regarding the 'Age of Debt,' there are noteworthy parallels in legal developments outside the European experience for the same time period: Joseph Schacht, *An Introduction to Islamic Law* (Oxford, The Clarendon Press, 1964), esp. 144–5; Dan Fenno Henderson, *Conciliation and Japanese Law: Tokugawa and Modern* (Seattle, University of Washington Press, 1965), I, 106–15, on 'Main Suits (Honkuji) and Money Suits (Kanekuji)' in sixteenth century Shogunate courts; and, Ronald C. Jennings, 'Loans and credit in early 17th century Ottoman judicial records: the Sharia court of Anatolian Kayseri,' *Journal of the Economic and Social History of the Orient*, XVI (1973), 168–216.

The King's Privy Chamber, 1547–1553

DALE E. HOAK*

When the duke of Northumberland captured control of Edward VI's government sometime in November 1549, he won the power virtually to be king: because he now governed access to the young prince and controlled the signet and stamp of his hand, he was able to order almost any action in Edward's name. The duke of Somerset had exercised this power officially as Governor of Edward's person, a title – the only title – which rationalized his self-assumed authority as England's Lord Protector. Since none of the conspirators who overthrew Somerset in 1549 could effect a claim to the office of Governor, the battle to succeed him, waged principally between Northumberland (then earl of Warwick) and the earls of Arundel and Southampton, really became a struggle for possession of the king's body, with both sides scrambling to position themselves and their clients in the royal apartments, next to the king's bedchamber, as close as possible to the king himself. Maintaining verbal contact with the king required access to, and eventually control of, the king's private lodgings, the suite of rooms in every royal residence known as the Privy Chamber.

In reconstructing these events, I once assumed that because Northumberland gained the upper hand in Council, he was able to infiltrate the various departments of the royal household and so finally to dominate the personnel of the Privy Chamber. The reverse probably describes the historical truth of the matter: in order to seize the machinery of government, Northumberland first needed to acquire Edward VI himself, and this he accomplished at the crucial moment by procuring, as an eye-witness later put it, 'great frendes abowte the king.'[1] And who were these 'frendes'

* The research for this paper was supported by grants from two sources that I gratefully acknowledge here, the Hays Fund of the American Philosophical Society and the Committee on Faculty Research in the College of William and Mary. I also wish to thank DeLloyd Guth, John McKenna and David Starkey for their helpful criticism of various parts of this paper.

1 BL, MS Add. 48126, fols. 15*v.*–16; Dale E. Hoak, *The King's Council in the Reign of Edward VI* (Cambridge, CUP, 1976), 249, 344 n. 4 and 348 n. 83.

who assured his eventual triumph? The designation of their standing ('great') and the timing of their joint appearance suggest that they were among the six lords and four knights appointed on 15 October 1549 to assume collectively the duties Somerset had discharged as Governor of Edward's person. If so, their appointment reveals a potentially important but neglected aspect of mid-Tudor government – the identity, organization and functions of the personnel of the king's Privy Chamber.

At least thirty-four men served Edward VI as Gentlemen of the Privy Chamber. Many have never been cited in published scholarship and none has been discussed in the context of this, the most important department of the royal household, the natural center of political life and power at the Tudor court. In his forty-page essay on the organization of the court (1923), E. K. Chambers passed silently over the years 1547–58.[2] An unpublished dissertation (1971) on office-holding in the royal household, 1540–60, unaccountably ignored the structure of the Privy Chamber and made no systematic effort to identify its personnel.[3] For this reason, Dr D. R. Starkey's pioneering work on the early Tudor Privy Chamber (1973), which brought the administrative story down to 1547, raised some very insistent questions about the organization of the whole household after that date,[4] but neither Neville Williams's few words on 'The Tudors' (1977)[5] nor Penry Williams's more exhaustive attempt to analyse *The Tudor Regime* (1979) filled in the gaps. Since a fuller study of the mid-Tudor household is already underway,[6] the present effort will be limited to identifying the Gentlemen of Edward VI's Privy Chamber and suggesting something of the significance of their office during the extraordinary period marked by the predominance of the dukes of Somerset and Northumberland. A brief consideration of the structure of the early Tudor court will serve as the background to this story.

I

By 1540 the king's household in England, excluding the stables and Chapel Royal, was divided into three departments corresponding to the geography and architecture of the various royal residences. These were

[2] Edward K. Chambers, *The Elizabethan Stage* (Oxford, Clarendon Press, 1923), I, 27–71.

[3] Robert C. Braddock, 'The Royal Household, 1540–60: study in office-holding in Tudor England' (Northwestern University, Unpublished Ph.D. thesis, 1971).

[4] David R. Starkey, 'The King's Privy Chamber, 1485–1547' (University of Cambridge, Unpublished Ph.D. thesis, 1973).

[5] Neville Williams, 'The Tudors,' in Arthur G. Dickens (ed.), *The Courts of Europe: Politics, Patronage and Royalty 1400–1800* (London, Thames and Hudson, 1977), 147–67.

[6] Mr John Murphy, a research student at Leeds University, is at work on this topic.

the Chamber, Privy Chamber and what is perhaps confusingly called the Household proper. In the Chamber the king played out his 'public,' official life, dining and entertaining in great state and formally receiving official visitors. For his private life the king withdrew, as it were, to his Privy (originally 'secret') Chamber. Here an adult king like Henry VIII surrounded himself with perhaps two dozen intimate body servants, including barbers and physicians, for example, and his sometimes boisterous boon companions. A much married king like Henry also maintained a separate suite of private rooms 'on the queen's side.' Below stairs the Household proper supplied the king and his resident entourage with the obvious necessities of food, drink, lighting, and fuel. The names of its twenty-one suboffices in Edward's reign identify the various types of provisions supplied or services rendered: pantry, buttery, cellar, ewry, kitchen, bake-house, spicery, confectionery, pitcher house, chandlery, larder, boiling-house, catery, poultery, scalding-house, pastry, scullery, laundry, wafery, and woodyard.

While this tripartite division corresponds to what we know about the organization of the royal household between about 1540 and 1553, the Tudors themselves usually referred to only two departments. A manuscript list of all 'Officers and servauntes in Household' of 1552 divides the personnel of the royal establishment between 'The Counting House' and 'The Chamber,' with 'Pensioners' and 'The Garde' and those in the offices below stairs listed separately.[7] This classification is instructive as it preserves a contemporary's sense of rank, order, and precedence within the household, but it does not accurately reflect either the honorific nature of the head officers' titles – as a minister of state, the Lord Great Master had nothing to do with household administration, for example – or the political importance and unitary nature of the Privy Chamber whose Gentlemen are here consigned to an already anachronistic conception of 'the Chamber.' Thus the Counting House was not a separate department of the household, but rather the cashier's office within that department known as 'the Household.' The head of the Household was the Lord Great Master (or Lord Steward of Elizabeth's reign). Administration of the financial affairs of the Household was the responsibility of the members

7 Society of Antiquaries, MS 125, fols. 29–39, part of a contemporary fair-copy of 'A booke of ffees and offices.' Although dated 1 August 1553 ('Primo Die Augusti Anno primo Regine Marie'), the book records Edward VI's household establishment *c.* mid-1552. BL, MS Stowe 571, fols. 29*v*–39 is an Elizabethan copy of the original material in the Library of the Society of Antiquaries. The watermark on the folios of the volume now in the British Library – a dog, mouth open, surmounting a scroll labelled 'Nivelle' – dates the Stowe extracts to the period 1563–81; see C. M. Briquet, *Les Filigranes* (Paris, 1907), I, nos. 3639, 3640, and 3642.

of the Board of Greencloth, assisted by various clerks and clerks comptrollers in the Counting House. In other words, on the administrative side, the officers and staff of the Household department in 1552 were ranked as follows: after the Lord Great Master (Northumberland) and the Treasurer (Sir Thomas Cheyne), came the two chief executive officers, the Comptroller (Sir Richard Cotton) and the Cofferer (Thomas Weldon),[8] followed by three so-called Masters of Household (Michael Wentworth, Edward Shelley, and James Gage) who acted as links between the Board of Greencloth and servants below stairs.[9] In the Counting House, beneath the officers and Masters, were five clerks, a yeoman, and a groom.[10] Below stairs, in the suboffices of supply, twelve serjeants and fourteen clerks supervised the day-to-day work of 73 yeomen, 50 grooms, 21 pages, 16 'children,' and 16 others whose titles aptly describe their laboring lives – a bread-bearer in the pantry, two master cooks and two surveyors of the dresser in the kitchen, a laundress, two 'gentlemen' of the ewry, six 'conductes' in the bake-house and two wood-bearers, a total of 176 servants. There were also ten porters and 'scurrers' (runners) at the gates.[11]

After naming the ranking officers and staff of 'The Counting House' in the Lord Great Master's department, the compiler of the list of 1552 proceeded to 'The Chamber' whose two chief officers, the Lord Chamberlain (Thomas Lord Wentworth) and Vice-Chamberlain (Sir John Gates), headed the next section of his report. At this point, however, he listed the names and titles of men who as a group clearly constituted (by his own designation) personnel of the Privy Chamber, returning without a break to the true officers and staff of what we should properly call the Chamber. In fact, the compiler's anachronistic method of listing the men in 'The Chamber' indicates the historically superior position of the Privy Chamber: in effect our anonymous clerk recognized that under Northumberland the Lord Chamberlain and Vice-Chamberlain functioned as head officers of the Privy Chamber. In the Chamber – the traditional, collective designation of the royal apartments – the Lord Chamberlain nominally organized the king's public life at court. Physically and ceremonially the Chamber really accommodated the officers of state whom the king had called into residence at court. Thus, independent lists of 'the ordinary of the King's chamber which have bouch of court and also their diets within the court' included pre-eminently the members of the Privy

[8] The compiler of the list erred in calling him John Weldon.
[9] *APC*, III, 137.
[10] Society of Antiquaries, MS 125, fol. 29.
[11] *Ibid.*, fols. 32*v*.–37; BL, MS Stowe 571, fols. 33–37.

Council.[12] Like the Treasurer and Comptroller of the Household, the Chamberlain and Vice-Chamberlain were themselves Privy Councillors *ex officio*, officers of state only nominally attached to the household establishment. Although (like the Master of the King's Horse) they were considered to be executive officers within their own department, the real administrative work was carried out by subordinates. Of course there were functional servants in the Chamber – sewers, grooms, yeomen ushers, pages, and messengers – but they are not to be confused with the cupbearers, carvers and sewers to the king who were prominent nobles or knights or royal favorites holding purely honorific Chamber titles.[13]

The one hundred yeomen of the royal guard nominally operated out of the Chamber, policing the precincts of the royal court under the command of the Vice-Chamberlain. In effect, the Chamber provided the king with a domestic security force, the Vice-Chamberlain acting (in Edward's reign) as a minister of internal security on orders from the Council. Thus at the height of the *coup* against Somerset, it was Sir Anthony Wingfield, in his capacity as Captain of the Guard, who 'was sent [by the Council at London] to the king at Windsor, and severed the Lord Protector from his person and caused the Guard to watch him till the Lords coming.'[14]

The pike-bearing yeomen, their coats jingling with the costly gold spangles ordered up by Northumberland's government,[15] were not the only armed force at court. Theoretically superior to them, and also operating out of the Chamber, were the spears, or poleaxe-wielding gentlemen pensioners. During May 1550 Northumberland reformed the pensioners' ranks, increased the number of yeomen and realigned the command of the entire household guard. Since the purpose of these moves was to provide greater security for himself and the king in the Privy Chamber, and since the Council had already reorganized the Gentlemen of the Privy Chamber to the same end, a discussion of these military developments at court in May 1550 conveniently prefaces the subject of the Privy Chamber itself.

II

The gentlemen pensioners were first organized in 1539 as an elite corps of fifty mounted guardsmen. Did they, as Professor Elton once thought,

[12] BL, MS Lansdowne 2, fol. 34, a list dated early 1545, printed in *LP*, XX(2), App. 2(1).
[13] Society of Antiquaries, MS 125, fol. 30.
[14] John Stow, *Annales, or a Generall Chronicle of England* (London, 1631), 600.
[15] The Council paid Peter Richardson, goldsmith, £180 12s. 6d. for 'spangles bestowed upon the coats of the Yeomen of the Guard'; *APC*, IV, 171.

exist only for display, their places creating fine opportunities at Henry's court for the promotion of young men from socially respectable families?[16] One suspects as much, since by February 1551 Northumberland had found it necessary to create another mounted guard, a brigade of twelve trained bands of some 850 cavalry. These were the fashionable new gendarmes, a mobile, fast-striking crew retained by individual Privy Councillors and paid for at debilitating cost out of the king's coffers. The gendarmes – the word itself suggests Northumberland's martial panache – were really the Council's own palace guard, and even one contingent of them must have rendered the gentlemen pensioners superfluous. Nonetheless the pensioners remained in wages throughout Edward's reign and the gendarmes, never a part of the ordinary household establishment, were abolished for lack of money at Michaelmas 1552.[17]

Although there is no evidence that the pensioners mounted their horses for more than ceremonial duty – together with the gendarmes they escorted the Dowager Queen of Scotland the last two and a half miles to Hampton Court on her journey through England in October 1551 – on foot they certainly did attend daily on the king at court, and in this capacity they constituted a showy royal bodyguard within the walls of the king's residence.[18] Moreover, since their captain, the Lord Great Chamberlain – William Parr, marquess of Northampton – was one of six nobles of the Council appointed on 15 October 1549 to be attendant in the Privy Chamber, the pensioners, originally part of the ordinary of the Chamber, suddenly became (at least during the period of Northumberland's rule) a special, if still somewhat ornamental, Privy Chamber guard.[19]

However, Northumberland's policy of peace with France dictated a reform in the ranks of the pensioners early in 1550, for when the government disbanded its garrison at Boulogne, it reassigned to Northampton's personal command sixty light horse and men-of-arms previously stationed there. The rationale for this was two-fold, to stifle potential discontent among the unemployed soldiers ('to thentent they shulde not have cause to murmour'), 'and that the Kinges Majestie may be the better furnisshed of men aswell about his person as for any other necessarie.'[20] Since the ranks of the pensioners had dwindled to thirty-eight by 1548[21]

[16] G. R. Elton, *The Tudor Revolution in Government* (Cambridge, CUP, 1953), 387–8.

[17] On the gendarmes, see Hoak, *King's Council*, 199–201.

[18] Wilbur K. Jordan (ed.), *The Chronicle and Political Papers of King Edward VI* (Ithaca, N.Y., Cornell University Press, 1966), 91; *CPR, Edward VI*, III, 290; IV, 106.

[19] William Tighe, a research student at the University of Cambridge, is writing a history of the Tudor gentlemen pensioners.

[20] *APC*, III, 29–30; Jordan, *Chronicle*, 30.

[21] *APC*, II, 182.

and were filled with too many disabled, over-aged veterans, Northumberland decided to dismiss them with life annuities[22] and put in their places the demobilized men-of-arms. In Council on 11 May 1550, 'upon mocion made by the Lord Great Chamberlaine [Northampton], it was agreed that from hensfoorthe the Gentlemen-at-Armes shulde be placed successively in the pencioners romes at everie avoidaunce and so give attendaunce on his Lordship as their Capitaine.'[23] These 'Gentlemen-at-Armes' (not to be confused with the gendarmes) thus supplanted the pensioners as a special security force attached to the Privy Chamber.

The redeployment of the Boulogne light horse followed that of Edward Lord Clinton, Chief Captain of Boulogne since 1548. 'Forasmuch as his service at Bulloigne deserved notable consideracion,' the Council moved the king on the same day (11 May 1550) to create Clinton High Admiral of England and 'accept him of his Privie Chambre.'[24] In Clinton's case, right of access to the Privy Chamber was not the merely honorable privilege clearly befitting a ranking officer of state. In the council register, on the page following the one recording Clinton's elevation and buried among other proceedings considered that day, is the clerk's dutiful observation that of 'such souldeours as had well served at Bulloigne and were nowe comme over . . . the Lord Admirall shulde choose out vj^c footmen of them (if they be so many) with capitaine, peticapitaine and standerde bearer, whereof cc [are to] attende on the Kinges person.'[25] The list of 'Officers and servauntes in Household' of 1552 confirms the Council's action of May 1550: 'The Garde' are there grouped as 'Ordinarie: Yeomen in number. CC' and 'Extraordinary: Yeomen in number. C.C. & vij.'[26]

By 11 May 1550, then, Northumberland had quadrupled the number of standing guardsmen by doubling those in 'ordinary' (from 100 to 200) and reinforcing them with another contingent of 200 yeomen. Sir Thomas Darcy, one of the four new 'principal' Gentlemen of the Privy Chamber (and probably one of the duke's 'great frendes'), had become Captain of the yeomen in 'ordinary.' The marquess of Northampton, one of the six new lords attendant in the Privy Chamber, had buttressed his own command of the pensioners with sixty active men-of-arms. And Lord Clinton, an experienced ex-commander, had been admitted to the Privy Chamber in conspicuous fashion at the head of 200 armed yeomen 'extra-

22 Thus Edward Vaughan, *CPR, Ed. VI,* III, 110 and IV, 106, and Edward Garrett, *ibid.*, IV, 174.

23 *APC,* III, 30.

24 *Ibid.*, 29.

25 *Ibid.*, 29–30; Jordan, *Chronicle,* 30.

26 Society of Antiquaries, MS 125, fol. 31*v*.; BL, MS Stowe 571, fol. 32.

ordinary.' Why the sudden concentration of armed forces around the king's person on 11 May 1550?

The answer is that on that day Northumberland had been forced, perhaps reluctantly, to readmit Somerset to the Privy Chamber.[27] When, earlier in November, Northumberland had discovered that Arundel and Southampton had linked his own fate to that of the imprisoned Protector, he had labored mightily to secure his rival's release from the Tower, and by April 1550 could no longer deny the king's uncle a preferred place at court. But would Somerset try to regain his former power at Northumberland's expense? The evidence would later show that Northumberland had good reason to suspect as much in May 1550. The Privy Chamber reforms of 11 May 1550 probably reflect his suspicion. After all, working through the London Council he himself had once ordered the household guard to 'sever' the king from Somerset at Windsor Castle, within the Protector's own encampment. The lesson was clear: Northumberland would make the king's Vice-Chamberlain his own man, station him officially in the Privy Chamber as one of the Chief Gentlemen there, and surround the Privy Chamber with new horse and foot sufficient to prevent any defections. Only then could Somerset be safely readmitted to the king's presence, a virtual prisoner within a palace now bristling with pike and arquebusiers. And of course Northumberland himself was one of the six lords of the Privy Chamber holding the governorship of the king in collective commission.

III

The foregoing discussion thus introduces us to the Privy Chamber, the object of the heretofore unnoticed military reforms of May 1550. But as the 1552 list of 'Officers and servauntes in Household' presents a picture of the Privy Chamber as it was reorganized in October 1549, it will be useful first to consider the organization and personnel of that department under the first two Tudors.

Dr Starkey has shown that the existence of the Privy Chamber as a small subdepartment of the English royal household dates from the reign of Henry VII. As a specialized branch of the Chamber, this 'Secret Chamber,' as it was then called, provided Henry VIII in his early years (1509–17) with his most intimate body servants, two Grooms of the Stole (stool), two Grooms of the Privy Chamber, various pages, and the king's barber. The year 1513 marks the first official reference to these servants as cor-

[27] *APC*, III, 29.

porate members of a 'privy chamber.' According to Dr Starkey, it is possible to speak of the Privy Chamber as an autonomous household department only after 1519: in that year the dual division of the medieval household gave way to the tripartite structure described above. For this reason, as Dr Starkey argues in a most convincing way, the Eltham Ordinances of 1526 simply confirmed what had already happened by 1519.[28] A further set of reforms in 1539 completed the development of the Privy Chamber by establishing formally the list of those in 'ordinary' there: that is, those provided board at court by putting the entire ordinary establishment of the Privy Chamber in wages and by transferring from the Treasurer of the Chamber to the Cofferer the responsibility for paying the wages of Privy Chamber personnel. At about the same time (1536–40), the Wardrobe of the Robes and the Wardrobe of the Beds left the Chamber, becoming separate suboffices within the Privy Chamber.[29]

Thus by 1540 the Privy Chamber had emerged as a formal department of the royal household. Since the functions of the Treasurer of the Chamber had gone out of court, the Groom of the Stole – now one of the Chief Gentlemen – took over the management of the king's Privy Purse. Since almost one-third (31%) of the Privy Purse expenditures at this time can be accounted expenditures of state, it is apparent that by 1547 the Chief Gentlemen had effectively become some of the king's most important ministers. As Dr Starkey has said, in matters financial this looks very much like medieval, household kingship.[30]

To meet the increased demands of business conducted there, the officers and staff of the Privy Chamber had increased in numbers and some of their functions had become more specialized. By 1545 the number of Gentlemen stood at eighteen. There were also two gentlemen ushers, four gentlemen ushers (daily waiters), four grooms, and two barbers. A yeoman, groom, and page filled out the Robes office and the Beds counted a yeoman, two grooms, and two pages. A groom porter rounded out the full complement of men in ordinary in the Privy Chamber.[31] Additionally, the Chief Gentlemen employed their own servants to relieve them of routine labor, and a specialized clerk now served as their secretary.[32]

If this represents a general picture of the organization of the Privy Chamber under Henry VIII, what happened to the department and the men in it following the accession of a nine-year-old boy? Obviously the

[28] Starkey, 'The King's Privy Chamber,' 24, 59, 68, 78, 121, 125, 174, 202.
[29] *Ibid.*, 202, 212–13, 274.
[30] *Ibid.*, 296, 305, 369, 384, 415–16.
[31] BL, MS Lansdowne 2, fol. 34, printed in *LP*, xx(2), App. 2(1).
[32] Starkey, 'The King's Privy Chamber,' 417.

personal needs of the child were not those of the man: without a king's beard to shave, for example, Henry VIII's barbers, Edward Harmen and John Penne, might well wonder what would become of their offices, now that their titles were as useless as their razors. In fact, the office and title of king's barber disappeared in 1547 and Harmen and Penne simply added to the existing list of 'Groomes of the Privie Chamber.'[33] Many other servants were simply dismissed. On Shrove Sunday, 27 February 1547, within hours of Edward's coronation, 'order was taken for all his servants being with his father and [with] him [while] being prince, and the ordinary and unordinary were appointed.'[34] During the next several months John Rither, Cofferer of the household, distributed almost £1000 in pensions to the gentlemen ushers, gentlemen waiters, sewers, yeomen, and grooms who had lost their places in the households of Prince Edward and King Henry.[35]

IV

Although the present study is concerned to identify only the Gentlemen of the Privy Chamber, the problem in doing so is the same for all of those whom the king retained in service, since the establishment list of 1552 remains the only source of its type for the years 1547–53. Hence, for the period of Somerset's Protectorate the Gentlemen's names must be retrieved from scattered references in a variety of official sources. Where the evidence has been lost or deliberately destroyed – the Protector's adherents removed papers from Westminster and cast them abroad after the *coup* – one must infer an individual's probable tenure in the Privy Chamber by comparing the last complete roster of personnel in Henry's reign, dated January–May 1545, with the only available one for Edward's.

Incontrovertible evidence exists for the tenures of seven men who had been Gentlemen in 1545: Sir Anthony Denny, Sir William Herbert, Sir Thomas Cawarden, Sir Anthony St Leger, Sir Ralph Sadler, Sir Thomas Speke, and Sir Thomas Paston.[36] The patent rolls and minutes of Council

[33] Society of Antiquaries, MS 125, fol. 30a; BL, MS Stowe 571, fol. 30*v*. References to Penne as a groom are dated 1548 and 1550: *APC*, II, 201 (28 May 1548) and *CPR*, *Ed. VI*, III, 243 (20 November 1550).

[34] Jordan, *Chronicle*, 5. BL, MS Royal 7. C. xvi, fols. 92–7, gives 'The Names of such officers in ordinary of the Chamber of the late Kynges Majestie as [are] now discharged.' I wish to thank DeLloyd Guth for providing me with a transcription of these folios.

[35] *APC*, II, 83.

[36] The following references are the earliest found for each individual. Denny: *APC*, II, 3, 31 January 1547. Herbert: *ibid.*, 31 January 1547. Cawarden: *ibid.*, 472, 7 April 1547. St Leger: *CPR, Ed. VI*, I, 117, n.d., probably 1547. Sadler: *ibid.*, 258, 30 June 1547. Speke: *ibid.*, II, 337, 25 June 1549. Paston: *ibid.*, I, 113, 23 July 1547.

meetings yield clear references to another five: Sir Michael Stanhope, Sir John Gates, Sir Philip Hoby, Sir Edward Bellingham, and William Fitzwilliams, Esq.[37] A muster roll of 'The privie chamber & certen of the counsell at large,' identifying those who were to be assessed horse and demi-lance in the middle of 1548, adds another four names: Sir Edward Rogers, Sir Thomas Darcy, Sir Francis Bryan, and Sir Maurice Berkeley.[38] Like Henry VIII, Somerset probably retained a fixed roster of eighteen Gentlemen in ordinary; Northumberland certainly did so, and there is no reason to suppose that between 1545 and 1553 this number was changed. (Northumberland merely added a superior, distinct group of 'The foure knights' to the 'Gentlemen of the privie chamber. xviij,' as the official list of 1552 so plainly classifies them.) If so, we must discover two more men to add to the sixteen already identified. On the assumption that as Governor, Somerset was not among them, five logical choices emerge: Sir Thomas Hennage, Thomas Lord Seymour, Northumberland (then earl of Warwick), Sir Anthony Browne, and Sir Peter Mewtas. All five were Gentlemen of the Privy Chamber in 1545, Hennage then being Chief Gentleman. More important is the observation that Northumberland, Hennage, and Mewtas were also counted among Edward VI's Gentlemen in 1552, suggesting that only death or political demise removed a man from the Privy Chamber in the intervening years.[39] The addition of the five appears to create a surplus of three, but Browne (whose tenure is assumed here) died on 10 May 1548, leaving a place open for Sir Edward Rogers who seems to have been appointed about then. Since St Leger and Bellingham served successively as Lords Deputy in Ireland (April 1547 to September 1548 and September 1548 to September 1550, respectively) and Hoby was the king's ambassador to the Emperor, the Gentlemen resident at court would have numbered eighteen by about June 1548. Whatever the case, Table 1 sets out the resulting list of the twenty-one Gentlemen for the period in question.

During the subsequent period of Northumberland's rule (12 October 1549 to 6 July 1553) the composition of the Gentlemen's ranks changed

[37] Stanhope: *APC,* II, 128, 13 September 1547. Gates: *CPR, Ed. VI,* I, 216–17, 16 September 1547. Hoby: *ibid.*, 225, 1 July 1547. Bellingham: *ibid.*, 232, 28 February 1548. Fitzwilliams: *APC,* II, 454, 15 March 1547.

[38] PRO, SP 10/5/fols. 55ff. Although the list does not distinguish those of the Privy Chamber from the rest, the first nine are clearly of greater eminence. In the order listed they are: Stanhope, Rogers, Bryan, Cawarden, Gates, Paston, Darcy, Speke, and Berkeley.

[39] Sir Henry Knevett, Sir George Carew, Sir John Wellesborne, and Sir Richard Long appear on the 1545 list. Knevett died on 20 August 1546. Carew drowned on 19 July 1545. I have found no evidence that Long or Wellesborne were Gentlemen of the Privy Chamber in Edward's reign. Long died before 4 August 1547 (*CPR, Ed. VI,* I, 188), Wellesborne before 6 May 1548 (*ibid.*, II, 3).

Table 1. *Gentlemen of the Privy Chamber, 28 January 1547–11 October 1549*[40]

1. Sir Michael Stanhope ('first Gentleman' by 18 August 1548)	11. Sir John Gates
2. Thomas Lord Seymour	12. Sir Ralph Sadler
3. Earl of Warwick	13. Sir Thomas Paston
4. Sir Thomas Hennage	14. Sir Thomas Darcy
5. Sir Anthony Denny	15. Sir Thomas Speke
6. Sir William Herbert	16. Sir Maurice Berkeley
7. Sir Anthony St Leger	17. Sir Peter Mewtas
8. Sir Edward Rogers	18. Sir Philip Hoby
9. Sir Francis Bryan	19. Sir Edward Bellingham
10. Sir Thomas Cawarden	20. Sir Anthony Browne
	21. William Fitzwilliams, Esq.

markedly. By the middle of 1552 ten of the ordinary Gentlemen had been replaced and three other new men had become 'principal' (or Chief) Gentlemen. By 17 October 1552 Sir Richard Blount, formerly a gentleman usher, had also been appointed one of the eighteen Gentlemen.[41] The ten vacancies in the Gentlemen's places, 1549–52, are to be explained by Thomas Seymour's arrest and execution (17 January and 20 March 1549, respectively), Stanhope's removal at the time of Somerset's arrest (12 October 1549), the promotion of Darcy, Gates, and Rogers, and the deaths of Denny (10 September 1549), Bellingham (before 10 July 1550),[42] Bryan (2 February 1550), Paston (by 13 December 1550),[43] and Speke (before 21 October 1551).[44] The list of 1552, which must have been penned before 17 October of that year (the date of the earliest independent reference to Blount, who is not on the list), records the appearance of eight replacements: Lord Robert Dudley, Barnaby Fitzpatrick, Sir Richard Morison, Sir Nicholas Throckmorton, Sir William Goring, Sir Anthony Cooke, Henry Wheler, and Sir Henry Nevill.

On 15 October 1549 there were also appointed four 'principal' Gentlemen of the Privy Chamber, Sir Edward Rogers, Sir Thomas Darcy, Sir Andrew Dudley, and Sir Thomas Wroth.[45] Rogers lost his new position some time in January 1550, perhaps because of his suspected con-

[40] Sources: PRO, SP 10/5/fols. 55ff.; *APC*; *CPR, Ed. VI.*

[41] The earliest dated reference to Blount's status as a Gentleman of the Privy Chamber is 17 October 1552: *CPR, Ed. VI*, v, 380. The other clear references are: 1 November 1552, *ibid.*, iv, 234; 15 February 1553, *ibid.*, v, 1; and 1 April 1553, *APC*, iv, 246.

[42] *APC*, iii, 70. [43] *CPR, Ed. VI*, iii, 402. [44] *Ibid.*, iv, 195. [45] *APC*, ii, 344–5.

nection with the earl of Arundel, and was pensioned off the following June.[46] Gates apparently moved into his place as one of the principal Gentlemen. According to Edward VI, Sir Henry Sidney and Sir Henry Nevill together became ordinary Gentlemen on 18 April 1550; when Darcy (then Vice-Chamberlain) became the king's Chamberlain (5 April 1551), Sidney took his place as one of the four Chief Gentlemen (22 July 1551).[47]

As already stated, both Bellingham and St Leger had served as Lords Deputy in Ireland; apparently the title and not the office of Gentleman was customarily bestowed as an honor on the king's Lord Deputy. Thus when St Leger was recalled to England in April 1551, the Council wrote to the new Lord Deputy, Sir James Crofte, 'signifying unto hym that the Kinges Majestie hath appointed hym to be one of his Privie Chamber.'[48] The letter was dated 23 November 1551, but St Leger's name, not Crofte's, appears on the list of Gentlemen in 1552, since St Leger (like Bellingham) had been a Gentleman before his appointment to the Irish post. Actually, St Leger's revocation almost cost him his standing in the Privy Chamber: the Council had barred his presence there from January to April 1552 while he underwent examination on the charge, which he successfully rebutted, that as Lord Deputy he had secretly favored the Pope's religion.[49]

It appears that courtesy also dictated honoring the king's ambassador to the Emperor with the title of Gentleman of the Privy Chamber. Sir Richard Morison, ambassador to Charles V, certainly held it, though, like Hoby before him, his residency overseas (1550–3) prevented any life for him in the Chamber itself.[50]

In addition to Blount, evidence seems to exist for the tenures of two others whose names are not on the 1552 list: Jean Belmaine, the king's 'scholemaster in the Frenche tonge,' and Sir John Cheke, the king's tutor since 1544. In a letter of 3 June 1552 to the chancellor of the court of Augmentations, the Council referred to 'John Belmayne, one of the Privie Chamber'; his earlier patent of denization (11 June 1551) had identified him as 'a gentleman of the Privy Chamber.'[51] Such references, however, do not necessarily imply that Belmaine held the office of Gentleman; the employment of 'gentleman' in the terms of the patent would be expected for anyone like Belmaine who had served a prince in

[46] *Ibid.*, 399; III, 52; Braddock, 'The Royal Household,' 169.
[47] Jordan, *Chronicle*, 25, 75.
[48] *APC*, III, 426.
[49] See St Leger's biography in the *DNB*, L, 163–7.
[50] Wilbur K. Jordan, *Edward VI: The Young King* (London, Allen & Unwin, 1968), 232; *APC*, III, 45, 94.
[51] *APC*, IV, 67; *CPR, Ed. VI*, IV, 180.

his capacity. The same holds true for Cheke. Although the king himself unquestionably associated Cheke with Sidney and Nevill – 'all three of the Privy Chamber' – and although other references make him out to be 'a gentleman' of the Privy Chamber,[52] such designations reflect the institutional courtesy of signet clerks who prepared the warrants for action in Chancery where those references are now to be found. Cheke's right of access to the king in the Privy Chamber did not confer upon him the office in question; as 'a gentleman' who frequented the Privy Chamber, he was, as the patent rolls also record it, 'the king's household servant.'[53] The distinction between the eighteen Gentlemen of the Privy Chamber and those who were merely 'gentlemen' needs to be emphasized, as it is often ignored or misunderstood.[54] (A parallel case is the equally clear distinction between the fixed membership of the Privy Council and the king's many 'councillors' at large.) In short, the absence of Cheke and Belmaine from the list of 1552 represents important negative evidence: they were not then and never had been Gentlemen of the Privy Chamber. Table 2 sets out all of those who have been identified as Gentlemen of the Privy Chamber under Northumberland.

As already noted, in abolishing the Protectorate and committing Somerset to the Tower, the Council transferred governorship of the king's person to a committee of Privy Councillors, all temporal lords of the realm. The official version of the event described the impact of this political revolution at Hampton Court on the organization of the Privy Chamber: thinking 'it requisite to have summe nobell men appointed to be ordynarely attendant about his Majestes person in his Prevey Chamber . . . [the Council] dyd chuse for that purpose one Marques, two Earles and thre Barrons,' that is the marquess of Northampton, the earls of Arundel and Warwick, and the Lords Wentworth, St John, and Russell, 'the same six or at least two of them to be alwayes attendant.' Ostensibly the six lords were 'to give order for the good gouvernement' of the king and promote 'the honorable educacion of his Hieghnes in thies his tender yeres.'[55] In fact all but Arundel were identified politically with Northumberland's cause. As the king's Chamberlain, Arundel logically merited a place among those who now governed access to the king, but Arundel's ties with Southampton cost him this office and right, and by 2 February 1550 he had been banished from court, the victim of Northumberland's

[52] Jordan, *Chronicle*, 86; *CPR, Ed. VI*, IV, 182 (6 May 1551); *ibid.*, 260–1, 404 (20 August and 12 September 1552); *ibid.*, V, 92–3 (22 May 1553).

[53] *CPR, Ed. VI*, III, 113 (3 January 1550).

[54] The author of the unpublished biography of Cheke in the History of Parliament Trust files (Tavistock Square, London) wrongly thought him a 'Gentleman' of the Privy Chamber by October 1547.

[55] *APC*, II, 344–5.

The King's Privy Chamber, 1547–1553

Table 2. *Gentlemen of the Privy Chamber, 12 October 1549–6 July 1553*[56]

Principal Gentlemen

1. Sir Edward Rogers (to January 1550)
2. Sir Andrew Dudley
3. Sir Thomas Wroth
4. Sir Thomas Darcy (to April 1551)
5. Sir John Gates (from *c.* January 1550)
6. Sir Henry Sidney (from 22 July 1551)

Gentlemen

1. John Dudley, duke of Northumberland
2. William Herbert, earl of Pembroke
3. Sir Anthony St Leger
4. Lord Robert Dudley (from 15 August 1551)
5. Sir Thomas Hennage
6. Sir Thomas Cawarden
7. Sir Philip Hoby
8. Sir Anthony Cooke (by 12 February 1551)
9. Sir Maurice Berkeley
10. Sir William Goring (by 28 April 1551)
11. Sir Richard Morison (from *c.* 27 July 1550)
12. Sir William Fitzwilliams
13. Sir Nicholas Throckmorton (before 6 May 1551)
14. Sir Henry Nevill (from 18 April 1550)
15. Sir Peter Mewtas
16. Henry Wheler (by October 1552)
17. Barnaby Fitzpatrick (from 15 August 1551)
18. Sir Ralph Sadler
19. Sir John Gates (until *c.* January 1550)
20. Sir Henry Sidney (18 April 1550 to 22 July 1551)
21. Sir James Crofte (from 23 November 1551)
22. Sir Richard Blount (by 17 October 1552)
23. Sir Edward Bellingham (d. 1550)
24. Sir Thomas Paston (d. 1550)
25. Sir Francis Bryan (d. 2 February 1550)
26. Sir Thomas Speke (d. 1551)

[56] Sources: Society of Antiquaries, MS 125, fol. 30; BL, MS Stowe 571, fol. 30; Jordan, *Chronicle; APC; CPR, Ed. VI.* References to the tenures of those not already cited in the text are as follows: R. Dudley and Fitzpatrick: Jordan, *Chronicle*, 77. Cooke: *CPR, Ed. VI*, IV, 107. Goring: *ibid.*, IV, 52. Throckmorton: *APC*, III, 271. As Wheler appears on the 1552 list he must have been appointed before the earliest dated reference to Blount's tenure as a Gentleman, 17 October 1552.

armed suspicion.[57] Wentworth immediately replaced Arundel as Chamberlain. As Wentworth was also one of the six attendant lords, the question arises as to who took Arundel's place in that group. Probably it was Clinton: it will be remembered that when Clinton was admitted to the Privy Chamber two months later, he brought with him 200 soldiers specially charged to attend on the king, probably in order to prevent the sort of blow against Northumberland that Arundel and Southampton were said to have been planning during November 1549. As will be seen, the designation of four men as 'principal' Gentlemen fits the same pattern.

After 15 October 1549 the Privy Chamber was expanded not only by the addition of ten new men at the top – six lords attendant and four principal Gentlemen (the 'foure knights') – but also by the creation of eighteen new positions in the ranks below the complement of eighteen Gentlemen. By 1552 there were three gentlemen ushers, or one more than in 1545; five gentlemen ushers (daily waiters), or an increase of two; a wholly new staff of eight gentlemen ushers (quarterly waiters); and twelve grooms, an increase of eight since 1545. The suboffice of the Robes still counted a yeoman, groom, and a page, and in the Beds there were now two yeomen (where there had been one) and a new clerk, with the number of grooms and pages (two each) remaining unchanged. Excluding the Robes and Beds, the Privy Chamber had almost doubled in size since Henry's last days, from thirty to fifty-six.

The increase in the number of gentlemen ushers and grooms is explained only superficially by the presence of a superior group of lords attendant and principal Gentlemen who, since some of their own servants were now denied access to the Privy Chamber, required the assistance of a larger staff. The real explanation lies in three quite specific developments. The first characterized almost every late-Renaissance court – the social and political pressure exerted by a place-seeking generation of would-be courtiers. In England, a royal minority temporarily allowed the governing nobility to satisfy the office-hunger of kinsmen and ambitious young clients by expanding the sovereign's Privy Chamber to a degree that would not be tolerated by Edward's adult sisters.[58] Secondly, the accident of the accession of a child quite literally created more space at court. On 22

[57] Hoak, *King's Council*, 241–58.

[58] Mary I retained four Gentlemen, two gentlemen ushers, and four grooms in her Privy Chamber, according to John Norrys, one of the gentlemen ushers; Francis Grose and Thomas Astle (eds.), *The Antiquarian Repertory . . .*, 2nd edn. (4 vols., London, Edward Jeffery, 1807–9), IV, 651. In 1558 Elizabeth I employed fourteen women and five men as follows: four Gentlewomen of the Bedchamber, seven Gentlewomen of the Privy Chamber, three female Chamberers, one Gentleman of the Privy Chamber, one gentleman usher and three grooms of the Privy Chamber; BL, MS Lansdowne 3, fol. 192.

October 1551 the exclusive zone defining the king's lodgings at Westminster was expanded to include the vacant rooms 'on the Queen's side.'[59] By a kind of 'Parkinson's Law' of the Tudor court, when these rooms were formally added to the Privy Chamber 'on the king's side,' the number of attendant grooms and ushers almost tripled (from ten in 1545 to twenty-eight by 1552). Finally, the stepped-up demands for security in May 1550 may well have stimulated the need for a reserve staff of ushers and grooms.

V

Since a full discussion of the politics of these developments lies beyond the scope of the present study, in what follows I shall try to sketch out the significance of the changes already mentioned with reference to the Gentlemen as a whole.

'Well languaged, experte in outward parts, and meete and able to be sent on familiar messages, or otherwise, to outward princes, when the case shall require . . . Doeing humble, reverent, secrett, and lowly service' about the king as well: such were Wolsey's qualifications for the Gentlemen of the Privy Chamber in 1526,[60] and the ideal very often described the reality. In their martial exploits, cultural achievements, diplomatic missions, and honorable pretensions, Edward's Gentlemen could lay legitimate claim to the collective title of 'men for all seasons.' A few of them had already won fame as 'Renaissance' courtiers in the continental style. Sir Francis Bryan, for example, had come close to putting Castiglione's theory into practice in the 1520s and 1530s. In their persons, however, the Gentlemen were supposed to be more than royal adornments or soldier-poets, creators of *belles lettres* and *bons mots*. By their birth, attainments, and preferment they were really extensions of a king's honor. As his personally chosen private companions, they fused, somewhat paradoxically, the ceremonial role of private body servant with that of bureaucrat and royal official.

An unforgettable picture of this fusion – or confusion – of the roles of statesman and servant, which is so characteristic of the sixteenth century, survives in a letter Sir Thomas Cheyne wrote to Henry VIII from Bordeaux, 14 April 1522, while on embassy to Francis I:

In my last Letters is mencioned of the Frenshe Kinge's commandement to me, that I should use myself at all hours in his Prevye Chambre, as I doo in Yours. Yet, that

59 *APC*, III 393.
60 *A Collection of Ordinances and Regulations for the Government of the Royal Household* (London, Society of Antiquaries, 1790), 155.

notwithstanding I wolde not be so presumptuous uppon his furst commaundement so to doo, wherefore this morning he sent Morrett to my lodging to bring me to him. At my comyng, the Kyng was but lately rysen, and in his nyght gowne was looking out a windowe. Please yt Your Grace, that when I came into his sayde chambre, and that he was ready to the wasshing of his handes, the Towell was brought to the Great Maister, and so he toke it to me, and made me gyve hit to the Kyng, saying, that your Grace used hym so, at his being in England.[61]

That an English king's Gentleman might do such service at the French king's court is no less interesting than the nature of the service itself. A Gentleman was to be in the Privy Chamber at the king's rising in order 'to apparrell and dresse his Highnesse.' Grooms delivered the morning's garments, hose and shoes as well, to a gentleman usher who in turn conveyed them to one of the Gentlemen. Only the Gentlemen 'ministered unto the King's person': only the Gentlemen could actually approach the king or presume 'to lay hands upon his royall person, or intermeddle with prepareing or dressing of the same.'[62] One naturally wonders if the prescription of 1526 really described what happened in Edward VI's 'raying' chamber. Apparently it did, since Sir Richard Blount's extraordinarily detailed account of 'The Gent. Ushers Office of the Privye Chamber,' 1547–53, specifically mentions that 'the Gent. Ushers, the Gent. of the Chamber, savinge those that bee of the Bedd Chamber, ought to go noe farther than the Privye Chamber, unlesse they bee called.' The ushers were to be always 'at the dore, yf the K. bee presente.'[63]

When Blount excepted 'those' of the bedchamber, he meant only those Gentlemen who had been appointed to sleep, armed, on pallets in a room next to the king's bedchamber. A new rotation for such duty, dictated by Northumberland's concern for security, was spelled out in an order of 20 April 1550. Together with Blount's report, this order offers concrete evidence of a division of the Gentlemen's duties.[64] By April 1550 various of the eighteen Gentlemen could be distinguished by the degree of their relative proximity to the king. Those who, like the four knights, were charged with personal attendance had come to be recognized as belonging to the 'inner' Privy Chamber. Architecturally, the inner Privy Chamber

[61] Quoted in Nicholas Carlisle, *An Inquiry into the Place and Quality of the Gentlemen of His Majesty's Most Honourable Privy Chamber* (London, Payne & Foss, 1829), 22–3. On the relationship between office in the Privy Chamber and ambassadorial duty, see David Starkey, 'Representation through intimacy: a study in the symbolism of monarchy and court office in early modern England,' in Ioan M. Lewis (ed.), *Symbols and Sentiments: Cross-cultural Studies in Symbolism* (London and New York, Academic Press, 1977), 201–2. On the contacts with the court of Francis I, see R. J. Knecht, 'The court of Francis I,' *European Studies Review*, VIII (1978), 8–9.

[62] *A Collection of Ordinances* (1790), 156.

[63] Grose and Astle, *Antiquarian Repertory*, IV, 648. [64] Jordan, *Chronicle*, 26.

comprised chiefly the royal bedchamber, probably a 'raying' (or dressing) chamber, a closet, or stool chamber, if it was separate from the bedchamber, a pallet chamber next to the bedchamber, and any other gallery, room or rooms of the Privy Chamber declared to be out of bounds to all but the select few. When Edward VI said that after 20 April 1550 'three of the *outer* Privy Chamber gentlemen should always be here,' he meant that the number of ordinary Gentlemen admitted to the inner Privy Chamber had been increased. Two of these three were now to 'fill the room of one of the four knights' who usually lay 'in the palat' chamber during the 'all night' service. The times required vigilance: those at the doors were to be 'diligent in their office,' and five grooms were always to be present, 'of which one to watch in the bed-chamber.'[65] In other words, the order of 20 April 1550 suggests that Northumberland intended the four principal Gentlemen to serve as Edward's bodyguards in the 'inner' Privy Chamber. Of the two who were always to be attendant, one was excused this duty on 20 April, his place being taken during the day by three Gentlemen of the 'outer' Privy Chamber, and during the night by two.

Now the Eltham Ordinances, which had prescribed a Gentleman's duties generally, did not distinguish between the Chief (or 'principal') Gentlemen and the ordinary ones. That distinction arose during the course of the 1530s when the Tudors borrowed the title of the office from the Valois court (*le premier gentilhomme de la chambre*) and gave it to the Groom of the Stool, thereby identifying him as the unquestioned head of the Privy Chamber. By 1536 there were two Chief Gentlemen (Bryan and Hennage), but one of them, the Groom of the Stool (Hennage), remained *ex officio* the 'first' Gentleman.[66] By 1547 the six Gentlemen (of the Eltham Ordinances) had become eighteen, and the Chief Gentlemen (Denny and Herbert), who were destined to play such a prominent role at Edward's coronation, were now also Privy Councillors.

By 13 September 1547, however, Somerset had made his brother-in-law, Sir Michael Stanhope, 'one of the Chief Gentilmen of the Privy Chamber' and by 15 August 1548, 'first' Gentleman.[67] As first Gentleman, Stanhope discharged duties both strategic and sensitive: a Chief Gentleman always stayed physically very close to the king, serving him intimately in the royal bedchamber and other Privy Chamber rooms; he held 'a pryvy key' to these rooms and so regulated all access to the king in the Privy Chamber; he administered such of the king's plate, jewels, linen, etc. as were in daily use; he was the king's most confidential mess-

[65] *Ibid.* [66] Starkey, 'The King's Privy Chamber,' 237–44.
[67] *APC*, II, 128; *CPR*, *Ed. VI*, I, 391.

enger.[68] And he, and not the king's secretaries, kept the dry stamp of Edward's signature – together with his control of the Privy Purse, the true basis of a Chief Gentleman's powers. Stanhope's autograph letters conveying 'my Lorde protectors pleasor' to the other Gentlemen leave little doubt about his status at court: after Somerset he was the most influential man about the king.[69] Well might the Protector's brother, Thomas Seymour, envy Stanhope his position next to the king, wishing even 'that he shulde have the gouvernaunce of him as Mr. Stanhope had.'[70]

As *de facto* Governor of Edward VI, Stanhope probably delegated to others some of the routine duties of a Chief Gentleman's attendance, but one he must have guarded jealously was the keepership of the king's Privy Purse. Stanhope's record of Privy Purse expenditures has not survived, so there is no way now to estimate whether the Privy Chamber operated as an agency of national finance during the Protectorate. Did Somerset channel funds through the Privy Purse in order to pay off some of the expenses of his war in Scotland? The informality and flexibility of such a method would be in keeping with what we know of his conduct of government generally: he preferred to run things through his own household on orders to his 'new council' of men like Stanhope and Edward Wolf, a former naval captain who owed his place in the Privy Chamber (as a gentleman usher?) to Somerset's patronage.[71]

Under Northumberland the Council regularly ordered warrants drawn on the various courts of revenue for the delivery of lump sums of money, ranging typically from £100 to £1000, into 'thandes of the Chief Gentlemen of the Kinges Majesties Privy Chamber, to be disbursed by them in suche paymentes as hathe been accustomed to passe oute of his Majesties pursse.'[72] And what customarily were these 'diffraymentes' of the Privy Purse? Typically they included £14 6s. 0d. for hay and oats for the deer in the king's park at Greenwich, various sums (£10 to £18) for 'wages of woorkemen, weders and other necessaries' in the king's gardens at Greenwich and Westminster, £40 in reward to John Knox, 'preacher in

[68] Starkey, 'The King's Privy Chamber,' 250–67; Starkey, 'Representation through intimacy,' 205–6.

[69] Folger Library, MS L. b. 290, Stanhope to Sir Thomas Cawarden, from Westminster, 5 February 1548; MS L. b. 48, Stanhope to Cawarden, from the court at Westminster, 13 August 1549. On the use of the stamp of Edward's hand, see Hoak, *King's Council*, 27, 66, 118, 149–51, 325 (nn. 39, 41, 44, 46), 326 n. 56, 328 n. 73.

[70] *APC*, II, 260.

[71] A list of the fleet of 10 August 1545 identifies Wolf as captain of the *Phenix Hertford*, described as 'The Erle of Hartfordes barke': *LP*, XX(2), 88 and 27(2).

[72] *APC*, III, 175, 10 December 1550.

the North,' etc.[73] All such specific references, however, constitute the Council's own warrants addressed to the Gentlemen; these are the only kinds of Privy Purse expenditures so described in the council books; they are usually for amounts not in excess of £20; and there are relatively few of them. What happened to the remainder of the money – tens of thousands of pounds sterling – diverted from the courts of revenue into the Privy Purse?

We know that almost £40,000 passed through the hands of Peter Osborne, clerk to the four principal Gentlemen, and that it was spent on the Council's orders in King Edward's 'special affairs' – for fortifications, the gendarmes, the repayment of foreign loans, as well as rewards and household expenses.[74] Osborne apparently stashed some of this money in the Privy Chamber whence he transferred it to the hands of the Chief Gentlemen, and especially to Sir John Gates, who in turn paid it out on Northumberland's orders. Occasionally account was taken 'of all suche sommes of monny as be cumme therefore to thandes of the . . . Chefe Gentlemen,' but the informality of Osborne's methods made record-keeping difficult. On 2 May 1553 someone actually stole £600 of the money brought by Osborne to Westminster palace and 'remayning in our chamber thear wheare we [the king] most accustomabley do heare the sermondes.'[75] In any case, we may be sure that at least during Osborne's tenure (January 1552 to May 1553) the Privy Chamber operated as a clearing-house or agency for the administration of national finance, for of the money paid into Osborne's account by the treasurers of the courts of revenue, Osborne regularly turned over large, single sums, sometimes totalling £3000 and £7000, to the treasurer of the Chamber (for example), who then disbursed smaller sums (for military expenses etc.) by warrant of the Council.[76] It is clear that the Council set the financial policy and directed the expenditures; it is equally clear that the Chief Gentlemen and their clerk managed this money in the privy chambers of the royal palaces.

VI

Nothing has been said here about the cultural life of the court, and very little of politics, religion, and the great issues of state. Evidence certainly exists for a history of the Privy Chamber to be written with respect to

[73] *Ibid.*, IV, 81, 234, 101, 157, 158; 154, respectively.
[74] *CPR, Ed. VI*, V, 85; Hoak, *King's Council*, 210–11.
[75] *APC*, IV, 58; III, 437; *CPR, Ed. VI*, V, 185. Thomas Mildmay and William Berners were commissioned to discharge Osborne of the £600.
[76] *APC*, III, 501–2, 503.

such topics. The burden of the foregoing remarks has been to suggest that for the reign of Edward VI an adequate history of politics and government cannot be written without reference to the Privy Chamber. It has been said that the succession of a minor and two women after 1547 'killed off' the Privy Chamber both as a household department and an administrative agency.[77] In light of what we are beginning to learn about Edward VI's Privy Chamber, it would be fairer to say that the premature death of the last Tudor king altered the development of the royal household, and hence the development of English central government, in ways that could not have been foreseen in 1547. A truer history of Tudor politics after that date remains to be written.

[77] Starkey, 'The King's Privy Chamber,' 419.

The place of women in Tudor government

MORTIMER LEVINE

I

The place of women in Tudor government cannot be deduced simply from the mere existence of two queens regnant. Mary I and Elizabeth I were exceptions, only biological accidents in the line of royal succession who happened to be females. Their attitude toward the participation of women aside from themselves in government seems to have been no different from that of their male predecessors. A recent writer, on the basis of hearsay evidence from the seventeenth century, indicates that Mary may have appointed a female justice of the peace and then asserts that Elizabeth, 'judging from available evidence, did not concern herself about other women in political positions of responsibility.'[1] Even if the hearsay was correct, a single appointment would hardly make Mary's feminine consciousness greater than her sister's. The sexual significance of Mary and Elizabeth in turn occupying the highest place in Tudor government may be different than it appears to be at first glance. Early in Mary's reign the authority of a queen regnant was declared by parliamentary statute. Though the wording of the act indicated that it was merely confirmatory, it really was more than that. A queen regnant was unprecedented in England, and statutes before Mary's accession attributed all royal power 'unto the name of King.' Now Parliament

> declared and enacted . . . that the kingly or regal office of the realm, and all dignities, prerogative royal, power, preeminences, privileges, authorities, and jurisdictions thereunto annexed, united, or belonging, being invested either in male or female, are and be and ought to be as fully, wholly, absolutely, and entirely deemed, judged, accepted, invested, and taken in the one as in the other; so that what and whensoever statute or law doth limit and appoint that the King of this realm may or shall . . . do anything as King . . ., the same the Queen . . . may by the same authority and power likewise . . . do.[2]

[1] Pearl Hogrefe, *Tudor Women: Commoners and Queens* (Ames, Iowa, Iowa State University Press, 1975), 34.

[2] Joseph R. Tanner (ed.), *Tudor Constitutional Documents, A.D. 1485–1603, with an Historical Commentary*, 2nd edn (Cambridge, CUP, 1930), 123–4.

This act can be viewed not only as making queens regnant the equal of a king but also declaring a woman, albeit a particular one, the equal of a man. It might even be called the royal 'women's liberation' statute of the sixteenth century.

There is another way of reading the statute, however. It specifically called the office now belonging to Mary and future queens regnant 'kingly,' and it authorized them to do anything a king was authorized to do 'as King.' This can be interpreted as meaning that Mary and Elizabeth were legally kings, that is, males, for the purpose of ruling. It is possible that Elizabeth came to think of herself as such. This would explain the curious wording of her 'golden speech' of 1601 where she referred to 'our kingly dignity' and 'my kingly bounties' before making what turned out to be a final statement in which, by word count if not by meaning, she was more king than queen:

> I know the title of a King is a glorious title; but assure yourself that the shining glory of princely authority hath not so dazzled the eyes of our understanding, but that we well know and remember that we also are to yield an account of our actions before the great Judge. To be a King and wear a crown is a thing more glorious to them that see it, than it is pleasant to them that bear it. For myself, I was never so much enticed with the glorious name of a King or royal authority of a Queen, as delighted that God hath made me His instrument to maintain His truth and glory, and to defend this Kingdom . . . from peril, dishonour, tyranny and oppression.[3]

II

A natural result of the in-the-eyes-of-some unnatural appearance of the queens regnant was the appearance of a literature on gynecocracy. This literature not only provided arguments for and against women rulers but indicated attitudes toward lesser women as well. The actual first blast against the rule of women came about three and a half years before John Knox published his famous charge. In the latter part of 1554, over a year after the Catholic Mary's accession, Thomas Becon, an English exile at Strassburg, published *An Humble Suplication unto God* in which he lamented God's having 'taken away from us' the sixteen-year-old Edward VI.

> For in the stead of that virtuous prince thou hast set to rule over us a woman, whom nature hath formed to be in subjection unto man, and whom thou by thine holy apostle [Paul] commandest to keep silence, and not to speak in the congrega-

[3] John E. Neale, *Elizabeth I and Her Parliaments, 1584–1601* (London, Jonathan Cape, 1953), 390–1.

tion. Ah, Lord! to take away the empire from a man, and to give it to a woman, seemeth to be an evident token of thine anger toward us Englishmen. For by the prophet [Isaiah] thou, being displeased with thy people, threatenest to set women to rule over them, as people unworthy to have lawful, natural, and meet governors to reign over them. And verily, though we find that women sometime bare rule among thy people, yet do we read that such as ruled and were queens were for the most part wicked, ungodly, superstitious, and given to idolatry and to all filthy abominations; as we may see in the histories of queen Jesebel, queen Athalia, queen Herodias, and such-like.[4]

This in essence is Knox's case against female rule written small.

Early in 1558 at Geneva John Knox published his *First Blast of the Trumpet Against the Monstruous Regiment of Women*. In this diatribe Knox provided more than a mere elaboration of Becon's case. The frustrated Scottish reformer had twice the reason his English counterparts had to oppose gynecocracy, what with the England he had fled ruled by the 'Jezebel' Mary Tudor and his native land under the regency of the 'idolatress' Mary of Guise. The tone of the *First Blast* indicated that with Knox, Calvinist zealot and revolutionary though he was, sexual rather than religious or political bigotry was the driving force. As a recent writer has put it, of all the Marian exiles who wrote against gynecocracy, 'only Knox despised female sovereignty for its own sake.'[5]

In the *First Blast* Knox maintained that the rule of women 'is repugnant to Nature; contumelie to God, a thing most contrarious to his reveled word and approved ordinance; and . . . the subversion of good Order, of all equitie and justice.'[6] Women are by nature unfit to rule; they are 'weake, fraile, impacient, feble, and foolish . . . unconstant, variable, cruell, and lacking the spirit of counsel and regiment.'[7] Knox followed Becon in citing Paul's command that 'women kepe silence in the Congregation' and added from Paul, 'I suffer not a woman to teache, nether yet to usurpe authoritie above man.'[8] While Becon, by condemning 'the most part' of women rulers, at least left room for 'godly' women rulers, Knox denied that biblical 'examples' like the illustrious Deborah held any political authority.[9] As for an existing woman ruler like Mary Tudor, Knox concluded that it is the duty of the estates and the people 'to remove from honor and authoritie that monstre in nature.'[10]

While Becon, Knox, and other Marian exiles published attacks on

[4] John Ayre (ed.), *Prayers and Other Pieces of Thomas Becon, S.T.P.*, for the Parker Society, IV (Cambridge, CUP, 1844), 227–8.

[5] P. L. Scalingi, 'The scepter or the distaff: the question of female sovereignty, 1516–1607,' *Historian*, XLI (1978), 75.

[6] David Laing (ed.), *The Works of John Knox* (6 vols., Edinburgh, Thin, 1846–64), IV, 373.

[7] *Ibid.*, 374. [8] *Ibid.*, 379. [9] *Ibid.*, 409. [10] *Ibid.*, 416.

gynecocracy, the only known English defense of female rulers written during Mary's reign was an anonymous passage that did not reach print until the 1563 edition of the *Mirror for Magistrates*.[11] The author made four points. 'The chiefest poynt of a princes offyce consysteth in obedience to god' and a woman can obey God as well as a man. 'The second poynt of a princes offyce is to prouyde for the impotent, nedy, and helples . . . . And seing women are by nature tender harted, mylde, and pytefull [compassionate], who maye better then they discharge this dutie?' Third, the examples of Deborah and others show that women have the courage to do battle with the enemy. And finally,

> as all wysedome and pollicie, seing it consisteth in folowing the counsayl of many godly, learned, & long experienced heades, it were better to have a woman, who consideringe her owne weaknes and inabilitye, should be ruled thereby, than a man which presuming vpon his owne fond brayne, wil heare no advise save his owne.[12]

The author's women are by nature tender-hearted, mild, and compassionate, but they are also by nature weak and lacking in ability. They are not like Knox's women by nature unfit to rule but, as should become evident, defenders of female rulers were not enthusiastic about their abilities.

The first English defense of gynecocracy published after Elizabeth's accession was John Aylmer's *An Harborowe for Faithful and Trewe Subiectes*. Aylmer wrote this answer to Knox's *First Blast* while still an exile but had returned to England at least a month before its publication on 26 April 1559.[13] He maintained that Knox was led into error by generalizing from the example of Mary Tudor, a particular woman ruler, that rule by any woman 'was vnnaturall, vnreasonable, vniust, and vnlawful.'[14] In the next breath Aylmer called Elizabeth Tudor, England's new woman ruler, 'a woman weake in nature, feable in bodie, softe in courage, vnskilfull in practise, [and] not terrible to the enemy.'[15] Aylmer regarded rule by men as normal, but he asserted, when God chooses to supply no male heir, 'it is a plain argument, that for some secret purpose he myndeth the female should reigne and gouerne.'[16] Of course the inevitable Deborah was among the women so advanced.[17] Another was Anne Boleyn: 'the mother of this blessed woman [Elizabeth], the chief, first, and only cause of

[11] Lily B. Campbell (ed.), *The Mirror for Magistrates* (Cambridge, CUP, 1938), 12–13.
[12] *Ibid.*, 419–20.
[13] Hastings Robinson (ed.), *The Zurich Letters*, for the Parker Society, L (2 vols., Cambridge, CUP, 1842–4), I, 11.
[14] John Aylmer, *An Harborowe for Faithfvl and Trewe Subiectes* (Strassburg [more likely London, John Day], 1559), sig. B2.
[15] *Ibid.*, sig. B2*v*. [16] *Ibid.*, sig. B3. [17] *Ibid.*, sig. B3*v*.

banyshing the beast of Rome, with all his beggerly baggage.'[18] In sum, the rule of a woman was not unnatural, but it was an exception that required a special act of God. In any case, in England having a female ruler was not as dangerous as men commonly thought it to be. There the laws ruled and not the queen. And she could only make laws in parliament with the consent of her lords and commons. If, Aylmer concluded, 'she were a mere monarch and not a mixed ruler, you might peraduenture make me feare the matter the more.'[19] So much for the principal Elizabethan defense of gynecocracy, which, if read by Elizabeth, might help to explain why Aylmer had to wait some eighteen years to receive his desired bishopric of London.

The only other Elizabethan defense of women rulers worth bringing up here is that in Lawrence Humphrey's *De Religionis Conservatione et Reformatione Vera*, published at Basle in September 1559. Like John Aylmer, Humphrey held that rule by men was normal, but God sometimes 'shows his strongest power in a woman, a very weak vessel.' Humphrey's example was the ever useful Deborah. But he went further and asserted that God sometimes gave authority to a boy such as Josiah. And in England God 'has accomplished incredibly and singularly' the restoration of the kingdom of Christ via 'a boy king [Edward VI] and a woman prince [Elizabeth].'[20] With Humphrey, one might say, a woman, 'a very weak vessel,' became the equivalent of a male child. Modern feminists should find the direct Knox, vituperation and all, less insulting than Humphrey and even Aylmer.

The last writer to be considered is Sir Thomas Smith whose *De Republica Anglorum* was first written in 1565 but not published until 1583, six years after his death. Till now our writers have been clerical controversialists; with Smith we have a secular scholar whose long experience in government began in Edward VI's reign. The difference was in approach more than conclusion. Smith did not quote Paul to reject female participation in government but he rejected it nonetheless:

> We do reject women, as those whom nature hath made to keepe home and to nourish their familie and children, and not to medle in matters abroade, nor to beare office in a citie or common wealth no more than children and infants.

It was a different matter, however, if a title to the crown, a duchy, or an earldom passed to a woman or child by right of blood:

[18] *Ibid.*, sig. B4*v*. [19] *Ibid.*, sig. H3.

[20] Lawrence Humphrey, *De Religionis*, translated in J. K. Kemp, 'Lawrence Humphrey, Elizabethan Puritan: his life and political theories' (West Virginia University, Unpublished Ph.D. thesis, 1978), 212–13.

> These I say have the same authoritie although they be women or children in that kingdome, dutchie or earledome, as they shoulde have had if they had bin men of full age. For the right and honour of the blood, and the quietnes and sueritie of the realme, is more to be considered, than either the tender age as yet impotent to rule, or the sexe not accustomed (otherwise) to intermeddle with publicke affaires, being by common intendment understood, that such personages never do lacke the counsell of such grave and discreete men as be able to supplie all other defectes.[21]

Smith, according to his modern biographer, 'simply did not like women very much.'[22] To Smith a woman's place was in the home. Women had no more role in government 'than children and,' as he saw fit to add, 'infants.' Smith would allow women and children the same authority as grown men if the crown, a duchy, or an earldom came to them by right of inheritance, mainly, one suspects from his language, because history taught the dangers involved in trying to meddle with hereditary titles. With Smith at least women were not quite the same as children: children were 'impotent to rule' while women were only 'not accustomed' to do so. But it was 'by common intendment understood' that women as well as children continually needed 'the counsell of such grave and discreete men as be able to supplie all other defectes.' Elizabeth would not have liked Smith very much for the last if it had come to her attention during his lifetime.

III

Sir Thomas Smith's *De Republica Anglorum* provides a convenient place at which to turn our primary interest from the matter of queens regnant to the question of participation by lesser women in government. With the exception of succession to dukedoms and earldoms by right of blood, Smith apparently held that such women could not hold any office 'in a citie or common wealth.' Smith's exceptions apart, his view had been anticipated in a work published in 1558 in Geneva by an ally of Knox, Christopher Goodman's *How Svperior Powers Oght to be Obeyd*. There Goodman asked:

> Yf women be not permitted by Ciuile policies to rule in inferior offices, to be Counsellours, Peers of a realme, Iustices, Shireffs, Bayliues and such like: I make

[21] Sir Thomas Smith, *De Republica Anglorum*, ed. Leonard Alston (Cambridge, CUP, 1906), 30.

[22] Mary Dewar, *Sir Thomas Smith: a Tudor Intellectual in Office* (London, Athlone Press, 1964), 172.

your selues iudges, wither it be mete for them to gouerne whole Realmes and nations?[23]

On the matter of women being peers in their own right in Tudor England, Goodman was wrong and Smith was too narrow in his hereditary restriction. Two notable cases suffice: Margaret Pole became countess of Salisbury, an earldom that had been held by her father and brother; Anne Boleyn was created marchioness of Pembroke, a marquisate to which she had no claim in blood. Aside from these instances the matter becomes more difficult.

The only general account of women office-holders in Tudor England is that of Miss Hogrefe, and it is necessarily slim. She could only state with certainty that a number of Tudor women served in the low-level and local office of churchwarden. She claimed with some justification that Tudor women could have been sheriffs and justices of the peace, admitted that none were sheriffs, and only offered hearsay evidence of three possible justices. More interesting, Hogrefe argued convincingly that Henry VII probably made his mother, Lady Margaret Beaufort, 'High Commissioner of the Council of the North.' The title she gave to the office may be anachronistic, but her main evidence for Lady Margaret heading a Council in the North was substantial. It was a memorandum that Thomas, Lord Darcy wrote on a petition of 1529 objecting to a commission that Henry VIII had given to his illegitimate son, Henry Fitzroy, duke of Richmond, whom he had made the nominal head of a Council in the North. In his memorandum Darcy referred to

how the like commission that my lady the king's grandam had, was tried and approved, greatly to the king's disadvantage, in stopping of many the lawful processes and course of his laws at Westminster Hall . . . and none gain commonly by any such commission but the clerks.[24]

Darcy, a northern lord, was old enough to be testifying from personal experience, but his testimony suggested the possibility that Lady Margaret's headship, like Richmond's, was merely nominal. Darcy was invoking Margaret's 'disastrous' commission in support of a petition to get rid of a council composed of low-ranking men, the majority of them clerics, which the fallen Cardinal Wolsey had used under the nominal headship of Richmond to enforce royal justice in the north.[25] It was cer-

[23] Quoted in J. E. Phillips, Jr, 'Spenser's attitude toward women rulers,' *Huntington Library Quarterly*, v (1941), 11.

[24] Hogrefe, *Tudor Women*, 27–36.

[25] F. W. Brooks, 'The Council of the North,' in Joel Hurstfield (ed.), *The Historical Association Book of the Tudors* (London, Sidgwick & Jackson, 1973), 176–7.

tainly possible that Henry VII used a similar council under the nominal headship of his mother for a similar purpose.

In the case of royal ladies like Lady Margaret Beaufort political influence may have been a more important consideration than the holding of an office. Lady Margaret could not take us far on this track. While it seemed likely that Henry VII sometimes consulted his mother about political matters,[26] we lack specific evidence. And there was no reason to believe that Henry's wife, Elizabeth of York, had any influence when it came to affairs of state. We may learn more by considering some of the wives of Henry VIII.

IV

The one woman, the queens regnant excepted, who certainly exerted real influence on the conduct of affairs of state in Tudor England over a number of years was Henry VIII's first wife, Catherine of Aragon. When the seventeen-year-old Henry married Catherine shortly after his accession in 1509, she was five years his senior and had been for two years Spain's accredited ambassador to England. For five years more she continued to be the real Spanish ambassador in England, skillfully steering her inexperienced husband towards a pro-Spanish policy. Even after Wolsey's rise Catherine continued to exert some influence until about 1520. In 1513 Henry, before embarking on his first invasion of France, had his wife proclaimed 'Governor of the Realm and captain-general of the forces for home defense.' Catherine was no figurehead regent. She governed England, raised supplies for Henry's army, and prepared to meet a Scottish invasion which the septuagenarian earl of Surrey and his men stopped at Flodden. Enough has been said to make the point; there is no need to go on with a story that has been well told by a master.[27] If the case of the early Catherine of Aragon stands alone, however, it does not take us far. Her influence then could be dismissed as no more than an accident, as a mere product of Henry's youth and inexperience. That would make her much like the queens regnant, an exception that proves little.

The only other of Henry VIII's queens to be appointed as regent was his sixth and last wife, Catherine Parr, who held the office in the summer of

[26] Stanley B. Chrimes, *Henry VII* (London, Eyre Methuen, 1972), 109; Michael van C. Alexander, *The First of the Tudors: a Study of Henry VII and His Reign* (Totowa, N. J., Rowman & Littlefield, 1980), 176.

[27] Garrett Mattingly, *Catherine of Aragon* (London, Jonathan Cape, 1950), 74–7, 105–8, 116–27, 152–6.

1544 when Henry campaigned in France for the last time. Catherine Parr's regency was hardly, as her biographer indicated, the equivalent of Catherine of Aragon's.[28] In the spring of 1544 Scotland had been devastated by an English army commanded by Edward Seymour, earl of Hertford, Henry's brother-in-law by his third marriage. This meant that the Scots were in no condition to launch their customary major strike from the north while the English were engaged in France. And that meant that it was safe to entrust the regency to the politically inexperienced Catherine Parr instead of a great nobleman or ecclesiastic whose acquisition of power might be dangerous. As regent Catherine was to use the advice of a council of five, namely, Archbishop Cranmer, Lord Chancellor Wriothesley, Hertford, Bishop Thirlby of Westminster, and Sir William Petre, one of Henry's principal secretaries. Wriothesley or Hertford was to be resident at court, and if neither of them could be there, Cranmer and Petre were to remain with Catherine. As it turned out, it was Cranmer and Petre who stayed with the regent and what business of government there was evidently was handled by Petre.[29] It would seem that Catherine Parr was little more than a figurehead regent.

But did Catherine Parr, her regency apart, come to exert real influence? It is true that a circle of humanists attached themselves to Catherine and that she provided from out of that circle tutors for Prince Edward and Princess Elizabeth who in varying degrees may have initiated their pupils in Protestantism. It is at least possible to say from this that Catherine had an indirect influence on England's Protestant future, but that is not the kind of influence we are looking for. Catherine, however, has been charged by her biographer with converting Henry VIII to 'the New Faith.'[30] And a distinguished historian has asserted that Catherine 'unquestionably' influenced Henry's belated decision that 'England was to be Protestant.'[31] What is lacking, of course, is genuine evidence of Henry's 'conversion' or 'decision.' The best word on Catherine Parr remains that written by a great historian a little over a quarter century ago: 'Henry's last queen, who apparently had protestant sympathies, managed on the whole to keep out of politics, so that she survived her husband.'[32]

[28] Anthony Martienssen, *Queen Katherine Parr* (London, Secker & Warburg, 1973), 174.
[29] Frederick G. Emmison, *Tudor Secretary: Sir William Petre at Court and Home* (London, Longmans, 1961), 53–4.
[30] Martienssen, *Queen Katherine Parr*, 221.
[31] Wilbur K. Jordan, *Edward VI: the Young King* (London, Allen & Unwin, 1968), 31–3.
[32] G. R. Elton, *England under the Tudors* (London, Methuen, 1955), 195.

V

The last, and for our purposes crucial, wife of Henry VIII to be considered is his second, Anne Boleyn. While it lasted, no woman ever had a greater hold on Henry than Anne. And she surely was not lacking in desire for power or in the will to go after it.

Anne Boleyn was not, as Aylmer implied, an English Deborah. Deborah was a prophetess who was accepted by the children of Israel as their judge. She and Barak led them into battle and delivered Israel from the twenty-year oppression of the king of Canaan.[33] Anne Boleyn was a woman who became a queen consort, not a ruler. If she alone was responsible for delivering England from 'the beast of Rome,' it was only because she refused to yield to Henry without assurance of matrimony and a queenly crown. And she was quite willing to let Wolsey get her what she wanted via Rome until it became clear that his efforts there had failed. If expedient resistance to the royal lust made Anne England's deliverer, it was only because the resistance finally led to action by Henry and his parliament under the guidance of Thomas Cromwell. Anne's resistance may have constituted the ultimate in political influence, but, if so, it was an anomalous instance.

Contemporary testimony, however, would have it that Anne's political influence was of long duration and of high order. A few examples should suffice. At the time of Wolsey's fall in October 1529 Jean du Bellay, the French ambassador, reported: 'The duke of Norfolk is made chief of the Council, Suffolk acting in his absence, and, at the head of all, Mademoiselle Anne.'[34] In 1531 the abbot of Whitby, according to his prior, 'said he hard say thatt my lord off Norffooke, the duke of Suffook, [and] my lady Anne was the hyest in fawor w^{t} the kyngeis grac and hath most miytt in all thys reyme.'[35] Shortly after Anne's coronation in June 1533 Ridolfo Pio, bishop of Faenza, wrote: 'All business passes through the hands of people who depend on the new Queen, and must therefore be settled according to her purpose.'[36] And as late as November 1535 Eustace Chapuys, the Imperial ambassador, reported: 'It is she [Anne] who now rules over, and governs, the nation, the King dares not contradict her.'[37]

The trouble with this testimony is not that those quoted, du Bellay

33 Judges 4–5. 34 *LP*, IV, 2679.
35 PRO, SP 1/2371, fol. 15. 36 *LP*, VIII, 358.
37 Gustav A. Bergenroth *et al.* (eds.), *Calendar of Letters, Despatches, and State Papers, Relating to Negotiations between England and Spain* (15 vols., London, HMSO, 1862–1954), V, pt 1, 571.

excepted, were hostile to Anne Boleyn. Their testimony doubtless reflected widespread opinion. It was natural to assume that Anne had great political power, considering her personal hold on Henry. But the assumption was not necessarily correct. Henry's early deference to Catherine of Aragon probably was no more than a youthful aberration. There is no reason to suppose that he did not share common prejudices with regard to women. It was one thing to yield to Anne in matters personal; it was another to let her have her way in matters of state. At any rate, convincing evidence of Anne's power is lacking, even in cases where one might most expect to find it.

A good illustration of this is the 'persecution' of Wolsey after his fall from power. Wolsey certainly blamed Anne for his plight. Some months after his fall he told his servant George Cavendish that he had only submitted to Henry and accepted his losses as a necessary means to recover the royal favor.

> [For] there was a continual serpentine enemy about the King that would, I am well assured, if I had been found stiff-necked, [have] called continually upon the King in his ear (I mean the night crow [Anne]) with such a vehemency that I should (with the help of her assistance) have obtained sooner the King's indignation than his lawful favor.[38]

Others apparently shared his view. In October 1530 Wolsey learned from Thomas Cromwell, who worked in his interest at court, that 'none dare now speak to the King on his part for fear of Madame Anne's displeasure.'[39] And at the time of Wolsey's final arrest in late November 1530 Chapuys reported that the duke of Norfolk, Anne, and her father, the earl of Wiltshire, 'have never ceased plotting against the Cardinal, especially the Lady.' He concluded, 'nothing would satisfy the Lady short of the Cardinal's arrest.'[40]

Anne undoubtedly desired Wolsey's utter ruin, but so did Norfolk, Suffolk, and Wiltshire, the triumvirate that came to power after his fall. Anne no doubt took every opportunity to prejudice Henry against Wolsey, but the evidence shows that it was Norfolk who was the effective aggressor against the cardinal. Though Norfolk was Anne's uncle, he must have been working primarily in his own interest. He had become chief minister on Wolsey's fall and quickly came to fear that Henry might restore the cardinal to power 'owing to his uncommon ability.'[41] On

38 George Cavendish, 'The life and death of Cardinal Wolsey,' in Richard S. Sylvester and D. P. Harding (eds.), *Two Early Tudor Lives* (New Haven and London, Yale University Press, 1962), 141.

39 Richard Fiddes, *The Life of Cardinal Wolsey* (London, J. Barber, 1724), Appendix, 208.

40 *Calendar of Letters . . . Spain*, IV, pt 1, 819. 41 *Ibid.*, 368.

being told by a colleague how this might happen, 'the Duke began to swear vehemently, declaring that sooner than allow the Cardinal's return to favor . . . he would eat him up alive.'[42] When Wolsey sought to go to his diocese of Winchester, which was 'so nigh the King,' instead of his far-off province of York, it was Norfolk who insisted that he go to York.[43] And when Wolsey was slow about proceeding to York, Norfolk sent word: 'I will, rather than he should tarry still, tear him with my teeth.'[44] Immediately after Wolsey's arrest at Cawood, his physician, Dr Augustine, was rushed to London where he was examined at Norfolk's house. There he made a deposition against Wolsey which probably would have enabled Norfolk to secure the cardinal's conviction for high treason if he had lived to reach London.[45]

At the end of October 1536, the first month of the so-called Pilgrimage of Grace, Jean du Bellay, then a cardinal and back in France, received word from a correspondent in England:

> At the beginning of the insurrection the Queen [Jane Seymour] threw herself on her knees before the King and begged him to restore the abbeys, but he told her, prudently enough, to get up, and he had often told her not to meddle with his affairs, referring to the late Queen [Anne Boleyn], which was enough to frighten a woman who is not very secure.[46]

About a month later the bishop of Faenza reported that when Queen Jane raised the matter of the dissolution, Henry told her 'to attend to other things, reminding her that the last Queen had died in consequence of meddling too much with State affairs.'[47]

It is quite likely that some such exchange between Jane and Henry did take place. The parts played fit the participants. As for Jane, there is hitherto unrecognized evidence that she had previously attempted to prevent the suppression of at least one religious house. It takes the form of a letter from the prioress of the Cistercian nunnery of Catesby to Thomas Cromwell soliciting his aid in saving Catesby. Here the prioress reminded Cromwell that 'the queen's grace hath moved the king's majesty for me, and hath offered his highness two thousand marks in recompense of that house of Catesby, and hath as yet no perfect answer.' The prioress also reminded Cromwell of 'the report that the commissioners did send unto you of me and my sisters.' She concluded by placing her trust in God and Cromwell 'to help forward that the queen's grace may obtain her request that it [the house] may stand.' Both of the nineteenth century editors who

[42] *Ibid.*, 449–50. [43] Cavendish, 'Cardinal Wolsey,' 125–8. [44] *Ibid.*, 130.
[45] E. A. Hammond, 'Doctor Augustine, physician to Cardinal Wolsey and King Henry VIII,' *Medical History*, XIX (1975), 222–4.
[46] *LP*, XI, 346. [47] *Ibid.*, 510.

printed the letter identified the queen referred to as Anne Boleyn.[48] This is impossible. The commissioners wrote their favorable report on Catesby on 12 May 1536[49] at which time Anne was in the Tower awaiting trial. Since Catesby was dissolved later in 1536,[50] the queen referred to could only have been Jane Seymour.

As for a Henry VIII confronted with insurrection, a plea from Jane to restore those abbeys that had been dissolved was bound to provoke an angry response. A claim that Anne had died for meddling too much with state affairs would serve as a warning to Jane to cease and desist. Of course, the claim would not actually mean that meddling with affairs of state was the reason for Anne's execution. Yet Henry's bringing it up when Jane asked him to restore the abbeys would not have to be accidental, for it now can be said that Anne was opposed to the despoiling of the religious houses.

VI

The source for this finding is a manuscript now at the Bodleian Library. The manuscript, entitled 'A briefe treatise or cronickill of the moste vertuous Lady Anne Bulleyne late quene of England,' was written early in Elizabeth I's reign by William Latimer the younger. Latimer's, like most Elizabethan writings on Anne, was an encomium no doubt written to impress her daughter. Latimer, however, should not be equated with, and discounted like, his fellow eulogists. He alone among them had first-hand knowledge of Anne. As a young man he had served Queen Anne as an ordinary chaplain, a preferment he may well have owed to his probable relative, Anne's principal chaplain, Hugh Latimer. There is good presumption that William Latimer was essentially honest in his account of Anne's activities with regard to the dissolution of the religious houses. Latimer, a Protestant whose language suggested Puritan inclinations, could have had no religious reason for falsely portraying his heroine of the Reformation as wanting to preserve the religious houses in any form.

According to William Latimer, when Queen Anne learned that 'all houses of Religion of the yearlye valewe of too hundrethe pounds and vnder' were to be suppressed, she told Hugh Latimer that in his next sermon before Henry VIII he should attempt 'to dissuade the vttere

[48] Mary A. E. Wood [Green] (ed.), *Letters of Royal and Illustrious Ladies* (3 vols., London, Henry Colburn, 1846), II, 184–6; Henry Ellis (ed.), *Original Letters Illustrative of English History* (11 vols. in 3 series, London, Richard Bentley, 1824–46), 3rd series, III, 50–2.

[49] Thomas Wright (ed.), *Three Chapters of Letters Relating to the Suppression of Monasteries*, Camden Society, old series, XXVI (London, 1843), 129–30.

[50] Joyce Youings, *The Dissolution of the Monasteries* (New York, Barnes & Noble, 1971), 51.

subuersion of the said houses and to induce the kinges grace . . . to converte them to some better vses.' Accordingly, the chaplain in his next sermon besought Henry 'to converte the Abbeys and Prioryes to places of studye and good letres and to the contynvall releve of the poore.' From that time on Anne took every opportunity to admonish other preachers in their sermons 'to make contynvall and earnest peticions for the staye' of the religious houses. William Latimer would have it that Anne's reputation became such that certain unspecified religious supplicated the queen to save their houses. She answered that their houses deserved to be suppressed because of their own manifest demerits. She indicated, however, that they could save their houses by mending their ways. She stressed the idea of their using their wealth to subsidize 'preachers of goddes word' and 'poore and nedye studentes in the vniuersities.' If we may believe Latimer, the frightened religious, after consultation among themselves, 'humblyd their selves to her highnes, most liberally offering to her grace large stipendes & exhibicions [scholarships] to be distributed yearely to preachers and scollars by the only assignemente of her ma^tie^.'[51] One wonders whether or not the stipends and exhibitions were invented by Latimer to suggest something he wanted Elizabeth to do.

This account suggested a good deal of activity that had to take place in a short time: the legislation suppressing the smaller houses passed in mid-March 1536; Anne was sent to the Tower on 2 May. So much activity could not have gone unnoticed at court. The idea of using monastic wealth for educational and charitable purposes was hardly dangerous; similar ideas were circulating in Thomas Cromwell's own circle.[52] But whatever the government's intention at the time regarding the larger houses, the act of 1536 had determined that the smaller houses were to be dissolved, and Anne's activities ran counter to that determination, a determination that meant the acquisition of property by Henry VIII. Anne's activities were really harmless; there was no way that she as queen could save a single house. To Henry, however, her activities could easily constitute meddling too much in affairs of state by a woman he had grown tired of.

In the spring of 1536 Thomas Cromwell deemed it a political necessity to get rid of Anne Boleyn and what might be called the Boleyn faction, that is, those friends of Anne who remained entrenched in positions of power at court after she had lost her hold on the king. To accomplish this

[51] Bodleian Library, MS Don c. 42, fols. 28*v*.–30. Concerning Latymer, see Arthur J. Slavin's essay, above, 13–20, esp. n. 66.

[52] G. R. Elton, *Reform and Reformation: England, 1509–1558*, The New History of England, II (London, Edward Arnold, 1977), 237–8.

Cromwell had to, and did, construct a case 'which would vilify Anne sufficiently to drive Henry into wanting to kill her.'[53] While modern investigators who are concerned about the niceties of justice may find the case so constructed unconvincing to say the least, it is not difficult to see Henry accepting the charges against his wife. But accepting those charges constituted an admission that majesty had been cuckolded by five men, which had to be disturbing to one of his ego. However, there was another, and not at all humiliating, explanation of Anne's death at hand, though it did not have to occur to Henry in the May of her execution, to wit, she had died for meddling too much with affairs of state. Five months later Henry could well have used this explanation to frighten a Jane Seymour who begged him to restore the abbeys.

Of course, Henry did not actually mean what he said, assuming that he said it. He knew that Anne had not died for meddling with state affairs and he obviously was not contemplating Jane's execution. In either case, meddling would have been an almost impossible 'crime' to construe as high treason. But there was a message in Henry's reported words. Anne, by wanting to save but change the religious houses, and Jane, who doubtless only wanted to restore those houses without change, were aligning themselves against the king's wishes in a matter of state that meant wealth for Henry. They had crossed the line where involvement, no matter how ineffective, was not to be tolerated. The message was that even queens consort, the highest placed women in Henry's England, could only involve themselves innocuously in affairs of state. Barring accidents like the two queens regnant and the younger Catherine of Aragon, the evidence would have it that what held true for queens consort surely held true for all women in Tudor England: they had no significant place in Tudor government.

[53] *Ibid.*, 253.

Part two

The Age of Elizabethan Polity

Parliament: the Elizabethan experience

WALLACE T. MacCAFFREY

Perhaps the most vigorous debate currently agitating English historical circles is the one raging around the parliaments of the early Stuarts.[1] The received wisdom on this subject has for generations reflected the dicta laid down by S. R. Gardiner in his monumental history. That view is now being contested by a new and radically different one, which – to state it oversimply – posits a healthy and soundly functioning parliamentary institution at least through the reign of James I and strongly discounts the existence of constitutional conflict before the late 1620s. Since the indefinite assumption behind this conception is that the Tudor Parliament represented a norm of institutional soundness and vigor; and since recent scholarship has focused on the years after 1603, it seems useful in this essay to ask in a very preliminary way what the norm had been and what was the character of Tudor, more particularly of Elizabethan, experience. This inquiry naturally challenges the received views, but it can do little more than raise questions and speculations in the hope of stimulating more far-reaching studies.

I

Gardiner portrayed an unfolding drama which began with the session of 1604 and steadily developed in a sequence of acts, each marking another stage in a mounting confrontation between royal prerogative and popular liberty; this reached its climax in 1642. Although capable of broadly sympathetic understanding for the motives of all the actors, Gardiner never concealed his conviction that the tides of history were flowing with heroic parliamentary leaders who successively challenged the encroachments of royal authority upon the ancient rights of Englishmen. His successors, less ardently partisan, assumed a more neutral and self-consciously objective stance, but did not abandon the notion of developing conflict, revealed in a tightly linked chain of cause and effect stretching from the

Fortescue–Goodwin Case to the raising of the standard at Nottingham. One of the first historians to sound a cautionary note was Professor Elton[1] in his essay on the Apology of 1604. Sensibly he pointed to the dangers of assuming that English history from 1603 to 1642 was, so to speak, 'programmed' in such a way as to lead inevitably from the arrival of the first Stuart to the outbreak of civil conflict. His adjurations have been taken to heart by the current generation of historians, who seek to escape the blinders of hindsight and to recover a vision of events more faithful to contemporaries' understanding of their own age.

Such re-examination is giving us a radically revised picture of early Stuart parliamentary history.[2] Gardiner's emphasis on the adversarial relationship of Crown and Parliament from 1604 onwards is being replaced by a subtler and more complex account in which misunderstanding, confusion, and drift are more apparent than a crisp drama of developing conflict between King and Commons. This version points up the normally cooperative relations between sovereign and Houses, resting on an assumption that they were laboring together to achieve common ends. Their cooperation was not unmarked by friction, but their expectations were of ultimate consensus rather than of disagreement. A second feature in the revisionist scheme stresses the importance of local interest as against national and on MPs' down-to-earth preoccupation with immediately pressing problems. The significance of 'constitutional' debates is strongly downgraded; they are seen as exceptional and often unintended episodes in the history of a parliamentary session. Less emphasis is laid on the personal deficiencies of the Stuart kings and much more on the ambitions of individual politicians in court and parliament. Parliamentary sessions, up to the late 1620s, are no longer pictured as contests of 'court' and 'country.' Much greater weight is given to the interplay of personal rivalries, particularly those of the greater courtiers, to the role of patronage, and to the pressure of special interest groups. In such a scheme direct confrontations on constitutional principles play a minor role – at least until 1628.

How much of these revisionist views will be accepted as a new corpus of received historical wisdom one cannot, at this stage, say for certain. Clearly a new historical landscape of the years 1603–42 is in the making,

[1] G. R. Elton, 'A high road to civil war?' in his *Studies in Tudor and Stuart Government* (2 vols., Cambridge, CUP, 1974), II, 164–82.

[2] Some of the more influential works are: Conrad Russell, *Parliaments and English Politics 1621–29* (Oxford, Oxford University Press, 1979); Kevin Sharpe (ed.), *Faction and Parliament: Essays on Early Stuart History* (Oxford, Oxford University Press, 1978); and Derek Hirst, *The Representative of the People?: Voters and Voting in England under the Early Stuarts* (Cambridge, CUP, 1975). And now see Rudolph W. Heinze's essay, below, 237ff., as well as Jack H. Hexter's, 369ff.

but as yet not all its features are clearly visible. Quite enough has been done to alert the Tudor parliamentary historian to a reconsideration of presently received judgments about that age. The older version of Stuart parliamentary history drew a sharp line between the two dynasties. Unflattering comparisons were drawn between the tact and managerial skills of Elizabeth and the bumbling ineptitude of James. More important his parliaments were viewed as inaugurating a new phase of the institution's history, marked by constant complaints, friction and, ultimately, confrontation. The revised version emphasizes continuity between the dynasties. The Jacobean rather than the Elizabethan decades are seen as the final phase of sixteenth century parliamentary practice. The sharp break now comes not in 1603 but in 1625.

II

An inquiry into Elizabethan parliamentary experience will receive only modest assistance from contemporary witnesses. Sixteenth century Englishmen rarely took the trouble to articulate their understanding of an institution which they took for granted. Their silence may well be a general testimony to their satisfaction with it. Certainly the straightforwardly descriptive account in Thomas Smith's famous book is entirely laudatory, not to say self-congratulatory, in tone. A very different document a generation later, the Apology of 1604, throws a more oblique light on the subject and suggests that in some quarters at least a growing dissonance was audible by 1603.

The paucity of reflective judgments about Parliament suggests an institution which was too familiar a fixture of Tudor political life to need discussion or justification, one with well-established ways of doing business and a generally understood repertory of activities. But our knowledge of parliamentary history also tells us that it was a very malleable – indeed protean – body which could be shaped, by the deliberate actions of its members, sovereign, Lords, or Commons, or by the sheer force of events, into varying and sometimes quite novel forms at different moments in its history. Clearly a photographic 'still' will not reveal much to us; we have to see our quarry in motion.

Smith's observations about Parliament, as he knew it in mid-century, are a useful starting-point. His dictum that the members were met 'to advertise, consult and shew what is good and necessarie for the common wealth, and to consult together'[3] echoes the words of the writs of summons

[3] Thomas Smith, *De Republica Anglorum*, ed. by Leonard Alston (Cambridge, CUP, 1906), 48–9.

and the sentiments of chancellors' opening addresses from Thomas More to Nicholas Bacon. There follows a catalogue of functions. After a general assertion that Parliament 'abrogateth olde lawes, maketh newe, giveth orders for thinges past, and for thinges hereafter to be followed,' he goes on to enumerate such specific powers as legitimizing bastards, altering weights and measures, defining doubtful rights for which there is no existing law and, of course, levying taxes. Shuffled in between bastards and weights is the power to establish forms of religion and – a little farther on in the list – is the right to give forms of succession to the Crown. This hodge-podge enumeration simply summarizes the main topics of legislation from preceding decades. Implicit in Smith's catalogue is, Parliament's corrective and remedial function within the body politic. In this high court men hoped to find relief for the multiple ailments which afflicted that body. The business of any meeting of Parliament was to find the means to restrain whatever forms of violence most immediately threatened civil peace, to promote the exercise of distributive justice within competing interests of individuals and of corporate groups, and in general to seek to ease existing social and legal frictions.

III

Such generalizations sum up the central concerns of a Tudor parliamentary assembly and justly emphasize its businesslike determination to show results and its expectation of fruitful collaboration. They also veil historical circumstances that had often in the past turned Parliament into an arena of struggle. In its earliest phase it had frequently served as an instrument by which the Commons – sometimes manipulated by the magnates, sometimes speaking in their own voice – sought to compel such monarchs as Richard II, Henry IV, or Henry VI to provide the fundamentals of good government. The decades between the Yorkist accession and the summons of the Reformation Parliament were ones of diminished parliamentary activity and of less frequent meetings. This reflected the relative contentment of the parliamentary classes with the conduct of the government, the fact of stronger royal leadership in Edward IV and Henry VII, the diminution of magnate faction after 1471, and royal pursuit of pacifying policies designed to diminish the fiscal pressures which were the usual occasion for a summons.

It would be a mistake to see in this an epoch of parliamentary decline. In the past strong initiatives from subjects had aimed not at reducing royal power but at prodding the sovereign into more effective performance of his duties. The relative effectiveness of the Yorkists and the first Tudor eliminated the needs for such initiatives from below. But the Houses did not surrender the effective checks on royal actions which their predecessors had achieved. The most important of these was of course their fiscal power. Although the king never came away empty-handed when he asked for money, he knew there were undefined yet well-understood limits as to what he might expect. An implicit bargain assured the monarch of support in wartime but yet set a band of limits as to the scale of his expenditure. Wolsey was able to expand that scale somewhat by experiments with the new parliamentary subsidy, but he soon ran up against the limits of taxpayers' willingness to contribute. Only the final seven years of Henry VIII's reign form an important exception to the generally narrow limits of parliamentary generosity.

In legislation it is harder to clarify the interplay of the Yorkist or early Tudor Crown with the parliamentary orders. Initiatives in particular acts are hard to identify. Probably those coming from the Crown predominated, but they were not necessarily always successful. Henry VII's effort in 1504 to prevent the loss of feudal incidents by limiting the effects of uses revealed the strength of parliamentary stubbornness when vital interests of the landed classes were touched.[4] The sixty years preceding 1530 were not a time of vigorous parliamentary activity nor of important innovation, but they were not marked by any real loss of institutional vitality. Since neither subjects nor monarchs were moved to utilize Parliament as an instrument for their ambitions, it did not become a center of important political activity. That epoch came to an abrupt end after 1529.

The dramatic change in the role of the Houses which occurred in that decade needs no retelling here. They now became the instrument, neither of a restive aristocracy nor of a dissatisfied Commons, but of a willful king increasingly bent on bludgeoning the whole ecclesiastical order into submission. In 1529 Parliament was not summoned to finance war but to participate, in a role still undetermined, in the confrontation between state and church. What followed was, to put it in the simplest terms, a total reversal of Parliament's traditional role. An institution hitherto used as a conservative force, remedial and restorative, was now made a vehicle for radical innovation. No skillfully designed guise could conceal this fact: statute was in practice used to pull down an ancient polity and to erect a new one in its place. Parliament was engaged not merely in tinkering with social machinery in an effort to patch up its defective parts, but in full-scale social engineering that would produce long-term structural change.

The great engineer was of course Thomas Cromwell, acting at the

[4] Stanley B. Chrimes, *Henry VII* (London, Eyre Methuen, 1972), 182–3.

behest of his royal master.[5] Not the least of his achievement lay in Cromwell's understanding that the program of his sovereign required important innovations in the parliamentary institution. He was the first identifiable practitioner of the delicate art of parliamentary management, of maneuvering and persuading in order to accomplish the aims of king and minister. But the members of the Houses may have learned as much as the minister, about management and compromise. Cromwell's persuasions awakened in members a stronger sense of their own powers to obstruct and to bargain. On the whole they seem to have accepted ministerial leadership in the king's great matters, in the legislation which carried through the break with Rome, the divorces and the changed order of succession. But on the minister's own initiatives, his program of legal and administrative reform, which touched more sensitively their own interests, the Houses were quick to resist displeasing demands.[6] The result was the growth of attitudes which, while certainly not adversarial in character, did assert the reciprocal roles of what (in American terminology) we may call the executive and the legislative branches within Parliament. While accepting the minister's right to initiate action, they carefully reserved their own rights to shape and to limit the precise forms of statute. Thomas Cromwell passed from the scene after less than a decade of power, but the imprint of that decade's experience on English political practice was permanent.

The parliamentary record of the years following Cromwell's fall is less distinctive.[7] To the truly staggering tax demands made by the king in the 1540s' Parliament proved surprisingly biddable, displaying none of the recalcitrance which Wolsey had encountered twenty years earlier. With the disappearance of Cromwell the flow of reforming proposals which he had sponsored gradually dried up. The record of Edward VI's reign in general resembles that of the 1530s. On the great issues of religion the initiatives of the Protector and of Northumberland met ready agreement in the Commons. It was largely the conservative bishops who, in the Upper House, objected to the new liturgy.[8] On the other hand the Chantries Act, particularly the clauses dealing with guilds and corporations, excited voluble protests from the boroughs and had to be sent back for

[5] For his most recent consideration of the work of Cromwell, see G. R. Elton, *Reform and Reformation: England, 1509–1558* (Cambridge, Mass., Harvard University Press, 1977).

[6] G. R. Elton, *Reform and Renewal: Thomas Cromwell and the Commonweal* (Cambridge, CUP, 1973); and, Stanford E. Lehmberg, *The Reformation Parliament, 1529–36* (Cambridge, CUP, 1970).

[7] Stanford E. Lehmberg, *The Later Parliaments of Henry VIII, 1536–47* (Cambridge, CUP, 1977).

[8] Wilbur K. Jordan, *Edward VI: the Young King* (London, Allen & Unwin, 1968), 318.

rewriting.[9] In Northumberland's time his attempt to deprive Bishop Tunstall by act of Parliament failed in the Lower House.[10] So did a series of bills, backed by the young king himself, aimed at abuses of patrons of livings and of incumbents as well as such familiar problems as regrating of merchandise and engrossment of farms.[11] Finally, the Houses showed considerable independence in their attitudes towards the economic and social measures which preceded the rising of 1549.[12]

Mary's parliaments displayed an even higher quotient of stubbornness than those of her predecessors. They refused to restore the diocese of Durham,[13] and in her second parliament a dangerous novelty appeared in the failure of proposed legislation because of factional disagreements within the Council. Religious legislation sponsored by Gardiner was checkmated in the Lords by Paget.[14] Her later parliaments continued to obstruct official policy, either by redrafting, as in the case of first-fruits and tenths or by outright rejection as in the case of the exiles' property bill.[15]

Between 1529 and 1558 Parliament had been summoned twelve times and sat for twenty-nine sessions. Not since the early fifteenth century had there been such a spate of parliamentary activity. Much of the business of these parliaments had involved the Houses in great matters of state – the changes in religion, the succession, and the attainder of ministers and magnates. Although in most of these matters, they had faithfully followed the lead given by Crown and Council, sheer involvement in high politics had an intangible although not easily measurable effect. Their self-image was also altered by their participation in the religious revolution. Once called to give initial assent to preliminary moves against Rome, mere logic (and ingrained custom) dictated their involvement in every successive alteration of religion. While they proved to be docile servants to three regimes with radically different religious programs, the notion was nevertheless taking root that the supreme headship of the Church rested, like the Crown's civil authority, in the King in Parliament.

[9] Wilbur K. Jordan, *Edward VI: the Threshold of Power; the Dominance of the Duke of Northumberland* (Cambridge, Mass., Belknap Press of Harvard University Press, 1970), 183–4; also, Alan Kreider, *English Chantries: The Road to Dissolution*, Harvard Historical Studies, XCVII (Cambridge, Mass., Harvard University Press, 1979).

[10] Jordan, *Threshold of Power*, 383.

[11] *Ibid.*, 340–1; and, Albert F. Pollard, *The History of England . . . (1547–1603)* (London, Longmans, Green & Co., 1923), 61.

[12] Michael L. Bush, *The Government Policy of Protector Somerset* (London, Edward Arnold, 1975), 50–1.

[13] David M. Loades, *The Reign of Mary Tudor: Politics, Government, and Religion in England, 1553–1558* (London, St Martin's Press, 1979), 156.

[14] *Ibid.*, 83. [15] *Ibid.*, 270–1.

Important as this experience proved to be, it was perhaps less significant than parliamentary participation in the more mundane aspects of lawmaking. The volume of statute law grew at an unprecedented pace under the impulse given by Thomas Cromwell and the bulk of it dealt with secular matters, primarily the awkward problems posed by a strained economy and an unstable social order. In such matters the Houses played a constructive and cooperative role. Their experience as local magistrates made them valuable informants and it was of course these same MPs, wearing their JPs' hats, who would have to enforce the acts of parliament.[16] Such cooperation involved not only acceptance of royal and ministerial direction, but the assertion of the reserve powers of the Houses to impose limits upon royal actions. Quite consistently resistance had risen, as in the case of uses, chantries, or the monastic lands, when rights in private property seemed threatened by the Crown's proposals. Such resistance did not imply an adversarial relationship between Crown and Houses, certainly no notion of concerted opposition to Crown policy. But there was a more marked sense of the Houses' watchdog function as the protectors of vested property interests which, it was well understood, ought to be inviolable. There was no need to put forward any doctrine of 'fundamental laws' where simply a tacit, pragmatic acceptance of underlying political realities would do. The Crown pressed as far as it could but not beyond the bounds of political prudence; the Houses defended immediate and tangible interests. Hence the political generation which surrounded Elizabeth at her accession enjoyed a parliamentary inheritance which comprehended both cooperation and obstruction. Even more paradoxically parliament combined a sense of permanence, balancing an immemorial antiquity with a malleability which made it responsive to an ever-changing present.

IV

During the next forty-five years parliament was to play a lively role in English political life. Some themes of the previous thirty years repeated, with variations and differing emphases, but new topics would add to the parliamentary repertory. Even more important was the marked change in the thrust of initiative. The character of parliament at any given time was determined by its constituent members. From 1529 to 1559 it had been the monarch (or his surrogates) who had shaped its actions. For the remainder of the century it was more often members of the Lords and Commons

[16] John H. Gleason, *The Justices of the Peace in England, 1558–1640: A Later Eirenarcha* (Oxford, Clarendon Press, 1969).

who sought to use parliament for their ends, while the sovereign stubbornly resisted most initiatives that they pressed on her. Hence, ironically, the most popular of the Tudors was also the one most often at odds with her parliaments.

At the opening of Elizabeth's reign circumstance compelled her to use parliament as her predecessors had done. Securing the religious settlement she desired necessarily required statutory action. In the classical account of this episode, that of J. E. Neale,[17] the queen is seen as shifting from her original intention of merely restoring the supremacy to a much bolder program which effectually resurrected the Edwardian Protestant settlement. The change in direction he ascribes partly to a more favorable international situation and partly to the pressure of a Commons dominated by an evangelical party for whom even the Second Book of Common Prayer was tainted with Popish remnants. Recent scholarship has shaken some of the assumptions on which Neale worked without providing a fully satisfactory alternative explanation.[18] We may never know what actually happened in 1559, but it is fair to guess that the queen was pushed farther and faster along the road from Rome than she would ideally have preferred. One thing is clear: having accomplished a religious settlement, the queen had no further use for parliament as an instrument of change. Parliament was, for Elizabeth, now useful primarily as a source of revenue. Since her policy was generally pacific in the early years of her reign, and since she was parsimonious to a fault in general fiscal policy, the parliamentary history of her reign might have resembled that of her grandfather. But events dictated otherwise. Their force, and the nagging insistence of some of her subjects speaking through the two Houses, made her reign a lively era in the history of the parliamentary institution.

In exploring these years we do well to recall the official view of parliament's functions set forth by the royal spokesman, the lord chancellor (or keeper). Nicholas Bacon in his opening speech of 1571 succinctly stated the familiar distinction between 'commonwealth' business and matters of state.[19] The former was the stuff from which most statutes were fashioned, those matters which arose within the national and local communities out of everyday frictions in society and economics. It belonged properly to the MPs to bring these matters to the attention of the Crown and its ministers, and indeed the latter were likely to be already alerted to

[17] John E. Neale, *Elizabeth I and Her Parliaments, 1559–81* (New York, St Martin's Press, 1958), pt I; and, his article 'The Elizabethan Acts of Supremacy and Uniformity,' *English Historical Review*, LXV, 304–32.

[18] Norman L. Jones, 'Faith by statute: the politics of religion in the parliament of 1559' (University of Cambridge, Unpublished Ph.D. thesis, 1977).

[19] BL, MS Cotton, Titus F 1, fol. 135.

most of these problems through the reciprocal relations of Council and JPs. Matters of state, however, remained the queen's exclusive concern. The Houses should not meddle, except 'such as should be proponed unto them' at the royal pleasure. These, of course, comprehended the whole range of executive actions, at home and abroad.

This simple distinction was a commonplace in Elizabethan political discourse, reflecting more nearly the experience of the recent past than the rapidly shifting practice of the years after 1560. Of course, the bulk of what appears on the statute book represented 'commonwealth' matters, and of that more will be said below, but the queen's intention that the agenda of parliamentary discussion should be defined by the Crown became less and less a matter of fact as the years rolled on. This shift represented no considered change of direction on the part of the Houses but the sheer force of circumstance. Queen Elizabeth was the last surviving Tudor and the uncertainties of succession should she die unmarried or childless were terrifying. From the beginning of the reign down to about 1570 the political community was preoccupied with this problem, and Parliament offered the natural forum for advertising their anxieties. The sessions that met in 1563 and again in 1566 were filled with this matter, almost to the exclusion of other business. The succession, as well as the marriage, issue could obviously not easily be dealt with by statute but another strategy remained open to the Houses: the ancient right of petition. No statute could force the queen into marriage, or compel her to recognize a successor, but the collective will of her political nation, speaking through the Houses, could exert formidable moral pressure. In both 1563 and 1566 a well-organized and pertinacious effort tried to put the queen under just such pressure, either to announce her intention to marry or else to allow the Houses to limit the succession.[20] Elizabeth evaded any direct answer in 1563; in 1566 she sought, unavailingly, to halt discussion. This only brought to the surface the even more sensitive subject of freedom of speech. She retreated gracefully, forgave the third payment of the subsidy, and palmed off the Houses with a graciously obscure half-promise. An attempt to tack that promise on to the subsidy bill as a prologue was turned back only by her determined opposition.

She used the same strategy when the awkward question of Mary Stuart's fate first came to the Houses in the session of 1572. Parliamentary impulses to petition for her death were checked initially by the queen but proved too strong for royal restraint. She could only divert their energies

[20] For a full account of these Parliaments see Neale, *Parliaments, 1559–81*, pts II and III. Throughout this essay, I rely on Neale's account of the Elizabethan Parliaments for basic narrative.

by allowing them the luxury of drawing up a bill on Mary's title. They did their best, under Council guidance, to disable the Scottish queen's claim but Elizabeth once more evaded both Parliament and councillors by declining either to approve or totally disapprove the measure. Their moral pressure did pay off when Norfolk, already judicially condemned, went to the block after a strong plea from the Houses for his death.[21]

More than a decade later, in the autumn session of 1586, Mary's fate again preoccupied the Houses, this time in the wake of her formal condemnation for participation in the Babington plot.[22] As in 1572 petition was the technique adopted by the Houses, although in this case the petitioners were simply seeking the execution of a judgment already rendered. Twice delegations appeared before the queen to belabor her with weighty reasoning in favor of Mary's death. The immediate result was publication of the sentence given against her, but as to how far their efforts weighed in the actual execution, performed in the interval between the two sessions, we can only speculate.

These episodes cast interesting light on the varying roles of the Houses and on the interplay of political forces within them. In 1572 and again in 1586 there was virtual unanimity among Lords and Commons in their enmity towards the Scottish queen. The petitions, however, were something more than the spontaneous motion of the assembly. The queen's councillors were as hostile to Mary as the parliamentarians, so in some measure the Houses were being used as a weapon by the Council to pressure the queen. Parliament is clearly revealed in these episodes not so much as a merely legislative body but as the effective vehicle for an organized and focused body of public opinion, embracing almost the whole of the political classes. As a petitioning body Parliament proved to be a somewhat blunt but serviceable instrument against the queen. Moreover, such menaces may not have been entirely unwelcome, because these parliamentary demonstrations effectively blocked Mary's hopes for an English following in the 1570s and drove her to the conspiracies that would ultimately destroy her. In 1586–7 they provided Elizabeth with a measure of justification when she had to defend the execution of her rival.

These interventions of the Houses into high matters of state illustrated the limitations of the queen's rule that Parliament should deal with such matters only upon her request. Their importunities with these matters could not be denied, and willy-nilly the queen had to allow their partici-

[21] *Ibid.*, 247–90.

[22] John E. Neale, *Elizabeth I and Her Parliaments, 1584–1601* (New York, St Martin's Press, 1958), 103–44.

pation. But this parliamentary intervention was in no sense adversarial, or even critical of royal policy. The petitioners did not seek redress of grievances for injustices suffered by the subject but rather warned the queen of grave dangers to her safety and that of the realm. The circumstances were unique and the issue died with Mary Stuart. The struggle against the Queen of Scots had been a vital and centrally important aspect of Elizabethan parliamentary experience, but it is hard to see in it a permanent effect on parliamentary practice or on the members' conception of their role.

The emergence of Mary Stuart in English politics had produced more or less spontaneous reactions among the political classes, and it had needed only a very modest amount of stimulation from conciliar sources to produce an effective agitation. The rise of the Catholic problem at the end of the 1570s and in the next decade produced somewhat similar reactions. Popular anti-Catholic sentiment had had to be restrained in the parliaments of the 1560s and 1570s, probably at the queen's bidding. But by 1581 the Council had woken, a little belatedly, to the fact of a Catholic renascence sparked by the missionaries of Douay. Mildmay gave a lead to the Commons in his denunciation of the Catholic menace at home and abroad.[23] Both Houses responded with proposals for radical repression, although the Commons clearly preferred enforcement by civil rather than ecclesiastical officials. They had to be restrained by royal intervention and, as in the proposed act against Mary Stuart of 1572, the Houses were racing ahead of government, or at least of royal intentions. A severe pull on the reins was necessary to keep them in check.

In these instances Parliament has appeared as the instrument of a vigorous public opinion which outran, although it did not contravene, the prevailing sentiment of councillors and did not stand altogether athwart the ambiguous wishes of the queen. But from the late 1570s the Crown and its ministers faced a problem of great seriousness for which the support of the political classes was crucial but where their opinions needed to be cultivated, indeed coaxed, rather than restrained. Relations with Spain, highly sensitive ever since the Dutch rising of 1572, became increasingly strained after the epoch of the 'Spanish fury' in 1576. Much more overt support for Philip's mutinous Low Countries' subjects awakened increasing Spanish resentment, and the more far-seeing of Elizabeth's coun-

[23] Simonds D'Ewes, *A Compleat Journal of the Votes, Speeches and Debates, Both of the House of Lords and House of Commons throughout the Whole Reign of Queen Elizabeth, of Glorious Memory*, 2nd edn (London, 1693), 285–7; and F. X. Walker, 'The implementation of the Elizabethan statutes against recusants, 1586–1603' (University of London, Unpublished Ph.D. thesis, 1961), 121–8.

cillors began to think anxiously of the probabilities of open hostilities. Hitherto the queen's pacific policy had kept the need for parliamentary subsidies at a low ebb. *Post hoc* appropriations had covered the expenses of the Scottish expedition of 1559–60 and the Newhaven venture of 1562–3. In 1566 Cecil had been apprehensive about seeking a grant in peacetime.[24] The queen then remitted the third payment of the subsidy as a sweetener for her evasion of the succession problem.[25] In 1571 the expenses of the Northern Rebellion and the raid into Scotland following the death of the Regent Moray justified the usual subsidy plus two tenths and fifteenths.[26] In 1572 no money was asked for.

The meeting of 1576 marked a momentous turning-point in Elizabethan foreign policy and in the ministers' handling of Parliament. In past sessions the need for money had been stated in a cursory retailing of recent history which required no reasoned justification. Now in 1576 it was a future contingency, not past events, which had to be dealt with. The ministers could not allege expenditures already made nor point to an immediate and concrete threat. They had to sell their conviction that the potential dangers of the coming years demanded a present supply of money, to be used if necessity demanded.

They therefore took the Houses into the government's confidence by giving them a far fuller and broader picture of English foreign relations and the government's policy than had been the case in the past. This was done by Sir Walter Mildmay in a masterful speech.[27] He began by laying out the queen's achievements: religious reform, decades of peace at home and abroad, careful economy in her own expenditures. By her endeavors the realm now stood in peace and security, but these achievements were threatened by the great tumults abroad. These endangered England because of the 'hatred that is borne us by the adversary of our religion.' For the moment there was calm, but 'the tail of these storms which are so bitter and so boisterous in other countries may reach us before they be ended.' The Great Council of the Realm, he continued, ought 'to consider beforehand the dangers that may come by malice of enemies and to provide in time how to resist them' by giving the queen sufficient treasure to maintain forces adequate 'to answer any thing that shall be attempted against her and us.' The subsidy passed without hesitation.

The two remaining peacetime parliaments, those of 1581 and 1584, saw the same strategy repeated. In 1581 Mildmay reiterated most of his

[24] Frederick C. Dietz, *English Public Finance, 1558–1641* (New York, The Century Co., 1932), II, 23.

[25] *Ibid.*; Neale, *Parliaments, 1559–81*, 160–1.

[26] Dietz, *Finance*, II, 392, fn. 23.

[27] BL, MS Sloane 326, fols. 1–8; D'Ewes, *Journal*, 246.

former arguments but this time he named England's enemies directly, not only the Pope but Spain, as sponsors of the two recent expeditions to Ireland. Pulling no punches, he warned that these were enemies who 'if their power be answerable to their wills this realm shall find at their hands all the miseries and extremities that they can bring upon it.'[28] Naval and land forces must be strengthened. In 1584 the country was still at peace and the queen still striving for accommodation, but the situation had measurably worsened. The ambassador Mendoza had been expelled for his participation in the Throckmorton plot. Mildmay warned the House of the *odium implacabile* of the Pope and his confederates. Hatton followed, mincing no words, and recited in detail the catalogue of Spain's hostile actions since the early years of the reign.[29]

In this series of speeches the ministers of the Crown had, during peacetime, openly named Spain as a potential enemy and asked for parliamentary support against an anticipated war. The purpose was, of course, more complex than the speeches themselves revealed. Ministers sought to achieve two alternative ends: a genuine intention of building up a financial reserve in case of war and a hope that this public defiance, coupled at least in 1581 with a diplomatic offensive for a French alliance, might persuade the King of Spain to the necessity of compromise. This latter hope proved a vain one, but at home the effect was to stir up deep public animosity against Catholic Spain which, in turn, would soon be shaped into a national myth of great power. It would provide psychological foundations enabling the Crown to sustain a long-drawn-out war, lasting in its various phases almost twenty years. The deep-lying fears of an international Catholic plot, with which Mildmay had chilled his listeners' blood, was to sink deep into the English national consciousness for a very long life of its own.

These new strategies of parliamentary management signalled an important shift in basic characteristics of English political life. Mildmay and Hatton and their colleagues were relearning, in a different context, the lesson which Thomas Cromwell had assimilated half a century earlier. Then, as that minister realized, a far-reaching alteration in the religious polity demanded not only formal statutory exactment but also an arduous campaign of persuasion if the support of the political classes was to be secured.[30] Now, in the 1580s, Elizabeth's councillors saw that the pros-

[28] BL, MS Sloane 326, fols. 19–29.

[29] Northampton Record Office, MS Fitzwilliam of Milton, fols. 2*v*.–5*v*. for both speeches.

[30] G. R. Elton, *Policy and Police: the Enforcement of the Reformation in the Age of Thomas Cromwell* (Cambridge, CUP, 1972); and, William Gordon Zeeveld, *Foundations of Tudor Policy* (Cambridge, Mass., Harvard University Press, 1948).

pect of a long, dangerous, and costly war required similar psychological mobilization to provide the intangible underpinning upon which such political enterprise must rest. More than once, in negotiations over Anjou's venture as leader of the Dutch rebellion, English diplomats had pleaded the unwillingness of English tax-payers to back a foreign war on behalf of a Catholic prince. What seems like convenient diplomatic evasion had a firm base: even in 1586–7 a parliamentary spokesman could express his distrust of the Dutch and urge an inexpensive 'blue-water strategy' against Spain.[31] Successful prosecution of what promised to be a long-drawn-out struggle required careful preparation of a firm base of focused national sentiment. How much the experience of the Elizabethan wars affected parliamentary consciousness did not become fully apparent until the possibility of major war loomed again after 1618. Parliament did not expect to direct foreign policy, but it had come to expect that it should be taken into the royal confidence in fairly large measure, that the aims of policy should be expounded, and the justification for them made explicit. The time when the Houses would more or less automatically respond to royal requests for taxation to pay for war was past.

V

Matters of state clearly consumed a good deal of parliamentary time and attention, but they are sparsely reflected in that permanent record of parliamentary achievement, the statute book. The central business of Parliament's activity was the passing of statutes, both public and private. These reflected those 'commonwealth' matters which were common concern of the councillors at Westminster and the knights and burgesses coming up to the capital. The largest category of such business was that which concerned regulation of the economy. The first parliament of Elizabeth found time, while debating the terms of the religious settlement, to deal with the shoemakers, the trade in tallow and hides, linen-making, cloth-making outside towns, fishing, and the transport of goods in English vessels.[32] Such a list might serve, *mutatis mutandis*, for most of the succeeding sessions of the reign. The statute of artificers in 1562–3 and the succession of poor laws, culminating in the act of 1601, are among the best remembered of Elizabethan statutes but they only represented many less comprehensive or less enduring enactments of similar character. How far the initiatives for such acts came from the Crown, how far from the floor of the House of Commons, is impossible to determine as a general

[31] Neale, *Parliaments, 1584–1601*, 179. [32] *SR*, IV, 367–79.

rule. The one act whose legislative history has been thoroughly investigated, the statute of artificers, illuminates the interplay of ministerial purpose and local interest which was probably characteristic of much other legislation.[33] The local exceptions which honeycomb so many of the statutes regulating the cloth trade serve to bear this out.

On the whole the very richness of statutory achievement suggests the frequency with which councillors and MPs were able to come to agreement on a viable enactment which reflected the needs and experiences of both parties. But this was not always so. The much less complete and often unsatisfactory journals of the Houses' business recall those bills which failed to pass into statute. A detailed study of such measures – and comparison with those which passed – would be illuminating. Even a cursory survey suggests that ministers did not always have their own way. In 1576 a bill for regulating apparel failed in the Commons, partly because of objections to the use of proclamations which it proposed, partly because the penalties were thought too severe. A bill to deal with fraudulent conveyance which included a shift from common law jurisdiction to Star Chamber resulted in an amendment maintaining the former's authority. Lord Burghley's favorite Wednesday fish-day statute failed of renewal in 1584.[34] Sometimes measures which satisfied both Houses, and even the royal officials concerned, failed to achieve royal approval because the queen felt that they trespassed on her prerogative.

On occasion submerged resentments burst on to the floor of the House. In 1571 a motion on the subsidy unleashed a rush of grievances about grants of privilege contrary to statute, the use of public funds by collectors of revenue, purveyance, and abuses in the Exchequer. This led to formation of a committee 'for motions of griefs and petitions.'[35] Of course the classic instance of such an outburst was the monopolies episode in 1601.

In general, one can only record the impression, without much more detailed investigation, that relations between the Houses and the monarch reflected the same general mixture of cooperation and obstructiveness which prevailed in earlier reigns. When councillors proposed legislation which offended parliamentary sensibilities, particularly in the Commons, they were likely to be rebuffed, and that range of sensibilities seemed to be growing. At different times the powers of prerogative courts, at other

[33] Stanley T. Bindoff, 'The making of the Statute of Artificers,' in *Elizabethan Government and Society*, ed. by Stanley T. Bindoff, Joel Hurstfield, and C. H. Williams (London, Athlone Press, 1961), 56–94; also, Margaret Gay Davies, *The Enforcement of English Apprenticeship: A Study in Applied Mercantilism, 1563–1642*, Harvard Economic Studies, XCVII (Cambridge, Mass., Harvard University Press, 1956).

[34] Neale, *Parliaments, 1584–1601*, 88–91. [35] Neale, *Parliaments, 1559–81*, 219–22, 224–5.

times religious questions, ignited a flash of resentment and of obstruction. It may be that, taken in all, the restlessness and sense of independence of the Lower House was expanding and correspondingly its willingness to accept the somewhat paternalistic direction of the Crown diminishing. All this suggested the normal frictions of a healthy organism rather than the abrasions of malfunction, at least until the last parliament of the reign.

The explosion of irritability which occurred in the monopolies episode of 1601 stood in contrast to the history of preceding parliaments. There had been occasional rumbles of discontent over administrative or legal procedure with appropriate committees of grievance, but nothing of the fierceness and passion of this occasion. For the first time there was bitter complaint about a major governmental practice and one which reflected immediately on ministers nearest the queen and indirectly upon the sovereign herself. It clearly touched prerogative, giving a familiar ring to students of Stuart parliamentary history and an introductory link to parliaments of the next reign. At the same time the response, both of Queen and Commons, provides a vivid reminder that the ancient conception of Parliament as a petitioning body, a glorified grand jury presenting the grievances of the nation, still had vitality. The particular grievance of monopolies was dealt with not by statute but by the queen's use of her prerogative to cancel offending patents. It was a very old-fashioned scene, in which a just and gracious monarch responded to the legitimate grievances of her subjects and by her prerogative provided remedy.

VI

Aside from this isolated episode, at the very close of the reign, there were two areas in which, over a long period of time, Crown and Commons jangled irritably without finding any ground for even tentative agreement. The first was the question of religion, the second that of the Commons' privileges, especially free speech. About religion much has been written and the subject is too large for full consideration here, but a few comments may be useful. To this historian the most baffling aspect of the problem is the persistence with which, in session after session, the evangelicals pushed measures for ecclesiastical alterations which were regularly rejected by a ruler who went to some trouble to make clear her unyielding opposition to any sort of change. These men were not political novices and they were ardently loyal to their sovereign. How then can we explain their obstinate insistence on batting their heads against a stone wall of royal disapproval?

First it should be noted that the Puritan campaign was very much extra-parliamentary in origin. At its center stood a group of zealous clergy who provided the ideas and the dynamism to egg on their lay supporters in the Commons. These single-minded men, moved by the conviction that they were doing God's revealed work, were not easily rebuffed about the rightness of their cause and the necessity for its triumph.

Much of their support in parliament came from men who sympathized with the general impulses of a vigorous Protestant piety without necessarily sharing the particular ecclesiastical goals of the clergy. They were anti-Papist and mildly anti-clerical, but the measures for which they voted did not touch them as secular measures did. It was one thing to oppose particular measures proposed by the government, to force ministers to compromise, even to defeat them, but it was quite another thing to fight with such energies for measures initiated privately. What did move the House more passionately was the closely related issue of their privileges. They were not prepared for a long-drawn-out wrestling match over liturgical revision but they were prepared to fight on the right of free speech and, by extension, to control their own agenda.

The issue was virtually a new one in Elizabeth's reign. The request for freedom of speech on the floor of the House was only added to the speaker's protestation in 1523 and became a regular feature of the protestation only from 1559.[36] In 1566 it became an issue between the House and the Crown when Elizabeth forbade discussion of her marriage. The royal command was challenged very directly by Paul Wentworth. The House stuck to its guns and formulated a petition which set forth their claim to 'an ancient laudable custom . . . a leeful sufferance and dutiful liberty to treat and devise of matters honourable for your Majesty and profitable for your realm.'[37] The queen backed away far enough to withdraw her original prohibition. In 1571 a speech by Robert Bell (Speaker in 1572) complaining of 'licenses,' i.e. grants exempting a favored subject from the restrictions of a particular statute, set off a whole string of angry complaints against other administrative practices of the Crown's servants and led to a committee on grievances. Bell was reprimanded by the Council for his speech and this in turn led to irritated disruption in the House.[38] These were apparently the only occasions, up to 1601, in which royal intervention was provoked by matters not touching religion. It was the latter which touched off not only royal prohibitions but the punishment

[36] John E. Neale, 'Free speech in Parliament,' in *Tudor Studies Presented . . . to Albert Frederick Pollard*, ed. by Robert W. Seton-Watson (London, Longmans, Green & Co., 1924), 267.
[37] Neale, *Parliaments, 1559–81*, 152–5. [38] *Ibid.*, 218–23.

of offending members and the respectful but obstinate resistance of the Commons.

As early as 1571, when Strickland was sequestered for a bill he had offered on religion, there was lively debate in the House, but before any action was taken Strickland was released.[39] In 1576 there occurred Peter Wentworth's passionate but carefully considered demand for free speech, particularly on questions of religion and on the Queen of Scots (for him a closely related question). His plain speaking was too much for the shocked House and at their initiative he was committed to the Tower.[40] After examination, a sojourn of a month in prison, and public acknowledgment of fault, Wentworth was readmitted to the House by the queen's command.

In 1584 the determined Puritan assault on Whitgift's new policy led to a forthright rebuke from the queen to the House, asserting her sole authority as supreme head and resolutely rejecting any 'motion of innovation' in the established order of the Church. The Puritan leadership in the Commons persisted and brought in more measures for ecclesiastical reform, some of which passed through the Lower House in spite of royal displeasure. These foundered in the Upper House. Two bills on religion which managed to get through both Houses were vetoed by the queen.[41] The climax of the Puritan campaign came in 1586–7. The queen's reaction to their bold attempt to undo the whole settlement of 1559 was to seize the bill by which they proposed to accomplish this revolution. Wentworth once more made a rousing oration in behalf of freedom of speech and once more, but this time at the royal command, was sent to the Tower with four other members. An attempt in the House to petition for their release led to a full-scale defense of the Crown's action and a skillful attack on the Puritan program by no less a personage than Sir Christopher Hatton. The prisoners remained in the Tower until at least the end of the session.[42] In the Parliament of 1593 no less than seven members were sequestered or imprisoned by the queen, for varying reasons, and the response of the House was far weaker than in the past. A brief discussion led to no action. Peter Wentworth had thought to bring forward a bill on the succession and had conferred with several other members on his proposed legislation. When the whole matter came to the Council's attention, there was no time to launch the bill and the whole clutch of would-be backers were imprisoned. Most were speedily released, but Wentworth was to die in the Tower after four years' incarceration.[43]

[39] *Ibid.*, 200–3. [40] *Ibid.*, 318–32.
[41] Neale, *Parliaments, 1584–1601*, 72–83. [42] *Ibid.*, 145–65. [43] *Ibid.*, 251–66.

This catalogue of clashes between the queen and the Commons is notable in several ways. The very fact that a ruler so popular and so politically shrewd as Elizabeth had to intervene overtly on so many recorded occasions revealed a striking novelty in parliamentary behavior. Although it was usually religious questions which triggered royal intervention, it was the control of their agenda which moved the House to respectful but persistent protest. Wentworth in his exuberance outpaced his colleagues and thereby shocked their sense of fitness. Nevertheless, the difference between him and them was one of degree not of substance. The idea was taking firm hold that the House was indeed a great national forum where any question of common concern to the local communities which collectively made up the realm was a proper matter for discussion. Members should not be prohibited from discussion of such issues nor punished – by external authority – for what they said on the floor of the House. It was a position which did not receive coherent formulation until the beginning of the next reign, in the Apology of 1604. It would be restated again in 1610 and 1621.

It was not altogether new nor was it a radical departure from the past in spite of the false reading of history which was sometimes used to justify it. Basically it extended the ancient use of Parliament as the place where grievances of a public character could be aired. What was new was the transformation from petition to debate. This marked a necessary, although perhaps delayed, effect of the Commons' promotion from petitioners to legislators. Such a status necessitated discussion, debate, and compromise. Clearly in 'commonwealth' measures the Crown accepted such procedure. The awkwardness arose when the Commons sought to extend the practice of discussion to other matters and, by so doing, effectively to gain control of the whole agenda of the House. It was not initially a self-conscious effort but it was one to which circumstances gave much momentum. On some issues, such as the fate of Mary Stuart, the Crown itself gave at least reluctant approbation to Commons debate; on others, the succession or religion, members of the House took the matter into their own hands.

What remains most striking is the tacit restraint displayed by both parties. The House contented itself with dignified pressure for the release of imprisoned members; and the queen usually responded by freeing her prisoners after varying periods of confinement. Both sides shrank from a confrontation in which rigid positions of principle would be taken. The result was a series of somewhat muted clashes, ending in truces. Neither party was prepared to yield its residual claims. The Crown insisted that it could, when necessary, limit the agenda of debate, while the Commons urged that they alone could set bounds to their own discussions. The matter remained for continued disagreement at the close of the reign.

VII

What can one say in summary as to the legacy left by Tudor parliaments to their successors? In the most general sense one can observe the gradual transformation of Parliament from something more than an occasion – a great deal more – into something a little less than an institution. Continuity of personnel, repeated consideration of the same public questions in successive sessions, the more intimate linkage between the Council and the members, all contributed to a growing sense of institutional self-consciousness. This was manifest in the Common's increasing insistence on the right to lay out their own agenda. Most important was the developing awareness of *national* politics, of involvement in problems which transcended the interests of a particular region or a particular trade and which looked outside the insular bounds of the kingdom. The significance of the succession problem, of religion, and of war speak for themselves, but statutes such as artificers or the poor laws also contributed to such an outlook.

Nevertheless, one should not overemphasize these changes. Perspectives, expectation, general awareness all changed, but practice did not. The general framework within which legislation was enacted and business done did not profoundly alter; above all the dependence on Crown initiatives did not change. Parliament was still in a very real sense the sovereign's great council, summoned at royal pleasure, to give advice on topics to be laid before it. Still, the widening gap between such practice and the actual experience in Tudor parliaments was creating latent tensions, which might or might not be heightened in the new era and dynasty.

The court of Exchequer comes of age

W. HAMILTON BRYSON

The Exchequer was well established as a court of law in the thirteenth century.[1] For the next three hundred years, the Exchequer court seems to have carried out its duties without much change in function or status.[2] At the beginning of the sixteenth century, the judicial business of the Exchequer amounted to about 200 cases per year as compared with about 2500 in the court of King's Bench and 10,000 in the Common Pleas.[3] However, during the middle period of the reign of Henry VIII, the first signs of growth since the thirteenth century appeared. This expansion of the court of Exchequer continued steadily through the reigns of the later Tudors to the beginning of the Interregnum. In 1649 the Exchequer court established itself as a high court of general jurisdiction in both common law and equity. At this point the Exchequer can be said to have come of age as a court of law. This development began during the reign of Henry VIII and can be seen as part of the Tudor Revolution in government.

I

The expansion of the judicial jurisdiction of the Exchequer paralleled the increase in its political and financial importance. Perhaps the court could

1 See Charles H. Jenkinson and Beryl E. R. Formoy (eds.), *Select Cases in the Exchequer of Pleas*, Selden Society, XLVIII (London, 1932); John H. Baker, *Introduction to English Legal History*, 2nd edn (London, Butterworths, 1979), 44–6; S. F. C. Milsom, *Historical Foundations of the Common Law* (London, Butterworths, 1969), 20–1, 53–4; Charles Gross, 'The jurisdiction of the Court of Exchequer under Edward I,' *Law Quarterly Review*, XXV (1909), 138–44.

2 There are no detailed studies of the court of Exchequer during the fourteenth and fifteenth centuries; so these generalizations should be accepted with caution, until the end of the era. Then see, DeLloyd J. Guth, 'Exchequer penal law enforcement 1485–1509' (University of Pittsburgh, Unpublished Ph.D. thesis, 1967) which gives detailed analyses of mesne process and quantified litigation. There is no published book on the Exchequer similar to Margaret Hastings, *The Court of Common Pleas in Fifteenth-Century England* (Ithaca, N.Y., Cornell University Press, 1947), and Marjorie Blatcher, *Court of King's Bench 1450–1550: A Study in Self Help* (London, Athlone Press, 1978).

3 DeLloyd J. Guth, 'Notes on the early Tudor exchequer of pleas,' in Arthur J. Slavin (ed.), *Tudor Men and Institutions* (Baton Rouge, Louisiana State University Press, 1972), 106.

not have increased the scope of its jurisdiction without the approval and support of the most powerful politicians of the kingdom. Even if their good wishes were not necessary, their self-interest would not have hindered the growth of the court.

The lord treasurer was the head of the Exchequer. Although he never sat on the common law side of the court, he did sit on the revenue and equity sides. During the middle ages the office of lord chancellor seems to have been more important politically than that of lord treasurer, and the chief advisors to the king, such as Cardinal Wolsey, preferred to be appointed to the former office. From 1547 to 1612, however, the men who held the office of treasurer – Edward Seymour, William Paulet, William Cecil, Thomas Sackville, and Robert Cecil – were far more prominent politically than the chancellors of the time. With powerful politicians as head of the Exchequer department, times were favorable for the expansion of the Exchequer court.[4]

The fact that Thomas Cromwell, the chief advisor to Henry VIII from 1533 to 1540, was not lord treasurer is noteworthy. The treasurer during this time was Thomas Howard, third duke of Norfolk, who had been given the office in 1522; his military skills made him indispensable to the king, and he was not removed in favor of Cromwell. Cromwell received instead the office of chancellor of the Exchequer, and he significantly increased its prestige and power.[5] The office of chancellor of the Exchequer became the second office in importance in the Exchequer during the sixteenth century, overshadowing the lucrative offices of the chamberlains of the Exchequer. This was significant in the expansion of the Exchequer court because the chancellor of the Exchequer sat with the barons of the Exchequer to hear suits brought on the equity side of the court. The earliest equity bill of complaint presently known to have been filed in the Exchequer is that in the case of *Capull* v. *Ardern* (1543–5).[6] This suit commenced shortly after the fall of Thomas Cromwell.

Several months after the accession of Elizabeth I, Sir Walter Mildmay was appointed chancellor of the Exchequer. He was an active politician in the middle rank of Tudor government. During his thirty-year tenure as chancellor of the Exchequer, the equity side of the Exchequer picked up a large amount of judicial business, and its office procedures and archives were established.[7] Between the appointment of Cromwell to this office

[4] W. Hamilton Bryson, *Equity Side of the Exchequer* (Cambridge, CUP, 1975), 34–41, 171.

[5] G. R. Elton, *The Tudor Revolution in Government* (Cambridge, CUP, 1953), 114–19, 266.

[6] PRO, E 111/14.

[7] Stanford E. Lehmberg, *Sir Walter Mildmay and Tudor Government* (Austin, University of Texas Press, 1964); Bryson, *Equity Side of the Exchequer*, 20–1, 41–6, 106–7, 173.

and the death of Mildmay, the equity jurisdiction of the court was initiated and firmly established.

The office of baron of the Exchequer was ancient. This is indicated by the use of that general word 'baron,' i.e. man, to describe the office. A baron of the Exchequer in the distant medieval past was an officer who did all tasks including the judging of disputes involving revenues. In the middle ages his judicial functions were not his most important duties. However, in the Tudor period, the barons of the Exchequer as judges became more significant. Before 1579 only the chief barons were appointed from the ranks of the serjeants; the puisne barons were usually barristers, but often they were men of only modest legal professionalism. After 1579 all of the barons were appointed from the lawyers of the rank of serjeant. As of this date the barons of the Exchequer were of equal education and social rank with the justices of the other high courts at Westminster, and this was very important for the prestige of the court of Exchequer.[8] When the barons were members of Serjeants Inn and served as justices of assize, the self-congratulating snobbery of the other high courts lost its force, and some very eminent jurists have sat in the Exchequer – men such as Hale, Gilbert, Parke, Alderson, and Pollock. The professional equality of the Exchequer bench by the end of the reign of Elizabeth I made it easier and perhaps more appropriate for the Exchequer court to expand its jurisdiction. Chief Baron Sir John Walter, who sat from 1625 to 1630, was a notable champion of the jurisdiction of his court.

The financial functions of the Exchequer were diminished in the first half of the sixteenth century by the use of the king's privy chamber and various other departments to handle much of the royal revenue. By 1550, however, the chamber as a treasury had ended.[9] In 1554 the financial functions of the court of Augmentations and the court of First Fruits and Tenths were given to the Exchequer, and these two institutions were suppressed.[10] This increased financial activity in the Exchequer in the second half of the sixteenth century drew attention and litigation to it.

It is submitted that the partial eclipse of the Exchequer in the first half of the sixteenth century was owing to its control by the second and third dukes of Norfolk, who were successively lords treasurer from 1501 to

[8] Bryson, *Equity Side of the Exchequer*, 48–51.

[9] Elton, *Tudor Revolution in Government*, 169–77; Walter C. Richardson, *History of the Court of Augmentations, 1536–1554* (Baton Rouge, Louisiana State University Press, 1961), 22–9; Walter C. Richardson, *Tudor Chamber Administration, 1485–1547* (Baton Rouge, Louisiana State University Press, 1952). But now see Dale E. Hoak's essay, above, 87ff., esp. 106–7.

[10] Elton, *Tudor Revolution in Government*, 230–43; Richardson, *Court of Augmentations*, 436ff.

1546. They were too useful to be removed from their offices, but they were too independent to be entrusted with any more power than was necessary. Thus, while they held the office of treasurer, their power, income, and patronage were kept in check by diminishing the activities and responsibilities of the Exchequer. In 1546 the third duke of Norfolk was arrested and stripped of his offices. Shortly thereafter the Exchequer under William Paulet began to be revived as the major financial institution of the kingdom. (Only the court of Wards and Liveries remained to handle any significant part of the revenues of the Crown.) From 1547 to the end of the Tudor period, the lord treasurer was one of the major ministers, if not the prime advisor, of the monarch. To say that the institution was the tool of its head would be an overstatement, but the political position of its head, the treasurer, directly affected its role in the national government.

II

The foundation of the judicial jurisdiction of the Exchequer was the settling of disputes between the Crown and a subject as to whether or how much money was due to the Crown. Informal negotiations quickly developed in the thirteenth century into formal legal proceedings. The Exchequer became what we might call a 'tax court'; the king was the plaintiff and the subject, the 'tax-payer,' was the defendant. (The word tax here includes not merely the medieval taxes due but also all other forms and types of income due to the king, private sources of income as well as public ones.) This was the theoretical foundation of the court's legal jurisdiction in the sixteenth century as in earlier times, and the sixteenth century lawyers never lost sight of it.

The duty of the Exchequer to collect the royal revenue naturally led to the determination of who owed the money. The next logical step was to assist the person who owed the money to collect it from his own debtor; otherwise he would be unable to pay his debt to the Crown or at least he would be less able to pay, a position that was logically unassailable. This second step, inaugurated in the thirteenth century, involved a separate lawsuit between the two private parties in order to assure that there was in fact a legal obligation on the part of the king's debtor's debtor. This separate lawsuit could be brought in the court of Exchequer by means of an allegation of *quo minus*, asserting that the plaintiff was 'less able' to pay the Crown because the defendant would not pay him. Thus a private party could sue another private party in the Exchequer, if the plaintiff was a debtor to the Crown and if that debt diminished his ability to settle with the Crown. If money was withheld, then logically the plaintiff was less able to pay, and this second requirement for Exchequer jurisdiction was legally unassailable.[11]

The plaintiff, in the thirteenth century and throughout the Tudor period, had to be a genuine debtor to the Crown to be able to sue in the Exchequer court. However, most people of any financial standing would have such obligations from time to time. The collection of the royal revenue was not very rigorously pursued, and many people owed the king some feudal due, rent, tax, duty, tallage, tenth, fifteenth, fine, amercement, scutage, fee, toll, hearth money, ship money, or the like. Any of these classes of debtors could have sued before the Exchequer, in contract or in tort, any other private person.

By the end of the thirteenth century, so many lawsuits between private parties, *placita communiae*, had been brought into the Exchequer court by writs of *quo minus* that a new office had to be set up to handle them. This was the office of pleas, under the supervision of the clerk of the pleas. That clerk and the sworn clerks under him handled the clerical aspects of the common law litigation between private parties; the barons sat as the judges, as they did in litigation directly involving the Crown.

To aid the king's debtors to recover from their debtors was a reasonably implied power of the Exchequer, and this extension of its jurisdiction was not questioned. Another equally valid extension of jurisdiction was to allow its officers to sue and be sued only in the Exchequer; otherwise the king's officers could be taken away from the performance of their duties, and the Exchequer would function less effectively. This privilege was in keeping with the practices of the other common law courts. The course of the common law was, or could easily be made to be, circuitous and dilatory. Some forms of action were begun with the arrest and imprisonment of the defendant by means of a writ of *capias ad respondendum*. An Exchequer officer could not properly serve the king in the Exchequer if he were busy litigating in another court. The privilege to sue and be sued only in the Exchequer, whether the litigation involved the Crown or not, was given not only to the high officials but to the minor employees as well, to anyone who was *de gremio scaccarii*.[12] This right was also extended to the personal servants of the Exchequer officers.[13]

[11] Jenkinson and Formoy, *Select Cases in the Exchequer of Pleas*, xxviii, xc–xci, c–cii; Harold Wurzel, 'Origin and development of *quo minus*,' *Yale Law Journal*, XLIX (1939), 39–64.

[12] Jenkinson and Formoy, *Select Cases in the Exchequer of Pleas*, xci–xcii, xcviii–xcix; *Stradling* v. *Morgan*, 1 Plowden 199, 208, 75 English Reports 305, 318 (Exchequer 1560); *Clapham* v. *Lenthall*, Hardres 365, 145 English Reports 499 (Exchequer 1664); that is, *The English Reports* (176 vols., London, Stevens & Sons, Ltd, 1900–30).

[13] E.g., *Abbot* v. *Sutton*, Year Book, Michaelmas 22 Henry VI, pl. 36, fol. 19 (Common

A third area of Exchequer jurisdiction was the privilege granted to public officials who were not officers of the Exchequer but who were collectors of the royal revenue or a part of it. One of the major duties of the sheriffs was to collect moneys due to the king and to account for them in the Exchequer; many other royal officers had similar responsibilities. In addition, many types of royal income were farmed out to private persons for collection. Sheriffs and farmers of revenues were not officers of the Exchequer, yet they were required to come into the Exchequer to make their accounts. Lest they be hindered in this process of paying money to the king, they were given the privilege at their option to sue and be sued only in the Exchequer. This similarly prevented these local officers and other accountants to the Crown from being tied up in the other courts.[14] After their accounts were settled but before the amounts found due were paid, these persons had the slightly less advantageous position of debtors to the Crown.[15] It is to be noted that common law suits involving accountants to the Crown, like those concerned with debtors to the Crown, were common pleas; the king was not a party to the suit, though he was indirectly concerned in the outcome.

III

Thus we see that the Exchequer court was hearing lawsuits from the thirteenth century onward. The barons sat as the judges in all cases, but different clerks handled the paperwork of the different branches of the court's jurisdiction. Where the litigation concerned the Crown directly, it was a part of the revenue jurisdiction of the court and would be handled by the king's remembrancer's office or the lord treasurer's remembrancer's office, depending on the nature or source of the revenue involved. The office of pleas dealt with litigation between private persons, who had the privilege to sue for common law claims in the Exchequer as debtors or accountants to the Crown. Here plaintiffs filed their writs of *quo minus*; here was handled the common law side of the court. In the middle of the sixteenth century, the equity side of the court arose within the king's remembrancer's office. As on other sides of the court, a suit in equity had

Pleas 1443), *dictum*; Leventhorp's Case, Year Book, Michaelmas 34 Henry VI, pl. 28, fol. 15 (Common Pleas 1455).

[14] Jenkinson and Formoy, *Select Cases in the Exchequer of Pleas*, xciii–xciv, cii–cviii; *Forde* v. *N.B.*, Year Book, Michaelmas 9 Edward IV, pl. 20, fol. 40 (Common Pleas 1469), *dictum; Young* v. *Clerk of the Hanaper*, Year Book, Hilary 9 Edward IV, pl. 18, fol. 53; Case 67, Jenkins 131, 145 English Reports 92 (Exchequer Chamber 1470); *Anon.*, 2 Bulstrode 36, 80 English Reports 939 (King's Bench 1612).

[15] *Clapham* v. *Lenthall*, Hardres 365, 145 English Reports 499, 500 (Exchequer 1664).

to concern the Crown or have been brought by someone privileged to sue in the Exchequer.[16]

In the thirteenth century the details of the procedure are unclear. By the beginning of the seventeenth century, however, the quantity of litigation required the development of specific formulae by which royal rights could be vindicated in the Exchequer. On the revenue side, if the action was an official suit to collect money, the attorney-general sued in the king's name (*viz. Rex* v. *Richard Roe*). If a private party was suing for the breach of a statute which gave him a share of the penalty and the Crown the other part, then he would sue in his own name *qui tam*, 'who as well as, the king was entitled to the penalty (*viz. John Doe qui tam* v. *Richard Roe*). On the equity side, if the suit directly touched the Crown, the attorney-general sued in his own name and office (*viz. Attorney-General* v. *Richard Roe*). If the suit in equity only concerned the king indirectly, the private person, who was the real party in interest, sued by a relator information (*viz. Attorney-General ex relatione John Doe* v. *Richard Roe*). In actions at law and suits in equity by mere debtors to the Crown, the king was not mentioned (*viz. John Doe* v. *Richard Roe*).

This brings us to the consideration of Exchequer privileges of suit in relation to the other high courts at Westminster. The courts of Chancery, King's Bench, and Common Pleas stood on an equal footing with the Exchequer regarding removal of suits out of one court and into another. The writ of prohibition, which lay to inferior courts, did not travel between them. The removal of suits was based on the various privileges of the courts which in turn related to their jurisdictions. Privileges were of two sorts: special and general. The officers of the Exchequer and accountants had the benefits of the special privilege of the Exchequer, but mere debtors to the Crown had only a general privilege.

General privileges gave a plaintiff only the right to sue in a certain court. A general, as opposed to a special, privilege could not be used by a defendant as the grounds for removing a case into another court.[17] Moreover, if a plaintiff had a general privilege and the defendant had a special privilege in another court, the general privilege deferred to the special, and the defendant could insist on being sued in his own court.[18] When both parties had special privileges but of different courts, then the

[16] Bryson, *Equity Side of the Exchequer*, 13–27.

[17] Hunt's Case, 3 Dyer 328, 73 English Reports 742 (Common Pleas 1573), *semble*: a *supersedeas* declaring the defendant to be a debtor to the Crown was not allowed.

[18] E.g., *Clapham* v. *Lenthall*, Hardres 365, 145 English Reports 499 (Exchequer 1664); *Castle* v. *Lichfield*, Hardres 505, 145 English Reports 570 (Exchequer 1669); Note, 3 Salk. 281, 91 English Reports 825.

court in which priority of suit was established heard the case.[19] The courts were not anxious to lose business in this way, and so they insisted on the general rule that such a jurisdictional point be raised before a general appearance or pleading to issue.[20] Moreover, where there was a plurality of defendants, all of them would have to be privileged in order for the request for removal to have prevailed.[21]

The traditional method of removing suits into the Exchequer was by a writ of *supersedeas*.[22] However, a *supersedeas* could not be sent to the King's Bench because the pleas there were held *coram rege* and writs could not lie against the king.[23] The problem was resolved by having the cursitor baron take the Red Book of the Exchequer into the King's Bench and assert that the defendant was an officer or accountant in the Exchequer and could be sued only there.[24] The cursitor baron showed the copy of the writ of privilege which was in the Red Book, an official record, at folio 36.[25] Thereupon the case was dismissed to the Exchequer without any plea or prayer from the defendant.[26]

There were alternative methods of asserting the Exchequer privilege in the seventeenth century. It could be pleaded by the defendant,[27] or the

[19] E.g., *Baker* v. *Lenthall*, Hardres 117, 145 English Reports 409 (Exchequer 1658); *Clapham* v. *Lenthall*, Hardres 365, 145 English Reports 499 (Exchequer 1664); Note, 2 Salk. 281, 91 English Reports 825.

[20] E.g., Note, Year Book, Michaelmas 22 Henry VI, pl. 9, fol. 7 (Common Pleas 1443); *Young* v. *Clerk of the Hanaper*, Year Book, Hilary 9 Edward IV, pl. 18, fol. 53; Case 67, Jenk. 131, 145 English Reports 92 (Exchequer Chamber 1470); Case 31, Dal. 36, 123 English Reports 253 (Common Pleas 1561); Jervas's Case, Sav. 33, 123 English Reports 996 (Exchequer 1582).

[21] E.g., *S.* v. *T.B.*, Year Book, Michaelmas 34 Henry VI, pl. 13, fol. 29 (Common Pleas 1455); *East* v. *Bittenson*, Cary 67, 21 English Reports 36; Cecil Monro (ed.), *Acta Cancellariae, or, Selections from the Records of the Court of Chancery, 1558–1624* (London, W. Benning and Co., 1847), 457, (Chancery, 1578); Powle's Case, 3 Dyer 377, 73 English Reports 846, Godb. 10, 78 English Reports 6 (Common Pleas 1581); *Vendall* v. *Harvey*, Nels. 19 at 22, 21 English Reports 779 (Chancery 1633); David E. C. Yale (ed.), *Lord Nottingham's Two Treatises: 'Manual of Chancery Practice' and 'Prolegomena of Chancery and Equity'* (Cambridge, CUP, 1965), 336.

[22] E.g., *Anon.*, Year Book, Michaelmas 21 Henry VI, pl. 44, fol. 22 (Common Pleas, 1442).

[23] Bracton, fol. 5b: George E. Woodbine (ed.), *Bracton De Legibus et Consuetudinibus Angliae* (4 vols., New Haven, Yale University Press, 1915–42), II, 33; trans. by Samuel E. Thorne (ed.), *Bracton On the Laws and Customs of England* (4 vols., Cambridge, Mass., The Belknap Press of Harvard University Press, 1968–77), II.

[24] E.g., *Walrend* v. *Winroll*, Noy 40, 74 English Reports 1010 (King's Bench 1601); *Guy* v. *Reynel*, 2 Brownl. and Golds. 266, 123 English Reports 934 (Common Pleas 1609), *dictum; Anon.*, 2 Bulstrode 36, 80 English Reports 939 (King's Bench 1612); *Foster* v. *Barrington*, 2 Sid. 164, 82 English Reports 1313, Hardres 164, 145 English Reports 433 (King's Bench 1659), *dictum; Lampen* v. *Deering*, 2 Show. K.B. 299, 89 English Reports 951 (King's Bench 1680).

[25] PRO, E 164/2; this has been transcribed by Hubert Hall, *The Red Book of the Exchequer*, Rolls Series, XCIX (3 vols., London, HMSO by Eyre and Spottiswoode, 1896), III, 823–4.

[26] *Anon.*, 2 Bulstrode 36, 80 English Reports 939 (King's Bench 1612).

[27] E.g., *Foster* v. *Barrington*, 2 Sid. 164, 82 English Reports 1313, Hardres 164, 145 English

Red Book could have been sent into the court of Common Pleas.[28] However, in the eighteenth century it became customary to assert the Exchequer privilege by means of an injunction out of the Exchequer to the plaintiff; this was a personal order not to sue in the other court, but with liberty to sue in the Exchequer.[29] This was a far superior procedure to the clumsy and embarrassing traditional methods of *supersedeas* and direct claim of jurisdiction *in facie curiae*.

IV

In the sixteenth century, the court of King's Bench, which like the Exchequer had considerably less business than the court of Common Pleas, consciously expanded its jurisdiction and its case load. This was done by use of the fiction in bills of Middlesex and writs of latitat and by the extension of the scope of actions on the case.[30] However, during the sixteenth century the court of Exchequer remained within its ancient, traditional boundaries.

The medieval Exchequer in its role as a court of law was explicitly circumscribed by statute. The Statute of Rhuddlan of 1284, the *Articuli super Cartas* of 1300, and the Statute of 1311 had limited the court to cases concerning the Crown and the officers of the Exchequer.[31] Thus the hearing of common pleas was generally forbidden to the Exchequer, but the affairs of debtors to the Crown concerned the Crown sufficiently to justify extending Exchequer jurisdiction to them. In the sixteenth century litigants attempted to expand the jurisdiction of the Exchequer court by means of fictions in pleading,[32] but the court did not allow this.[33]

From the beginning of the Interregnum, however, the allegation of the Exchequer general privilege, claiming that the plaintiff was a Crown debtor, came to be used fictitiously on the equity side of the court. Unfor-

Reports 433 (King's Bench 1659); *Wentworth* v. *Squibb*, 1 Lutw. 43, 125 English Reports 23 (Common Pleas 1701); *Phips* v. *Jackson*, 6 Mod. 305, 87 English Reports 1045 (King's Bench 1705).

28 E.g., *Wentworth* v. *Squibb*, 1 Lutw. 43, 125 English Reports 23 (Common Pleas 1701); also, Lawrence Squibb, 'A Book of All the Several Officers of the Court of Exchequer . . .,' ed. by William Hamilton Bryson, *Camden Miscellany XXVI*, Camden Society, 4th series, XIV (London, Royal Historical Society, 1975), 102–3, 112.

29 *Cawthorne* v. *Campbell*, 1 Anstr. 205, 145 English Reports 846 (Exchequer 1790); J. Manning, *The Practice of the Court of Exchequer, Revenue Branch*, 2nd edn (London, 1827), 191.

30 Baker, *English Legal History*, 38–41; Milsom, *Historical Foundations*, 54–7.

31 Parliamentary Statutes 12 Edward I [1284]; 28 Edward I [1300], c. 4; 5 Edward II [1311], c. 25: *SR*, I, 70, 138, 163.

32 John H. Baker (ed.), *The Reports of Sir John Spelman*, Selden Society, XCIV (London, 1978), 63, fn. 5.

33 *Ragland* v. *Wildgoose*, Savile 11, 15, 123 English Reports 984, 986 (Exchequer 1580); *Williams* v. *Griffin*, PRO E 126/2, fol. 176*v*. (1619).

tunately the first cases which allowed this fiction do not appear to have been reported. The fictive jurisdiction was asserted at the beginning of each bill by adding after the plaintiff's name the following phrase: '. . . *debtor and accountant to his majesty as by the records of this honorable court and otherwise it doth and may appear.*'[34] An examination of the files of the bills of complaint discloses that this formula of jurisdiction, which had been used occasionally during the latter years of Charles I's reign, became general after 1649 when most equity bills identify the plaintiff as a Crown debtor,[35] using this strict formula. Moreover, in many bills the formula appears as an interlinear addition. The evidence of the records thus points with some precision to the year 1649 for the introduction of the wider jurisdiction based on this fictitious and non-traversable allegation of indebtedness to the Crown.[36] The first references to the fictitious basis of the Exchequer equity jurisdiction appear in Matthew Hale's treatise of August 1665, 'Considerations Touching the Amendment or Alteration of the Lawes,'[37] and *The Compleat Sollicitor* (1666), page 389.

At the beginning of the Tudor period, therefore, the judicial jurisdiction of the court of Exchequer was limited to common law matters that affected the revenue of the Crown. By the end of the Tudor period the court had acquired an equity jurisdiction, and therefore was the only high court of justice in England to administer both general civil common law and equitable remedies. In 1649 the Exchequer extended its common law and equitable jurisdictions to all parties; at this point the court of Exchequer came of age as a full-fledged high court of general jurisdiction. Thus, although the courts of Common Pleas, Chancery, and King's Bench had developed earlier, the court of Exchequer ultimately embraced a lesser quantity but a greater scope of judicial action.

[34] David B. Fowler, *The Practice of the Court of Exchequer upon Proceedings in Equity* (2 vols., London, 1795), I, 29; Anon., *The Compleat Sollicitor* (1666), 389; William Bohun, *The Practising Attorney; or, Lawyer's Office* (London, 1724), 292; Anon., *The Compleat Clerk in Court* (1726), 149; Samuel Turner, *An Epitome of the Practice on the Equity Side of the Court of Exchequer* (London, 1806), 2.

[35] Or a debtor to the Commonwealth.

[36] This fits with the tentative conclusions in regard to the Exchequer common law fiction in Wurzel, 'The origin and development of *quo minus*,' 39, 61, 64. Furthermore no reported cases have been found after 1649 which challenge the general jurisdiction of the court. It is submitted that the Exchequer extended all of its jurisdictions to all litigants at the same time, 1649.

[37] In Francis Hargrave (ed.), *A Collection of Tracts Relative to the Law of England* (Dublin, for E. Lynch, etc., 1787), 278; the date is given in BL, MS Harleian 711, fol. 187*v*.

The Elizabethan Chancery and women's rights

MARIA L. CIONI

Lord Chancellor Christopher Hatton observed in 1587 that the law is 'the inheritance of all men.' But how beneficial was this bequest to Elizabethan women? The common law provided certain limited rights for the spinster and widow; married women, however, suffered from the fiction that they could have no proprietary rights separate from their spouses.[1] The law existed for all men but accessibility for women was strictly defined. The treatment of women in equity jurisdictions, and in particular in Chancery, became significant because relief was available there to both single and married women when, for numerous reasons, they could not go to the common law. Poverty, old age, uncertainty, confederacy, and maintenance were sufficient causes in Chancery but not at the common law.

Throughout the Elizabethan era Chancery increasingly entertained female litigants, and problems coming before that court precipitated a shift in its jurisdiction concurrent with a standardization of procedure. Chancery, like all other courts, was both a product and a reflection of its society. Recognition by the Elizabethan Chancery that women should be accorded some regularized course of action and rights indicates, therefore, that social attitudes toward women were changing.

I

Responding to the needs of society, Chancery evolved into a separate royal court which, by the end of the sixteenth century, administered its own body of substantive law, referred to as equity. Women sought and received Chancery's judicial aid in enforcing possessory rights and in

[1] Frederick Pollock and Frederic W. Maitland, *The History of English Law*, 2nd edn (2 vols., Cambridge, CUP, 1968), II, ch. 7; Theodore F. T. Plucknett, *A Concise History of the Common Law*, 5th edn (London, Butterworths, 1956), 546–57; T.E., *The Lawes Resolutions of Womens Rights* (London, 1632), Books 1 & 4: *STC* 7437.

recognizing their property rights because common law had been consistently unreceptive to their legal demands. Chancery could promise relief when the common law did not even entertain such suits. The widow who did not possess the evidences to claimed lands, the jointress whose lands and profits were being withheld by the trustee, the separated wife whose husband would not permit her to enjoy a share of what she brought into the marriage, these and more had no case at the common law but they made their way to Chancery. Willingness to give women security moved Chancery to protect future equitable interests and to develop a new instrument, the trust, to allow married women to have separate estates, free of their spouses' control. New requirements for testamentary cases rendered the position of personal representatives more secure and responsible, and in consequence were well-tailored to the needs of the court's female clientele.

The practical attitude of Chancery was realized in its procedure and its powers of enforcement. Rather than determine a specific right, action could be taken to force the defendant to comply with its orders, especially by employing the injunction. As well as being used to ensure a fair trial at common law, to restrain an infringement of rights[2] and to inhibit suits in other courts, Chancery increasingly used the injunction throughout Elizabeth's reign to restore a person expelled from an estate to 'quiet possession' of lands and tenements.[3]

The suit between Frances, lady Chandos and William, lord Chandos concerning the will and estate of the late Edmund, lord Chandos illustrates the many uses of the injunction.[4] At the hearing in May 1595, Lord Keeper Puckering assisted by Chief Justices Popham and Anderson and the then master of the rolls, Sir Thomas Egerton, agreed that three cases in the law had to be settled before the suit in Chancery could proceed. Consequently, an order was issued advising William to bring an action of trespass at the common law to decide the question of right. Shortly thereafter, Frances wrote Puckering that her in-laws were attempting to take possession of her estate.[5] An order in Chancery stipulated that Frances should enjoy possession of the estate.[6] When some tenants refused to pay

[2] William Tothill, *The Transactions of the High Court of Chancery (1559–1646): The English Reports, Chancery*, XXI (176 vols., London, Stevens & Sons, Ltd, 1900–30), I, 165: *Browne* v. *Bridges & Ley*, 1589–90.

[3] William J. Jones, *The Elizabethan Court of Chancery* (Oxford, Clarendon Press, 1967), 183–4.

[4] Tothill, *Transactions of Chancery*, I: *Dame Chandois* v. *Chandois*; PRO, C 33/90, fols. 152*r*.–*v*., *same* v. *same*, May 1595.

[5] BL, MS Harleian 6997, fol. 28 (Frances, lady Chandos to the Lord Keeper, 29 May 1595).

[6] PRO, C 33/90, fols. 416*v*.–417, *Frances, Lady Chandos* v. William, Lord Chandos, 12 June 1595; C 33/89, fol. 430, *same* v. *same*.

their rents, Frances obtained a further order from Chancery for her rents and arrears.[7]

William, stymied by Chancery's decision, subsequently brought a trespass action *eiectio firmae* at common law for damages. Chancery issued an injunction in 1596 to stay the suit.[8] Another year passed; Frances continued to enjoy the profits while William continued his action of trespass. After a two year impasse William forcibly entered certain copyhold lands which Frances enjoyed. She informed Chancery, whereupon the court put her in quiet possession of the same.[9] By bringing her case before Chancery, Lady Chandos had been able to enjoy the possession of and profits from disputed lands for four years while the defendant brought numerous and expensive actions at common law. Without providing a decree, the injunction afforded immediate relief to the litigant.

Another way in which Chancery provided aid without actually proceeding to a judicial order was by arbitration. Chancery's willingness to delegate certain cases to local gentlemen and women for conciliation became a touchstone of equity. The patience, perceptiveness, and talents of the arbitrators could effectively adapt equitable principles to community needs and, in so doing, enable them to participate in the functioning of the law.[10] A case might be sent to arbitration or it might also be referred to common law. Such referral occurred when the issue was not suited for equity or after Chancery had helped the litigant to secure the necessary requisites for legal action. These advantages attracted into Chancery female litigants who were unsure and perhaps unprepared to enter immediately into an action at common law. In a sense, Chancery could provide rudimentary experience for women who might later proceed to common law.[11]

Chancery's realistic attitude is most apparent in the handling of suits involving married women. During the 1590s petitions were increasingly exhibited by married women (a *feme covert*) for protection of their 'separate estate'. The common law fiction that a *feme covert* had no rights separate from her spouse was dismantled by a long process begun at the end of the sixteenth century in Chancery. That court, responding to changing social expectations, permitted married women to arrange for property

[7] PRO, C 33/90, fol. 452*v*., 7 Oct. 1595; fols. 528, 678*v*., 737*r*.–*v*., 21 Oct., 15 Nov., 17 Nov. 1595; C 33/89, fol. 738, 24 Nov. 1595.

[8] PRO, C 33/91, fol. 102, *same* v. *same*, May 1596.

[9] PRO C 33/90, fol 907*v*., *same* v. *same*, 15 Feb. 1597.

[10] See Jones, *Elizabethan Chancery*, 272.

[11] Cambridge University Library, MS Gg.2.26, fols. 80*v*.–81. 'It is usual in a Bill of Chancerye to obiect that the Case hath proper helpe at the Comon Lawe; . . . But these helpes be divers, and not the same: For by the one Chancery he seeketh the land, and in the other he demaundeth damages onely.'

secure from their husbands' control. Through the utilization of Chancery's new mechanism, the trust, property was given over to trustees who received the benefits for the wife only.[12] The chancellor declared:

> that if a *feme covert* doe purloyne her husbands money or goods and putteth such money into other mens hands whoe there with doe buy land to her vse he [the chancellor] will not releeve the heyre or Executor of the husband to haue the lands or the money restored neither such a husband himselfe.[13]

Recognition by Chancery of equitable uses and trusts thus became the basis for legal enhancement of the status of married women.

Decisions in Chancery bound the person, and punitive measures were adopted to enforce decrees. During his office, Nicholas Bacon introduced sequestration, limiting it to those things involved in the suit.[14] By the end of the century, the process extended to include lands and leases not pertaining to the cause, if the suit was for a personal debt.[15] The sequestration of lands bound the property, and consequently underscored the rights in the property. The progression in Chancery from the traditional basis of conscience into the realm of proprietary right was in part promoted by using sequestration. Informality, range of jurisdiction, relatively small cost, and fairly quick process made Chancery attractive to litigants. Then, too, the court's sympathy toward female litigants increased Chancery's popularity and helped to dispel their fears about involvement in legal matters.

II

By the close of Elizabeth's reign, the concept of equity had evolved a formulated body of rules and laws administered in Chancery. The changing nature of the court's business resulted in the formation of these rules; the more systematic the procedure became, the more able was the court to deal with new legal areas. Chancery's expansion from its traditional basis of conscience was manifest in the progression from contract to trust, from equity to equitable estates, and from moral duties to proprietary rights.[16]

[12] PRO, C 33/91, fols. 365*v*., 610*v*., 698*v*., 707.

[13] Cambridge University Library, MS Gg.2.31, fols. 445*v*., no. 68. The document is undated but in context the chancellor may be assumed to be Egerton.

[14] *A General Abridgement of Cases in Equity* . . . (2 vols., Dublin, J. Rice, 1792–3), I, 130.

[15] David E. C. Yale (ed.), *Lord Nottingham's Two Treatises: 'Manual of Chancery Practice' and 'Prolegomena of Chancery and Equity'* (Cambridge, CUP, 1965), 30; Richard O. Bridgman, *A Digest of the Reported Cases on Points of Practice and Pleading in the Courts of Equity* (London, H. Butterworth, 1824), 149, *Whareby* v. *St John*, Trinity 1599. The court was inclined to grant sequestration for money.

[16] George Spence, *The Equitable Jurisdiction of the Court of Chancery* (2 vols., London, V. and

Moreover, as the procedures and rules of the court became apparent to the populace they sought its justice in increasing numbers. Different types of litigant emerged during this period: the married woman seeking remedy in her own right or being sued (under mitigating circumstances) without her husband, the woman wanting to be put back in possession of her estate, and the executrix seeking equity's aid in a testamentary case. Although the ramifications of Chancery's dealing with these sorts of cases did not occur until fifty years later, the fact remains that such suits had been adjudged long before. The inveterate desire of women, single and married, to have some kind of security, whether in land, chattels or trust, was recognized by Chancery. In so doing the court expanded its jurisdiction to compensate women for disadvantages they might suffer at common law.

The majority of suits involving female litigants centered on issues regarding their present and future security. Inheritance was a major preoccupation of families. From the mid-sixteenth century there was added significance: the Statutes of Uses (1535) and of Wills (1540) had altered the existing forms of uses and conveyances with the result that such devices now came under the common law rather than Chancery. Chancery re-entrenched its jurisdiction during the latter half of the century by defining and enforcing equitable future interests which the common law did not recognize.[17] Concomitantly, landowners resorted to the creation of equitable future interests as an attempt to circumvent the restrictions of the common law. By this means their estates could be settled on more family members over a greater length of time. Anxiety about inheritance was therefore well-founded.

Land was the traditional basis of wealth, and any action involving partition, transfer or leasing of property aroused the interest of family, friends, and neighbors. When the head of a family died his will usually stipulated how and by whom the estate was to be handled. In the event that he died intestate, common law provided that an estate in fee simple should be divided allowing one-third to the widow for her dower, one-third to the children and the remainder to the Crown. Nuncupative (oral) wills were under the jurisdiction of ecclesiastical courts and could not be adjudicated at common law, but Chancery did rule on them with certain reservations.[18] In a state of anxiety about their futures, minors, widows,

R. Stevens and G. S. Norton, 1846–9), I, 424. And now, see the basic argument in DeLloyd J. Guth's essay, above, 69–86.

17 Ecclesiastical courts were experiencing increased difficulty enforcing orders concerning bequests.

18 Jones, *Elizabethan Chancery*, 407–8; PRO, C 2 D4/33, *Ellen Dunston* v. *Richard Ripton*, May 1593.

and female heiresses were vulnerable. They might not be aware that they could sue for recovery at the common law or even know if they were eligible to bring such a suit.

A young heiress in such a tenuous position depended solely upon her relatives or guardian for the management of her estate. The larger the estate the more vulnerable her position, particularly if she was a sole heir. It was common for the heiress to delay legal action until she married; she and her husband would then sue. If one co-heiress married, the others often took legal action. In the case of *Dockwray* v. *Poole*, for instance, a man had three daughters upon whom he entailed land. One sister married and agreed to accept £1000 in consideration of the land to which she had a right as co-heiress. After marrying, she decided to sue for her inheritance despite her sisters' protestation that she had already received adequate compensation. Chancery decided that the consideration was not a bar to the inheritance.[19] In other words, she should not be penalized for marrying.

Not all spinsters were prepared to wait until marriage to recover their inheritance. Those suing before were usually moderately wealthy and could afford professional advice. A spinster involved in business likely found it easier to protect her interests, as the case of Anne Norwich illustrates.[20] She sued her brother, Simon, for a £200 legacy that he had attempted to take for himself. First she sued him for recovery in Queen's Bench where it was found that she had a right to the sum as her inheritance. She then sued in Chancery for a decision to bind her brother to reimburse her. There it was decreed that Simon should pay his sister £80 and an annuity of £6 13s. 4d. for the duration of her life.[21]

According to common law, when the father died the eldest, single daughter could recover her appointed share as yet unpaid by the executors or the heir. The purpose was to aid her in marriage. This did not apply to the younger daughters, and those who had reached majority without receiving their inheritance had no relief at common law. These younger co-heiresses often came to Chancery to try to obtain their legacies.[22]

Inheritance of copyhold lands was more complex because this involved jurisdiction of the lord of the manor and the manor court. The plight of one such heiress is summed up in Agnes Butcher's plea before Chancery:

[19] Tothill, *Transactions of Chancery 98*, 135, Trinity 1609.
[20] PRO, C 3/132/8, *Anne Norwiche* v. *Symon Norwiche*.
[21] PRO, C 78/49/35, *same* v. *same*, 25 Nov. 1577.
[22] PRO, C 78/31/8, *Elizabeth, Kathryn, Anne and Florence Cassye* v. *William Reade and Gyles Reade*, 21 June 1564; C 2 B3/34, *Johan Broke* v. *Johan Walker*, 13 Feb. 1594; C 2 B3/3, *same* v. *same*.

In tender consideracion . . . for that your saide oratrix is a verye poore maiden and a stranger not well known in these parts, and the said Richard Butcher is a man of wealthe and in suche favoure with the lorde of the saide mannor, that your saide oratrix is out of all hope of annie indifferencye to be shewed her yf she shoulde attempte to try for her lawfull and iuste title in the court of the said manor . . . and she is without all remedye to be had in anie other of Quenes Courts at the comon lawe vnlesse she might obteyne licence of the Lorde of the said mannor which she can by noe meanes doe.[23]

Chancery was sympathetic toward young, single women coming before the court to seek their inheritance. If the legacy involved land, the court attempted to insure that the terms of the testator's will were fulfilled; and if he died intestate, equity sought to assure that all the relatives got an adequate share. The court even took the liberty of deciding that a plaintiff should be awarded more than was claimed, as in the case of a spinster who, because she was getting older and was unmarried, needed a supplement to her portion.[24]

Chancery also supported the widow. Upon the death of her spouse, a widow's legal status reverted to that of a single woman responsible for her own actions. Beside responsibility and recognition, a widow assumed the burden of supporting herself and her children. Usually she depended on the inheritance from her own family and her deceased spouse.

The presence of children involved increased responsibility for the widow and also raised potential for conflict with the heir. The matter between Alice Bewforrest and her son Luke shows the magnitude possible in such conflicts. They enjoyed a good relationship until Luke allegedly took the £80 that Alice had given him to purchase a lease and instead bought it in his own name. She also said that he had tricked her out of the title to her own farm.[25] In 1556, she obtained a Chancery decree ordering Luke to relinquish possession of the farm and permit her to enjoy the premises.[26] The son countered with suits at common law and in Chancery, maintaining that he had purchased the lease with his own money.[27] Further, he had agreed to relinquish his estate and allow his mother to receive all the profits from the farm if she would assign him a one-half share, with stock after she died. The common law adjudged the validity of his deed to the farm. Chancery, on the other hand, decreed that the mother was being cheated and consequently reaffirmed her possession in the farm and rents. Further, it was decreed that another son, Richard,

[23] PRO, C 2 B24/35, *Agnes Butcher* v. *Richard Butcher*, 28 Nov. 1586.
[24] PRO, C 78/94/18, *Katherine Walronde* v. *Thomas Gawyne*, 31 Jan. 1590.
[25] PRO, C 3/14/30, *Alice Bewforrest* v. *Luke Bewforrest*.
[26] PRO, C 78/35/27, *same* v. *same*, 7 May 1566.
[27] PRO, C 3/22/22, *Luke Bewforeste* v. *Alyce Bewforeste*.

should at his own expense and in his mother's name, bring an action at common law to ascertain if the deed was original or fraudulent. If valid, Luke would enjoy a moiety of the farm after Alice died; if invalid, Richard would inherit. Further, Alice was not to be charged for any trial of the suit.[28] Alice had taken her problem to Chancery and had obtained a decree; the court was adamant that she be protected in that decision. The suit brought by Luke at common law was, as far as equity was concerned, irrelevant to Alice's possession of the farm and should not be allowed to threaten her enjoyment. It was one thing for Chancery to refer a case to common law, but it was another matter when the court had issued an order or decree and the defendant tried to counter it with an action at common law.[29]

Marriage brought a woman into close contact with her in-laws, and before the marriage families usually made financial arrangements for the prospective wife: dower or jointure. The widening family circle presented a larger arena for conflict, particularly if the husband predeceased the wife. In one case, John Spencer attempted unsuccessfully to divest his mother-in-law, Dame Anne Catlin, of her jointure in the manor and warren of Sandy. Sir Robert Catlin, chief justice of Queen's Bench, had left a considerable estate to his daughter Mary, John's wife. Spencer, being in financial straits, attempted to bypass the widowed Anne and gain immediate possession, but her suit in Chancery checked his action. The widow continued to enjoy her life interest in the estate until her death in 1589.[30]

This Catlin–Spencer case deserves fuller scrutiny because it concerns future equitable interests, an area repudiated by the common law and embraced by Chancery. For instance, at the common law a lease to A and after his death to B, gave B a contingent interest that was highly suspect. The deviser could not be sure that the contingent remainder would work as intended. This consequently put B in an uncertain position. The uncertainty of this construction did not diminish its popularity although the problem of securing the estate fell to the person holding the contingent interest.[31] Equity followed the common law, but in its efforts to define and enforce the future interests it made detours and explorations far afield.

As mentioned earlier, the Statute of Uses transformed the majority of

[28] PRO, C 78/44/30, *same* v. *same*, 24 Jan. 1572.

[29] PRO, C 3/110/12, *Alice Lovell* v. *Alice Strowde* (to Bacon).

[30] PRO, C 78/109/2, *Dame Anne Catlin* v. *John Spencer*.

[31] William S. Holdworth, *A History of English Law* (12 vols., London, Methuen & Co., Ltd, 1924–38), VII, 116 and IV, 437–42.

uses previously under Chancery jurisdiction into legal estates triable at the common law. Not all categories were encompassed, but those remaining under Chancery auspices became equitable interests.[32] One such category was a term held in use. Terms of years differed from inheritance since they were intended to benefit some specific person or constructed for a specific purpose. The person who received the beneficial interest had a recognized right in equity, and the trustees were obliged to fulfill their obligations.[33] Creating a future interest by a lease for term of years was one method of providing security for a wife and children upon the death of the husband. The common law, by adopting the restrictive view that a term of years was a mere chattel interest, denied the possibility of limiting estates to a fixed term. Still, throughout Elizabeth's reign, landowners were attempting to settle the succession of their estates by preventing the heirs, who were tenants in tail, from barring such limitations. Chancery agreed in principle that an executory interest in a term of years should be indestructible,[34] but in 1597 Egerton 'forbore' to make an order to that effect since it would deprive the daughter, the heir apparent, of any estate.[35] The common law's drastic view of terms of years was fostered in part by its inveterate fear that these terms would lead to the creation of perpetuities. Chancery followed the same logic, but it was prepared to consider the length of time in the context of a particular case. When contention resulted concerning a lease for a lengthy period, it was consequently beneficial to bring the dispute to Chancery.[36]

Great care and consideration were taken to provide future security for a female child in particular, and here the term of years was often employed, as the case of the Catlin family illustrates. As a common law justice, Sir Robert Catlin knew that the common law would not acknowledge the legality of a future interest in a term of years; but as a concerned husband and father, he recognized the usefulness of such an interest in providing security for his family. He apparently had confidence that Chancery would uphold such interests. Mary, Sir Robert's only daughter, had married John Spencer in 1566, bringing with her lands spread throughout the counties of Leicester, Dorset, Bedford, and Northampton. Sir Robert's marriage settlement bestowed on Mary a life estate in all his properties in Leicestershire and a future interest in those leases of land which his wife

[32] *Ibid.*, VII, 117.
[33] Spence, *Equitable Jurisdiction*, I, 513.
[34] Plucknett, *Concise History of the Common Law*, 594–6. Not until 1612 did the common law recognize this point.
[35] PRO, C 33/93, fol. 503, *Long* v. *May*, 1597.
[36] PRO, C 78/43/32, *Isabel Wycombe* v. *William & Richard Mychell*, 11 Feb. 1573.

then enjoyed for her jointure.[37] In 1572, Sir Robert let various premises in Bedfordshire for a term of forty-one years to the use of himself, to his wife for her life, and the remainder to their daughter Mary. Dame Anne died in 1589 but John and Mary Spencer did not receive rents from the above leases for the remainder of the term. After John died in 1600, Mary presented her bill in Chancery.[38] If it had been a matter of securing the reversion of the inheritance or else suing for non-payment, Mary could have sued at common law. However, because a term of years was still valid her recourse was in Chancery.

As with property, the Elizabethan Chancery assumed the responsibility of protecting those who had an interest in a remainder of personal goods.[39] Early in the reign, Chancery entertained writs for such purposes.[40] The common law did not recognize the harm which a tenant for life could cause by assigning or disposing of the life estate until Mildmay's Case in 1606. Chancery's help, available from the mid-sixteenth century, was thus all the more significant.

III

The Statute of Uses did not encompass copyhold lands. A copyholder provided for the future of his wife by surrendering his holding and obtaining a lease for his life, then to his wife for her life, with the remainder to the heirs of his body.[41] If any problems with the copyhold of the widow arose as a result of actions taken by the lord of the manor, she could sue in Chancery. Although the husband might forfeit his copyhold, Chancery held that he could not convey away from the wife her life estate without her consent.[42] Action at common law against such ejectment was not possible until the latter part of Elizabeth's reign.[43]

[37] Mary E. Finch, *The Wealth of Five Northamptonshire Families 1540–1640*, Northamptonshire Record Society, XIX (Oxford, Oxford University Press, 1956), 50–1.

[38] PRO, C 2 S15/54, *Mary Spencer* v. *Henry Dowson et al.*, 15 Apr. 1600.

[39] *General Abridgement*, I, 360–1.

[40] Holdsworth, *History of English Law*, VII, 134; David E. C. Yale (ed.), *Lord Nottingham's Chancery Cases*, Selden Society, LXXIII and LXXIX (2 vols., London, B. Quaritch, 1957–61), I, lxxv. Both observed that by the latter part of Elizabeth's reign the one having a remainder of a term could exhibit a bill in Chancery to compel the holder of the life interest to be put in security not to bar his interest. Their observations are based on the case of *Price* v. *Jones* (26 Eliz.) and *Cole* v. *Moore* (6 James I). However, in 1559 Lady Isabel Ayleff was ordered to take a £400 bond not to bar her son, John, from his remainder interest. PRO, C 78/17/6, *Dame Isabell Ayleff* v. *John Ayleff*, 8 July 1559.

[41] Eric Kerridge, *Agrarian Problems in the Sixteenth Century and After* (London, Allen & Unwin, 1969), 33–41; and, Charles M. Gray, *Copyhold, Equity, and the Common Law* (Cambridge, Mass., Harvard University Press, 1963).

[42] Cambridge University Library, MS Gg.2.31, fol. 277.

[43] Jones, *Elizabethan Chancery*, 452–3.

Another area of contention concerned the custom of 'widow's freebench' as it was known on some manors. Essentially the custom acknowledged that the wife, after the death of her husband, could enjoy his copyhold until her demise or for as long as she remained unmarried. Common law forbade a tenant to sue the lord of the manor, assuming that the problem would be solved in the manorial court. Although Chancery would not attempt to abrogate the custom of the manor, by the later years of Elizabeth's reign the court usually decided for the widow.[44] Even if the lord protested that he could furnish proof, Chancery ordered that the widow enjoy possession until the new evidence was adjudged.[45] Sometimes the person having reversion attempted to claim the estate. The court's response was to grant the reversion but allow the widow an annuity and premises on which to live for the duration of her life.[46]

Heirs could also petition Chancery for release from unreasonable conditions. The devise of a remainder to a widow or even a single girl was often contingent 'as long as she shall remain sole and chaste.' At common law a conditional limitation, if violated, caused the estate to revert immediately.[47] Chancery's interpretation differed substantively. In the case of *Pexall Brokas* v. *Sir John and Dame Eleanor Savage*, Chancery considered whether the devise to Eleanor was a condition or a limitation, that is if absolutely for the term of her life.[48] There were 'fyftene presidents of decrees [made in Chancery] within fewe yeares past for defendants . . . beside many like presidents both in the Courts of Starre Chamber, Eschequer Chamber, Wards and Dutchie of Lancastre . . .' Chancery concluded that the estate had been devised to Eleanor for her life and that the condition, to remain single, did not bar her from enjoying the same.[49]

Equitable uses were frequently employed in creating family settlements. Such uses could be constructed only upon three considerations: for payment of money, in consideration of marriage, and for natural love and affection. This last was not admitted in Chancery until 1565. The common law held that at marriage the husband and wife became one; the husband therefore could not convey or grant any estate to his spouse

[44] PRO, C 78/35/3, *Rose Lodge* v. *Peter Francis*, 14 Nov. 1566; C 78/69/14, *Anne Jorden & Nicholas her son* v. *Wm Clement*, 20 Nov. 1588; C 78/70/21, *Elizabeth Jaye* v. *Richard Mode*, 27 May 1590.

[45] PRO, C 78/96/7, *Edithe Quytyne als Frier* v. *Bernard Drake*, 18 Nov. 1574; C 78/96/11, *same* v. *same*, 14 May 1575.

[46] PRO, C 3/141/1, *John Pope* v. *Christian Joyce*; C 78/44/28, *same* v. *same*, 13 Oct. 1571; C 3/167/5, *John Shepard* v. *Edith Shepard*; C 78/27/16, *same* v. *same*, 15 May 1564.

[47] Edward Coke, *The First Part of the Institutes of the Laws of England. Or, A Commentary upon Littleton* . . ., 13th edn, rev. by Francis Hargrave (London, 1788), 214b.

[48] PRO, C 33/76, fols. 735*r*.–*v*., *Pexall Brokas* v. *Sir John Savage and Lady Eleanor*, 25 June 1588.

[49] PRO, C 78/79/20, *same* v. *same*, 28 Nov. 1589.

either in possession, reversion or remainder.[50] After the Statute of Uses Chancery had acknowledged that a husband could convey to feoffees to the use of his wife in fee and thereby she could be seised of the inheritance. This equitable use was regularly employed to create a family settlement.[51] Landowners anxious to establish such land settlements caused a rather chaotic situation in litigation,[52] but Chancery was prepared to aid women and heirs who found themselves deprived of testamentary benefits.

Equitable use became popular during the latter half of the sixteenth century because it permitted greater latitude in establishing a family settlement than did a will. If a man held three acres in knight service he could devise two-thirds of it, but one-third had to be reserved for the heir. Yet this same man could convey all of the estate to his wife and children in his lifetime for a feoffment, fine or recovery, bargain and sale, or covenant to stand seised to uses, even to the exclusion of the heir.[53] Then, too, a single woman could make a feoffment of her estate to whomever she desired, whereas she was denied this right by the Statute of Wills. Chancery appreciated the importance attached to conveyancing by the landowners. Lord Chancellor Hatton, writing in 1587, advised a serjeant-at-law: 'In conveyances deal justly . . . for these touch all men's goods, possessions and lands [so] these, if they be duly done, work great help in the subject, and great benefit to all men.'[54]

During the 1590s, women often complained to Chancery that their husbands had made a covenant in consideration of their jointure which, since their spouses' deaths, had not been performed.[55] In 1603 the opinion of the court was 'that uses may be raysed by covenant for Ioyntures' but that the power to make leases of the jointure could not pass by the same means.[56] Jointure might be construed as consideration of marriage; as Chancery uncertainty changed to acceptance, more women were able to enjoy their security. There was a very fine distinction between the simple use, which came under the statute, and an active trust that did not. In practical terms, a simple trust was constructed by conveying land to some intermediary, who thereby had legal title exacting a promise to allow the

[50] **Coke . . .** *on Littleton*, 187b.
[51] PRO, C 2 U2/35, *Edmund Verney and Dame Awdreye his wife* v. *Anne Carewe and George Harvey*, 25 June 1588; C 2 U1/49, *William Upcrofte* v. *Isabael Upcrofte*, 12 May 1596.
[52] Alan W. B. Simpson, *An Introduction to the History of the Land Law* (Oxford, Oxford University Press, 1961), 186, 219.
[53] Cambridge University Library, MS Gg.1.35, fol. 42.
[54] Cecil Munro (ed.), *Acta Cancellariae, or, Selections from the Records of the Court of Chancery, 1558–1624* (London, W. Benning and Co., 1847), 566.
[55] PRO, C 2 B18/14, *Dame Dorothy Benger* v. *Greene et al.*, n.d.; C 2 S19/36, *Amy Scoley* v. *John Leigh et al.*, 7 Feb. 1593.
[56] Cambridge University Library, MS Gg.2.26, fols. 82*v*.–83, 27 Jan. 1603.

benefits of the land to accrue to a third party. Chancery knew and maintained the difference: the trust was its creature and over it the court exercised an original, peculiar, and exclusive jurisdiction.[57]

Proving that a trust had been agreed upon was not an easy task. And yet, by the end of the sixteenth century, the chancellor was prepared to take extreme measures if he believed that a trust did exist. In the case of *Mynn* v. *Cobb* it was noted that:

> The trust was not so fully proved as the Lord Chancellor [Egerton] would make a full decree thereupon, so as it should be a President for other causes, And yet so far forth proved as it satisfied him, as a private man. And therefore, in this case he thought fitt to wryte his Letters to the defendant to conforme himself to reason; And affirmed, that if he should find the defendant obstinate, then would he rule this cause specially against the defendant sans la tires consequence.[58]

IV

Landowners were quick to seek out means to circumvent the Statute of Uses, to separate legal and equitable ownership. Increasingly throughout Elizabeth's reign, springing and shifting trusts were employed. By means of a springing trust an equitable interest 'sprang' in the future without being supported by a particular estate, as the common law required. This equitable interest resided in the grantor until the condition for the spring vested it in the beneficiary. The shifting trust was arranged so that the equitable interest 'shifted' from one person to another at the occurrence of some specified future event.[59] The conveyancing and transactions of the Vaughan family illustrate the importance of trusts in family settlements. A properly executed trust could provide income for several people at different times and so ensure the family's security over several generations. In 1578 one John Morgan brought a Chancery bill against Frances, the daughter of John Vaughan, to perform a trust made by her father in 1574.[60] Vaughan had died in 1577 leaving Frances to administer his goods and chattels. Morgan alleged that Frances would not enforce the trust. She charged that Morgan was trying to take her estate even though she had agreed to uphold the trust. Twenty years later Frances reappears in Chancery records as Lady Burgh, the widow of Thomas, lord Burgh, Baron of Gainsburgh, former governor of Brill and Deputy of Ireland. As part of her campaign to secure maintenance during widowhood, Frances

[57] Spence, *Equitable Jurisdiction*, I, 491.
[58] Cambridge University Library, MS Gg.2.26, fol. 85*v*.
[59] PRO, C 78/60/9, *Johan Keate* v. *Richard Keate and Richard Estman*, 10 June 1581.
[60] PRO, C 2 M7/41, *John Morgan* v. *Frances Vaughan*, 5 June 1578.

brought suit against several for non-performance of another trust established by her father.[61]

The trust in this case appears to have been quite fragile.[62] Vaughan had sold his manor of Glastonbury in 1577 to his aunt, Blanch Perry (one lady of the queen's chamber) upon secret trust that after his death she should devise it to his mother, at a reasonable rate providing a 'competent maintenance to live upon.' When his mother died, Blanch was instructed to devise the same at a small rent to his brother, Robert, for his life. Finally, after Blanch's death, the manor was to be conveyed to his son, Francis and upon his death to the Lady Burgh. The story that unfolds is a tangled web of secret trusts, bargain and sale, and shifting and springing uses. Chancery considered that two problems had to be solved: one, whether the trust had been revoked by Blanch's actions, to enable the defendants to purchase the premises (the court said that the trust still existed); and second, six months later, whether Morgan held lawful title to the manor. The court agreed and ordered that he should receive the rents and profits without hindrance from other defendants. Further, since Morgan had title he must dispose of the trust concerning the lands to Lady Burgh. The court had unravelled a matter complicated by events over a twenty-three year span.

By the close of Elizabeth's reign, Chancery had dealt with enough cases pertaining to trusts and female property rights to adumbrate some general principles. The case of Sir Moyle Finch and Lady Elizabeth, his wife, was the catalyst in this formation.[63] In 1597, a Chancery bill against the Finches alleged that Sir Thomas Heneage had conveyed part of his estate to Finch and to John Audley in trust for himself, his wife and her heirs. When Sir Thomas died the countess of Southampton, his administratrix, claimed the estate in order to pay Heneage's debts. The court decided in the countess's favor, the defendants petitioned the queen, and she referred the matter to all the judges of England. Consequently, in 1601 the following points for rules in equity were resolved. The court would compel conveyance by the person who was seised and under an express trust to convey to a beneficiary. The judges affirmed that Sir Thomas had a trust, but decided that this could not be assigned to the plaintiff since it was 'a matter of privity' and not a 'power of the land.' Further, once the land had descended to the defendant, Elizabeth Finch, as heir to her mother Anne

[61] PRO, C 3/257/4, *Frances Burgh* v. *Robert Vaughan et al.*, 1599.

[62] PRO, C 78/109/7, *Lady Frances Burghe* v. *David Williams, Robert Vaughan, John Morgan et al.*, 22 Nov. 1600.

[63] PRO, C 2 W11/62, *Edward, Earl of Worcester; Mary, Countess of Southampton; Henry, Earl of Southampton; Sir John Fortescue* v. *Sir Moyle Finch and Lady Elizabeth, his wife*, 18 Apr. 1597.

Heneage, the trust was extinguished since the purpose of the conveyance had been fulfilled. Finally, the justices declared that litigants could sue in Chancery for evidences to lands as long as they did not make a claim to title, because questions of title remained under the jurisdiction of common law.

By James I's reign, the trust could be used to confer a benefit on a married woman to the exclusion of the spouse. Parents might create a trust if they feared that the daughter's husband 'would waste and consume' the benefit, a theme common to popular drama in this Shakespearean era. The estate would be conveyed to feoffees in trust to convey the estate to the daughter at her request.[64] The trust in this situation acted to bar the husband, if he survived the wife, from holding the estate by courtesy. A trust could also be constructed to benefit both the wife and her children. This meant that upon the beneficiary's death, the estate would continue to the use of the children. If the children were minors or deceased, the estate would be held by the wife's executors, not the widower.[65] Thus it became socially acceptable for a widow to have an estate in trust to her separate use especially if a prospective husband seemed grasping.[66] Chancery bills and orders in the 1590s show women increasingly presenting petitions to have such trusts enforced or to prevent the spouse from gaining estates which were intended for personal maintenance.[67] Juxtaposing the legal concept of married women (having no right apart from the husband) alongside the equitable perception that had now evolved exemplifies how vital was the latter in the establishment and advancement of a married woman's proprietary rights.

Separated or divorced women were accorded the benefits of both married and single status.[68] The one case that seems to found the concept of a married woman's separate estate is that of *Mary Sankey alias Walgrave* v. *Arthur Goldinge* (1581).[69] Chancery had now conceded that a married

[64] PRO, C 2 S16/23, *Joane Stanton* v. *Pierce Underhill*, 29 June 1601.

[65] PRO, C 2/L5/54, *Thomas Leadham et al.* v. *Hugh Fairdloughe and Faith his wife*, 20 Nov. 1601; C2 H6/55, *Sir Thomas Hoby and Dame Margaret his wife* v. *George, Earl of Huntingdon and Henry Smith*, 14 Oct. 1596.

[66] PRO, C 2/F9/16, *Katheryne Fisher* v. *George Ourde*, 5 Nov. 1586; C 2/P9/40, *William, Hugh, Margaret and Ann Price* v. *Humphrey David ap Price et al.*, 7 Oct. 1596. In 1586, Elizabeth ap Price remarried and enjoyed an estate worth £116 'not claymed or dealt withall by the same John David Lloyd her second husband but in truth reserved and kept by hir.'

[67] PRO, C 33/91 fol. 707*r.–v.*, *Henry Sacheverall and Jane his wife* v. *Sir Humphrey Ferrys*, 22 Feb. 1597; C 2 T6/59, *Thomas Tasburghe and Jane his wife* v. *Sir John Danvers*, 25 Jan. 1590.

[68] Cambridge University Library, MS Gg.2.31, fol. 407; Monro, *Acta Cancellariae*, 664–5.

[69] PRO C 2/W26/37, *Mary Walgrave* v. *Arthur Goldinge*, n.d.; Spence, *Equitable Jurisdiction*, I, 595–6; George W. Keeton, *The Law of Trusts*, 9th edn (London, Sir Isaac Pitman & Sons, 1968), 49.

woman, separated from her husband, had the right to bring a bill in her own name. Proceeds from any sale of her own inherited property were put in trust for her separate maintenance, thereby establishing an estate over which she alone had control. This case established that whenever an estate was conveyed to trustees, to the separate use of a married woman, Chancery would allow her prerogative to hold or dispose of that estate unhampered by her husband's interference.[70] Chancery's mechanism, the trust, enabled the evolution of the property rights of married women throughout succeeding centuries.

V

Concern for the security of a wife had spawned the twelfth century's temporal concept of dower, a voluntary premarital gift of up to one-third of the lands of the husband. By the fourteenth century this portion was defined by legal process.[71] Dower at common law was one-third of all lands to which the husband was seised during the marriage. Dower, which permitted the widow a life interest in land, rents, and offices, did not apply to copyhold. The custom of the manor, however, usually granted a widow 'freebench' for as long as she remained single. Kentish gavelkind and borough customs permitted a dower of as much as one-half of the husband's estate.

The widow's right could be defended by writ of dower at common law against both the heir and the lord. In effect, the law of dower delayed alienation and obstructed conveyances. Despite prior existence of the common law writ, Chancery's jurisdiction over dower became established during Elizabeth's reign. It rested primarily on the equitable procedure that enabled the widow to uncover details concerning her dower:[72] which of her spouse's estates applied? what encumbrances existed? were there other claims and rights? what was the true value of these estates? By means of injunction, Chancery could stay legal proceedings and actions harmful to a dowerable estate. The widow could thus be allotted a fair share, but Chancery did not want this to be to the heir's serious disadvantage.[73] Consequently, it did not uphold a widow's claim to both dower and a payment in lieu of dower: only the common law did.

[70] PRO, C 2/B8/58, *Thomas Bird* v. *Margaret Jewett et al.*, Feb. 1596.

[71] Simpson, *Land Law*, 65; Pollock and Maitland, *History of English Law*, II, 421, 394–5, 422–8; Plucknett, *Concise History of the Common Law*, 566.

[72] Tothill, *Transactions of Chancery 99*, 135: *Thomas* v. *Thomas*, 1571. The plaintiff sues to define her dower.

[73] Dower was intended to help the widow bring up her family, and Chancery upheld this rule: PRO, C 3/167/92, C3/169/78, *Henry Savell and Dorothy his wife et al.* v. *Margaret*

The prospect of a writ of dower could itself cause dissension. If a widow's dower was not immediately forthcoming after the husband died, she could sue out the writ. In a peaceful family this was unnecessary; in a feuding family, such action was mandatory. Between these extremes lay the majority, and even here bargaining might ensue. Some widows were convinced that there was no need to sue a writ, while others granted concessions to avoid the writ. The resulting distress was remedied in Chancery either after a case had been heard at common law or in place of the writ.

A husband might attempt to restrain dower. To remedy this, Chancery entertained bills from the widow for a fair share and acted to enforce her claim for a portion commensurate with the amount that she had brought into the marriage. This claim became known as the wife's 'equity to settlement,' the operation of which is seen in the case of Joanne Lyne against her brother-in-law, John.[74] Chancery found that the defendant had forced Joanne to renounce her executorship, relinquish authority over her children, and exclude herself from dower. Its judgment restored her rights and gave her a full third of the estate rather than the twenty marks allocated to her.

Divorce or legal separation dissolved a woman's right to dower at common law.[75] Elizabeth Broughen *alias* Fillam petitioned Chancery for aid, alleging that her divorced spouse, Nicholas, had conveyed the lease of Chigwell parsonage for a forty-one year term in trust to another for his use.[76] Since a premarriage contract involved that lease, Elizabeth claimed the parsonage but the defendant entered and took the profits, maintaining that she had no right since the divorce. It was decreed that Elizabeth should enjoy the parsonage and various tithes for the remainder of the term.[77]

Jointure evolved as a substitute for dower. In theory, jointure was a joint tenancy of husband and wife in lands which could only be alienated during marriage by consent of both parties; the survivor became the sole tenant of the entire estate. By the mid-sixteenth century, jointure usually operated on a proportional basis of ten per cent of the amount that the

Wilbram, 1558; C 78/30/3, *same* v. *same*, 24 May 1565; *Alexander Horden and Dame Dorothie* v. *Humphrey Mosley and Roger Barney*, 1559.

74 PRO, C 78/75/14, *Johane Lyne* v. *John Lyne*, 11 May 1590; also C 78/81/11, *Humfrey Samith & Anne, his wife, Anne Crane* v. *Anthony, Robert and Henry Crane et al.*, 26 Feb. 1584. The plaintiff, Anne Crane, sued her husband because he excluded her from a right to the goods and chattels that she inherited.

75 **Coke . . .** *on Littleton*, 33a.

76 PRO, C 3/23/58, *Elizabeth Broughen als. Fillam* v. *Robert and Thomas Speckman, c.* 1572.

77 PRO, C 78/46/30, *same* v. *same*, 22 Oct. 1573.

wife had brought to the marriage.[78] The author of *Lawes Resolutions*, a late-Elizabethan treatise, criticized dower and advised the use of jointure as the more modern method for securing a woman's living:

> Ioyntures saith Dyer are made for the most part to Baron and Feme onely . . . and they are made . . . without consideration of money, bargaine or any thing saving for love and affection of the Baron and his ancestors, and these Iointures are present possession: But Dower must be tarried for till the Husband be dead: It must be demanded, sometime sued for, sometime neither with suit or demand obtained.[79]

Occasionally, a woman might have both dower and jointure. If jointure was made prior to the marriage, the common law bound the widow to accept it.[80] However, if it was made far in advance of the marriage, Chancery held that it was not binding.[81] Problems obviously arose when a choice was possible.[82]

Jointure defined precisely what estate belonged to the widow; nevertheless, quarrels between the widow and the heir frequently arose culminating in suits before Chancery.[83] At the request of her husband, Sir John Zouche, lady Eleanor had relinquished her jointure worth £600 annually to her son John, in return for a smaller estate of £300 yearly. When Sir John died, she began to receive her annual income. To help her son further, Eleanor granted more lands to him in return for an additional £100 yearly. Shortly after that the payments ceased because, John alleged, the mother owed him £400 from his father's estate. Lady Zouche sued in Chancery. The court conceded that Eleanor owed the money but deemed that that was insufficient cause to withhold her annuities. Accordingly, John had to pay the £400 annuity while Eleanor, in turn, must pay the sum owing from her husband's estate.[84]

It was not unusual for the husband to join with his relatives to undo his

[78] Christopher Clay, 'Marriage, inheritance and the rise of large estates in England, 1660–1815,' *Economic History Review*, 2nd series, XXI (1968), 509–18.

[79] T.E., *The Lawes Resolutions of Womens Rights*, Sects. 29 and 30, 182–3: *STC* 7437.

[80] Edward Coke, *The Institutes of the Laws of England* (London, 1628), IV, 1a: *Vernon's Case*.

[81] Cambridge University Library, MS Gg.2.5, fol. 429*v*., Michaelmas 38 & 39 Elizabeth I (1596): 'If jointure is made to a female infant as heir and after the marriage is celebrated the husband dies. The widow may wave the former and decide for dower upon condition in law, it was held in Chancery.'

[82] PRO, C 2/H8/45, *Matthewe Herbert* v. *Sir William Wynter & Anne Herbert et al.*, 30 May 1580.

[83] PRO, C 2/S7/56, *Elizabeth Snagge* v. *Thomas Snagge et al.*, 20 Jan. 1598; C 78/97/16, *same* v. *same*, 12 July 1599; C 2/S23/51, *Francis, Countess of Sussex* v. *Henry, Earl of Sussex et al.*, 9 Feb. 1586; C 2/B13/21, *Dame Eleanor Broome* v. *Henry, Lord Windsor*, 21 July 1589; C 2/T5/48, *Dorothie Tappe* v. *John Tappe*, 10 May 1590.

[84] PRO, C 78/85/9, *Lady Eleanor Zouche* v. *John Zouche*, 21 Oct. 1589.

wife of her estate. If father and son were joint tenants of lands involved in jointure, the estate would remain with the son at his father's death.[85] Another strategy affirmed, that the estate in which the widow thought she had jointure was copyhold rather than freehold.[86] Alternatively, because an entail could not be cut off to provide jointure, such a claim could negate the widow's estate.[87] In all such circumstances, the jointress could turn to Chancery and successfully secure the jointure against the heir.

Physical possession of evidences was at the crux of many problems. At common law, evidences concerning the reversioner's estate were usually allowed to be either in his hands or retained by the tenant for life under the stipulation that the documents could not be used to prejudice either estate. Numerous petitions before Chancery suggest how impractical this procedure was in cases involving jointure. As a result '. . . my Lord Chancellor will not order that the heyre shall haue the sight of this deed during the woman's life, lest thereby her Joincture be defeated.'[88] If different documents validated the separate holdings, the jointress could exhibit a bill to recover the evidences that were being withheld; whereupon, an order was given to deliver them to the court for safe-keeping. Once deposited, the documents could be seen by the heir only with permission from the jointress.[89] In certain cases, Chancery would permit the jointress to possess the evidences for her estate, rather than her husband's executors.[90]

Lord Chancellor Egerton was not immune from the problems that he adjudged in court. His third marriage to Alice, the dowager countess for Derby, brought him financial complications and legal anguish. Compounding the difficulties was the marriage of his son and heir, John, to one of the daughters of the countess. He expressed his worry that '. . . the ende of my lyfe, will be the begynninge of troubls to my Sonne . . . The questions which are lyke to growe . . . can be noe other But either my money . . . Or for her right or title of loynture or dower of my Landes.' To avert controversy Egerton put his entire estate, except Alice's joint-

85 PRO, C 78/17/18, *Dame Mary Fulleshurst* v. *Robert Fulleshurst*, 13 May 1560. The son was considered to have possession of the estate but he was ordered to pay the widow an annuity in recompense for her dower.

86 PRO, C 2/S24/55, *Margaret Saunder* v. *Thomas James*, 29 Oct. 1599.

87 PRO, C 2/B7/26, *Dame Katherine Baskervyle* v. *John Baskervyle*, Nov. 1573; C 78/49/12, *same* v. *same*, 6 May 1574.

88 Cambridge University Library, MS Gg.2.31, fol. 440, no. 31, n.d.

89 PRO, C 2 A6/65, *William Andrew & Jane his wife* v. *Anthony Gouson*, Feb. 1584; C 33/75, fol. 240, *Earl of Lincoln* v. *Elizabeth, Countess of Lincoln*, 30 Nov. 1587; C 33/76, fol. 224*v*., *same* v. *same*, 30 Nov. 1587.

90 PRO, C 78/77/13, *Dame Margaret, Viscountess Byndon* v. *Boxe, Burton & Mannynge*, 27 June 1587.

ure, in trust to the use of himself and his son.[91] Further, he increased her jointure by about £300 annually during their marriage.[92] These precautionary measures succeeded, and after his death the son *alias* son-in-law and stepmother coexisted peacefully.

Jointure was intended to provide the wife with a satisfactory living while protecting the heir's estate. Throughout the sixteenth century the practice of making a jointure estate grew and was refined. The common law furnished a procedure for securing the right of dower but provided no such remedy for attaining an estate of jointure. Unless a contract existed, the jointress had no recourse at the common law, a situation which was exacerbated as the popularity of jointure grew. Thus, women exhibited bills in Chancery for two different purposes: either to supplement an action at common law or for grievances not specifically provided for by the law. In both instances, equity attempted to define and secure the widow's estate. Such cases also increased the perception of women as financially responsible within society. Women were frequently appointed executrices and administratrices, two areas over which the Elizabethan Chancery broadened its jurisdiction. As personal representatives for estates, women held a vital office which imposed duties and responsibilities but bestowed powers and benefits.

VI

The role of executor came under the auspices of the ecclesiastical courts until the late thirteenth century when statutes allowed actions at the common law.[93] By the reign of Elizabeth the office conveyed upon an executor:

> the propertie of all his [the testator's] goods, chattles wardshipps of land and body extents of statutes, Iudgments recognizances, and all debts and specialties as bills, bonds and covenantes of debts . . . and all right concerninge these things the executors may meddle with the goods, dispose them before they prove the will, but they cannot bring any accon for any debt or duty belonginge unto there Testator before they have proved the will.[94]

An estate was administered when a person died intestate, when the will did not appoint an executor, or when the executor appointed refused the

[91] Huntington Library, MS Ellesmere 213: 'An unpleasant declaracon of thinges passed betwene the Countesse of Derby and me, since our marriage . . .,' 27 July 1611, fols. 2*v*., 4–5.

[92] Huntington Library, MS Ellesmere 214.

[93] Pollock and Maitland, *History of English Law*, II, 334–52; Jones, *Elizabethan Chancery*, 400–13.

[94] Cambridge University Library, MS Gg.1.35, fol. 44*v*.

charge. That title was effective from the date of grant from the ordinary of an ecclesiastical court, whereas an executor's authority stemmed from the will and was valid from the moment of the testator's death. After the administrator's duties were accomplished he could retain the residue of the estate.

By the mid-sixteenth century both positions entailed similar duties and responsibilities. In a case of intestacy, the law had singled out the widow as the most likely candidate to administer the estate and, likewise, the husband often named his wife to execute his will. When problems arose the courts offered solutions. Estates involved both ecclesiastical and common law jurisdictions, but Chancery could help personal representatives by auditing accounts,[95] helping to collect the evidences, and rendering the representatives blameless. Only in Chancery were executors allowed to sue each other. As a result of these provisions many testamentary cases came to Chancery for confirmation, clarity, and compassion.

For some the most immediate problem was to secure the position itself. Even when an executor had been named other family members might attempt to claim the position.[96] If credentials were questioned Chancery could verify the status and licence the executor to proceed with the necessary duties.[97] There were funeral expenses to be paid, debts satisfied and legacies distributed. The personal representative had no control over real property unless it was devised for purposes of administration or the land was charged with payment of debts. The personal estate was available for the settlement of debts and other liabilities. Debts during this period could involve the various courts attempting to extend their jurisdiction at the litigant's expense.[98] Creditors could pursue charges of alleged debt against the executor, claiming to have bonds and obligations due upon the estate. The personal representatives could be 'rendered harmless' if Chancery directed the defendants to accept a bond and promised not to take advantage of the executor or administrator.[99] No such protection was available at common law since no wrongdoing had occurred. Chancery also permitted executors to obtain protection against their fellow executors, whereas common law did not.[100] Equity perceived that co-

[95] PRO, C 3/190/24, *Jane Wall* v. *George Wall* (addressed to Bacon); C 78/33/36, *same* v. *same*, 21 June 1564.

[96] PRO, C 2/A1/33, *Richard Ashburye & Jane his wife* v. *Elyns Walwyn et al.*, 10 May 1568; C 2/14/48. *Robert Jacob and Hammett Jacob* v. *Mary Castell*, 28 Nov. 1601.

[97] PRO, C 33/85, fol. 29, *Alice Cottingham et al.* v. *Henry Hardward and Anne Hardward*, 10 Nov. 1593.

[98] Plucknett, *Concise History of the Common Law*, 638–48.

[99] *Choyce Cases in Chancery, 1557–1606. The English Reports, Chancery*, XXI (176 vols., London, Stevens & Sons, Ltd, 1900–30), I, 75: *Byard* v. *Byard*, 1578/9.

[100] Cambridge University Library, MS Gg.2.31, fol. 404*v*.

executors were also responsible to fulfill any promises or duties agreed between themselves.[101] Further, if executors assumed the office and then changed their minds, the co-executors had recourse in Chancery to protect themselves and to determine the terms of withdrawal.[102]

Above all, Chancery helped the executrix and administratrix to maintain a secure position *vis-à-vis* the heir. Even though the heir had possession of the real estate, the representative controlled the chattels and leases and held all documents for the settlement of the estate. By equating a lease with a chattel and thereby allowing it to pass with the remainder of the testator's estate to the executrix, Chancery began fostering the idea of the precedency of an executor over the heir.[103] Indeed, the remainder of the personal estate residing in the personal representative was an attraction of the office; it supplemented the dower or jointure of the widow holding that position.[104]

The office of personal representative could be a lifetime commitment, as with the executrixship of Anne Gresham. Anne, the daughter of William Ferneley, citizen of London, married William Read, a Suffolk gentleman. Read died in 1544 leaving an estate worth £138 15s. 4d. yearly.[105] Within the year she married Thomas Gresham, a privy councillor, founder of the Royal Exchange, and popularly remembered for 'Gresham's Law.' Their son had died, and in 1579 Gresham himself died, leaving Anne with a clear income of £2388 10s. 6½d. yearly. Anne was his sole executrix and for the next sixteen years she occupied herself with accomplishing the will and consolidating the new estate.[106] Gresham's will, confirmed by a private act in parliament, listed lands and profits and then established the position of the heir, Henry Nevill, son of Sir Henry Nevill. It specified that Gresham's debts were to be satisfied by Easter term 1583, and thereafter a commission would sell lands to settle any outstanding debts and legacies.

As could often happen controversy developed, here concerning copyhold lands in the estate. Gregory Fiennes, lord Dacre, threatened to sue Anne on charges of trespass and waste; she went to Chancery alleging

[101] PRO, C 78/17/11, *Jane, Countess of Southampton* v. *Sir William Stamford and Roger Potter*, 7 Feb. 1560. It was ordered that the defendants (co-executors of the plaintiff) deliver bonds to the countess to render her harmless.

[102] PRO, C 2/S11/60, *Edward Stanhope, Michael Stanhope et al.* v. *Dame Margaret Stanhope*, *c.* 1596.

[103] Jones, *Elizabethan Chancery*, 401; C 78/91/7, *George Rotheram* v. *Anne Rotheram et al.*

[104] PRO, C 3/5/99, *Mary Askryge* v. *Raphell Symonds and Edward Arden* (addressed to Bacon); C 78/32/21, *same* v. *same*, 29 Oct. 1565.

[105] John W. Burgon, *The Life and Times of Sir Thomas Gresham* (2 vols., London, E. Wilson, 1839), I, 49–52.

[106] *Ibid.*, II, 488, 490.

that the seizure of her lands for non-payment of rent encroached upon her right within her own manor.[107] Chancery decreed that upon payment of £20 to Dacre, Anne should be readmitted to the premises and that he was to pay her £10 for the trouble he had caused. An uneasy peace ensued for some years, until Dacre presented a bill in Chancery charging Anne with about thirty counts of encroachment, trespass, and waste.[108] She countered that his charges were matters for common law and challenged him to sue her there. No further action has been recorded in that matter, but Anne was sued at common law by another, claiming a £400 sum on a bond that she was declared to have forfeited. She obtained a Chancery injunction to stay the proceedings at the common law, and a further order declaring the principal to be only £200.[109]

Anne, like many personal representatives, had difficulty obtaining the evidences pertaining to the deceased's estate. She presented bills against several stewards of the Gresham manors for the court rolls and other necessary documents, secured the evidences, and became actively involved in management of the manors. For example, she decided that the tenant holding one of the Yorkshire manors was paying too low a rent, so she demanded and secured verbal agreement doubling the rent. When the tenant defaulted Anne sued in Chancery despite lack of witnesses and evidences.[110] The court decreed that the tenant pay the old rent to date and a fine covering the remainder of his term as previously agreed.[111] After further default Anne petitioned Chancery, which iterated the decision and arranged a lease in return for further payment.[112]

The private act of parliament confirming the agreement between the executrix and heir for the payment of Gresham's debts had become a source of difficulty. Lands to be sold to pay estate debts included manors in Brecon, except for the land in which William Vaughan had an estate. Inevitably, both claimed the same land. Vaughan attempted to bring two assizes against Anne but no trial resulted. Anne went to the Court of Wards on the premise that the lands belonged to the heir, still a minor, but this was dismissed to common law. Anne did not proceed, choosing instead to lease the lands to an officer of the Exchequer who brought an action against Vaughan in that court. Delays there resulted in a non-suit.

[107] PRO, C 78/53/15, *Lady Anne Gresham* v. *Gregory Fynes, Lord Dacre*, 1585; C 33/69, fol. 340, 28 Jan. 1585.

[108] PRO, C 2/D12/48, *Gregory Fynes, Lord Dacre* v. *Lady Anne Gresham*, 1 Apr. 1591.

[109] BL, MS Hargrave 160, fol. 109, *Lady Anne Gresham* v. *Thomas Andrewes and John Barnard*, 30 Oct. 23 & 24 Elizabeth I (1581–2).

[110] PRO, C 2/G13/40, *Dame Anne Gresham* v. *George Creswell*, 23 Jan. 1584.

[111] PRO, C 33/76, fols. 434*r.–v.*, *same* v. *same*, 20 Jan. 1588.

[112] PRO, C 78/82/1, *same* v. *same*, 25 Nov. 1589.

Meanwhile, pressure mounted on Anne to satisfy her husband's debts. To settle the matter she presented a bill in Chancery in 1584 against the sisters and co-heirs of Vaughan and their husbands, alleging that they wrongfully entered her manors and detained evidences.[113] All in all, Anne's office as executrix had brought her into the Elizabethan Chancery so often during the sixteen years after Sir Thomas's death that she might have been considered a regular customer.

VII

From the mid-sixteenth century such jousting within and between law courts served to extend jurisdictions, especially increasing participation of Chancery in testamentary cases. That general area of inheritance specifically affected and involved females, and Chancery accordingly made itself accommodating. It was less formidable and less expensive than common law courts and perhaps less moralizing than spiritual courts. In successive actions, the executrix and administratrix seemed to mature in their role: as they brought problems before Chancery and received remedy, their confidence and litigiousness increased. Women found that Chancery litigation could be lucrative, it afforded authority, control, and security.

Equity guarded the Elizabethan widow where common law too often faltered, and it was left to Chancery to begin according female litigants recognition as responsible individuals. The majority of suits involving female litigants concerned their need to be assured of present or future security in estates and chattels. This desire for security was not new, but taken in the context of developments during the reign of Elizabeth, it brought judicial and social innovations. The unquestioned improvements in the status of propertied women, which are so marked a feature of English society in the seventeenth and eighteenth centuries, rested upon the consideration given to their needs by the Elizabethan Chancery.

[113] PRO, C 2/G15/26, *Dame Anne Gresham* v. *Rowland Vaughan et al.*, 14 July 1594.

Too good to be true: Thomas Lupton's Golden Rule

ELLIOT ROSE

It is natural to seek the mind of an age through the writings of its greatest men. It may be as informative to read the little men, the hacks, who took the stamp of their age rather than putting their mark on it. Derivative writers are most useful for this perspective, but the more creative writers, too, sometimes compete with the lesser in writing to please the public or to curry favor. It is a questionable advantage to have one's works revealing too low and ignoble a view of human nature, but if our concern is to define an era's attitude to crime and punishment, then the low, ignoble view is one that must be heard. And who so well qualified to express that view as Thomas Lupton?

The average educated person would hardly think of Lupton as the first writer to compose, in English, a dialogue describing an ideal commonwealth under a name that means 'Nowhere.' There is, however, no other candidate, apart from Ralph Robinson who translated More's *Utopia* in 1551 and, setting trick questions aside, Lupton at least seems to have the honor of being the first English imitator of More, and about the first in any language. His commonwealth is called 'Mauqsun' (More himself had tentatively used 'Nusquama' at one point),[1] and is described in his book *Too Good to be True* whose two parts appeared in 1580 and 1581.[2] Both parts are overwhelmingly concerned with the single problem

[1] Frank E. and Fritzie P. Manuel, *Utopian Thought in the Western World* (Cambridge, Mass., Harvard University Press, 1979), 1.

[2] *Too Good to be True* is clearly what Thomas Lupton meant his book to be called, but on the title page it appeared thus:

Siuquila: Too good, to be true
Omen: Though so at a vewe. . . .

and this consequently is how it appears in *STC* 16951 (London, H. Bynneman, 1580). Incidentally, Lupton throughout uses the feeble antithesis, 'Too evil to be false' to describe his description of Ailgna.

Part II appeared as *The second part and knitting up of the Boke entituled Too good to be true*: Wherein is continued the discourse of the wonderfull Lawes, commendable customes, & strange manners of the people of Mauqsun: *STC* 16954 (London, H. Binneman, 1581).

of how best to punish offenders: the same problem which was the starting point – but only the starting point – of More's dialogue.

I

About Lupton personally we know almost nothing except what can be inferred from his writings. Of these there was one brief flowering, from 1578 to 1583, after which he either died or got the appointment he was angling for, and so disappeared from the historical record. In that time his productions, and his choices of patron, were quite varied. *All for Money*, in 1578, was a play of the traditional 'interlude' type and undedicated.[3] *A Thousand Notable Things of Sundry Sortes* (1579), a compendium of household hints, quack remedies and superstitions compiled quite uncritically from printed sources, was dedicated to Margaret Clifford, countess of Derby, who may have been a kindred spirit. She would otherwise be a singularly inept choice of patron, for by the end of the year she was out of favor, under arrest and in debt. The countess was Elizabeth's cousin on the Suffolk side and had the dubious honor of being the last person named in Edward VI's Devise for the Crown; as if this was not enough, she had one son and an interest in astrology. Perhaps she had been casting the wrong people's horoscopes, but in any case she was in no position to help Lupton. The book, however, was his most successful, and at least the printers did well out of it. It was last reprinted in 1793.[4]

Too Good to be True (pt I, 1580) was dedicated to Christopher Hatton, again a more or less penniless patron but very much the rising star at court. *The second part and knitting up of the Boke entituled Too good to be true* (1581) was dedicated to William Cecil. Also in 1581, *A Persuasion from Papistrie*, although addressed to the Recusants (who it proved were

[3] *A Moral and pitieful comedie, Intituled, All for Money*: *STC* 16949 (London, R. Ward & R. Mundee, 1578); John S. Farmer (ed.), *The Tudor Facsimile Texts*, XLVI (London, 1910).

[4] *STC* 16955 (London, J. Charlwood, 1579). The book is described in the *DNB*, XXXIV, 287–8: Thomas Lupton. His main acknowledged source was 'Mizaldus.' For the misfortune of Margaret Clifford, *APC, 1578–80*, 316–17: 23 Nov. 1579 and 12 Mar. 1579/80. The Privy Council requested the lord mayor to 'use good means' with the countess' creditors until the queen allows her her liberty. William Camden, *The History of . . . Elizabeth, Late Queen of England*, ed. by Wallace T. MacCaffrey (Chicago, The University of Chicago Press, 1970), 529; this is the 1688 edn of *Annales Rerum Anglicarum et Hibernicarum Regnante Elizabetha*. Camden records that . . .

> out of her womanish Fancy and curiosity consulting
> with Wizards and Cunning men with a vain Credulity
> and out of I know not what ambitious Hope, did in a
> manner lose the Queen's Favour.

In her will she left her son 'my table with the 12 signs to it.' I am indebted for these references to the kindness of Ms Norah Fuidge.

'English Enimies, and extreme Enimies to England'), was dedicated to the queen herself.[5] It drew some passing attention from Father Robert Parsons in his attack on the renegade John Nicholls, *A Discoverie of I. Nicolls Minister*, which allowed Lupton to reply in 1582 with *The Christian against the Jesuits* (Parsons's tract was anonymous, so 'Jesuit' was a lucky guess).[6] The dedication was to Francis Walsingham. Lastly, Lupton returned to the subject of avarice with *A Dreame of the Devill and Dives* (1583), dedicated to Francis Russell, earl of Bedford, who was perhaps moved by it to relieve the poverty of its author, for we hear no more of him.[7]

II

Even from this we can see that Lupton was one – not by any means the only one – who expected credit and reward for denouncing things, like greed and popery, that everyone was against. Such credit and reward were only likely to be forthcoming if he attacked his tired old targets in a new and interesting way, or could put forward original remedies for old abuses. If Lupton ever did this he did it in *Too Good to be True*. In this, the admirable institutions of Mauqsun are described in a dialogue between a citizen, Omen, and one Siuqila, a traveller from Ailgna. Siuqila, sickened by the moral depravity of his own country, has searched the world for a better. When he finds it, its careful laws do not allow any stranger to enter, so he has to be content with Omen's description when they meet at the border. We might just as well call him Notpul; for the game of backward spelling adds proof that there is nothing of More's subtlety or ambiguity here. *Too Good to be True*, despite its title, is clearly intended to impress as a model for real reforms: in the language of the day, a 'platform.' This is the whole purpose of the book. Despite a promise of 'strange manners' on the title page of part II the reader is not entertained with any bizarre travellers' tales outside the context of law enforcement. Lupton shows no sign of technical legal knowledge and, indeed, little as we know about him it is pretty safe to say he was no lawyer. He shows the conventional distrust for lawyers, yet Mauqsun relies on a wholly profes-

5 *A Persuasion from Papistrie* Written chiefly to the obstinate, determined, and disobedient English Papists, who are herein named and proven English Enimies, and extreme Enimies to England: *STC* 16950 (London, H. Bynneman, 1581).

6 For the renegade, and the occasion of Parsons's attack, see *DNB*, XL, 441–3: John Nicholls. He was a fugitive from the English College in Rome, and at that moment (he returned to the Roman Church later) a much more dangerous anti-Catholic than Lupton, who merely happened to produce his pamphlet at the right time to attract Parsons's notice.

7 He may be the T.L. who published *Babylon is Fallen*, a millenarian prediction: *STC* 15111 (London, E. Allde, 1597); see Bernard S. Capp, *The Fifth Monarchy Men: A Study in Seventeenth Century English Millenarianism* (London, Faber, 1972), 26, fn 8.

sional judiciary, and he does not appear to realize what a massive change in the institutions of the actual Ailgna it would take to imitate such a system.

Lupton deals with problems of crime, sin and vagrancy, but apart from sin – he may, for all we know, have been a clergyman – he deals with them as an amateur, the concerned Elizabethan in the street, and that is where his significance lies. Naturally some of his concerns were shared by people with more qualification to speak as experts. Where their attitudes sharply differed from his, however, this may sometimes be because of differences of temperament rather than expertise. It may be well to review attitudes on one central question before we return to Mauqsun. The question is the role of severity of punishment in the repressing of crime.

Sir Thomas Smith, in *De Republica Anglorum*, commented on the mildness, as he saw it, of the English penal code:

> For any felonie, manslaughter, robberie, murther, rape, and such capitall crimes as touch not treason and *laesam maiestatem*, we have by the Lawe of England no other punishment, but to hang till they be dead . . . Heading, tormenting, demembring, either arme or legge, breaking upon the wheele, empailing, and such cruel torments, as be used in other nations by the order of their law, we have not; yet as few murthers commited as any where: nor it is not in the Judges or the Justices power, to aggravate or mitigate the punishment of the Lawe, but in the Prince onely and his privie Counsell, which is marvellous seldom done.[8]

Smith went on to qualify his statement, with such legal curiosities as the special penalty (boiling to death) for murder by poison, and to discuss the absence of judicial torture from English criminal procedure. His argument on this, which echoes Fortescue's *De Laudibus Legum Angliae*,[9] does not quite fit with his views on punishment. The freeborn Englishman, it would seem, had a particularly rooted objection to being tortured, whereas he hardly minded being killed, and would therefore be much too ready to confess. Fortescue had supposed this a universal human trait. If Smith was right, it is hard to see why Englishmen could be adequately deterred from crime by simple hanging, but Smith plainly thought this was so and that the lack of cruel torments, either in judicial process or in punishment, was to England's credit.

By contrast Sir Thomas More, or at any rate his mouthpiece Raphael Hythlodaeus, had argued that the English law of simple hanging for all

[8] Thomas Smith, *De Republica Anglorum*. *STC* 22857 (London, H. Midleton, 1583); a facsimile edn (Menston, Yorks., Scolar Press, 1970), 84ff.; and the standard edn by Leonard Alston (Cambridge, CUP, 1906). Smith's work, begun in the 1560s, was printed posthumously but had a considerable circulation in MS earlier.

[9] Fortescue denounces the use of judicial torture, especially in France, in his chapter 22. He does not discuss punishments: John Fortescue, *De Laudibus Legum Angliae*, ed. by Stanley B. Chrimes (Cambridge, CUP, 1942).

felonies alike was an inadequate deterrent for theft and a positive inducement to murder. The main argument in book I of *Utopia* takes its starting point from the observation that thieves were hanged in England with admirable zeal and regularity – lax enforcement of the law was not a problem – yet thieving continued. The law, according to Hythlodaeus, was too severe to be effective, although English lawyers stubbornly went on praising it on patriotic grounds. Before he ever got to Utopia proper he expounded the good customs of the Polylerites, who subjected their thieves to forced labor rather than death, with excellent results. His host, Cardinal Morton, thought this would be suitable treatment for vagabonds.[10]

Hythlodaeus was a spreader of idle tales: the Polylerites were a people of whom many lies were told and the name 'Utopia,' as well as More's own name when latinized to 'Morus,' contained conscious ambiguities.[11] We can never be sure how far Hythlodaeus speaks for the real More. But this is probably the single point in the whole fantasy when he comes closest to doing so. On the futility of hanging for theft, as on the need for attacking the root causes of theft, More's argument, though placed in another man's mouth, is too strongly worded not to involve More. This has to be what he really meant. (We may note, for whatever its evidential value, that this is regularly assumed whenever the passage on the causes of poverty is quoted.) More thought, then, that the English law was efficiently administered but failed to produce its desired effect because the punishments it laid down were too severe.

In this, surely, More was in a minority in his century and Hythlodaeus' fellow guests at the Cardinal's table were more typical and were meant to sound that way. Few would think that the laws of England were too severe. It was more patriotic to think that they were exactly severe enough, whether you chose to emphasize the contrast with foreigners who were more ferocious, as Smith did, or with foreigners who were more culpably lax. This I suppose was the point John Lyly made in *Euphues his England*, where the country that supplied his primary contrast was Italy but where there is no reason to suppose that his information about Italy was sound:

[10] Editions of *Utopia* are too numerous for a reference to be helpful, but this argument occupies the whole second half of Book I. The edition I consulted was the one edited by, strangely enough, Joseph H. Lupton (ed.), *The Utopia of Sir Thomas More* (Oxford, The Clarendon Press, 1895).

[11] These are the likeliest intended meanings of 'Hythlodaeus' and 'Polylerites'; 'Utopia' from More's time to our own has been capable of meaning 'Nowhere' or 'The Good Place.' More used 'Eutopia' in his prefatory notes, and this sense is of course presumed in the modern coinage 'dystopia.' 'Morus' meaning 'foolish' was a standing joke between him and Erasmus, as was Erasmus' own name, 'darling.'

Murtherers & thieves are hanged, witches burnt, al other villanies that deserve death punshed w^{t} death, insomuch that there are very fewe haynous offences practised in respecte of those that in other countries are commonly used.[12]

Lyly's statement about witches would seem to be wrong; at this date (1580) witchcraft, if used to compass a death, was ordinary felony, a hanging offense like theft. Other witchcraft was misdemeanor, a much commoner charge.[13] Lyly in fact exaggerated the severity of English law, as Smith somewhat exaggerated its mildness (there were cruel punishments he omitted to mention, and there sometimes was a little judicial torture).[14] It is hard to compare the two because Smith had more to say, and almost certainly knew more about the law, but plainly Lyly and Smith made different assumptions about what was creditable to a nation when praising the same nation in these opposite ways. One point to remember is that Smith, whose book did not see print in his lifetime, was not writing to please anybody in particular, whereas Lyly was seeking, very openly, to ingratiate himself with William Cecil,[15] and may have affected for the occasion attitudes and judgments that were not so much his own as Cecil's, or what he imputed to Cecil.

We get a perspective on Cecil's views from *The Execution of Justice in England*, published in 1583.[16] Lyly may have known the substance of this work earlier and had many means of forming an opinion about Cecil's views. The book dealt with only one aspect of the execution of justice, namely its execution against Catholic missionary priests, and it is generally regarded as a propagandistic work of arrant hypocrisy. For our

[12] John Lyly, *Euphues his England*: *STC* 17051 (London, J. Cawood, 1578); see, *The Complete Works of John Lyly*, ed. by Richard W. Bond (3 vols., Oxford, The Clarendon Press, 1902), II, 195, entitled 'Euphues' Glass for Europe.'

[13] Witches may have been burnt sometimes, legally or illegally. It would be legal if the offense was regarded as heresy or apostasy, but this was common on the continent and seems not to have happened in England. If witchcraft was used to cause the death of a husband or employer it would be petty treason, for which women were burnt as Smith duly notes in the passage cited above, n. 7. On the frequency of the misdemeanor, see Alan Macfarlane, *Witchcraft in Tudor and Stuart England: A Regional and Comparative Study* (London, Routledge & Kegan Paul, 1970), ch. 3.

[14] He did not mention hanging, drawing and quartering. On the occasional, and essentially extra-legal, use of torture in England, see John H. Langbein, *Torture and the Law of Proof: Europe and England in the Ancient Regime* (Chicago, The University of Chicago Press, 1977) who lists all the known cases in an appendix. At this period the victims were mostly Catholic missionaries.

[15] The book was dedicated to the earl of Oxford, Lyly's patron at the time, but it contains fulsome flattery of 'Burleigh,' uniquely given his own name unclassicized: Lyly, *Works*, II, 198.

[16] [Anon.], *The Execution of Justice in England*: *STC* 4902 (London, [C. Barker], 1583); it is never ascribed other than to William Cecil; reprinted, with William Allen's *Defense of English Catholics*, ed. by Robert M. Kingdon (Ithaca, N.Y., Cornell University Press for the Folger Shakespeare Library, 1965).

present purposes that is no disadvantage. It suited Cecil to maintain that the execution of justice, on these priests, was mild; and while he had to admit that they were tortured, they were only tortured reluctantly, as a last resort, and rightly considered it was all their own fault anyway. Cecil's concern was to urge that English justice was good and not too severe. Lyly evidently expected Cecil to be pleased with a suggestion that English justice was good and not too mild. The two positive statements concurred and the two negatives did not conflict.

Smith claimed for English justice that it was effective and therefore was to be commended for not being needlessly harsh. More, writing fifty years earlier but on broadly the same facts, claimed that it was needlessly harsh and consequently ineffective. All these, with the partial exception of Cecil who was only writing about part of the subject, agreed that English law was administered firmly, in a consistent and uncapricious way. They all take for granted that those criminals in England who were supposed to die by the law, by and large did die. This may have been truer in the sixteenth century than it would be in the eighteenth, but it was less than wholly true. An educated mind could entertain the notion that the law was laxly administered and the further notion that its penalties ought to be made more severe.

III

By the 1580s it is tempting, and to be avoided, to pin the name 'Puritan' on anybody who expressed such feelings. Puritans certainly held generally that virtuous behavior ought to be enforced. Their leading spokesmen invoked the Mosaic death penalty for adultery and blasphemy.[17] Puritans, however, did not mainly rely on a freer use of the gallows, and they were not alone in deploring the laxity of the age. It was a time when moral censoriousness was in fashion and could be adopted by people who had nothing of the true Puritan about them, people whose apparent motive was to curry favor with great men in government. Lyly was one example and so, in all probability, was Thomas Lupton.

Lupton was no Puritan in any useful sense of the word. In 1580 the fact that he dedicated his book to Hatton, later an active enemy to Puritans, was perhaps not conclusive, but on religious questions he was content to

[17] Notably Thomas Cartwright (who also urged it for incest), *A Reply to an Answere made of M. Doctor Whitgift agaynste the Admonition to the Parliament*: *STC* 4711 (London, *c.* 1574), 22. Clive S. Lewis, *English Literature in the Sixteenth Century, Excluding Drama,* The Oxford History of English Literature, III (Oxford, The Clarendon Press, 1954), 445–9, quoted this passage but curiously omitted to mention adultery in a discussion of Cartwright which is, as a whole, interesting to our subject.

give thanks that Ailgna enjoyed the liberty of the Gospel, and there was never a word of criticism of the Elizabethan settlement or ceremonies or bishops. He was a moral rigorist; he relied heavily on punishment to make people better and thought it should follow automatically on every offense, using the utmost ingenuity in making it fit the crime. This the laws of Mauqsun were designed to achieve. By contrast, the laws of Ailgna are likened to a cobweb, which the 'humble bee' breaks, though small flies are caught in it.[18] This makes it sound as though Siuqila–Notpul was more worried about the wrongdoings of the rich than of the poor. Actually he seems less interested in the poor, but he also seems to think that where common rogues and vagabonds are concerned the laws of Ailgna are harsh enough, and harshly enough administered, to satisfy anybody:

(*Omen*) What, have you no lawes to bridle them?
(*Siuqila*) Yes, the ydle roages are burned throughe the eares, and if they be taken after a roaging, they are hanged.
(*Omen*) Then you are sure that they will roag no more . . .[19]

Where enforcement is lacking is in providing work:

(*S.*) We have verye good statutes ordayned for them both, but if the statute for the sayde provision were as well prosecuted, as the statute for punishing of roages in some places is executed, then godly exercise shoulde be more used.[20]

Here at least Notpul broadly approves of the law of Ailgna. He may have slightly misunderstood what it said. The Act against Vagabonds of 1572 did make 'a roguing trade of life' felony for the second offense, but not automatically; it laid down the death penalty for a fourth offense of 'roguing' plus two offenses of breaking the conditions of pardon. The amending act of 1576 made this clause obsolete and did not mention death; it made it easier for a vagabond to become a felon, but still contemplated that the same vagabond could be convicted of this felony an indefinite number of times.[21] All this is very different from the picture Siuqila drew for Omen and illustrates the gap that could yawn in practice, even here in the mind of the legislator, between the assizes and the gallows.

On the treatment of the poor, Notpul draws no lessons from Mauqsun. He cannot; for in Mauqsun everybody is so charitable that there scarcely are any poor, although 'the poor' are always present as a convenient category of people to be done good to, and law after law imposes some form of alms-giving as a penalty. Herein Mauqsun sounds old-fashioned, and less modern than Ailgna where:

[18] Lupton, *Too Good to be True*, pt I, 9. [19] *Ibid.*, 33–4. [20] *Ibid.*, 34.
[21] 14 Elizabeth I, c. 6: *SR*, IV, pt I, 598–9; 18 Elizabeth I, c. 3: *ibid.*, 610–13.

(*S*.) Of all other people with us, the pore is the moste out of frame, especiallye the beggars, for they seldome or never come to the Church, neither heare the worde of God: whereby they are given to suche ydlenesse, drunkennesse, fighting, brauling, swearing, cursing, and most ungodlye living, that it greeves me to consider theyre estate.[22]

With this kind of attitude it is not surprising that *Too Good to be True* puts more emphasis than *Utopia* had done on crime and punishment, and less on 'Commonwealth matters.' In Utopia, of course, there were no unemployed, but in *Utopia*, the book, there was the suggestion that vagabonds should be treated the way the Polylerites treated thieves. It must be remembered that the suggestion was put in the mouth of Cardinal Morton and praised by his yes-men, not by Morus or Hythlodaeus. It could well have been praised by Notpul, had he been there.

Before coming to crime and punishment, one detail of 'Commonwealth matters' may be mentioned for the incidental light it casts on our author's view of his world. In economic affairs generally it is hard to draw lessons from Mauqsun that were applicable to Ailgna, since Mauqsun never suffered the sixteenth century price rise; the level of rents and of prices has remained stable for four or five thousand years.[23] But even Mauqsun has experienced economic change. Apparently recent to the time of the dialogue, the entire agricultural population, landlords and tenants alike, became convinced of the advantage of enclosures – that is, of converting champion ground and commons to several. Landlords divided the land with the consent of the tenants and normally bore the whole cost of ditching and quicksetting (where the lord's own share was a small one this cost was undertaken by the tenants, excluding the poor cottagers); a twentieth of all the land was reserved for previously landless cottagers, and even after that, every tenant's allotment was enough to feed twice as much stock as his old stint on the common. Everybody, lord and tenant, ended up richer than before.[24] Naturally in happy Mauqsun nobody was charged a higher rent as a result. Rents are never raised, and all tenants have the right to renew at a fine certain of one year's rent. There are no boondays or labor services.[25] Such fortunate tenants have no need to raise prices in the market; even natural calamities pass them by.

(O.) Nay we know not what scarcitie doth mean: for God doth so blesse the grounds, of our godlye and contented Landlords, that we never have but great aboundance of corne, victual, and other necessaries.[26]

[22] Lupton, *Too Good to be True*, pt I, 33.
[23] *Ibid.*, pt II, sig. I.i (*verso*). [24] *Ibid.*, sig. I.iv (*verso*) – K.iii (*verso*).
[25] *Ibid.*, sigs. E.iii, I.iii. [26] *Ibid.*, sig. E.ii.

Such fairyland economics might seem to belie what was earlier said about travellers' tales, but corroboration comes from Ailgna of all places. When Siuqila comes to think of it,

(*S.*) We have had likewise such a continuall plenty since we received the Gospel, that I believe our Country never tasted the like so long togither.

However, the happy relationship between landlord and tenant in Mauqsun is guaranteed by heavily punishing those who would seek to upset it. Any who offers to take another man's farm for higher rent or higher fine loses the bargain and a quarter of his goods, actually a mild penalty by local standards.[27]

This policy, it appears throughout, is the secret of Mauqsun's prosperity: there is a punishment for everything, and it is swift, automatic and inevitable. Omen stresses again and again that pardon is unknown. After explaining that the penalty for swearing is, for a first offense, admonition by a minister, for a second, a year's exile from a man's own house, and for a third, cutting out the tongue, he draws the moral:

(*O.*) Surely it is for wante of punishing of offendours, that you have so many offendors: and bycause we punishe withoute pardon, we have no swearers to crave pardon.[28]

Because they punish without pardon, it is somewhat unexpected that the Golden Rule is the foundation of their law:

(*O.*) *Whatsoever you woulde that men shoulde doe to you, even so do yee to them:* This sentence is painted on the postes of oure houses: and there is such a straighte Lawe with us, for the doing according to this saying, that if they folowe it not for the love of Christe, they dare not breake it for feare of the penaltie that belongeth to it.
(*S.*) How is that?
(*O.*) Forsooth as they do, they shall be done unto.[29]

In this version of the rule, not only is Mrs Bedonebyasyoudid considerably more prominent than Mrs Doasyouwouldbedoneby,[30] but it turns out that the law always demands something more than the simple eye for an eye or tooth for a tooth.

Omen illustrates the principle by a story of a rich man who refused to relieve a poor man; his clothes were given to the poor man and he was compelled to sit in the street all day in rags like a beggar, but not begging because all were forbidden to give him anything.[31] Such an order might give rise, among the general public, to some confusion about what the Golden Rule required of them. Omen had another story of a grasping

[27] *Ibid.*, sig. E.iii. [28] *Ibid.*, pt I, 78. [29] *Ibid.*, 31–2.
[30] Charles Kingsley, *The Water Babies* (London, Macmillan, 1863), ch. 5.
[31] Lupton, *Too Good to be True*, pt I, 32.

surgeon, who had to restore four times his extorted fee and then have other surgeons wound him and mistreat the hurt, which might be a problem for the other surgeons. There are many such stories, invoking the rule as a reason for inventing a punishment, and from them one would certainly not have gathered that the people of Mauqsun were as profoundly moved by the Gospel, as loving in their mutual dealings, and as complete strangers to vice and self-seeking, as Omen represents them. It would be tedious to multiply examples, and the stories themselves are tedious enough. I have no doubt Lupton thought of them as light relief, helping down the dry doctrine.

At an early stage Omen comments on what he has learned of Ailgna:

> (*O*.) I perceyve that you have many good lawes, and evill kept: but we have but fewe, and verye well kepte.[32]

I am not sure how far Notpul wished to commit himself to the view that the laws of Ailgna are, on paper, good ones, but it is astonishing to be told that the laws of Mauqsun are few. There is, indeed, a story in the Talmud of a proselyte who asked the great Hillel to teach him the entire Mosaic code while he stood on one leg. Hillel taught him: 'Never do to others what you would not wish them to do to you,' and explained that that was the whole of the Law; everything else was commentary on it.[33] No doubt in Lupton's mind the same held good of his code, but the principle is capable of infinite extension and its detailed application acquires an intricacy which we may suspect the author enjoyed for its own sake.

IV

It follows logically enough from the principle that there is virtually no relationship in human life too intimate, or too casual, to be brought under the control of law. Thus, the laws of Mauqsun regulate family life, punishing disobedient wives, brutal husbands, and parents who neglect to discipline their children. Between mere acquaintances there is a punishment for ingratitude. The regulation of the family is not so strange an idea as it may sound; Lupton is only seeking to have the state wield a power that many a reformed church tried to exercise and which was often usurped by the neighbors or the young men of the parish. Part of the intention is to suppress the disorder of Skimington Ride or *Charivari*.[34] Still, the power

32 *Ibid.*, 34.
33 Tractate *Shabbath* 31a; quoted in Abraham Cohen, *Everyman's Talmud* (New York, E. P. Dutton, 1949), 65.
34 For the *Charivari*, see Natalie Zemon Davis, 'The reasons of misrule: youth groups and charivaris in sixteenth-century France,' *Past and Prersent*, L (1971), 41–75.

assigned to the magistrate in such affairs is pretty sweeping. After a husband has failed to bring his wife to obedience by peaceful persuasion, the minister of religion is to try; after that, the magistrate will order her to wear a special ignominious dress and release her husband from all obligation to maintain her until she becomes obedient.[35] The husband has no right to enforce obedience by blows; if he should try, he is publicly beaten by the wives of four other men.[36] If a wife should beat her husband she is paraded on horseback through the town in her husband's clothes and then imprisoned for a month.[37] The principle of doing as you would be done by is less apparent here than the borrowing from traditional village rough justice.

Normally, of course, the wives of Mauqsun need no such sanctions. Their obedience is total, and their modesty such that they scarcely go out of the house except to church and market. When they go out, women of all classes wear a long linen mantle to the ground, which hides the face.[38] At home, they keep strict rule over servants and children; every child is put to some useful work at the earliest possible age and must be able to 'read or say' the Lord's Prayer and the Creed by the age of five. Omen is incredulous to hear how parents in Ailgna, 'especially the poorer sort,' spoil their children:

(*O.*) Have you not a lawe for the punishing of the Father that so brings up his children?
(*S.*) No truely.
(*O.*) Then we have. . .[39]

and an elaborate law it is: so elaborate as to suggest, in any but an imaginary country, that the problem was a serious one. If any child of five cannot say the Lord's Prayer and Creed, or any other child is 'ignorantly, rudely or disobedientlye brought up,' the rich father must pay for his own children's education in a special institution and for an equal number of poor men's children; and if poor, the father

(*O.*) . . . shall receyve twentie stripes, every moneth once, untill he have trayned hys children Christianlye and obedientlye, according to the order of our Country.[40]

Children who are disobedient to parents are bound apprentice, if under twenty, 'with such maisters as be able and will rule them,' and they become slaves to the King for life if they run away. If over twenty (to omit a few complications) they lose their inheritance if there is one, and

[35] Lupton, *Too Good to be True*, pt I, 46. [36] *Ibid.*, 47.
[37] *Ibid.*, 49–50. Siuqila claims that in the form of *charivari* used in Ailgna in such cases, a neighbor is made to ride around the town in place of the wife.
[38] *Ibid.*, 60. [39] *Ibid.*, 37–8. [40] *Ibid.*, 38.

their parents are forbidden to give them anything on pain of loss of all property. If there is no inheritance to be forfeited,

(*Q*.) they receyve on theyr bare skin thirtie stripes with a whip 30 days together.[41]

Both parties to adultery are stoned to death; Siuqila comments approvingly that this allows the wronged spouses to remarry.[42] If an unmarried girl was ever to have a baby, Omen is confident that she would be lynched by angry virgins: for once this seems to be his guess in an unheard-of case.[43] In the one case of simple fornication between unmarrieds, they were made to marry after wearing goatskin for a year.[44]

On ingratitude there is of course no law of Ailgna with which that of Mauqsun could be compared. Siuqila rightly guesses there is one, though Omen has forgotten it:

(*S*.) I pray you, Sir, (if I may be so bold to aske you) howe are unthankfull or Ingrate persons used wyth you?
(*O*.) I can not wel tel you how, for we have never an unthankful or ingrate person in al our Countrey.[45]

But after a story about ingratitude in Ailgna it comes back to him:

(*O*.) If such a one were handled as there was one with us, he woulde take heede howe to be unthankful after, as long as he lived.
(*S*.) Then belike you have a lawe for the bridling of ingrate persons.
(*O*.) Yea that we have. . . .

though it seems to have been needed only once. The ingrate in this case had been befriended by a stranger, and failed when opportunity offered to befriend the same man in return. He was made to wear a serpent badge, back and breast, for seven years; during that time, anybody who did him any favor was to incur the same penalty for a year, and four times a year he was bound to serve the other party for a week.

(*O*.) & we never had any unkinde or unthankfull person in our country since.[46]

This suggests that the case was a recent one, for Omen's other stories abound in examples of lurid and stony-hearted villainy, too prolix for quotation.

The discussion of ingratitude continues, and at a couple of points may shed light on Notpul, or at least on the impression he is seeking to make. Omen and Siuqila edify each other with much talk about gratitude to God, and His readiness to strike down sinners who fail to give Him credit for blessings bestowed. An outstanding example of ingratitude to God is to believe in salvation by works.[47] They also discuss public gratitude to

[41] *Ibid*., 40. [42] *Ibid*., 61–2. [43] *Ibid*., 64. [44] *Ibid*., 65. [45] *Ibid*., 154.
[46] *Ibid*., 164. [47] *Ibid*., 167.

benefactors of the state and it emerges that in Mauqsun, unlike Ailgna, a special degree of esteem and promotion is the lot of those who write virtuous books.[48] We learn in the sequel that books are the most acceptable of all gifts in Mauqsun, a stark contrast to Ailgna, where people frequently do not trouble to read them with due attention.[49]

It is a fate which could easily befall *Too Good to be True*, and it would be wearisome to reproduce the penal code of Mauqsun *in toto*. A few more examples may illustrate its salient features. We have seen a few laws, and there are others, which show that the happy citizens need to use care in doing as they would be done by, lest they incur penalties for doing it to an undeserving person. The laws, as indeed is the nature of laws, come closer to insuring that the guilty shall be done by as they did. Physical injury earns similar physical injury. False accusers suffer whatever penalty they sought their victim.[50] Those who injured others by a lie are ordered to keep silence for three months and to wear a badge on the sleeve with the letters HL for 'hurtful liar,' besides compensating the injured party. But the unhurtful lie is punished as well:

> (O.) Nay, Lying is so much detested with us, that if one lye in sporte, he shall be punished in earnest: for, if one make a pleasaunt lye, thoughe he hurt nobody therewith, for the firste suche lye he shall be reproved, for the second suche lye he shall be five days imprisoned, and for the third suche lye and every other suche lye after, he shall be banished from the place he dwelleth in for the space of three moneths.[51]

In Mauqsun you would think twice before telling tales that were 'too good to be true.' The penalty for hurtful lying, incidentally, applies to any lie in a law court and is thus incurred, on top of any other penalty, by just about every offender in Omen's stories. Perjurers in court have their tongues cut out and lose half their goods to the King.[52]

Usury is another offense that puzzles Omen at first, but when the meaning of the word is explained he remembers the law: a remarkable feat, for it is highly complex, with a scale of penalties for those who lent, borrowed, or failed to report the crime. For a first offense the lender on usury loses a hand and half his goods, the borrower or concealer of the fact a finger and a quarter of his goods. For a second offense the usurer is thrown to the bears, and although there is a great deal more of this law perhaps we may leave it with the observation that one of its objects is to encourage competitive informing and thus make the accomplices distrust each other.[53]

If an informer catches a merchant exporting valuable commodities

48 *Ibid.*, 169. 49 *Ibid.*, pt II, sig. Cc. iv. 50 *Ibid.*, pt I, 83–93.
51 *Ibid.*, 78. 52 *Ibid.*, 81–2. 53 *Ibid.*, 146–50.

from the homeland he gets half his fortune; the other half goes to the King, the merchant is torn in four pieces by horses – for the first offense – and his son or another representative must wear a viper badge for life.[54] If a man breaks his promise, he is made to perform it, and any promises made to him in the past year must be broken, which again shows how awkward it can be to do as you would be done by. The promise-breaker also wears a badge for a year.[55]

But the culmination of Notpul's ingenuity is to be seen in the law relating to corrupt judges. Thomas Preston's play *Cambises*[56] had made Elizabethans familiar with the story of the Persian tyrant whose one virtuous act was to have a corrupt judge beheaded and flayed. Inevitably, it comes up between Omen and Siuqila, but the law in Mauqsun is rather more carefully worked out:

> (O.) Oure lawe is, that if any Judge take any bribe or reward, or any other for him by his consent . . . & doth conceale it foure and twentie houres, . . . he shall die for it without any redemption. His death shall not be according to the execution of the common offenders: For first his hande shall be cutte offe, wherewith he received the bribe or rewarde: whyche hand shal be nayled on the seate or chayre where he did sit, to fear the Judges that shall sit there after him to do the like: And his tong shall be cut out of his head, and shall be nayled just over againste the Judges seat, and this shall be written under it: *This is the tong of the wicked Judge that gave false judgement*: that the Judges that shall sitte there after him, may thereby beware. . . .
>
> Forsooth all the golde and silver, that he shall receive to do wrong . . . shall be melted, and then his mouth shal be holden open, and it shal bee powred downe into his throate: whereby the money that he toke to defraude the Innocent of their rights, shal bereave the covetous and wicked Judge of his life.

Afterwards, the molten bullion is thriftily recovered from the corpse, and used to reward the informer.[57]

V

This brings us from particular laws of Mauqsun to the method of administering justice. Here more than anywhere it is plain that Lupton was a

[54] *Ibid.*, 136–7.

[55] *Ibid.*, 38–9. It was, of course, English practice to encourage informers by offering a share of the penalty, especially but not only in economic regulation. How this could work out is seen in G. R. Elton, *Star Chamber Stories* (London, 1958) ch. 3: 'Informing for profit.'

[56] *A Lamentable Tragedie mixed full of plesant mirth, containing The Life of Cambises, King of Percia, from the beginning of his kingdome, until his death, his one good deede of execution, after that many wicked deedes . . .*: *STC* 20287 (London, J. Alde, 1570?); entered at Stationers' Hall in 1569 but probably performed before then; Joseph Quincy Adams (ed.), *Chief Pre-Shakespearean Dramas* (Boston, Houghton Mifflin, 1924).

[57] Lupton, *Too Good to be True*, pt II, sigs. K.iv (*verso*) – L.i.

layman, lacking knowledge not only of the technicalities of law but of the practicalities of government. If in one way this makes his opinions less worth hearing than those of More or Smith, in another it gives him a special evidential value. The sixteenth century was beginning to see ignorance as a valuable quality in a juryman.[58] Lupton could perhaps bring to the problem of what was wrong with the law a mind unclouded by facts.

What he saw as wrong was not corrupt judges. Nothing in the gruesome passage just quoted suggests that corruption was rife in either Mauqsun or Ailgna. But Mauqsun has far more judges, with the risk of corruption that that involved. The country is covered by a network of courts so that no one need go more than ten or twelve miles to find one. Witnesses depose in their own local court, not that of the parties. In the ordinary way no case is allowed to run on for more than two months, insured in the usual way by enormous pecuniary pains on whoever, party, witness or judge, is held to be causing the delay.[59] It is clearly meant that all kinds of cases can be settled promptly and locally. Some kinds of cases should not be necessary at all: cheats and deceits in land transactions could be ruled out by keeping a deeds' registry in every market town.[60] Legal advice for the poor is easy and cheap in Mauqsun, although lawyers are few; we are not told how this was brought about.[61] But if lawyers are few, judges are many. It is plain that what Lupton has in mind is a wholly professional judiciary, and it would need to be huge. This is in contrast to More; Utopia also has prompt justice in local courts, but relies on lay magistrates.[62]

Although Siuqila had ranged the world looking for the perfect country, there is no indication that Lupton had done so. Unlike all the other authors named herein, he never brings another European state into com-

[58] The transition from an 'active' to a 'passive' conception of the jury's role is discussed in John H. Langbein, *Prosecuting Crime in the Renaissance: England, Germany, France* (Cambridge, Mass., Harvard University Press, 1974), sect. I: England.

[59] Lupton, *Too Good to be True*, pt I, 115–16 (courts everywhere within ten miles and cases to take no more than two months); pt II, sigs. L.ii (*verso*)–L.iii (courts everywhere within twelve miles; cases to take no more than three months, and sanctions against delay). For a comparison with the state of affairs in Ailgna, see Langbein, *Prosecuting Crime*; James S. Cockburn, *A History of English Assizes* (Cambridge, CUP, 1972); Cockburn (ed.), *Crime in England, 1550–1800* (London, Methuen, 1977), esp. John H. Baker, 'Criminal courts and procedures at common law'; William J. Jones, *The Elizabethan Court of Chancery* (Oxford, The Clarendon Press, 1967); and Joel Samaha, *Law and Order in Historical Perspective: The Case of Elizabethan Essex* (New York, Academic Press, 1974).

[60] Lupton, *Too Good to be True*, pt I, 141–4. [61] *Ibid.*, 114.

[62] In Utopia private disputes are settled by the Tranibori, one of whom is elected for every three hundred families, and who meet alternate days (*tertio quoque die*): *Utopia*, bk II: *De Magistratibus*.

parison or shows any awareness of their institutions. Thus we must suppose that his faith in centralized, supervised bureaucracy was a pure faith, uninfluenced by foreign experience or any garbled account of it.

He does have one remarkable notion about how his system could be made to work. It is a naive idea but does address a real difficulty. Both Ailgna and Mauqsun, as we have seen, normally depend on informers, and both encourage informers in much the same way. But if informers are lacking,

> (O.) our King hath his most trustie and privie Espials, that travel purposely through his whole Dominions, only secretely to learne and search out such notorious misdemeanours, who in their own persons, reveale secretely to the King, all such notable mischiefes: as they have truely learned, and surely searched out by their travel . . . to which privy Spials the King gives great livings, and also bountiful rewards. . . . These Spials are charged on paine of death, not to utter or reveale the cause of their travell . . . these Espials dare not certifie the King of any untruthe, for if they doe, they shall die for it . . . the moe matters that they have to certifie the King, the moe gifts and rewardes they shal have . . . and the King him self in his owne person, hath the hearing, determining and judging of every such notorious fact or matter, that is informed him by his said Espials.

It is also the duty of the Espials to report on good judges and officers who are worthy of promotion.[63]

How to insure that criminal process would be initiated in the absence of an accuser was a problem of the age and later.[64] How to keep the local agents of the state under constant surveillance would have been a worse problem than it actually was in the 1580s had Lupton's view of the state come to prevail. His is a drab, unromantic conception which may possibly seem a 'modern' one: Benthamism or Fabianism without the philanthropy! Mauqsun has a nobility and a gentry, but there is hardly room in such a commonwealth for the aristocratic idea of honor – one of the laws requires a man to run away from his enemy when attacked[65] – and it sounds like a world of officials. At best it has the virtues, along with the insensitivity, of a well-oiled, well-regulated machine.

We can get one further sidelight on Lupton from his play, *All for Money*, of 1578. This is in the 'interlude' mode, which derived from the older 'morality,' and is completely conventional.[66] Money, of course, is

[63] Lupton, *Too Good to be True*, pt II, sigs. R.ii (*verso*)–R.iii.

[64] Langbein, *Prosecuting Crime*; and Samaha, *Law and Order in . . . Essex*, ch. 4.

[65] Lupton, *Too Good to be True*, pt I, 51.

[66] Also, I should think, unfunny and unactable. The high moment of the piece is where Money 'shal make as though he would vomit, and with some fine conveyance pleasure shal appeare from beneath . . .' (sig. B.i.); whereupon Pleasure in turn sicks up Sin, who sicks up Damnation. Lupton's airy stage direction is only supplemented (A.iiii) by his advice to arrange a hollow place near the chair on which the sufferers sit.

the root of all evil. But the defense against this evil is not some moral quality or supernatural grace, but *learning*. Learning, not charity or humility or whatever, is the rich man's armor against the corruption of riches and the poor man's consolation against the canker of poverty. As for the unlearned, if poor they may be pitied, if rich they have no hope. Lupton throughout his work makes an ostentatious display of Protestant piety but he has an essentially secular mind.

VI

Let us turn finally to our other authors and compare More, Smith, Lyly, and Lupton on the laws of England. Two, the lesser two, are all for severity, but one thinks the laws are severe enough, the other not. Two are all for mercy, or what would then be reckoned mercy, and of these one thinks that the laws are merciful enough, the other not. The side of severity is maintained by less independent minds – both of them were seeking Cecil's favor – and has more claim to represent the conventional wisdom.

The two framers of ideal commonwealths both feel some need for a smoother judicial machinery, but here the gap in time, as well as mentality, between them means that they are not really talking about the same England.[67] Smith talks about the same England as Lupton but his original purpose was to explain it, and therefore defend it, to foreigners. He recognizes the inconveniences of the English judicial system only to shrug them off.[68] Lyly is not interested at all. One thing all four have in common: all assume that the purpose of punishment is deterrence pure and simple. Perhaps More would have refined on this theme if his argument had required it, but he as much as Lupton talks, or makes his characters talk, as if criminals acted on a rational calculation of risks. No doubt this should not surprise us. The less certainly punishment actually follows crime, the more unlike the real state is to Notpul's omniscient police state; thus, they all conclude, the more need there is to frighten possible offenders by making examples. That four such different minds should take this need for granted, and leave the question there, indicates a difference at least of degree between their age and our own.

[67] Changes in the meantime included the expansion of the court of Star Chamber and of the equity jurisdiction in Chancery, in which More himself had a hand, as well as the procedural statutes of 1554 and 1555, the rise in numbers and the revision of duties for JPs, plus the decline of benefit of clergy.

[68] Smith, *De Republica Anglorum*, bk II, chs. 11 and 17. He seems to be more offended, ch. 8, by barbarous legal Latin.

Towards petty sessions: Tudor JPs and divisions of counties

FREDERIC A. YOUNGS, JR*

Two statements, each a succinct appraisal of the work of justices of the peace at a specific time, define an intriguing chronological gap.

> The justices of the peace . . . were a well-established institution before the accession of the Tudors who greatly added to their administrative duties without really altering the nature of the office. But . . . during the sixteenth century this old system of local law-enforcement was vastly expanded and allowed to engross virtually all local government, to the exclusion of even older institutions.[1]

> By comparison, during the 1630s petty sessions had become a court *de facto* as well as *de jure* on which quarter sessions was beginning to rely for nearly all out-of-sessions work . . . Indeed, by 1640 . . . petty sessions had become indispensable to the divisional justices . . . and the machinery it had created was far too convenient to the magistrates themselves ever to pass into oblivion.[2]

What was the evolutionary bridge from Professor Elton's world of JPs who had individual and corporate duties in the early sixteenth century to that complete, regularized scheme of petty sessional meetings in the seventeenth century and after? The link was the Tudor practice of 'divisions' of counties.

The formation of divisions began in the 1520s and continued throughout the century. As might have been expected, the new divisions were mixtures of the old, the hundreds which had had a major role in medieval administration, and of the new, the grouping of hundreds into pairs and larger combinations to form divisions. Some elements of this sixteenth century process have attracted the interest and commentary of recent historians. A brief but bold sketch of the argument was stated by

* I would like to thank Messrs Ronald H. Fritze and William B. Robison III, for sharing with me their knowledge of Hampshire and Surrey, respectively, in the Tudor period, and for assistance in research.

1 G. R. Elton, *The Tudor Constitution* (Cambridge, CUP, 1960), 453.

2 Thomas G. Barnes, *Somerset 1625–1640* (Cambridge, Mass., Harvard University Press, 1961), 200.

two pioneers in the study of individual county communities, Thomas G. Barnes and A. Hassell Smith, whose respective studies of Somerset and Norfolk are outstanding examples of the genre.[3] Yet a full appreciation of the developments, of the extent to which they were employed, and of their importance in Tudor administration and justice is possible only when the scope of the study is broadened from individual counties to the entire realm, and when evidence which is necessarily fragmentary for this or that county is pieced into a whole.

I

The process had four main phases: financial, military, administrative, and judicial. When in the reign of Henry VIII new forms of royal parliamentary taxation developed, specifically the subsidy, new procedures for rating and collection also had to be devised, in which one finds the first evidence of divisions formed by groups of hundreds.[4] The next permanent advance came in the first muster of Elizabeth I's reign, when muster masters were told to form themselves into divisions in order to take the survey. In those instances where explicit details of their action remain, it can be seen that divisions first instituted for financial purposes were adapted to the new need. Throughout the remainder of Elizabeth's reign divisions were increasingly used for an expanding range of administrative concerns, so much so that they became ubiquitous elements of sophisticated conciliar orders. Finally, additional judicial sessions based on the divisions came to be used as supplements to the regular quarter sessions, thus forming the last link to regularized petty sessions in the Stuart period.

These developments over eighty years reveal an interesting interplay of central and local initiatives. As will be seen, the suggestions to use divisions came from the Crown's ministers, but the actual formation of the divisions rested on local decisions. And as can be expected in any study of Tudor governmental institutions over a period of time, there were occasional false starts and abandoned efforts.

This study is of necessity exploratory. A full appreciation of the extent to which divisions were used and of their changing composition by hundreds would require exceptionally broad research in local, personal and governmental archives. More importantly, the personnel assigned to the

[3] Barnes, *Somerset*, 82, and A. Hassell Smith, *County and Court: Government and Politics in Norfolk, 1558–1603* (Oxford, Clarendon Press, 1974), 103–4.

[4] Roger S. Schofield, 'Parliamentary lay taxation 1485–1547' (Cambridge University, Unpublished Ph.D. thesis, 1963).

divisions were more crucial than the divisions themselves. The death, incapacity or even laziness of justices in one locale might render a recently adopted scheme of divisions unsatisfactory. Even more important to the success of governmental efforts was the interplay of personal, factional and religious elements in a county's politics. Yet evidently an element of stability and permanence had developed by the end of Elizabeth's reign, both in the geographic constitutions of divisions and in the roles assigned the justices within them. Indeed, the composition of some petty sessions endured for centuries.[5]

The initial step was a false start, or at least one which has left no trace. An act in 1521 for the punishment of rogues and vagabonds also contained provisions to enable the impotent poor to beg under the supervision of local justices. The latter were 'to divide themselves' at their discretion, to search for those who truly needed alms, and then to issue the latter licenses which authorized begging within the limits of the division and not elsewhere.[6] The act was permissive rather than mandatory, and even if followed there would be few traces on the records of the time. It was later superseded by the act of 1536 which involved raising funds for the poor and the administration of relief.[7]

The first evidence of divisions appears in returns for the subsidy of 1523. Its enabling statute required commissioners to make assessment locally according to fixed rates. The commissioners in each shire must

> yearly during the said four years [the term over which payments were to be made] by their assents and agreement [to] sever themselves for the execution of their said commissions in hundreds, wards, lathes, rapes, wapentakes, towns, parishes and other places . . . as to them shall seem expedient to be ordered, and between them to be communed and agreed upon.[8]

Although subsequent accounts of collections never mention the process, there are occasional lists of divisions and mentions of divisions in certificates to the Exchequer, from which the results can be garnered.

The evidence about divisions, including the range of numbers adopted

[5] On a division of Salford hundred (the Bolton Division) which lasted to the nineteenth century, John Harland (ed.), *The Lancashire Lieutenancy under the Tudors and Stuarts*, Chetham Society, XLIX (Manchester, 1859), 32–3; in Middlesex, Diane K. Bolton, 'Edmonton Hundred,' in T. F. T. Baker (ed.), *VCH: Middlesex*, V (London, Institute of Historical Research, 1976), 129.

[6] 22 Henry VIII, c. 12: *SR*, III, 328–32.

[7] 33 Henry VIII, c. 10: *SR*, III, 841–4; on its implication for the later poor law, see E. M. Leonard, *The Early History of English Poor Relief* (Cambridge, CUP, 1900), 54–6, corrected by G. R. Elton, 'An early Tudor Poor Law,' *Economic History Review*, VI (1953), 55–67.

[8] 14 & 15 Henry VIII, c. 16: *SR*, III, 230–41. Later acts authorized the lord chancellor to appoint commissioners who would divide themselves when collectors had not been appointed locally as authorized, e.g., 32 Henry VIII, c. 50: *ibid.*, 812–24.

Tudor Divisions of Counties

English counties			Divisions		
	Square miles	Hundreds & liberties	Subsidies (1523–59)	List of 1575	Later lists
30 or more hundreds					
Kent (5 lathes)	1537	68	6–13	16	13 (1597)
Sussex (6 rapes)	1463	66	6	6	more than 6
Dorset	1005	55	5–6	5	
Hants	1628	48	6–8	6	7 (1582)
Somerset	1642	41	5–10	4	12 (1630)
Devon	2579	32	4–9 (32)	3	4 (1582)
Norfolk	2092	32	8–15	8	
20 to 29 hundreds					
Glos	1258	28	5–8	5	5 (1608)
Wilts	1379	28	5	6	6 (1592)
Suffolk	1512	21	HP-8	4	
Berks	726	20	5–7	5	
Essex	1532	20	9–18	6	6 (1594)
Northants	1017	20	7–13	2	
10 to 19 hundreds					
Cambs	858	18	5–6	4	
Lincs (Lindsey)	(**)	17	–	4	
Oxon	752	14	7–9	(***)	
Salop	1341	14	5-HP	9	5 (1590)
Surrey	758	14	4–12	2	
Yorks (N. Riding)	(+++)	12	8	H	
Heref	860	11	5–8	10	
Lincs (Kesteven)	(**)	10	4	2	
Staffs	1148	10	H	H	
Yorks (W. Riding)	(+++)	10	H	H	
9 or fewer hundreds					
Cornwall	1327	9	H	H	4 (1602)
Beds	463	8	3	3	
Bucks	740	8	H	H	
Herts	528	8	H	H	
Cheshire	1052	7	H	H	14 (17th cent)
Middx	282	7	4–7	4	
Derbys	1026	6	4–6	H	
Lancs	1831	6	H	H	more than 6
Leics	804	6	HP	7	
Northumb	1871	6	–	–	
Notts	837	6	HP	3	
Yorks (E. Riding)	(+++)	6	4	H	more than 4
Cumb	1478	5	–	H	
Worcs	780	5	H	H	
Durham	1061	4	–	H	
Hunts	370	4	2–4	H	
Rutland	142	4	undiv	2	
Warws	902	4	HP	H	
Westm	763	4	–	4	
Lincs (Holland)	(**)	3	H	2	

Notes to Tudor divisions of counties:

Abbreviations

H Hundred
HP Hundreds or pairs of hundreds
(+++) Yorks: 5961 sq miles
(**) Lincs: 2748 sq miles
(***) number unclear
undiv undivided

Counties
Separate commissions of peace (3 Ridings for York, 3 Parts for Lincs)

Hundreds
Wards in Cumb, Durham, Northumb, Westm; wapentakes in Notts, Yorks; hundreds and wapentakes in Lincs. Liberties counted as hundreds.

Sources
Square miles: Samuel Lewis, *A Topographical Dictionary of England* (5 vols., London, S. Lewis & Co., 1835).
Hundreds: Frederic A. Youngs, Jr, *Guide to the Local Administrative Units of England, I: Southern England*, Guides and Handbooks, no. 10 (London, Royal Historical Society, 1979), and research for volume II, in progress.
List of 1575: PRO, SP 12/104, with fair copy SP 12/96.
Later lists: Kent: William Lambarde, *A Perambulation of Kent* (London, Baldwin, Cradock and Joy, 1826), 22–7; Sussex, additional divisions, undated list, in Anthony Fletcher, *A County Community in Peace and War: Sussex 1600–1660* (London, Longman, 1975), 137–9; Hants: BL, MS Lansdowne 52/64; Somerset: Barnes, *Somerset*, 41; Devon: PRO, E 179/100/387; Glos: William Bradford Willcox, *Gloucestershire. A Study in Local Government, 1590–1640* (New Haven, Yale University Press, 1940), 79–80; Wilts: Joel Hurstfield, 'County government *c.* 1530–*c.* 1660,' in Ralph B. Pugh and Elizabeth Crittall (eds.), *VCH: Wiltshire*, V (London, Institute of Historical Research, 1957), 87–8; Essex: Sir Henry Ellis (ed.), *Speculi Britanniae Pars: an Historical and Chorographical Description of the County of Essex, by John Norden, 1594,* Camden Society, IX (London, 1840), 12–13; Salop: D. C. Cox, 'County government 1327–1603,' in George C. Baugh (ed), *VCH: Shropshire,* III (London, Institute of Historical Research, 1979), 73–4; Cornwall: Richard Carew, *The Survey of Cornwall* (London, 1602), 86; Cheshire: B. E. Harris, 'Palatine institution and county government 1547–1660,' in B. E. Harris (ed.), *VCH: Chester,* II (London, Institute of Historical Research, 1979), 52; Lancs: divisions within Salford hundred, John Harland (ed.), *The Lancashire Lieutenancy under the Tudors and Stuarts*, Chetham Society, XLIX, 32–3 (Manchester, 1859), 32–3; Yorks, E. Riding: division of Harthill wapentake into four divisions, K. J. Allison, 'Harthill Wapentake,' in K. J. Allison (ed.), *VCH: York East Riding*, III (London, Institute of Historical Research, 1976), 132.
Subsidy: All references from PRO, E 179 (this part of citation not repeated in what follows, and is to be supplied). Entries for most counties in 281/TG 12264, 281/TG 12486. Additional entries for specific counties as follows: Kent: 125/311, 126/355; Sussex: 190/221, 190/241; Dorset: 104/191, 104/196, 104/217; Hants: 174/292, 174/324, 174/303; Somerset: 169/140, 170/222, 170/225; Devon: 97/244, 96/170, 97/225, 98/249, 98/272, 98/295, 100/331, 100/340, 100/350; Norfolk, 151/336, 152/395; Glos: 113/195, 114/248, 114/268, 115/327, 11/335; Wilts: 239/159; Suffolk: 181/290; Berks: 74/189, 73/157, 73/184, 74/201, 74/219; Essex: 108/149, 108/194, 110/378; Northants: 155/163, 156/236, 156/274, 156/224, 156/279; Cambs: 82/164, 81/149A, 82/203, 82/212; Lincs (Lindsey): no entries beyond 281/TG 12486; Oxon: 161/188, 162/237, 162/305, 162/286, 164/535, 162/307; Salop: 167/16; Surrey: 184/183; Yorks (N. Riding) none beyond 281/TG 12486; Heref: 117/190, 117/183, 117/214, 118/241, 118/282; Lincs (Kesteven): none beyond 281/TG 12486; Staffs: none beyond 281/TG 12486; Yorks (W. Riding); none beyond 281/TG 12486; Cornwall: 87/135, 87/138, 87/142, 87/149, 87/152, 87/197; Beds: 71/131, 71/1494; Bucks: 79/167; Herts: none found; Cheshire: 85/31, 85/39; Middx: 141/118, 142/178, 141/156; Derbys: 92/165, 92/182, 94/188; Lancs: 130/95, 130/141, 131/173; Leics: none beyond 281/TG 12486; Northumb: none found; Notts: none beyond 281/TG 12486; Yorks (E. Riding): none beyond 281/TG 12486; Cumb: none found; Worcs: none beyond 281/TG 12486; Durham: none found; Hunts: 122/114, 122/121, 122/124; Rutland: none beyond 281/TG 12486; Warws: none beyond 281/TG 12486; Westm: none found; Lincs (Holland): 138/461.

over the years 1523–59, is summarized in the accompanying table, as is further information for the use of divisions in other matters. A few preliminary comments on the format of the table are in order. Since the divisions were almost always groups of hundreds, the number of hundreds becomes the single most important determinant and governs the arrangement of the table. The square miles in each county are given for references, but not lists for the number of justices in a county at a specified time (there were more justices in each county in the second half of the century than the first, and more in larger counties, but the figures were roughly proportionate in both instances). The abbreviation 'H' is used in the table when divisions were in fact single hundreds so that a recurrence of 'H' emphasizes those counties which did not group hundreds into divisions. Therefore every county with more than twelve hundreds grouped hundreds into divisions and most counties with fewer hundreds used the hundreds as divisions. To make the table more manageable, Welsh shires were omitted, although the discussion below will include evidence for those areas as well.

The degree of variation in the number of divisions in those early subsidy returns is striking. There are four lists from Kent, for example, showing that there were thirteen divisions in 1523, ten listed in an anticipatory list of 1546 (perhaps reflecting the divisions used in an earlier payment) while six appeared in the actual list of commissioners that year, and seven in 1555. A list for that county from 1575 (about which more below) as well as a list from 1597 are both comprised of divisions which in every case remain within the limits of a single lathe, but in none of the subsidy lists do all divisions respect those boundaries. Somerset was divided into ten in 1523, nine in 1524, five in 1546, and seven in a later but undated list from Henry VIII's reign. Devon was divided by hundreds or pairs of hundreds in 1526, in eight divisions in 1542 and 1545, in the thirty-two hundreds in 1544, in seven in an anticipatory list of 1546 and eight in the actual list of collectors in that year, in nine in 1552 and four in 1555. Less typical were counties with little variance, such as Sussex which in all reports was divided into the five rapes, and Berkshire which after an initial six in 1523 regularly thereafter reported five divisions. Stable numbers of divisions sometimes masked changes in constituent hundreds, as in Dorset where there were stable nuclei of hundreds in the five or six divisions but with constantly shifting hundreds beyond those.[9]

At the same time as these initial efforts were successfully inaugurated, an unsuccessful attempt was made to broaden the scope of divisions in a

[9] See sources cited in notes to the table.

thorough and important manner. In 1542 a parliamentary enactment 'concerning the execution of certain statutes' was passed which called for additional sessions on a hundredal basis; the law gave justices in those divisions powers to inquire into and punish offenders which went beyond the provisions of earlier laws. Thus in every quarter, at least six weeks before the quarter sessions, justices were to divide themselves into hundreds, make inquiry and receive presentments about offenses against the specified statutes, hear and determine offenses and punish offenders. The statute authorized the enforcement of laws regarding vagabonds, retainder and associated offenses, apparel, unlawful games, forestallers and other grain-related offenders, archery, and innkeepers.[10] Because the act specified that hundreds were to be used and that two justices were to be assigned per hundred, the result was an unsupportable burden on those in the commission of the peace. There was therefore considerable agitation for its repeal and in 1545 this was accomplished.[11] Had the experiment succeeded, petty sessions would have been a reality within twenty-five years from the first authorization for divisions; as it was, the bitter taste over the enactment persisted, calling forth denunciations as long as thirty-five years later from William Lambarde in his manual for justices, and perhaps also retarding any such imposed scheme before the following century.[12] It is noteworthy that the onus arose primarily because the act required the hundreds to be the basic units. One can only speculate that had there been some leeway to group hundreds into divisions the burden could have been substantially reduced in many shires, although probably not enough to save the proposal.

II

In Elizabeth's reign, however, the use of divisions was successfully extended to matters other than the subsidy. In the first month of her reign the Council ordered musters taken, appending articles to the commission which directed the commissioners to divide themselves in order to make the survey.[13] Here was an instance of a process to be repeated often: statutory provisions were supplemented by administrative orders aimed at a more effective result. In the few complete schedules of returns, divisions heretofore used for subsidies were adapted to serve the new pur-

[10] 33 Henry VIII, c. 10: *SR*, III, 841–4.
[11] 37 Henry VIII, c. 7: *SR*, III, 994–5.
[12] On the repeal of the act and reference to Lambarde: William S. Holdsworth, *A History of English Law* (16 vols., London, Methuen & Co., 1966), IV, 147.
[13] The articles cited in a return, for example, in PRO, SP 12/3/36.

pose.[14] Unfortunately the number of fully elaborated returns is not great enough to allow an appreciation of the divisions for most shires of the realm, but mustering by division thereafter became a seemingly unvarying procedure.[15]

There is a further and suggestive aspect arising from the timing of these orders in Elizabeth's reign. It was the responsibility of the principal secretary to be familiar with as many aspects of the realm's governance as possible, and in particular to gather precedents and surveys of information.[16] Elizabeth had entrusted the main direction of her affairs to Sir William Cecil who had first assumed the position of principal secretary under Edward VI in 1550, and who would therefore have had a number of years in that office before the hiatus of Mary I's reign. Ministers of Edward had, in the first month of his reign, issued a command for the justices to arrange themselves in divisions, a process which seems to have left only the most meager traces.[17] Yet when Cecil took charge, he issued an order within the first month of the queen's reign for the shires to be divided to take the musters. Had he revived a process which a predecessor of his had intended in the young king's reign, for which there was ample precedent in the financial sphere? Although there is no direct evidence to assign the impetus to Cecil, one can find elsewhere his fascination with divisions, notably in his annotation of several of them on the proofs of Saxton's county maps (first issued 1574–9), on which Cecil plotted the seats of the gentry of the 1570s.[18]

The most complete and therefore the most useful guide to divisions is in the returns of *custodes rotulorum* for the various counties in response to a conciliar letter of 13 June 1575 seeking information about the divisions

[14] E.g., Westminster in *ibid.*; Middlesex in PRO, SP 12/2/46 & 47. For the statutory basis, Lindsay Boynton, *The Elizabethan Militia 1558–1638* (London, Routledge & Kegan Paul, 1967), 8–11.

[15] E.g., Hants commissioners who wrote in 1574: 'We have accordingly performed the same by severing of ourselves in each division according to the accustomed order,' in PRO, SP 12/97/32, and Conyers Read (ed.), *William Lambarde and Local Government. His 'Ephemeris' and Twenty-Nine Charges to Juries and Commissions* (Ithaca, N.Y., Cornell University Press for the Folger Shakespeare Library, 1962), 15.

[16] On the types of records a secretary should possess, surely a statement of accustomed and earlier practice, see R. B. [Robert Beale], 'A Treatise of the Office of a Councellor and Principall Secretaries to her Ma[jes]tie,' in Conyers Read, *Mr Secretary Walsingham and the Policy of Queen Elizabeth* (3 vols., Cambridge, Mass., Harvard University Press, 1925), I, 423–43.

[17] *APC*, II, 28–9; notation in Hants in R. C. Anderson (ed.), *Letters of the Fifteenth and Sixteenth Centuries from the Archives of Southampton*, Southampton Record Society, XXII (Southampton, 1921), 68–9, noted also in D. E. Hoak, *The King's Council in the Reign of Edward VI* (Cambridge, CUP, 1976), 196.

[18] BL, MS Royal 18.D.III, on which, however, he noted divisions only for Devon (fol. 12), Hants (fol. 19) and Lincs (fol. 50); see also J. B. Harley, 'The map collection of William Cecil, first Baron Burghley 1520–98,' *Map Collector*, III (1978), 12–19.

and which justices resided in each.[19] The returns for the English shires (all responded except Northumberland) are displayed on the table; when added to the Welsh responses showing five counties with divisions of grouped hundreds,[20] a total of thirty-two counties was divided and twenty-six used individual hundreds as divisions. The former are nearly all concentrated in the south and the east, the latter in the north and west where the number of hundreds per county was relatively small. Where there were no resident justices in divisions or counties, the certificates provide evidence of *ad hoc* assignments of justices in adjacent units.[21]

Four returns state the exact time at which the county's justices had assigned the divisions: Shropshire officials reported that the divisions 'are not certain, but as by agreement among themselves from time to time,' and the Pembrokeshire justices explained that when commissions arrived they met at Haverfordwest to 'divide themselves as they be in number there in the country, sometimes two justices of the peace to two hundreds, otherwise time two to a hundred, and sometimes two to three hundreds, so as there is no certain division of any one place, where always one justice of the peace or more usually are tied.'[22] Ancient divisions of counties are sometimes reflected, as in Westmorland where the barony of Kendal was one undivided unit but the barony of Westmorland was in three divisions, and in Suffolk where the ancient liberties of Bury St Edmunds and St Audrey each formed one division while the Geldable in the east of the shire was divided in two.[23] There was a single instance of a division of a hundred into two units, considered necessary in the extensive hundred of Goscote in Leicestershire.[24]

The roles served by the divisions are mentioned in the certificate from Leicestershire: 'There is no ordinary divisions of the said justices of the peace except upon special cause for the service of the prince as at subsidies and at musters and such like when they for better expedition among themselves do sit in several hundreds, but their ordinary place of assembly at the assizes, gaol deliveries and sessions quarterly of the peace is at the castle of Leicester.'[25] Judicial concerns are not mentioned except perhaps in that the Lincolnshire divisions are each called 'sessions,' and in the very fact of the division of Rutland, where otherwise there would not have

[19] PRO, SP 12/104, with fair copy in SP 12/96.
[20] Caernarvon, Montgomery, Pembroke, Glamorgan, Monmouth.
[21] E.g. Bedfordshire and Cornwall: PRO, SP 12/104, fols. 89, 121.
[22] Earlier divisions, none earlier than 1572, in *ibid.*, fols. 37, 43, 51, 59; Salop, fol. 66; Pembroke, fol. 45.
[23] *Ibid.*, fols. 95, 117.
[24] *Ibid.*, fol. 79, a division which persisted thereafter.
[25] *Ibid.*

been two resident justices in most hundreds who could have exercised powers reserved by the statutes to groups of justices.[26]

From that time, however, to the end of Elizabeth's reign there was a striking multiplication of occasions when divisions were ordered and employed in administrative matters. Although here I offer no exhaustive survey of records to ascertain completely the use of divisions, enough can be noted in the following instances to show consistent use of such divisions throughout the realm before 1600. In military concerns there was a further use. In Cecil's draft of instructions to commissioners for a special muster of horses and geldings in 1565 there was an order to divide the shires and assign places for the animals to be viewed.[27] Commissioners in Devon assigned in 1584 to inquire into the decay of archery were instructed to be sure that 'in every of their divisions' all were trained in the use of the long bow as required by law.[28] There was a divisional quota in Kent in 1587 for men to be pressed into military service in the Low Countries.[29] In each of these cases, administrative procedures supplemented the statutes.

The relief of the poor and the punishment of rogues and vagabonds was a major concern of justices of the peace. The act of 1572 required justices to divide themselves, to search and inquire of the needy poor within their divisions, and then to appoint collectors for their relief – the sole instance known thus far where parliamentary statute mandated such divisions.[30] After the important enactments of 1597 and 1601 superseded earlier regulations and based poor relief on the parishes, justices had to supervise parochial officials, which became their major task in petty sessions in the seventeenth century.[31] Meanwhile, the justices assembled in quarter sessions in Devon in 1598 ordered the act for the punishment of vagabonds 'to be proclaimed by the several justice of peace in every their several market towns within their divisions in the said county.'[32] Levies for the expenses of houses of correction were made in divisional sessions in Kent, and in Norfolk there were special monthly Bridewell sessions for the management of the new institutions.[33]

Food-related matters exercised divisional justices in a number of ways.

[26] *Ibid.*, fols. 107–8, 81.

[27] PRO, SP 12/36/88. [28] PRO, SP 12/170/32.

[29] Read, *Lambarde's Ephemeris*, 47.

[30] 14 Elizabeth I, c. 5(16): *SR*, IV, Pt I, 593.

[31] Peter Clark, *English Provincial Society from the Reformation to the Revolution: Religion, Politics and Society in Kent, 1500–1640* (London, Harvester, 1977), 405.

[32] Devon County Record Office, MS Quarter Session Order Book 1592–1600, fol. 207.

[33] Clark, *English Provincial Society*, 311, 352; Read, *Lambarde's Ephemeris*, 29; Hassell Smith, *County and Court*, 104.

A division in south-west Kent heard presentments from constables about victuallers in a fairly formal session by 1565.[34] An order in 1585 requiring justices to enforce the statutory abstinence from meat in Lent for the maintenance of the navy commanded the justices to meet and inquire in divisions once every fourteen days.[35] The Council ordered the sheriff and justices in Norfolk in 1591 to look into the abuses of purveyors and commanded that the names of justices in the several divisions be certified so that their diligence in this matter could be evaluated. When five years later the county of Norfolk compounded to avoid the purveyors, the collections to defray the expense were made on a divisional basis.[36]

The onset of famine made action by the justices crucial. At these times of crisis the normal procedures – the prohibition of grain export at times of high prices and the punishment of forestallers[37] – were clearly inadequate. The severe situations in the late 1580s and the mid-1590s were complicated by the cupidity of those with grain supplies who would not bring corn to the markets, in anticipation of enhanced prices and profits. The Council in 1586 devised the most complex and elaborate set of regulations to date in order to see the markets served. Too long to be published in broadside form as a proclamation, and intended rather for officials than the public, the norms as the 'Book of Orders' were so valuable that they were reissued with elaborations in 1595 and again in 1630/1.[38]

The issue and enforcement of the orders need not concern us here, but it is germane to note that the key to success was the command that the justices divide themselves for the execution of the orders so as to bring local knowledge into tune with the conciliar directives. The orders in 1587 required the justices to meet and make inquiry in their divisions once every fourteen days, and the reissue in 1595 added the requirement for monthly certificates of compliance. The initiative of justices within their divisions is evident from their supplementary efforts: justices in Wiltshire, Shropshire and Suffolk were assigned the task of overseeing markets in their divisions, the Caistor sessions in Lincolnshire drafted

[34] Clark, *English Provincial Society*, 115.

[35] Southampton Record Office, MS Miscellaneous Letters SC15/30.

[36] W. H. Saunders (ed.), *The Official Papers of Sir Nathaniel Bacon of Stiffkey Norfolk as Justice of the Peace 1580–1620*, Camden Society, third series, XXVI (London, 1915), 64–5; Hassell Smith, *County and Court*, 104.

[37] For a justice's initiative in 1575 to proclaim the import of the Council's letters on grain within the divisions of Berkshire, see PRO, SP 12/106/2.

[38] The Elizabethan orders: *Orders deuised by the especiall commandement of the Queenes Maiestie, for the reliefe and stay of the present dearth of Graine Within the Realme* (London, 1586 [1587 new style]), issued and proclaimed in January 1587; *A New Charge giuen by the Queenes commandment, to all Iustices of Peace . . . for execution of sundry orders . . . for staie of Graine, With certaine additions nowe this present yeere to be well obserued and executed* (London, 1595).

supplementary orders,[39] and the Council added pressure for action within divisions in 1595–7.[40]

Three important dimensions besides grain arose from the Book of Orders. Administratively they were the most elaborate and sophisticated set of procedures devised to that date by a Tudor government, and as such have been hailed as the 'apogee of paternalism,' a position not without critics.[41] Constitutionally they provoked a conflict because the reissue in 1595 was enforced in the prerogative court of Star Chamber as well as in common law courts.[42] More to the point for this essay, though relevant directly to the seventeenth century, the reissue of the Book of Orders in 1630/1 commanded, formalized, and made permanent the monthly meetings of petty sessions. To this last point we shall soon return, only noting here that these seventeenth century orders made permanent and general those provisions which in the sixteenth century were temporary for particular crises and which fell into disuse when the famine eased.

A number of other administrative uses of divisions can be briefly noted. Because a statute of 1552 required alehouse keepers to be licensed, Shropshire keepers naturally applied to the nearest magistrate so that the practice arose early in that county of holding special divisional licensing sessions. Later in the reign there is evidence that the divisional justices devised supplementary articles binding alehouse keepers.[43] In Kent efforts were made on a divisional basis to determine the numbers of alehouse keepers, and of course licensing became a standard feature of both special and quarter sessions throughout the realm.[44] Among the uses for financial purposes were the collections of loans on privy seals for the queen's purposes, assessments for repairs to dykes, bridges and roads,[45]

[39] Cox, *VCH: Shropshire*, III, 72; use of divisions to control fairs, in Hurstfield, *VCH: Wiltshire*, V, 100; PRO, SP 12/198/74; PRO, SP 12/198/21; Diarmaid MacCulloch, 'Power, privilege and the county community: politics in Elizabethan Suffolk' (University of Cambridge, Unpublished Ph.D. thesis, 1977), 324.

[40] *APC*, XXV, 8; *ibid.*, XXVI, 99; and, *ibid.*, XXVII, 59–61.

[41] Claim by Norman S. B. Gras, *The Evolution of the English Corn Market from the Twelfth to the Eighteenth Century*, Harvard Economic Series, XIII (Cambridge, Mass., Harvard University Press, 1915), 236. For the critics and a study of the conditions leading to and the enforcement of the Book in the 1580s and 1590s, see Frederic A. Youngs, Jr, *The Proclamations of the Tudor Queens* (Cambridge, CUP, 1976), 114–17.

[42] Youngs, *The Proclamations*, 117–21. [43] Cox, *VCH: Shropshire*, III, 73–4.

[44] Read, *Lambarde's Ephemeris*, 20–1; special sessions, for example, in S. A. H. Burne (ed.), *The Staffordshire Quarter Sessions Rolls, I: 1581–1589*, Staffordshire Record Society, LIII (Birmingham, William Salt Archaeological Society, 1929), 281–91; quarter sessions, for example, in James Tait (ed.), *Lancashire Quarter Sessions Records, I: Quarter Sessions Rolls 1590–1606*, Chetham Society, LXXVII (Manchester, 1917), *passim.*

[45] Saunders, *Stiffkey Papers*, 95–6, 115–16; Read, *Lambarde's Ephemeris*, 21; S. A. H. Burne (ed.), *The Staffordshire Quarter Sessions Rolls, III: 1594–1597*, Staffordshire Record Society, LVI (Birmingham, William Salt Archaeological Society, 1932), 291–3.

and the collection of the statutory alms for maimed soldiers and the prisoners in the Marshalsea.[46] Although primary authority for searching out Catholic priests was statutory, supplemented by a royal commission, searches occurred as ordered on a divisional basis, including requests for recommendations regarding the secret sympathies of commission members, lest favorers of Catholicism be reappointed.[47] Lancashire justices had also to appoint overseers in each division to assist in enforcing the statutes against the stretching of cloth.[48]

III

The last link to petty sessions and the one most fraught with interpretative problems is the judicial aspect of the divisions. There are three problems here, the first of an evidential nature since so few quarter sessions records have survived, among which divisional papers can be found. The second problem is the statutory authority for sessions. Whereas the requirement to hold quarter sessions and the authorization to hold other needed sessions beyond four is explicit in the law, there were no statutory directives in the sixteenth century commanding petty sessions, nor were there prerogative efforts for general as opposed to special uses. On the other hand, an increasing number of new statutes gave legal authority to at least two justices acting in concert to carry on much business – work which was authorized regardless of whether it was done on a personal, informal basis or in a more formal session for which records were kept. The legal authority for business was therefore indirectly already in place, and even in the seventeenth century when petty sessions became formalized, they needed no additional statutory powers. The third problem has to do with regularity and permanence, and has been raised in the context of seventeenth century practice. Before turning to it, it will be useful to summarize the Tudor practice for the judicial aspects of divisions.

There is no evidence of the use of divisions in this sense before the 1560s. Subsidies and musters were handled by commissioners and not in sessions. The practice of holding meetings of justices on a divisional basis in Wiltshire dates from 1565, although the exact nature of the business cannot be determined.[49] There were meetings for victuallers at Kent, as earlier mentioned, which date from the 1560s, again probably of an

46 Tait, *Lancashire Quarter Sessions Records*, xiii–xiv, and 138.
47 PRO, SP 12/240/138; *APC*, XXII, 139–40; Saunders, *Stiffkey Papers*, 171, 174.
48 Tait, *Lancashire Quarter Sessions Records*, xiii, and 97–8.
49 Hurstfield, *VCH: Wiltshire*, v, 93.

administrative rather than judicial nature,[50] and there were meetings for minor business in north-east Suffolk in 1560.[51] The meetings to manage Bridewells in Norfolk date from the 1570s, again presumably of an administrative nature, while the provisions of the act for the poor in 1572 envisaged administrative work out of sessions and enforcement in quarter sessions.[52] But in the 1580s, as records of judicial business become more frequent, it is possible to identify judicial business on a divisional basis. Special sessions for the punishment of rogues and vagabonds occurred in the 1580s in Kent and charges to these sessions penned by William Lambarde himself survive,[53] while special sessions for a variety of purposes exist for Staffordshire and Wiltshire.[54] In the instance of Staffordshire there was the range of criminal offenses handled which were common to quarter sessions, most notably forcible entry and assault. It will also be recalled that the Book of Orders in 1587 authorized justices to act divisionally and punish offenders.

The 1590s witnessed a much wider use of judicial remedies, so much so that in Kent the period has been called one of 'marked formalisation,' with regular meetings for the JPs of a particular division noted.[55] There was a marked contrast in Staffordshire as well: the meetings in the 1580s had been concerned with crimes in a particular area so that juries were impanelled from the neighboring vicinity, but in the 1590s there were sessions and juries drawing on hundreds and pairs of hundreds, clearly of a divisional nature.[56] The 1590s witnessed limited sessions in Lancashire dealing with special crimes but also general sessions on a divisional basis which heard as wide a range of cases as the quarter sessions between which they were held.[57] In some instances the work done by justices in these special sessions looked to an ensuing meeting of the quarter sessions, but in other situations and times cases were handled completely in the

[50] Above, n. 33. [51] *Ibid.*, n.38. [52] *Ibid.*, nn. 29 and 32.

[53] Read, *Lambarde's Ephemeris*, 29, 153–76 (two each of the latter for riotous assembly, rogues and grain).

[54] Staffordshire: Burne, *Staffordshire Quarter Sessions Rolls, I*, 226–9 (1587), 229–30 (1587); Wiltshire: Hurstfield, *VCH: Wiltshire*, v, 91 (1584, 1586).

[55] Clark, *English Provincial Society*, 145.

[56] Burne, *Staffordshire Quarter Sessions Rolls, III*, 219–21 (1596), 291–3 (1597); other sessions, S. A. H. Burne (ed.), *The Staffordshire Quarter Sessions Rolls, II: 1590–93*, Staffordshire Record Society, LIV (Birmingham, William Salt Archaeological Society, 1930), 231, 375–7; Burne, *Staffordshire Quarter Sessions Rolls, III*, 3–6, 121–2, 342; S. A. H. Burne (ed.), *Staffordshire Quarter Sessions Rolls, IV: 1598–1602*, Staffordshire Record Society, LIX (Birmingham, William Salt Archaeological Society, 1935), 179, 251–2, 381.

[57] Tait, *Lancashire Quarter Sessions Records*, 47–8, 45–6, 47, 87–8. These juries were impanelled in cases outside the quarter sessions; DeLloyd J. Guth informs me that common law trial juries in the Exchequer a century earlier had to be impanelled out of correct hundreds, or be dismissed: e.g., PRO, E 159/268, r. XXII–XXIV (Hilary 1492) and PRO, E 159/284, r. XX (Trinity 1506).

divisional sittings. It will also be recalled that the decade of the 1590s included judicial determinations on the basis of the revised Book of Orders.

Clearly, then, such meetings qualified by authority, organization and nature as 'petty sessions,' but the limited sources used in this study suggested no judicial regularity. The first step towards that judicial permanence came in 1605 when the Council ordered magistrates in every county to meet in divisions once a quarter between quarter sessions.[58] This initial effort was taken to its completion in 1630/1 when the Book of Orders commanded monthly meetings and certifications from divisions. These actions fulfilled Professor Barnes's insistence: 'The establishment of permanent petty sessions as a distinct institution with regular times and meetings could only be accomplished by a sustained force so strong that the justices could never return to their former unevenness of out-of-sessions administration.'[59] Even though historians still debate the intention and effectiveness of the orders of 1630/1, a question which does not concern us here, it is clear that after the interruption of civil war petty sessions were reimposed and remained permanent until the late nineteenth century.

What then of Tudor divisional meetings and the law? They clearly did all that regularized petty sessions meetings would do later, given the degree of statutory imperatives at a given time. They emphatically existed and developed for central administrative efficiency, a point doubly important when it is remembered that the bulk of business done in quarter sessions was administrative and that major cases had been withdrawn from quarter sessions to the assizes. It thus seems that, if the practice surveyed here was typical of other counties (the usual and frustrating 'if' of local studies where records are not complete), every element except regularity existed.

IV

It is appropriate to step back and appreciate the importance of divisions in the context of government as a whole. Given the insistence of the Crown and Parliament in placing increasing burdens on the justices, it seems inevitable that there would be efforts to handle the new load. There must have been a gradual realization that the hundredal organization had to be adapted, in particular because the number and size of hundreds varied so

[58] Cited in Tait, *Lancashire Quarter Sessions Records*, xiii; in Barnes, *Somerset*, 82; and in other sources.

[59] Barnes, *Somerset*, 84–5.

greatly and the large numbers in the south and east made effective supervision unmanageable. The divisions were thus a convenient transition, retaining the essential geographic nature of the hundreds but providing where needed the means for reducing large numbers to more effective sizes.

Regularity had indeed been achieved to a much greater extent than has been realized before. Subsidies were collected frequently, not only because they were granted at nearly every session but also because the payments were spread out over a number of years. Musters were called frequently, at least every three years in the determination of one historian,[60] and the number of special military musters and presses was even larger. Our survey has shown that the multiplication of assignments of divisional responsibilities increased markedly in the 1580s and 1590s, the same decades which experienced the series of famine years which evoked the Book of Orders. Although not regular in a literal sense, they were regular in that the device was in place, used without hesitation in an ever larger number of matters, and spread throughout the entire realm. The divisions were therefore a convenient transition, easily susceptible to efforts to control them for Crown purposes, yet institutions of worth to royal and local officials alike. When by the end of the seventeenth century the Crown's ability to supervise and coerce local justices had been seriously weakened, petty sessions continued as preserves for an informed and self-confident county elite.

[60] Boynton, *Elizabethan Militia*, 14.

Binding the nation: the Bonds of Association, 1584 and 1696

DAVID CRESSY

I

The autumn of 1584 was a jittery time for the Protestant rulers of Elizabethan England. William the Silent had been assassinated in July, the Calvinist republic of Ghent had fallen late in the summer, and the Spanish armies under Parma were pressing victoriously into the Netherlands. The forces of antichrist seemed to be gathering strength while the prospects for international Protestantism were darkening. Catholic priests were secretly at work in the English provinces, Catholic fanatics were feared to be at large, while plots and rumors of plots revolved around the captive Mary. Throckmorton's conspiracy had recently been unravelled, while others were suspected. The queen's life was thought to be in imminent danger and the entire English Protestant achievement was at risk. The leadership in London was uncertain how the political nation might react in an emergency and was haunted by the twin spectres of disloyalty and disorder. To meet this problem Walsingham and Burghley devised and circulated 'the Instrument of an Association for the preservation of the Queen's majesty's royal person.' Its purpose was to alert and arouse the gentlemen of the political nation and to steel them to revenge any assassination attempt against the queen.[1]

Historians have not had much to say about the Elizabethan Association, apart from making clear their dislike of it. It has been treated, briefly, as an aberration from the usual Tudor lawfulness and good sense, as an ill-considered invitation to violence and vengeance, something to be conveniently set aside when calmer thoughts returned. The document which Walsingham and Burghley concocted in 1584 is an embarrassment to later analysts, especially to those who prefer a measure of *politesse* in their politics. Froude referred to 'the famous Bond of Association, which was a

[1] PRO, *SP* 12/174/1.

virtual suspension of law.'[2] Black called it 'this appeal to Texan justice'[3] (unfair to Texans). Neale likened 'the notorious Bond of Association' to 'lynch law'[4] (unfair to Virginians). For Hurstfield it was 'more appropriate to the Scottish than the English scene'[5] (unfair to the Scots). Elsewhere the Association has been called 'a naked appeal to the most primitive instincts of its signatories.'[6] When mentioned at all it is usually with some distaste and discomfort.

Yet the Association reveals more than the nervous paranoia of some councillors in 1584. Its history shows how the central government could mobilize political resources in distant parts of the realm, and demonstrates the care with which the Privy Council could cultivate its provincial agents. Walsingham and Burghley were concerned not just to draft the document but to impose it, and they were ready to awe and cajole, to instruct and demand, to secure widespread subscription to the pledges it contained. The Association was, in fact, a masterly piece of propaganda which served to bind the country to the Crown, to combat disorder, to focus the concerns of the political elite, and to achieve a dramatic and public attestation of loyalty to Queen Elizabeth. Not just the content of the Association but also the way in which it was administered bound the leaders of English society to the destiny of the English Protestant reformation and to the dynasty which had created it. Involving as it did solemn oaths and ritual display, the Bond of Association was significant as a matter of posture and symbol as much as it was a matter of text and law.

II

The Bond was drafted and refined for the Privy Council meeting on 19 October 1584. Its preamble reminded all subjects that they should 'love, fear and obey their sovereign princes, being kings or queens.' Passive obedience was not enough, however, since loyalty involved a commitment to active duty. It obligated all subjects 'to the uttermost of their power, at all times, to withstand, pursue and suppress all manner of persons that shall by any means intend and attempt any thing dangerous or

[2] James A. Froude, *The Reign of Elizabeth* (5 vols., New York, Everyman, 1930), v, 110.
[3] John B. Black, *The Reign of Elizabeth 1558–1603*, 2nd ed. (Oxford, Clarendon Press, 1959), 377.
[4] John E. Neale, *Elizabeth and Her Parliaments, 1584–1601* (2 vols., New York, Norton Library, 1966), II, 16; John E. Neale, *Queen Elizabeth I* (New York, Doubleday Anchor, 1957), 274.
[5] Joel Hurstfield, *Elizabeth I and the Unity of England* (New York, Macmillan, 1969), 125.
[6] Alison Plowden, *Danger to Elizabeth: the Catholics under Elizabeth I* (New York, Stein and Day, 1973), 204.

hurtful to the honours, estates or persons of their sovereign.'[7] This reminder primed the reader for the desperate action which might be called for in the current crisis.

An emergency was said to threaten both queen and country. In an early draft of the Association the threat was located in 'the wicked dispositions of some mischievous persons, moved by the instinct of the devil to execute their malice.' This was crude and vague and failed to suggest the interlock of dark conspiracy and providential discovery that characterized the crisis for Walsingham and others. The final text therefore spoke more pointedly of 'divers depositions, confessions, and sundry advertisements out of foreign parts, from credible persons well known to her Majesty's council.' Intelligence reports claimed that 'the life of our gracious sovereign lady Queen Elizabeth hath been most traitorously and devilishly sought,' and might even have been taken 'if almighty God, her perpetual defender, of his mercy had not revealed and withstood the same.'[8] Details were lacking but action was due. The Instrument of Association gave its readers a glimpse of intrigue and counter-intrigue not normally seen outside the highest state circles in London. As many of Elizabeth's successors learned, there was nothing like a good plot to outrage and mobilize opinion.

The Association offered native-born subjects the opportunity to perform their loyal duty. Subscribers pledged their lives and their wealth to 'withstand, offend and pursue, as well by force of arms as by all other means of revenge, all manner of persons, of what estate soever they shall be, and their abbettors, that attempt by any act, counsel or consent to any thing that shall tend to the harm of her Majesty's royal person.' They vowed 'never [to] desist from all manner of forcible pursuit against such persons, to [their] uttermost extermination.' Even more determined action was promised if the plotters were successful in their attempt against the Protestant protectress. Rather than transfer their allegiance to the queen's successor (almost certainly Mary Queen of Scots, who was thought to be deeply involved in the plotting as its obvious beneficiary), they swore 'never to accept, avow, or favour any such pretended successors, by whom or for whom any such detestable act shall be committed or attempted.' Furthermore, the Association denounced 'any that may any way claim by or from such a person or pretended successor,' thereby excluding James. The associators swore to prosecute all such persons 'to the death, with our joint and particular forces, and to take the uttermost revenge of them that . . . we . . . can devise.'[9]

[7] PRO, *SP* 12/174/1. [8] PRO, *SP* 12/173/81–3. [9] PRO, *SP* 12/173/1.

Exactly how to do this was not specified; it was a contingency without a plan. Retribution was to be violent and relentless, and the members of the Association bound themselves together 'jointly and severally, in the bond of one firm and loyal society' to carry it out. Patriotic enthusiasm was suffused with religious solemnity in a union of armed solidarity. A sacred oath sealed the bond 'in the presence of the eternal and ever living God . . . corporeally taken upon the Holy Evangelists.' Any who broke from the bond would be prosecuted by the rest, 'as perjured persons and as public enemies to God, our queen and our native country.'[10]

The Privy Council took the Association on 19 October (although the signatures and seals of some of its members were still being collected on 22 October) and immediately set about getting the principal people throughout the country to join them.[11] Burghley supposed that 'many sorts of persons by degrees of offices and callings are like to be parties in that society' and suggested that copies should be made for wider distribution. Walsingham agreed, adding 'the more public the matter is made, the better effect it is like to work.'[12] The councillors committed themselves to taking the Association to the nation, or at least to its most politically significant sections. Walsingham took command of the task, pressing the bond on the officials of every shire and taking charge of the completed returns. Burghley and Leicester were also busily involved.

The trick was to bind by oath every important person, while preserving the fiction that there was a spontaneous movement to join the Bond and that all subscriptions were voluntary. Walsingham fostered the impression of an unsolicited surge of support for the Association, while at the same time working hard to insure that the desired support was complete. In his letter to the various lords lieutenant, composed the day after the Association was approved by the Council and on the very day that he wrote to Burghley about its wider dissemination, Walsingham claimed that a movement was already afoot to join in the Bond. 'Divers good and well affected subjects . . . as the Judges of the realm, the City of London, the heads of the Inns of Court, and certain Lords and gentlemen of divers counties' were alleged to have 'got knowledge' of the document sworn at Hampton Court by the Council. How this breach of Council security was

[10] *Ibid.*

[11] *Ibid.*: on 21 October Burghley wrote to Walsingham, 'I will tomorrow send to you the instrument of the Association when I shall have Mr. Chancellor's hand and seal, having already the three Councillors' hands with their seals, as I am persuaded by their most earnest protestations and solemn oaths.' Conyers Read, *Lord Burghley and Queen Elizabeth* (New York, Knopf, 1960), 570, citing BL, MS Cotton Caligula C. viii, fol. 162.

[12] Burghley to Walsingham, October 19, PRO, *SP* 12/173/85; Walsingham to Burghley, October 20, PRO, *SP* 12/173/86.

supposed to have happened is beside the point; what mattered was that these loyal subjects, in an exemplary display of patriotism, petitioned 'that they might be permitted in their several charges and professions to subscribe and set their seals to like instruments.'[13] The hint was clear for others to do likewise.

In case the hint was missed Walsingham sent out copies of the Instrument of Association along with instructions for its local administration. The Secretary advised county officials that 'I would be loth in so necessary and dutiful a purpose there should be any slackness found in your Lordship (who have always heretofore been found careful of her majesty's safety).' The pressure was firm and irresistible. The county lieutenants were to present the document to such as might 'be inclined of their own voluntary accord and disposition to enter into this . . . Association.' Joining the Bond was a matter of free individual choice, 'for that it is not meant that any shall be drawn either by authority or persuasion to enter into this fellowship and society.' Yet the instructions stressed again that the Association was both 'necessary and dutiful.' Walsingham expressed his confidence that 'every good and well affected subject' would 'of their own voluntary accord for the care they have of her Majesty's preservation be most ready and desirous to join therein so soon as they shall be acquainted therewith.' This was an invitation that was hard to refuse. It was up to the lieutenants to get out the volunteers, and to satisfy the Council as soon as possible that the turnout was complete. How to accomplish this was a matter for local initiative. Walsingham's instructions concluded, 'touching the order of proceeding I shall not need to direct your Lordship in any course but reserve it to your discretion, upon conference with such gentlemen of that county as you shall think meet to communicate the same.'[14]

Other members of the Privy Council wrote letters promoting the Association, stressing its voluntary nature but making it difficult to refuse. Burghley sent a copy to Lord Cobham, lord lieutenant and warden of the Cinque Ports, asking him to make it known 'to such of your acquaintance there in Kent as you shall think convenient, leaving it voluntarily to their own judgements whether they will hereupon enter into the like union and association.' With examples of 'noblemen and others, principal gentlemen and officers . . . and Justices of Peace in sundry countries' before them it was difficult to imagine them declining. As for Lord Cobham himself, Burghley suggested he take the Association oath in London with other lords of parliament, 'but yet, all this that I write to

[13] PRO, *SP* 12/173/87. [14] *Ibid.*

your Lordship I pray you accept it as a matter that I leave to your own consideration.'[15] Cobham in turn passed the Association along to the leading gentlemen of Kent, and was gratified to receive from them six weeks later a completed return bearing close to one hundred hands and seals. The signatories for the most part overlapped with the county commission of the peace.[16]

III

The Council's correspondence over the next few months included reports from all parts of England on the progress of the Association. Local officials devised occasions of appropriate ceremony, fit for the solemnity of the undertaking and the danger of the moment. The north of England was especially diligent, as if to compensate for the rebelliousness of its leaders fifteen years before. The earl of Derby stage-managed a compelling spectacle of aristocratic loyalty at Wigan on 1 November. He summoned the 'Justices of the Peace and gentlemen of best haviour' of Lancashire to meet with him, in church, to receive the Association. There he made a speech about the importance of the Association, 'whereunto (as from your Lordship) I moved them, and freely myself before them all assented.' Derby reported his efforts to the earl of Leicester: 'I most reverently upon my knees bareheaded in the church took my oath first, ministered unto me by my Lord Bishop of Chester; afterwards I ministered the oath to my Lord Bishop and my son [Lord] Strange upon their knees bareheaded.'[17]

Thus moved and encouraged, the gentry of Lancashire pressed forward in groups of six, kneeling bareheaded before the bishop, to take the oath in the public view of their peers and betters. None refused. The whole business took three hours. A few days later a similar scene was played at Northwich, where the gentlemen of Cheshire had been assembled. They too enthusiastically entered the Association, 'none gainsaying or in any sort backsliding, to my great good liking and comfort.' No doubt London was equally pleased. By 5 November Derby had collected 66 subscriptions from Lancashire and 84 from Cheshire 'upon two long pieces of parchment,' and was making efforts to tender the oath to other gentlemen who could not be present at the two great ceremonies.[18]

[15] Burghley to Cobham, 27 October, in Edmund Lodge, *Illustrations of British History*, 3 vols. (London, 1791), II, 299–300; see, *HMC*: *Calendar of the MSS of the Most Honourable the Marquis of Salisbury, K.G., Preserved at Hatfield House, Hertfordshire*, III (London, HMSO, 1889), 72.

[16] *HMC*: *Salisbury*, III, 75, 77. [17] PRO, *SP* 12/175/4. [18] *Ibid.*

In Yorkshire Lord Darcy, 'as soon as he heard of it warned all the gentlemen of the best calling and dwelling within four wapentakes to meet him at Doncaster on the 14th instant [November], and they all agreed to engross the instrument on parchment, and there and then signed and by oath bound themselves to perform, and Lord Darcy gave the first example.' The earl of Huntingdon sent out a similar summons from York and was gratified that 'above 300 gentlemen have earnestly desired to be admitted into that honourable society, and have sealed, subscribed and sworn to perform its contents.'[19] Once again the leaders of the countryside took their cue from their noble superiors. The ceremony powerfully reaffirmed the social order, as the great magnates received pledges from the county elite on behalf of their distant sovereign.

In some areas subscriptions to the Association went well beyond the select community of gentlemen and officers originally envisaged. The principal townsmen of Lyme Regis, Blandford and Weymouth, twenty-two in all, joined in the Association with the gentlemen of Dorset. Nineteen townsmen of Ludlow subscribed from Shropshire, while the city of Worcester returned the names of over 200 inhabitants who had taken the Bond.[20] The decision to extend the Association to allow common citizens to join was apparently a matter of local initiative. In some cases the supervising official may have wished to create a good impression with a fat stack of subscriptions; elsewhere the publicity about the Association and rumors about threats to the queen may have stimulated a surge of popular patriotism, just as Walsingham had reported in London.

In Yorkshire enthusiasm for the Association ran so strong as to overwhelm the lord lieutenant's capacity for dealing with it. The earl of Huntingdon, who nurtured his own claims to the throne, may have stimulated this movement which challenged the Stuart succession. By the end of November over 2000 subscriptions had been taken in York and other corporations; some of the justices had 'admitted such of the meaner sort of gentlemen and of the principal freeholders and clothiers about them as sued to be accepted into the society'; and 5300 'of that sort' had taken the Association oath about Halifax, Wakefield, and Bradford. Huntingdon wrote to Walsingham that he would have sent up the completed instruments already, by 30 November, 'but as it will be too cumbersome to do so by post, there being 7,500 seals at the least, I retain

[19] Huntingdon to Walsingham, 22 November, *CSP, Domestic Series . . . Addenda, 1580–1625*, ed. Mary A. E. [Wood] Green (London, HMSO, 1872), 129.

[20] PRO, *SP* 12/174/7, 10, 11. An enumeration of the city of Worcester in 1563 found 937 families, so one in five of Worcester householders appear to have subscribed the Association: see Alan D. Dyer, *The City of Worcester in the Sixteenth Century* (Leicester, Leicester University Press, 1973), 26.

them until I hear from you.'[21] Three weeks later the problem had expanded. Huntingdon wrote on 22 December, 'since my last, divers gentlemen and a great number of inferior quality have signed, sealed and sworn to the Instrument of Association for preservation of Her Majesty's person. I wrote that from the number of seals it was too cumbersome to send by post, and now the number has so increased that it will fill a good big trunk.' Lord Scrope had lately delivered to him the Association lists for Cumberland, Westmorland, and for the towns of Carlisle and Kendal. Huntingdon expected to receive more at any moment from Newcastle and elsewhere, to compound his problems of shipping and storage. As an interim measure he arranged to have 'the names of all who have sworn to it to be engrossed in parchment rolls' and these he dispatched to London. Sadly, they do not survive; nor do the originals, with the seals and autographs of so many northerners. All that remains of Huntingdon's work on behalf of the Association is a fair copy list of 185 freeholders and farmers from Richmondshire in the North Riding, filed now among the State Papers.[22]

Walsingham ordered a complete record of the subscribers to the Association to be delivered to the Privy Council, with a duplicate 'to remain in the country under the custody of the custos rotulorum.' This local copy, in the view of a group of Kentish associators, would allow them better to proceed against backsliders.[23] A thorough search of local records might determine how many of these county returns are extant. Among the State Papers there are fourteen Association oath returns, their varying size and format reminding us that subscription was a matter of *ad hoc* local arrangement.[24] Most are on parchment, a few on paper. Some carry original signatures and seals, while others merely list the names of subscribers in a common secretarial hand. The return from Kent, for example, reports on three sheets of paper the names of 99 gentlemen who took the Association between 28 November and 7 December. The Flintshire Association appears on a parchment measuring 50 × 97 cm, and bears 158 autograph subscriptions, 28 of which are rendered by marks. Although not all associators were capable of signing their names, this deficiency by no means impugned their loyalty or their willingness to join

[21] *CSP, Domestic Series . . . Addenda, 1580–1625*, 130.

[22] *Ibid.*, 133. PRO, *SP* 12/174/13.

[23] PRO, *SP* 12/173/87; *HMC: Salisbury*, III, 77.

[24] PRO, *SP* 22/174/5–18. Besides Associations by the Privy Council and the leading clergy, there are returns from Cornwall (110 names), Devon (45), Dorset (70), Hertford (108), Somerset (30), Ludlow (19), Worcester (200), Kent (99), Richmondshire (185), Cardigan (48), Flintshire (158), Monmouth (42), Pembroke (95), and Caernarvon (39). None of the Associations so carefully collected by Derby, Scrope, and Huntingdon in the north is known to survive.

in a bond of revenge. In Hertfordshire, where 108 men subscribed, five made marks instead of signatures.[25]

IV

The treatment of the Association in Parliament is quite well known and needs little elaboration here.[26] Election writs had gone out on 12 October, a week before the Association came into being, and the new parliament met for the first time on 23 November, while subscriptions to the Bond were still being collected. By December the Council was more concerned with seeing the Association through the House of Commons than with following up its progress in the country. Legal scruples and moral misgivings, which had little chance of expression in the heightened atmosphere of public bond-swearing, now came out into the open in parliamentary debate. The Bill for the Queen's Safety, introduced on 1 December, closely resembled the Bond of Association and promised bloody revenge against any involved in a plot against the queen. Some members balked at the prospect of unregulated vengeance without due trial and judgment, and sought to make the Association more conformable to English law. There were second thoughts about victimizing the heir of any 'pretended successor' especially if he (unnamed, but obviously James) was not implicated in any crime. This would avoid punishing someone for the fault of another, and would also leave the way open for a possible Stuart succession. The queen supported this modification, but it posed a problem for some who had subscribed the original Association. They had sworn a sacred oath, joined a solemn bond, to pursue to the death both the claimant and the heir; but now they were asked to relax the terms of the Association and to expose themselves to perjury. The issue was unresolved when parliament adjourned before Christmas, not to reassemble until 4 February. Eventually a new Bill for the Queen's Safety appeared on 3 March, which would pass into law as 'An act for provision to be made for the surety of the Queen's most royal person' (27 Elizabeth I, c. 1). Those of tender conscience had to accept that parliamentary statute had overridden their sacred oaths, for James was exempted from the penalties of the act unless he was demonstrably 'assenting and privy' to a crime.

Almost a decade later the Jesuit Robert Parsons brought the Associa-

[25] For discussion of signatures, marks and literacy, see David Cressy, *Literacy and the Social Order: Reading and Writing in Tudor and Stuart England* (Cambridge, CUP, 1980), 55–9, 123, 143.

[26] This paragraph is based on Neale, *Elizabeth and Her Parliaments, 1584–1601*, II, 28–53, and Stanford E. Lehmberg, *Sir Walter Mildmay and Tudor Government* (Austin, University of Texas Press, 1964), 242–5, 250–7.

tion back to public attention. Writing as R. Doleman, and wilfully confusing the original Bond with the statute which modified it, he cited the existence of the Association as an obstacle to the claims of the king of Scots.[27] This was simply a smokescreen, an attempt to deflect the likely Stuart succession, but apparently it had some effect. Peter Wentworth noted 'a scruple bred in the minds of the common people, arising from I know not what buzzing report of an act of Association,' and he was moved to counter 'Doleman's objections' which had fueled this discussion. The enemies of Protestantism had abused and deceived the common people 'by misrepresenting the tenor and intent of the act of Association . . . by . . . whispering and muttering in the ears of the ignorant.'[28]

Wentworth's own account of the Association is somewhat confused. He claimed it was devised to suppress the 'great stirs and troubles' which might follow the execution of Mary, when in fact it was the threat to Elizabeth's life that prompted the Bond. His report of the Association's reception across the kingdom was tailored to present polemical purposes and may not be altogether trusted. Subscriptions, he claimed, 'were not freely and jointly given but secretly and severally urged and begged.' 'Many did yield for fear or facility,' while 'many of a preposterous zeal did readily yield' to the oath without thinking. The original Association, in this view, was a rashly sworn document, accepted under duress, and not a genuine expression of opinion. While subscribers were being pressured to grant their 'voluntary' approbation, 'divers of the wiser sort [like Wentworth?] . . . refused modestly to ratify and confirm that same, because by due examination hereof they perceived that the general words therein contained might easily be wrestled to a very hard construction, contrary to equity and to the minds of the makers themselves.'[29]

Wentworth was probably right in regarding the Bond of Association as a product of Privy Council persuasion, but he may be reading a scrupulous legal nicety into the autumn of 1584 which did not emerge until later. In any case, as Wentworth rightly observed, the Association 'was a private order, and no act of Parliament, and therefore could be of no force or strength to bind as a law before it was confirmed by Parliament.'[30] The statute, when it came the following year, took pains to leave open the possibility of a Jacobean succession.

[27] Robert Parsons (R. Doleman), *A Conference About the Next Succession* (Antwerp ?, 1594), pt II, 217: *STC* 19398.
[28] Peter Wentworth, *A Treatise . . . Concerning the Person of the True and Lawfull Successor*, appended to *A Pithie Exhortation to Her Majestie* (Edinburgh, R. Waldegrave, 1598), 16, 36: *STC* 25245
[29] *Ibid.*, 17 , 30, 29, 22.
[30] *Ibid.*, 30.

V

The Elizabethan Bond of Association was remembered again in 1696 when news of a Jacobite assassination plot reached the court of William III. Government strategy once again called for a binding oath and a nationwide collection of signatures, and once again the machinery of central government set to work to secure the required response from the localities. A comparison of this later seventeenth century episode with its Elizabethan prototype shows developments in administrative style and procedure, as well as a changed conception of who in England constituted the political nation. The fact that parliament was sitting at the time of the Williamite Association gave wider publicity to the oath and increased the speed and scale of the popular response. There was no need for privy councillors privily to inform their county agents or to arrange for the document to be tendered to the provincial gentry. Members of Parliament could distribute the document, while the *London Gazette* could report the results.

The king appeared in Parliament on 24 February to announce the breaking of the conspiracy and to point out the continuing dangers to the realm and to religion. He felt assured of Parliament's 'readiness and zeal to do everything which you shall judge proper for our common safety' and without suggesting what that was, he asked them to attend to it with 'all possible despatch.'[31] As the Lords and Commons discussed the crisis they found that Lord Keeper Somers had ready a document for them to sign, acknowledging King William to be 'rightful and lawful king' and promising 'to stand by and assist each other . . . in the support and defence of his majesty's most sacred person and government.' Sir Rowland Gwynne introduced this document in the Commons, apparently with the full connivance of the Whig junto. Echoing the Association of the sixteenth century, the subscribers to this new compact pledged themselves 'freely and unanimously . . . to unite, associate and stand by each other' to obtain revenge in case the king was killed.[32]

31 *The London Gazette*, no. 3161, 24–27 February 1696. On the plot, see Thomas B. Macaulay, *The History of England from the Accession of James the Second*, ed. by Charles H. Firth (6 vols., London, 1913–15), v, 2584–2619, with illustrations of the medals struck to commemorate it. For a modern narrative see Jane Garrett, *The Triumphs of Providence: The Assassination Plot, 1696* (Cambridge, CUP, 1980).

32 *The London Gazette*, no. 3164, 5–9 March 1969. James R. Jones, *Country and Court: England, 1658–1714* (Cambridge, Mass., Harvard University Press, 1979), 275. See also John H. Plumb, *The Growth of Political Stability in England, 1675–1725* (London, Macmillan, 1967), 137; and, Henry Horwitz, *Parliament, Policy and Politics in the Reign of William III* (Newark, University of Delaware Press, 1977), 175.

The idea and the text came straight from the Association of 1584. Somers had evidently searched the State Papers for records of the Elizabethan Association, and it was probably on this authority that a pamphlet appeared, 'A True Copy of the Instrument of Association that the Protestants of England entered into in the Twenty-seventh year of Queen Elizabeth, Against a Popish Conspiracy; with an Act made upon the same for the Security of the Queen's most Royal Person.' If nothing else this is a tribute to the filing system of the State Papers in the late seventeenth century and to Somers's efficiency in archival retrieval. The historical documents, printed without comment, prefaced the text of 'this Association drawn up and signed by the High Court of Parliament now assembled, on the 24th of February, 1695–6.'[33] What better way for the similarity of the situations to be implied, with William III cast as Queen Elizabeth?

In fact, the parliamentary response was neither unanimous nor immediate. The Commons adopted the oath on 25 February as did the Lords on 27 February, but by 3 March there were still 113 MPs and several dozen Lords who had not signed. The stumbling block for some Tories was the notion that William, who owed his throne to the gift of the Convention, was 'rightful and lawful king' and not just king *de facto*. The names of these non-associators were printed in 'A Summary Account of the Proceedings upon the happy Discovery of the Jacobite Conspiracy.' This partisan pamphlet quoted extracts from speeches delivered in the Lords and Commons, and not surprisingly it was quickly condemned as 'a violation of the rights and privileges of parliament.' It was part of a swelling campaign to gain support for the Association and to taint refusers or hesitators with disloyalty. The campaign was effective, and several of those named in the 'Summary Account' subsequently signed.[34] Like its Elizabethan precursor, the Association of 1696 was presented as a voluntary bond, but in practice there was intensive pressure to subscribe.

Those who followed public affairs were speedily informed of the Association by the press, by private correspondence, and by government action. Literacy was more widespread now, especially among the expanded trading and industrious classes, and a regular flow of printed material spread political information on a scale that would have been inconceivable to Elizabethans. 'The public prints' spread news of the Jacobite

[33] *A True Copy of the Instrument of Association* (1696) is reprinted in *The Harleian Miscellany* (12 vols., London, R. Dutton, 1808–11), II, 3–10; *CSP, Domestic Series . . . 1696*, ed. William J. Hardy (London, HMSO, 1913), 52.

[34] Horwitz, *Parliament, Policy and Politics*, 175–6. *HMC*: *House of Lords, 1695–1697*, new series, II (London, HMSO, 1903), 202–12. Dennis Rubini, *Court and Country 1688–1702* (London, Hart-Davis, 1967), 65.

conspiracy and its aftermath, inspiring readers to perform their patriotic duty and to show their zeal for their Protestant religion. As easly as 29 February a letter-writer in London could report to a correspondent in Manchester, 'I saw a printed paper today that mentions the Association and the justness and reasonableness of it.' Humphrey Prideaux saw the *Postboy*'s account of the Association in Norwich in April and reacted, 'every word of it is false.' *The London Gazette* dutifully carried reports of the Association from the first exposure of the plot to the last trickling in of oath rolls in September.[35]

With the Whig junto pulling the strings, the Association swept enthusiastically through the country at large. On 25 February, 750 warrants went out for dispatching the Association, and by the 26th a team of thirty-two messengers was delivering the text to county lieutenants and sheriffs.[36] The lord mayor, aldermen and most of the common council men of London took the oath on 25 February, within thirty-six hours of the first motion in Parliament. The militia officers, justices and grand jurors of Middlesex took the oath on 26 February, and within a week officials and notables in more distant places had signed.[37] There was no need to summon special assemblies of the sort Lord Derby had arranged in 1584. Those concerned could demonstrate their loyalty by subscribing the Association at one of the regular legal meetings of the county community, the quarter sessions or assizes. 'The high sheriff, justices of the peace, and many other gentlemen' of Berkshire took the oath at the Reading assizes on 2 March. Similar duty was done at the Winchester assizes on 3 March and at the assizes at New Sarum on 6 March, and so on throughout the spring.[38] By the act which made the Association law, officeholders within thirty miles of London were to swear the oath at the courts of Chancery or King's Bench, and the rest would subscribe at their local quarter sessions.[39]

The voluntary aspects of the Association was soon dropped, and it became not only a test of affection but a qualification for office. At a

[35] Sir George Fletcher to Sir Daniel Fleming, 24 March 1696, *HMC: Twelfth Report, App. Part VII, The MSS of S. H. Le Fleming* (London, HMSO, 1890), 342; Richard Edge to Roger Kenyon, 29 February 1696, *HMC: Fourteenth Report, App. Part IV, The MSS of Lord Kenyon* (London, HMSO, 1894), 406; Daniel Bret to earl of Huntingdon, 27 February 1696, *HMC: Report on the MSS of . . . Reginald Rawdon Hastings*, ed. Francis Bickley (London, HMSO, 1930), II, 258; H. Prideaux to John Ellis, 15 April 1696, *Letters of Humphrey Prideaux*, Camden Society, new series, XV (Westminster, 1875), 169. *The London Gazette*, nos. 3161–3217, 24 February–8 September 1696.

[36] Bret to Huntingdon, 27 February, *HMC: Hastings*, II, 258; Bret observed that Lord Gray of Wark and Lord Mordaunt were 'the chief court managers.'

[37] *The London Gazette*, no. 3164, 5–9 March 1696.

[38] *Ibid.*

[39] 7 & 8 William III, c. 27: *SR*, VII, 114–17.

meeting of the Privy Council on 12 March the king declared 'he thought it fit for his service that all who were in employment under him should sign the Association,' so the names of three non-associating councillors were stricken.[40] Like the first Elizabethan bond the Association at this stage lacked the force of law, but that would soon be remedied. A bill for the better security of his majesty's royal person and government, reminiscent of the Elizabethan act, was introduced in the Commons on 2 April, passed the Lords on 13 April, and received royal assent at the prorogation on 27 April. The text of Somers's Association was adopted unchanged. All existing officeholders were to take the oath before 1 August, and the Association, along with the oaths of supremacy and allegiance already required by 25 Charles II, c. 2, became a prerequisite for new appointments. By late July some 86 justices and 104 deputy lieutenants had lost their offices; some had actually taken the Association, but without sufficient enthusiasm or promptness.[41]

The Elizabethan Association was designed to unite the Protestant nation behind their undisputed monarch, but Somers and the junto used their Association to solidify Whig ascendancy and to purge their political enemies from Parliament and commissions of the peace. The oath readily became a test of loyalty for officeholders and gentlemen in the much-enlarged political nation, but it was not initially intended for ordinary people lower down the social scale. It was designed to bind the ruling class to William of Orange and to identify and isolate the Jacobites. However, it was not long before a widening circle of Englishmen joined the Association. Whether this was a response to popular clamor, a patriotic urge to participate in the defense of the king, or whether local agents for the Association took it upon themselves to pad the rolls, is not entirely clear. What is certain is that Kensington Palace was soon swamped with lists of subscribers containing not hundreds but thousands of names. From the beginning of March there was a regular traffic of civic and county leaders bearing humble addresses, expressions of subject-like concern, and sworn promises to avenge the king if he were assassinated. For example, the Association of 'the mayor, aldermen, bailiffs, town clerk, common council, burgesses and other inhabitants of the town of Cambridge' arrived on 29 March, at the same time that lists of subscribers came in from Warwick, East Sussex, and the Cinque Ports. Members of the lieutenancy or Members of Parliament usually presented the documents and performance of this duty was often an occasion for royal favor. Charles Turner,

[40] Horwitz, *Parliament, Policy and Politics*, 176, citing Privy Council memoranda and correspondence.

[41] 7 & 8 William III, c. 27: *SR*, VII, 114–17. Horwitz, *Parliament, Policy and Politics*, 176, 179.

Edward Seyward, and Joseph Tiley were among the MPs knighted by the king in March 'for the loyalty and good affection to his person and government' regarding the Association. Each had delivered an impressive list of subscribers from his local community. On 25 March the earl of Monmouth presented the king with an Association and humble address subscribed by the officers and 'about fourteen thousand freeholders of the country of Northampton.' On 1 April came in 'above 20,000 hands' from Westminster, and on 29 April an Association roll appeared with another 37,389 subscriptions from Westminster and Middlesex. Surrey turned in the names of 16,556 associators, Yorkshire delivered 'above 24,000 hands,' while the collected Association oath rolls from Suffolk boasted above 70,000 subscriptions.[42] Clearly the Association had reached out beyond the officeholders and gentlemen for whom it was originally intended, to embrace, in some areas, every adult male inhabitant. Perhaps it is fitting that the age of 'political arithmetic' should yield such a weight of numbers.

What to do with all this paper and parchment? Somers had created a monster, and the administration was faced with transportation and storage problems which made the earl of Huntingdon's difficulties in 1584 look trivial. On 3 April the king agreed to a suggestion by the Speaker of the House of Commons that all the Associations 'be lodged among the records in the Tower, to remain as a perpetual memorial of [their subscribers'] loyalty and affection.' The Association Act, a few weeks later, required the oath rolls to be hung up and displayed in the courts where they were signed. The Associations sworn in Chancery would remain in the office of the Petty Bag, those in King's Bench in the crown office of King's Bench, and the rest in some public place of every quarter session.[43] Some still exist, although not necessarily where they originally belonged. Between the county record offices and the PRO it is possible to reconstruct how the oath was disseminated and how local officials responded to the orders and suggestions of central government. The taking of the Association in 1584 had involved dramatic and ritual elements, displays of pageantry and manifestations of power. While these were not altogether lacking in 1696 the collecting of subscriptions was more like a dutiful chore that barely interrupted the administrative

42 *The London Gazette*, nos. 3170, 26–30 March; 3168, 19–23 March; 3169, 23–26 March; 3171, 30 March–2 April; 3179, 27–30 April; 3178, 23–27 April; 3180, 30 April–4 May; 3184, 14–18 May 1696.

43 *The London Gazette*, no. 3172, 2–6 April; 7 & 8 William II, c. 27: *SR*, VII, 114–17. The names of those who refused to take the oath were to be forwarded to the Council. See duke of Shrewsbury to the deputy lieutenants, 14 May, *CSP, Domestic Series . . . 1696*, 177.

routine. The scurrying of constables through parts of East Anglia, for example, may have been more a matter of bureaucratic reflex than of passionate loyalty for the lawful king.

The Suffolk quarter sessions, meeting at Beccles on 20 April, set aside the business of bastards and bridges, and the price of cheese and salt, to attend to the security of the realm. The Grand Jury made a written presentment about the assassination plot and the danger of invasion from France, 'and did desire that some effectual course may be taken to recommend to all the parishes of this county the speedy entering into the Association lately entered into by both houses of parliament.' Responding to this the courts ordered the chief constables to supervise the petty constables in tendering the oath to every householder and lodger in every parish, and to deliver the completed returns by 7 May.[44] At this time there was no statute directing anyone to take the Association, nor, so far as I can find, an official order requiring the oath to be taken parish by parish. Yet the Suffolk justices were not alone in this initiative. On the same day the Hertfordshire quarter sessions were sitting, ninety miles away, and they too ordered the local administrative chain of high and petty constables, tithing men and headboroughs, to press home the Association. The magistrates instructed local officials to carry the Association 'from house to house through the parish' and to secure the subscriptions of every householder and lodger. They were given until 6 June to return the lists of names to the clerk of the peace.[45] Both counties arranged for special parchment rolls to be printed with the text of the Association, with the cost of the business to be borne by the county stock. The names of refusers had to be taken down, with a note of their additions, callings and places of abode. The timing of this effort in Suffolk and in Hertfordshire, and the similarity of their instructions and preparations, suggests that both counties were responding to directives from London. Instead of being confined to officeholders and gentlemen, the Association was extending to all men, the humble as well as the prominent. The collection of names went well beyond anything attempted in 1584, and exceeded the terms of the statute awaiting King William's signature. Similar efforts were under way in other counties, and the results can be seen in the surviving returns from Cornwall, Yorkshire and Essex.[46]

Completed Association oath rolls survive for nearly every parish in Suffolk. It seems that every adult male over the age of sixteen was invited

[44] Suffolk Record Office, Quarter Sessions Order Book, MS 105/2/13, fols. 16–17*v*.

[45] William Le Hardy (ed.), *Hertford County Records: Calendar to the Sessions Book* (Hertford, 1930), v, 485–6.

[46] PRO, C/213/33–59, C/213/313–31. Essex Record Office, MS Q/RRo/2/1.

to subscribe, and there were very few refusers. The constable of Coney Weston certified that the oath had been tendered to 'householders and lodgers, young men and servants above the age of sixteen . . . we had not any did refuse to subscribe their names hereunto within our said town.' Community after community subscribed the Association rolls, some adding, like Ixworth, 'we have none that refuse, so God bless King William.' Where there were refusers the constables made note of their names. At Bardwell 'Thomas Turpin a quaker and Thomas Foster a journeyman tailor and Robert Tabell, labourer' refused the oath. Mr John Buxton , usher in the free school at Kelsale, would not subscribe, despite being 'asked several times by us constables.' And at Westhorpe there were two Quakers who refused the Association because they could 'not for conscience sake revenge for ourselves nor any man else.'[47] The Association statute excused Quakers from the oath, but many were willing to subscribe an alternative testimony of loyalty and peacefulness.[48] For the most part the Suffolk turnout was complete. A check against taxation returns, tithe books and other local records shows that for Suffolk at least the completed Association oath rolls constitute an approximate census of the adult male population. They can be used in demographic and community history, to estimate the size of the population or to certify the presence of an inhabitant, as well as to reconstruct in detail the local geography of illiteracy.[49] We still do not know whether Whig supporters were more literate than Tories, or whether dissenters were more literate than Anglicans, or even whether those categories are meaningful at the local level. Thanks to the assassination scare and the ebullient administrative response we have some of the materials with which to find out.

VI

In both episodes, in 1584 and in 1696, court and Council turned assassination scares to immediate political advantage. By cracking conspiracies, each government demonstrated the effectiveness of its security apparatus, while the deliverance of the monarchs from danger revealed the smiles of divine providence. It signified that the regime would survive. Each escape

47 PRO, C/213/264, rolls 20, 19, 17.

48 'The ancient testimony and principle of the people called Quakers, renewed with respect to the king and government, and touching the present Association,' subscribed by Quakers of Colchester is in PRO, C/213/473. Of 125 subscribers 24 made marks instead of signatures (19%).

49 Cressy, *Literacy and the Social Order*, 99–103. Association oath subscribers, people of communicant age, and hearth-taxed households are compared for 35 Essex parishes in David Cressy, 'Education and literacy in London and East Anglia 1580–1700' (Cambridge University, Unpublished Ph.D. thesis, 1972).

served further to legitimate the Crown, while exposing the diabolical machinations of its opponents. Each emergency presented an opportunity for propaganda. Properly managed, the scare could unite the country in a bond of outraged patriotism. At stake, aside from the life of a particular king or queen, was the whole future of Protestantism in England. Each Association warned Marian or Jacobite plotters that the country stood alert and vengeful. A single knife or bullet would not be enough to change the succession and reshape England's destiny.

Although they had much in common the Elizabethan and Williamite Associations differed in important ways. The Bond of 1584 originated with the Privy Council and its distribution was largely confined to the leading gentry. Taking the oath was a solemn, even a ceremonial act, giving one membership in an honorable society. In some cases the Association was broadened to include townsmen and freeholders, who occupied the fringe of the political nation, but there was no systematic attempt to secure the subscriptions of ordinary people. The Council knew exactly whose signatures counted, and wasted no more effort than was necessary to collect them. The Association of 1696 was more ambitious and less discriminating. In scale, target and application it was broader than its Elizabethan prototype, and relied for its success on the entire machinery of government. Whereas Walsingham and Burghley used the authority of their office and a handful of officials to coax the political nation into line, the Whig junto of William III employed Members of Parliament, lieutenants and deputy lieutenants, sheriffs, justices and constables to deliver their document. All officeholders had to take the oath as a matter of course, and tens of thousands of other men subscribed for good measure. The county elite could still take the oath in a formal setting, at assizes or sessions, but parish officers took the Association to the rest from door to door, like travelling salesmen. As a dramatic event it lacked finesse and substance, but as an ideological mustering it was fully as impressive as its earlier counterpart.

Part three

Early Stuart Variations

Proclamations and parliamentary protest, 1539–1610

RUDOLPH W. HEINZE

In July 1610 the House of Commons presented a petition to King James I protesting his use of royal proclamations. The Commons complained about the number of proclamations issued, penalties threatened, the methods of enforcement decreed, as well as their use as legislative instruments. They maintained that James was not only using proclamations more frequently than his predecessors but in a manner which violated his subjects' rights. As a result there was 'a general fear spread amongst your Majesty's people, that proclamations will by degrees grow up and increase to the strength and nature of laws' and 'in process of time bring a new form of arbitrary government upon the realm.' The petition concluded by listing seven specific grievances and citing nine proclamations as examples.[1] Although the Crown had used proclamations extensively throughout the Tudor period, and Parliament had occasionally expressed concern, Tudor parliaments do not seem to have protested their use as specifically and vociferously as did the House of Commons in 1610.

This new militance towards royal proclamations was once explained either by accepting the validity of the complaints in the petition or by viewing the attack on proclamations as another example of a more assertive Parliament encroaching upon royal authority.[2] In an age when the reign of James was viewed as the first step on the 'high road to civil war,' the complaints about proclamations seemed to be part of a general pattern, in which Stuart parliaments would witness more conflict between Crown and Parliament than had their Tudor counterparts. However, recent reappraisals of the early Stuart period, influenced by Professor Elton's provocative articles and reviews, suggest that conflict in Stuart

[1] Elizabeth R. Foster (ed.), *Proceedings in Parliament 1610* (2 vols., New Haven, Yale University Press, 1966), II, 258–61.

[2] Samuel R. Gardiner, *History of England from the Accession of James I to the Outbreak of the Civil War, 1603–1642* (10 vols., London, 1883–4), II, 86. George L. Mosse, *The Struggle for Sovereignty in England* (East Lansing, Michigan State University Press, 1950), 135.

parliaments has been overestimated and that its explanation is significantly more complex than earlier studies allowed.[3] Professor Esther Cope, in her doctoral dissertation on parliamentary reaction to royal proclamations during the period 1604 to 1629, maintains that there was more agreement between Crown and Parliament on the role of royal proclamations than had once been assumed.[4] If this is true, then the differences between Tudor and Stuart parliaments in their reactions to royal proclamations are more surprising, and this comparative study of parliamentary protest may help to clarify the issues and to explain the conflict which occurred.

I

The only major recorded debate about royal proclamations in the parliaments of the Tudor kings occurred in 1539 when the government introduced a bill apparently intended to define the role and power of proclamations, to provide statutory authority for them, and to improve enforcement by a special conciliar court for speedy and more certain punishment of offenders. The bill, eventually enacted in modified form as the Statute of Proclamations, probably did not include any limitations on penalties or provisions to protect statutory and common law from infringement by proclamations. The bill was debated extensively in both the Lords and the Commons, and both added amendments. Lords' amendments consisted largely of adding the words 'by authority of this act' at key places in the text, thereby emphasizing the role of Parliament in granting authority to royal proclamations. The Commons apparently amended more extensively, having rejected the original bill and then rewritten it. The major addition seems to have been a proviso protecting existing law from infringement by proclamations and severely limiting the penalties which could be imposed, stating that subjects could not have 'their enheritaunces, lawfull possessions, offices, libertyes, privileges, franchisies, goodes, or chattelles taken from them . . . nor by vertue of the said Acte suffer any paynes of Deathe, other than shal be hereafter in this Acte declared.' The full intent of the proviso is not entirely clear. Strictly interpreted, it seems to have prohibited even fines and forfeitures, but later the statute clearly

[3] G. R. Elton, 'A high road to civil war?' in his *Studies in Tudor and Stuart Politics and Government* (2 vols., Cambridge, CUP, 1974), II, 164–83; Elton, 'The unexplained revolution,' in *ibid.*, 183–99; Conrad Russell, 'Parliamentary history in perspective, 1604–1629,' *History*, LXI (1976), 1–27.

[4] Esther S. Cope, 'Parliament and proclamations 1604–1629' (Bryn Mawr College, Unpublished Ph.D. thesis, 1969). I am indebted to Professor Cope for the help she has given me on this project. Her dissertation originally provided the stimulus for this study.

stated that offenders convicted by the conciliar court would 'lose and paye suche penaltyes, forfeytures of somes of money, to be levyed of his or their londes, tenements, goodes and catalles to the Kinges use' as specified in the proclamations.[5] Despite limitations imposed, the proviso did not seem to have annulled the government's major purpose in seeking the act, because the revised bill was accepted. Although the debate appeared fierce, Crown and Parliament arrived at an equitable compromise protecting the major concerns of both parties.

The enactment of the Statute of Proclamations revealed that Parliament recognized the king's need to have extraordinary powers when 'soden causes and occasions . . . do require spedy remedyes' as they had in a series of earlier statutes granting specific powers to proclamations. These statutes delegated authority to proclamations in matters which could not be regulated effectively by Parliament, like price controls, because they needed periodic readjustment for economic changes. They also granted a discretionary power to suspend or alter statutory regulations on a variety of subjects when occasion warranted. Lack of evidence makes certainty difficult, but there is no sign that Parliament protested any of these acts.[6] There was, however, some debate over an act in 1543 which revised the Statute of Proclamations by lowering the quorum on the conciliar court in order to make it operate more efficiently. Although details of the debate are unknown, the Commons amended the bill by restricting its duration to the lifetime of Henry VIII, while the *Lords Journal* recorded one dissenting voice when the bill passed. Even though the Statute of Proclamations was repealed in 1547, there is no evidence that the repeal was motivated by parliamentary opposition.[7]

There was also some protest about proclamations in Elizabeth's reign, but it seems not to have reached serious proportions. One most revealing comment on proclamations in a parliamentary debate came in 1576 in

[5] 31 Henry VIII, c. 8: *SR*, III, 726–8. See G. R. Elton, 'Henry VIII's Act of Proclamations,' *English Historical Review*, LXXV (1960), 208–22; Stanford E. Lehmberg, *The Later Parliaments of Henry VIII, 1536–1547* (Cambridge, CUP, 1977), 75–9; Rudolph W. Heinze, *The Proclamations of the Tudor Kings* (Cambridge, CUP, 1976), 165–74 for detailed discussions of the statute.

[6] Examples of these statutes are 23 Henry VIII, c. 7, 24 Henry VIII, c. 6, 28 Henry VIII, c. 14 (wine prices); 25 Henry VIII, c. 2 (food prices); 25 Henry VIII, c. 1 (meat prices); 26 Henry VIII, c. 10 (exports and imports); 27 Henry VIII, c. 26, 28 Henry VIII, c. 3, 31 Henry VIII, c. 11, 34 & 35 Henry VIII, c. 26 (Wales); 33 Henry VIII, c. 15 (Sanctuary). The Lords actually added the proviso to 33 Henry VIII, c. 15 which allowed the king to change the sanctuary by proclamation. Lehmberg, *The Later Parliaments*, 159.

[7] 1 Edward VI, c. 12: *SR*, IV, Pt I, 18–22. The act may have been repealed because its restrictions inhibited the Duke of Somerset's use of proclamations. Heinze, *Proclamations*, 175–6.

opposition to a bill on apparel authorizing regulation by royal proclamation. Sir Walter Mildmay stated that some objected to the bill:

utterly grounding themselves specially upon this reason, That, where the subjectes of the Land have not byn heretofore bound to anything but unto such as should be certaynly established by the authority of Parliament, This Act proceeding a Proclamacion from the Prince should take the force of law which might prove a dangerous precedent in tyme to come . . .. Least by this example the authority of Proclamacions may extend to greater matters than theis are.[8]

This concern that precedent might encourage a more tyrannically inclined sovereign to extend the powers of proclamations must have been widespread enough to cause Robert Beale, in a treatise on the office of the principal secretary written in 1592, to include a warning about offending the subjects' sensitivities by carelessly drafted proclamations. He first pointed out that precedents of previous proclamations should be consulted and, if possible, the proclamation should be based on existing statute law. But 'as new evills require new remedies' where no previous law existed, 'then her Majestie by her prerogative may take order in mannie thinges by proclamacion.' He also suggested that edicts of the kings of France and Spain might be consulted, but he warned:

be circumspect in applyinge of those presidents to this Estate to avoide an opinion of beinge new fangled and a bringer in of new Customes. Shew the necessitie and cause and likewise the common benefitt, that it may not be thought to tende to anie private respects, and let the threateninge of the penalties be such as may not seeme strange or excessive, against the Lawe and libertie of the Lande.[9]

II

This was good advice and had James followed it, he might have avoided some problems over proclamations in his parliaments. James began his reign by issuing many more proclamations than any of his Tudor predecessors – 32 in the first nine months of his reign and 16 in the second year. Elizabeth had issued only five proclamations in the last full year of her reign and never issued more than 18 in a single year. Although a significant majority of James's early proclamations dealt with non-controversial matters, some touched very sensitive areas. The proclamation of 20 October 1604 announcing the new royal style is an example. It was part of the king's effort to advance the Scottish union. When James first came to England, he assumed that the union would be easy to achieve,

[8] BL, MS Sloane 326, fols. 15*v*.–16.

[9] Conyers Read, *Mr Secretary Walsingham and the Policy of Queen Elizabeth* (2 vols., Oxford, Clarendon Press, 1925), I, 439, printed from BL, MS Add. 48149.

because people of both kingdoms favored it. Consequently, one of his earliest proclamations, issued in May 1603, announced that 'his Highnes will with all convenient diligence with the advice of the Estates and parliament of both Kingdomes' take steps to perfect the union. In the meantime subjects were 'to repute, hold and esteeme both the two Realmes as presently united.'[10]

James quickly found that he had overestimated his English subjects' desire for the Scottish union. Parliament in 1604 received a proposal to change the royal style to King of Great Britain and to appoint commissioners to meet with Scottish commissioners to prepare details of the union. Although 1 James I, c. 1, did provide for the meeting of commissioners, it refused to sanction the alteration in royal style. James, severely disappointed by Parliament's reluctance to accept the Scottish union, sent an angry letter to Parliament reproaching them for their failure to act, and he ended the session with a speech on the same question.[11] Then James undiplomatically issued the proclamation assuming the style King of Great Britain on the very day the commissioners were scheduled to meet. Dudley Carleton noted this at the time, pointing out that although the king could legally assume the title by proclamation, it would have been wiser to wait until Parliament asked him to take the title.[12] The proclamation was even more controversial because it was involved in the decision by the commissioners that individuals born in Scotland after the English accession of James (the *post-nati*) were considered naturalized by common law throughout the king's dominions. This led to vigorous debate in the 1606–7 session of parliament in which the proclamation was questioned. Ellesmere noted that:

> It was discreetely and modestly saied by learned Gentlemen of the lower House, that it was of great respect, and much to be regarded; but yet it was not binding, nor concluding: for, Proclamations can neither make, nor declare Lawes. And beside, that this Proclamation was not grounded upon any Resolution of the reverend Judges; but upon the opinion of some skilfull in the Lawes of this Land.[13]

[10] James L. Larkin and Paul L. Hughes, *Stuart Royal Proclamations* (Oxford, Clarendon Press, 1973), no. 9 (hereafter Larkin and Hughes, *SRP*).

[11] *CJ*, I, 193–4; PRO, SP 14/8/93; see David H. Willson, 'King James I and Anglo Scottish Unity,' in William Aiken and Basil D. Henning (eds.), *Conflict in Stuart England: Essays in Honour of Wallace Notestein* (London, Jonathan Cape, 1960), 43–55 for a full discussion.

[12] PRO, SP 14/9A/82; Larkin and Hughes, *SRP*, no. 45.

[13] Louis A. Knafla, *Law and Politics in Jacobean England: The Tracts of Lord Chancellor Ellesmere* (Cambridge, CUP, 1977), 208. It was also said in the same debate that 'there is great difference between an act of Parliament and a proclamation. An Act of Parliament is the skin that closeth in the flesh, a proclamation is but a girtle that keeps in use.' BL, MS Harleian 1314, fol. 46*v*.

James defended his proclamation, arguing that it had been based on a decision of the judges. Although he accepted the possibility that 'judges may err, as men,' he noted that 'it is as possible, and likely, your own lawyers may err,' and he warned them 'to beware to disgrace, either my Proclamation or the judges.'[14] Even though the courts upheld James in Calvin's Case, it was a pyrrhic victory because proclamations had been associated with an unpopular and controversial matter.

Nevertheless, James's proclamation seems to have been treated with respect in the debates, and overall very little was said about proclamations in the first three sessions of James's first parliament. In the first session a bill authorizing the king to regulate apparel by proclamation was rejected; but, as has been noted, a similar bill had failed in Elizabeth's reign.[15] Furthermore, the same parliament enacted 1 James I, c.6, allowing the king to prohibit the export of corn by proclamation. Growing sensitivity to statutes that authorized use of proclamations might be indicated by efforts to repeal the section of 34 & 35 Henry VIII, c.26 which allowed the king to make laws for Wales. Bills were introduced in almost every session of parliament on this subject. In 1624, 21 James I, c.10 repealed this section of the act while confirming the rest of the statute. But the repeal did not seem to have been motivated by a belief that statutes delegating powers to proclamations were inevitably dangerous. Rather, a petition in 1610 argued that since power had been granted 'to meete onlie with the inconvenyense which might aryse by that newe government,' it was no longer necessary, because 'nowe length of tyme by the space of 68 yeres hath approved the same lawes be good and benificiall for the commonweathe.' Furthermore, it was maintained that 'the purpose of the lawe makers' was to empower only Henry VIII and not his successors.[16] This made good sense. Whatever emergency powers may have necessitated the statute then could certainly no longer be justified. Therefore, repeal did not necessarily indicate a change in Parliament's attitude to statutes which delegated powers to proclamations. In fact, the same parliament which enacted 21 James I, c.10 also passed 21 James I, c.28, renewing the king's right to limit grain export by proclamation.

At least one Member of Parliament viewed the Statute of Proclamations as a safeguard against misuse of proclamations. Edward Alford, probably the most outspoken critic of proclamations, made what may have been a reference to the Statute of Proclamations in April 1607.

[14] *CJ*, I, 360.
[15] *Ibid.*, 152.
[16] PRO, SP 14/55/59; see *CJ*, I, 265 (1605), 308 (1607), 468 (1614), and 539 (1621) for bills introduced in Parliament.

Although one cannot be certain from the cryptic statement in the *Journal*, he seems to have cited limitations in the Statute of Proclamations as a model for his own day: 'In H. VIII. Time, no Man to be touched in his Life, Goods, Liberty or Member, by any Proclamation.'[17] Curiously, James also expressed respect for those responsible for revising the original government bill in 1539. In January 1610 he told Yelverton: 'I comend Bacon who when Hen. 8th fought by parliament to make his proclamation a law, and this with such violence thrust on your house, or none durst stir his finger. Then did Bacon as reason would, stand up and speake with boldness against it, for the king's seeking in that point was tyranical.'[18]

Although Parliament had not expressed much concern about proclamations, dormant fears and resentments which may have been created by the king's foolish use of prerogative early in the reign, were stimulated anew by his actions in the months preceding the 1610 parliament. This helped to create the situation which produced the 1610 petition. In the previous 19 months James issued 22 proclamations. Three dealt with two controversial subjects which received the most attention in the petition, building in London and starch making.[19] Furthermore, in 1609 a book containing all proclamations issued since the beginning of the reign was published. Although a similar collection for Edward VI's reign had been published in 1550, the new book caused concern because it suggested that proclamations were intended as more permanent legislation.[20]

Salisbury knew Parliament's apprehensions about proclamations when the session began. In his opening speech on 15 February he specified the *Book of Proclamations* as he rebuked those 'who, hearing of a course taken to bind all the printed proclamations into a book to the intent there may be the better notice taken of those things which they command, have been content to raise a bruit that it was intended at this parliament to make the

17 *CJ*, I, 1035, Alford was probably complaining about a proclamation of 1 March 1605 (Larkin and Hughes, *SRP*, no. 51) restricting building in London which threatened offenders with fine and imprisonment. See Cope, 'Parliament and proclamations,' 33, 79–88 for a discussion of Alford and his opposition to proclamations.

18 Henry Yelverton, 'Narrative of Sir Henry Yelverton,' *Archaeologia*, XV (1806), 43.

19 Larkin and Hughes, *SRP*, nos. 86, 87, 107. The publication of John Cowell, *The Interpreter* (London, 1607), caused additional concern, because it seemed to attribute more power to proclamations and to magnify the king's powers at the expense of Parliament. The Commons complained about the book, and although James issued a proclamation during the session which condemned it (Larkin and Hughes, *SRP*, no. 110), a reference to the book was still included in the petition. Cowell: *STC* 5900; suppressed by *STC* 8446.

20 *A Book of Proclamations Published Since the Beginning of His Majesty's Most Happy Reign Over England etc. Until This Present Month of Feb. 3 Anno Dom. 1609*. The 1550 collection was Robert Grafton (ed.), *All Suche Proclamations as Have Been Sett Furth by the Kings Majiestie from the Last of January in the First Year of His Highness Reign unto the last Day of Januarri Beeying in the III yere of His Reigne* (London, 1550): *STC* 7758.

power of proclamations equal to the laws.' He defended the action by pointing out that 'our purpose was only to take care that one might not cross another.' Sir Edward Sandys accepted this in an interesting speech on 17 February:

> The proclamations were drawn together that one might not cross the other. And as in this case, a wrong bruit hath been raised that the King intended to make laws of proclamations, so in these demands for the King's relief there hath been wrong reports raised thereof. The prerogative of the King is given him for the utility of the people.[21]

The defense did not satisfy the House because the final version of the petition complained about printing proclamations 'in such form as acts of parliament formerly have been, and still are used to be, which seemeth to imply a purpose to give them more reputation and more establishment than heretofore they have had.'[22]

The petition presented to the king in July seems considerably more moderate than an earlier proposal. Professor Cope suggests that the original draft for the petition, discussed on 7 May, asked that 'in tyme of peace' proclamations 'be forborne or sparingly used, and that the force and extent of the same may resceive some certain lymitacion, and every proclamation whatsoever hereafter to be made or put in execution may be agreeable to lawe and may be no longer of any force then untill the next session of parliament.' The draft also listed a proclamation of 9 July 1607 as a grievance, because it reinstated 'penal statutes worthely repeled by this Parliament.'[23] The proclamation in question had revived that portion of 5 Richard II, st.1, c.2 which stated that none except nobles, merchants and the king's soldiers were to leave the realm without license. The statute had been repealed by 4 James I, c.1, as hostile to union with Scotland, because it inhibited free travel to Scotland. The proclamation was carefully drafted with a detailed explanation. It also specified that it had been issued after consultation with the judges and on the basis of precedents from the reigns of Edward I and Edward III.[24] The king could also have mentioned Fitzherbert's *La Novel Natura Brevium* and a decision by

[21] Foster, *Proceedings 1610*, II, 22. Salisbury's explanation is given in another version of the speech: *ibid.*, no. 49. For Sandys' speech, see *ibid.*, 357. Wallace Notestein, *The House of Commons 1604–1610* (New Haven, Yale University Press, 1971), 433–4 calls Sandys a moderate spokesman of the 'opposition.'

[22] Foster, *Proceedings 1610*, II, 259.

[23] BL, MS Harleian 6842, fol. 146. This document is included in a collection of the papers of Edward Alford. It is entitled 'Proclamations – Notes of Grievances Concerning Them.' See Cope, 'Parliament and Proclamations,' 18–27 for a full discussion of the debate and Appendix I, 75–7 for a transcription of the document.

[24] Larkin and Hughes, *SRP*, no. 73.

Elizabethan justices which cited Fitzherbert in support of the king's right to 'restrain his subjects from going out without his special licence';[25] so there was legal justification for his action. The Commons may have realized this, because on 10 May it was agreed that the king had acted 'upon just Cause,' and a reference to the proclamation was not included in the final petition. The Commons may also have been concerned about inhibiting royal power to restrain the travel of recusants. On 25 May, as the final petition was being prepared, parliament petitioned the king to take action against recusants by royal proclamation.[26]

Although the final petition contained far-reaching complaints, the action requested was considerably more moderate. The petition invoked

> that indubitable right of the people of this kingdom not to be made subject to any punishments that shall extend to their lives, lands, bodies or goods, other than such as are ordained by the common laws of this land, or the statutes made by their common consent in parliament.

Proclamations, it was argued, had become more frequent and:

> they are extended not only to the liberty, but also to the goods, inheritances, and livelihood of men, some of them tending to alter some points of law, and make a new, other some made shortly after a session of parliament for matter directly rejected in the same session, other appointing punishments to be inflicted before lawful trial and conviction; some containing penalties in form of penal statutes; some referring the punishment of offenders to courts of arbitrary discretion, which have laid heavy and grievous censures upon the delinquents; some, as the proclamation for starch, accompanied with letters commanding inquiry to be made against the transgressors at the quarter sessions; and some vouching former proclamations to countenance and warrant the latter, as by a catalogue hereunder written more particularly appeareth.[27]

As a result of these abuses there was 'a general fear conceived' that proclamations would 'by degrees grow up and increase to the strength and nature of Laws' and 'in the process of time bring a new form of arbitrary government upon the realm.' Consequently, Commons petitioned the king that, unless the offense violated statute or common law:

> henceforth no fine or forfeiture of goods or other pecuniary or corporal punishment may be inflicted upon your subjects other than restraint of liberty, which

[25] John Vailliant (ed.), *Reports of Cases in the Reign of Henry VIII, Edward VI, Queen Mary, and Queen Elizabeth Taken and Collected by Sir James Dyer Knt.* (London, 1794), II, 165; Antony Fitzherbert, *La Novel Natura Breviuim* (London, 1534), 85.

[26] *CJ*, I, 427; Foster, *Proceedings 1610*, II, 118–19 for the petition about recusants. The original concern about the proclamation may have reflected the issues raised in the debate about impositions over the king's right to restrain trade and travel, *ibid.*, 184–5, 204–5, 226–7, and 246–7.

[27] Foster, *Proceedings 1610*, II, 258–9.

. . . may be but upon urgent necessity, and to continue but until other order maybe taken by course of the law . . . (and that) for the greater assurance and comfort of your people, that it will please your Majesty to declare your royal pleasure to that purpose, either by some law to be made in this session of parliament or by some such other course whereof your people may take knowledge.[28]

The request for action contrasts markedly with the sweeping nature of the protest in the petition. What the petition actually asked for does not seem to have been a great deal more radical than the proviso which the Commons probably added to the Statute of Proclamations. It may have reflected an understanding of that proviso which was not uncommon in the Stuart period. Coke seems to have interpreted it in this fashion and Alford may have had a similar impression when he made his comment in 1607. Furthermore, the Commons suggested that the king should use a statute to apply these restrictions. Fears about the growth of arbitrary government and of proclamations increasing to 'the force of law' were not so different from those expressed by Mildmay in the Elizabethan debate over the apparel statute.[29]

III

Even if the petition's request differed little from similar actions by Tudor parliaments, the accusations about improper use of proclamations, supported by citing specific proclamations in a catalogue appended to the petition, suggested that more reason existed for concern about arbitrary government than in the Tudor period. Were these concerns well founded? The first two complaints – that proclamations were more numerous than before and that they had been printed in a book – were general in nature. Although James had issued an exceptional number of proclamations in his first two years, and again in the period preceding the 1610 parliament, he averaged for the first eight years of his reign approximately 1.3 proclamations per month. This surpassed the reign of Elizabeth (0.72 per month),

[28] *Ibid.*, 259–60.

[29] Coke made the following reference to the Statute of Proclamations in his printed report: 'that which cannot be punished without a proclamation, cannot be punished with it. Vide le Stat. 31 H 8. cap. 8 which Act gives more Power to the King than he had before, and yet there it is declared, that Proclamations shall nott alter the Law, Statutes, or Customs of the Realm, or impeach any in his Inheritance, Goods, Body, Life etc. But if a Man should be indicted for a Contempt against a Proclamation, he shall be fined and imprisoned, and so impeached in his Body and Goods.' Edward Coke, *The Twelfth Part of the Reports of Sir Edward Coke* (London, 1738), 75. In 1628 Coke again cited the limitations in the Statute of Proclamations reminding the Commons that: 'It was with a provision also, when it was on foot, that it should not extend to lives, lands, goods and liberties.' Robert C. Johnson, Mary Frear Keeler, Maija Jannson Cole, and William B. Bidwell (eds.), *Commons Debates 1628* (4 vols., New Haven, Yale University Press, 1977), I, 101.

but was only slightly higher than Mary's average (1 per month), not as high as Edward's (1.65 per month), and was a good deal less than the 2.4 proclamations per month issued when the Protector Somerset ruled. Furthermore, the average for the entire reign was only 1.01 per month. Especially if the 32 proclamations issued in his first nine months are discounted, James appeared a normal user of proclamations. Perhaps the problem was his sporadic use, those spurts of activity, plus misunderstandings about innovations in publishing a *Book of Proclamations*.[30]

Specific complaints began with a particularly serious accusation – 'proclamations importing alteration of some points of law and making new.' If this involved regular use of proclamations for long-term legislation, the Commons had good reason to be concerned about innovations. Although proclamations had been used extensively throughout the Tudor period, they dealt largely with sudden emergencies 'whiche do require spedy remedyes, and that abidinge for a Parliament in the mean tyme myght happen great prejudyce to ensue to the Realme.' This was the function described in the Statute of Proclamations, and in carrying out that role they were to 'be obeyed, observed and kept as thoughe they were made by Acte of Parliament for the tyme in them lymitted.' More permanent legislation was the purview of statutes, and with few exceptions Tudor governments recognized this.[31]

The first proclamation listed as making new law was issued before the meeting of James's first parliament. It forbade the election of outlawed or bankrupt men and specified that returns were to be certified to the Chancery where 'if any shall be found to be made contrary to this proclamation, the same to be rejected as unlawful and insufficient.'[32] It was probably included in the petition because of the controversy which arose over these issues in 1604. The questions of whether outlawed men could sit in Parliament and who would judge such disputed elections was extensively debated in *Goodwin* v. *Fortescue*. Both sides cited precedents, and it is difficult to be certain who had the best argument. But it seems clear that this proclamation was included primarily because its provisions had become a central issue in the debate, and memories of that debate had not been forgotten.[33]

30 Heinze, *Proclamations*, 5.

31 31 Henry VIII, c. 8; Heinze, *Proclamations*, 295; Frederic A. Youngs, Jr., *The Proclamations of the Tudor Queens* (Cambridge, CUP, 1976), 54.

32 Larkin and Hughes, *SRP*, no. 33.

33 Notestein, *House of Commons*, 60–78 for the debate. He points out that the Commons would have had great difficulty proving that they controlled returns of elections in the early Tudor period or before. Conrad Russell, *The Crisis of Parliaments* (London, Oxford University Press, 1971), 267, states that before 1406 Commons had judged disputed elections, but after that date the Chancery judged them.

The second proclamation listed was issued on 23 August 1607. It was one of two dealing with the manufacture of starch, and four of the seven specific grievances used one or the other of these proclamations as examples. Concerns may not have been exclusively constitutional, and the history of efforts to regulate the starch industry better explained why these proclamations were so unpopular.

The starch industry began in Elizabethan England. It seems to have been unpopular, because it consumed large amounts of grain and the smell created a public nuisance, but a bill had failed in the 1585–6 parliament to ban starch manufacture in England. In 1588 Elizabeth granted a monopoly for making starch. A proclamation in 1596 prohibited all but the patentees from making or selling starch and forbade the use of bran. Two years later the high price of grain probably motivated a proclamation which universally banned the making of starch. The starch patent was one of those complained about in the 1601 parliament, and during the session Elizabeth issued a proclamation which cancelled the patent.[34]

During the first three years of James I's reign the starchmakers twice petitioned the king for incorporation. They also asked that the use of wheat be prohibited. In 1604 the judges recommended statutory legislation 'whereupon it might be grounded for the better proceeding with the same.' A bill was submitted, but after two readings it was referred to the next session. In the third year of the reign the judges again suggested that 'the abuse of making starch of wheatt shold by an Act of parliament be prohibited. And that thereupon the corporacion might be lawfully granted.'[35] Even though parliament failed to enact legislation on the subject, in June 1605 a patent was granted for the sole making and selling of starch. This was called 'very grievous and unlawful' in a list of Commons' grievances. In February 1607 the mayor of London wrote the council presenting a petition from the grocers protesting the monopoly and arguing that the price of starch had doubled.[36] Cranfield led a group to establish a rival monopoly making starch from bran, which resulted in additional complaints. A bill supported by them to ban the use of wheat failed the Commons in May 1607, so they sought the king's aid. The

[34] Paul L. Hughes and James F. Larkin (eds.), *Tudor Royal Proclamations* (3 vols., New Haven, Yale University Press, 1964–9) nos. 781, 795, 812 (hereafter Hughes and Larkin, *TRP*). The 1585–6 bill is found in Maurice Bond (ed.), *The Manuscripts of the House of Lords: Addenda 1514–1714* (London, 1962), 20–1. See Youngs, *The Proclamations*, 146–7, for a discussion of Elizabethan regulations, and Joan Thirsk, *Economic Policy and Projects* (Oxford, Clarendon Press, 1978), 84ff., for a discussion of the starch industry in England.

[35] BL, MS Harleian 160, fols. 181–181*v*.; MS Titus BV, fols. 259–61; *CJ*, I, 212, 243, 252.

[36] David H. Willson (ed.), *The Parliamentary Diary of Robert Bowyer 1606–07* (Minneapolis, University of Minnesota Press, 1931), 132; Corporation of London Record Office, MS Rem. 2, fol. 305.

result was a proclamation of 23 August 1607, providing commissioners to license starchmakers and that starch be made only of 'Branne, and such like courser stuffe.' Although the proclamation was defended as an effort to correct abuses, it, in fact, prepared the way for a monopoly to the Cranfield syndicate. A complex series of arrangements followed, designed to profit both the Crown and the syndicate,[37] which all helped further to discredit the starch regulations. In June 1608 the mayor of London again wrote the council requesting that starchmaking be prohibited during the dearth and that starch be imported.[38] A proclamation in July 1608 may have been a partial response to this request, because it ordered that starch be made only of 'decayed & mustie Wheat, bare Bran or such other stuffe, not fit for man's sustenace' by authorized persons in or near London where such grains were available and where the proclamation could be enforced more effectively. This effort must have been unsuccessful, because in January 1610 a new proclamation cited the 'many and often complaints against a thing offensive so many ways,' and completely banned manufacture in England, while permitting unrestricted imports.[39]

This proclamation was not mentioned in the Commons' petition, but it was also unpopular. One commissioner assigned for enforcement reported in April 1610 that he had conferred with justices of the peace in Surrey and they were reluctant to enforce the proclamation during parliament 'least it might give occasion to the Commons the more both to oppose themselves against it, being one of the grievances formerly exhibited unto them.'[40]

Efforts to regulate the starch industry had clearly violated Beale's advice against using proclamations in ways appearing 'to tende to anie private respects.' Although the proclamations were probably intended partly to deal with a public nuisance and to preserve grain, here the major result was to profit the Crown and to reward favorites. It is, therefore, not surprising that they received so much attention in the petition. Although claims about constitutional concerns probably were not the major reasons why the Commons objected, James certainly had acted in a

[37] Larkin and Hughes, *SRP*, no. 75; Anthony F. Upton, *Sir Arthur Ingram* (Oxford, Oxford University Press, 1961), 19–20 for a detailed discussion of the efforts and plans of the Cranfield group.

[38] Corporation of London Record Office, MS Rem. 2, fol. 325.

[39] Larkin and Hughes, *SRP*, nos. 86, 107.

[40] BL, MS Lansdowne 152, fol. 117. An undated petition complained that the proclamation took employment from Englishmen and gave it to foreigners. It reported that starchmakers were so upset that they had prepared a bill against the restraint which they intended to introduce in Parliament: *ibid.*, fol. 123.

questionable and foolish manner by using proclamations after failing to obtain the parliamentary action which the judges had advised. However, he clearly would have preferred statutory legislation, a legal defense could be constructed for his right to act by proclamation,[41] and there were precedents in the reign of Elizabeth for the use of proclamations in a similar fashion.

The next two items in the catalogue – 'proclamations made shortly after Parliament for matter directly rejected the precedent session' and 'proclamations touching the freehold livelihood of men' – also cited unpopular proclamations as examples. All three proclamations listed attempted to control building in London. A fourth building proclamation was protested because it provided for enforcement by the court of Star Chamber and cited previous proclamations as precedents.[42] Efforts to control building in London originated in the reign of Elizabeth at the request of City government. Worried by the sprawling growth of London, which multiplied problems of disease, crime control, and an adequate supply of food, Elizabeth's proclamations had prohibited new building except on old foundations and the dividing of houses into several dwellings. Originally intended as emergency measures until parliament could deal with the issue, they were a laudable but unrealistic attempt to correct a serious problem. But parliament seemed reluctant to act in any way that might effectively restrict its own membership from building. The only statute on the subject exempted buildings erected by wealthier residents, failed to provide for effective enforcement and was limited in duration.[43] Consequently, if effective controls were to be introduced, the Crown had to rely on proclamations. Elizabeth had issued another proclamation after parliament failed to renew the statute in 1601, which included orders that illegal buildings be torn down.[44]

[41] A defense was offered in a document dated 4 July 1612 which argued in part that since the king had the right to collect customs on imported starch and starchmaking in England deprived him of that custom, he could prohibit it by proclamation 'without parliament' because 'to say and hold that the King cannot restrain the starchmakers to make starch but by parliament . . . is to grant and admit that the subjects shall doo wrong to the King's inheritance and yet it shall rest in the will and election of the subjects whether the King shall have remedy for that wrong.' BL, MS Lansdowne 152, fols. 127–127*v*.

[42] Larkin and Hughes, *SRP*, nos. 25, 51, 78, 87. See Thomas G. Barnes, 'The prerogative and environmental control of London building in the early seventeenth century: the lost opportunity,' *California Law Review*, LVIII (1970), 1332–63 for a detailed discussion of the building regulations.

[43] 35 Elizabeth I, c. 6: *SR*, IV, Pt II, 852–3. Elizabeth's first proclamation emphasized the temporary nature of the proclamation stating that it would 'serve until some further good order to be had in parliament or otherwise.' Hughes and Larkin, *TRP*, no. 649.

[44] Hughes and Larkin, *TRP*, no. 815. Although neither the statute nor the first proclamation had ordered destruction of illegal buildings, a Star Chamber decree in 1597 introduced this procedure: *Les Reports del Cases in Camera Stellata, 1593 to 1609, from the Original MS of*

Although James added standards for the construction of new buildings on old foundations, his proclamations did not significantly differ from the Elizabethan policy. He had clearly issued proclamations 'shortly after parliament for matter directly rejected,' but Elizabeth's last proclamation also had been issued shortly after the 1601 parliament failed to renew 35 Elizabeth, c. 5. One of his proclamations was issued in response to a request by the City government after a bill supported by them had failed in parliament. This indicated that such use of proclamations was not universally considered undesirable.[45] Furthermore, James always viewed proclamations as temporary legislation and regularly sought parliamentary action. Controls on building were, in fact, prominent among the matters he submitted to the 1610 parliament. A bill introduced in the 1621 parliament clearly stated that the king had 'bene enforced owt of Consideracions of state and for the publique good, in his highe wisdome and princely judgment' to use 'proclymations to give some stay to those growing evills untill some exact remedye might be provided in Parliament.' There is little reason to doubt his sincerity.[46]

Although the building proclamations might be defended by citing parliament's failure to act on a critical matter involving public welfare, their legality was certainly questionable and they did touch 'the freehold livelihood of men.'[47] Consequently, efforts to defend royal rights to regulate building by proclamations provoked the most extreme claim for prerogative from Lord Chancellor Ellesmere. He argued before sentencing in the court of Star Chamber for violation of a building proclamation in October 1607: 'where the Common state or wealthe of the people or

John Hawarde, ed. by William P. Baildon (London, privately printed, 1894), 79; see the discussion of Elizabethan regulations in Youngs, *The Proclamations*, 170–4.

45 Corporation of London Record Office, MS Rep. 27, fols. 366*v*., 395*v*.; *ibid.*, 28, fol. 93*v*. The proclamation of 1 March 1605 (Larkin and Hughes, *SRP*, no. 51), which was complained of in the petition, was promulgated after a bill had failed in the 1604 parliament (*CJ*, I, 181, 188, 251). The Proclamation of 12 October 1607 (Larkin and Hughes, *SRP*, no. 78), although not mentioned under this category in the petition, also followed the failure of a bill in Parliament (*CJ*, I, 1053–4). Petitions for action by proclamation after bills had failed were not limited to the building regulations. In September 1608 the merchants importing wine from Bordeaux requested a proclamation prohibiting imports of new wines before 1 December, because parliament had failed to act: PRO, SP 14/36/44.

46 Foster, *Proceedings 1610*, II, 280; Wallace Notestein, Frances Relf, and Hartley Simpson (eds.), *Commons Debates 1621* (7 vols., New Haven, Yale University Press, 1935), VII, 272. In May 1624 when the Commons again petitioned the king about the building proclamations, the king responded in what was clearly an angry and impatient fashion: PRO, SP 14/165/57.

47 Barnes, 'London building,' 1358, comments 'at no time in the history of Tudor and Stuart government was there a scintilla of authority in law for the position that buildings adhering to the realty could be demolished by virtue of a proclamation.' In the reign of Charles the destruction of illegal buildings was defended by arguing that they constituted a common nuisance since 'abatement of a common nuisance was well established in law.'

kingedome require it, the kinge's proclamation bindes as a law & neede not staye a parliament.' In late 1615 or early 1616 William Camden presented a more moderate defense, pointing out that the proper use of proclamations was 'to turne away a mischefe which is not provided for by lawe' and that 'so farr as they take not away other written lawes or received customs' proclamations 'are law.'[48] A similar argument was advanced in an undated manuscript probably written around 1610, where proclamations were described as 'part of that great power and policy imparted to kings, quickly and of a sudden to stopp the current that runnith the wrong way which in an ordinary course of Justice can not be prevented without longer span accompaned with more debates.'[49] Even though all of the statements attributed significant power to proclamations, they were still defended as emergency legislation. In a period when there were long intervals between parliaments, and when some were notoriously unproductive, the king certainly needed such a power if the commonwealth was to run efficiently and if remedies were to be found for problems that could not wait until parliament acted. Only when that power was used for long periods of time and in areas such as building and starch regulations, where parliament had refused to act, might there be reason for concern about arbitrary government. But neither the defenses offered nor James's actions suggested that proclamations were proper as permanent legislation or that they equalled statutes.

Three items in the catalogue dealt with penalties and enforcement. Item four complained of enforcement by local officials and seizures by people who had no authority to deal with those offenses 'inflicted before lawful trial and conviction.' The seizure of prohibited items was at times decreed in Elizabethan proclamations, but it was objected to even in her reign.[50] Since it was also used in the controversial starch proclamation of 23 August 1607, it is not surprising that it was included in the petition. The complaint also listed a proclamation of 18 June 1604, to prevent deceits in the winding of wool by uncertified wool winders, citing two statutes and similar proclamations in the reigns of Edward VI and Elizabeth. It was issued at the request of merchants of the Staple, clothiers and woolmen. There were, in fact, five previous proclamations on the subject with similar provisions.

John Croke, who drew up the proclamation, obviously followed Beale's advice, consulting previous proclamations and repeating sections

[48] Hawarde, *Reportes*, 329, for Ellesmere's comment: BL, MS Stowe 277, fol. 8*v*. for Camden.
[49] BL, MS Add. 14030, fol. 93*v*. The last proclamation mentioned was that of 15 July 1608.
[50] Youngs, *The Proclamations*, 43.

from them verbatim. Unfortunately, he failed to heed his advice on excessive penalties. Edwardian and Marian proclamations had included an extremely severe fine of £20 for officials who failed to enforce the proclamation; Elizabethan proclamations had deleted this and replaced it with a vague threat: 'answer to the contrary at their perils.' Croke reintroduced the heavy fine. Since those who sat in parliament might be vulnerable to such fines, perhaps the fine rather than the standard order for enforcement by local officials produced the protest.[51]

The same proclamation was listed under the next item, 'proclamations penned with penalties in the form of penal statutes,' with the £20 fine specified.[52] Also mentioned was forfeiture of illegally manufactured starch in the proclamation of 23 August 1607. Forfeiture was a mild penalty common in Tudor proclamations, so this probably was not the basis of the complaint. More likely the Commons worried about the provision which gave half of the forfeiture to the individual seizing the starch. This resembled procedure in penal statutes which promised informers a share of fines or forfeitures, a common method of enforcing Tudor proclamations.[53] The proclamation of 4 November 1603, which threatened confiscation for transporting goods between Scotland and England outside of authorized ports of entry, was also cited. But this was due to careless drafting. The penalty and prohibition were clearly based on 22 Edward IV, c. 8, which was not mentioned in the proclamation. When James issued another proclamation on this subject in May 1611, he had the oversight corrected.[54]

Another Commons' concern about enforcement was use of Star Chamber. Three building proclamations and one starch proclamation were cited as examples. Actually five proclamations had mentioned this court before 1610. The fifth stated that individuals guilty of abuses in pur-

[51] Larkin and Hughes, *SRP*, no. 38. Proclamations regulating wool winding attempted to control abuses by part time wool winders who were not certified, and who were often guilty of winding impurities into the wool to add weight. 27 Edward III, st. 1, c. 4: *SR*, I, 330–1, provided for the certification of wool winders. 23 Henry VIII, c. 17: *SR*, III, 381, imposed a penalty of 6d. for fraudulent practices. The proclamations added penalties for winding wool without certification and for hiring these winders, as well as for negligent local officials. The five proclamations are in Hughes and Larkin, *TRP*, nos. 253, 359, 453, 497, and 780. PRO, C66/1624/32 reveals that James' proclamation was 'drawn by Jo. Croke' and 'at the humble suit of the Staple, Clothiers and Woolmen.'

[52] The penalty of imprisonment and pillory for uncertified wool winders and those who hired them was also mentioned. It was included in both the Edwardian and Marian proclamations and in the first Elizabethan proclamation: Hughes and Larkin, *TRP*, nos. 359, 453, 497.

[53] Thirty-one early Tudor proclamations offered a reward to informers or enforcement officials: Heinze, *Proclamations*, 62.

[54] Larkin and Hughes, *SRP*, nos. 31, 116.

veyance should be prosecuted by the attorney-general in Star Chamber. Possibly the Commons omitted the fifth because it wanted those abuses corrected, while it opposed the regulations on starch and building. Even if this was not the reason, James had ample precedent for using Star Chamber to enforce proclamations. Although mentioned in only three early Tudor proclamations, the conciliar court defined in the Statute of Proclamations was mentioned in nine, and it seems in practice to have been identical with the court of Star Chamber. Elizabeth and Mary also used the court regularly to enforce proclamations. Although this procedure may have been unpopular, James surely did not innovate by decreeing enforcement there.[55]

The final complaint in 1610, that previous proclamations had been cited as precedents, noted both the wool winding and the building proclamation of 25 July 1608 as examples. If previous proclamations could be used as precedents, the implied assumption was that proclamations had greater legal permanence. The building proclamation should have been least offensive because it simply referred to two previous proclamations issued by James and complained that they were not being obeyed. Numerous Tudor proclamations had been issued on the same subject largely because previous proclamations were being ignored. The wool winding proclamation gave more cause for concern because it cited proclamations from previous reigns and decreed penalties 'according to the Tenour' of those proclamations. This suggested that the Crown saw these proclamations as still in force. However, this surely was not the intent, and the phraseology probably resulted from careless drafting.[56]

IV

In his response to the petition James indicated his limited view of the role and function of proclamations. On 23 July he briefly acknowledged that 'Proclamations are not of equal Force, and in like Degree, as Lawes,' but he maintained they were necessary to deal with 'such Mischiefs and Inconveniences as We see growing in the Common Weal, against which no certain Law is extant, and which may tend to the great Grief and Prejudice of Our Subjects, if there should be no Remedy provided until a Parlia-

[55] Heinze, *Proclamations*, 62, 289; Youngs, *The Proclamations*, 51. The purveyance proclamation was Larkin and Hughes, *SRP*, no. 65.

[56] Larkin and Hughes, *SRP*, nos. 87, 38. Elizabethan proclamations at times referred to proclamations issued in previous reigns (Hughes and Larkin, *TRP*, nos. 366, 531). It was generally held that proclamations expired with the death of the monarch who issued them: Youngs, *The Proclamations*, 31–2.

ment.' If proclamations had been used more extensively and in a more arbitrary manner 'than is warranted by Law, We take it in good Part to be informed thereof by Our Loving Subjects and take it to Heart as a Matter of great Consequence.' He also said that he would confer with the Privy Council, the judges and

> Learned Counsel, and will cause such Our Proclamations as are past to be reformed, where Cause shall be found; and for future Time will provide, that none be made but such as shall stand with the former Laws or Statutes of the Kingdom and such as, in Cases of Necessity Our Progenitors have by their Prerogative Royal used, in Times of the best and happiest Government of this Kingdom.[57]

The king kept his word. On 24 September he issued a proclamation which revoked all but one of the proclamations cited in the petition. It reaffirmed the king's right to use proclamations as his predecessors had

> in all cases of sodaine and extraordinary accidents, and in matters so variable and irregular in their nature, as are not provided for by Law, nor can fitly fall under the certaine rule of a Law; and yet may greatly import either the preservation and good of Us and our people, or the publique honour and ornament of Our Kingdom.

He then revoked all proclamations mentioned in the petition with the exception of the one dealing with goods conveyed between England and Scotland. In doing so James carefully avoided accepting the validity of any grievances advanced against them. The proclamation dealing with the 1604 parliament was revoked because 'it did referre properly to the summons of the Parliament now past longe since'; the wool winding proclamation went because the abuses 'are partly holped by the law, as it now standeth, and if anything be defective, it is more fit for remedie by Acte of Parliament'; revocation of the building proclamations was explained by stating that for 'better execution of the good thereby intended' it was thought best 'to draw all the said Proclamations into one briefe and cleare forme.' The king added a subtle criticism of parliament's failure to act by pointing out 'wee could wish that some things in that behalfe might be further considered by our Parliament, seeing the matter hath beene so often moved, and never effected.' Admittedly 'there may seeme to be some ambiguitie' in the starch proclamations; so they were revoked with the intention of publishing another 'for the repressing of so great an enormitie.' The proclamation concluded by pointing out the need for legislation on a series of topics provided neither 'by law nor proclamation,' stating that the king had not acted by proclamation 'because we are will-

[57] *Journals of the House of Lords 1578–1714* (22 vols., London, 1846), II, 659.

ing to make triall, whether the remedies for these great enormities may be reduced under some regular form of Law.'[58]

The king also consulted the judges, specifically about the legality of the building and starch proclamations. As Professor Cope has pointed out, the decision of the judges as recorded by Sir Edward Coke in his *Twelfth Part of the Reports* evidently was not made public at the time or published until 1656. Furthermore, Coke's published report may be somewhat embellished. The decision as reported by him stated that 'The King by his proclamation cannot create any Offense which was not an Offense before.'[59] But a manuscript dated 26 October 1610, which Professor Cope thinks may have been the actual decision, had a somewhat different emphasis and may well recognize the king's emergency power to act by proclamations. Although it also stated that the king could not make new law by proclamations, it included an important qualifier not in the published report:

Necessety makinge an offence in lawe the kinge may prohibit or command by proclamacion, but then the lawe upon necessety created the offence, and not the proclamacion for unless the offence be created by the lawe the lawe will not punishe yt.[60]

On 3 November, after parliament had reassembled, Edward Alford, who may have authored the original more radical draft of the petition, again brought up the subject of proclamations. Four days later another member complained: 'So long as an arbitrary power of government (of impositions of proclamations) shall remain, what heart can we have to go on to the business.' James responded by again promising that 'proclamations should be reviewed and those (if there were any) contrary to the law taken away.'[61] That seemed to end the debate over proclamations in the 1610 parliament. Some members were not satisfied with the king's response, but the matter was not brought up again and other members felt 'good satisfaction' had been received on proclamations.[62]

[58] Larkin and Hughes, *SRP*, no. 113. Included among the problems listed for legislation were: 'excesse of Apparel, for the inlarging the vent of Cloth, for furnishing of the Realme with serviceable Armour, for stay of transporting of Our Treasure into forraine parts, against selling of Ships, and for restraint and prevention of Depredations at Sea.'

[59] Coke, *Twelfth Report*, 76; Esther Cope, 'Sir Edward Coke and proclamations, 1610,' *American Journal of Legal History*, xv (1971), 217.

[60] BL, MS Harleian 1576, fol. 18.

[61] Foster, *Proceedings 1610*, II, 397, 319, 341 n. 4.

[62] *HMC: Twelfth Report, Appendix, Part IV: The Manuscripts of His Grace the Duke of Rutland, G.C.B., Preserved at Belvoir Castle* (London, HMSO, 1888), 425. The king met with 30 Members of Parliament in November in his council chamber. One report of the meeting states that 'of the four greavincis, Prohibitions, Proclamations, Wales four Shyres, Impositions. In the first three they receyved good satisfaction, but for impositions none.'

James was considerably more restrained in his use of proclamations during the period 1610–14 when the average number of proclamations issued per month dropped to 0.56. Only two of the proclamations issued during that period included enforcement in Star Chamber, and I have not found any prosecutions by the attorney-general in that court for the period 1610–14. After the débâcle of the 1614 parliament, however, James issued an average of one proclamation per month for the rest of his reign. In addition, 40 proclamations either specifically mentioned the court of Star Chamber or implied that offenses would be tried there, which was true for at least 51 prosecutions by the attorney-general in the period 1614–25.[63]

In view of this frequent use later in the reign, it is not surprising that all of James's remaining parliaments complained about proclamations but never as strongly or effectively as in the 1610 petition. Although the king's response to the 1610 petition was mentioned in those debates, and the building proclamations were the subject of a new petition in 1624, the right and need of the king to act by proclamation when the situation demanded was also recognized. Even though unpopular proclamations continued to stimulate protest, the prerogative power was not questioned.[64]

V

The 1610 protest was clearly more extensive than any recorded in Tudor parliaments. Some criticisms were valid, but others reflected either a misunderstanding of previous practices or objections to particular proclamations. However, they do not seem to indicate an attitudinal change towards proclamations by either Crown or Parliament. The fears expressed

[63] The two proclamations which mentioned the court of Star Chamber in the period 1610–14 were Larkin and Hughes, *SRP*, no. 129, which prohibited the use of base Spanish coins and no. 132, which prohibited duels. Although James issued two proclamations forbidding building in London in August and September 1611 (*ibid.*, nos. 120, 121), neither of them used the court of Star Chamber for enforcement. Both the increase in the number of proclamations and the extensive use of Star Chamber were noted by John Chamberlain in March 1619 and July 1620. Norman E. McClure (ed.), *The Letters of John Chamberlain* (2 vols., Philadelphia, American Philosophical Society, 1939), II, 222, 310.

[64] *CJ*, I, 491 (1614). In 1621 Alford was the source of another outburst against proclamations: 'We sit here in parliament to make laws, where our ancestors have sat who have made laws that we are governed by and not by proclamations.' Notestein, *Commons Debates 1621*, II, 120. But in the same debate others affirmed the king's right to make proclamations (*ibid.*, 121), and even Coke stated that 'proclamations are sometimes so necessary as that we cannot be without them' (*ibid.*, 118). In 1624 the petition addressed to the king reminded him of his 'gratious promises afforded your loyall subiects uppon consideracion of a peticion of greventaunces exhibited to your Matie in the 8th yere of your happie reign': PRO, SP 14/165/53(11).

in the petition arose from extensive use of proclamations early in the reign and especially their use in controversial matters such as the Scottish union and the building and starch regulations. When combined with his other actions on matters like impositions, James seemed to some to be 'a bringer in of new customes.' These fears were unfounded. There is no evidence that his understanding of the role of proclamations differed from his Tudor predecessors. He continued to hold to the limited role and function of proclamations and he clearly preferred statutory legislation. Although he often failed to obtain the desired parliamentary regulations, possibly because he could not manage Parliament effectively or the topics were too controversial, he continued to acknowledge statutes as the only proper instrument for long-term regulations.

Parliament, for its part, did not seem to have intended to challenge the royal prerogative. The petition revealed a primary interest in protecting against innovations. Although the petition cited practices common in the Tudor period, the complaints about the starch and building proclamations were not without substance. The Commons was reasonable in the debate and deleted both the more radical demands from the original draft as well as one of the proclamations which rested on well-defined rights. The list of proclamations at the end of the petition suggested that for many the major issue may have been particular proclamations rather than constitutional concerns.

Although the Commons requested that 'no fine or forfeiture of goods or other pecuniary or corporal punishment may be inflicted' outside of statute or common law, contemporary comments suggested that some believed that the Statute of Proclamations had imposed a similar limitation. Although it had not banned penalties involving fine or forfeiture, it had defined both the power of proclamations and specified some clear limitations. It had also provided for an enforcement procedure designed to assure that proclamations could effectively carry out their proper role in government.[65] Furthermore, the statute represented a compromise between the original desires of the Crown and the concerns of Parliament. As long as it was in effect Parliament did not have to be concerned about proclamations being used to 'bring in a new form of arbitrary government upon the realm,' and the Crown possessed sufficient means to deal with 'soden causes and occasions' which 'require spedy remedyes.' The phrase in the 1610 petition which suggested that James deal with the issues raised

[65] An undated tract addressed to James, which complained about failure to enforce the building proclamations, cited the Statute of Proclamations and pointed out that as a result proclamations were obeyed in Henry VIII's reign: BL, MS Harleian 305, fol. 339.

about proclamations 'by some law to be made in this session of Parliament' may have indicated a desire for similar legislation. James would have been wise to heed that advice. If he had, subsequent protests might have been avoided.

Diplomatic intervention in English law enforcement: Sarmiento and James I

CHARLES H. CARTER

The things that govern whether laws will be enforced severely, laxly, or not at all are mostly domestic: political factors, vested interests, and so forth. It is much rarer that the historian has a chance to observe the very different process of diplomatic intervention in the enforcement of domestic law. One reason is mechanical: a sustained example of diplomatic intervention, not just an isolated instance, requires that it involve a resident ambassador, and in the sixteenth and early seventeenth centuries states exchanged residents with only about half a dozen others. Another is circumstantial: country A must have one or more laws whose enforcement or non-enforcement country B is interested in. A third is motivational: some situation must exist that might lead the ruler or rulers of country A to accept that intervention.

It is not often that all of these elements are present at one time; in the reign of James I they were. Better still, not only was the other state involved the one most important to James's foreign policy, Spain, but the essential elements were present in both directions and were acted upon in both directions, with James intervening diplomatically in Spanish legal matters as well as the reverse. Both countries had overarching policy aims within which were many entanglements, some compatible with broad policy and some not, and some of which entailed an assumption of crown responsibility to defend some particular interest abroad. James's broad goal was to prevent the resumption of major war in Europe, a policy based on principle since England need not be caught up in such a war. His conduct of foreign policy was characterized by alterations and vacillation, but it was consistent in one respect: almost to the end it hinged on maintaining friendly relations with Spain.

Spain's policy was a good deal less irenic than James's, but she was exhausted from decades of conflict and currently in a badly needed period of retrenchment. Avoiding war was as much a goal for Spain as preventing war was for James. If war *did* resume on the continent (and in the early part of the period the truce with the Dutch had not yet been made), Spanish policymakers preferred to follow Charles V's old rule, *Con todo el mundo la guerra, y paz con Inglaterra*: 'War with the whole world, and peace with England.' This of course reflected not a fear of England's rather miniscule military strength, but recognition of the damage she could do on Spain's maritime flanks, in European waters and both Indies. Each had a motive for listening to the other's complaints. Although for different reasons, it was basically the same motive, a desire to maintain Anglo-Spanish relations on as good a footing as possible, though of course the price for doing so must not be too high.

This still leaves the circumstantial level. Under terms of the Treaty of London, English merchants were allowed to resume trading in the peninsula and very soon became entangled in the Spanish courts. Often enough the charges against them were valid: smuggling and counterfeiting were widespread, and the culprits included Englishmen as well as other nationalities. But many merchants could be victimized by a local court system whose rules were virtually an invitation to corruption: when a merchant was convicted for smuggling or some other contraband crime, his cargo and often his ship as well were immediately confiscated and sold, and the proceeds divided equally among the informer, the judge, and the Crown. False accusations and improper convictions were as common as one would expect. The conviction could be appealed, the higher courts had a well deserved reputation for honesty, and hardly a single English case had been appealed unsuccessfully. But that process took years, and the expense was apt to impoverish anyone who had not already been wiped out by the confiscation.[1] The merchants' bitter complaints aroused much sympathy in England – and of course stirred anti-Spanish feeling.

James approached the problem by having his ambassador to Spain present the government – either the Council of State or the chief minister, the duke of Lerma during most of this period – with pleas, petitions and demands for direct intercession by the Spanish Crown to get the glacial Spanish courts to move faster. This was 'successful' to a point, the point of of getting Philip III to order that it be done. But the phrase 'to obey without complying' was invented by Spanish officials: they of course obeyed – one always obeys one's sovereign – but it did not result in a faster resolution of the cases. Again the English ambassador petitioned the government,

[1] These matters are reported extensively in PRO, SP 94 (State Papers, Spanish) for the two decades after the peace. The best summary remains Samuel R. Gardiner, *History of England from the Accession of James I to the Outbreak of the Civil War, 1603–1642* (10 vols., London, 1883–4), II, 149–50, also 134–5 and 163.

again Philip gave the same orders, and again nothing happened. Over the years the same scenario played out over and over, to the frustration of the Spanish Crown, the English Crown, and of course the English merchants. This was a continuing source of friction, with both sides constantly irritated, the Spanish annoyed with the trouble English merchants seemed always to be involved in, and the English unhappy over what they saw as injustice.

But this is not the place to pursue James's continuing efforts to intervene. It is the corollary that I seek to examine: Spanish diplomatic intervention in comparable matters in England.

I

Before doing so, the subject and the materials seem to call for a word about method. In the cases mentioned here, the outcome is important to the intervening party (otherwise there would be no intervention), while the host ruler or rulers had no interest at stake and considered the matter a source of current nuisance and possible future trouble: the enforcement policy one was being asked to reverse was, after all, the product of prevailing political and social interests. As a result the ambassador wrote, besides petitions and such, extremely detailed reports to his home government about how the matter was going , while the hosts saw little need to keep extensive records. Thus the documentation is overwhelmingly on the side of the intervening party. This is especially true in the case of Spanish intervention in English legal matters, for while the English ambassador to Spain dealt with the Council of State, which recorded its discussions, the Spanish ambassador to England dealt directly with the king in private audience. James did not record these conversations, but the ambassador did, in minute detail. Thus the sources dictate our observing the matter mainly from the Spanish angle of view.[2]

The Spanish government had not one corollary concern but two: English piracy in the Indies, and the condition of Catholics in England. Their diplomatic intervention sought the enforcement of anti-piracy laws and the non-enforcement of anti-Catholic laws.

[2] This also conforms to the author's prejudice in favor of using foreign diplomatic documentation for a different look into domestic affairs. The practice in this essay rests on a 'control' system based on the network of diplomatic reports from English, Spanish, French and Brussels ambassadors to each of the other three capitals (a total of twelve lines of diplomatic correspondence), in which the reports of a given ambassador are checked against those of the other ambassadors to the same court (with their different biases and sources of information), plus such other sources as fit the occasion. (Published versions of documents are cited whenever possible.) Spain's ambassador sometimes dealt with the Privy Council, but it did not generate consultative documents as did the Council of State.

English raiders in the Indies were of three principal types: those who might be called 'pure pirates'; those merchants trading illegally in the Indies who engaged in piracy on the side; and merchants in the Iberian trade who had been victimized by the Spanish courts as described above and sought to recover their losses by force from other Spaniards, executing their own justice under the controversial but widely supported 'law of reprisal.' Under this 'law,' raiding the Indies was supposedly legitimized by possession of a 'Letter of Reprisal,' which purportedly exempted the raiders from punishment as pirates while they recovered damages by this alternative route.[3] Both the principle and the document were of course invented by non-colonial nations, particularly the English, Dutch, and French; as colonial powers, Spain and Portugal quite flatly refused to recognize either. But the losses this caused in the Indies were not limited to the actual merchant losses in Spain. A Letter of Reprisal was for the amount of damages claimed, but as only the raider was keeping score it was in practice a permanent license to rob. And of course anyone else charged with piracy claimed it was to recover damages from Spain, whether or not he held a Letter of Reprisal or had ever even traded to Spain. In any case, in English mainstream opinion robbing the Spanish was a socially acceptable, even laudable, thing to do, which apparently no one was much inclined to punish.

There was yet another alleged loophole. Beginning with the Treaty of Cateau-Cambrésis in 1559, anyone negotiating peace with Spain demanded the right to trade with the Indies, Spain always refused, and the impasse was resolved by simply leaving the matter out of the treaty. Anent which the interloping nations came up with still another 'principle'

[3] Both contemporaries and modern historians sometimes use the omnibus term 'Letters of Marque and Reprisal,' which telescopes two distinct actions. A Letter of Marque, mainly used in wartime, gave a private vessel the status of government warship. A Letter of Reprisal is as described; it is particularly important in peacetime, because a Letter of Marque is not usually available and because trading with the offending nation, the most frequent source of the trouble, was mainly a peacetime phenomenon.

Underlying the law of reprisal was the questionable principle of the collective responsibility of a nation for individual crimes of any of its members: in this case, that damages suffered at the hands of Spanish courts, if not redressed by regular means, could properly be recovered from *any* Spanish subject. The procedure was to seek a Letter of Reprisal from the appropriate authority in one's own nation, which at least gave the matter a certain symmetry.

James did not like piracy and could see the obvious injustice of recouping one's losses by robbing individuals who had nothing to do with causing those losses, so English merchants sometimes went elsewhere, especially to the United Provinces, for the justifying Letter of Reprisal. This was not really inconsistent with reprisal by an individual against a nation, but it did dilute any principle based on nationality, since a non-English Letter of Reprisal would surely have to be based on some non-national, presumably wider, principle. The rationale justifying Letters of Reprisal was thoroughly compromised in practice anyway.

(of course not accepted by the colonial powers), that since access to the Indies was not covered in the treaties, the treaties themselves covered only Europe and European waters: there was 'no peace beyond the line.' This did not affect a raider's status regarding piracy, but it did remove an important motive for government restraint of one's own subjects.

II

Wanting English pirates suppressed was a matter of self-interest, actually self-defense, but concern over the condition of English Catholics had a very different basis. Many policymakers felt that Spain had an obligation to try to protect Catholics living under repressive Protestant regimes, which in practice mainly meant England.[4] Spain of course had long been involved in the affairs of the English Catholics, ranging in intensity from supporting the 'English mission' in Elizabeth's time to later permitting English seminaries in Spain, which the government found a nuisance and only feebly supported.

The accession of the tolerant James to the English throne in 1603, the quick beginning of peace negotiations with Spain, and the conclusion of the treaty in 1604 all gave reason to hope for a moderate reign. But in 1605 – the year the treaty was ratified and the Spanish embassy re-established in London – James's beginning-of-reign honeymoon with his subjects ended suddenly for Catholics with the Gunpowder Plot. The old repressive laws against Catholics were revived, added to, and enforced with a vengeance. In 1606 all priests were banished,[5] many who remained were imprisoned, and some were hanged. Also in 1606 came the greatest source of bitterness for English Catholics, a mandatory oath of allegiance.[6]

It was difficult for a devout Catholic to swear to several parts of the oath, but the worst was the third part:[7]

I do further swear that I do from my heart abhor, detest and abjure, as impious and heretical, this damnable doctrine and position that princes which be excommuni-

[4] Many Protestants held that James had a similar responsibility, but it did not apply to Spain as there was no native Protestant population to speak of.

[5] Mark A. Tierney (ed.), *Dodd's Church History of England from the Commencement of the Sixteenth Century to the Revolution in 1688* (5 vols., London, C. Dolman, 1839–43), IV, Appendix, cxxxii. Charles Dodd is the pseudonym of Hugh Tootell.

[6] Joseph R. Tanner, *Constitutional Documents of the Reign of James I, A.D. 1603–1625* (Cambridge, CUP, 1930), 77, 86–109; George W. Prothero (ed.), *Select Statutes and Other Constitutional Documents Illustrative of the Reigns of Elizabeth and James I*, 3rd edn (Oxford, The Clarendon Press, 1906), li–liiii, 424–35. For the place of oaths of allegiance in European history see, e.g., Thomas Dunbar Ingram, *England and Rome: a History of the Relations between the Papacy and the English State and Church from the Norman Conquest to the Revolution of 1688* (London, Longman, Green, and Co., 1892), 329–75.

[7] Prothero, *Select Statutes*, 259. In some versions this is the fourth part, and in some there is no division into 'parts.'

cate or deprived by the Pope may be deposed or murdered by their subjects or any other whatsoever.

This required English Catholics to take a publicly sworn position on the decades-long tyrannicide debate, the lethal Counter-Reformation version of the old dispute over papal supremacy in temporal matters. Had James been satisfied with an oath of loyalty to himself as head of the state, and several such oaths were suggested by Catholics,[8] there would have been little trouble. But he insisted on an oath that specifically contradicted, even vilified, an established doctrine of the Roman Church. As a result, no Catholic could take the oath without participating in heresy or at least running the risk of it, and, the real crux of the difficulty, no subject could refuse to take it without at least tacitly supporting rebellion and regicide. Refusals led to oppression.[9] Oppression led to a dangerous situation in Ireland, with the rebel leader Tyrone busily seeking military aid abroad.

Then the whole matter went international. Paul V condemned the oath and forbade all Catholics to take it.[10] The question of the lawfulness of deposing and killing the king of England became the subject of open and serious discussion among Catholic scholars on the continent. When Henry IV of France was murdered in 1610 it was rumored that the Jesuits had had him killed, and oppression in England became even worse.[11] Spanish concern increased, while it became increasingly difficult for the Spanish ambassador to get a sympathetic hearing.

III

The first Spanish resident, Don Pedro de Zúñiga (1605–7), made the mistake of dealing directly with English Catholics, to try somehow to strengthen their resistance to the oath and to the anti-Catholic laws. But he had little to offer by way of real support or even credible promises. He actually worsened their position by seeming to demonstrate the subversive Catholic–Spanish tie that the enemies of both had long claimed

[8] Tierney, *Dodd's Church History*, IV, Appendix, cxc–cxci.

[9] *Ibid.*, IV, 160–80.

[10] On 22 Sept. 1606 and 13 Aug. 1607 (Old Style); Gardiner, *History of England*, II, 23–4.

[11] See, e.g., Sarmiento to Philip III, 6 Sept. 1613, in Antonio Ballesteros Y Beretta (ed.), *Correspondencia Oficial de Don Diego Sarmiento de Acuña, Conde de Gondomar*, in 'Documentos inéditos para le historia de España' (4 vols., Madrid, 1936–45), III, 60–1. Hereafter cited as Ballesteros, *DIE*; dates are New Style; separate dispatches often bear the same title and date. Though the editor does not say so, these are simply the sender's letter-books; but such differences as exist between this version and the reports themselves do not affect things they touch upon in this essay.

existed, and thus alienated James by seeming to tamper with his subjects. The result of such dabbling was that he could make no progress with James in the matter. Those who had accepted Spanish pensions prior to Zúñiga's becoming resident, and for whom he had arranged substantial increases, sometimes gave support, but it often proved a vain hope. That route held little promise anyway. For most things, successful diplomatic intervention would have to be with James himself, and the ambassador's direct dealings with James's Catholic subjects left him badly compromised before the king.

His replacement, Don Alonso de Velasco (1607–13), was no more successful. The Council of State firmly ordered that there be no more involvement with the English Catholic community, but any improvement this made in James's attitude was soon offset by a complex of international tensions that by 1612 had pushed both Spain and England close to a break in diplomatic relations.[12] But this was only the setting for the task; the task itself was the central problem. Even in the best of times, success in dealing directly with James, a distinctly idiosyncratic person, was as much a matter of chemistry as ability. Velasco was a reasonably able man but he struck no chords with James, and made little headway with him.

In 1612 the Spanish Council of State chose Velasco's replacement: Don Diego Sarmiento de Acuña, a somewhat legendary figure, especially in English demonology, better known by his later title as the count of Gondomar. After the Council had drawn up his credentials they spent a year deciding whether to send him, break off relations, or take the middle course of just letting the embassy stay vacant; he finally arrived in England in mid-1613.

Sarmiento came from an ancient noble family in Galicia, which was a sort of 'cradle of ambassadors' for Spain in the period; he was 46, just a year younger than James. Having served the Crown in military and administrative posts since the age of sixteen, he was no stranger to responsibility or to affairs of state but he had no diplomatic experience. He did have two assumptions that he proceeded to operate on. One was that diplomatic success depended on dealing from strength, which required maintaining the dignity of the Spanish Crown through his own conduct; he was helped in this by a rather stiff-necked sense of his own dignity when challenged, though on a personal basis he was a very affable person. The second, perhaps to be credited to his extensive reading of history and his strong sense of Spain's role in the world, was a firm belief that one

[12] The 1612 diplomatic documents indicate an international crisis that deserves the historian's attention beyond merely the Cleves–Julich dispute.

must always act boldly, especially in crisis, whether dealing from real strength or not. Sarmiento looked for guidance to that old maxim of the battlefield, *aventurar la vida y osar morir*: risk your life and dare to die.[13] His diplomatic intervention put both assumptions to the test. He soon adopted a third assumption, that if he was ever to gain James's confidence he would have to deal with him with *la llaneza de Castilla la vieja*, with the traditional openness of Old Castile.[14] He would be as truthful and forthcoming with James as possible, and at the same time never leave any doubt that he was first of all a loyal servant of his own sovereign. This also bore fruit.

IV

Relations started with a serious contretemps. The ships bringing Sarmiento, scheduled to arrive via the Thames, were forced by a Channel storm into Portsmouth, where the man in command of the port demanded that the Spanish colors be struck in accordance with custom. Sarmiento refused, the English threatened to blow the Spanish ships out of the water, and Sarmiento, who knew the ships were sitting ducks for the shore batteries, literally followed the maxim 'risk your life and dare to die' by demanding time to go back aboard before the bombardment began. The matter was settled when James overruled the commander. Later James gave him a friendly reception at the ambassador's first audience,[15] but he met a wall of opposition elsewhere.

Spain's principal enemies proved to be Thomas Ellesmere, lord chancellor of the Exchequer, whom D. H. Willson described as 'very Protestant and anti-Spanish,' George Abbott, archbishop of Canterbury, who came to hate Sarmiento thoroughly, and the earl of Southampton, 'the richest peer in England and a mortal enemy of Spain.'[16] Sarmiento concluded that Ellesmere was moved mainly by anti-Spanish sentiment and Abbott mainly by anti-Catholic sentiment. Whether he was right about these two or not, he had perceived an important aspect of the problem: with respect to English Catholics his leading opponents would be those motivated mainly by religion, and with respect to piracy by those motivated by non-religious considerations. Each would give the opposi-

[13] It was a favorite saying of his; see, e.g., Sarmiento to Philip III, 6 Sept. 1613: Ballesteros, *DIE*, III, 55–6.

[14] The beginning of this practice is shown further on.

[15] For the Portsmouth incident and first audience, Ballesteros, *DIE*, III, 71–85.

[16] David H. Willson, *King James VI and I* (London, Jonathan Cape, 1956), 335.

tion a different appearance, but in either case each would be supported by the other group.

From the beginning Sarmiento found Abbott, Bishop King of London and many of the other bishops working hard to turn James against him and Spain. They supported the agitation of those who sought war as an excuse for piracy and themselves specialized in carrying stories to James about the seditious activities of the Catholics and Sarmiento's rather limited contact with them. The turmoil they kept stirred up was especially dangerous because of the rash of pro-tyrannicide polemics, directed at James personally, that had lately been published in the Spanish Netherlands. The question at issue, of course, was whether James's Catholic subjects might not lawfully cut his throat. James was understandably vexed, and Abbott, ably supported by Ellesmere, worked hard to convince him that every Catholic was a traitor and a potential regicide.[17]

The one special subject Abbott and Ellesmere focused upon was Sarmiento's alleged (and certainly arguable) abuse of his diplomatic privileges. English Catholics frequented his private chapel, and Abbott and Ellesmere dilated on the vast number of the king's subjects who went there to hear mass and to pray. They pressed James to enforce the laws strictly, which they knew would prevent any rapprochement with Spain, and actually argued that war with Spain would be preferable to allowing Catholics to use Sarmiento's chapel.[18]

It happened that Abbott's personal *bête noir* was a forty-seven-year-old Spanish lady who lived at the embassy. The lady, Doña Luisa de Carvajal, was admirably suited to be a pawn through whom Abbott could strike simultaneously at Sarmiento, the papists, and Spain itself. She had come to England in 1605, the year oppression began anew, with the avowed intention of becoming a Catholic martyr and managed to make herself thoroughly obnoxious to the Protestants, the authorities, and the king himself.[19] She busied herself with a personal campaign of conversion, distributed alms for Philip III and the archbishop of Toledo, openly visited priests in jail for treason, and kept a house in Spitalfields, on the edge of London, where priests came and went in broad daylight. She had been arrested in 1608 for her scandalous conduct in Cheapside where she frequently got into loud and seditious arguments, among other things denying the legitimacy of Queen Elizabeth. She had been released to

[17] Sarmiento to Philip, 6 Sept. 1613: Ballesteros, *DIE*, III, 59, 64.

[18] *Ibid.*, 64.

[19] For her background and activities prior to this incident see *ibid.*, 127n–28. I have encountered some starry-eyed eulogies of her but no serious historical work.

satisfy Velasco, but only on condition that she stop her activities, which she had not done.

Doña Luisa had long since moved into a little house next to the Spanish embassy in the Barbican, and stayed on when Sarmiento replaced Velasco. She was one of those types the times produced: a well-connected woman of means, filled with religious zeal and an undirected passion to serve God, without training or realistic goal, intent mainly on proving the glory of her religion by throwing herself to the Protestant wolves and the devil take the hangman, while she earned a martyr's crown. Though she doubtlessly believed she was on a selfless mission, to the modern observer she seems on a spiritual ego trip, as H. R. Trevor-Roper has suggested was true of the Jesuit fathers in the English Mission. As a practical matter she was a pious version of the cannon loose on a rolling deck. But Sarmiento was also a product of his time. To him what she was doing somehow made sense, and he took to her right away. Besides her house next door he gave her three rooms in the embassy itself, and she quickly became a valued companion to his wife, Doña Constanza.[20]

Just a month after Sarmiento's arrival, Abbott had an order issued for her arrest. He could not touch her so long as she stayed under Sarmiento's protection, so the ambassador made a conspicuous show of driving her around London in his coach, foolishly aggravating the situation. A self-satisfied ambassador reported that this gave much encouragement to the Catholics,[21] but it made Abbott even more furious.

James seemed to lose interest after a time. The order for Doña Luisa's arrest was allowed to lapse, and Sarmiento's relations with the king seemed to be improving. Earlier James had instructed his ambassador John Digby to complain to Lerma about reports of Spanish interference in Ireland, and Digby had now relayed a conciliatory and reassuring reply from Lerma, who rejected the notion that James's Catholic subjects even wanted foreign support. If James treated them kindly, Lerma had said, he would find that they were the most loyal and faithful subjects he had. James praised Lerma highly before the Council and promptly invited Sarmiento to hunt and dine with him at Theobalds. There James took him aside and repeated his praises of Lerma; he was convinced, he said, that anyone who told him Philip was not his true friend was trying to deceive him.[22]

[20] Sarmiento to Philip, 16 Nov. 1613: *ibid.*, 149; same to same, same date, *ibid.*, 183.

[21] Sarmiento to Lerma, 5 Oct. 1613: *ibid.*, 127–9.

[22] Sarmiento to Philip, 5 Oct. 1613: *ibid.*, 114–17. Lerma's reply contained a veiled threat that friendship was conditional on treating English Catholics well; since James was very acute it seems possible that he simply chose not to notice.

For a while things looked much better. James showed Sarmiento great favor in public, and they began to discuss a suitable present to send Philip. Sarmiento heard that one day James told the bishop of Lichfield he had no doubt that the Roman Catholic Church was the true one and that the Pope had spiritual jurisdiction over princes who did not do as they should, and could admonish them and even proceed against them, but that the ambition of some of the pontiffs and their desire to interfere in temporal matters had led to many abuses he could not tolerate. Another night, in front of the whole Council, he said that if the pope would be moderate in the exercise of his temporal power they could easily get along.[23]

This show of good will toward Catholics incensed Ellesmere, the Archbishop, most of the Puritans, and the other '*enemigos de España*'; they 'held many conferences' to try to find a way to turn James from his tolerant attitude toward the papists. Then at this crucial juncture there came into James's hands a book that seemed to be just what they needed.[24]

This was Father Francisco Suárez's *De defensione fidei*, the latest entry in the acrimonious tyrannicide debate, a response to James's two published statements on the oath. The eventual English title gives a hint about the cause of James's wrath: *A defense of the Catholic and apostolic faith, in refutation of the errors of the Anglican sect, with reply to the Apologie for the oath of allegiance and to the admonitory preface of His Most Serene Majesty James, King of England.*[25] The contents leave no doubt. It is a long, comprehensive discussion of whether the pope had power of excommunication over the English king, and if so whether his subjects had a right to depose and murder him, once excommunicated. Suárez answered both questions in the affirmative, and went even further: any Catholic who took the oath was participating in heresy; every Catholic was obliged to deny obedience to the heretic king; a foreign army could be invited to invade England to aid in deposing the heretic; and, in a thorough discussion of the matter, he demonstrated that the present situation in England, even without excommunication, justified deposing the king and if necessary killing him, on

[23] Sarmiento to Philip, 16 Nov. 1613: *ibid.*, 144–5. It is unlikely that James meant any of this. He loved to tease people, to the confusion of contemporaries and historians. As one might expect the touchier Protestants took him seriously. Later Sarmiento drew hope from James's asserting that his religious views were 'catholic,' but it is clear that he was playing with words.

[24] *Ibid.*, 145.

[25] See, e.g., James B. Scott (ed.), *Selection from Three Works of Francisco Suárez, S.J.*, The Classics of International Law, XX (2 vols., Oxford, The Clarendon Press, 1944), I, Latin text, and II, English translation by Gwladys L. Williams, Ammi Brown, and John Waldron, 647–725.

simple grounds of self-defense and promotion of the public good. The work was published by the Jesuit academy of Coimbra, passed with high praise by three separate bishop-censors, and licensed by Philip III.

James was understandably beside himself.[26] Many such works had appeared on the continent of late; what made this one appear fatal to Sarmiento's cause was that James accepted Suárez as the official spokesman for what he considered the official doctrine of the Jesuits[27] and through them of all Catholics. Worse, even, it had been published in Portugal with the specific approval of Philip III, who had been pretending to be his friend. This last made James even more furious. With Abbott and Ellesmere to keep the pot boiling, people were soon calling Suárez's argument 'The Spanish Doctrine.' James began speaking ill of the Jesuits, and of all Catholics, in public; he complained loudly about Philip for having allowed its publication in his kingdom. This was just what Abbott and Ellesmere had so impatiently awaited. Then, two more books appeared, printed in the Spanish Netherlands, which argued as Suárez had for the deposition and murder of the English king. As with Suárez, they were not discussing a hypothetical situation involving *some* English king: they urged the deposition and murder, *now*, of James Stuart.[28]

By the time James had digested these last two books the archbishop and the lord chancellor decided the time was right. They went to the king, and finding him in the mood they had hoped for they started vilifying all papists. James should never trust any Catholic prince, least of all Philip, because they were always plotting against his kingdom and his life. They found James a willing listener, so they brought forth all the arguments they could find to persuade him to clamp down firmly and put an end to recusants forever.

At this point Doña Luisa de Carvajal played into the archbishop's hands. Her little house in Spitalfields was right on the edge of town, with

26 Sarmiento to Philip, 16 Nov. 1613: Ballesteros, *DIE*, III, 145. Actually the work is a major contribution to political thought: based on the Catholic doctrine of all men's equality before God, it argues that kingly power derives from the body of men and is a principal foundation of subsequent Catholic teachings on democracy. James's fury is sometimes attributed to this contradiction of his divine right position, but Sarmiento is surely correct in attributing it to the work's personal attack on him. Digby had been sending James sections of the work as they came off the press; this was presumably book III, which focuses on deposition and killing of tyrants. The Spanish king's license was simply for its importation into Castile, but James accepted it as approval. In any case Philip would have found nothing exceptionable in the work's thesis, *pace* Northern European ideas of Spanish kingship.

27 See, e.g., *APC, 1613–1614*, 152–3 (23 July 1613).

28 Sarmiento to Philip, 16 Nov. 1613: Ballesteros, *DIE*, III, 145.

the house of Antonio Foscarini, the Venetian ambassador, on one side and the open countryside on the other. Doña Luisa was not well and decided to go there to escape the unhealthy London air. Sarmiento warned her that he would no longer be able to extend her his protection, but she went anyway.

When Abbott learned that she was there (Sarmiento suspected Foscarini of tipping him off) he must have thought it especially fitting: he could not only take her now, but he could do it at the house she used so scandalously as a meeting place for Jesuits. He and Ellesmere paraded all their old accusations before the king once more and added some new ones, crowned by a charge that she was setting up a nunnery at her country house. They begged James to order her arrest, now that she was beyond Sarmiento's protection as ambassador. In his anger over Suárez's book and under the influence of their recent harangues, James readily agreed. On 18 October an order was issued for her arrest and the officials went to seize her.

When Sarmiento heard of this he gathered some staff and servants and hurried to Spitalfields, picking up Fernand Boischot, the ambassador from the Spanish Netherlands, on the way. When they got there he saw that the archbishop had made his attack on the poor lady a full-scale military operation: a large number of armed men had surrounded the place and attacked it from three sides as though storming a fortress, scaling the walls, and had broken down three doors to get to her room.

Sarmiento tried to stop them from taking her into custody, but was told they had orders to take her before the Privy Council. They warned him not to try to stop them. Boischot managed, at considerable risk to himself, to save a priest caught in the raid by claiming that he was one of his own servants sent there on an errand; but they could do nothing to prevent the lady's arrest or that of her servants. Sarmiento sent a member of his staff with her, and she was taken to the archbishop's palace in Lambeth. Sarmiento wrote immediately to the archbishop, but Abbott, who clearly meant business, sent him a curt reply and sent Doña Luisa to jail.

The wives of the two Habsburg ambassadors went to the prison to be with Doña Luisa. For two days Sarmiento tried to obtain her release by every means possible short of referring the matter to James in his present hostile mood. But Spain's friends in the Council were unable to prevail against the archbishop and the chancellor. Finally he wrote a letter to James protesting her innocence and begging her release, with a covering note to Rochester, then the king's favorite, asking his help, and sending his language secretary Francis Fuller to deliver them to the royal court then at Royston.[29]

Rochester had already assured Sarmiento that he was opposed to Catholic persecution,[30] and was dallying (to his eventual regret) with the daughter of the earl of Suffolk, a leader of the 'Spanish party' and one of the Spanish pensioners. Rochester himself, of course, was at the head of the list of pensioners, having inherited that honor from the recently deceased Robert Cecil. Rochester got Fuller the best reception he could, but was not able to do much else. When James had read the letter his answer was hardly encouraging. He said he had already heard of the fuss Sarmiento had been making since the arrest, and had ordered the Council to release her on condition she leave the country. James had had quite enough of Doña Luisa's intrigues and was very much out of patience with Sarmiento for having interfered in a routine matter involving the nation's laws and his own security. He was incensed at her openly preaching a faith that embraced the hateful doctrine of Suárez, stirring up his subjects against him. He repeated that she would be released only if Sarmiento promised to see that she left the country. Fuller tried to reason with him, suggesting that the archbishop had motives of his own for her arrest, but James would not listen. When Fuller begged him to believe what the ambassador had written, James turned his back rudely and the interview was over.

Fuller returned to London. Next morning a secretary of the Privy Council came to tell Sarmiento that the Council had orders, as James had said, to release Doña Luisa provided he would give his word that he would send her out of the country within eight days.

Sarmiento, however, was convinced that much more was at stake than the case in question and that, having gone this far, he could not back down now. *Aventurar la vida y osar morir*: he flatly refused the ultimatum. He said that what he would give his word on was that if she were forced to leave the country he would go with her, if that was the way the Council wanted it, and not in eight days. He would leave that same day, and within the hour if possible.

The secretary was much taken aback, and asked time to return to the Council. He said he thought they would want to send an answer to this, because there were some in the Council who favored the ambassador's side of the argument. So Sarmiento said to go and tell them. He and

[29] The foregoing from *ibid.*, 145–9, and the remainder of the incident from 149–56, unless otherwise noted; but see n. 31. (Robert Carr, viscount Rochester, had not yet been made earl of Somerset.)

[30] Sarmiento to Philip, Sept. 1613: *ibid.*, 59.

Boischot waited until late in the afternoon, long after he should have had a reply. Then the reason for the delay became clear. The Council's secretary arrived not with a message but with Doña Luisa herself. Sarmiento's friends in the Council, helped by his ultimatum, had prevailed so well that the man had been ordered to go directly to the jail and have her released. The Council sent word that she would not have to leave the country.

It seemed a Pyrrhic victory at best. Within the Privy Council it was a serious setback for Abbott and Ellesmere but, aside from this and the fact that Doña Constanza's companion was once again free, Sarmiento had little cause for elation. It was a definite victory for his enemies in the battle for James's mind. Already furious over the publishing of Suárez's doctrine of sedition, rebellion, and regicide under the seal of the king of Spain, he was now even more angry over what he considered the ambassador's obstinate and troublesome conduct.[31] And now, with relations with James at their worst, another major danger to peace came to a head.

[31] The Council of State agreed completely with James and was furious at Sarmiento's threat to leave his post, which a king's minister had no right to do without permission; one member wanted him reprimanded. He was definitely out of touch with the Council, e.g. when James's displeasure over her presence in England outweighted religious considerations or the lady's desires. Some had already written her trying to get her to leave, using flattering assurances that she had accomplished her mission; the Cardinal of Toledo, Abbott's Spanish counterpart as primate, had urged her to return to Spain and become a nun. Others noted that the Archduchess Isabel would be glad to have her in Brussels, but all agreed that she should get out of England. See *consulta* of 11 Jan. 1614, concerning Sarmiento's dispatches of 16 Nov. and 6 Dec. 1613: Archivo General de Simancas, MS Secretaria de Estado, vol. 844 (unfoliated) contains both a rough and fair copy of the minutes, a rough of the votes (which in Spain include an explanation of one's position), and the reply to be sent Sarmiento.

One Council concern was that if the English decision to drop the requirement that she leave were later changed or forgotten 'there would be nothing for Don Diego to do but go with her' because of his unfortunate ultimatum. They hoped to be able to ease her out of the country quietly so no one would recall the ultimatum, getting Sarmiento off the hook. They did not know that she had died two weeks before, on 23 December, of 'colic worsened by persecution' according to Sarmiento; he said she had been 'murdered by the evil Archbishop.' Sarmiento to Lerma, 2 Jan. 1614: Ballasteros, *DIE*, III, 208.

The letter Sarmiento sent James at Royston was a long, obsequious plea for mercy for a poor lady in trouble, playing down the religious side of her character. The version included in his 16 Nov. letter to Philip played up the religious side, accused the archbishop by name of trying to wreck the peace, and was otherwise very aggressive. He knew (see Sarmiento to Ciriza, 16 Nov. 1613: a duplicate is in Simancas, MS Secretaria de Estado, 2590 [unfoliated]) that his actions required justification, improved the story in the telling to lessen Council displeasure, and got the opposite result because they had opposite priorities (but regarding piracy he would be on safer ground). The Ballesteros, *DIE* letterbook version of the 16 Nov. report is at Simancas, MS Secretaria de Estado, 7023 fols. 47*v*.–54*v*.; *ibid.*, 2590 (unfoliated) has an original and a duplicate. The original of Sarmiento to James, 29 Oct. 1613, is at PRO, SP 94/20/117–18*v*.; the cover letter to Rochester, which was not communicated to Madrid, is at fol. 115 & *v*., identified in the PRO index as 'Gondomar to ? Lake.'

V

John Davis was a London merchant with a grudge against Spain, a number of ships, and a penchant for piracy.[32] The Carvajal incident had barely been settled and feelings were still running high when one of Davis's ships camc sailing into Portsmouth with a prize taken in the West Indies, a Portuguese caravel with a cargo of sugar. As soon as Sarmiento heard of it he claimed Spain's rights in the matter, putting up a bond for the ship and cargo so they could not be disposed of by the pirates while he sought to have them restored to their owners.[33]

When Sarmiento's opponents in the Privy Council[34] saw what he had done they immediately ordered the prize turned over to Davis. This put Sarmiento in a difficult position. His only recourse was to the king, but after the Carvajal affair and Suárez's book and the agitation of Abbott and Ellesmere, James was in a dangerous mood. Still, he had no choice. On 7 November, as soon as he heard of the order in Council, he requested an audience.

Although James had just returned from the country, Sarmiento received word that he was leaving town again next day and it would be impossible to see him. But Sarmiento insisted, and was finally granted an interview for the following day, at nine in the morning so that James could still leave town in the afternoon.

When Sarmiento arrived for the audience next morning he was still incensed over this latest act of piracy, and over collusion in it by the Council itself, but he opened the interview with intended moderation.

I don't marvel that the king is pleased to leave London for the chase, which is the best of entertainments, and flee the entertainment the ambassadors give Your

The Council praised James highly for his courteous reply to Sarmiento, and thought he had conducted himself admirably under severe provocation by the ambassador, which rather undercuts the muscular, traditional historians who think contemporaries took James's peaceful behavior as a sign of weakness: one should remember that that was in many ways a more civilized age.

32 Sarmiento to Philip, 3 July 1614: Ballesteros, *DIE*, IV, 183: 'a great merchant of this city, a great corsair, and the head of a large company of them'; he is not to be confused with the famous navigator John Davis, who was killed by Japanese pirates in 1605.

33 Unless otherwise indicated, this incident and the audience are from Sarmiento to Philip, 24 Nov. 1613, and same to same, same date, *ibid.*, III, 187–92, 193–95. *APC, 1613–1614*, XXXIII, shows nothing between 17 and 23 Oct.

As direct discourse is not usually used in historical scholarship, one perhaps should note that it is taken directly and faithfully from the source; Sarmiento begins with indirect discourse but quickly slides into direct quotation, though often preceded by the 'he said that' of indirect discourse.

34 It was rumored that some of the Spanish pensioners were more interested in profiting from piracy than in supporting Spain.

Majesty [he said]. I beg your pardon for being such a bother, but it is most certainly in Your Majesty's service that I did it, to inform the king of the truth so that false information will not be credited, nor evil designs against the good feeling I know your majesty has for my king and he for your majesty. When it comes to preserving that friendship I will venture at times to be tiresome, both with your majesty and with my own sovereign.

Keeping the peace was a matter James could readily agree on, and he replied very favorably to Sarmiento's apology. Then, remembering, he added,

His majesty was the first prince to send congratulations on my accession to this kingdom, although others were much nearer.

They spoke for a time about Doña Luisa de Carvajal. The archbishop was still making accusations against her, which Sarmiento claimed were lies and frauds. In the heat of the conversation he implored James to let everyone witness the punishment of those who had embarrassed their king and caused him unpleasantness with accusations of so little foundation.

But James was not convinced. He answered in the slow, deliberate way he had at times.

It was not just the Archbishop who told me about the scandal she was causing [he said]. But in any case, if there is to be peace between England and Spain, as I wish there to be, it would be better to drop the whole matter, since the Council and my people are so offended by it. There is nothing more I can do about it, and anyway I don't see why you had to make such an issue of it.

Having gotten this off his chest he became less serious.

I have been told very confidentially [he said] that she has not yet left the country, but I didn't believe it.

Sarmiento thought the king was pulling his leg.

How could she leave, [he asked] in this kind of weather, and not being well?

But then he saw that James had really thought she had gone, so he quickly changed the subject. He had not yet learned how unreadable James could be.

He shifted to the piracy with all the heatedness he thought necessary and justified. After he had told the whole story of the captured Portuguese caravel and the order in Council which had countenanced Davis's piracy he said,

Your majesty must tell me what I should write my sovereign about this, because if your majesty does not remedy what the Council has done – if the king does not only order the ship and cargo turned over to me but punish this Davis as an example – it will encourage others here to become pirates, and in Spain those who suffer from it will take their revenge and recover their losses from the English wherever they can, which would be small injustice.

He went into great detail about the ways the English with vulnerable interests in Spain would be made to pay for losses to English pirates.

James's words were filled with anguish when he replied.

I don't know what to do [he said]. It seems to me you are right. But my Council tells me the claims and complaints of my subjects are not being taken care of in the Spanish courts, though I know your king has ordered that they be given speedy hearings. And my Council has informed me that Davis's experience with the Spanish courts was very sad. He used to be a wealthy merchant, but he and his partner were ruined by a Spanish judge who had him arrested for passing counterfeit money. Investigation showed it had been passed by a Frenchman and that Davis was innocent, and the Council set him free, but the judge kept the money. Davis did not even get his own money back, much less any damages.

The only notice I have had of the case [Sarmiento said] is in my copy of a list of claims Your Majesty's ambassador gave my king. But there is no John Davis on the list, though there is a Nigel Davis, and the amount involved is only £250, so that should be proof that the story of his having been ruined is false. But even if it were true that he has damages coming, that has nothing to do with his robbing someone else not even connected with the case, in a wicked and insolent act of piracy that breaks his king's royal word.

(Certainly justice is on the side of this argument, but the high moral tone consorts badly with his earlier threat that losses to pirates would be recovered from innocent English merchants in Spain.)

They spoke of this for some time without reaching any definite conclusion; then the conversation inevitably turned to the printing in Philip's kingdom of Suárez's book against James. James had already sent Digby orders to make a strong protest, and had sent him a list of specific complaints about it. But he spoke now in moderate and courteous tones, and with a great sadness.

This doctrine is a wish that I should lose my life and my kingdom [he said]. If anything like this were written in my kingdom against the king of Spain I would punish whoever did it, and make a great example of him.

And then, thinking of the rude treatment Suárez had given him,

Even though kings may be sinners, they must be treated with more temperance. I could never speak of His Majesty your king, except about the goodness of his soul, of his conscience, and of his person. That seems right to me. Since I am still the same as when the peace was made between us, your king should not do me evil with books printed against me in his kingdom under his authority and with his license.

It was obvious that this issue had to be separated from politics or it would be an insuperable block to amity and all that depended on it. Sarmiento had not even read the book[35] but he knew the gist of it and tried his best to set James's mind at ease.

These are religious matters [he said]. They are theological disputes, and those who write about them ought to be obliged to keep them so. I can only regret that Father Suárez has been so excessive. I was astonished by it because he was thought to be a moderate and gifted man. But there is one thing Your Majesty can be sure of: there is no one in the world who wishes more than my sovereign that Your Majesty's life and kingdom be preserved, that Your Majesty enjoy many long years. And the king of Spain will back this up with the sword if need be, from the day Your Majesty said he was my sovereign's friend until Your Majesty says he is not. My sovereign has stated this clearly, and it is something he is well able to do.

This appeared to please James, and he seemed to be eager to talk. It was already noon, and James was to leave for the country after lunch, but although Sarmiento was ready to take his leave the king kept detaining him, making it plain that he wanted to linger and talk.

I am very pleased that you speak so frankly [James said]. I am the friend of men who do, because I think you do me as much service as you do your own king when you conduct your affairs in that way.

Sarmiento was not a man to let an opening like this go by.

Since Your Majesty has done me this kindness, [he said] to believe this of me – which I value because it is true – I beg that whenever someone complains to Your Majesty about Spain or myself, that the king will send for me and tell me, so I can tell Your Majesty the facts. There is no one from whom Your Majesty can be more certain to hear the truth.

This appealed to James, perhaps more so because plain-dealing was so rare in his court.

I promise you I will do so [he said]. And I should like to start right now.

They were already standing and Sarmiento was ready to take his leave, but James turned to him and slowly began ticking off the complaints he had had about him:

They tell me you keep four chaplains, and another who is English; that you have a bell in your chapel as big as a church bell, that is rung at masses and on the hour, and that it can be heard in several of the streets; and that your chapel has been much enlarged over what it was before. And they tell me you keep five or six rooms with beds in them reserved for English priests who come and go at your house.

[35] Sarmiento to Lerma, 25 Jan. 1614: Ballesteros, *DIE*, III, 248–9.

The quick answer and the ready list threw Sarmiento badly off stride. He decided it was time to demonstrate *la llaneza de Castilla la Vieja* as best he could, while trying not to compromise himself too badly.

It is true about the chaplains [he said]. But I have many servants, and their duties require that they hear mass at different times of the day. One of the four is a Dominican friar, a studious man, who says only the early mass, and another is my secretary, so there is nothing excessive in this. As for the English priest, he is a hundred years old, going back to the time of Henry VIII and Queen Mary, is so blind he already can't see, and has not celebrated mass for seven years. I keep him in my house just out of charity, since Don Alonso de Velasco left him with me. The chapel bell is the same one my predecessors had. The chapel has not been enlarged, though it has been refurbished. And one who so freely confesses all this would also tell Your Majesty of keeping English priests as guests if it were really true.[36] The king can reassure himself that he can be as sure of me as of his most trusted counsellor,[37] and has not me to thank for this but my sovereign, who has ordered it to be so, although it conforms very well with my own tastes and desires.

The king thanked him for this last and said he approved very much of the answers he had made to the charges against him.

Your charity to the old priest seems best of all to me [he said]. I myself maintain four or five in Scotland in the same way, they having been with my mother and her ancestors. So whenever you decide not to take care of him, [James said with great vigor] let me know and I'll take care of him myself.

Perhaps James's greatest interest, after hunting and theology, was the history of emperors and kings. Now Sarmiento's knowledge of the subject came into use.

Your Majesty's wish is like that of the Emperor Charles V [he said]. Once a noble who had fallen into disgrace went to the house of a friend to beg a horse on which to make his escape from the Emperor's wrath, but the friend did not want to give it to him from fear of falling afoul of the law. When the Emperor heard of this he said, 'If he had asked it of me, *I* would have given it to him.'

This came off very well with James; he was greatly pleased with the Emperor's remark. On this note the ambassador took his leave and waited on the terrace for James's reply to his request in the piracy matter while the king went to lunch. James was still talking about the Emperor's

[36] This is a useful example of Sarmiento's care to avoid lying to James, but it does not translate well. The Spanish of the document is not *verdad* but *cierto*, very ambiguous in context, and in conversation would have been a cognate in Latin (which they both spoke fluently). Sarmiento 'seems' to deny the charge, while really saying only that he would admit it if it were provable; then he quickly changes the subject.

[37] Specific reference to Carr has been suppressed here because of the distorting effect a knowledge of later events has on the intended meaning.

remark and kept repeating Sarmiento's story to those around him while he ate. After a time a secretary came out onto the terrace and told Sarmiento that the king would reply to his request that evening. In order to satisfy thc ambassador, he was not going to leave town that afternoon but would convene the Council instead, to discuss the matter with them.

James was as good as his word, and more. Sarmiento heard that in the Council meeting he spoke out strongly against Davis, better and more strongly, the ambassador thought, than he could have done himself. The order in Council was revoked and a decision was given in Sarmiento's favor. The prize was turned over to him, and Davis, a man with powerful friends, went to prison.

VI

Just a month after Doña Luisa's release from prison, less than two weeks after the 8 November audience, Suárez's *Defense of the Faith* was burned by the public hangman in London, along with two similar works. James was not present, but it was obviously done at his order and he had asked the French to do the same. It seemed very likely that they would, and Buisseaux, the French ambassador to London, declared himself against the book. As a result, the French daily gained in credit with both James and Rochester.[38] If the French, fellow-Catholics, should condemn the so-called 'Spanish Doctrine' it would make Sarmiento's task even harder.

In the case of piracy, however, Sarmiento had less to worry about, for the moment. He followed up the 8 November audience with a vigorous campaign to get pirates arrested, prizes restored, and in general to make piracy too unprofitable to be attractive as a motive for seducing James into war with Spain. James too was active in this. He had no love for piracy. He hated it on principle as a form of lawlessness, of insolent defiance of his personal laws. As a sincere lover of peace he wanted to end a practice that might well lead to war, and as a man of honor he could not let his subjects break the pledge of friendship he had given in the treaty of 1604. So Sarmiento's job was not to convince James that piracy was wrong, but to keep him convinced that something should be done about it in the face of all the blandishments of Spain's enemies at court. And besides keeping him convinced, the ambassador had also to keep him interested.

After Davis's arrest, James also had other cases brought before the Council. Within three weeks after the 8 November audience, six prominent raiders had been condemned to hang, and – more unusual – only one

[38] Sarmiento to Philip, 6 Dec. 1613: Ballesteros, *DIE*, III, 200–2.

of the six managed to escape the gallows through influence. Sarmiento found the greatest danger to keeping James in this course was the embarrassingly plausible argument of the English merchants. Though Philip had repeatedly issued orders that those cases be handled with dispatch, it was simply not being done. The merchants argued convincingly that if their money, goods, and ships, ensnared in the Spanish judicial system, plus the exorbitant cost of these delays, could not be collected in Spain then the loss should be collected from the Spanish on the high seas.

Sarmiento wrote often to Madrid urging that this needless source of bitterness be eliminated, but there was little else he could do to placate the merchants. He had a strong moral argument that James had no wish to deny, that lawsuits in Spain and English piracy were two distinct matters, that one could not justify the other, and that appeals in Spain and piracy cases in England, when they involved the same person, should be considered separately and tried on their merits alone. His success in obtaining convictions, exemplary hangings, and restoration of prizes depended on his success in keeping the two matters from being confounded.

This was no easy job. The merchants showered him with petitions and memorials, demanding satisfaction of their claims in Spain. It got so bad he could not open his door without facing a mob. They demanded quick satisfaction, which he knew he could not deliver, so he formed a set policy of refusing to accept any complaints at all.

The climax of the movement came when he went to the Council on business one day. More than three hundred merchants and others showed up with memorials and complaints against Spain. He found out that many of them had been sent for by his enemies in the Council, to cause a demonstration and damage his position as ambassador. Sarmiento would have none of it. He prevented the petitioners from entering the Council chamber and refused to talk to them. He said he would not discuss the matter except with the councillors. Both the merchants and his enemies in the Privy Council were left with an unsuccessful maneuver.[39]

Then there arose a complication on the piracy side of the matter. Marie de' Medici had written James that the French government accepted the legitimacy of raiding shipping 'beyond the line,' and urged James to take the same position. Spain's enemies at court argued that if this did not violate France's treaty with Spain then English raids would not violate England's similar treaty.[40] Nevertheless, Sarmiento continued to be suc-

[39] Sarmiento to Lerma, 6 Dec. 1613: *ibid.*, 206.

[40] See, e.g. Sarmiento to Lerma, 26 Oct. 1613: *ibid.*, 142–3; same to Philip, same date: *ibid.*, 174–6; 'Declaration': *ibid.*, 176–8; Marie d' Medici to James [*c.* 1 Nov. 1613]: *ibid.*, 181–3.

cessful in his fight against pirates. Davis managed to get a stay of the Admiralty Court order that the Portuguese ship and its cargo be turned over to Sarmiento, arguing that the prize was a just compensation for his losses in Spain. But James ordered the Council to reconsider the case and that body ordered the prize turned over to the ambassador.[41]

Perhaps Sarmiento's most important success against piracy was in the case of the *Pearl*, important because he won his case based on Portugal's exclusive rights in the East Indies, because the case involved not only an individual like John Davis but the East India Company, and because he was allowed an unusually large part in the handling of the booty.

The *Pearl*, a ship of the East India Company, had arrived in Ireland in mid-October with a valuable cargo of spices from the East Indies. Sarmiento claimed the cargo had been plundered from the Portuguese, but at the moment he was in the midst of the concerted attack of the archbishop, Ellesmere and their allies that was to culminate in the Carvajal affair, so he could get no immediate satisfaction. Now, however, with James cooperating against piracy, he was able to get action from the Privy Council. A warrant was issued for a new admiralty commission to find and seize the *Pearl*. Orders went out to search for the goods, which had long since been widely scattered, in Ireland and Wales; even church markets and other privileged places were to be scoured.

Before long a pinnace arrived in the Thames with some of the *Pearl*'s cargo. Sarmiento claimed it, and it was impounded by the Council. Then it was arranged that he might also have a hand in the inventory and safekeeping of the goods as they were collected. To make the inventory, two representatives were appointed by Sarmiento, two by a merchant named John Morris who claimed an interest in the goods, and two by the crown. Three separate locks were put on the warehouse, and one key was given to the king's appointees, one to Morris, and one to Sarmiento. The search for the rest of the goods continued, and part of the cargo continued to be delivered to the customs house for some time. The court of the East India Company, as the sequestered goods piled up, voted to try to intervene with the Council, claiming half interest in the cargo, based on their patent, but the case was delayed until the goods were all in.[42]

41 *APC, 1613–1614*, XXXIII, 317–18 (2 Jan. 1614) says Sarmiento had promised to get justice for Davis in Spain, but I have seen no other evidence of this, and it would be contrary to his practice of not becoming involved in that controversy, a practice he continually justified to Madrid.

42 Some historiographical problems in identifying which of the several *Pearls* is involved can be seen, *inter alia*, in *APC, 1613–1614*, XXXIII, 324, 337–8, 371, and in William Noel Sainsbury (ed.), *Calendar of State Papers, Colonial Series, East Indies, China and Japan, 1513–1616* (London, HMSO, 1862), I, nos. 620, 661, 680, 682.

For the moment Sarmiento's campaign against piracy was going very well. His position was so obviously strong that the *Pearl*'s captain and crew begged him for a pardon (which the law hardly gave him the power to grant) and offered to declare which part of the cargo had been taken from subjects of the Spanish Crown. There were three other armed ships in port ready to leave for a raid in the Indies; these were disarmed and sold. Pirated goods continued to be restored to their owners, sometimes from cases dating well into the past, and pirates continued to be executed. By the middle of January 1614 James had ordered all pirates to be caught and hanged.[43]

VII

Since this was little more than two months after Sarmiento first took up the matter in earnest, it seems convincing testimony to the potential effectiveness of diplomatic intervention in the enforcement of laws in the host country. There continued to be both successes and failures, but one cannot in an essay pursue the matter at length. Nor is there room to examine whatever effect it might in practice have had on Spain's and James's quest for larger foreign policy goals or, in a different arena, on James's political position at home. But we may end with a 'what if' question: what if English diplomatic intervention in Spain had been this effective?

[43] Sarmiento to Lerma, 25 Jan. 1614: Ballesteros, *DIE*, III, 244; same to Philip, 12 Feb. 1614: *ibid.*, 281.

Mr Hudson's Star Chamber

THOMAS G. BARNES

Almost a quarter-century ago, Geoffrey Elton amused and edified us with some tales, of riots at Cambridge and a fool at Oxford, of 'An illegal story' and 'A cautionary story,' of an abbot deposed and a parson undertithed. One must allow for the apparent acceptance by a Cambridge don of suffering at the hands of a company of rioters as being preferable to suffering the company of fools (though one ruefully remarks that a decade later there would be plenty of both at Both Places as well as elsewhere, and that the scholar to whom we pay homage, like the author of this piece, would be much beset in the midst of the *mêlée*). Indeed, on rereading Geoffrey Elton's *Star Chamber Stories*[1] sometime about 1968, the academic might well have yearned for reviving the Henrician Star Chamber; he would certainly have envied his counterparts of that simpler time when all the gown could battle all the town in Cambridge, 1534, rather than those of the short-gown braving the long-robes with non-negotiable demands while citizens looked on in wonderment and growing disgust at the war within the walls. It is not the object of this essay to dwell upon that history, but rather to testify to one other facet of the pioneering historian who, having revolutionized the study of Tudor government, turned his attention to the Henrician Council and Star Chamber. *Star Chamber Stories* was the first fruit of that central and continuing endeavor. And Geoffrey Elton has encouraged others to undertake that labor, supervising the young historian who has opened to us Wolsey's Star Chamber.[2] As one who has in his long study of the later Star Chamber enjoyed Geoffrey's sustained encouragement since a first, chance, meeting on the steps of the Public Record Office in 1958, the author affirms that he is no less a *discipulus* of Geoffrey Elton than those who have had the great privilege to be numbered among his *scholarii*.

[1] G. R. Elton, *Star Chamber Stories* (London, Methuen, 1958).

[2] John A. Guy, *The Cardinal's Court: The Impact of Thomas Wolsey in Star Chamber* (Hassocks, Harvester Press, 1977).

I

To grant possession of a whole court, palpably the greatest of its age, to a mere Reader of Gray's Inn – as the title above does – is both parlous and presumptuous. Of course, the High Court of Star Chamber was not Mr William Hudson's. Yet, for almost two centuries most scholarly perceptions (and all vulgar ones) of Star Chamber have depended heavily on the author of *A Treatise of the Court of Star Chamber*. Completed sometime late in 1621, though this work was not printed until 1792,[3] it was widely published in manuscript in the later 1620s and the 1630s and beyond. Over a score of copies are in libraries and archives, and many others in private hands, including Geoffrey Elton's. The British Library has six copies, the Harvard Law School Library has four, which constitute the largest collections of it. The use made of the treatise by later historians has not always been executed with sufficient subtlety to avoid anachronism; the editors of a recent selection of Council records for the reign of Henry VII relied too heavily upon it to describe the Star Chamber's procedure in that reign, for which purpose its application was somewhat misleading.[4] Moreover, unfortunately the treatise has never been analysed as an integral contribution to the legal scholarship of its age, serving rather as a reservoir of factual detail useful for interpreting Star Chamber records, to be dipped into as needed but not treated as a whole. This is not surprising.

Though it is comparable in size to Edward Coke's *Third Institutes*,[5] it is not as comprehensive or as intrinsically important as that work on pleas of the Crown, and Hudson was not Coke in either contemporary fame or later reputation. Hudson is certainly easier reading: he was a lively prose-stylist, and though occasionally elliptical the treatise seems almost limpid compared to the involved prose and turgidity of the *Institutes*. Yet Hudson's treatise has suffered less by comparison with Coke in terms of authority and subject (and has had little chance to gain by its clarity and vivacity) than by the fact that Coke's work dealt with permanent legal

[3] William Hudson, 'A Treatise of the Court of Star Chamber,' *Collectanea Juridica*, ed. by Francis Hargrave (2 vols., London, E. and R. Brooke, 1791–2), II, 1–240. Except where otherwise indicated, all references to the treatise are to this printed version and quotations are from it. Its availability has overcome my scruples against using such a corrupt text.

[4] C. G. Bayne and William H. Dunham, Jr (eds.), *Select Cases in the Council of Henry VII*, Selden Society, LXXV (London, Bernard Quaritch, 1958); upon reflection, I was too expansive in finding Bayne's introduction 'peculiarly free from anachronism' on this point in my review, *Speculum*, XXXIV (1959), 650. See Geoffrey Elton's review, *English Historical Review*, LXXIV (1959), 686–90.

[5] Edward Coke, *The Third Part of the Institutes*, 1st edn (London, 1644), 245 pages (excluding the table): *STC Wing* C4960.

institutions and Hudson's with a court that was destined to disappear into oblivion, marked by obloquy, within two decades of its writing. Hudson's treatise held for centuries only some antiquarian interest. Its author was stained by the taint that destroyed the Star Chamber; his work as a contribution to English legal scholarship could be roundly ignored if not soundly condemned by the monochromatic Whiggism that set into English legal scholarship in the centuries following the English revolutions.

It is not the purpose of this essay to deal either with the textual problems of the treatise or with the contributions it can make to our understanding of the working of Star Chamber in the early seventeenth century. The textual problems are enormous: the printed version is corrupt and unscholarly in redaction, none of the known extant manuscript copies appears to be 'the' original, and the destruction of the court's order and decree books makes it always difficult and in too many instances impossible to check the text's accuracy on discrete points. What the treatise tells us about Star Chamber, its history, the substantive law implemented (and sometimes created) in it, and its procedures requires many pages for useful treatment. Rather, as counsellor Hudson would himself have put it, this essay seeks to 'open' Hudson's work, both as treatise writer and as practitioner in Star Chamber, analysing his purpose in the former endeavor in the light of his experience in the latter occupation. On both counts, it might appear that 'Mr Hudson's Star Chamber' is an only slightly exaggerated title.

II

Of William Hudson's parentage and background, early education, early career and first marriage, we know nothing, beyond the names of his four sons by that marriage.[6] From his second marriage, to Anne Stodderd, relict of William Stodderd of St Michael le Querne, London, skinner, which took place at Islington some time about 3 April 1613, we learn that he was a widower, aged thirty-five years, which would place his birth date in 1577 or 1578.[7] It is possible that the William Hudson of Kent admitted to Corpus Christi College, Cambridge, in 1591, B.A. in 1595 and M.A. in 1598, was our man; Star Chamber attorney Hudson still had a Kent connection in the early 1600s, and three of his sons entered Corpus

[6] Will of William Hudson, proved in Prerogative Court of Canterbury, 12 January 1636, PRO, Probate, PCC 8 Pile.

[7] George J. Armytage (ed.), *Allegations for Marriage Licences Issued by the Bishop of London, 1611 to 1828*, Harleian Society, XXVI (2 vols., London, 1887), II, 19.

between 1619 and 1623, the last of these being 'of Kent.'[8] We do know for certain that our William Hudson was admitted to Gray's Inn on 4 May 1601, as 'gentleman' but without indication of provenance. He was called utter-barrister, less than five years later, on 28 January 1606.[9] The lack of provenance in his admission and the relative promptness with which he did his exercises for call (neither of which is entirely remarkable) and his age of twenty-four at admission (which is) hint at a degree of unusualness about Hudson that set him apart from most young men going to Gray's. He was, in fact, already well-known at Gray's and might even have had a chamber there, though he was not of the society. He was already advanced in legal learning at the time of his admission and well-launched in a legal career. In 1594 he had entered the office of one of the three Attornies of Star Chamber, as an underclerk. That a seventeen- or eighteen-year-old would begin a clerkly apprenticeship was no sign of precociousness, but that Lord Keeper Puckering should ask him 'what the order of the court was in that point . . .' and receive a reply from the lad, that the party 'ought to have sued out a *dedimus potestatem* and not to putt in any demurr by his attorney, whereupon my Lord [Keeper Puckering] confirmed that order to be henceforth observed' verged on the incredible.[10] Yet, Hudson was merely demonstrating at a very tender age that command of the procedures of Star Chamber which were the hallmark of his entire career. About Trinity Term 1604, he succeeded John Beere as one of the three Star Chamber Attornies. He continued in that office for two years after his call to the bar. Sometime in the spring of 1608 he gave up his attorneyship and began practice as a counsellor at the Star Chamber bar.

By contemporary standards of success at the bar Hudson achieved all that could be expected of a barrister whose practice was concentrated in one court. He was never called to be a serjeant-at-law, not from any lack of ability or want of clientage (he was as highly reputed for learning as most of the coif and enjoyed a clientage as extensive as any but the top leaders) but because he chose to practice only in Star Chamber and not at

[8] John & J. A. Venn, *Alumni Cantabrigienses* (4 vols., Cambridge, CUP, 1922–7), II, pt I, 424–5: William Hudson of Kent, admitted CCC, 1591; William Hudson, CCC 1691; Christopher Hudson, CCC 1691; Michael Hudson, CCC 1623. The last is not to be confused with the Royalist- warrior-divine, killed by Parliamentarian forces in Northamptonshire 1648. Edward Hasted, *The History and Topographical Survey of the County of Kent* (2 vols., Canterbury, 1797), II, 414–15, refers to a Hudson who held Combes manor in Swanscombe, Kent, but the reference is too ambiguous to be helpful. In *Robert Newman, D.D. rector of Staplehurst, Kent* v. *Robert Berrye, William Hudson, et al.* (bill November 1605), it is clear that our Hudson was closely connected with the Staplehurst parishioners who were the parson's nemeses: PRO, STAC 8/221/25.

[9] Gray's Inn, MS Pension Book, I, fol. 273.

[10] BL, MS Lansdowne 639, fol. 82*v*. (31 Oct. 1594).

all in Common Pleas. He was called to the Bench of Gray's Inn, first appearing at Pension in May 1625 following his Lent Reading that year.[11] Throughout his career at the bar he maintained chambers in Gray's Inn, hard by the Star Chamber office which was located there, and he lived in Hosier Lane in West Smithfield in a modest house held by lease from St Bartholomew's Hospital, a ten-minute walk from Gray's. He allowed himself the relative luxury of better chambers in Gray's as his practice waxed and he took a country seat at Muswell Hill in Hornsey, Middlesex, still close to the center of his professional life. He was, as a Bencher of Gray's, moderately active in the governance of the Inn, but no more than his large practice allowed. He was too busy to hold those public offices, remunerated or not, filled by leading members of the bar: he never served as a Middlesex magistrate or as a country JP. Significantly, he did serve in those ambitious commissions to restrain building in the metropolis during the 1620s of which Inigo Jones was the guiding light. His inclusion with a few other barristers indicates an appreciation of his usefulness in an enterprise intended to result in prosecution of builders in Star Chamber.[12]

Hudson enjoyed no leisure time; the rather sizable estate that he bought, complete with swans, at Mareham-on-the-Hill near Horncastle, Lincolnshire, was settled on his son and heir, Christopher, who seated himself there and maintained the port of a gentleman. In effect, Hudson worked arduously to endow his sons and grandchildren. He devised from 'some money' on security £3300 for the purchase of lands for Christopher, made extensive settlements *inter-vivos* for Edward and Michael (his third and fourth sons), provided amply for his relict, and slighted only his second son William by leaving him 20s. for a ring, 'havinge already given him more then I could well spare.'[13] These workmanlike provisions displayed considerable acumen. He does not appear to have held at death any lands in-chief. He preferred leasehold, copyhold, socage, and customary tenure land, mostly in London and environs, which would make money at least charge and risk. His holdings were considerable but fluid, more

[11] Gray's Inn, MS Pension Book, I, fol. 358. No trace of Hudson's reading can be found, not even its subject matter. Perhaps it was on 3 Henry VII, c. 1, the so-called Act Pro Camera Stellata (1487): *SR*, II, 509–10. I am grateful to Charles M. Gray, William J. Jones, Louis A. Knafla, and Wilfrid R. Prest for their help in searching for Hudson's reading.

[12] Thomas G. Barnes, 'The prerogative and environmental control of London building in the early seventeenth century: the lost opportunity,' *California Law Review*, LVIII (1970), 1342–3; and, Thomas Rymer (ed.), *Foedera, Conventiones, Literae et Cujuscunque Generis Acta Publica . . . ab Anno 1101 . . .*, 3rd edn (10 vols., Hagae Comitis, Joannem Neaulme, 1739–45), VII, pt II, 97: a commission to abate nuisances of building in Middlesex and liberties, 27 Jan. 1624.

[13] Will of William Hudson, PRO, Probate, PCC 8 Pile; Thomas Allen, *The History of the County of Lincoln* (2 vols., London, J. Saunders, Jr, 1834), II, 99.

monetary than territorial in nature. By any standard, Hudson was wealthy. Characteristic of the *arriviste*, he was also frugal, careful, and not given to indolence.

Hudson's wealth was made entirely in practice in Star Chamber. The extent of that practice was prodigious. Of something over 6000 cases for which pleadings are extant between February 1608 and March 1625, Hudson had signed as counsel in almost 16 per cent of them, about evenly balanced between prosecution and defense.[14] Among all counsel practicing in Star Chamber between 1603 and 1625, including those who practiced throughout that period, none came even close to the size of Hudson's practice save his two Gray's colleagues, Thomas Hughes (called 1585) and John Walter (called 1593).[15] Both these practiced throughout the period and yet attained to only about two-thirds the number of cases in which Hudson signed pleadings. The mark that Hudson had arrived to pre-eminence at the Star Chamber bar is the fact that during the attorney-generalship of Thomas Coventry (1621–5), Hudson signed jointly with Coventry 22 per cent of the 112 informations filed by that law officer. By the time of his death in December 1635, Hudson was not only the leader par excellence of the specialized bar practicing in Star Chamber – he had become that by the early 1620s – but he had also the distinction of being more highly practiced than any contemporary and probably any other barrister in the court's history.

Pleading, by the written bill or information for the plaintiff and by answer, demurrer, or plea-in-bar for the defendant, constituted the steady fare of practice in any English-bill court such as Star Chamber. But the spectacular part of the specialized practice in Star Chamber was advocacy at the hearing of that fraction of the cases begun that were prosecuted to trial, and the more numerous motions in court which dashed many cases at an early stage. Some 1250 counsel signed pleadings in Star Chamber cases between 1603 and 1625, many of them only once and few more than a few times; 5 per cent of the counsel signing accounted for about 40 per cent of the cases. This 5 per cent were the fifty-four leaders of the bar in Star Chamber, and if Hudson was pre-eminent among them as pleader, he was by the 1620s also pre-eminent among them as advocate.[16]

[14] Analysis of signed instruments, Public Record Office, STAC 8/1-314, as rearranged and listed in *List and Index to the Proceedings in Star Chamber for the Reign of James I*, ed. by Thomas G. Barnes (3 vols., Chicago, American Bar Foundation, 1975).

[15] John Walter, Gray's called 1593, should not be confused with the Inner Temple barrister called 1590 who was later chief baron of the Exchequer.

[16] Thomas G. Barnes, 'Star Chamber litigants and their counsel, 1596–1641, in *Legal Records and the Historian*, ed. by John H. Baker (London, Royal Historical Society, 1978), 25–6. Hudson commanded top fees at the height of his practice; for his appearance as one of

Activity as a quantity and ability as a quality in an advocate is most difficult to measure at this remove, given the nature of the evidence: such assessment relies upon various collections of reports of cases in Star Chamber, of uneven quality, innocent of any uniform standards for reporting, and not always the work of barristers or judges but often of students. One set of reports, giving very good coverage of both hearings and motions in Star Chamber, Easter Term 1625 to Hilary Term 1628, provides considerable information about the leading advocates practicing at that time.[17]

Of the appearance of counsel noted in 130 hearings and motions, Hudson appeared thirty-seven times, almost twice as many times as his nearest competitor, Serjeant Heneage Finch. While it is rash to come to any firm conclusions about the quality of advocacy on the basis of whether the advocate's party wins or loses, it is worth remarking that of nineteen cases which came to trial and in which Hudson is explicitly mentioned as advocate, his side won nine and lost ten![18] More remarkable is the fact that in all but one of these cases he led for the client. Of the other eighteen instances in which an appearance by Hudson was noted by the reporter, eleven were motions. In these, he was defeated only once. Success in motions was a much sounder measure of an advocate's ability. A motion was on a single issue, generally interlocutory, in which success depended largely on being procedurally correct. Having quite literally 'written the book' on Star Chamber procedure, commanding the precedents that constituted the course of the court, Hudson was not likely to fail very often. The instance in which he did is instructive. Hudson moved for the plaintiff that to demur in general without showing particular cause was against the course of the court, and therefore the defendant's demurrer was bad. Lord Keeper Coventry ruled that the demurrer should stand, 'for otherwise when the cause is heard wee should have an ill bill upon which wee could not proceed to sentence, as many times it falleth out.'[19] Hudson was clearly correct; but with his own concern for exactness in pleading – as we will note in a moment – he could hardly have faulted

three counsel instructed for the hearing *ex parte* the plaintiff in *Croyden* v. *Vanlore*, Easter 1633, he received £11, more than either of the others, including Edward Herbert, later Solicitor-General and Attorney-General; PRO, E 215/857: I am grateful to Dr Wilfrid R. Prest for this reference.

[17] BL, MS Lansdowne 620, 146 fols. Reporter is unknown; however, this copy of a relatively popular report, of which five copies exist in MS, was the property of Hudson's protégé, John Lightfoot.

[18] Hudson for the plaintiff won seven and lost six; for the defendant, he won two and lost four – the plaintiff usually enjoyed an advantage at trial.

[19] BL, MS Lansdowne 620, fol. 143.

Coventry's reasoning if the plaintiff's bill was as weak as it appeared to be to the lord keeper.

Seven of Hudson's appearances were in cases in which he was evidently not of counsel with either party in the cause. These were appearances by Hudson 'at bar.' Such an appearance was, as a general rule, usually made by the one barrister whose attendance at every sitting-day of Star Chamber was required *de virtute officii*: the attorney-general. It was an old established practice that when the court needed assistance it would call upon the attorney-general for his opinion on a point of law. However, the court was at liberty to call upon any counsel standing 'at bar' to render such assistance. By 1625–8, the attorney-general was not alone 'at bar.' Most of the eminent practitioners who composed the specialized sub-bar in Star Chamber would be present as a matter of course. And of these, none was more knowledgeable (or, one suspects, more constant in his attendance) than Hudson. When the court was puzzled as to whether or not a relator to the attorney-general, having lost his case, should pay costs, it called for a search of the precedents, and 'Hudson said that he had there ten severall presidentes fully to the point that hee should pay.'[20] The reporter appears to reassure his reader, in another case, when he noted that

> It was agreed by Coventrye [the Lord Keeper] and Hudson at barre to be the course of the court if the defendant stand out all proces and will not answer, hee shall be comitted close prisoner and a day prefixed to him to answer; hee may have liberty to consult with his councell and answer within a short day; and if at that day hee answer not, then let the bill be taken for confest.[21]

That same *Judex Maximus*, president of the court, and Hudson were similarly yoked as authorities in another matter.[22] And when Coventry allowed a party to examine *de bene esse* more witnesses after the completion of the proof-gathering in his case, Hudson 'at bar' said that 'then this examinacion ought to be before the day given for publicacion [of the proofs], to which the Lord Keeper agreed.'[23] Hudson doubtless derived great satisfaction from Coventry's concurrence: he was strenuously opposed to examination *de bene esse* post-publication because of the unfair advantage it gave to the party who was already knowledgeable of the proof against him.[24] It was clear that Coventry considered Hudson the oracle of the court. As attorney-general, Coventry had gotten the measure of Hudson, and his respect waxed accordingly. Indeed, it was Lord Keeper Coventry's recognition of Hudson's stature which confirmed his pre-eminence at the Star Chamber bar among his fellow counsel, the court's clerical officers, and the litigants.

[20] *Ibid.*, fol. 124. [21] *Ibid.*, fols. 63–4. [22] *Ibid.*, fol. 122.
[23] *Ibid.*, fol. 123. [24] Hudson, 'Star Chamber,' 214.

By the last decade of his life and career, Hudson was distinguished not only by the size of his practice but also by the quality of his clients. Of these the attorney-general was the most eminent. Perhaps more correctly the king was his most eminent client, because the cases in which Hudson was engaged with the attorney-general increasingly were cases *pro Rege*, brought by the attorney-general on behalf of the king, rather than on relation by a private party. In relator actions, the attorney-general did not have much say in counsel associated with him; the relator generally was allowed counsel of his choice, and indeed it was his own counsel who would approach the attorney-general to have the case taken on relation. In cases in which the king and the state were directly interested, the attorney-general chose the associate counsel. This would often include one of the king's serjeants-at-law, in part to give weight to the information with the two chief justices sitting in Star Chamber with Privy Councillors. If the information raised complex procedural issues or, significantly, required a command of the precedent of Star Chamber, Hudson was retained.

Thus it was that Hudson appeared with the attorney-general in the prosecution of Bonham Norton for scandalizing Lord Keeper Coventry by accusing him of taking a bribe.[25] In February 1634, Hudson opened the case against William Prynne for writing and publishing *Histrio-mastix*.[26] Only the absence of proceedings for the reign of Charles I and the relative paucity of counsel noted in most reports of the period preclude us from discovering more causes of this sort in which Hudson was engaged. 'Cases of State,' as Hudson called them, also attracted an even larger clientele of eminent litigants, many of whom apparently considered him a track to the attorney-general accepting a cause on relation. By the same token, a defendant under fire from the attorney-general would find retaining Hudson a way to spike his adversary's gun, for whatever the direct advantage of having Hudson on his side there was the oblique advantage of denying his services to the other side. Yet, given the paucity of evidence for Charles I's reign, Hudson does not appear to have ever become a kind of 'Crown counsel,' either *pro Rege* or on relation by the attorney-general. In the same year that he appeared against Norton, he appeared for the defense in two notorious cases: the *Attorney-General* v. *Richard Carrier*,

[25] Samuel R. Gardiner (ed.), *Reports of Cases in the Courts of Star Chamber and High Commission*, Camden Society, new series, XXXIX (London, 1886), 94.

[26] John Rushworth (ed.), *Historical Collections of Private Passages of State, Weighty Matters in Law, Remarkable Proceedings . . . 1618, and Ending . . . 1648*, 2nd edn (8 vols., London, D. Browne, etc., 1721–2), II, 220.

clerk, and *Attorney-General* v. *James Cason, attorney*, which while both on relation saw a very active prosecution by Attorney-General Heath.[27]

Hudson built his reputation as a pleader on special pleading, that is a defense raised not by answering or traversing the matters of fact in the plaintiff's bill, but by objecting to the bill in point of law. This might be by demurrer, either to the sufficiency of the matter or to sufficiency of form. It could also be by a plea-in-bar: to the ability of the plaintiff, to the jurisdiction of the court, to foreign matter of record, or to the justice of twice convicting a defendant for the same crime or convicting him for a crime for which he had already been acquitted. In either demurrer or plea-in-bar the defendant did not answer the factual allegations until the special plea had been ruled upon. Special pleading might be merely dilatory, and so it was much used and the court thus much abused. In the hands of one as skillful and as knowledgeable as Hudson, it often proved sudden death to a plaintiff's case; he would pay good costs and be much discouraged from trying again. From the Jacobean Star Chamber proceedings, it is evident that in the majority of the 450 plus cases in which Hudson signed pleadings for the defense, he chose initially to plead specially. His successes were greater than his failures. Indeed, Hudson probably showed the way to increased use of special pleading between the early years of James's reign and his last years, whereby the amount of special pleading almost doubled.[28] Special pleading put a premium on economical pursuit of a narrow issue. Prolixity was death in a special plea. Hudson's finest demurrer was short and sweet: in lightheartedly dismissing the color of the plaintiff's hen and whether or not it came from an egg that was the plaintiff's own property, by abundant ridicule he persuaded the court that the bill had no future.[29] The medicine the physician prescribed for others, he could use to cure his own pains. Hudson, as defendant to a suit by the Archbishop of Canterbury brought by information in the Common Pleas in 1630, demurred to the sufficiency of the writ, and by establishing that it was founded upon a statute that gave the action only to the king and not to a private party, quashed it.[30] In this he bested the eminent Serjeant Edward Henden – but on Hudson's own ground, after all, since maintenance was a staple of Star Chamber's trade.

[27] Gardiner, *Reports*, 97 and 125.

[28] Between 1604 and 1624, the percentage of special-pleading to the number of bills put in rose from *c.* 16% to *c.* 30% per annum, Barnes, 'Star Chamber litigants and their counsel,' 17.

[29] PRO, STAC 8/257/24 (bill November 1614).

[30] *Abp. of Canterbury* v. *William Hudson* (Michaelmas 1630), reported in Littleton 349, 124 English Reports 279 and Hetley 164, 124 English Reports 424: that is, *The English Reports, Common Pleas*, CXXIV (176 vols., London, Stevens & Sons, Ltd, 1900–30), II, 279, 424.

Similarly, in answering (by traversing each charge and pleading not-guilty to it) precision and concision worked best. Hudson's answers were usually shorter than those of other counsel and always to the point. Yet, even when he answered Hudson seldom failed to plead specially, whether by that peculiar English-bill monstrosity called a 'plea, demurrer, and answer' or merely by an answer in which most of the charges were traversed and the remainder excepted to. Again, the physician-as-patient, when an attorney in Star Chamber, was charged with perjury in a bill in Star Chamber in November 1605, responded by answer to 'the falce, injurious, lewd, slaunderous' bill of Robert Newman, D.D., rector of Staplehurst, Kent, not only by a not-guilty to all allegations, but by excepting to the charge of perjury by alleging that he had not been sworn when he 'affirmed' before a local JP and later before special referees that Newman had spoken treasonous words. Hudson added that he had not even been present at the assizes where a true-bill was found against Newman. His 'answer' was effectual, for the Star Chamber case went no further.[31]

Hudson had a personal as well as professional impact on the practice of the law in Star Chamber. If he was the model barrister whom a legion of others emulated as well as, one supposes, envied, he produced in one young man a disciple, admirer, and worthy successor in his practice. John Lightfoot was admitted to Gray's in 1617. He was probably called to the bar by Hudson at his Lent 1625 Reading. He opened his first bill in Star Chamber in Hilary 1627.[32] Until Hudson's death he was closely associated with him, sometimes in concert, and sometimes as in Prynne's *Histriomastix* case on the other side. Following Hudson's death he succeeded to his practice and appeared in many of the most notable cases in that notable decade that was Star Chamber's last. An assiduous reporter in his own right, Lightfoot had Hudson's scholarly bent.[33] The closeness of master and pupil is attested by Hudson's will appointing Lightfoot a trustee for a residual settlement in favor of the n'er-do-well son William.[34] More significantly, Lightfoot came into much of Hudson's manuscript collection,

[31] PRO, STAC 8/221/25. Rhetorical analysis establishes that Hudson's answer is his own work; ostensibly signed by John Ferrour, a Gray's Inn barrister, the signature is not Ferrour's, but probably Hudson's rendering, albeit with Ferrour's allowance.

[32] *Fawcett* v. *Grice*, Harvard Law School, MS L.1128, no. 3: 'Ceo fuit le primer bill que Jeo avoy open en move le court.' British Library, Lansdowne MS 620, fol. 80: 'I was of councell with the plaintiff in this cause, which was the first bill that [I] opened in that court, J.L.'

[33] Harvard Law School, MS L.1128, 'Reports of cases in the Star Chamber during the reign of K. Charles I,' by an 'eminent practicer in that court, formerly a member of Grays Inne,' *viz*. John Lightfoot.

[34] Will of William Hudson, PRO, Probate, PCC 8 Pile.

and it is through Lightfoot's agency that we can come to a better appreciation of Hudson's work as treatise writer. In a note in a manuscript copied from Hudson's collection an affectionate compliment is paid the master, and in the process considerable light is thrown on the provenance of Hudson's treatise:

Note here that by the word 'My' is meant William Hudson, Esq., an ancient practiser and most and best experienced councellor attending this court, my patron, the composer and collector of the matters contayned in this booke. Hee hence and from other his observacions compyled the manuscript now in many handes touching this court, which is divided into three bookes, and those into severall consideracions. Hee presented it to the Lord Bishop of Lincolne at his first comeing to the Seale, for whose use it was originally prepared and digested into that method. Hee departed this life in the month of December last. For his memorie is this here put.

10 Junii 1636, by John Lightfoot.[35]

III

Hudson's avowedly didactic purpose in addressing his treatise to a non-lawyer and ecclesiastic, who became lord keeper of the Great Seal on 10 July 1621 and therefore had come to preside over the High Court of Star Chamber, and the treatise's apparent and, in the event, proven value to other practitioners in the court must not blind us to Hudson's larger purpose in writing it. Hudson sought to extol a court which his professional involvement, intellectual acumen, moral sensibility, and even emotional attachment led him to believe was the greatest court in the kingdom, truly the High Court of Star Chamber. It was also a tribunal which he perceived was imperilled by the general threat to all English-bill courts, central and regional, growing from increasing assertiveness by the common-law courts of King's Bench and Common Pleas to exclusive and pre-eminent jurisdiction in any instance where a litigant sought the extension of the privilege of the common law court as a protection against a cause in an English-bill court. He also recognized the existence of a growing current of popular contumelious criticism aimed at Star Chamber. This fed upon practices which both detracted from the grandeur of that high court 'well called *Schola Reipublicae*, the discipline whereof doth not only enter all the other courts of justice and ministers thereof, but all the subjects of the

[35] BL, MS Lansdowne 639, fol. 99*v*. This MS of 112 folios comprises a copy of Isaac Cotton's brief treatise on Star Chamber procedure presented 20 September 1622 to the new clerk and deputy clerk of the court, extracts from the order and decree books, notes of cases, and collections of precedents, all of which Hudson apparently compiled for his own use.

kingdom,' and furnished ammunition to its popular enemies to impugn the reputation of a court which 'in justice, it is, and hath been ever, free from the suspicion of injury and corruption.'[36] Throughout the treatise, but particularly in part III (on procedure), Hudson was unsparing in castigating those practices which in justice demanded reform and in fact fed contumelious criticism of Star Chamber. From his own abundant experience, he suggested how those practices should be reformed.

One might reasonably ask, if Hudson's greater purpose was to counter the court's detractors, why he did not publish the treatise in print. He was not niggardly in allowing its widespread reproduction in manuscript and in that sense he did indeed publish it. Moreover, he makes very clear in the first words of his treatise his reluctance to rush to print:

> I cannot but with admiration reverence the grave judgment of the sages of the common law of England who have been abstinent in publishing their meditations and arguments in their professions, either holding it as a flag of vain-glory unworthy their gravity, or as one of Lycurgus' maxims, or their ancestors' Druides' prescripts, *mandare memoriae, et disciplinae potius quam scriptis*; unlike to this cracking age, when all men in all professions *quicquid subito crepant omnino a statu Apollinis credunt*; who, for fear of burying their talent, post to the press to publish to others that which they well understand not themselves . . .[37]

and who in so doing furnish 'the multitude' with 'shifts to cloak their wickedness' by covering 'their dishonesty under some colour of law or justice.' The latter concern was conventional. But the scathing attack on contemporary lawyers who rushed into print reflected a grave professional reservation tainted with disrespect for one of the two most published lawyers of that 'cracking age' and disapproval of the other, Francis Bacon and Edward Coke, respectively. Coke he considered a threat to Star Chamber. Bacon, recently put from his place as its president, Hudson saw as the author of its growing misfortunes, a man whom he could seldom bring himself to refer to by name – the 'old lord chancellor' without any respectful adjective served – and the author of brilliantly ambitious works (*Instauratio Magna* was published two years before). One of Hudson's intellectually conservative sensibilities and animus toward their author might well move him to characterize Bacon as one who did 'well understand not' himself what he published.

It is likely that Hudson did not want to give undue prominence to his fears, whereby he might fuel contumely rather than damp controversy. Bacon was a broken man when Hudson presented the treatise to his successor. Sir Edward Coke, member for Liskeard, was already a marked

[36] Hudson, 'Star Chamber,' 22. [37] *Ibid.*, 1.

man for his increasingly strident opposition in the House; either shortly after or at the time the treatise was completed, Coke would be stripped of his seat on the Privy Council and therefore in Star Chamber, which he had enjoyed and made abundant use of since his post-judicial rehabilitation in 1617. Neither Bacon nor Coke could do any further mischief *in* Star Chamber. Bacon's successor, John Williams, bishop of Lincoln, had the potential to return the Star Chamber to its old ways and its old glory, arresting the erosion which Hudson believed had set in with Bacon's presidency. By addressing his work to Williams, by urging him to recognize his responsibility for the health of the High Court of Star Chamber, Hudson conceived that he might accomplish directly, and with least risk of giving comfort to its detractors, those reforms requisite to the court's recovery from the bad years of the 'old lord chancellor.'

Hudson's agenda for Lord Keeper Williams was nothing less than to return Star Chamber to the institution that it was in the days of Thomas Egerton, lord Ellesmere, who from 1596 until 1617 had held the Great Seal. In his peroration, leaving his labor 'to men of better judgments,' Hudson hoped that he had

> pursued so near as I can in all things the direction and opinion of that famous *lord chancellor Egerton*, whose memory I ever reverence, and to whom I must attribute all my observations, being glad to shroud myself under the protection of his name, *tanquam sub Ajacis clypeo*; by whose favour, yea private and particular fatherly directions, I have been enabled both in my poor understanding and weak estate . . .[38]

Such an encomium vitiates any surprise that the treatise contains exactly seventy explicit references to Egerton as president of Star Chamber. All are respectful in the extreme, and 'reverend *lord Egerton*,' 'most reverend and learned lord chancellor,' and 'wise chancellor' are the usual appellations.[39] Hudson wore his heart on his sleeve, but his hand on the page makes clear that Egerton was the model for all that could be desired in a judge, especially one who presided over the High Court of Star Chamber.

Much of Hudson's admiration for Egerton had to do with judicial style. In comparing the 'Dignity of this Court' to the Roman Senate – and perhaps half in jest bemoaning the fact that England had no Cicero or Hortensius to make a defense for the accused – and noting how large an arena Star Chamber was for the exercise of oratory, he noted that Egerton,

> affecting matter rather than affectation of words, tied the same to laconical brevity; an honour to the court of justice, to be swayed rather by ponderous reasons than fluent and deceitful speeches.[40]

[38] *Ibid.*, 238–9. [39] *Ibid.*, 93, 95, 131–2. [40] *Ibid.*, 18.

Hudson lauded Egerton's practice in perceptibly showing an apologetic concern when he called upon a counsellor to speak – especially if it was one whom he was known to favor – and the 'public grace' which he extended to counsel of note and merit and also to 'towardly and hopeful young men in their industrious inceptions' at the bar.[41] This, Hudson indicated, was in marked distinction to 'latter times [which] have rather introduced favourites or kinsmen as subjects for the judge's favour.'[42] Egerton was also tender of the Privy Councillors, who had to await his presence before the court could sit, never being late but usually arriving well before them.[43] Above all else Hudson admired Egerton for his fine impartiality and sense of justice, recalling with approval that 'the reverend *lord Egerton* would often remember,' *Vendere injustitiam insania est, vendere justitiam nequitia*: To sell injustice is madness, to sell justice, vile.[44]

The contrast between the revered Egerton and the despised Bacon is only implicit, but it is clear. Bacon as counsel, Hudson knew well, and it will doubtless shock us to have it intimated that that towering intellect might have been better known for 'fluent and deceitful speeches' than for 'ponderous reasons' in his advocacy. As for 'favourites or kinsmen as subjects for the judge's favour,' the shaft's target is clear: four Bacons practiced in Star Chamber, two of them prominently, during Francis Bacon's presidency.[45] Neither was Bacon noted for punctuality nor much sensitivity to his fellow councillors; how friendless he was, how many slights to so many powerful men, especially peers, came back to stalk him to destruction, was manifest at his impeachment. And though Hudson referred to embracery of jurors when recalling Egerton's maxim on selling justice, the point is susceptible of another meaning in the aftermath of a lord chancellor dashed for doing just that.

Much of Hudson's contempt for Bacon had to do with judicial style, a style diametrically different from that of Egerton. There is an elliptical passage in the treatise where, in discussing embracery of juries, Hudson writes:

But sure it is, that if a counsellor or attorney will take upon him to compass a jury, that is punishable. And so it was held in *Bradley's* Case, who escaped by faint proof; he being assuredly the greatest and most notorious preparer of juries of any

[41] *Ibid.*, 27. [42] *Ibid.*, 26. [43] *Ibid.*, 25.

[44] *Ibid.*, 93. For 'Vendere . . .' etc., I have followed Boalt Hall's MS of the treatise, fol. 103: the printed version has 'Vendere justitiam . . . vendere injustitiam,' which makes less sense. See James S. Cockburn's essay, below, 322, concerning Bacon.

[45] Nathaniel Bacon, Gray's 'ancient' 1576; William Bacon, Gray's 'ancient' by 1605; Francis Bacon, Gray's called 1616 (Justice of King's Bench, 1642); Nathaniel Bacon, Gray's called 1617. Of these, the two Nathaniels were closely related to the lord chancellor: the older being his elder brother of the full blood, the younger his brother of the half blood.

attorney in that part of the kingdom [the Marches of Wales]; under the burthen of whose corruption by that practice the county of Salop hath groaned many years, and if the lord *Egerton* had lived, would have been delivered ere this time.[46]

There is a long Hudson history behind this passage. Between 1618 and 1621, Hudson was counsel for four different plaintiffs in four different cases in which John Bradley, of Staple Inn, an attorney of the Common Pleas, was prosecuted in Star Chamber for jury embracery. Hudson's first bill, filed in June 1618, which came to trial in Easter Term 1620 came within a breath of convicting Bradley.[47] Through no fault of Hudson, the case was weak: most of the charges against the principal conspirators were trivial, the plaintiff was suspect in his motivation, and Bradley's laboring of the talesmen was sufficiently circumspect (he merely moved them to appear, not how to find) that he escaped. Most of the court, including Sir Edward Coke, Privy Councillor, found Bradley's actions distasteful but not amounting to embracery. Alone, the last to speak, as precedence in the court demanded, felt impelled to cuteness and a levity which seemed to condone Bradley's actions, Lord Chancellor Bacon: 'For the embracery, wee muste bee tender, naye, curious. Little charmes maye enchante. Butt here I cannot finde anie embracerie.'[48] Small wonder that Hudson concluded that had Egerton lived . . ., even if the outcome of the case had been no different.

Hudson's two score references to Egerton's assiduity in procedural regularity is no less an attack on Bacon. Throughout, not merely in part III, 'Of the Course of the Court of Star Chamber,' which comprises almost half the treatise, Hudson repeatedly provides Bishop Williams with the lodestar to follow in order to arrest the tendency to procedural deceleration and its attendant injustices, which he intimates had set in with Bacon's presidency. Indeed, Hudson draws a quite explicit contrast between Egerton and Bacon in the matter of pleading an outlawry. Egerton, unlike Bacon, required the whole record under the Great Seal to be pleaded, 'because the plea was in delay of the plaintiff.'[49] Was Hudson's concern ill-founded? We can, even at this remove, establish that it was not. Egerton's herculean efforts at speeding up Star Chamber proceedings, though they did not accomplish all that he – and, one supposes,

[46] Hudson, 'Star Chamber,' 94, also 117.

[47] PRO, STAC 8/162/11; the other three actions were STAC 8/165/21 (*Harryes* v. *Harryes and Bradley*, bill Nov. 1618), STAC 8/236/7 (*Powell* v. *Hixon and Bradley*, bill April 1619), STAC 8/311/24 (*Yonge* v. *Bradley*, bill Feb. 1621).

[48] Cambridge University Library, MS I.i.6.51, fol. 54 (report, 26 May 1620).

[49] Hudson, 'Star Chamber,' 162.

Hudson – desired, were not matched by Bacon. Unhappily, Williams did little better.[50]

The full extent of Hudson's displeasure with Bacon is, however, to be found in again as many complaints of recent shortcomings in the court as there are explicit references to Egerton and his virtues. These *dyscolii* remarks are distributed with remarkable evenness throughout the treatise. Many of them are directed at those procedural abuses which Egerton had striven against and which, implicitly, Bacon had permitted to flourish. Of these, no less than eleven are directed at ill-practices that had recently crept into the court's clerical establishment. The sharpest complaint was directed at the proliferation of underclerks to the clerk of the Council in Star Chamber: the clerk of appearances and certificates and the keeper of the records were the prime targets.[51] Hudson emphatically condemned the addition of a fourth attorney in Star Chamber as 'most unnecessary,' an addition instituted shortly after he gave up his attorneyship in 1608.[52] He feared that multiplying offices had increased fees and introduced disorder in the keeping of records;[53] increased fees had already become a grievance in the parliament of 1621 and would be subject to growing, though not always effectual, action by commissioners for exacted fees. Frivolous and insufficient pleas, carelessly drawn by 'ignorant clerks' of the attorneys, resulting in badly drawn issues for trial constituted a notorious abuse in Hudson's eyes.[54] In his complaints against the clerical establishment, Hudson was obliquely attacking Bacon not so much as holder of the Great Seal – though it was that officer's responsibility to order the clerical establishments – as clerk of the council in Star Chamber from 1608 to 1617. With William Mill's death in July 1608, the reversion of the Star Chamber clerkship fell in to Sir Francis Bacon; he would continue to hold the office, as the first sinecurist clerk, until he received the Seal on Egerton's resignation of it in March 1617. It was Bacon, as clerk, who introduced the new offices of clerk of the appearances and certificates and the keeper of the records, who appears to have encouraged the creation of the fourth attorneyship, and who through his neglect and possibly his cupidity (we will never be able to determine which or what mix of both) had allowed the Star Chamber office to become a luxuriant bureaucratic garden.

It can reasonably be argued that such condemnations of Bacon, both as president and formerly as clerk of Star Chamber, constituted relatively

[50] Thomas G. Barnes, 'Due process and slow process in the late Elizabethan–early Stuart Star Chamber,' *American Journal of Legal History*, VI (1962), 319–21.
[51] Hudson, 'Star Chamber,' 37–8, 41, 46, 158–60.
[52] *Ibid.*, 45. [53] *Ibid.*, 41. [54] *Ibid.*, 160 and 191.

small change. Slow process is the denial of justice, excessive fees discourage litigants' seeking justice, and slackness, silliness, and the show of favor in a chief judge demeans justice. Yet none of this amounts to a palpable miscarriage of justice. Any Jacobean legal commentator would feel constrained to exercise great circumspection in accusing a judge or a court of miscarrying justice, even if the judge had fallen so precipitously, so far as had Bacon. As directly as discretion allowed, Hudson implicitly condemned Bacon for miscarriage of justice in one notable case. *Attorney-General* v. *Philip Jacob and other Alien Merchants* provides no less than eleven explicit citations of the over five hundred cases cited in the treatise: the single most heavily cited case in a work which was very much in the new style of legal writing of the age, in which there was abundant use of cases both as illustration and even as precedent. The Dutch Case (as Hudson refers to it) proved the later adage that hard cases make bad law.

In June 1618, Attorney-General Yelverton filed an information *pro Rege* against thirty-two London merchants and others and thirteen alien merchants; in the course of pleading and proofs other alien merchants were added as defendants.[55] The charge was subversion of the realm by the exportation of bullion in violation of proclamations prohibiting the same. Star Chamber heard the case on 8 December 1619, twenty alien merchants (though no Englishmen) were fined in sums from £1500 to £20,000 for a total of £151,500 – the largest amount of fines ever imposed in Star Chamber in a single case – and the fines were estreated into the Exchequer three days later.[56] Hudson, who probably was engaged in the defense in this case and was the most prominent counsel defending a number of the sentenced defendants and others in a subsequent case to the same purpose,[57] put the point of the case succinctly and voiced a despairing hope:

> But that [Dutch] Case was a Case of State, wherein the Commonwealth was much interested, and I hope will be no precedent for future times.[58]

His criticism of the case was explicit: denying the defendants the benefit of the general pardon because they had not pleaded it in answer to the information because they were not citizens but aliens though they paid subsidy;[59] refusing them the benefit of the four-day rule, whereby they would have been admitted to attorney without examination because interrogatories had not been put in timely;[60] denying the defendants the

[55] PRO, STAC 8/25/19.
[56] PRO, E 159/457, Michaelmas 17 James I, r. 148.
[57] PRO, STAC 8/25/23, *Attorney-General pro Rege* v. *John de Munsey et al.* (information Feb. 1620).
[58] Hudson, 'Star Chamber,' 209. [59] *Ibid.*, 174–5. [60] *Ibid.*, 180.

right to impeach the testimony of witnesses against them, a 'liberty [that] is not denied but in the Dutch cause, wherein are many precedents tending to the overthrow of the antient courses';[61] forcing the defendants' servants to depose as witnesses by committing them for their contempt, though some years before Egerton on Hudson's motion had held that 'he knew no law to compel a witness to speak more than he would of his own accord';[62] giving insufficient time for the defendants to examine their witnesses which 'was no small scandal to the justice of the kingdom in the Dutch case';[63] and, sentencing one of the defendants on post-publication testimony on the grounds that the defendant had implied consent to this unusual procedure.[64] The only good that Hudson could say for a case in which the 'antient course' was so grievously mauled was that the court held strictly to individual service of mesne process to rejoin (or else be served anew) and to hear judgment (or else be dismissed, as some were).[65] Each one of these substantial denials of justice, and the two accordings of procedural strictness, were the work of only one member of the Star Chamber, the president of it, Lord Chancellor Bacon. Hudson's condemnation of these rulings goes beyond any distaste he had for Bacon, beyond the fact that he might well have been of counsel with those abused. We need not credit him with much sentiment for a parcel of the king's principal creditors who were lighted upon as so many convenient (i.e. foreign) abundantly golden fleeces to be shorn to the discharge of the king's heavy debts. That the case established many dangerous precedents to the 'antient course' of a court renowned for its justice based upon that steady 'course' troubled Hudson deeply.

The 'antient course' of Star Chamber is a recurring theme in the treatise. Thus, leaving to a committee composed of a common law judge full determination of both the form and the substance of a bill Hudson saw as encouragement to vexatious litigation. 'But if antient course might prevail, all would be redressed': a question of form would be settled either by the committee or the lord chancellor, and a question of substance would be heard in open court with counsel on both sides heard, which 'taketh away all possibility of grievance, and restoreth the court to their antient splendor.'[66] Bacon's failure in Hudson's eyes was above all else that he did not preserve the 'antient course.'

Hudson did not intimate that Bacon was in any wise disaffected towards the court or that he was critical of it and its role in judicature.

61 *Ibid.*, 201. 62 *Ibid.*, 209 and 78. 63 *Ibid.*, 137.
64 *Ibid.*, 211. See text above at n. 24. 65 *Ibid.*, 191 and 219.
66 *Ibid.*, 30. Hudson warned that, despite the court's 'great and sovereign arm' in exercise of discretion, it should not be 'stretched out in all cases, for that would destroy order and course, but must be rarely used, and in great and weighty causes.' *Ibid.*, 214–15.

Indeed, the palpable miscarriages of Bacon in the Dutch Case grew from an excess of zeal for the court's power and the king's interest. Bacon's fault was to give a handle to Star Chamber's enemies, and Hudson perceived that the court had no more dangerous foe than Bacon's inveterate rival, Sir Edward Coke. If Hudson's intention was that Williams should play the president to Egerton's measure, it was also to identify for him the enemy and the peril. Though Coke was dashed, his legacy lived on in the persons of his brethren on the benches of the common law courts and in the precedents reductive of Star Chamber's authority, which dated from his long dominance of Common Pleas and King's Bench, and his seat at the board in Star Chamber.

Hudson despised Bacon, but he held Coke in the conventional respect that virtually all lawyers of the age accorded him. Hudson was not loath to notice Coke's discomfiture at Egerton's hands when the former was attorney-general, where the latter awarded costs to the defendants against the attorney-general's relator 'although *sir Edward Coke* opposed it with all his power.' A very disapproving note was struck in reporting that Coke picked up a prosecution *de virtute officii* after the private plaintiff's case had been dismissed, thus wronging the defendants, by which 'the court [was] something dishonoured.'[67] And Coke as litigant, on relation to the attorney-general against Coke's estranged second wife's protector, John Holles, lord Houghton, received sharp reproof from Hudson for receiving costs for Houghton's dilatory demurrer before Coke was entered of record as relator.[68] But in no reference to Coke in the treatise is there a hint of any personal animus on Hudson's part.

Coke was the enemy because as chief justice of the King's Bench from 1613 until his famous fall in 1616 he had led that court in repeated disallowances of Star Chamber's writ of privilege. Hudson saw this as an all-out attack on the eminence of Star Chamber:

> But now of late the judges of the king's bench have refused to give allowance to the writ [of privilege] which hath been antiently allowed to the plaintiff which here followeth his cause, for that the words are *pendente placito in eadem curia*, making the interpretation thereof to be, that then no man should be sued in any other court, whilst he had any suit here depending; where the meaning of the writ is, that his privilege is to be allowed unto him at any time hanging the suit.[69]

Hudson noted with unconcealed smugness that unlike Common Pleas or

[67] *Ibid.*, 135–6. With respect to relator paying costs, see text above at n. 20.

[68] *Ibid.*, 135. Hudson was of counsel with Houghton in this case, but did not demur for him – he answered for him after the demurrer was overruled, Public Record Office, STAC 8/28/20.

[69] See Hudson, 'Star Chamber,' 121; I follow the Boalt Hall MS of the treatise in this quotation, fol. 132–132*v*.

King's Bench practice in writs of privilege, where the writ was awarded upon 'every suggestion,' in Star Chamber it was allowed only upon proof put in on oath.[70]

Indeed, the whole of part I, wherein Hudson sought to establish by historical evidence that the court of Star Chamber 'is a settled ordinary court of justice,' of great 'antiquity,' surpassing 'dignity,' its judges 'the great senators of this state,' and its ministerial officers 'principal' officers responsible to the greatest officer of state, the lord chancellor,[71] is a defense of Star Chamber's pre-eminence against Coke's disparagement of it. Where Coke is prepared to find precedents for Star Chamber from the reign of Edward III (but no earlier), Hudson argues that Star Chamber is the continuation of Henry II's *Curia Regis*.[72] Tolling Bracton and Britton – bells that could make only an uneven, even tremulous, sound – Hudson argued that 'all courts of justice have flowed out of this court, as out of a fountain; the king and the council having distributed these causes . . .' to King's Bench, etc.[73] That 'reverend judge sir Edward Coke' is turned to Hudson's own purposes when, with considerable disingenuousness cloaked as mere afterthought, Hudson cites 'the three *corams*' in 28 Edward III with which Coke's treatment of Star Chamber opens in the *Fourth Institutes* as proof of Star Chamber's antiquity, but studiously avoids Coke's comment, 'And of all the High and Honourable Courts of Justice, this [*coram nobis in Camera Stellata*] ought to be kept within his proper bounds and jurisdiction.'[74] He takes head-on Coke's denial of English-bill courts as being 'courts of record,' by stressing Star Chamber's concern for formality.[75] And Hudson does not fear to attack the lion under the throne in his own den. In condemning Star Chamber's reliance upon the single common law judge committee for fully determining the adequacy of special pleading – 'an insufferable indignity to that great court' – he points out that

> The committee for the most part being a judge of the inferior courts, doth willingly lessen the growth of this high court, as being desirous to uphold his own proper jurisdiction.[76]

There is no proof, beyond Hudson's own assertion based upon his experience, that this longtime common practice of the court was any more abused of late than formerly from the motives ascribed to the judges, but it does make patent Hudson's fear of the common law courts' erosion of Star Chamber's authority.

70 *Ibid.*, 121. 71 *Ibid.*, 3, 9, 17, 22, 37.

72 Edward Coke, *The Fourth Part of the Institutes*, 4th edn (London, 1669), 60–1: *STC Wing* C4931; Hudson, 'Star Chamber,' 11.

73 Hudson, 'Star Chamber,' 10. 74 *Ibid.*, 13; Coke, *Fourth Institutes*, 60.

75 Hudson, 'Star Chamber,' 5–6. 76 *Ibid.*, 20.

An unusually elliptical reference near the end of the treatise, in which Hudson refers to a case in 1614 in which 'I was more than *oculatus test.* for I can say without boasting, *quorum pars magna fui* . . .' follows an exhortation to Williams to 'maintain this power to execute the sentence, which was so worthily regained by the industry of the *lord chancellor Egerton* . . .'[77] In *Attorney-General ex rel. Sir Richard Egerton* v. *Richard Brereton et al.* (Trinity 1614), Star Chamber had split five to four on the issue of whether or not the court had as great a power as common law courts to issue process of extent to levy damages and costs upon parties sentenced in the court.[78] Chief Justice Coke led the minority which would have denied Star Chamber that power, carrying with him Chief Justice Hobart and Justice Croke of the Common Pleas as well as the senior lay Councillor, William Lord Knollys. James I, two years later in 1616, sitting in full regal panoply in his Council in the Star Chamber for the settlement of the dispute between the common law jurisdictions and Chancery, launched into a defense of Star Chamber in which he noted that that court 'hath bene likewise shaken of late, and . . . had receiued a sore blow, if it had not bene assisted and caried by a few voyces.'[79] So close had been the judgment in Brereton's Case. Ironically, the principal adversaries as to the Star Chamber's powers were those two whose influence on the court seemed most pernicious to Hudson: Coke from his seat at the board and Sir Francis Bacon, attorney-general at the bar, whose reliance upon precedent – much of it supplied by Hudson evidently – might have been more persuasive if his forensic rhetoric had been more muted. Hudson, the staunch defender of Star Chamber, found himself in Brereton's Case ground between friend and foe: so, too, did Star Chamber.

IV

It would be simple, and erroneous, to characterize Hudson as an upholder of the 'prerogative' against the 'common law.' If that whole dichotomy is

[77] *Ibid.*, 231.

[78] Thomas G. Barnes, 'A Cheshire seductress, precedent, and a "sore blow" to Star Chamber,' *On the Laws and Customs of England: Essays in Honor of Samuel E. Thorne*, ed. by Morris S. Arnold, Thomas A. Green, Sally A. Scully, and Stephen D. White (Chapel Hill, University of North Carolina Press, 1981), 359–82. Hudson's treatise, pt III, sect. xxiv, 'Of the execution of the sentence,' 228–31, contains virtually all of the precedents argued in Brereton's Case, indicating that though Hudson was not counsel of record in that case he was more than '*oculatus test.*' precisely in having searched out the precedents submitted by Attorney-General Bacon.

[79] James I, *The Political Works of James I*, ed. by Charles H. McIlwain (Cambridge, Mass., Harvard University Press, 1918), 326.

suspect, nowhere should it be given less credit than in the case of William Hudson. In referring to his travail in Brereton's Case, Hudson hoped that his labor 'doth not detract at all from the honour and dignity of the common law, as some without just ground have conceived.'[80] In explaining why he would not dispute *de jure* and *de facto* the jurisdiction of Star Chamber, but set down only what matters were usually determined there, he stated that he must

> steer a course full of peril betwixt *Scylla* and *Charybdis*; for if on the one side I shall diminish the force or shorten the stretching arm of this seat of monarchy, I should incur not only the censure of gross indiscretion and folly, but also much danger of reprehension; and if on the other side I should extend the power thereof beyond the due limits, my lords the judges, and my masters the professors of the common law will easily tax me for encroaching upon the liberty of the subject, and account me not only unworthy of the name of my profession, but of the name of an Englishman . . .[81]

The metaphor was hackneyed, but the peril real enough. Moreover, his perception of the peril was perspicacious, even precocious, from the vantage point of 1621. Star Chamber was a long way from coming under direct attack, and two decades away from abolition. All the great, notorious, cases which would be laid at its door, picked up and used in the Long Parliament to batter down that door, all of the prosecutions to essentially fiscal ends which in the course of the 1630s would alienate virtually every segment of political society, were at least a decade away. Certainly, Hudson detected a rising popular contumely directed at Star Chamber: *his* recognition of it is the best evidence for its existence, for elsewhere there is little indication of it. In arguing that the court was a settled ordinary court of justice he met head-on 'two several contentions': that the court was only a usurpation of monarchy upon the common law in derogation of the liberties granted subjects by Magna Carta, and that it was only an assembly for consultation at the king's command in cases where other courts lacked power.[82] Neither of these propositions found any support in respectable legal literature, least of all in Coke's writings. Hudson recognized that Star Chamber could be defended against this rising tide of calumny only by internal reform of its procedures and resistance to the encroachment of the common law court judges whose attacks fed popular misconception even though they did not intend to do so. In 1621, Hudson saw clearly what was needed and what must be done to protect Star Chamber.

If in Bishop Williams he saw who would do it, then William Hudson

[80] Hudson, 'Star Chamber,' 231. [81] *Ibid.*, 49. [82] *Ibid.*, 3.

was soon to be disillusioned. There was little to choose between Williams's presidency and Bacon's. Cynical, lazy, insouciant of legal affairs, Williams neither took up Hudson's agenda nor apparently perceived the peril it was meant to avert. By the time of Williams's removal in 1625, practices and precedents in the court from Bacon's tenure were further solidified. Only with Thomas Coventry's accession to the Great Seal in 1625 did Hudson, and Star Chamber, find the champion up to the motives if not the measure of Thomas Egerton. It can be argued that by then it was too late. More correctly, it should be argued that Coventry was not Egerton, that he never wielded the power over Privy Councillors and judges that Egerton had, never exercised the influence over Charles I that Egerton had had over James I. In this, Coventry's failings were merely a part of the greater failure that stalked Charles's governors and his governance.

Hudson's perspicacity grew from his sensitivity to a dilemma in which all lawyers would find themselves by 1641, whereby legal institutions came under selective attacks that ultimately broadened into a wholesale attack on all of them and even the law itself. That he took up arms to defend Star Chamber, having perceived the danger, was only to be expected. In Mr Hudson's eyes, it was in truth *his* court.

The spoils of law: the trial of Sir John Hele, 1604

JAMES S. COCKBURN*

On 10 October 1604 the High Court of Star Chamber met to consider a case which, even in the dramatic record of that famous tribunal, may well be unique. Four full days were spent in considering testimony which runs to 278 large membranes in the trial record and to an unprecedented five pages in Baildon's edition of John Hawarde's reports.[1] Ostensibly, the central issue was a relatively innocuous piece of sharp practice. But among the inflammable matters aired during the proceedings were subornation, bribery, perjury, intimidation, usury, murder, and treason. Closer examination suggests, too, the existence of a substratum of vendetta and conspiracy embracing prominent members of the court itself. When judgment was rendered on 19 October, Hawarde noted that a majority of the judges voted for acquittal or a modest fine. Yet within hours the defendant – sixty-two years old, the king's senior serjeant, an assize judge and a leading contender for the realm's highest legal offices – had been fined £1000, suspended from office and imprisoned in the Fleet, his career permanently ruined. Baildon, in editing Hawarde's version of the trial, was troubled by ambiguities in the reporter's account.[2] Almost four hundred years later the uncomfortable feeling persists that there was more to the trial of Sir John Hele than meets the eye.

I

The broad outline of Serjeant Hele's career suggests few problems. He

* I am grateful to J. H. Baker and L. A. Knafla for their advice on an earlier draft of this essay.

[1] The surviving interrogatories and answers are in PRO, STAC 8/9/4. Hawarde's account of the trial is printed in *Les Reportes del Cases in Camera Stellata, 1593 to 1609, from the Original MS of John Hawarde*, ed. by William P. Baildon (London, privately printed, 1894), 171–6. The hearing occupied two days in each of two consecutive weeks, 10, 12, 17 and 19 October 1604.

[2] *Ibid.*, 176, n. 1.

was born in 1541 or 1542,[3] the son of William Hele of Hele, Devon, and admitted to the Inner Temple in 1564.[4] During the 1570s he built up a lucrative legal practice, both at Westminster and in the traditionally litigious West Country. By 1578 he was in the peace commission for Devon and recorder of Plympton, which he represented in the parliament of 1584.[5] His most enduring ties, however, were with the cities of Plymouth and Exeter. During the early 1580s Hele served as 'town counsel' for Plymouth, and in 1585 was appointed recorder. He obtained a second recordership, that of Exeter, in 1592 and represented this city in the parliaments of 1593, 1597 and 1601.[6] Although the direct remuneration from these civic offices was modest, by 1591 Hele had amassed a fortune sufficient to purchase Wembury manor near Plymouth, and to build there, at a reputed cost of more than £20,000, one of the finest houses in the county.[7]

And though Wembury remained his principal residence, the focus of Hele's career was by this point shifting decisively to London. His prominence in the profession was institutionalized in 1594 when he was created a serjeant-at-law.[8] Throughout the 1590s he appeared regularly in Star Chamber, both as litigant and counsel.[9] His 'exquisite pleas' in the complicated case of *Beverley* v. *Pittes* in 1597 drew a public commendation from the Lord Keeper, Thomas Egerton,[10] and by 1600, when he was first

[3] Hele's monument in Wembury church, Devon, records that he was 66 at his death on 4 June 1608.

[4] Anon., *Students Admitted to the Inner Temple 1547–1660*, n.d. [1887], 53. There is considerable confusion in accounts of Hele's career with a second John Hele, admitted in 1578: *ibid.*, 89. In 1591 Serjeant Hele recited in an action for defamation that he had studied the law as a fellow of the Inner Temple for 29 years. This would date his admission to 1562: John H. Baker, 'Counsellors and barristers: an historical study,' *Cambridge Law Journal,* XXVII (1969), 217–18.

[5] PRO, STAC 5/B7/21.

[6] *Report and Transactions of the Devon Association for the Advancement of Science, Literature, and Art*, XVI (1884), 515; LXI (1929), 201, 209; Plymouth City Library, MSS W 359/45, 46; W 361/48; Exeter City Library, MS City Act Book, V, fol. 10; VI, fol. 99. I am grateful to the city librarians of Exeter and Plymouth for their help in establishing the details of Hele's civic connections.

[7] *Transactions, Devonshire Association*, XLII (1910), 528–37; J. Price, *The Worthies of Devon* (1810), 484–90. Prior to the Dissolution the estate had belonged to the priory of Plympton: Joyce Youings (ed.), *Devon Monastic Lands: Calendar of Particulars for Grants 1536–1558*, Devon and Cornwall Record Society, new series, I (1955), 50, 97–8.

[8] PRO, CP 45/92, m. 3. His patrons were distinguished: Henry Herbert, earl of Pembroke, Sir Christopher Hatton, John Popham, CJKB, William Peryam, CB, and Francis Gawdy, J. I owe this information to Dr J. H. Baker. It was probably about this time that Hele purchased the house at Kew from which most of his later correspondence is addressed.

[9] Hawarde, *Reportes*, 1, 2, 6, 10–11, 13–14, 29–30, 41, 42, 82, 94, 115–16, 126, 144, 158; see below pp. 318.

[10] *Ibid.*, 84.

tipped to succeed Egerton as Master of the Rolls.[11] Hele's professional standing was extremely high. Two years later he was appointed queen's serjeant and rode the summer circuit as an assize judge.[12] He was knighted in July 1603, rode the Home Circuit again in the spring and summer of that year[13] and acted with Sir Edward Coke as prosecution counsel at the trial of Sir Walter Raleigh.[14] Rumors that the serjeant was in trouble multiplied swiftly during the winter of 1603–4, but few were prepared for the crushing finality of his disgrace. Any possibility that the case might be reopened disappeared in the aftermath of the Gunpowder Plot, and Hele retired to Wembury where he died in 1608, still protesting his innocence.

II

Nothing in this brief biography prepares us for the complex tale of ambition and graft unfolded by Serjeant Edward Phillips in opening the Star Chamber proceedings against Hele.[15] Essentially, the Crown's case was as follows. In 1600 Hele, 'corruptly to obtain . . . the mastership of the Rolls,' advanced to Henry Brooke, lord Cobham, a loan of £3500. Hele himself contributed £2000 and guaranteed the balance, outstanding in debts to three Londoners.[16] The Crown claimed that Hele had agreed to the loan and to forfeit interest on it only after Cobham had undertaken to promote the serjeant's claim to the Rolls. By 1603, however, Hele was 'out of hope and despairing to attain the mastership of the Rolls,' and in May he approached Cobham for settlement of the debt. An agreement was drafted and sent to Cobham for his approval. Despite the original understanding, the reckoning included interest, and the debt totalled £4666 13s. 4d., which Cobham agreed to pay in four installments between October 1603 and October 1604.[17] He assumed that fulfillment of the agreement would cancel all his obligations. But counsel alleged that Hele had 'cautiously and craftily' amended his clerk's draft, deliberately introducing subtle errors so that he would have grounds for taking out execution against Cobham's estate, if necessary. Nevertheless, the draft was

[11] PRO, SP 12/275/100 and 12/278/27 (John Chamberlain to Dudley Carleton, 21 Oct. 1600, 3 Feb. 1601).
[12] PRO, SP 12/285/23 (Chamberlain to Carleton, 2 Oct. 1602).
[13] James S. Cockburn, *A History of English Assizes 1558–1714* (Cambridge, CUP, 1972), 268.
[14] PRO, SP 14/4/83; Thomas B. Howell (ed.), *A Complete Collection of State Trials . . .* (34 vols., London, T. C. Hansard, 1809–28), II, 1–59 (Raleigh was tried on 17 Nov.).
[15] Hawarde, *Reportes*, 172–4.
[16] There are some slight discrepancies between the amounts recorded by Hawarde and those in other, more reliable, accounts: see below p. 330.
[17] £1475 13s. 4d. on 18 Oct. 1603; £1075 on 19 Jan. 1604; £1050 on 22 Apr. 1604; £1050 on 23 Oct. 1604. There are slight discrepancies in the various accounts.

returned to Hele without amendment, and subsequently sealed and engrossed.

Three months before the first payment was due, Cobham was arrested on suspicion of treason. The Crown claimed that Hele knew that Cobham would be convicted, anticipated that as a consequence of attainder his estate would escheat to the Crown, and realized that he, Hele, would probably forfeit the debt and certainly lose the interest. In an attempt to recover his money Hele immediately instructed his attorney, William King, to institute process against Cobham's estate. Since the Trinity law term had already ended, he advised King to obtain antedated writs of *scire facias*[18] from the Common Pleas. These were quickly but irregularly returned, enabling Hele to procure writs of *elegit* and to begin proceedings upon them during the vacation.

Early in September the serjeant participated in a conference at Maidenhead where the king's counsel agreed that the evidence supported a charge of treason against Cobham and his brother, George Brooke. Hele himself was appointed to frame the indictments, was present when they were returned on 21 September and formally introduced the charge upon which Lord Cobham was eventually convicted on 25 November 1603.[19] Nevertheless, during September the serjeant continued to execute process against Cobham's Kent estate. According to the Crown, he sent one of his servants, William Brown, to persuade Cobham's retainers, the sheriff of Kent and the valuation jury to undervalue the estate. At Maidstone assizes on 29 September, Hele himself, sitting as an assize judge, personally thanked at least one member of a jury that had valued property at a fraction of its market value.

Hawarde reported that so much background material had been introduced 'by way of inducement to the matter.'[20] But he did not indicate why such an elaborate recital was necessary. The answer lies in the nature of contemporary notions of fraud. Although the law condemned in general terms attempts to take advantage of another's misfortune or any misuse of legal rights to obtain an advantage, the common law courts had no power to cancel documents obtained by fraudulent means. Moreover, in normal circumstances the law did not penalize a creditor who had undervalued property in the course of obtaining satisfaction for a debt owing to him. Only if the undervaluation was proved to be a deliberate act of fraud could an equitable remedy be sought in Chancery or Star

[18] Requiring matter to be brought to the attention of one who might then, if he wished, appear to defend his rights: Giles Jacob, *A New Law Dictionary*, 7th edn (London, Henry Lintot, 1756).

[19] BL, MS Stowe 396, fols. 83–6.

[20] Hawarde, *Reportes*, 172.

Chamber. But fraud itself could not be presumed; it had to be inferred from the attendant circumstances of the transaction. These had therefore to be set out in extended detail.[21] Thus the prosecutors sought to associate Hele, and his co-defendants, King, Dun and Brown, with sharp practice and breach of trust generally and then to establish, mainly by inference, the serjeant's involvement in several specifically fraudulent episodes. Our principal task therefore is to flesh out Hawarde's version of the proceedings with such collateral evidence as has survived in an attempt to establish the details and, more importantly, the context of the accusations against Hele.

III

Serjeant Hele's quest for the mastership of the Rolls was first mentioned – by John Chamberlain, the court gossip – in a letter of 21 October 1600.[22] Since 1596 the mastership had been held by Lord Keeper Egerton, and by this point he was under increasing pressure to surrender the office. Since it was estimated to yield as much as £2000 a year in fees, in addition to extensive patronage,[23] it is not really surprising that Egerton was unwilling to surrender the mastership or that Serjeant Hele was one of several candidates for the position. Chamberlain's letter indicates that Hele's interest was common knowledge and that at this date he was thought the most likely to succeed. Hele never denied that he had sought the Rolls, and it seems certain that late in the spring of 1600 he embarked on a serious campaign to secure this lucrative office.

Few contemporaries were under any illusion about the realities of preferment to high legal or administrative positions: Chamberlain cynically concluded that in this instance Egerton 'would make friends with the meetest mammon.'[24] Hele could hold his own in any auction, but to ensure success he needed also an influential voice to press his claim at court. Normally, such patronage had to be carefully cultivated over an extended period. Lord Cobham, however, represented an investment ripe for immediate exploitation: the influential courtier heavily in debt.[25] The details of Cobham's tangled finances were no doubt well known in legal circles and, in the swirl of predatory activity which routinely attended

[21] For a helpful discussion of fraud, in the context of Chancery's equitable jurisdiction, see William J. Jones, *The Elizabethan Court of Chancery* (Oxford, Clarendon Press, 1967), ch. XII.

[22] PRO, SP 12/275/100.

[23] Jones, *Elizabethan Chancery*, 51–5, 91–2.

[24] PRO, SP 12/275/100.

[25] For some of the political background to Cobham's overspending see Peter Clark, *English Provincial Society from the Reformation to the Revolution: Religion, Politics and Society in Kent, 1500–1640* (Hassocks, Harvester Press, 1977), 261–5.

financial embarrassment, Hele's approach probably attracted little attention. Details of the preliminary negotiations are lacking, but during May and June 1600 Hele assumed responsibility for three separate debts totalling £1500 and advanced Cobham two short-term loans of £1000 each.[26] Later correspondence between Hele and Cobham indicates clearly that Cobham promised to press Hele's claims at court, and there is every reason to accept the insinuation that their suddenly blossoming friendship was fertilized by mutual convenience and the expectation of quick profits.

At Hele's trial his attempt to oil the machinery of preferment would be characterized as 'corrupt.'[27] In the prevailing climate of corruption, however, it was nothing more than a routine and relatively straightforward attempt to insure promotion.[28] A suspicion that the stance adopted by Hele's detractors was essentially hypocritical is considerably strengthened by discovery that the Cobham agreement was not the only such bargain struck during this period. On 14 November 1600 Hele wrote privately to Sir Thomas Egerton. 'You know,' he reminded the Lord Keeper, 'how I came first to entertain the hope of the Rolls, and [I] have followed your own directions. I find now that my hope through your hard conceit against me is desperate. I shall therefore pray your lordship to deliver to this bearer my bonds, and at your lordship's pleasure to send me the £400 you owe me.'[29] The implications are startlingly clear: in consideration of a loan of £400, the Lord Keeper himself had undertaken to advance Hele's candidacy for the Rolls. Now that Egerton had withdrawn his support, Hele regarded their agreement as dead and was therefore calling in his debt.

Egerton was notoriously unsympathetic towards creditors who tried to collect their debts,[30] and one can only speculate on the reasoning behind the serjeant's apparently ill-timed move. Hele may have reasoned that, with Cobham's support apparently guaranteed, the unpredictable Lord Keeper was expendable.[31] In this connection, the date of Hele's letter is particularly interesting. On the same day as he wrote to Egerton, 14

[26] Details taken from Hele's evidence: PRO, STAC 8/9/4, m. 278. The amounts printed in Hawarde, *Reportes*, contain minor inaccuracies.

[27] Hawarde, *Reportes*, 172.

[28] See Lawrence Stone, 'The fruits of office: the case of Robert Cecil, first earl of Salisbury, 1596–1612,' Frederick J. Fisher (ed.), in *Essays in the Economic and Social History of Tudor and Stuart England* (Cambridge, CUP, 1961), 89–116.

[29] Huntington Library, MS Ellesmere 2691.

[30] One man who loaned Egerton £217 was too frightened to collect in his debtor's lifetime: *ibid.*, 61 (R. Meyrick to John Egerton, 26 May 1617).

[31] Hele's letter suggests that the agreement with Egerton predated, indeed stimulated, his approach to Cobham. This would place it earlier than May 1600, when Hele began to assume Lord Cobham's debts.

November, the first of the Cobham debts assumed by the serjeant fell due.[32] Cobham was unable to satisfy his creditor, Sir Robert Lee, who eventually recovered his money from Hele, to whom he surrendered the cancelled bond. Any lawyer could have anticipated this sequence, and Hele knew that possession of the bond would immeasurably strengthen his hold over Cobham. The pressure being brought to bear upon the Lord Keeper to surrender the Rolls[33] may have encouraged Hele to think also that Egerton's influence in the disposal of the office was declining. Nevertheless, Hele still believed that the mastership would go, conventionally, to the highest bidder, and early in 1601 he apparently made the Lord Keeper an improved offer for the office. Writing to Cobham on 22 January, he grumbled that, with the general decline in the profits of office, the returns would now hardly justify his investment in the Rolls. Complaining that he had 'many children very chargeable to me, and my estate not so much as the common opinion holdeth,' he urged Cobham to press his suit vigorously with the queen. A single sentence hints darkly at his smouldering resentment and fear that Cobham too might betray him: 'I hope I have no cause to think ill of any other that have seemed to wish me well.'[34]

Cobham's reply must have been immediate. Judging by Hele's urgent and agitated response on 23 January,[35] it may also have contained the first definite information that Egerton's hostility had taken a new and dangerous turn. 'Imputations' questioning Hele's fitness for public office had reached the queen's ears, and although Hele's letter did not specify their nature, he was in no doubt about their origin. Significantly, he urged Cobham to bring matters into the open by encouraging the queen to appoint a committee to sift the allegations. There is no evidence that a formal inquiry was mounted, but during the last week of January the debate over the mastership of the Rolls seems to have reached a crescendo. Egerton was given 'some schooling' about the appointment but, according to Chamberlain, he was now interested only in denying it to Hele.[36]

Up to this point, there is no evidence that Egerton's animosity towards Hele had expressed itself in detailed charges. As long as the Lord Keeper's personal prejudice coincided with the queen's own wish to avoid rivalry between the Cecil and Essex factions over the Rolls,[37] unsubstantiated

32 PRO, STAC 8/9/4, m. 278.
33 PRO, SP 12/278/27 (Chamberlain to Carleton, 3 Feb. 1601).
34 PRO, SP 12/278/16 (Hele to Cobham, 22 Jan. 1601). Hele appears to have had eight sons and two daughters by his wife Mary, daughter of Ellis Warwick of Holbeton, Devon.
35 PRO, SP 12/278/20.
36 PRO, SP 12/278/27 (Chamberlain to Carleton, 3 Feb. 1601).
37 Jones, *Elizabethan Chancery*, 92–3.

suggestions of Hele's unsuitability were probably enough to maintain a politically convenient status quo. The events of February 1601 altered the situation drastically. The destruction of the Essex faction removed Elizabeth's principal reason for delaying the appointment of a new Master of the Rolls. This realization almost certainly prompted Egerton to step up his campaign to discredit Hele. But when Essex went to the scaffold on 25 February, he also took with him between £4000 and £5000 in debts owing to Hele, a fact which only aggravated the serjeant's impatience to recoup some of his losses through the Rolls.[38] At the same time, he realized that an intensification of Egerton's opposition was now inevitable. Writing to Cobham on 10 April, he tried halfheartedly to fight back by suggesting that Egerton had made himself rich by impoverishing the Rolls. But his dominant preoccupation was with the imminent attack: 'god defend me, poor wretch, from the violence of him that was no better than myself before her majesty advanced him.'[39]

Hele's fears were realized almost immediately. On 26 April 1601 Lucy Paulet, marchioness of Winchester, wrote to her uncle, Robert Cecil, on behalf of 'her very good friend and neighbour' Benjamin Tichborne. She claimed that Tichborne had been publicly insulted by Serjeant Hele at Winchester assizes and that he was now petitioning the Council for satisfaction. Since Tichborne was the son of a prominent Hampshire papist and Hele apparently sympathetic to Puritanism, the source of their disagreement is not hard to imagine.[40] On learning of Tichborne's petition, Hele himself wrote to Cecil to acquaint him with his own version of the affair.[41] This action apparently succeeded in heading off a formal inquiry.

The episode introduces several additional complexities. Of at least three letters written by Hele to Cecil on this issue, only one survives. Disappearing correspondence will continue to cloud our understanding of the relationship between Hele, Cecil and Cobham. That is particularly unfortunate in view of the fact that Cobham was Cecil's brother-in-law, a relationship which leads, inevitably, to speculation about the Secretary's knowledge of Cobham's affairs and Hele's involvement in them. At Hele's trial Cecil would pretend ignorance, but in fact he appears to have been fully informed almost from the beginning. Certainly he discussed

[38] PRO, SP 12/279/61 (Hele to Cobham, 10 Apr. 1601); *HMC: Calendar of the MSS of the Most Honorable the Marquis of Salisbury, K.G., Preserved at Hatfield House, Hertfordshire* (London, HMSO, 1899), VII, 375; *ibid.*, IX (London, HMSO, 1902), 425.

[39] PRO, SP 12/279/61.

[40] *HMC: Salisbury*, XI (London, HMSO, 1906), 177; Cockburn, *English Assizes*, 207–8; see also below, p. 335, n. 122.

[41] *HMC: Salisbury*, XI, 188 (Hele to Cecil, 1 May 1601).

the Tichborne petition and Hele's reply with his brother-in-law,[42] and it is a reasonable assumption that Cobham in turn explained at least some of the background to Hele's current difficulties.

Under Egerton's careful orchestration, the campaign to embarrass Hele gathered momentum rapidly. A few days after the Tichborne episode, the Council received a second petition against the serjeant – this time from Sir William Dethick, the Garter King of Arms. Dethick's complaint closely resembled Tichborne's petition: allegations of public defamation at assizes, this time in Exeter, over a long period, and a further exchange of insults following a case of dangerous riding in the environs of Westminster.[43] The riding incident, in itself, was trivial: Dethick certainly gave as good as he received and, in Hele's version, had provoked the argument by striking the serjeant's horse. Hele alleged, moreover, that the incident had occurred almost six months ago. The altercation at assizes was, he claimed, even more stale, having taken place almost a decade earlier; and it had already been the subject of an unsuccessful petition.[44]

Dethick's stance as the victim of Hele's unprovoked hostility sits uncomfortably on the known facts of the herald's personality. Described by the official historian of the College of Arms as, at best, 'hot tempered and overbearing,'[45] he was associated with irrational violence throughout his career.[46] Not surprisingly, his fellow heralds sought to have him removed from office, and from at least as early as 1584 he was under almost constant pressure to resign. He was not formally suspended, however, until 1603, and a further three years elapsed before he was finally dismissed.[47] Even more revealing than evidence of Dethick's violent nature is the suggestion that he was connected to Egerton through members of the Lord Keeper's extensive clientele.[48] Among the many patents of arms said to

[42] *Ibid.*: Cobham told Hele that the serjeant had forgotten to sign one of the letters to Cecil.

[43] PRO, SP 12/279/98–100.

[44] To Charles Howard, earl of Nottingham, and the Lord Chamberlain in 1593 or 1594. Nottingham was Lord Cobham's father-in-law: see below p. 335, n. 123.

[45] Anthony R. Wagner, *Heralds of England: A History of the Office and College of Arms* (London, HMSO, 1967), 201.

[46] Folger Library, MS x.d.313: 'Detections and abusesse of William Dericke of some called Garter kinge of Armes' (n.d.); BL, MS Stowe 568, fols. 90*v*.–94*v*.: 'A Remembrance of Sir William Dethick . . . his abuses . . .' (*temp.* Jas I). In 1591 he was indicted in KB for attacking a man in St Paul's churchyard, but escaped on a technicality: William Leonard, *Reports and Cases of Law . . . Queen Elizabeth, from the 18th to the 33rd Year of Her Reign* (2 vols., London, W. Hughes, 1658), I, 248–9; George Croke, *The First Part of the Reports of . . .*, rev. by Harbottle Grimston (London, 1661), 224, 542.

[47] PRO, SP 12/175/25; Huntington Library, MS Hastings 15602; Wagner, *Heralds of England*, 221.

[48] Huntington Library, MS Hastings 15602 (William Ravenscroft to Sir John Davies, 13 Feb. 1604). For the composition of Egerton's organization see Louis A. Knafla, *Law and*

have been granted illegally by Dethick was one in 1594 to Serjeant Peter Warburton.[49] Warburton was not only Egerton's relative and Cheshire neighbor, but as vice-chamberlain of the Exchequer court of Chester, a key figure in the Lord Keeper's scheme to control the palatine courts.[50] At Hele's trial Warburton, by that time a justice of the Common Pleas, would be one of the judges.

Egerton was also able to capitalize on hostility generated by Hele's aggressive use of wealth and influence in his native Devon. Like the Lord Keeper's own operation to secure land and influence in Cheshire, Hele's relations with his Devon neighbors carefully balanced patronage, opportunism, intimidation and, of course, litigation. During the 1590s more than one of the serjeant's West Country adversaries was forced to make the long and costly journey to Star Chamber.[51] Hele's aggressive and ingenious use of legal process to vex, distract, and intimidate his opponents was hardly novel, but it made him many enemies.[52] Egerton, it seems, had already made contact with one of these, Sir Richard Champernon of Modbury, perhaps through his colleague Chief Justice Popham, Champernon's father-in-law.[53] After almost exhausting his patrimony by a 'high splendid way of living,' the rather unstable Champernon was, like Lord Cobham, peculiarly vulnerable to manipulation.[54] Enmity between Champernon and Hele existed earlier than 1598 when the serjeant complained to Robert Cecil that Champernon, 'an indifferent man,' was utilizing his position as a militia captain to pay off old scores

Politics in Jacobean England: The Tracts of Lord Chancellor Ellesmere (Cambridge, CUP, 1977). Dethick had apparently been acquitted of another wounding in 1591 – in Westminster Abbey – through the intervention of William Fleetwood, recorder of London and father-in-law of Sir Thomas Chaloner, another of Egerton's clients: BL, MS Stowe 568, fols. 90*v*.–94*v*., substantiated by John C. Jeaffreson (ed.), *Middlesex County Records* (4 vols., London, The Middlesex County Record Society, 1886–92; reprinted 1972), I, 194, 197.

49 Folger Library, MS v.a.156 (unfoliated volume of coats of arms illegally granted by Dethick).

50 Knafla, *Law and Politics*, 145–6; William J. Jones, 'The exchequer of Chester in the last years of Elizabeth I,' in Arthur J. Slavin (ed.), *Tudor Men and Institutions* (Baton Rouge, Louisiana State University Press, 1972), 123–70; and, Huntington Library, MSS Ellesmere 86, 1402a.

51 E.g. PRO, STAC 5/H3/6; 5/H28/36; 5/H51/36; 5/H58/1; 5/H59/32 (*Hele* v *Ambrose Rowse*, 1596–7); 5/H2/11; 5/H13/1; 5/H34/17; 5/H43/11; Hawarde, *Reportes*, 149–50, 154 (*Hele* v *George Prestwood*, 1599–1600).

52 The vexatious use of the law is discussed in Michael J. Ingram, 'Communities and courts: law and disorder in early-seventeenth-century Wiltshire,' in James S. Cockburn (ed.), *Crime in England 1550–1800* (London, Methuen, 1977), 110–34.

53 Price, *Worthies of Devon*, 192–4; Knafla, *Law and Politics*, 159.

54 Price, *Worthies of Devon*, 193. He attempted to restore his fortunes by prosecuting in Star Chamber a fatuous claim to the earldom of Devon: Hawarde, *Reportes*, 338–41, 444. Edward Courtenay, earl of Devon, had died unmarried in 1556.

and to 'triumph over [Hele] as an enemy.'[55] Clearly their relationship had not improved by 19 June 1601 when Champernon wrote a sycophantic letter to the Lord Keeper.[56] Acknowledging himself bound to Egerton 'for your honourable favours heretofore received,' he accused Hele, his relations and their supporters of persecuting Arthur Vowell, a Devon JP, in order to have him excluded from the Devon peace commission. Hele's 'settled malice' had expressed itself in petitions to the Privy Council and 'unjust suits in law,' the standard techniques, as we have seen, for political in-fighting.

There is no doubt that Hele and Vowell were engaged in a complex and protracted factional struggle, only one episode of which is reflected in Champernon's letter. Vowell and his relations had sided with George Prestwood, another of Hele's neighbors, in a bitter dispute over rights of pasture and way on Hele's manor of Langford Leicester. The Vowells had encouraged Prestwood and his men to resort to violence and, in June 1599, there was a pitched battle during which several of Hele's tenants were injured. Hele countered by having Prestwood and his faction subpoenaed to appear in Star Chamber and by mounting a full-scale campaign to vex and discredit Vowell.[57] This included not only the exploitation of legal process alleged by Champernon, but also a Star Chamber suit during which Hele accused Vowell, and by implication Champernon too, of irregularities in apportioning militia service. Champernon reacted by writing a second letter to Egerton,[58] in which he claimed that Vowell had uncovered a murder committed by Hele's brother and that that had so fuelled the enmity between them that local justice was in danger of being overwhelmed by factional strife. In turn, Hele had encouraged one Waterman, 'a baggage bailiff,' to file a Star Chamber suit against Vowell and had himself underwritten Waterman's costs.[59] He had also, according to Champernon, 'reviled the mayor of Exeter,'[60] terming him 'fool and ass' for refusing to support the Hele faction in sessions. 'His usury, misery, law and pride of his purse' had, Champernon concluded,

[55] *HMC: Salisbury*, VIII (London, HMSO, 1899), 27 (Hele to Cecil, 28 Jan. 1598).

[56] Huntington Library, MS Ellesmere 2698.

[57] PRO, STAC 5/H2/11; 5/H13/1; 5/H34/17; 5/H44/39; 5/H57/5; 5/H70/15; Hawarde, *Reportes*, 149–50, 154.

[58] Huntington Library, MS Ellesmere 2699 (Champernon to Egerton, 10 Dec. 1601), supported by *ibid.*, 2700 (an undated petition).

[59] This suit was to drag on into 1603: Hawarde, *Reportes*, 166, 167; PRO, STAC 5/R1/22; 5/R21/18; 5/R28/12; 5/R38/32; 5/P66/39; 5/P12/35; 5/R10/34; 5/R22/6; 5/R25/28; 5/R29/11; 5/P12/35; 5/P66/39.

[60] Egerton's notes refer consistently to the *bishop* (William Cotton) rather than the *mayor* of Exeter, and this identification seems, on balance, more likely.

'brought him to that height of insolence, as he is grown insufferable in our country.'

Egerton must have been particularly irritated to learn also that the serjeant had confidently threatened to make Arthur Vowell 'his porter of the Rolls.' Shortly after receiving Champernon's intelligence, the Lord Keeper marshalled his evidence and set out his reasons for rejecting Hele as a candidate for the mastership of the Rolls.[61] He took it, he said, as an insult that his twenty years of public service should be 'put in balance' with 'Hele and his purse.' Now that he had been commanded to admit him against his better judgment he would 'set down what I have heard Serjeant Hele charged with, that thereupon her majesty may make judgment how unworthy this man is for so worthy a place as he seeketh.' He gave four reasons for rejecting Hele: he was a usurer; he commonly took excessive fees and was a notorious ambidexter; he was 'puffed up to such extreme height of pride' that he was 'insolent and outrageous . . . offensive and intolerable'; and, finally, he was a notorious and violent drunkard, 'a vice ill becoming a serjeant, but in a judge or public magistrate intolerable.'[62]

In the light of what we already know of Egerton's informants and their motives for embarrassing Hele, these charges merit closer examination. That the serjeant was a usurer was surely common knowledge long before he became a candidate for the Rolls. In addition to Cobham, Essex and of course Egerton himself, his distinguished debtors included the earl of Rutland, Lord Compton, Anthony Cooke, grandson of Sir Anthony Cooke, John Killigrew, captain of Falmouth castle, and Arthur Hall, the troublesome member for Grantham.[63] The sums involved were large and, although such matters were handled discreetly, the nature of Hele's second profession demanded that it be fairly well known. Egerton cited several pieces of anonymous gossip in an attempt to demonstrate that

[61] Huntington Library, MSS Ellesmere 2706–9, 2712, 2713. The drafts are undated but the inclusion in them of material from Champernon's correspondence indicates that they were completed after 10 Dec. 1601.

[62] *Ibid.*, 2708. Two additional faults – that he spent less than a month each year with his wife and family, and was a notorious liar – were omitted from the final draft. Hele's long absences from home were apparently a source of concern even to his friends: Robert P. Sorlien (ed.), *The Diary of John Manningham of the Middle Temple, 1602–1603* (Hanover, N.H., University Press of New England for the University of Rhode Island, 1976), 74.

[63] *HMC: Twelfth Report, Appendix, Part IV: The MSS of His Grace The Duke of Rutland, G.C.B., Preserved at Belvoir Castle* (London, HMSO, 1888), 412; Lawrence Stone, *The Crisis of the Aristocracy 1558–1641* (Oxford, Clarendon Press, 1965), 532ff.; Edwin F. Gay, 'The rise of an English country family. Peter and John Temple to 1603,' *Huntington Library Quarterly*, I (1937–8), 387; Huntington Library, MSS Stowe, oversized letters (Anthony Cooke to John Temple, 5 Dec. 1595); *APC, 1598–99*, XXIX, 535–6; *HMC: Salisbury*, VIII (London, HMSO, 1899), 155; XI, 370, 376, 512–13; PRO, SP 14/59/21 (proceedings against the Killigrew estate by Hele's executors).

even for a usurer Hele's behavior was greedy and unethical.[64] But the surviving correspondence suggests, rather, that Hele's dealings with his debtors (unlike those of Egerton towards his creditors) were generally cordial and always businesslike. Moreover, he was not the only serjeant-at-law practicing usury.[65] Oddly, Egerton cited only two witnesses (neither of them known to be Hele's debtors) to the serjeant's usury, one Nicholson and John Davies of the Middle Temple. About Nicholson we know nothing, but John Davies is of course identifiable as the attorney-general in Ireland, reporter and minor poet, who was said to have reached the Bar 'by studying [and] noble men.'[66] The reference may well have been to Egerton, whose protégé Davies was. A few months earlier in fact he had been readmitted to the Middle Temple, after being disbarred in 1598, only after the Lord Keeper had exerted considerable pressure on the Benchers.[67] In return, Davies was no doubt prepared to testify as instructed.

One other piece of evidence deserves notice at this point. Writing to Robert Cecil from the Fleet on 5 December 1601, Arthur Hall claimed that his attempts to reach agreement with Hele and his other two creditors had been frustrated by the Lord Keeper, who had deliberately misinformed the queen in order to delay settlement.[68] Hall, particularly when in prison, is perhaps not the most reliable of sources. But in the context of the Lord Keeper's vendetta against Hele, both the date and substance of his allegation are interesting.

Complaints about the avarice of lawyers were a constant theme in the later sixteenth century, and much of the criticism was justified. Egerton collected a persuasive body of documented evidence testifying to the fact that Hele had commonly taken fees which were thought excessive or had acted for both plaintiff and defendant in the same cause. Several examples

[64] Huntington Library, MS Ellesmere 2707.

[65] *HMC: Salisbury*, VIII, 155 (Sergeant Harris); *ibid.*, 451 (Sergeant Spurling). One contemporary source lumped together lawyers and usurers as twin plagues of the commonwealth: PRO, SP 12/288/65.

[66] Quoted in Wilfrid R. Prest, *The Inns of Court under Elizabeth I and the Early Stuarts 1590–1640* (Totowa, N.J., Rowman and Littlefield, 1972), 58, n. 36. For further, highly unflattering, contemporary comments on Davies see, Sorlien, *Manningham's Diary*, 7–8, 235.

[67] Huntington Library, MS Hastings 2522 (Egerton to Middle Temple Benchers, 30 June 1601). For evidence of their continuing relationship see MS Hastings 2523; MS Ellesmere 129; Virgil B. Heltzel, 'Sir Thomas Egerton as Patron,' *Huntington Library Quarterly*, XI (1948), 105–27. In the preface to his *Reports* (dedicated to Egerton) Davies acknowledged that the Lord Chancellor's 'favour hath been (as it were) a good angel unto me, and to whom I stand bound for so many benefits as that which might carry a show of adulation in another must needs be thought but duty and gratitude in me.'

[68] *HMC: Salisbury*, XI, 512, 513.

from Winchester assizes had no doubt been provided by Benjamin Tichborne, Hele's Hampshire adversary.[69] Although the fact hardly excuses the practice, Hele was certainly not alone in taking what were thought to be excessive fees: only two years earlier Serjeant Edward Heron had been accused of sharp practice and taking exorbitant fees; at least one incumbent judge, Justice Fenner, was thought to have accepted bribes; and Manningham's casual reference to Serjeant Harris's ambidexterity suggests that this practice too was fairly common.[70] Indeed, Egerton himself was no novice at utilizing legal process to his own profit.[71]

The accusation of 'pride' and 'insolence' was taken almost verbatim from the petition of Sir Richard Champernon and, naturally enough, Champernon was cited as a source of the charge. Four of the remaining five witnesses had already been identified with attempts to discredit Hele: Benjamin Tichborne, Sir William Dethick, Sir Edmund Morgan, a supporter of Dethick's petition, and the bishop of Exeter, William Cotton. The fifth was a familiar figure – the sycophantic and unscrupulous Francis Bacon. He too was indebted to the Lord Keeper, for the beginning of his career, like its end, was troubled by financial scandal. In 1598 he had been arrested for debt and was forced to solicit Egerton's protection against his creditors.[72] Thus Bacon, like John Davies, entered the Lord Keeper's web of obligation and doubtless he too could be relied upon to support his patron.[73] At Hele's trial Bacon, in his capacity as king's counsel, would appear for the Crown.[74]

No other source alludes to Hele's drunkenness. Egerton cited three authorities for the charge: Justice Walmesley, Lawrence Hyde of the Middle Temple and, once more, the bishop of Exeter.[75] Beyond the fact that he was a bencher of his Inn and uncle of the first earl of Clarendon, we know little of Hyde. Thomas Walmesley (b. 1537) had been a bencher of Lincoln's Inn and was a judge of the Common Pleas from 1589. In the course of an undistinguished career he had amassed a large fortune and

[69] Huntington Library, MSS Ellesmere 2706, 2707. See also *HMC: Salisbury*, XIII (London, HMSO, 1915), 463. Tichborne was sheriff of Hants in 1602–3 and in charge of ceremonial arrangements for the trial and execution of Lord Cobham and his fellow conspirators: *HMC: Salisbury*, XV (London, HMSO, 1930), 304–7, 313, 319–20.

[70] PRO, SP 12/271/134; 12/254/74; and, Sorlien, *Manningham's Diary*, 76.

[71] Louis A. Knafla, 'New Model lawyer: the career of Sir Thomas Egerton 1541–1616' (University of California, Los Angeles, Unpublished Ph.D. thesis, 1965), ch. v.

[72] Thomas Birch, *Memoirs of the Reign of Queen Elizabeth, from the Year 1581 Till Her Death* (2 vols., London, Printed for A. Millar, 1754), II, 107–8.

[73] For their relationship see, Heltzel, 'Egerton as patron,' as well as Thomas G. Barnes' essay, above, 297–306.

[74] Hawarde, *Reportes*, 171.

[75] Huntington Library, MS Ellesmere 2706.

extensive estates in his native Lancashire. He was also a suspected papist, whose wife and brother Robert were both Catholic recusants.[76] Thomas Egerton and Robert Walmesley had been contemporaries at Lincoln's Inn, where both were suspected of Catholicism.[77]

In what form, and precisely when the Lord Keeper presented his charges we do not know. On 27 April 1602 Cobham wrote to Robert Cecil to find out 'what answer you have received from my Lord Keeper touching Serjeant Hele.'[78] This suggests that Egerton had just published his objections or, less probably, that a vain attempt was being made to persuade him not to do so. Their impact on the queen and her advisers can only be guessed at. Although Egerton worked up his notes with customary care, he must have realized that the evidence against Hele smacked of personal enmity and partisan bias. Except on the unclear question of legal fees, the charges relied heavily on hearsay evidence supplied by adherents of the Old Faith and men who were both morally undistinguished and clearly obligated to the Lord Keeper. This too cannot have escaped notice. Although Hele was not in fact to have the Rolls, the events of May and June 1602 suggest that his detractors were not taken too seriously by those in authority. On 16 May Hele was appointed queen's serjeant and on 4 June, despite the Lord Keeper's assertion of his unfitness to be 'a judge or public magistrate,' was commissioned to ride the Home Circuit as an assize judge. His conduct on circuit stimulated a mixed response. Immediately after the Essex assizes, Sir Henry Maynard wrote to tell Robert Cecil that Hele, although 'exceeding tormented with the stone,' had 'discharged his duty in his place with good liking.'[79] Three months after the event John Chamberlain reported that the serjeant had 'played such pranks and so demeaned himself' on circuit 'that he is become both odious and ridiculous.'[80] Attempts to discredit Hele were, apparently, by no means ended.

In February 1603 Hele again rode the Home Circuit as an assize judge: on this occasion his proceedings appear to have excited little comment. On 24 March, less than a month after the circuit ended, the queen died. But well before that it must have become quite clear to Hele that his

[76] *DNB*, LIX, 159–60; Cockburn, *English Assizes*, 214–17.

[77] PRO, SP 12/118/68–71. For a suggestion of hostility between Walmesley and Hele see, Sorlien, *Manningham's Diary*, 96 and n. (p. 342).

[78] *HMC: Salisbury*, XII (London, HMSO, 1910), 126.

[79] *Ibid.*, 240–1 (Maynard to Cecil, 22 July 1602).

[80] PRO, SP 12/285/23 (Chamberlain to Carleton, 2 Oct. 1602). The bitter encounter between Hele and Egerton recorded by both John Manningham and Roger Wilbraham apparently took place shortly after Hele's elevation to queen's serjeant: Sorlien, *Manningham's Diary*, 70–1; Folger Library, MS M.b.42, fol. 99.

embassy had failed. Indeed, there is not a scrap of evidence after 27 April 1602 of any further attempt to promote Hele, or anyone else, as a candidate for the Rolls. All parties seem to have accepted that the Lord Keeper's blast had terminated both Hele's chances and any further debate about possible alternatives. After a final exhortation to Cobham and Cecil in January 1602, backed up by a gift to the queen which would later be the subject of bitter recriminations,[81] Hele's surviving correspondence contains no further reference to the Rolls. The appointment of Edward Bruce, baron Kinloss, to the mastership by the new sovereign on 18 May 1603 formally terminated what had long been merely a technical possibility. To the pragmatic and always businesslike Hele it was the logical moment at which to call Cobham to account: their settlement was engrossed and sealed on the same day as Kinloss was appointed to office.

IV

Up to this point, nothing in Hele's conduct was sufficiently out of the ordinary to justify examination in Star Chamber. Irrespective of its origin, the debt was, as the serjeant insisted and Cobham himself admitted, a 'just' obligation: there was no suggestion of deceit, duress, or other irregularity. Since the genesis of Cobham's obligation was not at issue, the history of Hele's efforts to obtain the Rolls was relevant only insofar as it could be interpreted as evidence of the serjeant's fraudulent disposition.

The settlement agreement between Hele and Cobham thus assumes considerable importance as the context within which Hele was first associated with attempts to gain unfair advantage. In essence, the prosecution alleged that Hele (who claimed to have been preoccupied with term business at the time) instructed his clerk, Henry Dun,[82] to draft an agreement under which Cobham would be discharged completely on payment of the debt, interest and costs. Counsel claimed that Hele himself penned a fair copy of Dun's draft and sent it to Cobham for his approval. The Crown's law officers had also sought evidence to support allegations that Dun had bribed Cobham's advisers to allow the draft to pass unchallenged and that Hele himself had encouraged Cobham to seal the agreement without taking legal advice. Egerton's own notes on the case include what was obviously intended to be a key quotation: 'Take no counsel; I will draw it [the agreement] indifferently.' Prosecution counsel

[81] PRO, SP 12/279/111 (Hele to Cobham, 17 Jan. 1602); see below p. 338.
[82] One source refers to Dun as Hele's 'chief man': Folger Library, MS Cecil Papers 82/47 (W. Elston to John Prideaux, 5 Dec. 1600).

also alleged that after Cobham was arrested the serjeant tried to get possession of his copy of the agreement and to suppress all references to it. This line of inquiry had been stimulated by the discovery that the instrument contained three errors which, counsel claimed, had been introduced 'cautiously and craftily' to negate the agreement and to allow Hele to take out execution against Cobham's estate in the event of his default. Not surprisingly, the serjeant denied any irregularity, insisting that the draft had been forwarded, routinely, for inspection by Cobham's counsel. Several days later the document was returned, without comment, and Hele had it engrossed and sealed on 18 May 1603.

The charge, as eventually outlined by Serjeant Phillips, made no reference to attempts to prevent the draft agreement being scrutinized. Hawarde's version of the proceedings in fact allows that Hele sent the agreement to Cobham 'to peruse by his counsel, who after two or three days returned [it] back again to the serjeant; and thereupon [it] was sealed and delivered.' When he was questioned in July 1604, Henry Dun insisted on oath that *he* had drafted the agreement; that he had no special instructions from Hele; that he intended no irregularity; and that he himself had consigned the document to a messenger for delivery to Cobham. If Dun had maintained his line in court, his evidence would have seriously undermined the case against Hele. But sometime between 2 July 1604, when the deposition was taken, and 10 October, Dun died. At the opening of the trial the attorney-general, Edward Coke, informed the court that he had committed suicide, a suggestion immediately challenged by Hele who offered to produce a letter from Dun's wife and to call 'the preachers and physicians that were present at his death and [are] now in court.' We have no further information on this curious encounter. But on the evidence available, it looks suspiciously like a crude attempt to discredit by innuendo testimony which seriously damaged the prosecution's case. No explanation was put forward to account for the troublesome fact that although Cobham's advisers scrutinized the draft, or at least had ample time to do so, it was nevertheless returned unchallenged. Thus the allegation that Hele had tampered with the document in the privacy of his chamber rested wholly on inference. Although counsel sought to paper over this crack with innuendo ('*clausulae inconsuetae inducunt suspicionem*'), beyond the fact that the instrument was found to be technically defective, no evidence could be adduced to link Hele directly with malfeasance.

For almost two months after conditions for its repayment had been fixed nothing occurred to suggest that Hele's debt was in any danger. But on the last day of Trinity Term, 13 July 1603, George Brooke was arrested on suspicion of complicity in the Main Plot. Two days later his brother, Lord Cobham, followed him to the Tower. The details of the conspiracy to place Arabella Stuart on the English throne remain confused and uncertain, but clearly the train of events which led to the arrest of the conspirators began considerably earlier. During investigations prior to Hele's trial, his prosecutors apparently sought to establish that rumors of Cobham's intention to leave the country reached the serjeant in April or May 1603. At Raleigh's trial the Crown would allege that Cobham agreed to solicit help on the continent at a meeting on 9 June 1603, and that he did not write to the Austrian ambassador until 17 June.[83] This timetable satisfactorily accommodates the known facts. But the compressed chronology adopted by Hele's prosecutors served two useful purposes: it allowed them not only to suggest a motive for tampering with the settlement, but also to introduce the damaging inference that Hele himself was implicated in the conspiracy. Thus they sought evidence to substantiate a report that Hele and Cobham had planned to meet on the day Raleigh was arrested – a development which prompted Cobham abruptly to cancel the rendezvous.

Beyond the insinuation underlying this line of inquiry, no contemporary source alludes to Hele's involvement in the Cobham conspiracy.[84] He had represented Raleigh in a professional capacity;[85] and both were Devon men. Hele had also, of course, been acquainted with Lord Cobham for at least three years. In his formal answer to the Star Chamber accusation the serjeant was cautiously vague about the nature of their relationship. About the time that he and Cobham had reached a settlement (on 18 May) he had learned, he said, that his debtor was 'much discontented' and 'proposed to go beyond the seas.'[86] He was careful to omit the source of this information and to avoid speculation on the reasons for Cobham's departure. At another point in the same document Hele asserted that he knew nothing of Cobham's treason until 5 September when he was officially informed in his capacity as Crown counsel. Obviously both statements leave much unsaid. Hele was well placed to learn that the Brookes were under suspicion; at the very least he must have been able to put two and two together as soon as he heard of the arrests. On the other hand, it seems most unlikely that Hele, the hardened professional, would risk everything by associating himself with the ill-conceived schemes of a man

83 Howell, *State Trials*, II, 1–59.

84 The assertion to the contrary in Knafla, *Law and Politics*, 63, is not supported by the sources cited.

85 Sorlien, *Manningham's Diary*, 342.

86 PRO, STAC 8/9/4, m.278.

whom he knew to be politically weak and personally unreliable. The serjeant had no difficulty in identifying treason with personal misfortune. Less than three years earlier the Essex fiasco had cost Hele more than £4000 in undischarged debts. He did not need Crown counsel to remind him that if Cobham were attainted for treason, his estate would escheat automatically to the Crown, and that the future of outstanding claims upon it would depend solely on the king's goodwill.

Faced with the prospect of losing a second substantial sum in almost identical circumstances, Hele moved swiftly to recover his debt. On 17 or 18 July the serjeant instructed his attorney, William King, to institute process against the Brooke estates. Six months later King, an attorney of the Common Pleas, recalled how he had been summoned to Hele's chamber in Serjeants' Inn and instructed to sue out writs of *elegit* against Cobham's property. King pointed out that *elegits* could not be obtained unless writs of *scire facias* had first been sued and returned.[87] Since vacation had now begun, no writs could be returned until the following Michaelmas law term, which began in October. Faced, so he said, with an angry and increasingly impatient client, King suddenly thought of antedating *scire facias* writs and having the sheriff of Middlesex return them as of the Trinity Term which had just ended. Such antedating was, he assured the serjeant, common practice. 'Sue them out and see if you can get the sheriff to return them,' said Hele cautiously, 'but do no more than you may do justly.' Mindful of this warning, King consulted both Zachary Scott, second prothonotary of the Common Pleas, in whose office he was a clerk, and the deputy sheriff of Middlesex. Neither voiced any objection, whereupon King drafted the necessary *scire facias*. The prothonotary read and signed them; they were sent to the sheriff, returned by Robert Bright, his deputy, and filed in the Common Pleas. The prothonotary then instructed King to enter them on the remembrance, which he did, adding in the margin appropriate dates in Trinity Term. He then drafted writs of *elegit* and delivered them to Hele or his appointed agents. The entire process took less than a week.

Early investigations concentrated almost exclusively upon the propriety of antedating judicial process. Writing to Cecil in February 1604, Sir Edward Coke characterized the device as 'a horrible forgery . . . of a

[87] *HMC: Salisbury*, XVI (London, HMSO, 1933), 22–3 (Coke to Cecil, 6 Feb. 1604), containing a résumé of King's deposition in PRO, STAC 8/9/4, m.277. An *elegit*, directed to the sheriff, allowed the distraint and delivery to the creditor of lands and goods in lieu of an undischarged debt. The writ *scire facias*, applied to these circumstances, simply allowed the debtor an opportunity to show cause why legal action should not be taken to recover the debt. Giles Jacob, *A New Law Dictionary*.

judicial proceeding which ought to be most sacred.'[88] But in court Hele contended flatly that antedating was 'not only usual in this case but in many other, and there be many precedents of antedating writs and process.' At least fifteen Common Pleas clerks, recalling the court's practice as far back as 1566, were examined, and all concurred that antedating had long been common. Ultimately, John Hawarde was forced to record that the course of action taken by Hele was 'good by the advice of prothonotary Scott, so as there be neither practice, fraud nor prejudice.'[89]

Of the events between the third week in July, when Hele successfully obtained the writs of *elegit*, and the beginning of September we know little. In normal circumstances Hele would have remained in London to prepare for the Home Circuit, in which he had again been commissioned as a judge, and which usually began in mid-July. Because of plague in and around the capital, the Home Circuit was postponed and did not in fact begin until 23 September. Counsel inferred that the serjeant had put this unexpected break to sinister use, leaving London late in July for an undisclosed destination. It seems likely, however, that he simply returned for a few weeks to the West Country to visit his family and, perhaps, to ride part of the Western Circuit. He set out again for London no later than the beginning of September, because on the 5th[90] he attended the conference at Maidenhead during which the judges and king's counsel decided that the evidence supported charges of treason against Lord Cobham and his brother. Their decision, of course, virtually destroyed any chance that Cobham would escape to satisfy his creditors.

We can fairly assume that as the serjeant made his way from Maidenhead to, presumably, his house at Kew he was preoccupied with the implications of this decision. His prosecutors were to allege that even before reaching his destination the serjeant demonstrated his fraudulent intentions by spreading a rumor that Cobham was *not* to be indicted for treason. The evidence upon which this accusation was based constitutes a curious and, perhaps, revealing episode. Lord Cobham's steward, Richard Mellersh, later described how he had met John Brewster, a Middle Temple lawyer and Fine Office official, near Dartford sometime late in the summer of 1603. Brewster told Mellersh that he had encountered Hele on his way from Maidenhead and that the serjeant had

88 *HMC: Salisbury*, XVI (London, HMSO, 1933), 22. For a similar instance (1601) involving Justice Warburton, see *ibid.*, XI, 423–4. Egerton himself, while attacking the antedating of mesne process, admitted that it was common practice: Knafla, *Law and Politics*, 279–80.

89 Hawarde, *Reportes*, 173.

90 The chronology of Hawarde's account is compressed and garbled. These dates are taken from PRO, STAC 8/9/4.

assured him that Cobham would not be charged with treason. Rather unexpectedly, Mellersh made a written note of this casual conversation and filed it among his papers, where it was said to have been discovered following his arrest in October 1603.[91]

Beyond the facts that he was Lord Cobham's steward, emerging as a key figure in precipitating the Hele investigation, we know frustratingly little about Richard Mellersh. However, as steward he obviously was closely acquainted with Cobham's affairs and had access to his financial and estate documents. He later alleged that shortly after Cobham was arrested Serjeant Hele borrowed Cobham's receipt book and copied some sections. Mellersh also claimed that subsequently the serjeant offered him £100 for his master's copy of the settlement agreement. He agreed to produce the document but instead complained to the Privy Council about Hele's extent of the estate in Kent. At a later meeting Hele was said to have angrily accused Mellersh of opening his letters to Cobham. Mellersh admitted that he had never intended to deal honestly with the serjeant: he and his master had connived to encumber the estate with Hele's extent in order to frustrate 'those who should attempt to beg any of it.'

Attempts to establish the chronology and context of Mellersh's evidence led to a second critical figure in the investigation – Sir John Leveson.[92] Leveson, a Kent JP, was a confidant of Henry, Lord Cobham and executor under the will of Henry's father William, Lord Cobham (d. 1597).[93] He was also on good terms with William Lambard, a co-executor and fellow JP, who was, in turn, an old friend of one of Hele's persecutors, Thomas Egerton.[94] Until his death in 1601 Lambard had doubtless kept the Lord Keeper informed of developments relating to the Cobham estates. A second Privy Councillor, Robert Cecil, continued to be informed by Leveson himself. Cecil was not only Henry Brooke's brother-in-law but also one of his father's executors, and it was in his capacity as a fellow executor that Leveson felt obliged to keep him informed of proceedings against the Cobham estates. He had, he said, been alerted to possible problems by Richard Mellersh who had visited him shortly before the proceedings to execute Hele's *elegits*. They had talked at

91 See below, p. 331.

92 Leveson appears in Baildon's version of Hawarde as 'Sir John Lucen': Hawarde, *Reportes*, 171.

93 John H. Gleason, *The Justice of the Peace in England, 1558–1640: A Later Eirenarcha* (Oxford, Clarendon Press, 1969), 32; *HMC: Salisbury*, XVI, 9, 256. For the political relationship between Leveson and Henry, Lord Cobham see Clark, *English Provincial Society*, 262–6. A few routine estate documents relating to the administration of the Cobham estates survive among Leveson's deputy-lieutenancy papers in the Staffordshire Record Office, MS D593.

94 Knafla, *Law and Politics*, 156.

length about Cobham's affairs: Mellersh said that he had examined the records and found that most of the estate was entailed. Hele intended, Mellersh said, to encumber the remaining property. Thus forewarned, and despite being weakened by a 'tertian ague,' Leveson maintained daily contact with the extent proceedings which were conducted at Rochester in September 1603 before the sheriff of Kent, and a valuation jury drawn from the locality.[95] Counsel alleged that these jurors were bribed or coerced to undervalue by Hele's agent, William Brown. But the sheriff himself insisted that Brown had behaved correctly throughout, and none of the jurors could be persuaded to associate him with impropriety. Cobham retainers, including a Dutch 'arras worker,' were equally adamant in countering suggestions of interference. Nevertheless, the jury's appraisal prompted Leveson to write urgently to Cecil when the proceedings ended on 25 September 1603. Everything, he reported, had been grossly undervalued: Cobham's lands in Kent, worth £2030 yearly, at £649 per annum and the contents of Cobham Hall, worth more than £1000, at £400. Copies of the extent drawn up later for use in the proceedings against Hele[96] demonstrated an attempt to defraud the Crown of, in all, £4766 15s. 8d. Cecil replied on 1 October, commending Leveson for his care. Hele, he said carefully, would have to answer any complaints.

Leveson preserved Cecil's letters, together with copies of his own, but neither copies nor originals have come to light. Their disappearance is not entirely unexpected. For Leveson's account not only underlines the role played by Richard Mellersh in fuelling the investigation, but also reinforces the notion that Robert Cecil was fully informed about matters of which he would later deny all knowledge. From this point onwards the possibility of a conspiracy to turn Hele's interest in the Cobham estates to corrupt use cannot be entirely disregarded.

Sir John Leveson was too ill to attend the Kent assizes, which opened at Maidstone on 29 September 1603,[97] and therefore did not witness the final act in the valuation of Cobham's property. Counsel alleged in Star Chamber that Hele himself, sitting as an assize judge, caused jurors to be impanelled and taken to an inn where William Brown was waiting. There they appraised two pieces of brass ordinance, and valued at £66 a nine-

[95] Leveson's accounts include a claim for counsel engaged to attend the three-day proceedings at Rochester: Staffordshire Record Office, MS D593/S/4/62.

[96] Two copies survive: PRO, SP 14/10/85; Huntington Library, MS Ellesmere 2705. Both give the valuation of Cobham's lands at £657 3s. and of the goods in Cobham Hall as £411 8s.

[97] PRO, ASSI 35/45/5, m. 51.

teen-year lease worth £400. Hele was said to have thanked a juryman personally and to have promised one of Cobham's retainers 'to be as good unto him as his lord was.' Egerton's case notes also associate with this episode yet another provocative quotation: 'Find at a low value, for else some Scot will beg it.'[98]

Encounters with plague delayed the completion of the Home Circuit, and it was not until 13 October that Hele, writing from Kew, was able to send Cecil his circuit report,[99] more than half of which was devoted to a plea for the Secretary's assistance. Cecil already knew, Hele said, what had induced him to loan money to lord Cobham. It was true that he had 'caused much of . . . Cobham's land . . . and some of his goods in Kent . . . to be extended and delivered to me.' This had been done in his absence by a servant 'according to the law and without any indirect course of means.' Anyone in his position would have acted similarly. Nevertheless, 'the case standing as it doth,' he was taking this opportunity to seek the Secretary's help and protection.

Exactly how the case stood at this point is not clear. On 27 October, one of Lord Cobham's counsel revealed that Richard Mellersh was organizing Cobham's defense and had regular access to him in the Tower.[100] Mellersh was arrested on the following day and his chambers searched. The documents found there were first taken to Sir Thomas Egerton, and he and Sir Edward Coke 'spent an afternoon in perusing them.' Many, as Egerton reported to Robert Cecil, were 'very important and material' and confirmed that Mellersh and others had regularly visited the imprisoned Cobham. Mellersh himself behaved 'very audaciously,' and Egerton asked Cecil's advice on how best to deal with him.[101]

The full impact of these developments on the case against Hele remains, to some extent, a matter of conjecture. Mellersh, as an accessory to treason, was now vulnerable to intimidation, and Hele would later imply that his evidence was perjured.[102] Suspicion certainly attaches to the con-

[98] Huntington Library, MS Ellesmere 2710. In Hawarde's version (*Reportes*, 174) the remark is attributed to William Brown, Hele's agent. Given the seriousness of these accusations, one further peculiarity merits attention at this point. Midway through the section dealing with events at Maidstone assizes Hele's formal reply to the charges against him has been cleanly cut off: PRO, STAC 8/9/4, m.278. The missing portion cannot now be traced. Pieces of parchment were of course commonly reused for a variety of purposes, but it is very unusual to find court records defaced in this fashion. In fact, 'imbeciling' records was a statutory felony; 8 Henry VI, c.12: *SR*, II, 248–9. Moreover, out of 278 membranes in the relevant file, this is the only one to show signs of deliberate damage. One cannot help but speculate on the location of and motivation behind such exceptional mutilation.

[99] PRO, SP 14/4/16. [100] Folger Library, MS Cecil Papers, 102/1. [101] *Ibid.*, 102/5.

[102] PRO, STAC 8/9/4, m.212.

veniently preserved memorandum of the serjeant's conversation with John Brewster and its 'discovery' during the search of Mellersh's papers. Within a short time of Mellersh's arrest Lord Cobham, too, became convinced that his steward was no longer trustworthy. Writing to Cecil early in 1604, he castigated Mellersh as 'a false knave, and to no man so much as to yourself.' Mellersh, he objected, was now privy to all correspondence between Cobham and Cecil, and was attempting to turn Cecil's trust to advantage.[103] For two months before Hele's trial Mellersh was said to be sick and apparently did not appear in public.[104] Subsequently, he was again vilified by Lord Cobham who sent several servants to testify to his steward's dishonesty before the official auditor of the Cobham estates.[105] Nevertheless, his accounts were accepted and shortly afterwards as part of the general settlement of Cobham's debts he was paid £325.[106] His complicity in his master's treason was apparently overlooked.

Following the arrest of Richard Mellersh, rumor may well have begun to link Serjeant Hele with irregularity. Strictly speaking, however, any discussion of fraud was hypothetical until Lord Cobham had been formally attainted for treason. He was tried and convicted at Winchester on 25 November 1603.[107] At this point his estate escheated to the Crown, and the responsibility to investigate any actions threatening the king's interest in it was assumed by the Treasurer. Thus Sir John Leveson's later assertion that he was ordered to investigate the extent by the Treasurer and other Privy Councillors[108] suggests that a formal inquiry was not instituted until after Cobham's trial. This is consistent with indications that the matter was considered at a Privy Council meeting in either December 1603 or January 1604.[109]

Leveson began his investigation, quite logically, with a search of the records. His attention focused on the prothonotaries' office in Common Pleas, and his inquiries there apparently alerted Zachary Scott – with whom Leveson sat on the peace commission for Kent[110] – to the possibility that he himself was in danger. According to Leveson's account, the prothonotary met him outside Lincoln's Inn one evening in Hilary Term (which began on 20 January). 'Sir,' he began, 'there is an honest young

103 Folger Library, MS Cecil Papers, 189/86.
104 *Ibid.*, 107/68 (Andrew Gofton to Robt Cecil, 18 Oct. 1604).
105 *Ibid.*, 104/89 (Gofton to Cecil, 13 Mar. 1605).
106 PRO, SP 14/12/81.
107 BL, MS Stowe 396, fols. 83–6.
108 PRO, STAC 8/9/4.
109 Huntington Library, MS Ellesmere 2702. A January date is suggested by Folger Library, MS Cecil Papers, 97/150 (Leveson to Cecil, 20 Jan. 1604).
110 James S. Cockburn (ed.), *Calendar of Assize Records: Kent Indictments, Elizabeth I* (London, HMSO, 1979), nos. 2872, 2920, 2960, 2999.

man called King . . ., a proper clerk and one to whom I wish well. It may be there has been some slip or thing done not justifiably. I pray you to procure him what favour you can.' If King revealed the whole truth, replied Leveson, he would do what he could to protect him. On the following evening, with the possibility of a bargain established, Leveson interviewed King in Scott's office. There the attorney confessed that the writs against Lord Cobham's property had been sued out after the end of Trinity Term on Hele's instructions. During his formal examination on 5 February before king's counsel King played down Hele's part in the episode, while firmly implicating Zachary Scott. 'Do no more than you may do justly,' the serjeant had said; it was Scott who had confirmed the legitimacy of antedating process. Forwarding the examination to Cecil on 6 February, Edward Coke recommended only the 'exemplary punishment [of] such as shall be found delinquent.'[111]

Within a few days Westminster rumor firmly associated delinquency with Sir John Hele.[112] The serjeant himself tried desperately to head off further speculation. Sometime in February he petitioned the king. He was particularly grieved, he said, by a rumor that he had 'dealt indirectly' and would in consequence lose the debt and be fined, imprisoned, and suspended from office. He did not speculate on the origin of this report, but its similarity to his eventual punishment serves as some guide to its authorship. The letter strongly implies that at this stage the only matter under suspicion was the antedating of legal process. That, the serjeant insisted, was a point of law which ought to be referred to the common law judges. On 24 February the king responded by ordering a judicial examination to determine whether Hele was 'to be touched with any undue or indirect practice and whether they shall find any cause that he should not be satisfied his debt.' Pending the judges' report, everything was 'to stay as now it is.'[113]

Whether the judges ever met to consider the case against Hele is uncertain. Thus the formal decision to prosecute the serjeant in Star Chamber can be dated only loosely to the period between 24 February[114] and 29 May 1604, when the first deposition was taken. Between that date and

[111] *HMC: Salisbury*, XVI, 22–3.

[112] *HMC: Seventh Report, pt* I, *Report and Appendix; The MSS of George Alan Lowndes, Esq., of Barrington Hall, co. Essex* (London, HMSO, 1879), 524 (Philip Gawdy to his father, 19 Feb. 1604).

[113] Two copies of the letter and endorsement survive: Huntington MSS Ellesmere 2702–3; MS Ellesmere 2704 is a copy of Hele's formal petition to James I.

[114] Although Gawdy and Hele once again issued precepts for the winter circuit, by the time the formal commission was issued on 13 Feb. 1604 Hele had been replaced as assize judge by Justice Daniel: PRO, ASSI 35/46/2, mm.51–2.

18 July depositions were taken from more than sixty people, and this testimony was presumably utilized in framing the formal charge. The relationship between the charge set out by Serjeant Phillips and the extensive notes on the case made by Lord Chancellor Egerton[115] is not clear. Egerton's outline is substantially the same as that presented by Serjeant Phillips. But his notes also include incriminating remarks which did not find their way into the charge – or at least into Hawarde's report of it – as well as marginalia which appear to have been made during or after the trial.[116] But use of the notes on more than one occasion is of course not inconceivable. Given the history of their relationship, we can safely assume that Egerton played a central role in drawing up the case against Hele.

Nothing further need be said about the Star Chamber hearing itself. But in order to understand the sentence with which it terminated, one needs to know something of the composition of the court. Twelve Privy Councillors attended throughout; a thirteenth, Thomas Cecil, Lord Burghley, on the final days.[117] At the close of the four-day hearing, each of the thirteen passed judgment on the three surviving defendants. Hele's attorney, William King, was unanimously acquitted. But only two judges voted for the acquittal of William Brown; the remainder recommended a fine ranging from £40 to £200.

Opinions on Hele's guilt and punishment varied widely. Only two members of the court exonerated the serjeant completely: the Archbishop of Canterbury, Richard Bancroft, and Chief Justice John Popham. Little can be read into their decision. Bancroft, whose contemporary reputation was not uniformly high, has been characterized as hostile toward Puritanism:[118] perhaps his judgment was influenced by Lord Cobham's reputation as an 'atheist.'[119] Chief Justice Popham was, as we have seen, father-in-law to Sir Richard Champernon, one of Hele's detractors. But he was also a patron at Hele's call to the coif in 1594, a fact which suggests respect if not friendship for the accused.[120] He seems, on the evidence of Hawarde, to have taken the view that the practice of antedating process was on trial; that the law tolerated this; and that in any case Star Chamber

[115] Huntington Library, MS Ellesmere 2710.
[116] See above p. 331. [117] Hawarde, *Reportes*, 171, 175–6.
[118] Sorlien, *Manningham's Diary*, 235; Patrick Collinson, *The Elizabethan Puritan Movement* (Berkeley, University of California Press, 1967), 387.
[119] Sorlien, *Manningham's Diary*, 235.
[120] PRO, CP 45/92, m.3. One source credits Hele with contributing to Popham's law reports: Bodleian Library, MS Rawlinson C.647, fols. 148–162*v*. ('Un abstract del Chidley's case et auters cases report par Popham, Chief Justyce, et Serjeant Heale').

was not competent to pass judgment on the issue.[121] A further six members of the court voted to fine Hele in respect of the 'misdemeanour' and to revoke his extent of Cobham's property. Of these, John Savile, an Exchequer baron and near contemporary of Hele, apparently based his leniency on the fact that in the event no one had been harmed by Hele's extent. Robert Cecil adopted a similar stance, but compromised it immediately by protesting that 'if he had known the offence to be of such a nature, he would never have agreed to have a public hearing.' Since we now know that the Secretary was better informed than even the principals in the affair, his protestation will need further examination later. The two courtier earls, of Devonshire (Charles Blount) and Northampton (Henry Howard), both newly created, simply echoed Robert Cecil 'in everything.' Thomas Cecil, Lord Burghley, in voting for a fine of only £500, was probably guided more by his brother's opinion than by memories of his own embarrassment at the hands of Hele's friend and colleague, Christopher Yelverton.[122] However, Charles Howard, earl of Nottingham, voted to fine the serjeant £2000, double that recommended by the other four members of this group. Possibly his position as Lord Cobham's father-in-law inclined him to greater severity.[123]

Particular interest attaches to the remaining five men – a clear minority of the court – who voted to fine, suspend and, in two cases, to imprison Serjeant Hele. The president of the court, Lord Chancellor Egerton, did not in fact recommend imprisonment; but this was his only concession to leniency. He pronounced Hele guilty of 'corruption and ambition, craft and covetous practises,' for which he ought to be fined £2000 and suspended from office. Egerton's judgment comes as little surprise. Although he had no particular interest in Lord Cobham or his property, his animosity towards Hele transcended professional respect or the dictates of judicial consistency.[124] Given his implacable hostility towards all who offended him,[125] Egerton no doubt viewed Hele's conviction as both a vindication

121 Hawarde, *Reportes*, 175.

122 Two years earlier Thomas Cecil had, with his brother's help, finally triumphed over Yelverton after a bitter dispute over precedence on the Northern Circuit: Cockburn, *English Assizes*, 41–2. For evidence of the friendship between Hele and Yelverton see BL, MS Hargrave 403, fol. 1 ('my brother Hele is to give me a case of counters of silver with my arms in them if he and I do live together till Michaelmas term 1604'); PRO, PROB 11/112, fol. 240*v*. ('Yelverton, in whom I have always found true kindness'): Sorlien, *Manningham's Diary*, 74.

123 His daughter Frances, widow of the earl of Kildare, had married Cobham sometime before May 1601: Sorlien, *Manningham's Diary*, 396. In the king's settlement of Cobham's debts she was granted an allowance of £733: PRO, SP 14/12/81.

124 For possible inconsistency between Egerton's general attitude to the morality of fraud and his stance in Hele's case see Jones, *Elizabethan Chancery*, 425.

125 As described in BL, MS Add. 35957, fol. 81*v*.

and culmination of his own campaign to disgrace the serjeant. In these circumstances, it seems reasonable to assume also that the Lord Chancellor's opinion heavily influenced the decision of his relative and client, Justice Peter Warburton, who recommended both a fine and imprisonment. The secretary of state, Sir John Herbert, also voted for imprisonment, in addition to suspension and a £2000 fine. His severity is less easily explained: Herbert had no particular axe to grind and, although he had been an outside candidate for the Rolls in 1601,[126] there is no evidence that he participated in efforts to discredit Hele. The two remaining judges, Thomas Sackville, the Treasurer, and Henry Percy, earl of Northumberland, have both been identified as Catholics.[127] Sackville had, in addition, some reputation among contemporaries for dishonesty and corruption,[128] and there is reason to think that he may have conspired with Robert Cecil against Hele as early as November 1600.[129] Northumberland patronized John Davies, the lawyer–poet, and like Egerton, was 'highly sensitive to slights, real or imagined.'[130]

William Baildon was confused by Hawarde's assertion that a majority of the judges 'acquitted the serjeant of all note and blemish of infamy,' and felt obliged to point out that his report does not support that conclusion.[131] In fact there is no contradiction. If a vote for the serjeant's suspension is taken to indicate a conviction that he was guilty of fraud in his professional capacity, only four members of the court – Egerton, Sackville, Herbert, and Northumberland – found him guilty of an attempt to defraud the Crown. Even if one includes in this group Justice Warburton, who did not vote for suspension, only five men were prepared to convict Hele for 'infamy.' The remaining eight found, or pretended to think, him guilty only of utilizing a dubious procedural device to obtain records which were a necessary but technical preliminary to the recovery of a legitimate debt. Robert Cecil characterized it as a 'misdemeanour.' Chief Justice Popham considered that legal convention had not been offended. Several seem to have been influenced by the fact that no one's rights had in fact been prejudiced: the attainted Cobham could

[126] Jones, *Elizabethan Chancery*, 92.

[127] Roger B. Manning, *Religion and Society in Elizabethan Sussex: A Study of the Enforcement of the Religious Settlement, 1558–1603* (Leicester, Leicester University Press, 1969), 233, n. 1; Sorlien, *Manningham's Diary*, 235; Prest, *Inns of Court*, 179.

[128] Sorlien, *Manningham's Diary*, 235.

[129] In a letter to Cecil, dated 27 Nov. 1600 (Folger Library, MS Cecil Papers, 250/76), Sackville wrote, 'I will take order touching Hele, according to your letter.' Cecil's letter has not survived, but its presumed date – a few days after the first of Cobham's debts to Hele fell due on 14 Nov. (see above p. 315) – may be significant.

[130] Sorlien, *Manningham's Diary*, 353–4. [131] Hawarde, *Reportes*, 176.

not, by definition, be victimized; the king's interest in the entailed property had been safeguarded before the trial began.[132] Thus only five of the thirteen judges publicly recommended that Serjeant Hele be sentenced for fraud. Although the group contained a powerful caucus in the persons of Egerton, Herbert, and Sackville, this fact alone cannot explain either the severity of Hele's punishment or the continuation of attempts to discredit him.

We can only guess at the process by which the disparate judgments passed upon the serjeant in Star Chamber were translated into a sentence which brought together the harshest elements of each: a fine of £1000, imprisonment, and suspension from office. Hele, writing from the Fleet Prison the day after the trial ended, was undoubtedly correct in attributing his predicament to the 'insatiable malice' of the Lord Chancellor.[133] Nevertheless, knowledgeable contemporaries and Hele himself assumed that his disgrace would be temporary and not necessarily damaging to his chances of professional advancement. Only four days after the trial, Philip Gawdy reported that the serjeant, even though he was imprisoned and under suspension, was a strong contender for the vacant office of chief baron and offered a good price for the position.[134] Three weeks later, however, Hele was still in the Fleet and becoming increasingly concerned about his future.[135] In accordance with the judgment of Star Chamber he had, he assured Cecil, voided all the disputed writs, and was ready to surrender the Cobham goods and leases. Nevertheless, he was still being closely restrained, and four petitions to the king had not been acknowledged. He was eventually released at the end of November after 'six weeks hard imprisonment, whereby being an old and corpulent man the state of my body and health is much impaired.'[136] The fine he was forced to pay in full.[137] Sometime in 1605, as part of a general settlement of Cobham's debts, Hele was repaid the £3500 which he had loaned to Cobham.[138] But his suspension was not lifted.

Significantly, one of Hele's first moves following his release was to try and make peace with Thomas Egerton.[139] Although he cannot have enter-

132 *HMC: Salisbury*, XVI, 225 (agreement dated 11 Aug. 1604).
133 *Ibid.*, 333 (Hele to Cecil, 20 Oct. 1604).
134 *HMC: Seventh Report, Part I . . . Lowndes*, 527.
135 *HMC: Salisbury*, XVI, 352 (Hele to Cecil, 10 Nov. 1604).
136 BL, MS Add. 36767, fol. 58 (petition to Jas I) and fol. 59 (covering letter to Sir Julius Caesar, 17 Dec. 1604).
137 Hawarde, *Reportes*, 411.
138 PRO, SP 14/12/81 ('Lord Cobham's debts paid by the king,' n.d.).
139 Huntington Library, MS Ellesmere 2714 (Hele to Egerton, 5 Jan. 1605).

tained any serious hope that Egerton would accept his overture, Hele was undoubtedly correct in attributing his continuing suspension to the Chancellor's animosity. What he apparently did not appreciate was that Robert Cecil, in whom he had consistently confided and on whom his hopes now focused, had been and was still at one with the Chancellor in attempts to disgrace Hele. Not until 1606 would the serjeant begin to suspect that Cecil had duped him: and by then it was of course too late.

Meanwhile, Hele concentrated his efforts on demonstrating that Cobham had acted in bad faith and, incidentally, in making out a case for the recovery of a further sum from Cobham's estate. Late in 1605 he apparently accused Cobham before the Privy Council of having embezzled £400, demanded in the queen's name to further Hele's claim to the Rolls. Writing to his brother-in-law from the Tower, where in 1619 he would eventually die, Cobham vehemently denied this 'barbarous scandal.'[140] But an almost illegible note, written in Hele's own hand on 17 January 1602, contains a very strong indication that Cobham had indeed profited in more ways than one from the serjeant's ambition.[141] The realization that these revelations were getting uncomfortably close to home may have prompted Robert Cecil to the hostile response which finally revealed to Hele that the Secretary, too, had deceived him. There is a new distance in the dispirited letter in which on 31 January 1606 Hele again asked Cecil to intercede with the king to have his suspension lifted.[142] Cecil did not respond, and Hele probably realized at this point that his career was finished. Five months later, in one of his last letters to Cecil, he conceded that his 'disasters [had] almost brought him to his grave.'[143] In October 1605 he resigned the recordership of Exeter[144] and in September 1606 that of Plymouth.[145] Although he shortly afterwards offered Cecil some halfhearted advice on The Prince's Case,[146] his vitality never returned. On 8 February 1608 a docket dispensing Serjeant Hele

[140] *HMC: Salisbury*, XVII (London, HMSO, 1938), 15 (Cobham to Cecil, 15 Jan. 1606); *ibid.*, XVI, 410 (Cobham to Cecil, n.d.).

[141] PRO, SP 12/279/111. The reference is to 'a jewel of some three or four hundred pounds' which Hele had given to Cobham for presentation to the queen.

[142] *HMC: Salisbury*, XVII, 40.

[143] *Ibid.*, XVIII (London, HMSO, 1940), 167 (Hele to Cecil, 14 June 1606).

[144] Exeter City Library, MS City Act Book, VI, fol. 99.

[145] His resignation was not in fact accepted: Plymouth City Library, MSS W 359/45 and W 361/48. In 1616 Hele's arms joined those of Drake and Hawkins in the windows of the Plymouth guildhall: Richard N. Worth (ed.), *Calendar of the Plymouth Municipal Records* (Plymouth, 1893), 150.

[146] *HMC: Salisbury*, XVIII, 337–8 (Hele to Cecil, 1 Nov. 1606).

from further service formally terminated a career which had in fact ended on 19 October 1604.[147]

Efforts to disgrace Serjeant Hele did not end with his conviction in Star Chamber. Egerton's client and former private secretary, the poet John Donne,[148] satirized Hele in his mock *Courtier's Library*.[149] The allusion is almost certainly to Hele's alleged attempt to obtain documents from Cobham's servants, an identification which would date Donne's lampoon to the period of the Star Chamber trial. Two further attacks can be identified through a stray letter from Sir John Harrington to Sir Thomas Chaloner, son of the Elizabethan poet and diplomat.[150] Writing in September 1607, Harrington noted with disapproval the reference to Serjeant Hele in a sermon preached at Chelmsford by one Rowley. This was almost certainly the assize sermon preached on 20 July 1607;[151] but further details are lacking. In the same letter Harrington also referred coldly to Hele's misfortune in being mentioned in Chaloner's 'book,' which he was now returning.

Since Chaloner was hitherto known to have written only one work – a published tract on the medicinal properties of nitre – the reference is, on the face of it, totally inexplicable. But among Egerton's papers is an undated and, strictly speaking, anonymous manuscript treatise entitled 'The Usurer Reformed . . .'[152] Inside the front cover is a loose sheet containing, in Egerton's hand, the note 'Sir Tho. Challoner Agaynst usurye,' and comparison with letters in Chaloner's hand confirms that he was indeed the unlikely author of the work, of which only one copy has apparently survived. Further investigation reveals that Chaloner, having served the earl of Essex as a continental spy in the 1590s, entered the extensive clientele of Thomas Egerton, for whom he performed a variety of functions in the early Jacobean years.[153] As a favorite of James I and tutor to Henry, prince of Wales, Chaloner was peculiarly well placed to

147 *Calendar of State Papers, Domestic Series . . . 1603–1610*, ed. by Mary A. E. [Wood] Green (London, Longman, Brown, Green, Longmans, & Roberts, 1857), 402.

148 Knafla, *Law and Politics*, 54.

149 '21. *A Manual for Justices of the Peace*, comprising many confessions of poisoners tendered to Justice Manwood, and employed by him in his privy; these have now been purchased from his inferior servants and collected for his own use by John Hele': Evelyn M. Simpson (ed.), *The Courtier's Library, or Catalogus Librorum Aulicorum Incomparabilium et non Vendibilium, by John Donne* (London, The Nonesuch Press, 1930), 49, 69.

150 Folger Library, MS Cecil Papers, 193/148 (Harrington to Chaloner, 6 Sept. 1607).

151 PRO, ASSI 49/9/2 (before Croke, J., and Snigge, B.).

152 Huntington Library, MS Ellesmere 2468. I hope to treat both Chaloner and this treatise more fully elsewhere.

153 For evidence of their association see, in particular, Huntington Library, MSS Ellesmere 129 and 219. I am indebted to L. A. Knafla for confirming this relationship.

represent his patron's interests at court and to disseminate propaganda among the educated and influential. Harrington, another of the prince's tutors, apparently received Chaloner's blast against usury sometime in 1607, and his letter indicates that this copy contained specific reference to Hele. Egerton's copy, which is clearly a very early draft,[154] does not in fact mention Hele by name. But there are at least four allusions which fit the serjeant precisely; and it is conceivable that the inclusion of Hele's name in a later version was suggested by Egerton himself. Be this as it may, it seems certain that the Lord Chancellor continued to orchestrate the harassment of his beaten adversary until the final months of the serjeant's life. Little wonder that Hele's epitaph bitterly records a spite ended only by death.[155]

V

What, then, can be learned from this reconstruction of the trial of Sir John Hele? Insofar as many blind passages and tantalizing questions remain, the episode illustrates only too well the difficulties facing any attempt to penetrate the substrata of court politics at the turn of the sixteenth century. In that twilight world where politics, profit, and personal enmity met in uneasy interaction, destroyed correspondence, shifting alliances, and carefully concealed motives were the rules of the game: the dice is heavily loaded against the historian. Nevertheless, this case study serves at least two useful purposes. Not only does it constitute a model for the techniques of high-level in-fighting during an unusually tense and confused period, but it also sharpens and extends the established but largely impressionistic picture of a serious decline in official morality in the twenty or so years after 1595.[156]

Sir John Hele himself remains an essentially unsympathetic figure.[157]

[154] Extra leaves have been pasted in at mid-page at several points, and in at least two places earlier drafts have been pasted over with pieces of paper.

[155] 'De vita rogitas, et de virtute? sed ista Invidiam peperit: dum fuit ergo fuit.' For the full inscription, with translation, see W. Jones, 'Wembury Church and Sir John Hele,' *The Western Antiquary*, x (1891), 1.

[156] See in particular, Stone, 'The fruits of office.' For a graphic contemporary description of the economic climate see, Folger Library, MS Cecil Papers, 82/47 (W. Elston to John Prideaux, 5 Dec. 1600): 'The world runs here [in London] crabwise, sidelong, driving every man out of his bias, so that if eight men sit at table, you shall hear seven of them complain of this corrupt time, and such as have lands wish money in their purses for it. The city is growing to great misery, both with the artificer and merchant groaning under the burden of exactions; in a word, hold that you have, and do not be outfaced in right.'

[157] The only known portrait of Hele was, in 1967, in the possession of Mrs Paul Hamlin of Montclair, New Jersey. It was described as Sir Matthew Hale, but was identified by Dr J. H. Baker. The sitter, whose features compare readily with those of the effigy at

Ruthless in his pursuit of material advancement, he cynically abused the law of which he was a custodian and capitalized on the misfortunes of others through the device of usury. This undemanding sideline brought him considerable returns. But it also drew him into an unfamiliar world of high stakes in which his routine trust in the 'power of his purse' proved a fatal miscalculation. However, it would be misleading to overemphasize Hele's cynicism towards the law and the parasitic nature of his second profession. Perversions of legal process had long been common and by the early seventeenth century few at court were prepared to sacrifice personal advantage to principle or the letter of the law. Usury, in a period of unusual stringency, was an essential and widely used financial service provided by, among others, a number of senior lawyers. Against this background, Hele appears very much a creature of the times, playing the game by the rules as he understood them.

Much the same might be said of Hele's principal adversary, Chancellor Thomas Egerton. A strict contemporary, Egerton shared the serjeant's willingness to harness their common profession to the cart of personal advancement and his preference for Star Chamber prosecution as a means of intimidating and discrediting opponents. Indeed, as Hele himself pointed out (with perhaps more truth than he realized), only the accident of royal favor distinguished their respective careers.[158] At least one contemporary isolated the reliance on weak and manipulated men which characterized the Chancellor's vendetta against Hele and criticized him as not only ambitious, but also cowardly and vindictive.[159] His conduct in the Hele affair also confirms the suggestion in other sources that when personally slighted he was an unprincipled, indiscriminate, and vicious adversary. Since the essential motivation for his hounding of Hele was private malice rather than personal gain, it should not perhaps be viewed as 'corrupt' except in a general sense. Nevertheless, Egerton's conduct in the Hele affair heavily qualifies recent characterizations of the Lord Chancellor as a public servant of high moral standards and unimpeachable integrity,[160] and suggests that the burden of responsibility for moral bankruptcy in the early Jacobean establishment should not fall on Sir Robert Cecil alone.

Wembury, is shown wearing a scarlet serjeant's hood with white fur and a white coif covered by a black square cap. On his finger is a ring with the arms of Hele (five fusils in bend). The similarity of name explains the confusion with Hale. In 1977 neither the portrait nor its owner could be traced.

158 PRO, SP 12/279/61.

159 BL, MS Add. 35957, fol. 81*v*. ('memorandum' on Egerton's death).

160 See Jones, *Elizabethan Chancery;* Knafla, *Law and Politics;* and Thomas G. Barnes' essay, above, 298–9.

The possibility that Robert Cecil actively worked to dispossess his brother-in-law, Lord Cobham, was first raised by Professor Stone twenty years ago. Faced with the undeniable fact that by 1610 Cecil had acquired the bulk of his imprisoned relative's property at a fraction of its market value, Stone concluded that, initially, Cecil's motives were mixed and that 'only at a later stage did he succumb to the temptation to take over the Brooke estates altogether.'[161] Cecil's stance in the Hele affair, however, suggests a calculated, long-term intention to acquire the Cobham inheritance, formulated shortly after the arrest of the Brookes in July 1603. Of several possibilities raised by evidence uncovered during the Hele investigation, the most plausible appears to be that Cecil connived in a plan to protect the estate against dismemberment in the early months of the new reign by allowing it to be encumbered with Hele's extents. Lord Cobham's steward, Richard Mellersh, was clearly aware of the possibilities of this device,[162] and his critical contributions to the Hele inquiry, cryptic allusions to 'his master' and repudiation by Cobham himself could well indicate that he was working for Cecil throughout. The intentions of Cecil himself can be inferred from the fact that he carefully concealed and at the trial publicly denied his detailed knowledge of Hele's affairs and his own developing interest in the Cobham property. In any event, the fact remains that the Brooke estates, though vulnerable, survived the critical period intact. After Hele had served his purpose, it was a relatively simple matter to sever him from the property. There is a satisfying symmetry in the probability that Cecil capitalized on Egerton's vendetta against Hele in essentially the same way as Egerton had utilized Hele's enemies in the struggle over the Rolls.

Against this background, the trial of Sir John Hele emerges as relatively insignificant. Like the serjeant's antedating of legal process, his Star Chamber condemnation was simply a necessary incidental in a grander design: Robert Cecil's plot to acquire the Cobham inheritance. That a trial would also serve Egerton's personal interest, and be widely interpreted as a manifestation of his malice, was no doubt a critical consideration in Cecil's adhering to a public posture of the concerned but ignorant arbitrator. There are strong indications that Hele could have survived the Lord Chancellor's spite, of which contemporaries appear to have been well aware, but Egerton's vindictiveness and Robert Cecil's self-interest were a combination too potent for even the tough serjeant to take on. In

161 Stone, 'The fruits of office,' 109. For some pertinent remarks on 'corruption' generally and Robert Cecil in particular see, Joel Hurstfield, *Freedom, Corruption and Government in Elizabethan England* (Cambridge, Mass., Harvard University Press, 1973), 137–62.
162 See above p. 329.

the circumstances, the outcome was a foregone conclusion. Ostensibly, in punishing a corrupt lawyer Star Chamber simply discharged its traditional role as guardian of the prestige and integrity of the law. But, as we can now see, the successful prosecution of Serjeant Hele in fact represented a triumph for hypocrisy, graft, and ambition. That it demonstrates yet again the degree to which perversions of power and process dominated official life during the ascendency of Robert Cecil is both the final irony of and an appropriately cynical conclusion to the trial of Sir John Hele.

Prohibitions and the privilege against self-incrimination

CHARLES M. GRAY

It is a constitutional principle in the United States and a fundamental one in modern English law that no person may be compelled to testify under oath to matters that might expose him or her to criminal prosecution or conviction. The predominant historical tradition on this subject holds that common law judges in Tudor and early Stuart England reinforced the principle by requiring non-common law courts to observe it.[1] That is not strictly correct. The misunderstanding derives mainly from an inadequate contextual sense of the relationship between the different jurisdictions.

Medieval common law did not contain a straightforward 'privilege against self-incrimination.' It had little place for one because trial was normally by jury, and the jury was conceived as the source of truth from

[1] The major recent work is, Leonard W. Levy, *Origins of the Fifth Amendment: The Right against Self-Incrimination* (New York, Oxford University Press, 1968). Although useful for the larger political and intellectual history of the privilege against self-incrimination, Levy clearly misreads the aspect discussed in this essay. Much the best treatment is John H. Wigmore's great *A Treatise on the [Anglo-American] System of Evidence in Trials at Common Law* (Boston, Little, Brown and Company, 1904), sect. 2250. Here I hope to supplement Wigmore in two ways: (*a*) with some MS material, especially the most important single case on self-incrimination (Maunsell and Ladd); and, (*b*) with a different and wider context of contemporary civil cases concerning jurisdiction which, I shall argue, have considerable analogical force.

I shall not document general points of law and legal history in this essay, knowing that when it comes to refinements of emphasis and contextual placement practically nothing in legal history is beyond controversy. Much in this essay depends on my extensive, unpublished study of Prohibitions in Tudor–Stuart England and is too multifarious to document briefly. Sources directly on self-incrimination are of course cited and printed law reports are cited by the reporter's name (5 Coke 1 = Coke's *Reports*, vol. 5, p. 1). Unprinted ones are all from the British Library MSS collections and are cited by name of the collection (e.g. BL, MS Harleian 1631, fol. 365 = British Library, Harleian MS no. 1631, folio 365). Unprinted reports carry as much historical authority as printed ones, since publication was either an accident of the publishing business or the result of a few lawyers publishing their private collections (and at least in Sir Edward Coke's case of conscious intent to teach the law as he conceived it to be, not always accurately). Unprinted reports often supply links in legal topics that are missing from the printed corpus, and their quality is as various as that of those in print.

its own knowledge. Ideally, jurors would know the matter at issue; if they did not know enough, they were free to supplement the evidence presented at a trial with their direct knowledge; if they knew nothing, they were morally obliged to go by the evidence, but they were subject to no effective controls. There was no compulsory testimony by witnesses until Elizabeth I's reign,[2] and parties – civil or criminal – were not compellable to testify. Voluntary sworn witnesses, including civil parties and criminal defendants, simply had to answer truly any questions they were asked or take the consequences. Criminal defendants were under strong *de facto* pressure to testify under oath, since the jury was free to draw adverse conclusions from unwillingness to do so, and verdicts based on no visible evidence, or none but inference from the defendant's silence, were unimpeachable. For the common law's ordinary purposes, these features did not change until after the civil war.

Non-common law jurisdictions, however, compelled testimony by parties and witnesses. Their law did not as a general rule forbid demanding self-incrimination. Common law courts had a procedural basis for intervention, primarily in the ancient writ of Prohibition. This offered the means by which a common law court said to non-common law and inferior courts, 'You have exceeded your jurisdiction. ('And invaded the common law's' can often be added, but that was not always a clear implication.) Therefore stop proceedings.'

There are jurisprudential problems about stretching authority to control jurisdiction into authority to control the law and procedure of other courts (e.g. jumping from 'This is a case or question of title to property exclusively within common law jurisdiction' to 'The subject matter of this suit belongs to you, but you must desist from demanding that the defendant testify against himself'). Nevertheless, the common law courts had the naked procedural power to stop what they did not like in non-common law courts. This essay will illustrate some of the ways it was used in the late sixteenth and early seventeenth centuries, when Prohibitions were issued most abundantly.

I

In the middle ages, the Prohibition was almost exclusively an instrument against ecclesiastical courts. In the early modern period it was also fre-

[2] The Perjury Act of 5 Elizabeth I, c. 9: *SR*, IV, pt I, 436–8, is the conventional landmark for the compulsion of witnesses at common law. The statute appears only to contemplate the practice, perhaps as something already commenced. Incidence of involuntary witnesses was probably low until much later.

quently used against equity and Admiralty courts, but only the common law *vs.* church law relationship is significant for self-incrimination. An equity or Admiralty court might in its civil business ask an incriminating question incidentally, but there is very little case law on that.[3] The Church courts, however, did a regular criminal business.[4]

The civil–criminal line in the ecclesiastical sphere was not precisely analogous to the common law distinction between Pleas of the Crown and Common Pleas, but a line did exist. People were liable to be prosecuted and punished in ecclesiastical courts for various misbehaviors, just as they were liable to be sued there for declaratory and injunctive relief for the benefit of a private party. In their criminal category fell offenses against religious orthodoxy, starting with heresy, offenses concerning disorderly or disrespectful behavior in church and toward churchmen, as well as behavior by clergymen that was unbecoming or unlawful to their status. Ecclesiastical law certainly included moral offenses, mainly sexual misconduct, as well as offenses that were often private wrongs, e.g. certain forms of defamation, thought to merit both punishment for unchristian conduct and an apology or retraction for the benefit of the defamed party.

Prosecution on this criminal side could be either private or public, the latter either *ex officio*, on the initiative of the ecclesiastical judge, or by presentment at a visitation. With a qualified exception for the post-Reformation Court of High Commission, ecclesiastical sanctions were 'spiritual.' In other words, excommunication was at once both the highest punishment and the coercive sanction by which attendance on the courts and execution of lesser sentences were enforced. There is no sign that ecclesiastical crimes were thought of as less than criminal because only excommunication could as a rule punish those found guilty. In fact, excommunication could be turned into imprisonment by the lay arm

[3] See my note 17, for one case in which an equity court (Requests) was prevented from exposing someone to self-incrimination in such an incidental way.

A trace of evidence suggests that at least once the Chancery tried on its own initiative to temper incriminating interrogation: one accused of violating a decree will at once be subjected to interrogatories (i.e. asked to convict himself of contempt out of his own mouth) if the accusation comes within a year of the decree; thereafter, the party in whose favor the decree was made must bring a new bill: Dalison 91 (15 Elizabeth I).

[4] Though confined to misdemeanors, the Star Chamber administered a large share of 'criminal' law and was Prohibition-proof, probably because judges regarded it as a necessary supplement to the common law, using civil law methods under auspices of the King's Council and with regular participation by the chief justices.

One report hints that the Star Chamber, like the Chancery, while fundamentally relying on incriminatory interrogation, sought to contain it: Coke stated, without context, that Star Chamber refused bills brought by private informers on 'penal' statutes in order not to give such plaintiffs the benefit of the inquisitorial procedure employed 'for the King' in pure criminal cases: BL, MS Harleian 4817, fol. 191 (undated).

through the ancient writ *De excommunicato capiendo*, and excommunicants were also subject to civil disabilities.

Procedural law in the ecclesiastical system put no barrier in the way of asking witnesses and parties under oath questions which, if answered truly, would convict them of crime or furnish a basis for charges. Were the common law courts disposed, and in an intellectually defensible position, to do anything about this? We perhaps assume that prevailing common law opinion regarded incriminatory questioning as morally objectionable and therefore that the courts intervened to stop it. Moral objection, expressed in the often repeated maxim *Nemo tenetur seipsum prodere*, was no doubt widespread. The sentiment that civil–canon procedure violated a natural right akin to the right of self-preservation had a long history. Acting judicially on that sentiment was not, however, easily justifiable.

Indirectly, common law judges wielding the Prohibition (and the *Habeas Corpus*) curbed the ecclesiastical courts' capacity to exact confessions and incriminating information. They were able to do so because ecclesiastical interrogation that tended to demand self-incrimination was sometimes beyond ecclesiastical jurisdiction in one of several ways. There remained cases in which such interrogation could not plausibly be analysed as a violation of jurisdiction, like violations in other areas of law, and it was permitted in such cases. This outcome is consistent with early modern jurisdictional law at large. Across the board, the non-common law courts were taken seriously as components of a 'federal' legal system under the King and Parliament. Although common law judges did not always treat those courts as fellow members in such a mixed system, they did not ride roughshod over them. The law of Prohibitions thus provided the means for much debate over how to distinguish between regulating the jurisdiction of non-common law courts and invading their due autonomy. In the matter of self-incrimination, the ecclesiastical courts could have been more restricted than they were, with some analogical support from other branches of jurisdictional law. It would have been hard to restrict them less in view of analogous practice.

Such questions as 'May a criminal defendant in an ecclesiastical court be forced to testify against himself?' are a species of a larger question. The general question is 'May common law courts prohibit non-common law courts from applying whatever rules they like in cases within their jurisdiction in the simplest sense, when the subject matter of the dispute or prosecution concededly belongs to the non-common law court?' An affirmative answer is correct for two situations, beyond which a negative one is preferable: (*a*) if, in the opinion of a common law court, a statute prescribes rules for non-common law courts, the common law court may enforce the statute against the non-common law court, by Prohibition or otherwise; and (*b*) if an ecclesiastical rule contradicts the common law its application may be blocked. Whether this second principle has any practical meaning depends on whether *contrasting* rules can be analysed as *contradictory*, or only as functions of undisputedly legitimate purposes and procedures different from those of the common law.[5]

A number of difficult cases raised the question whether particular substantive standards insisted on by ecclesiastical courts should be vetoed by common law courts.[6] It was procedurally possible to seek a Prohibition (in the early modern period, a judicial writ obtained by showing cause) with the allegation that one's plea in an ecclesiastical court had been improperly disallowed, conceding that one's being sued there in the first place was unobjectionable. For example, suppose A is properly sued for ecclesiastical defamation and the Church court disallows A's plea that the defamatory words were true. Should the ecclesiastical court be prohibited unless it will change course and allow the defense of truth, which was good against common law defamation? From cases of this sort, one prin-

[5] With respect to statutes, it was a good metaphysical question why common law courts should have the last word on their meaning, and why non-common law courts should not be allowed to enforce statutes on themselves (subject to appeals and ultimately to parliamentary correction), as common law courts did. Common law judges made good, however, on their claim to a special guardianship over the statutory law. The rule that ecclesiastical law must not contradict the common law was statutory, 25 Henry VIII, c. 19: *SR*, III, 460–1, but perhaps not dependent on the statute.

[6] This paragraph is based on analysis of 43 cases. A few Elizabethan cases suggest willingness to intervene when ecclesiastical decisions were merely foolish and probably untenable by ecclesiastical law. Greater restraint was shown by seventeenth century courts. The principle that conflicts with common law, as opposed to injustice and appealable error, is the sole legitimate basis for intervention was first stated by counsel in *Agarde* v. *Porter* (BL, Add. MS 25203, fol. 467, and Add MS 25213, fol. 31: Easter 44 Elizabeth I, Queen's Bench). The principle moved some judges but was not decisively approved in that case; it gained ground later.

A group of seven cases about the legal incapacities of married women will serve to illustrate the cross-currents of rule-conflict situations. An ecclesiastical rule that a husband's release of his wife's interests does not bind her would seem clearly at odds with the common law. One ecclesiastical court was prohibited from disallowing such a release *quoad* a legacy: *Stephens* v. *Totty*, Croke Elizabeth 905, and Noy 45; BL, Add. MS 25203, fols. 548*v*. 609*v*.; BL, Add. MS 25213, fol. 35: Trinity 44 and Michaelmas 44/45 Elizabeth I, Queen's Bench. But *quoad* defamation, three cases held the contrary: *Glanvyle* v. *Newport*, BL, MS Lansdowne 1065, fol. 42: Hilary 42 Elizabeth, Common Pleas; *Motam* v. *Motam*, 1 Rolle 426, and 3 Bulstrode 264, and BL, MS Harleian 4561, fol. 266: Michaelmas 14 James I, King's Bench; and, *Fenton* v. *Edwards*, BL, Add. MS 25208, fol. 73: Michaelmas 7 James I, King's Bench. That is, a woman's ecclesiastical interest in her reputation and the ecclesiastical court's interest in criminal prosecution of defamation are not releasable; pecuniary interests, which would accrue to the husband, are: to that extent conflict of rules is intolerable. These cases were flatly contradicted in *Vincent* v. *Genis*, BL, MS Hargrave 15, fol. 227: Michaelmas 8 James I, Common Pleas under Coke's chief justiceship; but see also, Anonymous, Croke Charles I 222.

ciple emerges strongly, though not unanimously: ecclesiastical courts should not be prohibited merely because they were mistaken, either in the sense that they misapplied their own law or in the sense that their decisions quarreled with morality or natural law. The ecclesiastical system allowed generous appeals. The common law judges did not usually preempt the role of ecclesiastical appeals, and they were willing to presume that appeals would correct miscarriages of justice as well as technical errors. Common law intervention must, therefore, be based on establishing that the ecclesiastical court had violated a duty to keep its rules in reasonable conformity with the common law, not to contradict it when a head-on collision of rules was perceptible. Cases in which an attempt was made to justify Prohibition, by showing such intolerable conflict of rules, are tangled and do not suggest sharp conclusions. On the whole, on close scrutiny of the fit between the common law and church law, they show that head-on collisions were hard to find, but some were discovered. (There are a few intimations in the cases that truth in defamation might be an instance, but that was never clearly held.)[7]

Cases on substantive rule conflicts are relevant for self-incrimination because they endorse the point that moral disapproval of ecclesiastical practices was insufficient grounds for interference. By the general standards of jurisdictional law, incriminatory questioning could be more safely prohibited by showing, if possible, that such procedure violated the common law than by relying on *Nemo tenetur* as a maxim of natural justice. More directly relevant for self-incrimination are the many cases on a procedural rule that Church courts frequently applied: that transactions must be proved by at least two witnesses. Common law sentiment may have disapproved of the two witness rule more than of incriminating

[7] The central reason for Prohibition in *Ambler* v. *Metcalfe* (BL, MS Lansdowne 1099, fol. 38; Add. MS 25198, fol. 210; and MS Harleian 1631, fol. 155; Michaelmas 38/39, Hilary 39, and Easter 39 Elizabeth I, Queen's Bench) was probably that the ecclesiastical court appeared to have rejected the truth defense. Defendant called plaintiff a bastard; defendant sought to plead that plaintiff *was* a bastard. The case was not definitively decided here but Prohibition was granted; the usual motion to reverse the Prohibition was made; the judges put off a final decision and there is no later report. There were complications: whether 'bastard' is always actionable at common law and never at ecclesiastical law and whether, if it is actionable at ecclesiastical law, the word must be given its common law meaning, *viz.* 'born out of wedlock' *simpliciter*. See *Webb* v. *Cook* (Croke James I 535, and 2 Rolle 82; BL, MS Lansdowne 1080, fol. 74*v*.; and BL, Add. MS 25213, fol. 232: Easter 17 James I, King's Bench) and a similar case (Anon., BL, MS Hargrave 30, fol. 114*v*.: Michaelmas 19 James I, King's Bench). Ecclesiastical courts were prohibited, not for rejecting the truth defense as such, but for refusing to take the findings of justices of the peace as conclusive support for that defense. Defendant said plaintiff begot a bastard, and pleaded that plaintiff did beget a bastard *because* justices of the peace had so found in the course of their statutory duty to identify fathers of bastards and make them contribute to the child's support.

interrogation in criminal cases. The bias of the judges was hardly against prosecution of moral and religious offenses, and effective prosecution without inquisition was difficult in view of the typically secret character of the crimes. The two witness rule, on the other hand, was widely regarded as a foolish or unfair formalism, embarrassingly at odds with the common law. For example, an executor sued at ecclesiastical law for a legacy might be required to support by two witnesses his plea that he had already paid the legacy; persons claiming to have paid money owed at common law, including the same executor in appropriate circumstances, were subject to no such burden. Save where wager of law or conclusive proof by sealed documents figured, claims brought to issue at common law simply went to the jury, and there were no rules as to the kind or quantity of evidence the claimant must produce. Some lawyers clearly believed that asking people to have certain transactions witnessed, and not others of comparable value and complexity, was too burdensome. They also held that common law process for settling factual disputes implied a sort of 'national choice' in favor of letting the trier of facts draw his conclusions from whatever evidence or lack thereof the parties put before him, a choice so important that ecclesiastical courts should not contradict it (as they should arguably not contradict so basic a chosen principle as 'truth excuses defamation').[8] In a number of cases, application of the two witness rule was blocked by Prohibition without apparent further grounds.

The weight of cases on the two witness rule, however, tends to the other side. The better opinion, after several decades of experience, is best construed as follows:[9] ecclesiastical courts are generally free to demand two witnesses to support claims made in infra-jurisdictional litigation;

[8] Jurisprudentially, 'choice' is the important concept here. A two witness rule is hardly objectionable morally, whether or not it is impractical and whatever may be true of incriminatory questioning. See, Charles M. Gray, 'Reason, authority, and imagination: the jurisprudence of Sir Edward Coke,' in Perez Zagorin (ed.), *Culture and Politics from Puritanism to the Enlightenment* (Berkely, University of California Press, 1980), 25–66.

Against the point that common law chose 'in favor of letting the trier of facts draw his conclusions,' it may be urged that jurors are not triers of fact analogous to ecclesiastical judges, i.e. triers of evidence. It may be said that the English method was also trial by witnesses, except that twelve rather than two were required. One can also argue that the common law had formalisms functionally like the two witness rule, e.g. in the law of treason.

[9] Construction of the 'better opinion' here is admittedly delicate. It may be a stricter reading of the cases to say: (*a*) the belief never died that the two witness rule should simply be banned when a party complains of it, although seventeenth century cases tend against it in contrast to earlier ones; (*b*) there was probably a vein of opinion that application of the two witness rule should never be banned and it is more than possible that this was Coke's view (he was particularly concerned lest two witness rule Prohibitions be abused by fictitious pleading, to the unfair detriment of ecclesiastical jurisdiction); and (*c*) what I describe in the

but they may not do so when enforcement of the ecclesiastical rule might prejudice interests within the common law's protection. Suppose that a release is pleaded in an ecclesiastical case. The release is a single document in which a number of claims are relinquished, some ecclesiastical, such as legacies, some temporal, such as debts and rents. The ecclesiastical court would probably be prohibited from insisting on two witnesses to authenticate the release. By making it harder to establish it, the odds on its being disauthenticated are increased; if the ecclesiastical court holds that the release is inauthentic, it may be more difficult for its beneficiary to convince a jury of its authenticity in subsequent common law litigation about the temporal interests. The principle that ecclesiastical proceedings, perfectly proper in themselves, may be arrested to prevent prejudice to common law interests was well-based in other contexts as well, notably in cases on wills containing both bequests of chattels and devises of land under the Statute of Wills (1540). Probate of such wills was commonly held up, at least when the will was contested, lest an ecclesiastical determination on the authenticity of the will prejudice litigation about the land.

This principle is important for self-incrimination. Owing to legislation, there was a limited area of concurrent ecclesiastical and secular jurisdiction in criminal matters.[10] In several cases, ecclesiastical courts were prohibited from interrogation when the effect would be to force someone

text as the better opinion represents the middle ground and may have been primarily the invention of Chief Justice Popham. My observations on the two witness rule are based on 34 cases, the most important being: The Elizabethan *Bagnall* v. *Stokes* (Croke Elizabeth, 89, and Moore, 907; BL, Add. MSS 25194, fol. 58, and Add. MSS 25196, fol. 109*v*: Hilary 30 Elizabeth I, Queen's Bench), upholds (though only by dictum) Prohibitions to prevent application of the two witness rule in apparently comprehensive terms. Coke criticized this opinion in his notebook (BL, MS Harleian 6687, fol. 739) and later recorded there that his own Common Pleas had reversed it (Peppe's Case, Michaelmas 4 James I; well-reported anonymously in BL, Add MSS 25215, fol. 36*v*.; briefly reported at Noy, 12, and cited by name in several other cases). Courts presided over by Coke indulged the two witness rule to a much greater extent than any others. King's Bench opinion was sharply divided in *Brown* v. *Wentworth* (Yelverton, 92; BL, MS Lansdowne 1111, fol. 241*v*., MS Harleian 1631, fol. 329*v*., and Add MS 25205, fol. 46*v*.: Trinity 4 James I), a majority of three favoring the Bagnall v. Stokes position, Popham and another dissenter defending the 'middle position'. Later decisions in both principal courts probably tend to Popham's side. In the latest pre-Civil War case (Anon., BL, MS Hargrave 39, fol. 35: Trinity 5 Charles I, King's Bench) the Popham position prevailed but disagreement continued.

[10] The character of such legislation was to create a secular offense where an ecclesiastical one already existed, with an express or implied saving of ecclesiastical jurisdiction. I use 'criminal matters' here to include 'penal' in the sense 'prosecutable by *Qui tam* action for a set penalty.' Whether activities made so prosecutable by statute are strictly 'criminal,' or whether a given one is *malum in se* or not, are questions we need not go into. It is just as real to be exposed to a £10 *Qui tam* suit as to be exposed to prosecution for felony.

to supply sworn confessional evidence that could be used against him in a secular prosecution for the same offense. It would have been anomalous for secular prosecution of some offenses (usury, say) to be easier than prosecution of others (say murder) merely because the former happened to be simultaneously ecclesiastical offenses. Preventing that anomaly is not the same as preventing inquisitorial investigation generally. It is closely analogous to other forms of checking accidental and unfair encroachment of ecclesiastical procedures on the temporal sphere. For example, it is anomalous for A to have a harder time establishing his release of debts at common law than B when the only difference between their cases is that A's release includes legacies as well as debts and an ecclesiastical court has previously disallowed the release for want of two witnesses.

The better opinion on two witness cases was in part the work of Chief Justice Coke. Some late Elizabethan authority supports the proposition that ecclesiastical courts may simply not enforce the two witness rule, owing to the absence of any equivalent in the common law system. Coke's Common Pleas reversed that law deliberately, and most seventeenth century opinion, including all subsequent cases that Coke sat on, sustains the view that the rule is enforceable in purely ecclesiastical litigation, where there is no incidental encroachment on temporal interests. Coke's role is noteworthy as a corrective to his reputation as the judge who most freely prohibited, and otherwise interfered with, non-common law courts. The reputation is a misleading projection from his high visibility as a leader opposing political attacks on the independence of the bench by ecclesiastical officials and others well connected with the Jacobean government. In fact, most of Coke's decisions unfavorable to the church were precedented in Elizabethan practice. Whether favorable or not his views were often shared by his colleagues but not always, for the bench in his day was not unnaturally unanimous. If there is a pattern across the whole field of jurisdictional law, it corresponds to the pattern in common law cases on the two witness rule: late Elizabethan judges tended to be less solicitous of the rights of non-common law courts in their sphere, less careful and lawyerly about justifying interference, than early Stuart judges. Coke's decisions do not always fit that pattern, but they sometimes do. Cases on self-incrimination are essentially outside the pattern because they are untypically, compared to more commonplace topics of jurisdictional law, concentrated in the early seventeenth century. I shall, however, show that Coke was not the hero-founder of a 'privilege against self-incrimination.' His position on the two witness rule may not have practical advantages over the competing one, but it reflects greater sensitivity to the problems of coordination intrinsic to mixed legal systems.

Most cases on self-incrimination involved the Court of High Commission. There were some involving ordinary ecclesiastical courts, which I shall discuss separately below. Though few, they are valuable as a model alongside the High Commission cases, for the latter were complicated in several ways. For one thing, numerous High Commission cases arose on *Habeas Corpus* rather than Prohibition, because the Commission purported to have authority to fine and imprison. The question of whether it was entitled to use incriminatory interrogation sometimes arose as an incident of the question whether someone imprisoned by its authority was lawfully imprisoned. Questions about self-incrimination tended to be mixed with other issues about the court's powers. That could be true in Prohibition, but it was especially true in *Habeas Corpus*, where the issue was by definition spare (has the jailer's return on the writ stated sufficient cause to hold the prisoner?), and the information available to the court (and hence to the historian) was often confined to returns written to reveal as little as possible.

On the High Commission's powers generally, there are many reported Prohibition and *Habeas Corpus* cases, leading to two main problems: (*a*) could the Commission be given by royal patent any and all forms of ecclesiastical jurisdiction, or only certain forms?; and (*b*) could it be given power to use secular sanctions? Both questions were essentially about the construction of the Elizabethan Supremacy Act, which authorized the monarch to set up an extraordinary ecclesiastical court.[11] Although decisions on these questions are complicated, prevailing opinion held that the Commission could only be given jurisdiction over major ecclesiastical crimes but that within its jurisdiction it could fine and imprison.[12] In quite

[11] Caudrey's Case (5 Coke 1, for the best-known of several reports) held that the monarch's power to create an ecclesiastical court like the High Commission was not dependent on statutory authorization. This doctrine had little influence outside the complex circumstances of Caudrey's Case itself. The monarch could have created a Commission by prerogative, but what jurisdiction and powers he could give it if he were to act alone was in practice not discussed. Parliament *had* authorized him and what, if any, limits it meant to attach to the authorization was the question the courts considered repeatedly. Regarding sanctions, an act of parliament was clearly necessary for powers beyond the regular ecclesiastical ones to be conferrable on the Commission.

[12] My conclusions here are based on analysis of eighty-odd cases uncomplicated by a self-incrimination element. In general: Elizabethan authority is sparse and divided. The Elizabethan court of Common Pleas came to the view that the Commission could never use secular sanctions, a position inherited and modified by Coke's Common Pleas. The Queen's Bench disagreed sharply. A few decisions on particular heads of jurisdiction point to the idea that not all ecclesiastical jurisdiction could be conferred on the Commission, to the potential overthrow of local justice, but the courts did not generalize. The text states essentially what Coke's Common Pleas held, subject to dissent by Justice

a few cases there was no reason for common law courts to debate the Commission's power to use inquisitorial procedure, even if counsel seeking a Prohibition (or a release of prisoners) brought it up. The Commission was prohibitable, or an imprisonment could be judged unlawful, simply because it had exceeded its jurisdiction.[13] A further complication of High Commission cases arose from the possibility, mainly hypothetical as it turned out, that that court could be (by the statute behind it) and was (by the patents constituting it) given greater power to conduct inquisition than ordinary ecclesiastical courts, as it was given sanctions they lacked.

Finally, the High Commission was more likely than ordinary ecclesiastical courts to prosecute crimes *ex officio* and therefore to employ the *ex officio* oath. That is, it could cite people and require of them an oath to answer all questions truthfully prior to formal specification of charges or notification of the questions to be asked. Issues about the legitimacy of the oath and proceedings connected with it were focused on the High Commission; other Church courts could use the procedure, but most of their less intense and lower-level criminal business arose from private prosecution or presentment wherein charges preceded any demand for an ap-

Walmesley, and did generalize. A divided King's Bench was meanwhile somewhat less restrictive toward the Commission than the Common Pleas, but more so than the same court in Elizabeth's reign. Coke as chief justice of the King's Bench after 1613 brought the two courts into conformity, and there they substantially remained. Coke once defined by dictum the serious or 'enormous' offenses appropriate to the Commission (Darrington's Case, 2 Brownlow and Goldesborough 3): heresy, schism, recusancy, polygamy, and incest. Decisions, however, do not suggest that there was consensus on quite so narrow a list. Post-Cokean courts loosened the list to allow the Commission to discipline clergy for offenses less than 'enormous,' but its exclusion from civil cases and petty ecclesiastical misdemeanors by laymen held up. The courts' strongest practical motive for curbing the Commission was to prevent it from becoming a domestic affairs court with the teeth to cause serious inconvenience to 'wife-abusers.' Puritan activity was almost never held beyond the Commission's reach.

13 A collection of MS Prohibition cases, precedents drawn from official records rather than reports of arguments and reasons for decisions (BL, MS Stowe 424, fol. 158), has been given considerable weight towards showing that incriminating interrogation as such was blocked by common law courts: Levy, *Origins of the Fifth Amendment*, 245. Levy recognizes that Prohibitions to High Commission were more often than not based on grounds other than objection to incriminating examination. He by no means connects all these Stowe MS cases with protection against self-incrimination but he associates some too clearly with that function. My analysis of these seventeen cases, all from Coke's Common Pleas, concludes that they are worthless for that purpose. Nearly all present commonplace questions about the Commission's substantive jurisdiction, and reports of a few of the cases show that nothing but jurisdiction was considered by the court. Those not independently reported add to the evidence that Coke's Common Pleas often prohibited the Commission from meddling with low-level offenses. By showing complaints written by lawyers seeking Prohibitions, such 'precedents' show instructively that incriminating procedure was often complained of in general terms, with invocations of Magna Carta, but they do not prove that the court attended to that aspect of the complaints when the cases were more easily disposable.

pearance or an oath. There is good common law authority that before a person is examined he must be informed of the questions, or at least of their topics, in order that he might complain to a common law court that the examination touched on matters beyond ecclesiastical jurisdiction, and in order that the court might judge whether it did. The notice requirement was regarded as enforceable *per se*: complainant to a common law court did not have to show that an *ultra vires* question had actually been put to him, but only that he had been asked to swear, or subjected to examination, without sufficient notice. The principle was that an ecclesiastical court may not tell a man he is accused of, for example, schism (if it tells him that much), then make him swear to answer truly any and all questions he is asked, because there is no assurance that he will be asked about schism or anything relevant to proving if he is a schismatic. For all a common law court knows, the ecclesiastical court intends to, or might, examine him about secular crimes or anything else outside of its authority.

This doctrine was a fairly inevitable function of jurisdictional control. Obviously ecclesiastical courts should be prohibited if it is apparent that they are not dealing with, or sticking to, ecclesiastical business. It goes a step farther, however, to say that they should be prohibited if it is *not* apparent that they *are* confining themselves to ecclesiastical business. It would be possible to presume that they are within their jurisdiction until the contrary is positively shown or to presume in the High Commission's favor on the ground that it enjoyed statutory privileges. But such presumptions would have been at odds with the prevalent vigilance lest Church courts reach beyond their borders, even incidentally. Most Prohibitions in civil cases were issued because the ecclesiastical court appeared to be out of bounds; but some of those were based on the judgment that nothing in tradition or common practice suggested that a claim belonged to ecclesiastical cognizance, even though nothing suggested the contrary. For example, the claim would not be recognized by the common law, did not fall in an area the common law reserved to itself (contract law, say), and was not ruled out by any specific customary or statutory restriction on ecclesiastical courts.[14] In any event, banning interrogation in a form

[14] The civil cases referred to form a small and anomalous category. All one can really say is that sometimes the judges looked at an ecclesiastical suit and said, 'You simply may not sue for that; it is unheard of, in an ecclesiastical court or anywhere else. The suit does not encroach on the common law, it is not inappropriate to an ecclesiastical court in its general flavor, but because it is not a known kind of ecclesiastical suit it is *ultra vires*.' It is important in principle that the judges were occasionally willing to say that (i.e. to arrest the proliferation of ecclesiastical liabilities, to leave people at liberty until parliament or

that could lead to violation of jurisdiction is not the same as banning incriminatory questioning.

II

We may now review the cases, taking first those confined to ordinary Church courts. Two late Elizabethan Prohibition cases, though skimpily reported, are good authority that at least a lay defendant to a criminal charge of pure ecclesiastical cognizance (incontinency in both cases) may not be asked to convict himself on sworn examination.[15] A third case, exceptional in form, cuts partly in the other direction.[16] An attempt was made to indict an ecclesiastical official for subjecting a defendant to incriminatory examination on a charge of incontinency. In an advisory opinion presumably taken before the indictment was returned, the chief justices and chief baron held in general terms that the ecclesiastical court was entitled to its inquisitory procedure within its jurisdiction. At a later hearing in the Queen's Bench, presumably on the validity of the indictment, the point was qualified: inquisition is permissible only if the charge is made by presentment of at least two men at a visitation, as it had been in this case. It does not follow that an ecclesiastical court is prohibitable, or not, because the ecclesiastical official is, or is not, indictable. Nothing in the judges' language suggests a distinction. The suggestion in the case, for which no rationale is reported, is that sworn inquisition is a permissible method of trial, but only when the method of accusation is putatively more reliable and more analogous to common law procedure than private or *ex officio* accusation. If the charges in the two cases above were not on presentment there is no inconsistency.

the common law itself has imposed liability). But this is analytically puzzling: why should common law courts have a monopoly in interpreting statutes (see note 5)? Why should the common law control the ambit of liability when its own interests and specialties are not concerned, and where there is no violation of a specifiable statutory or customary rule on the limits of ecclesiastical jurisdiction and the manner in which it must be exercised? I would not press the analogy with *ex officio* oath cases very hard but the point remains: prohibiting ecclesiastical courts did not always require saying that they had gone beyond their powers in a positive sense, only that they were not evidently within them.

15 See (*a*) BL, Add. MS 25196, fol. 213*v*. and Harleian 1633, fol. 63: Michaelmas 31/32 Elizabeth I, Queen's Bench; and (*b*) *Collier* v. *Collier*, Croke Elizabeth 201, Moore 906, 4 Leonard 194, and BL, MS Harleian 1633, fol. 160: Michaelmas 32/33 Elizabeth I, Queen's Bench.

16 Dr Hunt's Case, Croke Elizabeth 262: Michaelmas 33/34 Elizabeth I, Queen's Bench. That such misuse of an ecclesiastical official's powers was indictable as an 'oppression' (a recognized, if vague, category of misdemeanor by officials) is asserted in the extrajudicial opinion of Popham and Coke below.

Of seventeenth century cases, two fall under the principle that ecclesiastical inquisition may not be used to exact confessions so as to expose to secular prosecution.[17] One of these involved a civil suit in the ecclesiastical court. By implication of the opinion, there is no more right there than in a criminal suit to ask questions that will expose the examinee to criminal or 'penal' danger in the temporal sphere. A third case extends the principle:[18] pursuant to an incontinency suit, the ecclesiastical court required the defendant to enter a bond against consorting with a certain woman. It was later prohibited from forcing him to testify under oath as to whether he had broken the obligation, i.e. from exposing him to secular civil detriment through loss of the penalty stipulated in the bond. There is nothing surprising in that result, in view of the courts' propensity to prevent ecclesiastical events from encroaching on temporal interests. In a complex Elizabethan case, however, whether protection against civil detriment is among the limits on compulsory sworn examination was treated ambiguously.[19]

An extrajudicial opinion of 1606 speaks more decisively than these scanty Elizabethan cases.[20] The opinion was given by Chief Justice

[17] See (*a*) *Bullocke* v. *Hall*, BL, MS Harleian 1631, fol. 365: Easter 5 James I, Common Pleas. In the only case involving a non-ecclesiastical court, the court of Requests was prohibited from examining under oath to determine whether an obligation was fraudulent, a legitimate equitable function employed to prevent use of a fraudulent bond in common law proceedings, in a claim against an estate. The report is not explicit, but there is no evident basis for the Prohibition except protection against criminal, meaning 'penal,' fraud charges. Also (*b*) *Spendlow* v. *Sir William Smith*, Hobart 84: undated, but probably James I, Common Pleas. An ecclesiastical suit against a parson's executor by his successor for dilapidations (causing or suffering diminution of the capital value of the living), involving a fraudulent lease in which the executor was personally complicit. Prohibition was expressly granted to prevent examination about the fraud because the executor would be in danger of a 'penal' statute.

[18] Gammon's Case, Hetley 18, and BL, MS Harleian 5148, fol. 142, Easter 3 Charles I, Common Pleas. Decision rested clearly on exposure to forfeiture of the bond, though answering the question might expose to fresh charges of incontinency.

[19] Anon., Moore 906, and BL, MS Lansdowne 1073, fol. 108, Add. MSS 25194, fol. 6*v*. and 25196, fol. 199*v*.: Trinity 31–Michaelmas 31/32 Elizabeth I, Common Pleas. The intricate web of issues can be simplified: defendant in an ecclesiastical suit to revoke letters of administration objected that she was being put to examination about the estate's indebtedness on several scores. If she were to win the suit and remain administratrix, she would have been forced to confess certain debts and therefore would have trouble contesting them at common law. Two judges thought the examination should be prohibited. Two thought it probably should not but, perhaps, should if the questions were irrelevant for deciding whether to revoke administration. The party seeking revocation claimed that he should be administrator because he would be liable as heir for certain types of debt, and hence questions about the debts were relevant. The court got together on a type of Prohibition that was little more than admonitory: the examination was prohibited insofar as the questions were irrelevant. The main suggestion of the case is that ecclesiastical power to examine in testamentary matters, which the revocation suit presumably counts as, was not absolute, even when there was no risk of temporal criminal exposure.

[20] 12 Coke 26: Easter, 4 James I.

Popham and Coke, still attorney-general but shortly to be appointed chief justice of the Common Pleas. They gave the opinion at the request of Parliament and the Privy Council. It relates in terms to the ordinary ecclesiastical courts and contains nothing on special problems concerning the High Commission. Four limits on inquisition are laid down. Two are those that follow from general canons of jurisdictional law: 'secular detriment' and the doctrine that oaths may not be administered to answer wholly indeterminate or unannounced questions. The third limit points to a real, but qualified, 'privilege against self-incrimination.' According to Popham and Coke, regular ecclesiastical courts may compel laymen to be examined only in testamentary and matrimonial cases (by the letter, not even in other civil suits); clergymen, on the other hand, are examinable in criminal as well as civil cases. The opinion says nothing about the few judicial precedents that could be used to support this proposition and proceeds from a lame rationale to the real reason for it:[21] the ancient 'statute' *Articuli Cleri* limited examination of laymen to matrimonial and testamentary causes, and language of a Henrician statute suggested parliamentary objection to inveigling unlearned laymen and exacting shameful admissions. For the purposes of an advisory opinion, Popham and Coke gave the right advice: a good case could be made against at least all criminal examination of laymen on the positive basis of *Articuli Cleri*, and the best way for ecclesiastical courts to avoid trouble would be to avoid examining laymen. Whether opinion would hold up in contemporary Prohibition and *Habeas Corpus* cases, with counsel and judges giving close attention to the meaning and relevance of

[21] 'Lame' does not seem to me excessive. The alleged reasons were:

(*a*) Examination is necessary in testamentary and matrimonial causes because of the secret nature of the facts (is less really discoverable without testimony of the party in those cases than in others?);

(*b*) Examinees in such cases will not be made to confess anything 'shameful' ('shameful,' and potentially criminal, matter is more likely to be revealed in marital litigation, at any rate, than in most other forms of civil litigation); and

(*c*) Laymen, being 'unlettered,' can be entrapped and inveigled, especially into confessing religious offenses (perhaps valid for examination of orthodoxy, even assuming the rest of the Popham–Coke limits, but not convincing otherwise, except for the truism that a stupid witness may be tricked by clever questions). The reasons are not so lame as those contemplated by the authors of *Articuli Cleri*; they may have been the best justification for conceding something to ecclesiastical courts while conceding as little as possible, the activities, claims, and disputed areas of ecclesiastical jurisdiction being what they were in the early fourteenth century. The status of *Articuli Cleri* (9 Edward II) is itself vulnerable: an administrative order with local reference in form, though reputed a statute. Popham and Coke may have realized that, for they relevantly put a good deal of reliance on 25 Henry VIII, c. 14: *SR*, III, 454–5. That act repealed the famous *De heretico comburendo* (2 Henry IV, c. 15: *SR*, II, 125–8), which gave ecclesiastical courts power of examination in heresy and related offenses. The Henrician Parliament expressly objected to the dangers of inveiglement and extraction of 'shameful' confessions.

old authority, can unfortunately only be tested through the morass of complicating issues about the High Commission.

The fourth limit stated by Popham and Coke is that examination may not be about 'secret thoughts.' Some overt act must be charged and questioning must go to whether the act occurred; acts of speech of course count but one may not be forced to reveal one's beliefs or intentions. This principle was of little practical importance because defendants, benefiting from the required notice of questions, were usually charged with doing something: I have found it invoked only once. Its justification, not spelled out in the opinion, would seem virtually logical. It is an odd notion of a legal proceeding to say to a man, 'You are rumored to be a heretic, but we have no information, even on rumor, that you have ever said anything heretical; we must test whether you are a heretic by running through the articles of faith and asking you whether you believe in them.' There was little danger of that, though an occasional interrogatory might slip into mere beliefs. Secular courts, watchful lest ecclesiastical courts overstep their bounds in all sorts of ways, would of course have prevented them from straying into the grotesque.

The first major High Commission case was the *Habeas Corpus* of Maunsell and Ladd in 1607.[22] It was preceded by a few early cases frequently and undisputedly cited for the proposition that the High Commission, like ordinary Church courts, may not examine so as to expose to secular prosecution for concurrent offenses.[23] There was also a decision that the High Commission may not evade whatever limits on its examining powers there are by compelling the accusee to put in a bond obliging him to submit to unrestricted sworn interrogation.[24] Maunsell and Ladd has all the marks of a headline political case. The most concerted assault ever made on inquisition of any sort by any court was made by counsel for the

[22] BL, Add. MS 25206, fols. 55 and 59*v*., and MS Harleain 1631, fols. 353*v*. and 358*v*. These good reports have not, so far as I know, been used before. The only printed document of the case is Fuller's published argument: *The Argument of Master Nicholas Fuller in the Case of Thomas Lad, and Richard Maunsell, his Clients. Wherein it is plainly proved, that the Ecclesiastical Commissioners have no power, by vertue of their Commission, to Imprison, to put to the Oath Ex Officio, or to fine any of his Maiesties Subjects: STC* 11460 (London, 1607).

[23] Leigh's Case (9/10 Elizabeth I, Common Pleas), Mitton's Case and Hynde's Case (Michaelmas 18 Elizabeth I, referred to in another case at Dyer 175*v*.). These cases were often cited, and were accepted by the majority judges in Maunsell and Ladd's Case, for the proposition stated in the text. They were sometimes also cited for the proposition that laymen are not examinable at all except in testamentary and matrimonial cases. In the absence of independent reports, it is questionable whether they can be used for anything beyond 'temporal detriment'; they were never essential authority for any broader decision. The first two concerned Mass-attendance, the third usury, both offenses subject to 'penal' statutes.

[24] Berry's (or Birry's) Case, Godbolt 147; BL, Add. MS 25205, fol. 22: Michaelmas 3 James I, King's Bench.

Puritan prisoners in this case. Counsel were Nicholas Fuller and Henry Finch, the former the most prominent 'liberal lawyer' of his day and the latter also a lawyer of ability and reputation. In consequence of his role in the case, Fuller was unconscionably prosecuted for schism in the High Commission, and common law courts were unable to relieve him.[25] From jail, he wrote up and published his arguments in the case, improving them a bit in the character of a grandiose plea for the liberty of the subject, though his account is also useful as a supplement to other reports.

Owing to the blind spots typical of *Habeas Corpus* cases, Maunsell and Ladd is hard to reconstruct. As I construe it from the extensively reported remarks of counsel and judges, it presents fairly cleanly the question whether the High Commission may employ incriminatory inquisition in a case within its jurisdiction (participating in an unlawful religious conventicle) where there is no risk of exposure to secular detriment and the party is given sufficient notice of the subject of interrogation. The prisoners were jailed for refusing to answer a relevant question in the course of such examination. One prisoner was a cleric, but the other was a layman, and no distinction is reflected in the outcome.

Though not definitively reported, the result is clear from the judges' opinions: the prisoners lost the case. Three judges (Chief Justice Popham, Williams, and Tanfield, the last being the most undecided member of the court, who swung the decision) were against the prisoners; two (Fenner and Yelverton) were in their favor. The heart of the majority position was that the Supremacy Act intended to permit the High Commission to use sworn examination. The majority made a conscious effort to focus the issue on what the statute meant. The three judges were probably unimpressed by counsel's arguments that if the statute had a pro-Commission meaning it as good as repealed Magna Carta and the law of nature. The majority avoided saying whether or not there was a fundamental policy against self-incrimination, such that ordinary Church courts, without an enabling statute, might be flatly banned from requiring it, even of clergy. The speeches of the dissenters are not strongly reasoned. Perhaps some or all of Fuller's and Finch's arguments impressed them. Or perhaps they were simply firm in the plausible and precedented opinion, applicable also to the High Commission's sanctions, that the Supremacy Act did not authorize the Commission to do anything more than ecclesiastical courts generally could do. In that case the prisoners were improperly committed, whether or not ecclesiastical courts were prohibitable from demanding sworn examination in all circumstances.

[25] Fuller's Case is reported at 12 Coke 41, and Noy 127; BL, MS Hargrave 33, fol. 119 (the full record), and Add. MS 25213, fol. 81: Trinity–Michaelmas 5 James I, King's Bench.

Some of the arguments by Fuller and Finch go high. Those arguments have the look of playing to the gallery and were so perceived, irritably, by the majority judges. The lawyers can perhaps be criticized for never quite getting down to the chapter and verse of the Supremacy Act, for not saying enough in terms of pure construction to counter several judges' inclination (not itself very text-based) to think that parliament's setting up an extraordinary tribunal without any extraordinary powers would have been odd. My estimate, however, is that the lawyers' strategy was intelligent. The chances of proving by narrow arguments that the statute had the narrowest possible meaning were not good. Showing a massive commitment against self-incrimination deeply rooted in the English legal system, which it would be almost inconceivable for parliament to mean to contradict, was probably the best tactic, though quixotic.

The most striking feature of counsel's argument is their successful attempt to show that the common law contained a 'privilege against self-incrimination' in a sense specific enough to manage. While Fuller devoted time to pleading from Magna Carta, and Finch to arguing that the law of nature forbade demands that threatened self-incrimination, the lawyers clearly realized that the moral questionableness of requiring self-betrayal and the fact that the common law had no routine need to require it were insufficient reasons to deny inquisitorial procedure to ecclesiastical courts. Fuller set out to find a hard sense in which there was a common law rule against incriminatory questioning, so that ecclesiastical courts employing it could be said to contradict a common law rule, and parliament must have meant to permit such contradiction if it intended to permit its employment by the Commission. He discovered the rule that challenged jurors were examined on oath if the challenge was based on a blameless disqualification (e.g. kinship with a party) but were examined without oath if challenged for wrongdoing (e.g. taking a bribe). This and a few further close-grained arguments were not enough, however, to overcome three judges' intuitive and historical sense of what the authors of the Supremacy Act had had in mind.

III

The Maunsell and Ladd case was in the King's Bench. In the years immediately following, there were no complaints about High Commission examinations in that court, at least in reported cases. All complaints were brought in courts presided over by Coke, the Common Pleas up to 1613 and the King's Bench from 1613 to 1616. Lawyers representing the Commission's victims clearly expected greater favor from Coke and his colleagues than from other judges, which accords with Coke's reputation. How much did they get? Did Coke's courts reverse Maunsell and Ladd? The strict answer to the second question is No. From Coke's Common Pleas there are a few dicta reiterating the position that clergymen, not laymen, are examinable, with the clear but unargued implication that the Commission had no more power than the regular courts on that score.[26] The judges did not, however, face any head-on cases in which they had to consider carefully the bearing of the Supremacy Act on self-incrimination. They once applied the 'secret thoughts' limit on a minor point[27] and invoked 'secular detriment' a couple of times.[28] One clergyman accused of a serious religious offense failed on *Habeas Corpus*, confirming that the court did not accept an all-embracing 'privilege.'[29] Coke's court was undoubtedly the place to go if one had a complaint against the High Commission, since that court articulated and affirmed more clearly than had been done before the doctrine that the Com-

[26] See (*a*) Darrington's Case as reported in BL, MS Hargrave 52, fol. 20*v*. (note 12 above for the printed report on another point); (*b*) In *Huntley* v. *Clifford*, generalization by way of dictum (note 28); and (*c*) In Parson Wransfield's Case (note 29 below).

[27] Edwards' Case, 13 Coke 9: Michaelmas 6 James I, Common Pleas. High Commission was prohibited from proceeding against Edwards on several counts purely for want of substantive jurisdiction. For one count, the court gave an additional reason: Edwards was in effect accused of defaming an ecclesiastical dignitary as a cuckold by drawing a horn on a letter referring to him. The Commission proposed to ask him whether he intended the horn to have that meaning, thus violating the restriction on questions about 'secret thoughts.'

[28] See (*a*) *Huntley* v. *Clifford* (or Cage), 2 Brownlow and Goldesborough 14; BL, MS Hargrave 15, fol. 239. A case of record-breaking misconduct by the Commission: (1) it exceeded its jurisdiction (complaint of proposing to marry A in breach of a contract to marry B); (2) defendant was improperly imprisoned; (3) she was improperly forced to enter a bond against marrying A; and (4) it was then proposed to examine her so as to expose her to forfeiture of the bond. (Trickily – she objected to being so exposed, so the interrogatory was revised to ask her, not whether she had married A, but whether she lived with him in an unmarried condition. Thereby, the Commission recognized the 'temporal detriment' doctrine but note its non-recognition of an incapacity to examine a layman as to fornication. The illegality of (4) was given as a separate reason for Prohibition, and the trick was of course seen.)

Also (*b*), *Parson Latters* v. *Sussex*, Noy 151, Common Pleas, not dated but Cokean. A clergyman was declared unexaminable for simony because, by the statute 31 Elizabeth I, c. 6: *SR*, IV, pt II, 802–4, simoniacs were *ipso facto* deprived and therefore ousted from their temporal interest in the living.

[29] Parson Wransfield's Case, BL, MS Hargrave 52, fol. 15: Hilary 7 James I, Common Pleas. Basically: a clergyman is examinable as to inveighing against the Prayer Book, expressly called an 'enormous' offense. This is one of the few cases providing exposition of limits on examination when it is lawful as such: (1) while the examinee must be informed of the contents of the examination in advance, he need not be shown the actual questions: 'summary' information (not further explained) is enough; (2) after examination, examinee must be given a copy of the interrogatories (and presumably his answers); and (3) taking the *ex officio* oath to answer all questions does not bind the examinee to answer particular *ultra vires* questions and taking the oath (assuming the notice requirement as expounded is satisfied) is not a waiver of objection to the jurisdiction.

mission's statutory jurisdiction and secular sanctions were limited to a small number of 'enormous' crimes. It often prohibited the Commission on straight jurisdictional grounds. Counsel commonly threw generalized objections to inquisitorial examination into their complaints seeking Prohibitions, but the Prohibitions were almost always grantable by reason of jurisdiction without discussing self-incrimination. The motives for defining narrow bounds to the Commission's substantive jurisdiction probably came down to the belief that parliament could not have meant to undermine the regular ecclesiastical courts and to subject civil parties and trivial offenders to the inconvenience of non-local justice. This was true especially in view of another unrepealed statute whose purpose was to keep ecclesiastical justice local.[30] The Commission was considered an instrument against religious subversive activity beyond the capacity of the ordinary courts to handle, Papist at the time of the Supremacy Act, Puritan now. Coke's conduct as chief justice of the King's Bench testifies to his lack of tenderness for Puritans.

The only substantial case from Coke's King's Bench is the *Habeas Corpus* of Burrowes *et al.*[31] This case has virtually the opposite signifi-

[30] 23 Henry VIII, c. 9: *SR*, III, 377–8, was designed to protect diocesan jurisdiction against archdiocesan pre-emption. It was enforced and interpreted through many Prohibition cases, sometimes expressly cited as a reason for doubting that the Supremacy Act meant to permit the High Commission to take over routine diocesan business.

[31] The only other cases are rather tangled in reporting: *Sir William Boyer* v. *High Commission* (2 Bulstrode 182: Hilary 11 James I, King's Bench) upholds examination for simony as a crime, when the living will not be lost or the patronage rights affected. Here the clergyman who gained by simony was dead. The prosecution was apparently against someone else complicit in the simoniacal contract and simony is called 'enormous.' If the examinee was a layman, as he would appear to be, the case contradicts immunity for laymen as against the High Commission and agrees with Maunsell and Ladd's Case. In *Bradshawe* (or Bradstone) v. *High Commission* (2 Bulstrode 300; BL, Add. MS 25213, fol. 163: Michaelmas 12 James I, King's Bench) the Commission committed as many illegalities as in *Huntley* v. *Clifford* (see note 26), including examination exposing to forfeiture of an improperly exacted bond. Bradshawe was still only bailed on *Habeas Corpus* and told to reconcile himself with the Church: see, Burrowes *et al.*, which is variously named in the reports. Taken together, three prisoners besides Burrowes are named (Holt, Cox, and Dighton) and some report there were more: 3 Bulstrode 49, 1 Rolle 220, 337, and 410, Croke James I 388, and Moore 840; BL, MS Hargrave 47, fols. 60 and 114, MS Harleian 4561, fol. 251*v*., and Add. MS 25211, fol. 146*v*.: Trinity to Hilary 13 and Trinity 14 James I, King's Bench. The case receives radically different treatment in Levy, *Origins of the Fifth Amendment*.

A sequel to the case is covered by some reports. Two terms after being bailed, at least some of the prisoners were back in jail and attempting a *Habeas Corpus* again through a new lawyer. They essentially claimed that the Commission made improper demands on them when they went to 'make submission' according to the instructions of the King's Bench. The second round is not a self-incrimination case, since the prisoners were not asked to take an oath. It has some affinities, however, since the prisoners claimed that they were asked to express their submission in excessively general terms and in effect to accuse themselves of schism if they refused to. They got nowhere with the judges, Coke included.

cance from that which has been attributed to it, for it has been acclaimed as Coke's finest hour in broad opposition to self-incrimination. In fact, it shows Coke and his brethren leaning over backwards to avoid being harder on the High Commission than they could help. The case was all but open and shut on the merits. The prisoners were threatened with examination about offenses against the Prayer Book which, though proper to ecclesiastical courts and not disputed as appropriate to the High Commission, were also punishable by secular authorities under the Uniformity Act. Secular detriment should have sufficed to discharge them. Finch, counsel for these prisoners as for Maunsell and Ladd, urged that uncontroverted reason on his first appearance. In addition, he maintained that the prisoners were not apprised of the subject of the interrogation, a point that may not have been clearly inferrable from the brief and vague return on the writ but which came out in the course of the case as probably correct. Finally, while forgoing the altitude of his arguments in Maunsell and Ladd, Finch urged the rule that lay defendants are not examinable. On first hearing, Coke unsurprisingly expressed sympathy with the last argument. Thereafter, he did not advert to it, declining the opportunity to hold that the Supremacy Act did not take away the layman's exemption. His avoiding that was good judicial practice, since at no stage of the case did he or any other judge doubt that the prisoners were improperly committed, by virtue of secular detriment reinforced by insufficient notice of the articles of inquiry.

So believing, Coke allowed the case to drag on through two rounds of reargument, until the prisoners had spent some nine months in jail. His motives were frankly political. He wanted to give the Commission every chance to present its side of the case before releasing its prisoners; eventually the civilian Dr Martin was heard, with a legally unconstructive argument that unlimited powers for the Commission were a necessity of state. Coke told colleagues that he preferred to persuade the Commission, and expected he could, rather than use the *Habeas Corpus* against it. He advised the Commission from the Bench that it did not need inquisitorial powers for its laudable anti-Puritan purpose as much as it supposed and then bragged that he was its best friend. After so long a delay, Coke and the court bailed the prisoners and advised them to make their peace with the church, which did not release them outright. This half-measure rested on secular detriment and a new argument that, whatever powers the Commission had, it could not have power to imprison people forever for contempt, i.e. refusal to answer questions. In effect, discharge on the basis of secular detriment, which even the majority in Maunsell and Ladd conceded, was held off until the prisoners had served a substantial sentence. The conclusion had to be that the Commission's exceptional statutory power to imprison must have some quantitative limits. Coke's handling of the case may have been statesmanly rather than cowardly, and his private opinion on the Commission's examining powers may have been more restrictive than the accidents of litigation would ever force him to declare in a decision. Burrowes *et al.* definitely was not a triumphant moment for the 'privilege against self-incrimination.' Rather, the case reflected judges caught between sympathy, either politic or sincere, for some of the Commission's activities and a web of jurisdictional law that narrowed the scope for those activities.

After Coke's dismissal from the bench in 1616, there were very few cases on self-incrimination, none significant, and cases on the High Commission generally fell off. It seems dubious to explain this by the hypothesis that, without Coke, the courts lapsed into such indulgence of the Commission that complaining against it was futile. Although the Commission was never cut off from use of inquisition, limits to that, as to its jurisdiction and other procedures, were reasonably settled. Jurisdictional law on other subjects would be continuous right up to the civil war. Church interests and the autonomy of non-common law courts benefited from something of a conservative trend, as the bench shifted toward the generation of the Ship Money judges. This was mostly confined to a margin of difficult issues, with settled Elizabethan and Jacobean law consistently applied. The better hypothesis may therefore be that the High Commission grew more cautious and gave less occasion for legally plausible complaint. That need not mean it became less effective or less offensive to those it prosecuted. If by staying in its substantive bounds, refraining from inquisition when that was open to easy objection and stopping to think whether it was really necessary, it deprived its enemies of the forum of the common law courts. In so doing, it would have been following Coke's advice.

The bearing of jurisdictional cases from the sixteenth and early seventeenth centuries on self-incrimination for later law is tenuous. If one asks whether there was strong historical gravitation toward a privilege, such that not adopting one in new contexts would have to be seen as an anomalous failure to extend a traditional and expected feature of the legal system, then the answer is ambiguous. Opinion in favor of a comprehensive privilege, indeed the view that a privilege was part of the time-honored fundamental law, has deep historical roots. Such opinion did not start with, but was most vehemently articulated in, Puritan and politically 'left' circles in the seventeenth century. Like many attitudes, it passed into full respectability later. At the level of technical law, the acts of courts and the policies of the legislature, a general privilege cannot be asserted. One can still argue that a privilege was part of the common law, with as good (or no better) a claim to be binding on non-common law courts as other features.

The case from such sources as Magna Carta was as imaginative as most anachronistic cases from feudal law. It made as little impression on the courts as it deserved to. A narrower case could be patched together from miscellaneous aspects of the law, to stand against the larger truth that the absence of incriminating procedures at common law was mostly a result of the whole way the system worked, like the absence of a two witness requirement. The larger truth prevailed, in the sense that the courts never said that jurisdictions using civil–canon procedure could not expose individuals to self-incrimination. Had they done so, the argument would be strengthened that a common law which had traditionally had little need for a privilege must adopt one in later circumstances. It is largely an accident of the mixed legal system in England, and the law for regulating it developed by the early modern courts, that opportunities for incriminatory investigation were kept in narrow bounds. The fact that there was little space for it must have contributed to the future's impression that it was more decisively struck down than it was.

Quoting the Commons, 1604–1642

J. H. HEXTER

Some months ago I had a chance to talk shop with my old friend Geoffrey Elton. He suggested that the editorial work formerly done by Professor Wallace Notestein and his associates and students, more recently by the Yale Center for Parliamentary History and those associated directly or indirectly with it, should not be thought of as solving but raising certain problems. The one that concerned him went like this:

From recent and current editorial efforts we have had and are about to have floods of readily accessible information about who did and said what in the English parliaments of the early Stuarts. It is fuller information than survives – probably more than was ever recorded – for any representative assembly at any time or place in history before the early seventeenth century, fuller than exists for such an assembly anywhere for a century and a half thereafter. For each parliament from 1604 to the outbreak of the civil war in 1642, we have two or more, often many more, independent accounts of what went on in the House of Commons. For certain days at the peak of the recording mania, there are eleven such accounts. How, Professor Elton wondered, does one evaluate what these enterprising record-keepers got around to recording? From the 1620 parliaments there survive records of proceedings from the hand and mind of Nathaniel Rich, son of a byblow of the first baron Rich, the unequivocally Puritan adviser of his equivocally Puritan cousin, Robert Rich, second earl of Warwick; from John Pym, client of the earl of Bedford, future leader of the House of Commons in the Long Parliament; from Sir Thomas Wentworth, Yorkshire magnate, future earl of Strafford, who by the contrivance of the House which Pym led was brought to the block in 1641; from Sir John Eliot, the eloquent Cornishman whose long feud with Wentworth ended only when Eliot died in the Tower in 1632, unwilling to seek pardon for his part in disrupting the 1629 session of the House. These were men of significant stature, men whose intervention in debate or shrewdness won them eminence in the assemblies the proceedings of which they recorded. When we look into what they tell us about the doings of the House of Commons, we must keep in mind that we are not looking at transcriptions from a tape recorder. Instead, we have before us what men who were engaged participants in the events saw fit to record about them.

This is especially so in the case of documents like Pym's journals, or Sir John Eliot's *Negotium Posterorum*. Both men wrote their accounts not during but after the events they describe, presumably working from notes supplemented by memory. What we have is not their notes on speeches, taken as they heard them, but later reflections on those speeches; in the case of Eliot, considerably later. To catch the surface manifestations of the difference this makes, one need only compare the record of a day's proceedings in 1621 in the diary of John Pym with a record of the same day in the diary of Sir Thomas Barrington. The latter tried to get down everything that was said when it was said. He gives us more information about what was actually said and done than Pym does. Sometimes, however, he makes less good sense of a speech than the man who made it probably did. On the other hand, after reflection Pym probably made rather better sense of a speech than the speaker himself had done *ex tempore* when he addressed the House.

Moreover, what holds for the more eminent members of the House of Commons who recorded its proceedings holds as well for more obscure diarists. Consider Sir Richard Grosvenor's diary for 1628, for example. On casual examination, it appears to be an extensive and unselective *omnium-gatherum* of hasty notes, as much as Grosvenor could get down about what went on. Yet Grosvenor's own contributions to the debate are remarkably consistent in tone.[1] In the first debate on supply on 4 April he wryly expressed the hope that the king wished only to shear the members of his flock, not to skin them. All his later interventions – there were only four in all – express dislike of the actions of the king's government in the past or distrust of it in the future. Can it be that the hostility which Grosvenor so consistently displays in his speeches in parliament, does not seep through into his notes?

This, I take it, is a particular example of the question that Elton in-

[1] A speech is assigned to Grosvenor on 4 April 1628 by BL, MS Stowe 366, on 7 May by himself, on 24 May by Proceedings and Debates and himself, on 2 June by himself, and on 14 June by Newdegate: Robert C. Johnson, Mary Frear Keeler, Maija Jansson Cole, William B. Bidwell (eds.), *Commons Debates 1628* (4 vols., New Haven, Yale University Press, 1977–8), II, 308; III, 310, 596, 600; IV, 54, 326. For the location of 'Proceedings and Debates', see *ibid.*, I, 5 and 86.

tended to raise.[2] As to Grosvenor and most of the other men who recorded proceedings in the parliaments held from 1604 to 1649, the answer to Elton's question is, 'We do not know.' We do not know because in only one case does the political attitude of the writer show itself conspicuously in the account – Eliot in the *Negotium Posterorum*; and in only one has the sort of intensive scrutiny of the work been undertaken that makes the identification of the political inclination of the diarist feasible – Sir Simonds D'Ewes in his journal of the Long Parliament.[3]

I

Formulations of historical problems by scholars whose acuity I admire seem to affect me by sending me off on lines of inquiry tangential to the ones they propose. Professor Elton's statement of the problem of discovering the biases in the accounts of parliaments under the early Stuarts fixed my attention on a problem I had hitherto skirted by pretending it was not there; how ought one to go about *quoting* these accounts? Or more precisely, in drawing on the accounts of early Stuart parliaments, when is a historian justified in employing those standard conventions of quotation which almost all historians use in their scholarly work?

These conventions may turn out to be inconvenient, deceptive, or unduly restrictive with respect to the records of the parliaments between 1600–1649. Should we not then modify them in applying them to these records? Perhaps, but nothing that follows should be construed as a general attack on these conventions. The nearly unanimous and consistent adherence of historians to the conventions of quotation is itself the best certification of their convenience and soundness. So is the protection that historians throw around the conventions by publicly censuring in the

[2] The preceding paragraphs are not a reproduction of Professor Elton's remarks at the time of our encounter, but rather an inferential extension of them with concrete instances supplied. I hope I have done justice to Professor Elton's perplexity. Our actual exchange was less linear and somewhat more halting than what I have written. It was rendered discontinuous by the frequent and irrelevant interventions of Jack Daniels. I cannot in all candor claim that at the time either Geoffrey Elton or I complained of or showed any signs of resentment at the interruptions. To the contrary, we positively encouraged them.

[3] The scrutiny of D'Ewes was conducted by editors of two segments of his Journal: Wallace Notestein (ed.), *The Journal of Sir Simonds D'Ewes, from the Beginning of the Long Parliament* . . . (New Haven, Yale University Press, 1923), x–xi; Willson H. Coates (ed.), *The Journal of Sir Simonds D'Ewes, from the First Recess of the Long Parliament* . . . (New Haven, Yale University Press, 1942), xli–xliv; also, J. H. Hexter, *The Reign of King Pym* (Cambridge, Mass., Harvard University Press, 1941), 31–2, 52, 65–6. An investigation into that peculiar account, 'Proceedings and Debates,' pursued in connection with the introduction to *Commons Debates 1628*, I, 8–20, was neither intensive enough nor purposefully directed enough to make out the political slant of the compiler or compilers of that work.

review pages of their trade journals fellow historians who are careless about keeping strictly to those conventions. So much is this the case that casualness about conformity to the conventions of quotation is enough to undermine confidence in any historical study in which such casualness is frequent. The most meticulous adherence to the conventions will not make a writer of history a good historian. Frequent lapse of quotation from the standard that the conventions help insure does make a bad historian.[4]

What are these conventions?

The conventions involve the use of four sorts of special typographic signals:

(1) The two quotation indicators, either

(*a*) quotation marks or inverted commas '[quotation begins . . . quotation ends],' or

(*b*) indentation of the entire quoted passage and decrease of the space between the lines.

Both indicators set off the quoted material from the rest of the text.

(2) The ellipsis (. . .) which within quotation indicators indicates

(*a*) at the beginning of the quoted passage, that the beginning of the quoted sentence is there omitted, or

(*b*) at the end of the passage, that the end is there omitted, or

(*c*) in the middle, that between the word preceding the ellipsis and the word following, a word or words from the source quoted have here been omitted.

(3) The brackets ([ ]) which indicate that the words or letters between the brackets are not in the source quoted, but have been inserted by the writer in the interest of clarity or syntactical propriety.

(4) The superscript number in the text (text^{n}) which indicates that among the footnotes or endnotes readers will find a note of corresponding number, and that if the superscript number appears at the end of a quotation, the footnotes will contain a reference guiding readers accurately and precisely to the quoted matter.[5]

Clearly the conventions of quotation are designed to keep the historian honest at a basic level. They signal to the reader exactly what words the historian claims are in the document, whether he has omitted words from it or inserted words in it, and where one can find the quotation. This enables anyone to verify whether the words quoted are actually what and

[4] Refusal to employ the conventions does not make a bad historian. In *The Armada*, Garrett Mattingly refused to employ them. Nevertheless, he meticulously complied with the rules of which the conventions stand as a guarantee. *The Armada* (Boston, Houghton Mifflin, 1959), is a great historical work made no greater by its rejection of the conventions.

[5] There is a fifth, less compelling convention that some historians adhere to: when a source frequently resorts to elisions internal to words, spell out the words putting the elided letters in brackets.

where the writer says they are, and whether in its original context (n *op. cit.*, p. 77) the quoted passage will bear the construction that the historian has placed on it. These are elementary matters, indeed; so elementary that with respect to conventions of quotation, the more spacious intellects in the profession may consider insistence on precise protocol a symptom of the unfortunate propensity to triviality and pedantry of the profession itself. There may be some justice in this view. Still, that protocol helps to impose honest care on a cluster of people, the professional historians, whose natural propensity to carelessness and dishonesty is of the ordinary human dimension and who, though not propelled toward cheating by love of gain (not much is offered by way of a money payoff), may be steadily moved toward it by sloth and powerfully by pride or vanity.

II

Suppose then two historians, one reporting on what Robert Cecil said in the debate in the Commons on monopolies on 27 November 1601, the other on what William Hakewill said in the debate in the Commons on the Lords' addition to the Petition of Right on 22 May 1628. The first historian writes:

> On 27 November Secretary Cecil began his intervention in the debate on monopolies by saying, 'I promised to be as silent as I could. Amongst much speech of the wise, there wants not much folly.'[122]
>
> [122]Hayward Townshend, *Historical Collections*, p. 257.

Simple and forthright, although not perhaps entirely clear. A historian might be inclined to explicate the quotation in the interest of clarity. He would not want to alter or modify it. Nor does he feel impelled to the pedantry of writing 'Hayward Townshend says Cecil began his speech by noting . . .'[6]

Now the second historian – perhaps he writes:

> I. Hakewill began his speech by noting, 'Either this addition is idle or operative. If it be idle, it is not worthy either of the Lords' or our wisdom.'*
>
> **Commons Debates 1628*, III, 532.

[6] Nor being an honest man does he try to confirm the Townshend version by citing the D'Ewes version of Cecil's speech from that early seventeenth century scholar's edition of the proceedings of the parliaments of Elizabeth. He knows that the D'Ewes version offers no independent witness, but merely a transcription of Townshend's journal: Hayward Townshend, *Historical Collections: or, An Exact Account of the Proceedings of the Four Last Parliaments of Q. Elizabeth . . .* (London, T. Basset, W. Crooke, and W. Cademan, 1680).

But then, he could have written:

II. Hakewill began his speech by noting, 'This addition either is idle or operative. If it be an idle addition it is neither fit for them to offer or us to receive . . .'*

Commons Debates 1628, III, 545

or

III. Hakewill began his speech by noting, 'This addition is either idle or operative. If idle, one, it is neither worthy of the wisdom of the Lords to offer or us to accept . . .'*

Commons Debates 1628, III, 547

or

IV. Hakewill began his speech by noting, 'Either this addition is idle or operative. If idle, then not worthy of the wisdom of the Lords to offer, nor ours to receive . . .'*

Commons Debates 1628, III, 551

'Well,' one might be inclined to say, 'what's the difference? The statements are not absolutely identical; still they all say much the same thing.' For a moment we will leave these obviously sensible remarks aside in order to bring attention to a more conspicuous difficulty. On the face of the evidence, our notional historian might as well have written:

V. Hakewill began his speech by noting, 'I fear we err in our proceedings. If every man should speak at large and of several matters I fear our pains would prove fruitless. We should rather now treat by logic than rhetoric.'*

Commons Debates 1628, III, 537

or

VI. Hakewill began his speech by noting, 'Touching the method of our proceedings, some have made objections to the Lords' reasons, some have added reasons. Moved that we should be rather logicians than rhetoricians.'*

Commons Debates 1628, III, 541–2

Or finally, our historian could have written:

VII. Mr Hakewill took no part in the debate in the House about the Lords' additions.*

Commons Debates 1628, III, 546–7

MS Harleian 5324 does not give Hakewill any part in the debate that day.

But of course that is nonsense, a particularly clear instance of the fallacy of the *argumentum ex silentio*. Six diarists recorded a speech by Hakewill. Together they note twenty-one members speaking. The diarist of MS Harleian 5324 who omits Hakewill also omits ten other members quoted by the others. We take his omission of Hakewill for evidence of his lapse, not of Hakewill's silence. This implies a rule: when six other sources record a member as speaking, and one does not, it is reasonable to suppose that he spoke.

Yet surely to persuade us of the 'quotability' of a passage we do not demand five confirmations that something of the sort was said. In four of the accounts (I–IV) the first remark ascribed to Hakewill raises the either/or issue: the clause that the Lords wanted to latch on to the Petition of Right was either idle or operative. In V and VI Hakewill first suggests that the members discuss the Lords' addition to the Petition logically and concisely rather than rhetorically. But then accounts V and VI both go on 'Either the addition is idle or operative (V)'; 'Either this addition is idle or operative (VI).' Without trying to decide between the wordings of the writer of MS Stowe 366 (V) and of Sir Richard Grosvenor (VI) surely we must agree that in an account of the proceedings on 22 May 1628, a sentence that started 'Hakewill began his speech by noting . . .' could only properly go on by quoting V or VI, not by quoting I–IV. The evidence is that Hakewill *may* have said either V or VI first, that he surely did *not* say any of I–IV first. We can think of no plausible reason why two narrators, MS Stowe 366 and Grosvenor, should have collaborated on a frivolous fraud.

So V and VI are mutually confirming as to what Hakewill said first. Is such mutual confirmation a condition, a *sine qua non* of the use of quotation indicators after 'Hakewill began his speech by noting . . .'?

On at least three grounds we should hesitate to lay down such a rule. First, although it reduces the proper choices in the case of Hakewill's speech from six to two, it does not enable us to choose between the two, which are not identical: do we use indicators of quotation with V or VI, or both, or neither? Second, it would have the curious effect of barring a good deal of quotation from Grosvenor's diary, the account of proceedings in 1628 which offers us more information on those who spoke in the House than any other. During five sampled weeks, Grosvenor's diary records 60 per cent more speeches than the account with the next highest number.[7] Of a good many of those speeches he alone provides us with any evidence. Are we barred from quoting a member because only one independent witness, Grosvenor, ascribes a speech to him? One may hesitate to say so. If one does say so, by parity of reason one must never quote from Hayward Townshend in 1601 since he is the sole surviving witness to the words used in the debate. In effect that first historian, with whom

[7] *Commons Debates 1628,* I, 24.

we launched this inquiry, confidently 'quoted' Cecil's 'speech' in 1601 not because he knew so much about what Cecil said in the House, but because he knew so little. It is because the second historian knew so much more about Hakewill's 'speech' that we are in trouble about how to 'quote' it.

One more point, trivial perhaps, but designed to mark sharply the dilemma that Hakewill's speech confronts us with, as do hundreds of other speeches of which *Commons Debates 1628* offers us divergent versions from several different accounts. Suppose after dealing with Hakewill's prefatory remarks one decides to quote his remark on the addition to the Petition. How does one decide which of the similar but not identical six versions to quote? Roll the dice? All right, but suppose the roll comes up with III, Edward Nicholas's version? According to him remember, Hakewill said:

> . . . This addition is either idle or operative. If idle, one, it is neither worthy of the wisdom of the Lords to offer or us to accept.

At this point one might want to pull away from one's precommitment to crap-shooting. Why? Well, what about that 'If idle, *one* . . .?' One *what*? Nicholas does not say. There is no 'two,' so the 'one' dangles with no rational syntactical function. Perhaps someone has misread Nicholas's always ill-written text. One writes to the editors of *Commons Debates 1628*: 'In the speech that Nicholas ascribes to Hakewill on 22 May, did you by any chance omit "an" between "if" and "idle," and insert a comma between "idle" and "one"? Should it read "If an idle one, it is," etc.? Answer from the editors: 'May we refer you to *Commons Debates 1628*, I, 47, Editorial Conventions: Punctuation. "We have . . . modernized punctuation." There is no punctuation in Nicholas's MS between "idle" and "one." Nor is there an "an" between "if" and "idle." Yours sincerely, the Editors.'

So much for that. But stop a moment. Why did we send a query to the editors in the first place? What assumption underlies the query? Inexplicit but unmistakably present in the question is the assumption that if we achieve a wholly coherent and syntactically proper emended text for the Nicholas entry, we will have come closer to what Hakewill actually said on 22 May 1628. This is to commit ourselves to a peculiar view of the character of oral discourse. We imply that such discourse standardly meets the exacting criteria of clarity, coherence, and syntactical tidiness that intellectuals or pedants demand of *written* expository prose. That is why we want to anchor that floating 'one' to an article 'an' and an adjective 'idle.' Yet from daily experience with ordinary oral discourse we know that in actual speech 'one' is about as likely to be floating the way it is in the Nicholas version as it is to be syntactically anchored. On the face of our general knowledge and our daily experience, the assimilation, as above, of oral discourse to formal expository prose is flat absurd; that is not at all the way people talk to each other.

III

During the past few decades we have been made acutely conscious of the gap between oral communication and written discourse. We have read transcriptions of verbatim reports of testimony taken by trained court stenographers, so we know that not only witnesses but their interrogators, trying to phrase telling questions, speak not in riddles but in muddles. Above all, we know from those perfectly faithful minute-to-minute transcripts minus eighteen minutes, the Nixon tapes, that the exchanges of a president with his closest advisers reached a level of precision and clarity only slightly superior to what could be attained by pre-kindergarten kids high on pot.

And so circuitously, via the manifold reports of debates in the parliaments of England in the 1620s, we have come to a reformulated general question. We have moved from 'What *are* the rules for quotation of speech found in historical sources?' to 'What *should be* the rules for quotation of speech found in historical sources?' The reformulation is appropriate and timely because, as far as I know, there currently exists no considered answer to the question. There is none because *the orientation of the conventions of quotation worked out by professional historians and properly imposed by them on fledgling scholars and amateur historians lies toward written utterance intended from the start by its writer to be read by someone and to be intelligible to that reader.* Such, for example, in the 1600s are a dispatch of the Venetian ambassador, the Statute of Monopolies, the last will and testament of William Shakespeare. When we employ the conventions of quotations on these items, we are claiming that at such and such a time and place, such and such words, the ones enclosed in quotation marks, were set down – that dispatch, that statute, that will; and that in the repository or edition indicated in the footnote and at the indicated place, page, or folio; anyone who chooses can verify the internal accuracy and contextual propriety of the quotation. If we put quotation indicators around the reports of speeches of the members of the House of Commons in the 1620s that we find in the contemporary accounts of its sessions, they do not have the same or an analogous signification. They do not signify that inside the quotation marks are the words of a member of the House precisely as he spoke them. They do not mean that by referring to an actual record of the member's spoken words, an inquirer can check on whether the report is accurate. There is no such record to refer to. All the indicators mean is that one historian, for reasons he usually leaves unexplained, has decided to grace with the authority and added rhetorical force of quotation one among three, or six, or ten, alternative and, on the face of it, equally authoritative versions of the same speech. In such circumstances, from being a pointer to the single authentic record, the quotation indicators become a pointer only to a historian's whimsical choice. If the accompanying footnote adheres to the conventional form of citation for the quotation from sources originally written, it will make it easy for the skeptical reader to check on whether the historian has copied the version he selected accurately. Ironically, however, it will not make it easy to check that version against the *prima facie* equally good alternative versions since the latter will not be cited at all. Nor will it make it easier for a reader to find those versions.

The question of what the rules of quotation ought to be is particularly poignant to me because I am about to spend the little time that is left me for the practice of my craft amid the apparently roiling anarchy created by the survival of several accounts of proceedings of the House of Commons for each parliament under the early Stuarts. This situation, however, is only an acute instance of a chronic problem. Historians who use taped interviews, full stenographic transcripts, or the 'improved' versions of the speeches that representatives and senators have placed by a due exercise of privilege in the Congressional Record have to face difficulties of a different species, but of the same genus. I have by no means seen my way to the bottom of my own problem. Still, it won't go away. Moreover, in varying forms and at varying levels of intensity, many historians encounter it, whether or not they are conscious of the encounter. So perhaps the best thing for me to do is to think through some ways that have occurred to me for dealing with the particular form the problem takes for historians of early Stuart England. Proposals which are the fruit of that effort will then be available for modification or rejection by historians who deal with oral discourse of different times and involving a different sort of record. It will also be available for rigorous criticism by historians who deal with the debate of English parliaments in the early seventeenth century. By such a dialectical procedure we historians may eventually arrive at a common view of the etiquette and the conventions of quotation for oral discourse. Those conventions may be as clear, efficient, and codifiable as the ones all historians hold to with respect to formal written communication. We certainly have not got so far yet, and we will never get there at all until we begin to think our way toward the solution of this historiographic problem.

IV

The foundation doctrine is clear-cut. Rules for quoting records of speech, as those for quoting records of writing, should aim at maximum verisimilitude. Since the end is the same, our first inclination may be to believe that the method of achieving it should be the same. The method in the case of written records is a cluster of techniques for establishing the 'original text,' for finding the 'authoritative source' of the texts. This will usually be what the persons who set down the texts wrote or had written for them and authorized. The extraordinary pains and patience that scholars invest in establishing the original text of, say, *The Canterbury Tales*, testify to their view that the closer we get to that text, the closer we are to what six hundred years ago Geoffrey Chaucer meant for his readers to read and to accept as signifying his intention.

When we face the written reports of speech our first impulse will be to follow the rule we follow with respect to written communication. That rule would require us in the interest of verisimilitude to seek out the 'original text' of the speech, the report of it which most exactly reproduces the sounds made by the speaker, as the best written source reproduces the original text of the writer. How simply and how effectively such a rule would resolve our perplexities about whom to quote when as in 1628! Although we have several reports of the same speech, according to that rule we would almost always quote from the parliamentary diary kept by Sir Richard Grosvenor, knight of the shire that session for his county, Cheshire. Of the reports of proceedings of the House that are the notes taken by members as the events of the day unfolded, Grosvenor's is ordinarily the fullest by a good deal. Consider, for example, the record for the week of 5 May. Of the five diarists who left notes during that span, the next fullest diary is only one-third as long as Grosvenor's, and all the other four taken together are not significantly longer than his alone. On no single day during that week does any other diary attain the length of Grosvenor's.[8] For one day, Thursday 8 May, MS Stowe 366, one of the narratives written up after the debate it reports, is a bit longer. Both of the narratives, MS Stowe 366 and 'Proceedings and Debates,' however, must be deemed corrupt by the standard of proximity to the spoken word. They are both mainly the products of memory, probably refreshed by

[8] *Commons Debates 1628*, II, 250–364.

jottings, written down several hours or days after the events they describe. On the analogy of the rules for identifying or reconstructing the original written document such narratives stand at two removes of authenticity from an original source, the speech itself; they are the analogues of mere copies of copies.

Do we really want to cling to the analogy to written communication, however, when our source is a written record of oral communication? Compare the Stowe account of Robert Phelips's speech on 8 May with Grosvenor's notes, by that analogy, the most 'authentic' source. According to Grosvenor, what Phelips said went this way:

Though the country be unstable, yet in this way they
will pay cheerfully.
2 subsidies in July
1 subsidy in October papists double these[9]
1 subsidy in January
1 subsidy in April

According to the MS Stowe 366 diarist, Phelips (characteristically) called attention to the general point that the turning of the Commons to provision of supply refuted charges that the House was unready to provide for the king's needs.

I am marvellous glad to see this prisoner break loose, to the confusion of all such reports as have cast censures and misinterpretations on the proceedings of this House. There are 2 things considerable: his Majesty's occasions and the people's poverty. Yet I doubt not but in these necessitous times we shall proceed with cheerfulness.[10]

Only after that does the MS Stowe set down Phelips's proposed calendar of payment, the only thing recorded by Grosvenor. Here a doctrinaire attempt to adhere to the rules for quoting written communication would deprive us of the better part of what Phelips was recorded as saying on 8 May. Among seven recorders of the debate that day, only one, a man who wrote up his notes after the day's sessions and is therefore barred by our rule, bothered to do justice to Phelips's concern.

Or consider the following passages in which Grosvenor and MS Stowe 366 are reporting the same segment of a speech by the able lawyer and experienced MP, John Glanville. First Grosvenor:

There is in the King concerning some statute laws a trust, of others not; no trust in him to dispense or be above the common law. The statutes where in he is trusted are some penal laws prohibiting such things as are not *mala in se*. He may grant to

[9] *Commons Debates 1628*, III, 330.
[10] *Commons Debates 1628*, III, 337b–8a.

particular persons with a *non obstante* to transpose well, set at such a price, etc. . . .[11]

Then Stowe:

. . . now there is in a king for some statute laws some trust, in others none, for he cannot be above common law. There is a trust of some penal laws, not *mala per se* but *mala prohibita*; this has been long executed by kings with a *non obstante*. . . .[12]

These passages have two things in common. First, the men who wrote them down made a serious effort to get what they heard Glanville say straight. Second, to render what Glanville said intelligible to most readers, either passage will require some explication. They both try to report accurately the distinction Glanville made between two kinds of laws. There are laws that forbid certain action. The right of the authority that declares those actions wrong to forbid them renders the actions wrong (*mala prohibita*). In a rightful exercise of his prerogative, the king can set such laws aside by dispensing men from their penalties. On the other hand, there are actions that are intrinsically wrong (*mala in se*). From the penalties of laws against such actions the king has no right to dispense, for example, from the law of trespass, because to do so is to deprive an injured party of his common law rights and remedies.

Here is an instance where quotation is desirable because explication is necessary. Explication demands a passage to explicate. An apt quotation from the debate provides the firm foundation on which a structure of explication can be reared without wobbles or waste. For purposes of explication, the Stowe version of the passage in Glanville's speech is better than the Grosvenor version because whatever needs clarification in it bears directly on Glanville's allusion to a conception not easy to grasp, the conception of a prerogative that is at once absolute and limited by law. In explicating Grosvenor's version, one would have to explain that the phrase 'no trust in him to dispense or be above the common law' did not mean that the king had no prerogative to dispense with the penalties exacted by the statute law, but only, as the following sentence appears to indicate, that that authority stops at the point where it would deprive men of remedies that are theirs by common law. This indicates that for clarity's sake we should insert 'with' between 'dispense' and 'or.' This point is actually made economically and exactly by Nathaniel Rich in his version of Glanville's speech. 'Laws that confer a right upon the subject

11 *Commons Debates 1628*, III, 539; one might be inclined here to check in the MS whether 'transpose well' might not as well have read, 'transport wool.'

12 *Commons Debates 1628*, III, 536.

are in the nature of common law, and never was there a trust left to the King to dispense or to go above them.'[13]

And here we arrive at the crux of a problem concerning quotation from the record of spoken communication that one who writes about early Stuart parliaments is continuously confronted with. Grosvenor's record of Glanville's speech is the fullest *direct* record of it. It consists of notes taken as Glanville spoke. Yet it does not make one significant position expounded in that speech as clear as does a 'compiled' account, MS Stowe 366, set down in its present form at least several hours after Glanville spoke. Moreover, we have no way of knowing whether this inferior clarity was the result of Grosvenor's inadequacy as a note-taker or of his fidelity to what he heard Glanville say. In short, it may be that while Grosvenor got closest to what Glanville actually said, Stowe ended up closer to what he really meant.

This is a consequence of a difference between the record of oral communication and the record of written documents. The written record of a written document should *be* that document, or should reproduce it exactly enough to enable a user to quote the record confident that he is in no significant way deviating from the precise array of signs that appear in the original document.[14] It enables Reader A to say, 'That is exactly what X wrote,' and to validate his allegation by reference to the document, leaving B only to counter with, 'But that is not *really* what X meant.' This will be difficult for B to demonstrate, because the very process of writing creates a presumption that one means to write precisely what one writes. Thus writing usually produces an 'authentic' document.

No such presumption holds with respect to oral communication, particularly with respect to extemporary oral communication. Until about a half century ago, oral, or perhaps better, face-to-face communication could not be fully recorded. Only then did it become possible by videotape to reproduce the gestures of hands, face, and torso – the body language – that accompanied (and clarified) the sound sequences of speech. The technique of making an adequate sound track is less than a century old. Before that time, there is no audio record of any person's words to give us direct evidence of how the words sounded.[15] If therefore we insist

[13] *Commons Debates 1628*, III, 349.

[14] The qualification 'in no significant way' is necessary to allow for the American practice of modernizing spelling and punctuation, which the writer endorses.

[15] Occasionally a skillful recorder of debate such as the man who recorded debates in the House of Commons for Hansard in 1811 could convey a powerful impression that a speaker was drunk, as Mr Fuller appears to have been when he assailed Catholic Emancipation on 22 February: Thomas C. Hansard (ed.), *The Parliamentary Debates from the Year 1803 . . .* (London, 1812), XIX, 49–50.

on the exact sequence of sounds made by speakers as the foundation of our conventions of quotation for spoken discourse, we are in deep trouble. We would nearly have to limit ourselves to surviving copies of formal addresses and orations, that is, to those rare instances of oral discourse that are most like, indeed nearly identical to, written discourse, the kind of oral discourse to which the written is usually antecedent.

And here we need to reflect on the asymmetries we keep encountering when we try to treat the record of spoken discourse as analogous to that of written discourse. In respects significant to the task of a historian, the analogy is a misperception. It holds only in the rare case of the set speech based on script or memorization. Oral discourse ordinarily diverges so sharply from written discourse that our structure of psychological expectations for receiving the two, and our psycho-sensory procedures for understanding them, are also drastically divergent. Ordinarily, a certified true copy of a written communication – a letter, a writ, a short story – provides a reader with an exact view of just what the writer intends to say in writing. In contrast, a stenographer who takes down all the words emitted by a speaker in the course of an ordinary discussion will not produce just what the speaker intends in speaking. The reason is that although the *process* of ordinary speaking is like the *process* of ordinary writing, compared with the process of writing, that of speaking suffers severe disadvantages. The process of both is *editorial*. The careful writer stops to think of the just word or phrase in the course of writing, strikes out words or sentences, puts others in their place, drops whole paragraphs as redundant or otiose, shifts word order to achieve emphasis. Such a writer makes whatever changes he needs to achieve whatever effects he intends, often with complete success if the composition is a clause in a contract, less often if it is a line in a sonnet. Scarcely any of this editorial work appears in the final document. And of course, with any moderately apt writer, the bulk of the editorial work does not reach paper at all, even in the roughest first draft. The writer does his editing in the pauses between the physical acts of writing. The pause may be momentary, or a break for coffee, or an hour or so break for lunch. Where circumstances permit, the stop may even be days or weeks while the writer lets things sort themselves out. On a tighter schedule a writer will select one line of thought to follow among the several that come to his mind, pull one set of synonyms from his memory bank out of the many on deposit there, choose a particular syntactical structure among a half-dozen possible ones – all in a few minutes. The final document, the one the historian uses, bears no marks of editorial work. That has all ended in the waste basket, or has never gotten written down at all.

In *ex tempore* or impromptu oral communication, a great deal of this editorial work – both what would appear in a rough written draft, and what would not appear at all – is audible in the sound track recording of speech and becomes visible in any verbatim stenographic report – the hesitations, the repetitions, the restatements, the confusions, the syntactical gaffes, the ill-chosen words, the failures to follow through. The speaker ordinarily does not have the luxury of a week's reflection in which to tidy up his ideas, and set them in neat array. His audience won't sit still for a week. They won't even sit still for a minute. Most oral communication does not result in disastrous misunderstanding only because, by relying on the sensitivity of his audience, a competent speaker can make a mass of inexplicit deletions from what he has already said. These work well enough face-to-face. The audience sees, hears, and senses the speaker's shifts. In verbatim transcription, however, these shifts take on the look of random convulsions. One of the standard interjections of speakers in conversation underlines the editorial intention that accompanies much oral discourse. Fourth only to 'er,' 'umm,' and 'uh' is 'I mean.' And 'I mean' is there to say to the audience, 'I didn't quite mean what I just said. I more nearly mean what I am about to say – I hope.' This sort of amendment is inevitable because the circumstances of dialogue do not allow an active participant the pauses to reflect that are commonplace in composing a written document.

Of course, any competent listener knows all this. In following oral discourse, all of us all the time filter out not only random external noise – the backfiring of motorcycles, the whistling of the wind, the whir of the air-conditioning – but also the so-to-speak random internal noises the speaker himself makes – his hesitations, his false starts, his implicit deletions. And that is precisely what the speaker wants and expects us to do. He wants those who hear him to carry away the best formulation of his intentions that he achieves in the course of his oral meandering, not the sound track that registers the slow-crawling, staggering course of those meanderings vocal inch by vocal inch.

There are procedures that in order to produce a valid record do justice to what we know about the relation of performance to intention in oral discourse, or to put it in Platonic terms, of actuality to reality. In organizing and managing a conference participated in by articulate intellectuals, a friend of mine with wide experience records the entire conference on tape. He also has relays of pairs of skilled note-takers – often junior law school faculty – take notes on the discussion among the conferees. After the conference, each pair write up a smooth version of their notes, ironing out divergences. Then with the write-up in hand, they listen to the tapes.

From them they draw anything that they missed in their note-taking which appears to express the intention of a speaker better – that is, more fully, clearly, and cogently – than their notes do, and fit it into the final write-up. It is this final write-up that becomes the record of the conference. I assume that conferees prefer a record so arrived at to the earlier write-up of the proceedings from the notes, to the rough notes taken by each note-taker, and certainly to the incoherent sound track of the meeting. They do so because without saying what they did not say, without putting words into their mouths, a write-up so arrived at comes as close as practicable to doing justice to what they *really* meant to say.[16]

V

In deciding on the ground rules for quoting from records of speech in the parliaments of the early Stuarts, these conference procedures seem to provide a functional analogue to work from in contrast to the mechanical analogue of the written document. They do so because those records actually yield documents roughly corresponding to the materials described above. First, there are the analogues to the reworked notes of the skilled note-takers – the reworked notes of the clerk of the official Journal of the House of Commons for 1604, the anonymous journal and John Pym's account for 1621, Pym again for 1624, Pym and (to be used with caution) Eliot's *Negotium Posterorum* for 1625, and Proceedings and Debates and MS Stowe 366 for 1628 – all reworkings of rough notes that no longer survive except in the case of the Diarium, the clerk's rough notes for some of the sessions of James I's first parliament. Second, there are notes of proceedings taken in the House while it was in session, between eight and ten of these for each of the parliaments of 1621, 1624 and 1628. Neither individually nor collectively are these notes the equivalent of a tape recording of the proceedings or of a transcript of such a recording. The better sets of notes are probably a good deal more orderly and intelligible than such a transcript would have been; that is to say, the note-takers

16 'Really' is one of the words that historians do well to avoid ordinarily. I am turned off by commentators who tell me what I 'really mean' by what I have written; or even by what I have spoken. Such people seem to be suggesting that they have a better notion of what I mean than I do. The text and context here, however, may make the use of 'really' legitimate. The surviving diaries come close in varying degrees to what speakers actually said. The narrative accounts ordinarily aim to make the sense of what speakers said coincide with what the narrators construed the speakers themselves as 'really' meaning rather than 'actually' saying. Given two such narratives and a half-dozen diaries, why shouldn't a twentieth century scholar come closer to what speakers 'really' meant than any single seventeenth century recorder of their speeches?

in early Stuart parliaments – like those my friend uses – were skillful enough to pre-edit and eliminate a good bit of the hemming and hawing, chopping and changing, that is so large a part of impromptu speech even by practiced speakers.

The men who prepared their accounts of proceedings from notes supplemented by memory a day or a few days after the events they detail are analogous to the note-takers who listen to tape recordings to catch what they missed in their initial notes. These writers of narratives of parliament perforce relied on their memories rather than on a tape recorder. Those memories are less accurate instruments, but especially in the case of attention-seizing episodes not contemptible ones. Such reconstructors of the course of debate were even better able than the diarists to capture the meaning and intention of those who took part in it. Most obviously, when they set about writing up a speech from notes, they already knew – as diarists did not – how it ended. That is to say, as they organized their notes into an account, they had in mind – as diarists could not have – what each speaker's point was, what he was getting at, what he meant, what he intended. Therefore, to the extent that the men who returned to their notes later in the day or week succeeded in making sense of them, they provide us with a *more coherent* account of what participants in debate meant by saying what they did. They also provide us with a historically *more accurate* account, one that gives us a sense of how a speech and a whole debate registered in the mind of a competent auditor committed not to catching as many words as possible, but to recapturing the sense of what the speakers said. In these terms the narratives that appear to have been worked out by members shortly after the events they describe – for example, Pym and X for 1621, 'Proceeding and Debates' and MS Stowe 366 for 1628 – should have preferred status when one is quoting from the debates of the House of Commons of the early seventeenth century.[17]

[17] This sort of narrative is superior to the long delayed eye-witness account in its verisimilitude to the happenings it records. The two instances of delayed accounts among the many recorded narratives of sessions of the Houses of Parliament in the early seventeenth century confirm this judgment. Sir John Eliot appears to have written his 'Apologetical Narration' of the proceedings in the parliament of 1625 between four and seven years after the events it describes. The intervening years were among the most significant in the history of the English Parliament. They were fatally decisive for Sir John Eliot, involving the consummation of his breach with the Duke of Buckingham and his speaking to the impeachment of the Duke before the Lords in 1626. The last three and a half years of his life he spent in prison for inciting the House to riot in 1629, for resisting the adjournment, and for violence to the Speaker. His experience in transit from intimate to enemy of the Duke markedly colors the 'Apologetical Narration,' his account of what happened in the House of Commons of 1625. In intent that book is primarily an apologia for himself and the House, a vindication of both, not a straightforward record of what went on in the House in 1625. To a lesser degree, the same reservation applies to Sir

Whatever the individual outlooks of the several members who made narratives from their notes shortly after the occasions the notes record, they took a bad second place behind the dominating motive of recorders: to have to hand an intelligible, coherent account of the day-to-day proceedings in the House of Commons. This does not mean that scrutiny will fail to reveal any biases or mind-traits of the recorders. 'Proceedings and Debates,' for example, focuses more tighly on the constitutional issue in 1628 and pays less heed than does MS Stowe 366 to less elevated matters such as who said what in the debates on subsidies.[18] Often Pym's record of the order, structure, and direction of an argument may have been a bit more precise than the words of the man who made the argument in the first place, but one suspects that most of those who spoke would have been happy to accept Pym's formulation as a true expression of their meaning. Indeed, whether they take the form of on-the-spot notes or of accounts written up from such notes shortly after the event described, narratives of the proceedings of deliberative bodies ordinarily are made in order to serve one function only. They exist to remind their compilers or to inform others of what went on in those bodies. Only if they strive for verisimilitude, only if they aim steadily at accuracy, do they achieve the purpose of those who went to the trouble to create them.[19]

Of course a narrator may have biases[20] or defects inherent or accidental as a note-taker,[21] or he may be narrowly focused in his interests,[22] the refraction of which affect in detail and in scope the matters he gives attention to. Nevertheless, unless the views a narrator attributes to a speaker contradict what others ascribe to him, his general overriding interest in versimilitude permits us to accept what he writes as coming close to what the speaker meant to say.

Simonds D'Ewes. A considerable portion of his smooth account of proceedings in the Long Parliament reached final draft in the shadow of his disillusion with the course the House of Commons took down dangerous by-ways that ended in civil war. That longer vision affected what he made of his notes when he had his clerk set down the smooth version of his journal.

18 In the first large subsidy debate in 1628 on 4 April, MS Stowe 366 records nearly forty more members as speaking than 'Proceedings and Debates' does: *Commons Debates 1628*, II, 297–309.

19 The occasional exceptions to this rule such as Eliot's 'Apologetical Narration' in the earlier seventeenth century or Richard Crossman's apologia in the later twentieth are not hard to identify.

20 Pym had a bias in favor of business-like dealings.

21 Newdegate appears to have been not very bright, or inexperienced, when he came to the House in 1628, or badly seated in the House for hearing what was said, or generally hard of hearing.

22 The man who wrote BL, MS Harleian 5234 seems to have been more concerned to keep a reminder of what legal precedents the members cited in the debates on the liberties of the subject in 1628 than with what the members said about those liberties.

In connection with the narratives, the rules for the use of indicators of quotation would simply be:

(1) Use indicators of quotation in connection with any passage directly excerpted from any narrative of any session of parliament from 1604 to 1649 unless there is strong positive evidence to doubt its authenticity. In general, select from the various versions of a passage the most intelligible and effective one. This means starting with the best organized and effective 'delayed' acount and scavenging the other narratives for particular bits that complement or supplement that basic version.

(2) Abandon altogether the use of the ellipsis and the bracket. They are appropriate to the quotation of written sources, because the original written source survives, and the quotation can be checked against it for an accuracy which the writer himself intended. Prior to the invention of recording devices, no oral equivalents to written original sources exist. If they did, we would not want to use them anyway, because as we have seen, they would give us only the sequences of sounds that speakers made and would not tell us – as the surviving records actually do – what several witnesses took the speakers to mean.[23] Given the nature of the oral record, therefore, the use of ellipsis and bracket becomes merely pretentious. Consider the complication of using them in quoting from, say, Pym's accounts. By analogy with the conventions of quotation for written sources, they are signals that one is altering by omission or addition what precisely the speaker said. But of course we have no record at all of what *precisely* the speaker said. For that reason, if we bound ourselves to the analogy of quotation from written sources, we should be obliged to put *everything* in Pym's accounts in brackets since everything stands at two removes from what men actually said in the House. That is one remove further than even a present-day historian is from his written source when in the interest of rhetorical convenience or propriety he 'improves' the source with ellipses and brackets. In our view of course the analogy is false and irrelevant. An account written only a little after the event is not at any numerically stateable stage away from what a speaker *meant*. It deserves

[23] A difficult problem about quoting is worth mentioning here. A few 'speeches' survive that are remarkable for their quality, but they almost certainly were not delivered in the form in which we know them. Instances of this are the great 'addresses' of Hakewill, Whitelocke, and Hedley on impositions in 1610, Cresheld's opening speech in the Committee of the Whole House on 27 March 1628, and Mason's on 22 May 1628. The five men named no doubt gave speeches at the times indicated since other sources than those of the full texts indicate that they spoke. That, however, they spoke the words of the 'full text' is far less certain. Indeed, those texts are so full that it is reasonably certain they were not given as is in the House. Deciding how to deal with them when we are 'quoting speeches' in the parliament of the early seventeenth century is different from the problem we have dealt with in this paper and would need separate treatment.

indicators of quotation because its writer aims to set down what people meant by what they said with the scurf of misspeaking, misfollowing, and bad note-taking got rid of. *Ceteris paribus* it should be the version of what was said that comes nearest to what the speaker had in mind in the end, though it may not have been on the tip of his tongue as he spoke.

(3) Finally, the last convention of quotation is the least altered in the area we have concerned ourselves with. The superscript number will still be matched with a footnote or endnote guiding the reader to the sources – the various narratives – from which the language of the quotation was drawn. And this marks a strict limit to what it is permissible for a historian to do to his sources in constructing his quotation of spoken language from the evidence available to him. In constructing a quotation he must make verisimilitude to the language ascribed by the sources to the speaker his first imperative. Occasionally this may be difficult, often it is very easy. Consider the passage from Hakewill's speech of which I earlier printed variants from six diaries. In all six versions eleven specifying words appear: *addition, idle, operative, Lords, receive/accept, offer/gave, worthy/fit,* and *wisdom.*[24] Consider the frequency with which the terms appear, taking into account an occasional occurrence of synonyms in different versions.

addition	6		offer	4	5
idle	6		gave	1	
operative	6		worthy }	3	6
Lords	5		fit }	3[24]	
receive }	4	5	wisdom	3	
accept }	1				

A closer accord on the specifying terms among six independent narratives (all of which differed slightly on non-specifying terms and on word order) is hard to imagine. In such a case surely no specifying terms other than the eleven should appear in a quotation; 'suitable' must not take the place of 'fit,' 'effective' of 'operative.' We may want to paraphrase the quotation using specifying terms similar to but not identical with the ones the speaker used. If we do, we should renounce the quotation indicators. Between quotation in which verisimilitude to what the speaker intended

[24] Two other specifying terms, 'vain' and 'works somewhat' occur in one source only: Grosvenor. They occur in a phrase appositional to one that appears in all the texts. The phrase patently adds no substance to what all the narrators describe Hakewill as saying. On the other hand, for that very reason it is in harmony with what he meant to say, and it seems quite likely that he actually said of the addition something very like 'it is either vain or works somewhat.' It is not unlikely that a note-taker like Grosvenor who combined high speed with deficient selectivity would have caught a redundant phrase that the other recorders missed.

to say is paramount and paraphrase in which maximizing intelligibility, perception, and impact for the reader is paramount, the line must be kept clear and distinct.

In the case of the passage we considered earlier, the rule on the rhetorical structure for a quotation is as clear as the above rule for the selection of words: if, as in this instance, a consensus on a clearly defined syntactical–rhetorical schema emerges from an inspection of the narratives, follow it when quoting. Suppose a historian wrote, 'Either this addition is idle, or it is operative. If it is idle, it is not worthy of the wisdom of the Lords to offer it nor of our wisdom to receive it.' If one accepts that in the quotation of written speech the signs of quotation are due to matters in the substantive terms and the rhetorical form the speaker used, would any one deny those signs to the above sentences? If the rhetorical schema is not so manifest, then the historian should structure the quotation so as to maximize intelligibility while doing as full justice as possible to the speaker's meaning.[25]

These seem to me at least to be reasonable conventions of quotation for a historian to follow when using the records of the parliaments of the early Stuarts. Whether and how those conventions would need to be modified in dealing with other records of extemporary speech I do not know. Nor am I sure how well they will work even on the material that occasioned the attempt to elicit them. *Faute de mieux* – since the sound conventions of quotation developed for written communication just will not suit the case and are therefore irrelevant – I will have to learn by doing, that is, by writing. Of course, I will also make the nature of the conventions explicit when I use them in writing. I will be able to refer readers to this essay for their rationale.

VI

One more matter. I return to the beginning, Professor Elton's concern about the sources on the parliaments of the early Stuarts and understanding of the points of view embedded in their creation and compilation. The situation reverses the usual cliché on these matters. It loomed so ominously at first that we preferred to turn away and write about something else. Having done so and now turning back to it again, it appears on the far horizon, a cloud scarcely the breadth of a man's hand. What a little reflection suggests and a little sampling of the surviving records of one of the

[25] One should not try to dodge the implication that two historians quoting the same spoken passage might not use the identical words. If they footnoted adequately, I (at the moment) see no harm in this.

early Stuart parliaments confirm is that Elton's problem is a bit of a non-starter. For if a man keeping a record of a meeting wants that record to be of use to him or others for reference, his prime object will be verisimilitude, and in a record of oral discourse, verisimilitude is an approximation, not of the sequence of noises a sound-producing device – the human voice – makes, but of the sense a human being makes. Simultaneously note-takers in the House of Commons with varying degrees of competence and zeal pursued the same end of verisimilitude. The axes along which it turns out to be worth grading the narratives of the early Stuart parliaments therefore are completeness, competence, and coherence. Bias and point of view enter the picture occasionally but rarely. Any problems that may rise on those scores, as in the case of Eliot's *Negotium Posterorum*, are best dealt with *ad hoc*.

So Geoffrey, not to worry. *Vale!*

Bibliography of the writings of G. R. Elton, 1946–1981

Locations of reviews are given in detail sufficient to make finding them reasonably convenient. Items marked ⋆ are reprinted in the collected *Studies* (1974).

Abbreviations

ARG	*Archiv für Reformationsgeschichte*
BIHR	*Bulletin of the Institute of Historical Research*
CHJ	*Cambridge Historical Journal*
EcHR	*Economic History Review*
EHR	*English Historical Review*
HJ	*Historical Journal*
JEH	*Journal of Ecclesiastical History*
JTS	*Journal of Theological Studies*
TES	*Times Educational Supplement*
THES	*Times Higher Education Supplement*
TLS	*Times Literary Supplement*
TRHS	*Transactions of the Royal Historical Society*

1946

⋆'The date of Caesar's Gallic proconsulate,' *Journal of Roman Studies* 36, 18–42

1949

⋆'The evolution of a Reformation statute,' *EHR* 64, 174–97

'Two unpublished letters of Thomas Cromwell,' *BIHR* 22, 35–7

1950

'A note on the First Act of Annates,' *BIHR* 23, 203–5

1951

⋆'The Commons' Supplication of 1532: parliamentary manoeuvres in the reign of Henry VIII,' *EHR* 66, 507–34

⋆'Thomas Cromwell's decline and fall,' *CHJ* 10, 150–85

Reviews:

S. T. Bindoff, *Tudor England (Cambridge Journal*, January)

W. Schenk, *Reginald Pole, Cardinal of England* (*Cambridge Journal*, June)

D. Hay (ed.), *The Anglica Historia of Polydore Vergil* (*EHR*)

A. C. Chibnall & A. Vere Woodman (eds.), *The Subsidy Roll for the County of Buckingham Anno 1524 (EHR)*

T. M. Parker, *The English Reformation* (*Cambridge Journal*, August)

B. H. G. Wormald, *Clarendon – Politics, History and Religion* (*Cambridge Review*, 3 Nov.)

1952

*'Parliamentary drafts 1529–40,' *BIHR* 25, 117–32

'The Sixteenth Century' in *Annual Bulletin of Historical Literature* (Historical Association)

Reviews:

John Clapham, *Elizabeth of England*, ed. E. P. & C. Read (*Cambridge Review*, 9 Feb.)

A. G. Dickens (ed.), *The Register of Butley Priory, Suffolk, 1510–1535* (*EHR*)

D. Hay, *Polydore Vergil: Renaissance Historian and Man of Letters* (*EHR*)

D. Forbes, *The Liberal Anglican Idea of History* (*Lady Clare*)

J. D. Mackie, *The Earlier Tudors* (*Cambridge Review*, 29 Nov.)

1953

The Tudor Revolution in Government: Administrative Changes in the Reign of Henry VIII (Cambridge University Press)

*'An early Tudor poor law,' *EcHR* 2nd ser. 6, 55–67

'The Sixteenth Century' in *Annual Bulletin of Historical Literature* (Historical Association)

Reviews:

*J. D. Mackie, *The Earlier Tudors* (*EHR*)

H. E. Bell, *An Introduction to the History and Records of the Court of Wards* (*EcHR*)

J. E. Neale, *Elizabeth I and her Parliaments 1559–1581* (*Cambridge Review*, 30 May)

Christopher Morris, *Political Thought in England: Tyndale to Hooker* (*Cambridge Review*, 14 Nov.)

A. L. Rowse, *An Elizabethan Garland* (*Listener*, 29 Oct.)

1954

*'A further note on parliamentary drafts in the reign of Henry VIII,' *BIHR* 27, 198–200

'Informing for profit: a sidelight on Tudor methods of law-enforcement,' *CHJ* 11, 149–67

*'King or minister? The man behind the Henrician Reformation,' *History* 39, 216–32 [under this date but appeared 1956]

'The Sixteenth Century' in *Annual Bulletin of Historical Literature* (Historical Association)

Reviews:

J. A. Williamson, *The Tudor Age*, and L. Paul, *Sir Thomas More* (*Listener*, 14 Jan.)

C. V. Malfatti (ed.), *Two Italian Accounts of Tudor England* (*EHR*)
J. S. Roskell, *The Commons in the Parliament of 1422* (*Listener*, 22 Apr.)
G. Connell-Smith, *Forerunners of Drake: a Study of English Trade with Spain in the Early Tudor Period* (*Listener*, 11 Nov.)
A. Steel, *The Receipt of the Exchequer, 1377–1485* (*Cambridge Review*, 6 Nov.)

1955

England under the Tudors (London: Methuen)
'The Sixteenth Century' in *Annual Bulletin of Historical Literature* (Historical Association)

Reviews:
E. Auerbach, *Tudor Artists* (*Listener*, 13 Jan.)
P. Hughes, *The Reformation in England*, vol. 3 (*Listener*, 23 June)
F. Caspari, *Humanism and the Social Order in Tudor England* (*EHR*)
G. D. Ramsay (ed.), *Two Sixteenth-Century Taxation Lists, 1545 and 1576* (*EHR*)
C. Read, *Mr Secretary Cecil and Queen Elizabeth* (*Listener*, 12 May)
W. Weston, *The Autobiography of an Elizabethan*, ed. P. Caraman (*Listener*, 13 Oct.)
A. L. Rowse, *The Expansion of Elizabethan England* (*Listener*, 6 Oct.)
P. M. Dawley, *John Whitgift and the Reformation* (*Listener*, 8 Dec.)
C. Falls, *Mountjoy: Elizabethan General* (*Listener*, 29 Dec.)

1956

*'The political creed of Thomas Cromwell,' *TRHS*, 5th ser. 6, 69–92
'The quondam of Rievaulx,' *JEH* 7, 45–60
'Thomas Cromwell,' *History Today* (August)
'Fifty years of Tudor history at London,' *TLS* (6 Jan.)
'The Sixteenth Century' in *Annual Bulletin of Historical Literature* (Historical Association)

Reviews:
D. H. Willson, *James I and VI* (*Listener*, 16 Feb.)
C. Devlin, *The Life of Robert Southwell, Poet and Martyr* (*Listener*, 14 June)
J. W. F. Hill, *Tudor and Stuart Lincoln*, and L. Stone, *Sir Horatio Pallavicino* (*Listener*, 9 Aug.)
T. S. Willan, *The Early History of the Russia Company* (*Listener*, 6 Sept.)
Sir Winston Churchill, *A History of the English-Speaking Peoples*, vol. 2 (*Listener*, 6 Dec.)
B. Winchester, *Tudor Family Portrait* (*History*)

1957

Reviews:
C. Hill, *Economic Problems of the Church from Archbishop Whitgift to the Long Parliament* (*Cambridge Review*, 21 Jan.)
Lord Leconfield, *Sutton and Duncton Manors* (*Listener*, 31 Jan.)

J. S. Ridley, *Nicholas Ridley* (*Listener*, 2 May)
J. E. Neale, *Elizabeth I and her Parliaments 1584–1601* (*Listener*, 14 Feb., and *CHJ*)
J. G. A. Pocock, *The Ancient Constitution and the Feudal Law* (*Listener*, 20 Sept.)
I. Morgan, *Prince Charles's Puritan Chaplain* (*Cambridge Review*, 23 Nov.)
I. Grimble, *The Harrington Family* (*Listener*, 19 Dec.)

1958

(ed.) *The New Cambridge Modern History*, vol. 2: *The Reformation* (Cambridge University Press). Contributed: 'Introduction: the age of the Reformation' (1–22); 'The Reformation in England' (226–50); 'Constitutional development and political thought in Western Europe' (438–63); 'A note on constitutional developments in Germany' (477–80)
Star Chamber Stories (London: Methuen)
*'Henry VII: rapacity and remorse,' *HJ* 1, 21–39

Reviews:
T. Woodruffe, *The Enterprise of England* (*Manchester Guardian*, 15 Apr.)
H. Trevor-Roper, *Historical Essays* (*History*)
G. N. Clark, *War and Society* (*Manchester Guardian*, 18 Apr.)
A. Tindal Hart, *The Country Clergy in Elizabethan and Stuart Times* (*Listener*, 22 May)
W. McElwee, *The Wisest Fool in Christendom: the Reign of King James I and VI* (*Listener*, 14 Aug.)
H. C. Porter, *Reformation and Reaction in Tudor Cambridge* (*Listener*, 11 Sept.)
E. Burton & F. Kelly, *The Elizabethans at Home*, and G. B. Harrison, *A Second Jacobean Journal* (*Manchester Guardian*, 3 Oct.)
H. W. Chapman, *The Last Tudor King*, and E. Jenkins, *Elizabeth the Great* (*Manchester Guardian*, 11 Nov.)
R. H. Tawney, *Business and Politics under James I* (*Manchester Guardian*, 21 Oct.)
C. Ferguson, *Naked to Mine Enemies: the Life of Cardinal Wolsey* (*Listener*, 13 Nov.)
J. E. Neale, *Essays in Elizabethan History* (*Manchester Guardian*, 28 Nov.)
C. Hill, *Puritanism and Revolution* (*Manchester Guardian*, 12 Dec.)
J. Hurstfield, *The Queen's Wards* (*Listener*, 25 Dec.)

1959

'The records of the conciliar courts in the 16th century,' *The Amateur Historian* 4, 89–94

Reviews:
C. Ogilvie, *The King's Government and the Common Law, 1471–1641* (*Cambridge Review*, 24 Jan.)
R. L. Mackie, *King James IV of Scotland* (*EHR*)
*C. G. Bayne & W. H. Dunham (ed.), *Select Cases in the Council of Henry VII* (*EHR*)
A. H. Bourne & P. Young, *The Great Civil War* (*Guardian*, 3 Apr.)

P. Williams, *The Council in the Marches of Wales under Elizabeth I* (*HJ*)
L. C. Hector, *The Handwriting of English Documents* (*Cambridge Review*, 23 May)
H. Thieme, *Die Ehescheidung Heinrichs VIII. und die europäischen Universitäten* (*ARG*)
H. C. Porter, *Reformation and Reaction in Tudor Cambridge* (*ARG*)
E. C. Williams, *Bess of Hardwick* (*Listener*, 9 July)
T. S. Willan, *Studies in Elizabethan Foreign Trade* (*Guardian*, 26 June)
P. M. Handover, *The Second Cecil*, and G. Huxley, *Endymion Porter* (*Listener*, 28 May)
J. Burckhardt, *Judgments on History and Historians* (*Listener*, 30 July)
G. Mattingly, *The Defeat of the Spanish Armada*, and A. L. Rowse, *The Elizabethans and America* (*Observer*, 25 Oct.)
D. Knowles, *The Religious Orders in England*, vol. 3 (*Listener*, 3 Dec.)
A. G. Dickens, *Thomas Cromwell and the English Reformation* (*Listener*, 31 Dec.)

1960

The Tudor Constitution: Documents and Commentary (Cambridge University Press)
*'Henry VIII's Act of Proclamations,' *EHR* 75, 208–22

Reviews:

*W. K. Jordan, *Philanthropy in England 1480–1660* (*HJ*)
G. Cavendish, *The Life and Death of Cardinal Wolsey*, ed. R. S. Sylvester (*History*)
C. Read (ed.), *Bibliography of English History: the Tudor Period*, 2nd edn (*EHR*)
W. M. Wallace, *Sir Walter Raleigh* (*Listener*, 17 Mar.)
M. Lee, *John Maitland of Thirlestane* (*AGR*)
S. A. Fischer-Galati, *Ottoman Imperialism and German Protestantism* (*JTS*)
H. W. Chapman, *Two Tudor Portraits* (*Listener*, 9 June)
G. Donaldson, *The Scottish Reformation* (*Listener*, 23 June)
M. Lewis, *The Spanish Armada* (*Observer*, 16 Oct.)
J. Hurstfield, *Elizabeth I and the Unity of England* (*Listener*, 1 Dec.)

1961

*'The Elizabethan Exchequer: war in the Receipt,' in *Elizabethan Government and Society*, ed. S. T. Bindoff, J. Hurstfield, C. H. Williams (London: Athlone), 213–48
*'Henry VII: a restatement,' *HJ* 4, 1–29
*'State planning in early-Tudor England,' *EcHR* 2nd ser. 13, 433–9
'Stuart Government' [review article], *Past and Present* 20, 76–82

Reviews:

A. McNalty, *Mary Queen of Scots* (*Cambridge Review*, 11 Mar.)
Britannica et Americana, vol. 5 (*EHR*)
R. Marchant, *Puritans and Church Courts in the Diocese of York* (*JTS*)
C. S. Meyer, *Elizabeth I and the Religious Settlement of 1559* (*JEH*)
J. M. Osborn (ed.), *The Autobiography of Thomas Whythorn* (*Listener*, 9 Mar.)
W. K. Jordan, *The Charities of London* (*HJ*)

E. Doernberg, *Henry VIII and Luther* (*TLS*, 23 June)
F. L. Carsten (ed.), *The New Cambridge Modern History vol. 5*, and C. Hill, *The Century of Revolution* (*New Statesman*, 4 Aug.)
F. G. Emmison, *Tudor Secretary: Sir William Petre at Court and Home* (*Listener*, 20 July)
J. H. Hexter, *Reappraisals in History* (*Listener*, 23 Nov.)

1962
The Reformation (BBC Publications)
Henry VIII: an Essay in Revision (Historical Association, Pamphlet G 51)
'1555: a political retrospect' (talk on BBC Network Three, 14 March)

Reviews:
J. P. Dawson, *A History of Lay Judges* (*History*)
A. L. Rowse, *Raleigh and the Throckmortons* (*Listener*, 11 Apr.)
G. Cavendish, *Thomas Wolsey* (Folio Society) (*Listener*, 16 Aug.)
N. L. Williams, *Sir Walter Raleigh* (*Listener*, 6 Sept.)
C. H. and K. George, *The Protestant Mind of the English Reformation, 1570–1640* (*HJ*)
L. B. Smith, *A Tudor Tragedy* (*EHR*)
G. A. Holmes, *The Later Middle Ages* (*Biblion*, no. 1)
M. Strachan, *The Life and Adventures of Thomas Coryate* (*Listener*, 6 Dec.)

1963
Reformation Europe (London: Collins)
(ed.) *Ideas and Institutions in Western Civilization*, vol. 3: *Renaissance and Reformation* (New York: Macmillan)
(ed. with G. Kitson Clark) *Guide to the Research Facilities in History in the Universities of Great Britain and Ireland* (Cambridge University Press)
'The teaching of history,' *Cambridge Review* 84, 250
'Anglo-French relations in 1522: a Scottish prisoner of war and his interrogation,' *EHR* 78, 310–13

Reviews:
P. Ramsey, *Tudor Economic Problems* (*The Teacher*, 19 Apr.)
H. A. Enno van Gelder, *The Two Reformations of the 16th Century* (*JTS*)
E. F. Rogers (ed.), *St Thomas More: Selected Letters* (*Notes & Queries*, May)
S. E. Lehmberg, *Sir Thomas Elyot* (*ARG*)
F. Wendel, *Calvin* (*Listener*, 8 Aug.)
H. Lutz, *Ragione di Stato und christliche Staatsethik im 16. Jahrhundert* (*EHR*)

1964
'The Tudor Revolution: a reply,' *Past and Present* 29, 26–49

Reviews:
W. C. Richardson, *History of the Court of Augmentations* (*EHR*)
L. V. Ryan, *Roger Ascham* (*Listener*, 20 Feb.)

R. Peters, *Oculus Episcopi: Administration in the Archdeaconry of St Albans 1580–1625* (*JTS*)
N. Williams, *Thomas Howard, fourth Duke of Norfolk* (*Listener*, 9 Apr.)
B. W. Beckingsale, *Elizabeth I*, and L. B. Wright (ed.), *Life and Letters in Tudor and Stuart England*, and E. W. Talbert, *The Problem of Order* (*History*)
C. Hill, *Society and Puritanism in Pre-Revolutionary England* (*Observer*, 12 Apr.)
Mary Dewar, *Sir Thomas Smith* (*Listener*, 9 July)
A. G. Dickens, *The English Reformation* (*Listener*, 1 Oct.)
A. J. Krailsheimer, *Rabelais and the Franciscans* (*JEH*)

1965

*'Why the history of the early Tudor Council remains unwritten,' *Annali della Fondazione Italiana per la Storia Amministrativa* 1, 268–96
*'A high road to civil war?' *From the Renaissance to the Counter-Reformation: Essays in Honor of Garrett Mattingly*, ed. Charles H. Carter (New York: Random House), 325–47
*'The problems and significance of administrative history in the Tudor period,' *Journal of British Studies* 4/2, 18–28
*Introduction to J. N. Figgis, *The Divine Right of Kings* (repr. Harper Torchbooks)
*Introduction to A. F. Pollard, *Wolsey* (repr. Fontana Library)
'1555: a political retrospect,' in *The Reformation Crisis*, ed. J. Hurstfield (London: Arnold)
*'Government by edict?' [review article], *HJ* 8, 266–71
'A revolution in Tudor history?' *Past and Present* 32, 103–9

Reviews:
P. Williams, *Life under the Tudors* (*Listener*, 7 Jan.)
F. Raab, *The English Face of Machiavelli*, and J. Bowle, *Henry VIII* (*Listener*, 28 Jan.)
L. Stone, *The Crisis of the Aristocracy 1558–1641* (*Daily Telegraph*, 11 Mar.)
H. Aveling, *The Catholic Recusants of the West Riding of Yorkshire, 1558–1790* (*JTS*)
C. H. S. Fifoot (ed.), *The Letters of F. W. Maitland* (*Cambridge Review*, 21 May)
G. H. Cook (ed.), *Letters to Cromwell and Others on the Suppression of the Monasteries* (*Listener*, 15 July)
S. E. Lehmberg, *Sir Walter Mildmay and Tudor Government* (*Canadian Historical Review*)
D. M. Loades, *Two Tudor Conspiracies* (*Listener*, 23 Sept.)
H. S. Bennett, *English Books and Readers 1558–1603* (*Listener*, 30 Sept.)

1966

*Introduction to M. Creighton, *Queen Elizabeth* (repr. Crowell)

Reviews:
E. G. Leonard, *History of Protestantism* (*New Society*, 31 Mar.)

D. S. Chambers, *Faculty Office Registers 1534–1549* (*Cambridge Review*, 23 Apr.)
R. D. Linder, *The Political Ideas of Pierre Viret* (*EHR*)
C. C. Weston, *English Constitutional Theory and the House of Lords* (*HJ*)
D. S. Chambers, *Cardinal Bainbridge in the Court of Rome* (*EHR*)
J. E. Oxley, *The Reformation in Essex to the Death of Mary* (*JTS*)
La Renaissance et la Réformation en Pologne et en Hongrie (*HJ*)

1967
The Practice of History (Sydney University Press)
*'Thomas More and the opposition to Henry VIII,' *Moreana* 15 & 16, 285–303; repr. *BIHR* 41 (1968), 19–34
Storia del Mondo Moderno, vol. II (Italian translation of *New Cambridge Modern History*)

Reviews:
A. B. Ferguson, *The Articulate Citizen and the English Renaissance* (*EHR*)
J. H. Hexter & E. Surtz (eds.), *Complete Works of St Thomas More*, vol. 4: *Utopia* (*EHR*)
C. Cross, *The Puritan Earl*, and M. Prestwich, *Cranfield* (*Daily Telegraph*, 2 Mar.)
J. K. McConica, *English Humanists and Reformation Politics under Henry VIII and Edward VI* (*HJ*)
H. S. Herbrüggen (ed.), *Sir Thomas More: Neue Briefe* (*EHR*)
C. G. Cruikshank, *Elizabeth's Army*, 2nd edn (*HJ*)

1968
Ideas and Institutions in Western Civilization: Renaissance and Reformation, 2nd edn (New York: Macmillan)
The Future of the Past (Inaugural lecture: Cambridge University Press)
'The law of treason in the early Reformation,' *HJ* 11, 211–36
*'Reform by statute: Thomas Starkey's *Dialogue* and Thomas Cromwell's policy,' *Proceedings of the British Academy* 54, 165–88
*'Review article (G. E. Aylmer, *The Struggle for the Constitution*), *Annali della Fondazione Italiana per la Storia Amministrativa* 2, 759–65
'Interdisciplinary courses,' *Cambridge Review*, 26 January.
'Graduate studies in the humanities,' *Cambridge Review*, 18 October

Reviews:
R. B. Wernham, *Before the Armada* (*EHR*)
P. M. Hembry, *The Bishops of Bath and Wells 1540–1640* (*HJ*)
H. R. Trevor-Roper, *Religion, Reformation and Social Change* (*N.Y. Times Review of Books*, 31 Mar.)
G. W. O. Woodward, *The Dissolution of the Monasteries* (*EHR*)
L. R. Shelby, *John Rogers: Tudor Military Engineer*, and J. Crofts, *Packhorse, Waggon and Post* (*Cambridge Review*, 31 Mar.)
H. Aveling & W. A. Pantin (eds.), *The Letter Book of Robert Joseph* (*EHR*)
H. R. Trevor-Roper (ed.), *The Age of Expansion* (*The Times*, 31 Aug.)

J. Ridley, *John Knox* (*New Statesman*, 27 Sept.)
H. Koenigsberger & G. L. Mosse, *Europe in the Sixteenth Century* (*History*)
P. Collinson, *The Elizabethan Puritan Movement* (*HJ*)

1969

The Sources of History: England 1200–1640 (London: Sources of History Ltd)
*'*The Body of the Whole Realm': Parliament and Representation in Medieval and Tudor England* (Charlottesville: University Press of Virginia)
'Literaturbericht über die englische Geschichte der Neuzeit,' *Historische Zeitschrift*, Sonderheft 3
*'The King of Hearts' [review article], *HJ* 12, 158–63
*'The Good Duke' [review article], *HJ* 12, 702–6
'A reply [to a review of *Practice of History*],' *Journal of Historical Studies*, Winter 1968–9, 49–59
'Second thoughts on history in the Universities,' *History*, 54, 60–7
'Personal view,' *Listener*, 27 March

Reviews:
J. G. Russell, *The Field of Cloth of Gold* (*New Statesman*, 14 Feb.)
N. F. Cantor, *The English*, vol. 1 (*Political Science Quarterly* [1968])
A. G. Dickens, *The Counter Reformation* (*New Statesman*, 14 Mar.)
W. J. Jones, *The Elizabethan Court of Chancery* (*EHR*)
L. B. Smith, *Zwielicht einer Zeitenwende* (*Historische Zeitschrift*)
J. M. W. Bean, *The Decline of English Feudalism 1215–1540 (Revue d'histoire de loi)*
G. Williams, *Welsh Reformation Essays* (*Welsh History Review*)
L. W. Levy, *Origin of the Fifth Amendment* (*EHR*)

1970

Political History: Principles and Practice (New York: Basic Books)
Modern Historians on British History 1485–1945: a Critical Bibliography (London: Methuen)
'Reformation in Church and State 1485–1603,' *Encyclopaedia Americana* ('England')
'What sort of history should we teach?' *New Movements in the Study and Teaching of History*, ed. M. Ballard (London: Temple Smith), 221–30

Reviews:
W. T. MacCaffrey, *The Shaping of the Elizabethan Regime* (*Journal of Modern History*)
P. Zagorin, *The Court and the Country* (*Encounter*, July)
A. R. Myers (ed.), *English Historical Documents*, vol. IV: *1327–1485* (*HJ*)
J. H. Gleason, *The Justice of the Peace in England 1558–1640* (*Archives*)
P. L. Hughes & J. F. Larkin (eds.), *Tudor Royal Proclamations*, vols. 2 and 3 *(EHR)*
Paul S. Seaver, *The Puritan Lectureships* (*HJ*)

1971

'Government and Society in Renaissance and Reformation Europe,' in N. F. Cantor (ed.), *Perspectives on the European Past: Conversations with Historians* (New York: Macmillan), 228–51

*'Studying the history of parliament,' *British Studies Monitor* 4, 3–12

'Tudor historians,' *Listener*, 30 September

Europa im Zeitalter der Reformation, 2 vols. (German translation of *Reformation Europe:* Siebenstern)

Reviews:

W. K. Jordan, *Edward VI: the Threshold of Power* (*Spectator*, 26 Feb.)

G. Leff, *History and Social Theory* (*EHR*)

R. C. Barnett, *Place, Profit and Power: a Study of the Servants of William Cecil, Elizabethan Statesman* (*EcHR*)

R. B. Smith, *Land and Politics in the Reign of Henry VIII* (*HJ*)

C. Russell, *The Crisis of Parliaments: English History 1509–1660* (*Spectator*, 14 May)

P. W. Musgrave (ed.), *Sociology, History and Education: a Reader* (Journal of Educational Administration and History)

E. Shulin, *Handelsstaat England* (*Historische Zeitschrift*)

A. L. Rowse, *The Elizabethan Renaissance* (*Spectator*, 6 Nov.)

1972

Policy and Police: the Enforcement of the Reformation in the Age of Thomas Cromwell (Cambridge University Press)

*'Thomas More, councillor,' *St Thomas More: Action and Contemplation*, ed. R. S. Sylvester (New Haven: Yale University Press), 86–122

*'The rule of law in the sixteenth century,' *Tudor Men and Institutions*, ed. A. J. Slavin (Baton Rouge: Louisiana State University Press), 260–84

'Reply [to J. H. Hexter],' *British Studies Monitor* 3, 16–22

Reviews:

J. M. Headley (ed.), *Complete Works of St Thomas More*, vol. 5: *Responsio ad Lutherum* (*EHR*)

D. H. Fisher, *Historians' Fallacies* (*History*)

W. Notestein, *The House of Commons 1604–10* (*HJ*)

J. H. Hexter, *Doing History* (*Archives*)

R. E. Ruigh, *The Parliament of 1624* (*HJ*)

1973

Reform and Renewal: Thomas Cromwell and the Common Weal (Cambridge University Press)

Reviews:

W. Steglich (ed.), *Deutsche Reichstagsakten unter Karl V.*, vol. 8 (*EHR*)

Liber Memorialis Georges de Lagarde (*EHR*)

L. Stone, *The Causes of the English Revolution* (*HJ*)

A. Fraser, *Cromwell – Our Chief of Men* (*Spectator*, 9 June)

Saeculum Weltgeschichte, vol. 5 (*ARG*)
S. B. Chrimes, *Henry VII* (*HJ*)
G. Connell-Smith & H. A. Lloyd, *The Relevance of History* (*History*)
C.-P. Clasen, *Anabaptism: a Social History*, and I. Horst, *The Radical Brethren* (*EHR*)
L. A. Clarkson, *The Pre-Industrial Economy in Britain 1500–1750* (*Journal of Economic Literature*)

1974

England under the Tudors, 2nd edn (London: Methuen)
Studies in Tudor and Stuart Politics and Government, 2 vols. (Cambridge University Press)
La Europa de la Reforma (Spanish translation of *Reformation Europe*: Siglo veintuino)
Political History: Japanese translation
'Consultants' Report on Graduate Programs in History in the Province of Ontario'
'Tudor Politics: the points of contact. I. Parliament,' *TRHS* 5th ser. 24, 183–200
'The early Journals of the House of Lords,' *EHR* 89, 481–512
'Thomas Cranmer,' 'Thomas Cromwell,' 'Henry VIII,' in *Encyclopaedia Britannica* (15th edn)

Reviews:
B. Worden, *The Rump Parliament* (*Spectator*, 9 Mar.)
C. Russell (ed.), *The Origins of the English Civil War*, and B. P. Levack, *The Civil Lawyers in England 1603–1641* (*HJ*)
L. A. Schuster, R. C. Marius, J. P. Lusardi, R. J. Schoeck (eds.), *Complete Works of St Thomas More*, vol. 8: *The Confutation of Tyndale's Answer* (*EHR*)
H. Hearder & H. Loyn (eds.), *British Government and Administration: Studies presented to S. B. Chrimes* (*THES*, 7 June)
J. H. Langbein, *Prosecuting Crime in the Renaissance* (*TLS*, 20 Sept.)
J. A. Stayer, *Anabaptists and the Sword* (*EHR*)
J. Hurstfield, *Freedom, Corruption and Government in Elizabethan England* (*Reviews in European History*, 1/2)

1975

'Taxation for peace and war in early-Tudor England,' *War and Economic Development: Essays in Memory of David Joslin*, ed. J. M. Winter (Cambridge University Press), 33–48
'Thomas Cromwell and reform,' *Annual Report of Friends of Lambeth Library*
'Tudor Politics: the points of contact. II. The Council,' *TRHS* 5th ser. 25, 195–211

Reviews:
F. Yates, *Astraea* (*THES*, 10 Jan.)
C. Hill, *Change and Continuity in Seventeenth Century England* (*Spectator*, 8 Feb.)
C. Ross, *Edward IV* (*New Statesman*, 7 Feb.)
F. Engel-Janosi *et al.* (eds.), *Denken über Geschichte* (*History*)

W. R. D. Jones, *The Mid-Tudor Crisis* (*History*)
J. H. Shennan, *The Origins of the Modern European State* (*European Studies Review*)
M. E. James, *Family, Lineage and Civil Society* (*History*)
C. Carlton, *The Court of Orphans* (*HJ*)
A. Hanham, *Richard III and his Early Historians* (*TLS*, 10 Oct.)
C. R. Thompson (ed.), *Complete Works of St Thomas More*, vol. 3: *Translations of Lucian* (*EHR*)
A. Hassell Smith, *County and Court: Government and Politics in Norfolk 1558–1603* (*History*)
H. A. Oberman (ed.), *Luther and the Dawn of the Modern Era* (*JTS*)
O. Ranum (ed.), *National Consciousness, History and Political Culture in Early-Modern Europe* (*HJ*)

1976

Ideas and Institutions in Western Civilization, vol. 3: *Renaissance and Reformation*, 3rd edn (New York: Macmillan)
'Publishing history,' *TLS*, 25 June
'Tudor Politics: the points of contact. III. The Court,' *TRHS* 5th ser. 26, 211–28
(ed.) *Annual Bibliography of British and Irish History: Publications for 1975* (Brighton: Harvester Press)

Reviews:
M. L. Bush, *The Government Policy of Protector Somerset* (*TLS*, 6 Jan.)
G. A. J. Hodgett, *Tudor Lincolnshire* (*TLS*, 2 Apr.)
C. S. L. Davies, *Peace, Print and Protestantism* (*TLS*, 23 July)
B. L. Beer, *Northumberland: the Political Career of John Dudley, Earl of Warwick and Duke of Northumberland* (*EHR*)
E. Gasquet, *Le courant machiavelien dans la pensée et la littérature anglaises du XVIe siècle* (*EHR*)
Propyläen Geschichte Europas, vols. 1 & 3 (*TLS*, 5 Nov.)

1977

Reform and Reformation: England 1509–1558 (London: Arnold)
'Introduction: Crime and the historian,' in J. S. Cockburn (ed.), *Crime in England 1550–1800* (London: Methuen), 1–14
'The historian's social function, *TRHS* 5th ser. 26, 197–211
'Mid-Tudor finance' [review article], *HJ* 20, 737–40
'Thomas Cromwell redivivus,' *ARG* 68, 192–208
'A new venture in history publishing,' *British Book News* (December)
(ed.) *Annual Bibliography of British and Irish History: Publications for 1976* (Brighton: Harvester Press).

Reviews:
H. M. Colvin *et al.*, *The History of the King's Works III/1* (*EHR*)
G. R. Potter, *Zwingli* (*TLS*, 4 Mar.)
H. A. Kelley, *The Matrimonial Trials of Henry VIII* (*JTS*)
J. H. Hexter *et al.* (eds.), *Commons Debates 1628*, vols. 1–3 (*TLS*, 24 June)

C. Tilly (ed.), *The Formation of National States in Western Europe* (*Journal of Modern History*)
R. D. Edwards, *Ireland in the Age of the Tudors* (*History*)

1978

'The sessional printing of statutes, 1484–1547,' in *Wealth and Power in Tudor England: Essays presented to S. T. Bindoff*, ed. E. W. Ives *et al.* (London: Athlone), 68–86
'England und die oberdeutsche Reformation,' *Zeitschrift für Kirchengeschichte*, 3–11
(ed.) *Annual Bibliography of British and Irish History: Publications for 1977* (Brighton: Harvester Press)

Reviews:
J. Lorz, *Bibliotheca Linckiana* (*JTS*)
J. P. Kenyon, *Stuart England* (*New Statesman*, 4 Aug.)
L. L. Martz *et al.* (eds), *Complete Works of St Thomas More*, vols. 12–14: *The Dialogue of Comfort; Treatise on the Passion; De Tristitia Christi* (*EHR*)
R. Ashton, *The English Civil War* (*New Statesman*, 25 Aug.)
D. Gunning, *The Teaching of History* (*TLS*, 8 Sept.)
Propyläen Geschichte Europas, vols. 2, 4–6 (*TLS*, 20 Oct.)
B. W. Beckingsale, *Thomas Cromwell* (*TLS*, 3 Nov.)
V. F. Snow (ed.), *Parliament in Elizabethan England: John Hooker's Order and Usage* (*History*)
R. E. Ham, *The County and the Kingdom: Sir Herbert Croft and the Elizabethan State* (*History*)
J. H. Langbein, *Torture and the Law of Proof* (*Journal of Modern History*)

1979

'The Rolls of Parliament 1449–1547,' *HJ* 22, 1–29
'Reform and the "Commonwealth-Men" of Edward VI's reign,' in *The English Commonwealth 1547–1640: Essays in Politics and Society presented to Joel Hurstfield*, ed. P. Clark *et al.* (Leicester University Press), 23–38
'Parliament in the sixteenth century: function and fortunes,' *HJ* 22, 255–78
'England and the continent in the sixteenth century,' *Studies in Church History, Subsidia* 2, 1–16
English Law in the Sixteenth Century: Reform in an Age of Change (London: Selden Society)
'Catching up British history: 1. Tudors and early Stuarts,' *TLS*, 23 Nov.
(ed.) *Annual bibliography of British and Irish History: Publications for 1978* (Brighton: Harvester Press)

Reviews:
T. A. Brady, *Ruling Class, Regime, and Reformation at Strasbourg* (*JTS*)
J. T. Kelly, *Thorns on the Tudor Rose: Monks, Rogues, Vagabonds and Sturdy Beggars* (*The Historian*, Feb.)
B. Moeller, *Deutschland im Zeitalter der Reformation* (*ARG*)
J. D. Tracy, *The Politics of Erasmus* (*JTS*)

1980

'The real Thomas More?' in *Reformation Principle and Practice: Essays in Honour of A. G. Dickens*, ed. P. N. Brooks (London: Scolar Press), 21–31. Reprinted in *Psychological Medicine* 10 (1980), 611–17

'Politics and the Pilgrimage of Grace,' *After the Reformation: Essays in Honor of J. H. Hexter*, ed. B. Malament (Philadelphia: University of Pennsylvania Press). 25–56

'Enacting clauses and legislative initiative 1559–1581 [*sic*: not 1571],' *BIHR* 53, 183–91

(ed.) *Annual Bibliography of British and Irish History: Publications for 1979* (Brighton: Harvester Press)

Reviews:

K. Egan, *Educational Development* (*TES*, 11 Jan.)

J. E. Bellamy, *The Tudor Law of Treason* (*EHR*)

R. F. Atkinson, *Knowledge and Explanation in History* (*History*)

Penry Williams, *The Tudor Regime* (*TLS*, 15 Feb.)

J. B. Trapp (ed.), *Complete Works of St Thomas More*, vol. 9: *The Apology of Sir Thomas More* (*EHR*)

A. Pritchard, *Catholic Loyalism in Elizabethan England* (*JTS*)

W. J. Mommsen *et al.* (eds.), *Stadtbürgertum und Adel in der Reformation* (*Bulletin of the German Historical Institute in London*, 4)

R. Houlbrooke, *Church Courts and the People during the English Reformation* (*JEH*)

G. Williams, *Religion, Language and Nationality in Wales* (*Welsh History Review*)

1981

'Cranmer, Thomas,' *Theologische Realenzyklopädie*, vol. 8

'Arthur Hall, Lord Burghley and the antiquity of parliament,' in *History and Imagination: Essays in Honour of H. R. Trevor-Roper*, ed. H. Lloyd-Jones *et al.* (London: Duckworth), 83–103

'Thomas More,' in *Gestalten der Kirchengeschichte, Reformationszeit I*, ed. M. Greschat (Stuttgart: Kohlhammer), 89–103

(ed.) *Annual Bibliography of British and Irish History: publications for 1980* (Brighton: Harvester Press)

Reviews:

D. Bebbington, *Patterns in History* (*History*)

O. Handlin, *Truth in History* (*History*)

J. Cannon (ed.), *The Historian at Work* (*History*)

M. V. C. Alexander, *The First of the Tudors* (*TLS*, 27 Feb.)

W. Prest (ed.), *Lawyers in Early Modern Europe and America* (*TLS*, 6 Mar.)

A. B. Ferguson, *Clio Unbound: Perception of the Social and Cultural Past in Renaissance England* (*History & Theory*)

M. St Clare Byrne (ed.), *The Lisle Letters* (*London Review of Books*, 16 July)

L. Stone, *The Past and the Present* (*TES*, 17 July)

J. R. Lander, *Government and Community: England 1450–1509* (*American Historical Review*)

E. Le Roy Ladurie, *The Mind and Method of the Historian* (*London Review of Books*, 14 Oct.)

H. Butterfield, *The Origins of History* (*History Today*, Nov.)

B. Mansfield, *Phoenix of his Age: Interpretations of Erasmus 1550–1750* (*JTS*)

W. D. J. Cargill-Thompson, *Studies in the Reformation: Luther to Hooker*, ed. C. W. Dugmore (*JEH*)

Index of persons

Index of persons

Index of persons

Index of places